CODE OF FEDERAL REGULATIONS

Title 46
Shipping

Parts 140 to 155

Revised as of October 1, 2013

Containing a codification of documents
of general applicability and future effect

As of October 1, 2013

Published by the Office of the Federal Register
National Archives and Records Administration
as a Special Edition of the Federal Register

U.S. GOVERNMENT OFFICIAL EDITION NOTICE

Legal Status and Use of Seals and Logos

The seal of the National Archives and Records Administration (NARA) authenticates the Code of Federal Regulations (CFR) as the official codification of Federal regulations established under the Federal Register Act. Under the provisions of 44 U.S.C. 1507, the contents of the CFR, a special edition of the Federal Register, shall be judicially noticed. The CFR is prima facie evidence of the original documents published in the Federal Register (44 U.S.C. 1510).

It is prohibited to use NARA's official seal and the stylized Code of Federal Regulations logo on any republication of this material without the express, written permission of the Archivist of the United States or the Archivist's designee. Any person using NARA's official seals and logos in a manner inconsistent with the provisions of 36 CFR part 1200 is subject to the penalties specified in 18 U.S.C. 506, 701, and 1017.

Use of ISBN Prefix

This is the Official U.S. Government edition of this publication and is herein identified to certify its authenticity. Use of the 0–16 ISBN prefix is for U.S. Government Printing Office Official Editions only. The Superintendent of Documents of the U.S. Government Printing Office requests that any reprinted edition clearly be labeled as a copy of the authentic work with a new ISBN.

 U.S. GOVERNMENT PRINTING OFFICE

U.S. Superintendent of Documents • Washington, DC 20402–0001

http://bookstore.gpo.gov

Phone: toll-free (866) 512-1800; DC area (202) 512-1800

Table of Contents

	Page
Explanation	v

Title 46:

Chapter I—Coast Guard, Department of Homeland Security (Continued)	3

Finding Aids:

Table of CFR Titles and Chapters	333
Alphabetical List of Agencies Appearing in the CFR	353
List of CFR Sections Affected	363

Cite this Code: **CFR**

To cite the regulations in this volume use title, part and section number. Thus, 46 CFR 147.1 refers to title 46, part 147, section 1.

Explanation

The Code of Federal Regulations is a codification of the general and permanent rules published in the Federal Register by the Executive departments and agencies of the Federal Government. The Code is divided into 50 titles which represent broad areas subject to Federal regulation. Each title is divided into chapters which usually bear the name of the issuing agency. Each chapter is further subdivided into parts covering specific regulatory areas.

Each volume of the Code is revised at least once each calendar year and issued on a quarterly basis approximately as follows:

Title 1 through Title 16..as of January 1
Title 17 through Title 27..as of April 1
Title 28 through Title 41..as of July 1
Title 42 through Title 50...as of October 1

The appropriate revision date is printed on the cover of each volume.

LEGAL STATUS

The contents of the Federal Register are required to be judicially noticed (44 U.S.C. 1507). The Code of Federal Regulations is prima facie evidence of the text of the original documents (44 U.S.C. 1510).

HOW TO USE THE CODE OF FEDERAL REGULATIONS

The Code of Federal Regulations is kept up to date by the individual issues of the Federal Register. These two publications must be used together to determine the latest version of any given rule.

To determine whether a Code volume has been amended since its revision date (in this case, October 1, 2013), consult the "List of CFR Sections Affected (LSA)," which is issued monthly, and the "Cumulative List of Parts Affected," which appears in the Reader Aids section of the daily Federal Register. These two lists will identify the Federal Register page number of the latest amendment of any given rule.

EFFECTIVE AND EXPIRATION DATES

Each volume of the Code contains amendments published in the Federal Register since the last revision of that volume of the Code. Source citations for the regulations are referred to by volume number and page number of the Federal Register and date of publication. Publication dates and effective dates are usually not the same and care must be exercised by the user in determining the actual effective date. In instances where the effective date is beyond the cut-off date for the Code a note has been inserted to reflect the future effective date. In those instances where a regulation published in the Federal Register states a date certain for expiration, an appropriate note will be inserted following the text.

OMB CONTROL NUMBERS

The Paperwork Reduction Act of 1980 (Pub. L. 96–511) requires Federal agencies to display an OMB control number with their information collection request.

Many agencies have begun publishing numerous OMB control numbers as amendments to existing regulations in the CFR. These OMB numbers are placed as close as possible to the applicable recordkeeping or reporting requirements.

PAST PROVISIONS OF THE CODE

Provisions of the Code that are no longer in force and effect as of the revision date stated on the cover of each volume are not carried. Code users may find the text of provisions in effect on any given date in the past by using the appropriate List of CFR Sections Affected (LSA). For the convenience of the reader, a "List of CFR Sections Affected" is published at the end of each CFR volume. For changes to the Code prior to the LSA listings at the end of the volume, consult previous annual editions of the LSA. For changes to the Code prior to 2001, consult the List of CFR Sections Affected compilations, published for 1949-1963, 1964-1972, 1973-1985, and 1986-2000.

"[RESERVED]" TERMINOLOGY

The term "[Reserved]" is used as a place holder within the Code of Federal Regulations. An agency may add regulatory information at a "[Reserved]" location at any time. Occasionally "[Reserved]" is used editorially to indicate that a portion of the CFR was left vacant and not accidentally dropped due to a printing or computer error.

INCORPORATION BY REFERENCE

What is incorporation by reference? Incorporation by reference was established by statute and allows Federal agencies to meet the requirement to publish regulations in the Federal Register by referring to materials already published elsewhere. For an incorporation to be valid, the Director of the Federal Register must approve it. The legal effect of incorporation by reference is that the material is treated as if it were published in full in the Federal Register (5 U.S.C. 552(a)). This material, like any other properly issued regulation, has the force of law.

What is a proper incorporation by reference? The Director of the Federal Register will approve an incorporation by reference only when the requirements of 1 CFR part 51 are met. Some of the elements on which approval is based are:

(a) The incorporation will substantially reduce the volume of material published in the Federal Register.

(b) The matter incorporated is in fact available to the extent necessary to afford fairness and uniformity in the administrative process.

(c) The incorporating document is drafted and submitted for publication in accordance with 1 CFR part 51.

What if the material incorporated by reference cannot be found? If you have any problem locating or obtaining a copy of material listed as an approved incorporation by reference, please contact the agency that issued the regulation containing that incorporation. If, after contacting the agency, you find the material is not available, please notify the Director of the Federal Register, National Archives and Records Administration, 8601 Adelphi Road, College Park, MD 20740-6001, or call 202-741-6010.

CFR INDEXES AND TABULAR GUIDES

A subject index to the Code of Federal Regulations is contained in a separate volume, revised annually as of January 1, entitled CFR INDEX AND FINDING AIDS. This volume contains the Parallel Table of Authorities and Rules. A list of CFR titles, chapters, subchapters, and parts and an alphabetical list of agencies publishing in the CFR are also included in this volume.

An index to the text of "Title 3—The President" is carried within that volume.

The Federal Register Index is issued monthly in cumulative form. This index is based on a consolidation of the "Contents" entries in the daily Federal Register.

A List of CFR Sections Affected (LSA) is published monthly, keyed to the revision dates of the 50 CFR titles.

REPUBLICATION OF MATERIAL

There are no restrictions on the republication of material appearing in the Code of Federal Regulations.

INQUIRIES

For a legal interpretation or explanation of any regulation in this volume, contact the issuing agency. The issuing agency's name appears at the top of odd-numbered pages.

For inquiries concerning CFR reference assistance, call 202-741-6000 or write to the Director, Office of the Federal Register, National Archives and Records Administration, 8601 Adelphi Road, College Park, MD 20740-6001 or e-mail *fedreg.info@nara.gov*.

SALES

The Government Printing Office (GPO) processes all sales and distribution of the CFR. For payment by credit card, call toll-free, 866-512-1800, or DC area, 202-512-1800, M-F 8 a.m. to 4 p.m. e.s.t. or fax your order to 202-512-2104, 24 hours a day. For payment by check, write to: US Government Printing Office – New Orders, P.O. Box 979050, St. Louis, MO 63197-9000.

ELECTRONIC SERVICES

The full text of the Code of Federal Regulations, the LSA (List of CFR Sections Affected), The United States Government Manual, the Federal Register, Public Laws, Public Papers of the Presidents of the United States, Compilation of Presidential Documents and the Privacy Act Compilation are available in electronic format via *www.ofr.gov*. For more information, contact the GPO Customer Contact Center, U.S. Government Printing Office. Phone 202-512-1800, or 866-512-1800 (toll-free). E-mail, *ContactCenter@gpo.gov*.

The Office of the Federal Register also offers a free service on the National Archives and Records Administration's (NARA) World Wide Web site for public law numbers, Federal Register finding aids, and related information. Connect to NARA's web site at *www.archives.gov/federal-register*.

The e-CFR is a regularly updated, unofficial editorial compilation of CFR material and Federal Register amendments, produced by the Office of the Federal Register and the Government Printing Office. It is available at *www.ecfr.gov*.

CHARLES A. BARTH,
Director,
Office of the Federal Register.
October 1, 2013.

THIS TITLE

Title 46—SHIPPING is composed of nine volumes. The parts in these volumes are arranged in the following order: Parts 1–40, 41–69, 70–89, 90–139, 140–155, 156–165, 166–199, 200–499, and 500 to end. The first seven volumes containing parts 1–199 comprise chapter I—Coast Guard, DHS. The eighth volume, containing parts 200– 499, includes chapter II—Maritime Administration, DOT and chapter III—Coast Guard (Great Lakes Pilotage), DHS. The ninth volume, containing part 500 to end, includes chapter IV—Federal Maritime Commission. The contents of these volumes represent all current regulations codified under this title of the CFR as of October 1, 2013.

For this volume, Bonnie Fritts was Chief Editor. The Code of Federal Regulations publication program is under the direction of Michael L. White, assisted by Ann Worley.

Title 46—Shipping

(This book contains parts 140 to 155)

	Part
CHAPTER I—Coast Guard, Department of Homeland Security (Continued)	147

CHAPTER I—COAST GUARD, DEPARTMENT OF HOMELAND SECURITY (CONTINUED)

SUBCHAPTER N—DANGEROUS CARGOES

Part		Page
140–146	[Reserved]	
147	Hazardous ships' stores	5
147A	Interim regulations for shipboard fumigation	11
148	Carriage of bulk solid materials that require special handling	15
149	[Reserved]	

SUBCHAPTER O—CERTAIN BULK DANGEROUS CARGOES

150	Compatibility of cargoes	45
151	Barges carrying bulk liquid hazardous material cargoes	125
152	[Reserved]	
153	Ships carrying bulk liquid, liquefied gas, or compressed gas hazardous materials	192
154	Safety standards for self-propelled vessels carrying bulk liquefied gases	268
155	[Reserved]	

SUBCHAPTER P—MANNING OF VESSELS [RESERVED]

CHAPTER 15: COAST GUARD, DEPARTMENT OF HOMELAND SECURITY (CONTINUED)

SUBCHAPTER N—DANGEROUS CARGOES

PARTS 140–146 [RESERVED]

PART 147—HAZARDOUS SHIPS' STORES

Subpart A—General Provisions

Sec.
147.1 Purpose; applicability; preemptive effect.
147.3 Definitions.
147.5 Commandant (CG–OES); address.
147.7 Incorporation by reference.
147.8 OMB control numbers assigned pursuant to the Paperwork Reduction Act.
147.9 Waivers.
147.15 Hazardous ships' stores permitted on board vessels.
147.30 Labeling.
147.33 Right of appeal.

Subpart B—Stowage and Other Special Requirements for Particular Materials

147.35 Purpose of subpart.
147.40 Materials requiring Commandant (CG–OES) approval.
147.45 Flammable and combustible liquids.
147.50 Fuel for cooking, heating, and lighting.
147.60 Compressed gases.
147.65 Carbon dioxide and halon fire extinguishing systems.
147.66 Inert gas fire extinguishing systems.
147.67 Halocarbon fire extinguishing systems.
147.70 Acetylene.
147.85 Oxygen.
147.90 Refrigerants.
147.95 Explosives.
147.100 Radioactive materials.
147.105 Anesthetics, drugs, and medicines.

AUTHORITY: 46 U.S.C. 3306; E.O. 12234, 45 FR 58801, 3 CFR, 1980 Comp., p. 277; Department of Homeland Security Delegation No. 0170.1.

EDITORIAL NOTE: Nomenclature changes to part 147 appear at 74 FR 49235, Sept. 25, 2009, and 77 FR 59782, Oct. 1, 2012.

SOURCE: CGD 84–044, 53 FR 7749, Mar. 10, 1988, unless otherwise noted.

Subpart A—General Provisions

§ 147.1 Purpose; applicability; preemptive effect.

(a) This part prescribes regulations designating what hazardous materials may be on board vessels as ships' stores and prescribes requirements for the labeling, stowage, and use of those materials.

(b) This part applies to all vessels listed in 46 U.S.C. 3301 as subject to inspection under part B of 46 U.S.C. Subtitle II. On foreign vessels in the navigable waters of the United States, the Captain of the Port or District Commander may prohibit the unsafe use or stowage of hazardous ships' stores under 33 CFR 160.109.

(c) All certifications previously issued by the Coast Guard under this part permitting the use of particular materials or products as ships' stores are null and void.

(d) The regulations in this part have preemptive effect over State or local regulations in the same field.

[CGD 84–044, 53 FR 7749, Mar. 10, 1988, as amended by USCG–2006–24797, 77 FR 33885, June 7, 2012]

§ 147.3 Definitions.

As used in this part:

Accommodation, control, or service spaces means living quarters, including walkways, dining rooms, galleys, pantries, lounges, lavatories, cabins, staterooms, offices, hospitals, cinemas, and game and hobby rooms; areas containing controls for equipment and navigation; workshops, other than those forming part of machinery spaces; and store rooms adjacent to these spaces.

Combustible liquid means *combustible liquid* as the term is defined in 49 CFR 173.120(b).

Compressed gas means *compressed gas* as the term is defined in 49 CFR 173.115.

Consumer commodity means a commodity, such as a polish, insecticide, cleaning compound, or distillate, that is packaged and distributed in a form and quantity intended for sale through retail sales establishments.

Flammable liquid means *flammable liquid* as the term is defined in 49 CFR 173.120(a).

Hazardous material means *hazardous material* as the term is defined in 49 CFR 171.8.

Hazardous ships' stores means ships' stores that are hazardous materials.

§ 147.5

Proper shipping name means the name of the hazardous ships' stores shown in Roman print (not in italics) in 49 CFR 172.101.

Ships' stores means materials which are on board a vessel for the upkeep, maintenance, safety, operation, or navigation of the vessel (except for fumigants under part 147A of this chapter, for fuel and compressed air used for the vessel's primary propulsion machinery, or for fixed auxiliary equipment) or for the safety or comfort of the vessel's passengers or crew.

Technical name means the recognized chemical name used in scientific or technical publications.

[CGD 84–044, 53 FR 7749, Mar. 10, 1988, as amended by CGD 97–057, 62 FR 51048, Sept. 30, 1997]

§ 147.5 Commandant (CG–OES); address.

Commandant (CG–ENG) is the Office of Design and Engineering Standards. The mailing address is Commandant (CG–ENG), Attn: Office of Design and Engineering Systems, U.S. Coast Guard Stop 7509, 2703 Martin Luther King Jr. Avenue SE., Washington, DC 20593–7509; telephone 202–372–1372.

[USCG–2013–0671, 78 FR 60154, Sept. 30, 2013]

§ 147.7 Incorporation by reference.

(a) Certain material is incorporated by reference into this part with the approval of the Director of the Federal Register under 5 U.S.C. 552(a) and 1 CFR part 51. To enforce any edition other than that specified in this section, the Coast Guard must publish notice of change in the FEDERAL REGISTER and the material must be available to the public. All approved material is available for inspection at Coast Guard Headquarters. Contact Commandant (CG–ENG), Attn: Office of Design and Engineering Systems, U.S. Coast Guard Stop 7509, 2703 Martin Luther King Jr. Avenue SE., Washington, DC 20593–7509. The material is also available from the sources listed below. It is also available for inspection at the National Archives and Records Administration (NARA). For information on the availability of this material at NARA, call 202–741–6030 or go to *http:// www.archives.gov/federal_register/ code_of_federal_regulations/ ibr_locations.html*.

(b) American Boat and Yacht Council, Inc. (ABYC), 613 Third Street, Suite 10, Annapolis, MD 21403, telephone 410–990–4460, *www.abyinc.org*.

(1) ABYC H–25–81, Portable Fuel Systems and Portable Containers for Flammable Liquids, (May 12, 1981), ("ABYC H–25–81"), IBR approved for § 147.45.

(2) [Reserved]

(c) American Society of Heating, Refrigerating, and Air-Conditioning Engineers, Inc. (ASHRAE), Publication Sales Department, 1791 Tullie Circle NE., Atlanta, GA 30329, telephone 404–636–8400, *www.ashrae.org*.

(1) ANSI/ASHRAE 34–78, Number Designation of Refrigerants (approved 1978), ("ANSI/ASHRAE 34–78"), IBR approved for § 147.90.

(2) [Reserved]

(d) National Fire Protection Association (NFPA), 1 Batterymarch Park, Quincy, MA, 02169–7471, telephone 617–770–3000, *www.nfpa.org*.

(1) NFPA 2001, Standard on Clean Agent Fire Extinguishing Systems, 2008 Edition, ("NFPA 2001"), IBR approved for §§ 147.66 and 147.67.

(2) [Reserved]

(e) Public Health Service, Department of Health and Human Services (DHHS), Superintendent of Documents, U.S. Government Printing Office, Washington, DC 20402.

(1) DHHS Publication No. (PHS) 84–2024, The Ship's Medicine Chest and Medical Aid at Sea (revised 1984), ("DHHS Publication No. (PHS) 84–2024"), IBR approved for § 147.105.

(2) [Reserved]

(f) Underwriters Laboratories, Inc. (UL), 333 Pfingsten Road, Northbrook, IL 60062, telephone 847–272–8800, *www.ul.com*.

(1) UL 30, Standard for Metal Safety Cans, 7th Ed. (revised March 3, 1987), ("UL 30"), IBR approved for § 147.45.

(2) UL 1185, Standard for Portable Marine Fuel Tanks, Second Edition, revised July 6, 1984, ("UL 1185"), IBR approved for § 147.45.

(3) UL 1313, Standard for Nonmetallic Safety Cans for Petroleum Products, 1st Ed. (revised March 22, 1985), ("UL 1313"), IBR approved for § 147.45.

(4) UL 1314, Standard for Special-Propose Containers, 1st Ed. (revised February 7, 1984), ("UL 1314"), IBR approved for § 147.45.

[USCG–2006–24797, 77 FR 33885, June 7, 2012, as amended by USCG–2013–0671, 78 FR 60154, Sept. 30, 2013]

§ 147.8 OMB control numbers assigned pursuant to the Paperwork Reduction Act.

(a) *Purpose.* This section collects and displays the control numbers assigned to information collection and recordkeeping requirements in this subchapter by the Office of Management and Budget (OMB) pursuant to the Paperwork Reduction Act of 1980 (44 U.S.C. 3501 *et seq.*). The Coast Guard intends that this section comply with the requirements of 44 U.S.C. 3507(f), which requires that agencies display a current control number assigned by the Director of the OMB for each approved agency information collection requirement.

(b) *Display.*

46 CFR part or section where identified or described	Current OMB control no.
§ 147.9	1625–0034
§ 147.30	1625–0034
§ 147.40	1625–0034
§ 147.60(c)(2)	1625–0034

[CGD 88–072, 53 FR 34298, Sept. 6, 1988; 88–072, 53 FR 37570, Sept. 27, 1988, as amended by USCG–2004–18884, 69 FR 58349, Sept. 30, 2004]

§ 147.9 Waivers.

(a) Any requirement in this part may be waived on a case by case basis if it is determined by Commandant (CG–ENG) that the requirement is impracticable under the circumstances and that an acceptable level of safety can be maintained.

(b) Requests for issuance of a waiver must be in writing and contain a detailed explanation of—

(1) Why the requirement is impracticable; and

(2) What measures will be taken to maintain an acceptable or equivalent level of safety.

[CGD 84–044, 53 FR 7749, Mar. 10, 1988, as amended by CGD 95–072, 60 FR 50465, Sept. 29, 1995; CGD 96–041, 61 FR 50731, Sept. 27, 1996; USCG–2013–0671, 78 FR 60154, Sept. 30, 2013]

§ 147.15 Hazardous ships' stores permitted on board vessels.

Unless prohibited under subpart B of this part, any hazardous material may be on board a vessel as ships' stores if the material—

(a) Is labeled according to § 147.30; and

(b) Meets the requirements, if any, in subpart B of this part applicable to the material.

§ 147.30 Labeling.

(a) Except as provided in paragraph (b) of this section, all immediate receptacles, containers, or packages containing hazardous ships' stores must be labeled in English with the following information concerning the contents:

(1) Technical name or proper shipping name.

(2) For hazardous ships' stores other than liquid fuels, manufacturer's or supplier's name and address.

(3) Hazard classification under 49 CFR 172.101, 173.2, and 173.2(a).

(4) For hazardous ships' stores other than liquid fuels, step by step procedures for proper use.

(5) First aid instructions in the event of personnel contact, including antidotes in the event of ingestion.

(6) Stowage and segregation requirements.

(b) Hazardous ships' stores that are consumer commodities labeled in accordance with the Federal Hazardous Substances Act Regulations in 16 CFR part 1500 need not be labeled as specified in paragraph (a) of this section.

[CGD 84–044, 53 FR 7749, Mar. 10, 1988, as amended by CGD 97–057, 62 FR 51048, Sept. 30, 1997; USCG–2005–22329, 70 FR 57183, Sept. 30, 2005]

§ 147.33 Right of appeal.

Any person directly affected by a decision or action taken under this part, by or on behalf of the Coast Guard, may appeal therefrom in accordance with subpart 1.03 of this chapter.

[CGD 88–033, 54 FR 50381, Dec. 6, 1989; 55 FR 21386, May 24, 1990]

Subpart B—Stowage and Other Special Requirements for Particular Materials

§ 147.35 Purpose of subpart.

This subpart prescribes special requirements applicable to particular, named materials. These requirements are in addition to the general requirements in subpart A applicable to those materials.

§ 147.40 Materials requiring Commandant (CG–OES) approval.

(a) Commandant (CG–ENG) approval is required before the following hazardous materials may be on board a vessel as ships' stores:

(1) Poison gases of Class 2, Division 2.3 and toxic liquids of Class 6, Division 6.1 which are poisonous by inhalation in Hazard Zone A.

(2) Explosives of Divisions 1.1 or 1.2.

(3) Flammable gases, other than those addressed specifically in this subpart.

(4) Forbidden materials listed in 49 CFR 172.101.

(b) Request for approval must be submitted to the Commandant (CG–ENG), identify the material, and explain the need for its use.

(c) Upon approval, the material is added to the list of materials approved under this section. A copy of this list is available from the Commandant (CG–ENG) at the address in § 147.5.

[CGD 84–044, 53 FR 7749, Mar. 10, 1988, as amended by CGD 95–072, 60 FR 50465, Sept. 29, 19955; CGD 96–041, 61 FR 50731, Sept. 27, 1996; CGD 97–057, 62 FR 51048, Sept. 30, 1997; USCG–2013–0671, 78 FR 60154, Sept. 30, 2013]

§ 147.45 Flammable and combustible liquids.

(a) This section applies to the stowage and transfer of flammable and combustible liquids (including gasoline and diesel oil), other than liquids used as fuel for cooking, heating, and lighting under § 147.50.

(b) No flammable or combustible liquids may be stowed in any accommodation, control, or service space (other than a paint locker).

(c) No more than 19 liters (five gallons) of flammable liquids may be stowed in any machinery space. The flammable liquids must be in containers of 3.8 liters (one gallon) or less.

(d) No more than 208 liters (55 gallons) of combustible liquids may be stowed in any machinery space.

(e) An aggregate of more than 7.6 liters (two gallons) of flammable or combustible liquids stowed outside of an accommodation, control, or service space (other than a paint locker) or outside of a machinery space must be stowed in a paint locker that is marked with a warning sign indicating flammable or combustible liquid storage.

(f) Flammable and combustible liquids used as fuel for portable auxiliary equipment must be stored in—

(1) Integral tanks that form part of the vessel's structure;

(2) An independent tank meeting the requirements of subpart 58.50 of Part 58 of this chapter;

(3) A non-bulk packaging authorized for Class 3 (flammable) liquids or combustible liquids under 49 CFR 173.201, 173.202, or 173.203, as referenced for the specific liquid in column 8B of the Hazardous Materials Table of 49 CFR 172.101.

(4) A portable outboard fuel tank meeting the specifications of ABYC H–25–81 (incorporated by reference, see § 147.7) or one identified by Underwriters Laboratories as meeting the specifications of UL 1185 (incorporated by reference, see § 147.7);

(5) A portable safety container identified by Underwriters Laboratories as meeting the specifications of UL 30 or UL 1313 (both incorporated by reference, see § 147.7); or

(6) A portable safety container identified by Underwriters Laboratories as meeting the requirements of UL 1314 (incorporated by reference, see § 147.7).

(g) Each portable container of flammable or combustible liquid used for portable auxiliary equipment must be stowed in a paint locker or an open location designated by the master.

(h) Fuel tanks for portable auxiliary equipment using flammable or combustible liquids may only be refilled on a vessel—

(1) By using a container described in paragraph (f)(2), (f)(3), or (f)(5) of this section which has a capacity not exceeding 23 liters (6 gallons); or

(2) In the case of portable outboard fuel tanks described in paragraph (f)(4) of this section, in accordance with paragraph (i) of this section.

(i) Portable containers or portable outboard fuel tanks may be refilled from a larger container of flammable or combustible liquid on the weather deck of a vessel, other than a small passenger vessel subject to Subchapter T of this chapter, provided that—

(1) A drip pan of adequate size is used to collect any drippings; and

(2) At least one Coast Guard approved Type B, Size I, fire extinguisher is within three meters (9.75 feet) of the refilling location.

[CGD 84–044, 53 FR 7749, Mar. 10, 1988, as amended by CGD 92–100, 59 FR 17001, Apr. 11, 1994; CGD 97–057, 62 FR 51048, Sept. 30, 1997; USCG–2006–24797, 77 FR 33885, June 7, 2012]

§ 147.50 Fuel for cooking, heating, and lighting.

(a) Flammable and combustible liquids and gases not listed in this section are prohibited for cooking, heating, or lighting on any vessel, with the exception of combustible liquids on cargo vessels.

(b) Fluid alcohol is prohibited for cooking, heating, or lighting on ferry vessels. Fluid alcohol burners, where wet primed, must have a catch pan not less than ¾ of an inch deep secured inside the frame of the stove or have the metal protection under the stove flanged up ¾ of an inch to form a pan.

(c) Containers of solidified alcohol must be secured on a fixed base.

(d) Liquefied or non-liquefied gas is prohibited for cooking, heating, and lighting on ferry vessels, but may be used on other inspected vessels if the system in which it is used meets the applicable requirements of subpart 58.16 or subpart 184.05 of this chapter, as appropriate, or is approved by the Commandant (CG–ENG).

(e) Kerosene and commercial standard fuel oil No. 1, No. 2, and No. 3 are prohibited for cooking, heating, or lighting on ferry or passenger vessels, unless the following conditions are met:

(1) Pressure or gravity feed must be used.

(2) Where wet priming is used in a cooking device, the device must have a catch pan not less than three fourths of an inch deep secured inside the frame of the device or a metal protector under the device with a least a three fourths inch flange to form a pan.

(3) Where wet priming is used, a non-flammable priming liquid must be used.

(4) Fuel tanks for fixed stoves must be separated from the stove and mounted in a location open to the atmosphere or mounted inside a compartment with an outside fill and vent.

(5) Fuel lines must have an easily accessible shut-off valve at the tank.

(6) If the fuel tank is outside of a stove compartment, a shut-off valve must be fitted at the stove.

[CGD 84–044, 53 FR 7749, Mar. 10, 1988, as amended by CGD 83–013, 54 FR 6402, Feb. 10, 1989; CGD 95–072, 60 FR 50465, Sept. 29, 1995; CGD 96–041, 61 FR 50731, Sept. 27, 1996]

§ 147.60 Compressed gases.

(a) *Cylinder requirements.* Cylinders used for containing hazardous ships' stores that are compressed gases must be—

(1) Authorized for the proper shipping name of the gas in accordance with 49 CFR 172.101 and 49 CFR part 173;

(2) Constructed in accordance with subpart C of 49 CFR part 178 or exempted under 49 CFR part 107;

(3) Filled, marked, and inspected in accordance with 49 CFR 173.301 through 173.308; and

(4) Except as provided in 46 CFR 147.65, 147.66, and 147.67, maintained and retested in accordance with 49 CFR 180.

(b) *Stowage and care of cylinders.* (1) Cylinders must always be secured and, when not in use, they must be stowed in a rack in an upright position, with the valve protection cap in place.

(2) Lockers or housings must be vented to the open air near the top and bottom for positive circulation of vapors.

(3) Cylinders must be protected from all sources of heat which may cause the cylinders to be heated to a temperature higher than 130 °F.

(c) *Pressure vessels other than cylinders.* Pressure vessels, other than cylinders subject to paragraph (a) of this section, used for containing ships' stores that are compressed gases must—

§ 147.65

(1) Be constructed and inspected in accordance with part 54 of this chapter; and

(2) Carry only nitrogen or air, unless permission is granted by Commandant (CG–ENG) to do otherwise.

[CGD 84–044, 53 FR 7749, Mar. 10, 1988, as amended by CGD 95–072, 60 FR 50465, Sept. 29, 19955; CGD 96–041, 61 FR 50731, Sept. 27, 1996; USCG–2006–24797, 77 FR 33886, June 7, 2012; USCG–2013–0671, 78 FR 60154, Sept. 30, 2013]

§ 147.65 Carbon dioxide and halon fire extinguishing systems.

(a) Carbon dioxide or halon cylinders forming part of a fixed fire extinguishing system must be retested, at least, every 12 years. If a cylinder is discharged and more than five years have elapsed since the last test, it must be retested before recharging.

(b) Carbon dioxide or halon cylinders must be rejected for further service when they—

(1) Leak;

(2) Are dented, bulging, severely corroded, or otherwise in a weakened condition;

(3) Have lost more than five percent of their tare weight; or

(4) Have been involved in a fire.

(c) Cylinders which have contained carbon dioxide or halon and have not been tested within five years must not be used to contain another compressed gas on board a vessel, unless the cylinder is retested and re-marked in accordance with § 147.60 (a)(3) and (a)(4).

(d) Flexible connections between cylinders and distribution piping of semi-portable or fixed carbon dioxide fire extinguishing systems and discharge hoses in semi-portable carbon dioxide fire extinguishing systems must be renewed or tested at a pressure of 6.9 MPa (1000 psig). At test pressure, the pressure must not drop at a rate greater than 1.03 MPa (150 psi) per minute for a two minute period. The test must be performed when the cylinders are retested.

(e) Flexible connections between cylinders and distribution piping of fixed halon fire extinguishing systems must be tested at a pressure of one and one-half times the cylinder service pressure as marked on the cylinder. At test pressure, the pressure must not drop at a rate greater than 1.03 MPa (150 psi) per minute for a two minute period. The test must be performed when the cylinders are retested.

§ 147.66 Inert gas fire extinguishing systems.

(a) Inert gas cylinders forming part of a clean agent fixed fire extinguishing system must be retested every five years, except that cylinders with a water capacity of 125 pounds or less may be retested every 10 years in accordance with 49 CFR 180.209(b).

(b) An inert gas cylinder must be removed from service if it:

(1) Leaks;

(2) Is dented, bulging, severely corroded, or otherwise weakened;

(3) Has lost more than 5 percent of its tare weight; or

(4) Has been involved in a fire.

(c) Flexible connections between cylinders and discharge piping for fixed inert gas fire extinguishing systems must be renewed or retested in accordance with section 7.3 of NFPA 2001 (incorporated by reference, see § 147.7).

[USCG–2006–24797, 77 FR 33886, June 7, 2012]

§ 147.67 Halocarbon fire extinguishing systems.

(a) Each halocarbon cylinder forming part of a clean agent fixed fire extinguishing system must be:

(1) Retested at least once every 12 years and before recharging if it has been discharged and more than five years have elapsed since the last test; or

(2) As an alternative, a cylinder conforming to the requirements of 49 CFR 180.209(g) may be given the complete external visual inspection in lieu of hydrostatic testing provided for by that section.

(b) A halocarbon cylinder must be removed from service if it:

(1) Leaks;

(2) Is dented, bulging, severely corroded, or otherwise weakened;

(3) Has lost more than 5 percent of its tare weight; or

(4) Has been involved in a fire.

(c) Flexible connections between cylinders and discharge piping for halocarbon fire extinguishing systems must be renewed or retested in accordance with section 7.3 of NFPA 2001 (incorporated by reference, see § 147.7).

[USCG–2006–24797, 77 FR 33886, June 7, 2012]

§ 147.70 Acetylene.

(a) Seventeen cubic meters (600 standard cubic feet) or less of acetylene may be stowed on or below decks on any vessel.

(b) More than 17 m³ (600 standard cubic feet) of acetylene may be on board a vessel engaged in industrial operations, if it is stowed on deck.

§ 147.85 Oxygen.

(a) Eighty five cubic meters (3000 standard cubic feet) or less of oxygen may be on board any vessel.

(b) More than 85 m³ (3000 standard cubic feet) of oxygen may be on board a vessel engaged in industrial operations, if it is stowed on deck or in a well ventilated space.

§ 147.90 Refrigerants.

(a) Only refrigerants listed in ANSI/ASHRAE 34–78 may be carried as ships' stores.

(b) Refrigerants contained in a vessel's operating system are not considered as being carried as ship's stores.

§ 147.95 Explosives.

(a) *Explosives—general.* Except as provided for elsewhere in this subchapter, explosives, as defined in 49 CFR 173.50, which are hazardous ships' stores must be stowed in accordance with 49 CFR 176.116 through 176.138.

(b) *Small arms ammunition.* (1) No person shall bring, have in their possession, or use on board a vessel any small arms ammunition, except by express permission of the master of the vessel.

(2) All small arms ammunition must be stowed and locked in a metal closed cargo transport unit for Class 1 (explosive) materials as defined in 49 CFR 176.2. The key to the cargo transport unit must be kept in the possession of the master or a person designated by the master.

(c) *Ships' signals and emergency equipment.* (1) Explosive ships' signals and emergency equipment, including pyrotechnic distress signals and line throwing equipment, must be stowed in watertight containers or wood lined magazine chests.

(2) All pyrotechnic distress signals, rockets, and line throwing guns must be stowed in accordance with the requirements of 49 CFR 176.140 through 176.146.

[CGD 84–044, 53 FR 7749, Mar. 10, 1988, as amended by CGD 92–100, 59 FR 17001, Apr. 11, 1994; CGD 97–057, 62 FR 51048, Sept. 30, 1997; USCG–2013–0671, 78 FR 60154, Sept. 30, 2013]

§ 147.100 Radioactive materials.

(a) Radioactive materials must not be brought on board, used in any manner, or stored on the vessel, unless the use of the materials is authorized by a current license issued by the Nuclear Regulatory Commission (NRC) under 10 CFR parts 30 and 34.

(b) Stowage of radioactive materials must conform to the requirements of the NRC license.

§ 147.105 Anesthetics, drugs, and medicines.

Anesthetics, drugs, and medicines must be stowed and dispensed in accordance with the DHHS Publication No. (PHS) 84–2024.

PART 147A—INTERIM REGULATIONS FOR SHIPBOARD FUMIGATION

GENERAL

Sec.
147A.1 Purpose.
147A.3 Applicability.
147A.5 General requirement.
147A.6 Right of appeal.
147A.7 Definitions.
147A.9 Persons in charge of fumigation and the vessel; designation.
147A.10 Notice to Captain of the Port.

BEFORE FUMIGATION

147A.11 Person in charge of fumigation; before fumigation.
147A.13 Person in charge of the vessel; before fumigation.

DURING FUMIGATION

147A.21 Person in charge of fumigation; during fumigation.
147A.23 Person in charge of vessel; during fumigation.
147A.25 Entry.

AFTER VENTILATION

147A.31 Removal of fumigation material and warning signs.

§ 147A.1

SPECIAL REQUIREMENTS FOR FLAMMABLE FUMIGANTS

147A.41 Person in charge of fumigation; flammable fumigants.
147A.43 Other sources of ignition; flammable fumigants.

AUTHORITY: 46 U.S.C. 5103; Department of Homeland Security Delegation No. 0170.1.

SOURCE: CGD 74–144, 39 FR 32998, Sept. 13, 1974, unless otherwise noted.

GENERAL

§ 147A.1 Purpose.

The purpose of this part is to prescribe the requirements for shipboard fumigation that are critical for the health and safety of the crew and any other person who is on board a vessel during fumigation. These are interim rules pending further study and promulgation of comprehensive regulations on shipboard fumigation.

§ 147A.3 Applicability.

This part prescribes the rules for shipboard fumigation on vessels to which 49 CFR parts 171–179 apply under 49 CFR 176.5.

[CGD 86–033, 53 FR 36026, Sept. 16, 1988]

§ 147A.5 General requirement.

No person may cause or authorize shipboard fumigation contrary to the rules in this part.

§ 147A.6 Right of appeal.

Any person directly affected by a decision or action taken under this part, by or on behalf of the Coast Guard, may appeal therefrom in accordance with subpart 1.03 of this chapter.

[CGD 88–033, 54 FR 50381, Dec. 6, 1989]

§ 147A.7 Definitions.

As used in this part:

(a) *Qualified person* means a person who has experience with the particular fumigant or knowledge of its properties and is familiar with fumigant detection equipment and procedures, or an applicator who is certified by the Environmental Protection Agency if his certification covers the fumigant that is used.

(b) *Fumigant* means a substance or mixture of substances that is a gas or is rapidly or progressively transformed to the gaseous state though some non-gaseous or particulate matter may remain in the space that is fumigated.

(c) *Fumigation* means the application of a fumigant on board a vessel to a specific treatment space.

§ 147A.9 Persons in charge of fumigation and the vessel; designation.

(a) The person, including any individual, firm, association, partnership, or corporation, that is conducting a fumigation operation shall designate a person in charge of fumigation for each operation.

(b) The operator of each vessel shall designate a person in charge of the vessel for each fumigation operation.

§ 147A.10 Notice to Captain of the Port.

Unless otherwise authorized by the Captain of the Port, at least 24 hours before fumigation the operator of the vessel shall notify the Coast Guard Captain of the Port, for the area where the vessel is to be fumigated, of the time and place of the fumigation, and the name of the vessel that is to be fumigated.

BEFORE FUMIGATION

§ 147A.11 Person in charge of fumigation; before fumigation.

(a) The person in charge of fumigation shall notify the person in charge of the vessel of:

(1) The space that is to be fumigated;

(2) The name, address, and emergency telephone number of the fumigation company;

(3) The dates and times of fumigation;

(4) The characteristics of the fumigant;

(5) The spaces that are determined to be safe for occupancy paragraph (b)(1)(i) of this section;

(6) The maximum allowable concentration of fumigant in spaces, if any, that are determined to be safe for occupancy under paragraph (b)(1)(i) of this section;

(7) The symptoms of exposure to the fumigant; and

(8) Emergency first aid treatment for exposure to the fumigant.

(b) The person in charge of fumigation shall ensure that:

(1) A marine chemist or other qualified person who has knowledge of and experience in shipboard fumigation evaluates the vessel's construction and configuration and determines:

(i) Which spaces, if any, are safe for occupancy during fumigation; and

(ii) The intervals that inspections must be made under § 147A.21(a)(1);

(2) No persons or domestic animals are in the space that is to be fumigated or the spaces that are designated as unsafe for occupancy under paragraph (b)(1)(i) of this section;

(3) There is proper and secure sealing to confine the fumigant to the space that is to be fumigated, including blanking off and sealing any ventilation ducts and smoke detectors;

(4) The personal protection and fumigation detection equipment for the fumigant that is to be used is on board the vessel;

(5) Warning signs are:

(i) Posted upon all gangplanks, ladders, and other points of access to the vessel;

(ii) Posted on all entrances to the spaces that are designated as unsafe for occupancy under paragraph (b)(1)(i) of this section; and

(iii) In accordance with 49 CFR 173.9(c) or section 8.10 of the *General Introduction of the International Maritime Dangerous Goods Code*. The word "unit" on the warning sign may be replaced with "vessel," "barge," "hold," or "space," as appropriate.

(6) Watchmen are stationed at all entrances to:

(i) Spaces that are not determined to be safe for occupancy under paragraph (b)(1)(i) of this section; or

(ii) The vessel, if no spaces are determined to be safe for occupancy under paragraph (b)(1)(i) of this section.

[CGD 74–144, 39 FR 32998, Sept. 13, 1974; 39 FR 37771, Oct. 24, 19745; CGD 96–041, 61 FR 50731, Sept. 27, 1996; CGD 97–057, 62 FR 51048, Sept. 30, 1997]

§ 147A.13 Person in charge of the vessel; before fumigation.

(a) After notice under § 147A.11 (a)(5), the person in charge of the vessel shall notify the crew and all other persons on board the vessel who are not participating in the fumigation of the spaces that are determined to be safe for occupancy under § 147A.11(b)(1)(i).

(b) If no spaces are determined to be safe for occupancy under § 147A.11 (b)(1)(i), the person in charge of the vessel shall ensure that the crew and all persons who are not participating in the fumigation leave the vessel and remain away during fumigation.

DURING FUMIGATION

§ 147A.21 Person in charge of fumigation; during fumigation.

(a) Until ventilation begins, or until the vessel leaves port, the person in charge of fumigation shall ensure that a qualified person inspects the vessel as follows:

(1) He must use detection equipment for the fumigant that is used to ensure that the fumigant is confined to:

(i) The space that is fumigated, if partial occupancy is allowed under § 147A.11(b)(1)(i); or

(ii) The vessel, if no space is determined to be safe for occupancy under § 147A.11(b)(1)(i).

(2) He must make inspections at the intervals that are determined to be necessary by the marine chemist or qualified person under § 147A.11 (b)(1)(ii).

(b) If leakage occurs, the person in charge of fumigation shall:

(1) Notify the person in charge of the vessel that there is leakage;

(2) Ensure that all necessary measures are taken for the health and safety of any person; and

(3) Notify the person in charge of the vessel when there is no danger to the health and safety of any person.

(c) After the exposure period, if the vessel is in port, the person in charge of fumigation shall ensure that fumigators or other qualified persons ventilate the space that is fumigated as follows:

(1) Hatch covers and vent seals must be removed, other routes of access to the atmosphere must be opened, and if necessary, mechanical ventilation must be used.

(2) Personal protection equipment that is appropriate for the fumigant that is used must be worn.

(d) If ventilation is completed before the vessel leaves port, the person in charge of fumigation shall:

§ 147A.23

(1) Ensure that a qualified person, who is wearing the personal protection equipment for the fumigant that is used if remote detection equipment is not used, tests the space that is fumigated and determines if there is any danger to the health and safety of any person, including a danger from fumigant that may be retained in bagged, baled, or other absorbent cargo;

(2) Notify the person in charge of the vessel of this determination; and

(3) If it is determined that there is a danger:

(i) Ensure that all measures are taken that are necessary for the health and safety of all persons; and

(ii) Notify the person in charge of the vessel when there is no danger to the health and safety of any person.

§ 147A.23 Person in charge of vessel; during fumigation.

(a) The person in charge of the vessel shall ensure that the crew and all other persons on board the vessel who are not participating in the fumigation restrict their movement during fumigation to the spaces that are determined to be safe for occupancy under § 147A.11(b)(1)(i).

(b) The person in charge of the vessel shall ensure that the crew and all other persons who are not participating in the fumigation follow any instructions of the person in charge of fumigation that are issued under § 147A.21(b)(2) or (d)(3)(i) and that the vessel does not leave port if he is notified under:

(1) Section 147A.21(b)(1) that there is leakage, unless the person in charge of fumigation notifies him under § 147A.21(b)(3) of this subpart that there is no danger; or

(2) Section 147A.21(d)(2) that there is a danger after ventilation, unless the person in charge of the fumigation notifies him under § 147A.21(d)(3)(ii) that there is no danger.

(c) If fumigation is not completed before the vessel leaves port, the person in charge of the vessel shall ensure that personal protection and fumigant detection equipment for the fumigant that is used is on board the vessel.

(d) If the vessel leaves port before fumigation is completed, the person in charge of the vessel shall ensure that a qualified person makes periodic inspections until ventilation is completed and this person shall use detection equipment for the fumigant that is used to determine if:

(1) There is leakage of fumigant; or

(2) There is a concentration of fumigant that is a danger to the health and safety of any person.

(e) If the qualified person determines under paragraph (d) of this section that there is leakage or a concentration of fumigant that is a danger to the health and safety of any person, the person in charge of the vessel shall take all measures that are, in his discretion, necessary to ensure health and safety of all persons who are on board the vessel. If the danger is due to leakage, he shall also ensure that qualified persons immediately ventilate in accordance with paragraphs (c)(1) and (2) of § 147A.21.

(f) If the vessel leaves port during the exposure period, the person in charge of the vessel shall ensure that the space that is fumigated is ventilated by qualified persons after the exposure period in accordance with paragraphs (c)(1) and (2) of § 147A.21.

(g) If ventilation is completed after the vessel leaves port, the person in charge of the vessel shall ensure that a qualified person, who is wearing the personal protection equipment for the fumigant that is used if remote detection equipment is not used, tests the space that is fumigated to determine if there is a danger to the health and safety of any person, including a danger from fumigant that may be retained in bagged, baled, or other absorbent cargo. If the qualified person determines that there is a danger, the person in charge of the vessel shall take all measures that are, in his discretion, necessary to ensure the health and safety of all persons who are on board the vessel.

§ 147A.25 Entry.

(a) No person may enter the spaces that immediately adjoin the space that is fumigated during fumigation unless entry is for emergency purposes or the space is tested and declared safe for human occupancy by a marine chemist or other qualified person and is inspected under § 147A.21(a)(2) or § 147A.23(d).

(b) If entry is made for emergency purposes:
(1) No person may enter the space that is fumigated or any adjoining spaces during fumigation unless he wears the personal protection equipment for the fumigant that is in use;
(2) No person may enter the space that is fumigated unless the entry is made by a two person team; and
(3) No person may enter the space that is fumigated unless he wears a lifeline and safety harness and each life-line is tended by a person who is outside the space and who is wearing the personal protection equipment for the fumigant that is in use.

AFTER VENTILATION

§ 147A.31 Removal of fumigation material and warning signs.

After ventilation is completed and a marine chemist or other qualified person determines that there is no danger to the health and safety of any person under § 147A.21(d) or § 147A.23(g), the person in charge of fumigation, or, if the vessel has left port, the person in charge of the vessel, shall ensure that all warning signs are removed and fumigation containers and materials are removed and disposed of in accordance with the manufacturer's recommendations.

SPECIAL REQUIREMENTS FOR
FLAMMABLE FUMIGANTS

§ 147A.41 Person in charge of fumigation; flammable fumigants.

(a) The person in charge of fumigation shall ensure that:
(1) Before the space that is to be fumigated is sealed, it is thoroughly cleaned, and all refuse, oily waste, and other combustible material is removed;
(2) Before fumigation, all fire fighting equipment, including sprinklers and fire pumps, is in operating condition; and
(3) Before and during fumigation, electrical circuits that are in the space that is fumigated are de-energized.
(b) [Reserved]

§ 147A.43 Other sources of ignition; flammable fumigants.

While the space that is fumigated is being sealed or during fumigation, no person may use matches, smoking materials, fires, open flames, or any other source of ignition in any spaces that are not determined to be safe for occupancy under § 147A.11(b)(1)(i).

PART 148—CARRIAGE OF BULK SOLID MATERIALS THAT REQUIRE SPECIAL HANDLING

Subpart A—General

Sec.
148.1   Purpose and applicability.
148.2   Responsibility and compliance.
148.3   Definitions.
148.5   Alternative procedures.
148.7   OMB control numbers assigned under the Paperwork Reduction Act.
148.8   Incorporation by reference.
148.9   Right of appeal.
148.10 Permitted materials.
148.11 Hazardous or potentially dangerous characteristics.
148.12 Assignment and certification.

Subpart B—Special Permits

148.15 Petition for a special permit.
148.20 Deadlines for submission of petition and related requests.
148.21 Necessary information.
148.25 Activities covered by a special permit.
148.26 Standard conditions for special permits.
148.30 Records of special permits issued.

Subpart C—Minimum Transportation Requirements

148.50 Cargoes subject to this subpart.
148.51 Temperature readings.
148.55 International shipments.
148.60 Shipping papers.
148.61 Emergency response information.
148.62 Location of shipping papers and emergency response information.
148.70 Dangerous cargo manifest; general.
148.71 Information included in the dangerous cargo manifest.
148.72 Dangerous cargo manifest; exceptions.
148.80 Supervision of cargo transfer.
148.85 Required equipment for confined spaces.
148.86 Confined space entry.
148.90 Preparations before loading.
148.100 Log book entries.
148.110 Procedures followed after unloading.
148.115 Report of incidents.

Subpart D—Stowage and Segregation

148.120 Stowage and segregation requirements.

148.125 Stowage and segregation for materials of Class 4.1.
148.130 Stowage and segregation for materials of Class 4.2.
148.135 Stowage and segregation for materials of Class 4.3.
148.140 Stowage and segregation for materials of Class 5.1.
148.145 Stowage and segregation for materials of Class 7.
148.150 Stowage and segregation for materials of Class 9.
148.155 Stowage and segregation for potentially dangerous materials.

Subpart E—Special Requirements for Certain Materials

148.200 Purpose.
148.205 Ammonium nitrate and ammonium nitrate fertilizers.
148.220 Ammonium nitrate-phosphate fertilizers.
148.225 Calcined pyrites (pyritic ash, fly ash).
148.227 Calcium nitrate fertilizers.
148.230 Calcium oxide (lime, unslaked).
148.235 Castor beans.
148.240 Coal.
148.242 Copra.
148.245 Direct reduced iron (DRI); lumps, pellets, and cold-molded briquettes.
148.250 Direct reduced iron (DRI); hot-molded briquettes.
148.255 Ferrosilicon, aluminum ferrosilicon, and aluminum silicon containing more than 30% but less than 90% silicon.
148.260 Ferrous metal.
148.265 Fish meal or fish scrap.
148.270 Hazardous substances.
148.275 Iron oxide, spent; iron sponge, spent.
148.280 Magnesia, unslaked (lightburned magnesia, calcined magnesite, caustic calcined magnesite).
148.285 Metal sulfide concentrates.
148.290 Peat moss.
148.295 Petroleum coke, calcined or uncalcined, at 55 °C (131 °F) or above.
148.300 Radioactive materials.
148.310 Seed cake.
148.315 Sulfur.
148.320 Tankage; garbage tankage; rough ammonia tankage; or tankage fertilizer.
148.325 Wood chips; wood pellets; wood pulp pellets.
148.330 Zinc ashes; zinc dross; zinc residues; zinc skimmings.

Subpart F—Additional Special Requirements

148.400 Applicability.
148.405 Sources of ignition.
148.407 Smoking.
148.410 Fire hoses.
148.415 Toxic gas analyzers.
148.420 Flammable gas analyzers.

148.435 Electrical circuits in cargo holds.
148.445 Adjacent spaces.
148.450 Cargoes subject to liquefaction.

AUTHORITY: 33 U.S.C. 1602; E.O. 12234, 45 FR 58801, 3 CFR, 1980 Comp., p. 277; 46 U.S.C. 3306, 5111; 49 U.S.C. 5103; Department of Homeland Security Delegation No. 0170.1.

SOURCE: 75 FR 64591, Oct. 19, 2010, unless otherwise noted.

EDITORIAL NOTE: Nomenclature changes to part 148 appear at 77 FR 59783, Oct. 1, 2012.

Subpart A—General

§ 148.1 Purpose and applicability.

(a) This part prescribes special handling procedures for certain solid materials that present hazards when transported in bulk by vessel.

(b) Except as noted in paragraph (c) of this section, this part applies to all domestic and foreign vessels in the navigable waters of the United States that transport bulk solid materials requiring special handling.

(c) This part does not apply to an unmanned barge on a domestic voyage carrying a Potentially Dangerous Material (PDM) found in Table 148.10 of this part. All barges on international voyages must follow the requirements for PDM.

(d) The regulations in this part have preemptive impact over State law on the same subject. The Coast Guard has determined, after considering the factors developed by the Supreme Court in *U.S.* v. *Locke*, 529 U.S. 89 (2000), that in directing the Secretary to regulate the safe transportation of hazardous material and the safety of individuals and property on board vessels subject to inspection, as well as the provision of loading information, Congress intended to preempt the field of safety standards for solid materials requiring special handling when transported in bulk on vessels.

§ 148.2 Responsibility and compliance.

Each master of a vessel, person in charge of a barge, owner, operator, shipper, charterer, or agent must ensure compliance with this part. These persons are also responsible for communicating requirements to every person performing any function covered by this part.

§ 148.3 Definitions.

As used in this part—

A–60 class division means a division as defined in § 32.57–5 of this chapter.

Adjacent space means any enclosed space on a vessel, such as a cargo hold, cargo compartment, accommodation space, working space, storeroom, passageway, or tunnel, that shares a common bulkhead or deck with a hatch, door, scuttle, cable fitting or other penetration, with a cargo hold or compartment containing a material listed in Table 148.10 of this part.

Away from means a horizontal separation of at least 3 meters (10 feet) projected vertically is maintained between incompatible materials carried in the same hold or on deck.

Bulk applies to any solid material, consisting of a combination of particles, granules, or any larger pieces of material generally uniform in composition, that is loaded directly into the cargo spaces of a vessel without any intermediate form of containment.

Bulk Cargo Shipping Name or *BCSN* identifies a bulk solid material during transport by sea. When a cargo is listed in this Part, the BCSN of the cargo is identified by Roman type and is listed in Column 1 of Table 148.10 of this part. When the cargo is a hazardous material, as defined in 49 CFR part 173, the proper shipping name of that material is the BCSN.

Cold-molded briquettes are briquettes of direct reduced iron (DRI) that have been molded at a temperature of under 650 °C (1,202 °F) or that have a density of under 5.0 g/cm^3;.

Commandant (CG–ENG–5) means the Chief, Hazardous Materials Division of the Office of Design and Engineering Systems. The mailing address is: Commandant (CG–ENG–5), Attn: Hazardous Materials Division, U.S. Coast Guard Stop 7509, 2703 Martin Luther King Jr. Avenue SE., Washington, DC 20593–7509; telephone 202–372–1420 or email hazmatstandards@uscg.mil.

Compartment means any space on a vessel that is enclosed by the vessel's decks and its sides or permanent steel bulkheads.

Competent authority means a national agency responsible under its national law for the control or regulation of a particular aspect of the transportation of hazardous materials.

Confined space means a cargo hold containing a material listed in Table 148.10 of this part or an adjacent space not designed for human occupancy.

Domestic voyage means transportation between places within the United States other than through a foreign country.

Hazard class means the category of hazard assigned to a material under this part and 49 CFR parts 171 through 173.

HAZARD CLASS DEFINITIONS

HAZARD CLASSES USED IN THIS PART ARE DEFINED IN THE FOLLOWING SECTIONS OF TITLE 49

Class No.	Division No. (if any)	Description	Reference (49 CFR)
1	1.1, 1.2, 1.3, 1.4, 1.5, 1.6	Explosives	§ 173.50
2	2.1, 2.2, 2.3	Flammable Gas, Non-Flammable Compressed Gas, Poisonous Gas	§ 173.115
3		Flammable and Combustible Liquid	§ 173.120
4	4.1, 4.2, 4.3	Flammable Solid, Spontaneously Combustible Material, Dangerous When Wet Material.	§ 173.124
5	5.1	Oxidizer	§ 173.127
5	5.2	Organic Peroxide	§ 173.128
6	6.1	Poisonous Materials	§ 173.132
6	6.2	Infectious Substance	§ 173.134
7		Radioactive Material	§ 173.403
8		Corrosive Material	§ 173.136
9		Miscellaneous Hazardous Material	§ 173.140

Hazardous substance is a hazardous substance as defined in 49 CFR 171.8.

Hold means a compartment below deck that is used exclusively for the stowage of cargo.

§ 148.3

Hot-molded briquettes are briquettes of DRI that have been molded at a temperature of 650 °C (1,202 °F) or higher, and that have a density of 5.0 g/cm^3 (312 lb/ft^3) or greater.

IMSBC Code means the English version of the "International Maritime Solid Bulk Cargoes Code" published by the International Maritime Organization (incorporated by reference, see § 148.8).

Incompatible materials means two materials whose stowage together may result in undue hazards in the case of leakage, spillage, or other accident.

International voyage means voyages—

(1) Between any place in the United States and any place in a foreign country;

(2) Between places in the United States through a foreign country; or

(3) Between places in one or more foreign countries through the United States.

Lower flammability limit or *LFL* means the lowest concentration of a material or gas that will propagate a flame. The LFL is usually expressed as a percent by volume of a material or gas in air.

Master means the officer having command of a vessel. The functions assigned to the master in this part may also be performed by a representative of the master or by a person in charge of a barge.

Material safety data sheet or *MSDS* is as defined in 29 CFR 1910.1200.

Person in charge of a barge means an individual designated by the owner or operator of a barge to have charge of the barge.

Potentially Dangerous Material or *PDM* means a material that does not fall into a particular hazard class but can present a danger when carried in bulk aboard a vessel. The dangers often result from the material's tendency to self-heat or cause oxygen depletion. Materials that present a potential danger due solely to their tendency to shift in the cargo hold are not PDMs. For international shipments prepared in accordance with the IMSBC Code (incorporated by reference, see § 148.8), equivalent terminology to PDM is Material Hazardous only in Bulk (MHB).

Readily combustible material means a material that may not be a hazardous material but that can easily ignite and support combustion. Examples are wood, straw, vegetable fibers, and products made from these materials, and coal lubricants and oils. The term does not include packaging material or dunnage.

Reportable quantity or *RQ* means the quantity of a hazardous substance spilled or released that requires a report to the National Response Center. The specific RQs for each hazardous substance are available in 49 CFR 172.101, Appendix A.

Responsible person means a knowledgeable person who the master of a vessel or owner or operator of a barge makes responsible for all decisions relating to his or her specific task.

Seed cake means the residue remaining after vegetable oil has been extracted by a solvent or mechanical process from oil-bearing seeds, such as coconuts, cotton seed, peanuts, and linseed.

Shipper means any person by whom, or in whose name, or on whose behalf, a contract of carriage of goods by sea has been concluded with a carrier; or any person by whom or in whose name, or on whose behalf, the goods are actually delivered to the carrier in relation to the contract of carriage by sea.

Shipping paper means a shipping order, bill of lading, manifest, or other shipping document serving a similar purpose.

Stowage factor means the volume in cubic meters of 1,000 kilograms (0.984 long tons) of a bulk solid material.

Threshold limit value or *TLV* means the time-weighted average concentration of a material that the average worker can be exposed to over a normal eight-hour working day, day after day, without adverse effect. This is a trademark term of the American Conference of Governmental Industrial Hygienists (ACGIH).

Transported includes the various operations associated with cargo transportation, such as loading, off-loading, handling, stowing, carrying, and conveying.

Trimming means any leveling of a cargo within a cargo hold or compartment, either partial or total.

Tripartite agreement means an agreement between the national administrations of the port of loading, the port of discharge, and the flag state of the vessel, on the conditions of carriage of a cargo.

Ventilation means exchange of air from outside to inside a cargo space and includes the following types:

(1) *Continuous ventilation* means ventilation that is operating at all times. Continuous ventilation may be either natural or mechanical;

(2) *Mechanical ventilation* means power-generated ventilation;

(3) *Natural ventilation* means ventilation that is not power-generated; and

(4) *Surface ventilation* means ventilation of the space above the cargo. Surface ventilation may be either natural or mechanical.

Vessel means a cargo ship or barge.

[75 FR 64591, Oct. 19, 2010, as amended by USCG–2013–0671, 78 FR 60154, Sept. 30, 2013]

§ 148.5 Alternative procedures.

(a) The Commandant (CG–ENG–5) may authorize the use of an alternative procedure, including exemptions to the IMSBC Code (incorporated by reference, see § 148.8), in place of any requirement of this part if it is demonstrated to the satisfaction of the Coast Guard that the requirement is impracticable or unnecessary and that an equivalent level of safety can be maintained.

(b) Each request for authorization of an alternative procedure must—

(1) Be in writing;

(2) Name the requirement for which the alternative is requested; and

(3) Contain a detailed explanation of—

(i) Why the requirement is impractical or unnecessary; and

(ii) How an equivalent level of safety will be maintained.

§ 148.7 OMB control numbers assigned under the Paperwork Reduction Act.

The information collection requirements in this part are approved by the Office of Management and Budget, and assigned OMB control number 1625–0025.

§ 148.8 Incorporation by reference.

(a) Certain material is incorporated by reference into this part with the approval of the Director of the Federal Register under 5 U.S.C. 552(a) and 1 CFR part 51. To enforce any edition other than that specified in this section, the Coast Guard must publish notice of change in the FEDERAL REGISTER and the material must be available to the public. All approved material is available for inspection at the National Archives and Records Administration (NARA). For information on the availability of this material at NARA, call 202–741–6030 or go to *http://www.archives.gov/federal_register/code_of_federal_regulations/ibr_locations.html.* Also, it is available for inspection at the Coast Guard Headquarters. Contact Commandant (CG–ENG–5), Attn: Hazardous Materials Division, U.S. Coast Guard Stop 7509, 2703 Martin Luther King Jr. Avenue SE., Washington, DC 20593–7509. The material is also available from the sources listed in paragraphs (b) and (c) of this section.

(b) International Maritime Organization (IMO), 4 Albert Embankment, London SE1 7SR, United Kingdom, +44 (0)20 7735 7611, *http://www.imo.org.*

(1) International Maritime Solid Bulk Cargoes Code and Supplement, 2009 edition ("IMSBC Code"), incorporation by reference, excluding supplemental materials, approved for §§ 148.3; 148.5(a); 148.15(d); 148.55(b); 148.205(b); 148.220(b) and (c); 148.240(h); 148.450(a), (d), and (g).

(2) [Reserved]

(c) United Nations Publications, 2 United Nations Plaza, Room DC2–853, Dept. C089, New York, NY 10017, (800) 253–9646, *http://unp.un.org.*

(1) Recommendations on the Transport of Dangerous Goods, Manual of Tests and Criteria, Fifth revised edition (2009) ("UN Manual of Tests and Criteria"), incorporation by reference approved for §§ 148.205(b); 148.220(b) and (c).

(2) [Reserved]

[75 FR 64591, Oct. 19, 2010, as amended by USCG–2013–0671, 78 FR 60154, Sept. 30, 2013]

§ 148.9 Right of appeal.

Any person directly affected by enforcement of this part by or on behalf of the Coast Guard may appeal the decision or action under Subpart 1.03 of this chapter.

§ 148.10 Permitted materials.

(a) A material listed in Table 148.10 of this section may be transported as a bulk solid cargo on a vessel if it is carried according to this part. A material that is not listed in Table 148.10 of this section, but which is hazardous or a Potentially Dangerous Material (PDM), requires a Special Permit under § 148.15 of this part to be transported on the navigable waters of the United States.

(b) For each listed material, Table 148.10 identifies the hazard class and gives the BCSN or directs the user to the preferred BCSN. In addition, the table lists specific hazardous or potentially dangerous characteristics associated with each material and specifies or references detailed special requirements in this part pertaining to the stowage or transport of specific bulk solid materials. The column descriptions for Table 148.10 are defined as follows:

(1) *Column 1: Bulk Solid Material Descriptions and Bulk Cargo Shipping Names (BCSN).* Column 1 lists the bulk solid material descriptions and the BCSNs of materials designated as hazardous or PDM. BCSNs are limited to those shown in Roman type. Trade names and additional descriptive text are shown in italics.

(2) *Column 2: I.D. Number.* Column 2 lists the identification number assigned to each BCSN associated with a hazardous material. Those preceded by the letters "UN" are associated with BCSNs considered appropriate for international voyages as well as domestic voyages. Those preceded by the letters "NA" are associated with BCSNs not recognized for international voyages, except to and from Canada.

(3) *Column 3: Hazard Class or Division.* Column 3 designates the hazard class or division, or PDM, as appropriate, corresponding to each BCSN.

(4) *Column 4: References.* Column 4 refers the user to the preferred BCSN corresponding to bulk solid material descriptions listed in Column 1.

(5) *Column 5: Hazardous or Potentially Dangerous Characteristics.* Column 5 specifies codes for hazardous or potentially dangerous characteristics applicable to specific hazardous materials or PDMs. Refer to § 148.11 of this part for the meaning of each code.

(6) *Column 6: Other Characteristics.* Column 6 contains other pertinent characteristics applicable to specific bulk solid materials listed in Column 1.

(7) *Column 7: Special Requirements.* Column 7 specifies the applicable sections of Part 148 of this chapter that contain detailed special requirements pertaining to stowage and/or transportation of specific bulk solid materials in this part. This column is completed in a manner which indicates that "§ 148." precedes the designated numerical entry.

(c) The following requirements apply to combinations of bulk solids carried at the same time and in the same compartment or hold:

Combinations of bulk solid materials	Requirements
(1) Material listed in Table 148.10 carried with any other non-hazardous bulk solid material.	Requirements specified in Table 148.10 for the listed material.
(2) Material carried under Special Permit with any non-hazardous bulk solid material.	Requirements specified in the Special Permit.
(3) Two or more materials listed in Table 148.10	Must apply for a Special Permit.

(d) An owner, agent, master, operator, or person in charge of a vessel or barge carrying materials listed in Table 148.10 of this section must follow the requirements contained in 46 CFR part 4 for providing notice and reporting of marine casualties and retaining voyage records.

TABLE 148.10—BULK SOLID HAZARDOUS MATERIALS TABLE

Bulk solid material descriptions and bulk cargo shipping names	I.D. No.	Hazard class or division	References	Hazardous or potentially dangerous characteristics (see § 148.11)	Other characteristics	Special requirements (§ 148.* * *)
(1)	(2)	(3)	(4)	(5)	(6)	(7)
Aluminum Ferrosilicon Powder.	UN1395	4.3, 6.1	....	2, 3	Fine powder or briquettes.	135, 255, 405(b), 407, 415(a) & (e), 420(b), 445
Aluminum Nitrate	UN1438	5.1	....	4	Colorless or white crystals.	140
Aluminum Silicon Powder, Uncoated.	UN1398	4.3	....	2, 3	....	135, 255, 405(b), 407, 415(a) & (e), 420(b), 445
Aluminum Smelting Byproducts or Aluminum Re-melting Byproducts.	UN3170	4.3	....	1, 2, 3	Includes aluminum dross, residues, spent cathodes, spent potliner, and skimmings.	135, 405(b), 420(b), 445
Ammonium Nitrate	UN1942	5.1	....	5, 27	....	140, 205, 405(a), 407, 410
Ammonium Nitrate Based Fertilizer.	UN2067	5.1	....	5, 27	....	140, 205, 405(a), 407, 410
Ammonium Nitrate Based Fertilizer.	UN2071	9	....	6	Nitrogen, Phosphate, or Potash.	140, 220, 405(a), 407
Barium Nitrate	UN1466	5.1, 6.1	....	4, 7	....	140
Brown Coal Briquettes	....	PDM	....	11, 12, 14, 25	....	155, 240, 405(b), 407, 415(b), 420(a), 445
Calcium fluoride	....	....	See Fluorospar.	....	.	
Calcium Nitrate	UN1454	5.1	....	4	White crystals or powder.	140, 227
Calcium Oxide	....	....	See Lime, Unslaked.	....	.	
Castor Beans	UN2969	9	....	10	Whole beans	150, 235
Charcoal	....	PDM	....	1, 11, 12	Screenings, briquettes.	155
Chili Saltpeter	....	....	See Sodium Nitrate.	....	.	
Chilean Natural Nitrate ...	....	....	See Sodium Nitrate.	....	.	
Coal	....	PDM	....	11, 12, 13, 14, 25	....	155, 240, 405(b), 407, 415(b), 420(a) & (c), 445, 450
Copra	UN1363	4.2	....	11, 12	Dry	130, 242
Direct reduced iron (A) with not more than 5% fines.	....	PDM	....	1, 2, 12	Hot-molded briquettes.	155, 250, 420(b)
Direct reduced iron (B) with not more than 5% fines.	....	PDM	....	1, 2, 12	Lumps, pellets, and cold-molded briquettes.	155, 245, 405(b), 407, 420(b), 445
Environmentally Hazardous Substances, Solid, n.o.s..	UN3077	9	Hazardous substances listed in 40 CFR part 302.	15	....	150, 270
Ferrophosphorous	....	PDM	....	2, 3	Including briquettes	155, 415(e), 445

§ 148.10

TABLE 148.10—BULK SOLID HAZARDOUS MATERIALS TABLE—Continued

Bulk solid material descriptions and bulk cargo shipping names	I.D. No.	Hazard class or division	References	Hazardous or potentially dangerous characteristics (see § 148.11)	Other characteristics	Special requirements (§ 148.* * *)
(1)	(2)	(3)	(4)	(5)	(6)	(7)
Ferrosilicon with *30–90%* silicon.	UN1408	4.3, 6.1	....	2, 3	....	135, 255, 405(b), 407, 415(a) & (e), 420(b), 445
Ferrosilicon *with 25%– 30% silicon or 90% or more silicon.*	....	PDM	....	....	....	155, 255, 405(b), 407, 415 (a) & (e), 420(b), 445
Ferrous Sulfate	....	....	See Environmentally Hazardous Substances, Solid, n.o.s.	....	.	
Ferrous Metal Borings, Shavings, Turnings, or Cuttings.	UN2793	4.2	....	11, 12	....	130, 260
Fish Meal Stabilized or Fish Scrap, Stabilized.	UN2216	9	....	11, 12	Ground and pelletized (mixture), anti-oxidant treated.	150, 265
Fluorospar	....	PDM	....	8, 24	....	155, 440(a), 450
Garbage Tankage	....	....	See Tankage.	....	.	
Iron Oxide, Spent or Iron Sponge, Spent.	UN1376	4.2	....	3, 11, 12, 14	....	130, 275, 415(c), (d) & (f), 445
Iron Swarf	....	....	See Ferrous Metal Borings, Shavings, Turnings, or Cuttings.	....		
Lead Nitrate	UN1469	5.1, 6.1	....	4, 7, 22, 26	....	140, 270
Lignite	....	....	See Brown Coal Briquettes.	....	.	
Lime, Unslaked	....	PDM	....	1	....	155, 230
Linted Cotton Seed *containing not more than 9% moisture and not more than 20.5% oil.*	....	PDM	....	11, 12	....	155
Magnesia, Unslaked	....	PDM	....	1	Lightburned magnesia, calcined magnesite.	155, 280
Magnesium Nitrate	UN1474	5.1	....	4	....	140
Metal Sulfide Concentrates.	....	PDM	....	8, 11, 12, 22, 24	Solid, finely divided sulfide concentrates of copper, iron, lead, nickel, zinc, or other metalliferous ores.	155, 285, 450
Peat Moss *with moisture oontent of more than 65% by weight.*	....	PDM	....	8, 12, 13, 14, 24	Fine to coarse fibrous structure.	155, 290, 450
Pencil Pitch	....	....	See Pitch Prill.	....	.	

§ 148.10

TABLE 148.10—BULK SOLID HAZARDOUS MATERIALS TABLE—Continued

Bulk solid material descriptions and bulk cargo shipping names	I.D. No.	Hazard class or division	References	Hazardous or potentially dangerous characteristics (see § 148.11)	Other characteristics	Special requirements (§ 148.* * *)
(1)	(2)	(3)	(4)	(5)	(6)	(7)
Petroleum Coke *calcined or uncalcined at >55 °C (131 °F)*.	....	PDM	....	11	....	155, 295
Pitch Prill	....	PDM	....	14, 16	....	155
Potassium Nitrate	UN1486	5.1	....	4	....	140
Prilled Coal Tar	....	....	*See* Pitch Prill.	....	.	
Pyrites, Calcined	....	PDM	....	8, 9, 24	Fly ash	155, 225, 450
Pyritic ash	....	....	*See* Pyrites, Calcined.	....	.	
Quicklime	....	....	*See* Lime, Unslaked.	....	.	
Radioactive Material	UN2912	7	....	17	Low specific activity	145, 300
Radioactive Material	UN2913	7	....	17	Surface contaminated objects.	145, 300
Rough Ammonia Tankage.	....	....	*See* Tankage.	....	.	
Saltpeter	....	....	*See* Potassium Nitrate.	....	.	
Sawdust	....	PDM	....	12, 18	....	155, 405(a), 407
Seed Cake	UN1386	4.2	....	12, 19	Mechanically expelled or solvent extractions.	130, 310
Seed Cake	UN2217	4.2	....	12, 19	Solvent extractions	130, 310
Silicomanganese *with silicon content of 25% or more*.	....	PDM	....	2, 3, 12	With known hazard profile or known to evolve gases.	155, 405(b), 407, 415(a) & (d), 420(b), 445
Sodium Nitrate	UN1498	5.1	....	4	....	140
Sodium Nitrate and Potassium Nitrate Mixture.	UN1499	5.1	....	4	Mixtures prepared as fertilizer.	140
Steel Swarf	....	....	*See* Ferrous Metal Borings, Shavings, Turnings, or Cuttings.	....	.	
Sulfur	UN1350	4.1	....	14, 20	Lumps or coarse-grained powder.	125, 315, 405(a), 407, 435
Sulfur	NA1350	9	....	14, 20	Not subject to the requirements of this subchapter when formed into specific shapes (i.e., prills, granules, pellets, pastiles, or flakes).	125, 315, 405(a), 407, 435
Tankage	....	PDM	....	11	....	155, 320
Tankage Fertilizer	....	....	*See* Tankage.	....	.	
Vanadium Ore	....	PDM	....	21	....	155
Wood chips, Wood Pellets, Wood Pulp Pellets.	....	PDM	....	12	....	155, 325
Zinc Ashes	UN1435	4.3	....	2, 3, 23	Includes zinc dross, residues, and skimmings.	135, 330, 405(b), 407, 420(b), 435, 445

§ 148.11 Hazardous or potentially dangerous characteristics.

(a) General. When Column 5 refers to a code for a hazardous material or PDM, the meaning of that code is set forth in this section.

(b) Table of Hazardous or Potentially Dangerous Characteristics.

Code	Hazardous or potentially dangerous characteristic
1	Contact with water may cause heating.
2	Contact with water may cause evolution of flammable gases, which may form explosive mixtures with air.
3	Contact with water may cause evolution of toxic gases.
4	If involved in a fire, will greatly intensify the burning of combustible materials.
5	A major fire aboard a vessel carrying this material may involve a risk of explosion in the event of contamination (e.g., by a fuel oil) or strong confinement. If heated strongly will decompose, giving off toxic gases that support combustion.
6	These mixtures may be subject to self-sustaining decomposition if heated. Decomposition, once initiated, may spread throughout the remainder, producing gases that are toxic.
7	Toxic if swallowed and by dust inhalation.
8	Harmful and irritating by dust inhalation.
9	Highly corrosive to steel.
10	Powerful allergen. Toxic by ingestion. Skin contact or inhalation of dust may cause severe irritation of skin, eyes, and mucous membranes in some people.
11	May be susceptible to spontaneous heating and ignition.
12	Liable to cause oxygen depletion in the cargo space.
13	Liable to emit methane gas which can form explosive mixtures with air.
14	Dust forms explosive mixtures with air.
15	May present substantial danger to the public health or welfare or the environment when released into the environment. Skin contact and dust inhalation should be avoided.
16	Combustible. Burns with dense black smoke. Dust may cause skin and eye irritation.
17	Radiation hazard from dust inhalation and contact with mucous membranes.
18	Susceptible to fire from sparks and open flames.
19	May self-heat slowly and, if wet or containing an excessive proportion of unoxidized oil, ignite spontaneously.
20	Fire may produce irritating or poisonous gases.
21	Dust may contain toxic constituents.
22	Lead nitrate and lead sulfide are hazardous substances; see code 15 of this table and § 148.270.
23	Hazardous substance when consisting of pieces having a diameter less than 100 micrometers (0.004 in.); see code 15 of this table and § 148.270.
24	Cargo subject to liquefaction.
25	Subject to liquefaction if average particle size of cargo is less than 10 mm (.394 in.).
26	This entry is considered a Marine Pollutant in accordance with 49 CFR 172.101 Appendix B.
27	This entry is considered a certain dangerous cargo in accordance with 33 CFR 160.204.

§ 148.12 Assignment and certification.

(a) The National Cargo Bureau is authorized to assist the Coast Guard in administering the provisions of this part by—

(1) Inspecting vessels for suitability for loading solid materials in bulk;

(2) Examining stowage of solid materials loaded in bulk on board vessels;

(3) Making recommendations on stowage requirements applicable to the transportation of solid materials in bulk; and

(4) Issuing certificates of loading that verify stowage of the solid material in bulk meets requirements of this part.

(b) Certificates of loading from the National Cargo Bureau are accepted as evidence of compliance with bulk solid transport regulations.

Subpart B—Special Permits

§ 148.15 Petition for a special permit.

(a) Each shipper who wishes to ship a bulk solid material not listed in Table 148.10 of this part must determine whether the material meets the definition of any hazard class, or the definition of a PDM, as those terms are defined in § 148.3 of this part.

(b) If the material meets any of the definitions described in paragraph (a) of this section, the shipper then must submit a petition in writing to the Commandant (CG–ENG–5) for authorization to ship any hazardous material or PDM not listed in Table 148.10 of this part.

(c) If the Commandant (CG–ENG–5) approves a petition for authorization, the Commandant (CG–ENG–5) issues the petitioner a Coast Guard special permit. The permit allows the material to be transported in bulk by vessel and outlines requirements for this transport.

(d) A tripartite agreement developed in conjunction with the United States and in accordance with the IMSBC Code (incorporated by reference, see §148.8) may be used in lieu of a special permit.

§148.20 Deadlines for submission of petition and related requests.

(a) A petition for a special permit must be submitted at least 45 days before the requested effective date. Requests for extension or renewal of an existing special permit must be submitted 20 days before the date of expiration.

(b) Requests for extension or renewal must include the information required under §148.21(a), (f), and (g) of this part.

§148.21 Necessary information.

Each petition for a special permit must contain at least the following:

(a) A description of the material, including, if a hazardous material—

(1) The proper shipping name from the table in 49 CFR 172.101;

(2) The hazard class and division of the material; and

(3) The identification number of the material.

(b) A material safety data sheet (MSDS) for the material or—

(1) The chemical name and any trade names or common names of the material;

(2) The composition of the material, including the weight percent of each constituent;

(3) Physical data, including color, odor, appearance, melting point, and solubility;

(4) Fire and explosion data, including auto-ignition temperature, any unusual fire or explosion hazards, and any special fire fighting procedures;

(5) Health hazards, including any dust inhalation hazards and any chronic health effects;

(6) The threshold limit value (TLV) of the material or its major constituents, if available, and any relevant toxicity data;

(7) Reactivity data, including any hazardous decomposition products and any incompatible materials; and

(8) Special protection information, including ventilation requirements and personal protection equipment required.

(c) Other potentially dangerous characteristics of the material not covered by paragraph (b) of this section, including—

(1) Self-heating;

(2) Depletion of oxygen in the cargo space;

(3) Dust explosion; and

(4) Liquefaction.

(d) A detailed description of the proposed transportation operation, including—

(1) The type of vessel proposed for water movements;

(2) The expected loading and discharge ports, if known;

(3) Procedures to be used for loading and unloading the material;

(4) Precautions to be taken when handling the material; and

(5) The expected temperature of the material at the time it will be loaded on the vessel.

(e) Test results (if required under Subpart E of this part).

(f) Previous approvals or permits.

(g) Any relevant shipping or accident experience (or any other relevant transportation history by any mode of transport).

§148.25 Activities covered by a special permit.

(a) Each special permit covers any shipment of the permitted material by the shipper and also covers for each shipment—

(1) Each transfer operation;

(2) Each vessel involved in the shipment; and

(3) Each individual involved in any cargo handling operation.

(b) Each special permit is valid for a period determined by the Commandant (CG–ENG–5) and specified in the special permit. The period will not exceed 4 years and is subject to suspension or revocation before its expiration date.

§148.26 Standard conditions for special permits.

(a) Each special permit holder must comply with all the requirements of this part unless specifically exempted by the terms of the special permit.

§ 148.30

(b) Each special permit holder must provide a copy of the special permit and the information required in § 148.60 of this part to the master or person in charge of each vessel carrying the material.

(c) The master of a vessel transporting a special permit material must ensure that a copy of the special permit is on board the vessel. The special permit must be kept with the dangerous cargo manifest if such a manifest is required by § 148.70 of this part.

(d) The person in charge of a barge transporting any special permit material must ensure that a copy of the special permit is on board the tug or towing vessel. When the barge is moored, the special permit must be kept on the barge with the shipping papers as prescribed in § 148.62 of this part.

§ 148.30 Records of special permits issued.

A list of all special permits issued, and copies of each, are available from the Commandant (CG–ENG–5).

Subpart C—Minimum Transportation Requirements

§ 148.50 Cargoes subject to this subpart.

The regulations in this subpart apply to each bulk shipment of—

(a) A material listed in Table 148.10 of this part; and

(b) Any solid material shipped under the terms of a Coast Guard special permit.

§ 148.51 Temperature readings.

When Subpart D of this part sets a temperature limit for loading or transporting a material, apply the following rules:

(a) The temperature of the material must be measured 20 to 36 centimeters (8 to 14 inches) below the surface at 3 meter (10 foot) intervals over the length and width of the stockpile or cargo hold.

(b) The temperature must be measured at every spot in the stockpile or cargo hold that shows evidence of heating.

(c) Before loading or transporting the material, all temperatures measured must be below the temperature limit set in Subpart D of this part.

§ 148.55 International shipments.

(a) *Importer's responsibility.* Each person importing any bulk solid material requiring special handling into the United States must provide the shipper and the forwarding agent at the place of entry into the United States with timely and complete information as to the requirements of this part that will apply to the shipment of the material within the United States.

(b) *IMSBC Code.* Notwithstanding the provisions of this part, a bulk solid material that is classed, described, stowed, and segregated in accordance with the IMSBC Code (incorporated by reference, see § 148.8), and otherwise conforms to the requirements of this section, may be offered and accepted for transportation and transported within the United States. The following conditions and limitations apply:

(1) A bulk solid material that is listed in Table 148.10 of this part, but is not subject to the requirements of the IMSBC Code, may not be transported under the provisions of this section and is subject to the requirements of this part. Examples of such materials include environmentally hazardous substances, solid, n.o.s.

(2) Zinc Ashes must conform to the requirements found in § 148.330 of this part.

(3) Exemptions granted by other competent authorities in accordance with the IMSBC Code must be approved by the Commandant (CG–ENG–5) in accordance with § 148.5 of this part.

(4) Tripartite agreements granted by other competent authorities in accordance with the IMSBC Code must be authorized for use in the United States by the Commandant (CG–ENG–5).

§ 148.60 Shipping papers.

The shipper of a material listed in Table 148.10 of this part must provide the master or his representative with appropriate information on the cargo in the form of a shipping paper, in English, prior to loading. Information on the shipping paper must include the following:

(a) The appropriate BCSN. Secondary names may be used in addition to the BCSN;
(b) The identification number, if applicable;
(c) The hazard class of the material as listed in Table 148.10 of this part or on the Special Permit for the material;
(d) The total quantity of the material to be transported;
(e) The stowage factor;
(f) The need for trimming and the trimming procedures, as necessary;
(g) The likelihood of shifting, including angle of repose, if applicable;
(h) A certificate on the moisture content of the cargo and its transportable moisture limit for cargoes that are subject to liquefaction;
(i) Likelihood of formation of a wet base;
(j) Toxic or flammable gases that may be generated by the cargo, if applicable;
(k) Flammability, toxicity, corrosiveness, and propensity to oxygen depletion of the cargo, if applicable;
(l) Self-heating properties of the cargo, if applicable;
(m) Properties on emission of flammable gases in contact with water, if applicable;
(n) Radioactive properties, if applicable;
(o) The name and address of the U.S. shipper (consignor) or, if the shipment originates in a foreign country, the U.S. consignee.
(p) A certification, signed by the shipper, that bears the following statement: "This is to certify that the above named material is properly named, prepared, and otherwise in proper condition for bulk shipment by vessel in accordance with the applicable regulations of the U.S. Coast Guard."

§ 148.61 Emergency response information.

The shipper of a material listed in Table 148.10 of this part must provide the master or his representative with appropriate emergency response information. This information may be included on the shipping papers or in a separate document such as a material safety data sheet (MSDS). The information must include preliminary first aid measures and emergency procedures to be carried out in the event of an incident or fire involving the cargo.

§ 148.62 Location of shipping papers and emergency response information.

(a) The shipping paper and emergency response information required by §§ 148.60 and 148.61 of this part must be kept on board the vessel along with the dangerous cargo manifest required by § 148.70 of this part. When the shipment is by unmanned barge the shipping papers and emergency response information must be kept on the tug or towing vessel. When an unmanned barge is moored, the shipping paper and emergency response information must be on board the barge in a readily retrievable location.

(b) Any written certification or statement from the shipper to the master of a vessel or to the person in charge of a barge must be on, or attached to, the shipping paper. See Subparts E and F of this part for required certifications.

§ 148.70 Dangerous cargo manifest; general.

(a) Except as provided in paragraph (b) of this section and in § 148.72 of this part, each vessel transporting materials listed in Table 148.10 of this part must have a dangerous cargo manifest on board.

(b) This document must be kept in a designated holder on or near the vessel's bridge. When required for an unmanned barge, the document must be on board the tug or towing vessel.

§ 148.71 Information included in the dangerous cargo manifest.

The dangerous cargo manifest must include the following:
(a) The name and official number of the vessel. If the vessel has no official number, the international radio call sign must be substituted;
(b) The nationality of the vessel;
(c) The name of the material as listed in Table 148.10 of this part;
(d) The hold or cargo compartment in which the material is being transported;

§ 148.72

(e) The quantity of material loaded in each hold or cargo compartment; and

(f) The signature of the master acknowledging that the manifest is correct, and the date of the signature.

§ 148.72 Dangerous cargo manifest; exceptions.

(a) No dangerous cargo manifest is required for—

(1) Shipments by unmanned barge, except on an international voyage; and

(2) Shipments of materials designated as potentially dangerous materials in Table 148.10 of this part.

(b) When a dangerous cargo manifest is required for an unmanned barge on an international voyage, § 148.71(d) of this part does not apply, unless the barge has more than one cargo compartment.

§ 148.80 Supervision of cargo transfer.

The master must ensure that cargo transfer operations are supervised by a responsible person as defined in § 148.3 of this part.

§ 148.85 Required equipment for confined spaces.

When transporting a material that is listed in Table 148.10 of this part, each vessel, other than an unmanned barge, must have on board the following:

(a) Equipment capable of measuring atmospheric oxygen. At least two members of the crew must be knowledgeable in the use of the equipment, which must be maintained in a condition ready for use and calibrated according to the manufacturer's instructions.

(b) At least two self-contained, pressure-demand-type, air breathing apparatus approved by the Mine Safety and Health Administration (MSHA) or the National Institute for Occupational Safety and Health (NIOSH), each having at least a 30-minute air supply. Each foreign flag vessel must have on board at least two such apparatus that are approved by the flag state administration. The master must ensure that the breathing apparatus is used only by persons trained in its use.

§ 148.86 Confined space entry.

(a) Except in an emergency, no person may enter a confined space unless that space has been tested to ensure there is sufficient oxygen to support life. If the oxygen content is below 19.5 percent, the space must be ventilated and retested before entry.

(b) In an emergency, a confined space may be entered by a trained person wearing self-contained breathing apparatus, suitable protective clothing as necessary, and a wire rope safety line tended by a trained person outside the hold or in an adjacent space. Emergency entry into a confined space must be supervised by a responsible person as defined in § 148.3 of this part.

§ 148.90 Preparations before loading.

Before loading any material listed in Table 148.10 of this part, in bulk on board a vessel, the following conditions must be met:

(a) If a hold previously has contained any material required under Subpart D of this part to be segregated from the material to be loaded, the hold must be thoroughly cleaned of all residue of the previous cargoes.

(b) If the material to be loaded is Class 4.1, 4.2, or 5.1, then all combustible materials must be removed from the hold. Examples of some combustible materials are residue of previous cargoes, loose debris, and dunnage. Permanent wooden battens or sheathing may remain in the hold unless forbidden by Subpart E of this part.

(c) If the material to be loaded is classified as Class 4.3, or is subject to liquefaction, the hold and associated bilge must be as dry as practicable.

§ 148.100 Log book entries.

During the transport in bulk of a material listed in Table 148.10 of this part, the master must keep a record of each temperature measurement and each test for toxic or flammable gases required by this part. The date and time of each measurement and test must be recorded in the vessel's log.

§ 148.110 Procedures followed after unloading.

(a) After a material covered by this part has been unloaded from a vessel, each hold or cargo compartment must be thoroughly cleaned of all residue of such material unless the hold is to be reloaded with that same cargo.

(b) When on U.S. territorial seas or inland waters, cargo associated wastes, cargo residue, and deck sweepings must be retained on the vessel and disposed of in accordance with 33 CFR parts 151.51 through 151.77.

§ 148.115 Report of incidents.

(a) When a fire or other hazardous condition occurs on a vessel transporting a material covered by this part, the master must notify the nearest Captain of the Port as soon as possible and comply with any instructions given.

(b) Any incident or casualty occurring while transporting a material covered by this part must also be reported as required under 49 CFR 171.15, if applicable. A copy of the written report required under 49 CFR 171.16 must also be sent to the Commandant (CG–ENG–5), Attn: Hazardous Materials Division, U.S. Coast Guard Stop 7509, 2703 Martin Luther King Jr. Avenue SE., Washington, DC 20593–7509, at the earliest practicable moment.

(c) Any release to the environment of a hazardous substance in a quantity equal to or in excess of its reportable quantity (RQ) must be reported immediately to the National Response Center at 800–424–8802 (toll free) or 202–267–2675; or online at *www.nrc.uscg.mil.*.

[75 FR 64591, Oct. 19, 2010, as amended by USCG–2013–0671, 78 FR 60154, Sept. 30, 2013]

Subpart D—Stowage and Segregation

§ 148.120 Stowage and segregation requirements.

(a) Each material listed in Table 148.10 of this part must be segregated from incompatible materials in accordance with—

(1) The requirements of Tables 148.120A and 148.120B of this section that pertain to the primary or subsidiary hazard class to which the materials belong. Whenever a subsidiary hazard may exist, the most stringent segregation requirement applies; and

(2) Any specific requirements in Subpart D of this part.

(b) Materials that are required to be separated during stowage must not be handled at the same time. Any residue from a material must be removed before a material required to be separated from it is loaded.

(c) Definitions and application of segregation terms:

(1) *"Separated from"* means located in different cargo compartments or holds when stowed under deck. If the intervening deck is resistant to fire and liquid, a vertical separation, i.e., in different cargo compartments, is acceptable as equivalent to this segregation.

(2) *"Separated by a complete cargo compartment or hold from"* means either a vertical or horizontal separation, for example, by a complete cargo compartment or hold. If the intervening decks are not resistant to fire and liquid, only horizontal separation is acceptable.

(3) *"Separated longitudinally by an intervening complete cargo compartment or hold from"* means that vertical separation alone does not meet this requirement.

TABLE 148.120A—SEGREGATION BETWEEN INCOMPATIBLE BULK SOLID CARGOES

Bulk solid materials	Class	4.1	4.2	4.3	5.1	6.1	7	8	9/PDM
Flammable solid	4.1	X							
Spontaneously combustible material	4.2	2	X						
Dangerous when wet material	4.3	3	3	X					
Oxidizer	5.1	3	3	3	X				
Poisonous material	6.1	X	X	X	2	X			
Radioactive material	7	2	2	2	2	2	X		
Corrosive material	8	2	2	2	2	X	X	X	
Miscellaneous hazardous material and potential dangerous material	9/PDM	X	X	X	X	X	2	X	X

Numbers and symbols indicate the following terms as defined in § 148.3 of this part:
2—"Separated from".

§ 148.125

3—"Separated by a complete hold or compartment from".
X—No segregation required, except as specified in an applicable section of this subpart or Subpart E of this part.

TABLE 148.120B—SEGREGATION BETWEEN BULK SOLID CARGOES AND INCOMPATIBLE PACKAGED CARGOES

Packaged hazardous material	Bulk solid material							
	Class	4.1	4.2	4.3	5.1	6.1	7	8	9/PDM
Explosives	1.1	4	4	4	4	2	2	4	X
	1.2								
	1.5								
Explosives	1.3	3	3	4	4	2	2	2	X
	1.6								
Explosives	1.4	2	2	2	2	X	2	2	X
Flammable gas	2.1	2	2	1	2	X	2	2	X
Non-flammable compressed gas	2.2	2	2	X	X	X	2	1	X
Poisonous gas	2.3	2	2	X	X	X	2	1	X
Flammable liquid	3	2	2	2	2	X	2	1	X
Flammable solid	4.1	X	1	X	1	X	2	1	X
Spontaneously combustible material	4.2	1	X	1	2	1	2	1	X
Dangerous when wet material	4.3	X	1	X	2	X	2	1	X
Oxidizer	5.1	1	2	2	X	1	1	2	X
Organic peroxide	5.2	2	2	2	2	1	2	2	X
Poisonous material	6.1	X	1	X	1	X	X	X	X
Infectious substance	6.2	3	3	2	3	1	3	3	X
Radioactive material	7	2	2	2	1	X	X	2	X
Corrosive material	8	1	1	1	2	X	2	X	X
Miscellaneous hazardous material	9	X	X	X	X	X	X	X	X

Numbers and symbols indicate the following terms as defined in § 148.3 of this part:
1—"Away from".
2—"Separated from".
3—"Separated by a complete hold or compartment from".
4—"Separated longitudinally by an intervening complete compartment or hold from".
X—No segregation required, except as specified in an applicable section of this subpart or Subpart E of this part.

§ 148.125 Stowage and segregation for materials of Class 4.1.

(a) Class 4.1 materials listed in Table 148.10 of this part must—

(1) Be kept as cool and dry as practical before loading;

(2) Not be loaded or transferred between vessels during periods of rain or snow;

(3) Be stowed separated from foodstuffs; and

(4) Be stowed clear of sources of heat and ignition and protected from sparks and open flame.

(b) Bulkheads between a hold containing a Class 4.1 material and incompatible materials must have cable and conduit penetrations sealed against the passage of gas and vapor.

§ 148.130 Stowage and segregation for materials of Class 4.2.

(a) Class 4.2 materials listed in Table 148.10 of this part must—

(1) Be kept as cool and dry as practical before loading;

(2) Not be loaded or transferred between vessels during periods of rain or snow;

(3) Be stowed clear of sources of heat and ignition and protected from sparks and open flame; and

(4) Except for copra and seed cake, be stowed separate from foodstuffs.

(b) The bulkhead between a hold containing a Class 4.2 material and a hold containing a material not permitted to mix with Class 4.2 materials must have cable and conduit penetrations sealed against the passage of gas and vapor.

§ 148.135 Stowage and segregation for materials of Class 4.3.

(a) Class 4.3 materials listed in Table 148.10 of this part which, in contact with water, emit flammable gases, must—

(1) Be kept as cool and dry as practical before loading;

(2) Not be loaded or transferred between vessels during periods of rain or snow;

(3) Be stowed separate from foodstuffs and all Class 8 liquids; and

(4) Be stowed in a mechanically ventilated hold. Exhaust gases must not penetrate into accommodation, work or control spaces. Unmanned barges

that have adequate natural ventilation need not have mechanical ventilation.

(b) The bulkhead between a hold containing a Class 4.3 material and incompatible materials must have cable and conduit penetrations sealed against the passage of gas and vapor.

§ 148.140 Stowage and segregation for materials of Class 5.1.

(a) Class 5.1 materials listed in Table 148.10 of this part must—

(1) Be kept as cool and dry as practical before loading;

(2) Be stowed away from all sources of heat or ignition; and

(3) Be stowed separate from foodstuffs and all readily combustible materials.

(b) Special care must be taken to ensure that holds containing Class 5.1 materials are clean and, whenever practical, only noncombustible securing and protecting materials are used.

(c) Class 5.1 materials must be prevented from entering bilges or other cargo holds.

§ 148.145 Stowage and segregation for materials of Class 7.

(a) Class 7 material listed in Table 148.10 of this part must be stowed—

(1) Separate from foodstuffs; and

(2) In a hold or barge closed or covered to prevent dispersal of the material during transportation.

(b) [Reserved]

§ 148.150 Stowage and segregation for materials of Class 9.

(a) A bulk solid cargo of Class 9 material (miscellaneous hazardous material) listed in Table 148.10 of this part must be stowed and segregated as required by this section.

(b) Ammonium nitrate fertilizer of Class 9 must be segregated as required for Class 5.1 materials in §§ 148.120 and 148.140 of this part and must be stowed—

(1) Separated by a complete hold or compartment from readily combustible materials, chlorates, hypochlorites, nitrites, permanganates, and fibrous materials (*e.g.*, cotton, jute, sisal, *etc.*);

(2) Clear of all sources of heat, including insulated piping; and

(3) Out of direct contact with metal engine-room boundaries.

(c) Castor beans must be stowed separate from foodstuffs and Class 5.1 materials.

(d) Fish meal must be stowed and segregated as required for Class 4.2 materials in §§ 148.120 and 148.130 of this part. In addition, its temperature at loading must not exceed 35 °C (95 °F), or 5 °C (9 °F) above ambient temperature, whichever is higher.

(e) Sulfur must be stowed and segregated as required under §§ 148.120 and 148.125 of this part for a material of Class 4.1.

§ 148.155 Stowage and segregation for potentially dangerous materials.

(a) A PDM must be stowed and segregated according to the requirements of this section and Table 148.155 of this section.

(b) When transporting coal—

(1) Coal must be stowed separate from materials of Class/division 1.4 and Classes 2, 3, 4, and 5 in packaged form; and separated from bulk solid materials of Classes 4 and 5.1;

(2) No material of Class 5.1, in either packaged or bulk solid form, may be stowed above or below a cargo of coal; and

(3) Coal must be separated longitudinally by an intervening complete cargo compartment or hold from materials of Class 1 other than Class/division 1.4.

(c) When transporting direct reduced iron (DRI)—

(1) DRI lumps, pellets, or cold-molded briquettes, and DRI hot-molded briquettes, must be separated from materials of Class/division 1.4, Classes 2, 3, 4, 5, Class 8 acids in packaged form, and bulk solid materials of Classes 4 and 5.1; and

(2) No material of Class 1, other than Class/division 1.4, may be transported on the same vessel with DRI.

(d) Petroleum coke, calcined or uncalcined, must be—

(1) Separated longitudinally by an intervening complete cargo compartment or hold from materials of Class/divisions 1.1 and 1.5; and

(2) Separated by a complete cargo compartment or hold from all hazardous materials and other potentially dangerous materials in packaged and bulk solid form.

§ 148.200

TABLE 148.155—STOWAGE AND SEGREGATION REQUIREMENTS FOR POTENTIALLY DANGEROUS MATERIAL

Potentially dangerous material	Segregate as for class listed [1]	"Separate from" foodstuffs	Load only under dry weather conditions	Keep dry	Mechanical ventilation required	"Separate from" material listed	Special provisions
Aluminum Smelting Byproducts or Aluminum Remelting Byproducts.	4.3	X	X	X	X	Class 8 liquids	
Brown Coal Briquettes.						See paragraph (b) of this section.	See paragraph (b) of this section.
Charcoal	4.1			X		Oily materials	
Coal						See paragraph (b) of this section.	See paragraph (b) of this section.
Direct reduced iron (A).						See paragraph (c) of this section.	See paragraph (c) of this section.
Direct reduced iron (B).						See paragraph (c) of this section.	See paragraph (c) of this section.
Ferrophosphorus.	4.3	X	X	X	X	Class 8 liquids	
Ferrolilicon	4.3	X	X	X	X	Class 8 liquids	
Fluorospar		X				Class 8 liquids	
Lime, Unslaked				X		All packaged and bulk solid hazardous materials.	
Linted Cotton Seed.				X			
Magnesia, Unslaked.						All packaged and bulk solid hazardous materials.	
Metal Sulfide Concentrates.	4.2	X				Class 8 liquids	
Petroleum Coke		X					See section 148.155(d).
Pitch Prill	4.1						
Pyrites, Calcined.		X	X	X	X		
Sawdust	4.1			X		All Class 5.1 and 8 liquids.	
Silicomanganese.	4.3	X	X	X	X	Class 8 liquids	
Tankage	4.2	X	X				
Vanadium	6.1	X					
Wood chips	4.1						
Wood pellets	4.1						
Wood pulp pellets.	4.1						

[1] See Tables 148.120A and B.

Subpart E—Special Requirements for Certain Materials

§ 148.200 Purpose.

This subpart prescribes special requirements for specific materials. These requirements are in addition to the minimum transportation requirements in Subpart C of this part that are applicable to all materials listed in Table 148.10 of this part.

§ 148.205 Ammonium nitrate and ammonium nitrate fertilizers.

(a) This section applies to the stowage and transportation in bulk of ammonium nitrate and the following fertilizers composed of uniform, non-segregating mixtures containing ammonium nitrate:

(1) Ammonium nitrate containing added organic matter that is chemically inert towards the ammonium nitrate; containing at least 90 percent ammonium nitrate and a maximum of 0.2 percent of combustible material (including organic material calculated as carbon); or containing less than 90 percent but more than 70 percent of ammonium nitrate and a maximum of 0.4 percent combustible material;

(2) Ammonium nitrate with calcium carbonate and/or dolomite, containing more than 80 percent but less than 90 percent of ammonium nitrate and a maximum of 0.4 percent of total combustible material;

(3) Ammonium nitrate with ammonium sulfate containing more than 45 percent but a maximum of 70 percent of ammonium nitrate and containing a maximum of 0.4 percent of combustible material; and

(4) Nitrogen phosphate or nitrogen/potash type fertilizers or complete nitrogen/phosphate/potash type fertilizers containing more than 70 percent but less than 90 percent of ammonium nitrate and a maximum of 0.4 percent of combustible material.

(b) No material covered by this section may be transported in bulk unless it demonstrates resistance to detonation when tested by one of the following methods:

(1) Appendix 2, Section 5, of the IMSBC Code (incorporated by reference, see § 148.8);

(2) Test series 1 and 2 of the Class 1 (explosive) in the UN Manual of Tests and Criteria, Part I (incorporated by reference, see § 148.8); or

(3) An equivalent test satisfactory to the Administration of the country of shipment.

(c) Before loading a material covered by this section—

(1) The shipper must give the master of the vessel written certification that the material has met the test requirements of paragraph (b) of this section;

(2) The cargo hold must be inspected for cleanliness and free from readily combustible materials;

(3) Each cargo hatch must be weathertight as defined in § 42.13–10 of this chapter;

(4) The temperature of the material must be less than 55 °C (131 °F); and

(5) Each fuel tank under a cargo hold where the material is stowed must be pressure tested before loading to ensure that there is no leakage of manholes or piping systems leading through the cargo hold.

(d) Bunkering or transferring of fuel to or from the vessel may not be performed during cargo loading and unloading operations involving a material covered by this section.

(e) When a material covered by this section is transported on a cargo vessel—

(1) No other material may be stowed in the same hold with that material;

(2) In addition to the segregation requirements in § 148.140 of this part, the material must be separated by a complete cargo compartment or hold from readily combustible materials, chlorates, chlorides, chlorites, hypochlorites, nitrites, permanganates, and fibrous materials; and

(3) The bulkhead between a cargo hold containing a material covered by this section and the engine room must be insulated to "A–60" class division or an equivalent arrangement to the satisfaction of the cognizant Coast Guard Captain of the Port or the Administration of the country of shipment.

§ 148.220 Ammonium nitrate-phosphate fertilizers.

(a) This section applies to the stowage and transportation of uniform, nonsegregating mixtures of nitrogen/phosphate or nitrogen/potash type fertilizers, or complete fertilizers of nitrogen/phosphate/potash type containing a maximum of 70 percent of ammonium nitrate and containing a maximum of 0.4 percent total added combustible material or containing a maximum of 45 percent ammonium nitrate with unrestricted combustible material.

(b) A fertilizer mixture described in paragraph (a) of this section is exempt if—

§ 148.225

(1) When tested in accordance with the trough test prescribed in Appendix 2, Section 4, of the IMSBC Code or in the UN Manual of Tests and Criteria, Part III, Subsection 38.2 (incorporated by reference, see § 148.8), it is found to be free from the risk of self-sustaining decomposition.

(2) [Reserved]

(c) No fertilizer covered by this section may be transported in bulk if, when tested in accordance with the trough test prescribed in Appendix 2, Section 4, of the IMSBC Code or in the UN Manual of Tests and Criteria, Part III, Subsection 38.2 (incorporated by reference, see § 148.8), it has a self-sustaining decomposition rate that is greater than 0.25 meters per hour, or is liable to self-heat sufficient to initiate decomposition.

(d) Fertilizers covered by this section must be stowed away from all sources of heat, and out of direct contact with a metal engine compartment boundary.

(e) Bunkering or transferring of fuel may not be performed during loading and unloading of fertilizer covered by this section.

(f) Fertilizer covered by this section must be segregated as prescribed in §§ 148.140 and 148.220(d) of this part.

§ 148.225 Calcined pyrites (pyritic ash, fly ash).

(a) This part does not apply to the shipment of calcined pyrites that are the residual ash of oil or coal fired power stations.

(b) This section applies to the stowage and transportation of calcined pyrites that are the residual product of sulfuric acid production or elemental metal recovery operations.

(c) Before loading calcined pyrites covered by this section—
(1) The cargo space must be as clean and dry as practical;
(2) The calcined pyrites must be dry; and
(3) Precautions must be taken to prevent the penetration of calcined pyrites into other cargo spaces, bilges, wells, and ceiling boards.

(d) After calcined pyrites covered by this section have been unloaded from a cargo space, the cargo space must be thoroughly cleaned. Cargo residues and sweepings must be disposed of as prescribed in 33 CFR parts 151.55 through 151.77.

§ 148.227 Calcium nitrate fertilizers.

This part does not apply to commercial grades of calcium nitrate fertilizers consisting mainly of a double salt (calcium nitrate and ammonium nitrate) and containing a maximum of 15.5 percent nitrogen and at least 12 percent of water.

§ 148.230 Calcium oxide (lime, unslaked).

(a) When transported by barge, unslaked lime (calcium oxide) must be carried in an unmanned, all steel, double-hulled barge equipped with weathertight hatches or covers. The barge must not carry any other cargo while unslaked lime is on board.

(b) The shipping paper requirements in § 148.60 of this part and the dangerous cargo manifest requirements in § 148.70 of this part do not apply to the transportation of unslaked lime under paragraph (a) of this section.

§ 148.235 Castor beans.

(a) This part applies only to the stowage and transportation of whole castor beans. Castor meal, castor pomace, and castor flakes may not be shipped in bulk.

(b) Persons handling castor beans must wear dust masks and goggles.

(c) Care must be taken to prevent castor bean dust from entering accommodation, control, or service spaces during cargo transfer operations.

§ 148.240 Coal.

(a) The electrical equipment in cargo holds carrying coal must meet the requirements of Subpart 111.105 of this chapter or an equivalent standard approved by the administration of the vessel's flag state.

(b) Before coal is loaded in a cargo hold, the bilges must be as clean and dry as practical. The hold must also be free of any readily combustible material, including the residue of previous cargoes if other than coal.

(c) The master of each vessel carrying coal must ensure that—
(1) All openings to the cargo hold, except for unloading gates on self-unloading vessels, are sealed before loading

the coal and, unless the coal is as described in paragraph (f) of this section, the hatches must also be sealed after loading;

(2) As far as practical, gases emitted by the coal do not accumulate in enclosed working spaces such as storerooms, shops, or passageways, and tunnel spaces on self-unloading vessels, and that such spaces are adequately ventilated;

(3) The vessel has adequate ventilation as required by paragraph (f) of this section; and

(4) If the temperature of the coal is to be monitored under paragraph (e)(2)(i) of this section, the vessel has instruments that are capable of measuring the temperature of the cargo in the range 0°–100 °C (32 °–212 °F) without entry into the cargo hold.

(d) A cargo hold containing coal must not be ventilated unless the conditions of paragraph (f) of this section are met, or unless methane is detected under paragraph (h) of this section.

(e) If coal waiting to be loaded has shown a tendency to self-heat, has been handled so that it may likely self-heat, or has been observed to be heating, the master is responsible for monitoring the temperature of the coal at several intervals during these times:

(1) Before loading; and

(2) During the voyage, by—

(i) Measuring the temperature of the coal;

(ii) Measuring the emission of carbon monoxide; or

(iii) Both.

(f) If coal waiting to be loaded has a potential to emit dangerous amounts of methane, for example it is freshly mined, or has a history of emitting dangerous amounts of methane, then:

(1) Surface ventilation, either natural or from fixed or portable non-sparking fans, must be provided; and

(2) The atmosphere above the coal must be monitored for the presence of methane as prescribed in paragraph (h) of this section. The results of this monitoring must be recorded at least twice in every 24-hour period, unless the conditions of paragraph (m) of this section are met.

(g) Electrical equipment and cables in a hold containing a coal described in paragraph (f) of this section must be either suitable for use in an explosive gas atmosphere or de-energized at a point outside the hold. Electrical equipment and cables necessary for continuous safe operations, such as lighting fixtures, must be suitable for use in an explosive gas atmosphere. The master of the vessel must ensure that the affected equipment and cables remain de-energized as long as this coal remains in the hold.

(h) For all coal loaded on a vessel, other than an unmanned barge, the atmosphere above the coal must be routinely tested for the presence of methane, carbon monoxide, and oxygen, following the procedures in the Appendices to the schedules for Coal and Brown Coal Briquettes as contained in the IMSBC Code (incorporated by reference, see § 148.8). This testing must be performed in such a way that the cargo hatches are not opened and entry into the hold is not necessary.

(i) When carrying a coal described in paragraph (e) of this section, the atmosphere above the coal must be monitored for the presence of carbon monoxide as prescribed in paragraph (h) of this section. The results of this monitoring must be recorded at least twice in every 24-hour period, unless the conditions of paragraph (m) of this section are met. If the level of carbon monoxide is increasing rapidly or reaches 20 percent of the lower flammability limit (LFL), the frequency of monitoring must be increased.

(j) When a cargo of coal has a potential to self-heat or has been observed to be heating, the hatches should be closed and sealed and all surface ventilation halted except as necessary to remove any methane that may have accumulated.

(k) If the level of carbon monoxide monitored under paragraph (i) of this section continues to increase rapidly or the temperature of coal carried on board a vessel exceeds 55 °C (131 °F) and is increasing rapidly, the master must notify the nearest Coast Guard Captain of the Port of—

(1) The name, nationality, and position of the vessel;

(2) The most recent temperature, if measured, and levels of carbon monoxide and methane;

§ 148.242

(3) The port where the coal was loaded and the destination of the coal;
(4) The last port of call of the vessel and its next port of call; and
(5) What action has been taken.

(l) If the level of methane as monitored under paragraph (h) of this section reaches 20 percent of the LFL or is increasing rapidly, ventilation of the cargo hold, under paragraph (f) of this section, must be initiated. If this ventilation is provided by opening the cargo hatches, care must be taken to avoid generating sparks.

(m) The frequency of monitoring required by paragraph (f) of this section may be reduced at the discretion of the master provided that—
(1) The level of gas measured is less than 20 percent of the LFL;
(2) The level of gas measured has remained steady or decreased over three consecutive readings, or has increased by less than 5 percent over four consecutive readings spanning at least 48 hours; and
(3) Monitoring continues at intervals sufficient to determine that the level of gas remains within the parameters of paragraphs (m)(1) and (m)(2) of this section.

§ 148.242 Copra.

Copra must have surface ventilation. It must not be stowed against heated surfaces including fuel oil tanks which may require heating.

§ 148.245 Direct reduced iron (DRI); lumps, pellets, and cold-molded briquettes.

(a) Before loading DRI lumps, pellets, or cold-molded briquettes—
(1) The master must have a written certification from a competent person appointed by the shipper and recognized by the Commandant (CG–ENG–5) stating that the DRI, at the time of loading, is suitable for shipment;
(2) The DRI must be aged for at least 3 days, or be treated with an air passivation technique or some other equivalent method that reduces its reactivity to at least the same level as the aged DRI; and
(3) Each hold and bilge must be as clean and dry as practical. Other than double bottom tanks, adjacent ballast tanks must be kept empty when possible. All wooden fixtures, such as battens, must be removed from the hold.

(b) Each boundary of a hold where DRI lumps, pellets, or cold-molded briquettes are to be carried must be resistant to fire and passage of water.

(c) DRI lumps, pellets, or cold-molded briquettes that are wet, or that are known to have been wetted, may not be accepted for transport. The moisture content of the DRI must not exceed 0.3 percent prior to loading.

(d) DRI lumps, pellets and cold-molded briquettes must be protected at all times from contact with water, and must not be loaded or transferred from one vessel to another during periods of rain or snow.

(e) DRI lumps, pellets, or cold-molded briquettes may not be loaded if their temperature is greater than 65 °C (150 °F).

(f) The shipper of DRI lumps, pellets, or cold-molded briquettes in bulk must ensure that an inert atmosphere of less than 5 percent oxygen and 1 percent hydrogen, by volume, is maintained throughout the voyage in any hold containing these materials.

(g) When DRI lumps, pellets, or cold-molded briquettes are loaded, precautions must be taken to avoid the concentration of fines (pieces less than 6.35mm in size) in any one location in the cargo hold.

(h) Radar and RDF scanners must be protected against the dust generated during cargo transfer operations of DRI lumps, pellets, or cold-molded briquettes.

§ 148.250 Direct reduced iron (DRI); hot-molded briquettes.

(a) Before loading DRI hot-molded briquettes—
(1) The master must have a written certification from a competent person appointed by the shipper and recognized by the Commandant (CG–ENG–5) that at the time of loading the DRI hot-molded briquettes are suitable for shipment; and
(2) Each hold and bilge must be as clean and dry as practical. Except double bottom tanks, adjacent ballast tanks must be kept empty where possible. All wooden fixtures, such as battens, must be removed.

(b) All boundaries of a hold must be resistant to fire and passage of water to carry DRI hot-molded briquettes.

(c) DRI hot-molded briquettes must be protected at all times from contact with water. They must not be loaded or transferred from one vessel to another during periods of rain or snow.

(d) DRI hot-molded briquettes may not be loaded if their temperature is greater than 65 °C (150 °F).

(e) When loading DRI hot-molded briquettes, precautions must be taken to avoid the concentration of fines (pieces less than 6.35mm in size) in any one location in the cargo hold.

(f) Adequate surface ventilation must be provided when carrying or loading DRI hot-molded briquettes.

(g) When DRI hot-molded briquettes are carried by unmanned barge—
(1) The barge must be fitted with vents adequate to provide natural ventilation; and
(2) The cargo hatches must be closed at all times after loading the DRI hot-molded briquettes.

(h) Radar and RDF scanners must be adequately protected against dust generated during cargo transfer operations of DRI hot-molded briquettes.

(i) During final discharge only, a fine spray of water may be used to control dust from DRI hot-molded briquettes.

§ 148.255 Ferrosilicon, aluminum ferrosilicon, and aluminum silicon containing more than 30% but less than 90% silicon.

(a) This section applies to the stowage and transportation of ferrosilicon, aluminum ferrosilicon, and aluminum silicon containing more than 30 percent but less than 90 percent silicon.

(b) The shipper of material described in paragraph (a) of this section must give the master a written certification stating that after manufacture the material was stored under cover, but exposed to the weather, in the particle size in which it is to be shipped, for at least three days before shipment.

(c) Material described in paragraph (a) of this section must be protected at all times from contact with water, and must not be loaded or unloaded during periods of rain or snow.

(d) Except as provided in paragraph (e) of this section, each hold containing material described in paragraph (a) of this section must be mechanically ventilated by at least two separate fans. The total ventilation must be at least five air changes per hour, based on the empty hold. Ventilation must not allow escaping gas to reach accommodation or work spaces, on or under deck.

(e) An unmanned barge which is provided with natural ventilation need not comply with paragraph (d) of this section.

(f) Each space adjacent to a hold containing material described in paragraph (a) of this section must be well ventilated with mechanical fans. No person may enter that space unless it has been tested to ensure that it is free from phosphine and arsine gases.

(g) Scuttles and windows in accommodation and work spaces adjacent to holds containing material described in paragraph (a) of this section must be kept closed while this material is being loaded and unloaded.

(h) Any bulkhead between a hold containing material described in paragraph (a) of this section and an accommodation or work space must be gas tight and adequately protected against damage from any unloading equipment.

(i) When a hold containing material described in paragraph (a) of this section is equipped with atmosphere sampling type smoke detectors with lines that terminate in accommodation or work spaces, those lines must be blanked off gas-tight.

(j) If a hold containing material described in paragraph (a) of this section must be entered at any time, the hatches must be open for two hours before entry to dissipate any accumulated gases. The atmosphere in the hold must be tested to ensure that there is no phosphine or arsine gas present.

(k) After unloading material described in paragraph (a) of this section, each cargo hold must be thoroughly cleaned and tested to ensure that no phosphine or arsine gas remains.

§ 148.260 Ferrous metal.

(a) This part does not apply to the stowage and transportation in bulk of stainless steel borings, shavings, turnings, or cuttings; nor does this part apply to an unmanned barge on a voyage entirely on the navigable waters of United States.

(b) Ferrous metal may not be stowed or transported in bulk unless the following conditions are met:

(1) All wooden sweat battens, dunnage, and debris must be removed from the hold before the ferrous metal is loaded;

(2) If weather is inclement during loading, hatches must be covered or otherwise protected to keep the material dry;

(3) During loading and transporting, the bilge of each hold in which ferrous metal is stowed or will be stowed must be kept as dry as practical;

(4) During loading, the ferrous metal must be compacted in the hold as frequently as practicable with a bulldozer or other means that provides equivalent surface compaction;

(5) No other material may be loaded in a hold containing ferrous metal unless—

(i) The material to be loaded in the same hold with the ferrous metal is not a material listed in Table 148.10 of this part or a readily combustible material;

(ii) The loading of the ferrous metal is completed first; and

(iii) The temperature of the ferrous metal in the hold is below 55 °C (131 °F) or has not increased in eight hours before the loading of the other material; and

(6) During loading, the temperature of the ferrous metal in the pile being loaded must be below 55 °C (131 °F).

(c) The master of a vessel that is loading or transporting a ferrous metal must ensure that the temperature of the ferrous metal is taken—

(1) Before loading;

(2) During loading, in each hold and pile being loaded, at least once every twenty-four hours and, if the temperature is rising, as often as is necessary to ensure that the requirements of this section are met; and

(3) After loading, in each hold, at least once every 24 hours.

(d) During loading, if the temperature of the ferrous metal in a hold is 93 °C (200 °F) or higher, the master must notify the Coast Guard Captain of the Port and suspend loading until the Captain of the Port is satisfied that the temperature of the ferrous metal is 88 °C (190 °F) or less.

(e) After loading ferrous metal—

(1) If the temperature of the ferrous metal in each hold is 65 °C (150 °F) or above, the master must notify the Coast Guard Captain of the Port, and the vessel must remain in the port area until the Captain of the Port is satisfied that the temperature of ferrous metal has shown a downward trend below 65 °C (150 °F) for at least eight hours after completion of loading of the hold; or

(2) If the temperature of the ferrous metal in each hold is less than 88 °C (190 °F) and has shown a downward trend for at least eight hours after the completion of loading, the master must notify the Coast Guard Captain of the Port, and the vessel must remain in the port area until the Captain of the Port confirms that the vessel is sailing directly to another port, no further than 12 hours sailing time, for the purpose of loading more ferrous metal in bulk or to completely off-load the ferrous metal.

(f) Except for shipments of ferrous metal in bulk which leave the port of loading under the conditions specified in paragraph (e)(2) of this section, if after the vessel leaves the port, the temperature of the ferrous metal in the hold rises above 65 °C (150 °F), the master must notify the nearest Coast Guard Captain of the Port as soon as possible of—

(1) The name, nationality, and position of the vessel;

(2) The most recent temperature taken;

(3) The length of time that the temperature has been above 65 °C (150 °F) and the rate of rise, if any;

(4) The port where the ferrous metal was loaded and the destination of the ferrous metal;

(5) The last port of call of the vessel and its next port of call;

(6) What action has been taken; and

(7) Whether any other cargo is endangered.

§ 148.265 Fish meal or fish scrap.

(a) This part does not apply to fish meal or fish scrap that contains less than 5 percent moisture by weight.

Coast Guard, DHS § 148.280

(b) Fish meal or fish scrap may contain a maximum of 12 percent moisture by weight and a maximum of 15 percent fat by weight.

(c) At the time of production, fish meal or fish scrap must be treated with an effective antioxidant (at least 400 mg/kg (ppm) ethoxyquin, at least 1000 mg/kg (ppm) butylated hydroxytoluene, or at least 1000 mg/kg (ppm) of tocopherol-based liquid antioxidant).

(d) Shipment of the fish meal or fish scrap must take place a maximum of 12 months after the treatment prescribed in paragraph (c) of this section.

(e) Fish meal or fish scrap must contain at least 100 mg/kg (ppm) of ethoxyquin or butylated hydroxytoluene or at least 250 mg/kg (ppm) of tocopherol-based antioxidant at the time of shipment.

(f) At the time of loading, the temperature of the fish meal or fish scrap to be loaded may not exceed 35 °C (95 °F), or 5 °C (9 °F) above the ambient temperature, whichever is higher.

(g) For each shipment of fish meal or fish scrap, the shipper must give the master a written certification stating—

(1) The total weight of the shipment;

(2) The moisture content of the material;

(3) The fat content of the material;

(4) The type of antioxidant and its concentration in the fish meal or fish scrap at the time of shipment;

(5) The date of production of the material; and

(6) The temperature of the material at the time of shipment.

(h) During a voyage, temperature readings must be taken of fish meal or fish scrap three times a day and recorded. If the temperature of the material exceeds 55 °C (131 °F) and continues to increase, ventilation to the hold must be restricted. This paragraph does not apply to shipments by unmanned barge.

§ 148.270 **Hazardous substances.**

(a) Each bulk shipment of a hazardous substance must—

(1) Be assigned a shipping name in accordance with 49 CFR 172.203(c); and

(2) If the hazardous substance is also listed as a hazardous solid waste in 40 CFR part 261, follow the applicable requirements of 40 CFR chapter I, subchapter I.

(b) Each release of a quantity of a designated substance equal to or greater than the reportable quantity, as set out in Table 1 to Appendix A of 49 CFR 171.101, when discharged into or upon the navigable waters of the United States, adjoining shorelines, into or upon the contiguous zone, or beyond the contiguous zone, must be reported as required in subpart B of 33 CFR part 153.

(c) A hazardous substance must be stowed in a hold or barge that is closed or covered and prevents dispersal of the material during transportation.

(d) During cargo transfer operations, a spill or release of a hazardous substance must be minimized to the greatest extent possible. Each release must be reported as required in paragraph (b) of this section.

(e) After a hazardous substance is unloaded, the hold in which it was carried must be cleaned thoroughly. The residue of the substance must be disposed of pursuant to 33 CFR 151.55 through 151.77 and the applicable regulations of 40 CFR subchapter I.

§ 148.275 **Iron oxide, spent; iron sponge, spent.**

(a) Before spent iron oxide or spent iron sponge is loaded in a closed hold, the shipper must give the master a written certification that the material has been cooled and weathered for at least eight weeks.

(b) Both spent iron oxide and spent iron sponge may be transported on open hold all-steel barges after exposure to air for a period of at least ten days.

§ 148.280 **Magnesia, unslaked (lightburned magnesia, calcined magnesite, caustic calcined magnesite).**

(a) This part does not apply to the transport of natural magnesite, magnesium carbonate, or magnesia clinkers.

(b) When transported by barge, unslaked magnesia must be carried in an unmanned, all-steel, double-hulled barge equipped with weathertight hatches or covers. The barge may not carry any other cargo while unslaked magnesia is on board.

(c) The shipping paper requirements in §148.60 of this part and the dangerous cargo manifest requirements in §148.70 of this part do not apply to unslaked magnesia transported under the requirements of paragraph (b) of this section.

§ 148.285 **Metal sulfide concentrates.**

(a) When information given by the shipper under §148.60 of this part indicates that the metal sulfide concentrate may generate toxic or flammable gases, the appropriate gas detection equipment from §§148.415 and 148.420 of this part must be on board the vessel.

(b) No cargo hold containing a metal sulfide concentrate may be ventilated.

(c) No person may enter a hold containing a metal sulfide concentrate unless—

(1) The atmosphere in the cargo hold has been tested and contains sufficient oxygen to support life and, where the shipper indicates that toxic gas(es) may be generated, the atmosphere in the cargo hold has been tested for the toxic gas(es) and the concentration of the gas(es) is found to be less than the TLV; or

(2) An emergency situation exists and the person entering the cargo hold is wearing the appropriate self-contained breathing apparatus.

§ 148.290 **Peat moss.**

(a) Before shipment, peat moss must be stockpiled under cover to allow drainage and reduce its moisture content.

(b) The cargo must be ventilated so that escaping gases cannot reach living quarters on or above deck.

(c) Persons handling or coming into contact with peat moss must wear gloves, a dust mask, and goggles.

§ 148.295 **Petroleum coke, calcined or uncalcined, at 55 °C (131 °F) or above.**

(a) This part does not apply to shipments of petroleum coke, calcined or uncalcined, on any vessel when the temperature of the material is less than 55 °C (131 °F).

(b) Petroleum coke, calcined or uncalcined, or a mixture of calcined and uncalcined petroleum coke may not be loaded when its temperature exceeds 107 °C (225 °F).

(c) No other hazardous materials may be stowed in any hold adjacent to a hold containing petroleum coke except as provided in paragraph (d) of this section.

(d) Before petroleum coke at 55 °C (131 °F) or above may be loaded into a hold over a tank containing fuel or material having a flashpoint of less than 93 °C (200 °F), a 0.6 to 1.0 meter (2 to 3 foot) layer of the petroleum coke at a temperature not greater than 43 °C (110 °F) must first be loaded.

(e) Petroleum coke must be loaded as follows:

(1) For a shipment in a hold over a fuel tank, the loading of a cooler layer of petroleum coke in the hold as required by paragraph (d) of this section must be completed before loading the petroleum coke at 55 °C (131 °F) or above in any hold of the vessel;

(2) Upon completion of the loading described in paragraph (e)(1) of this section, a 0.6 to 1.0 meter (2 to 3 foot) layer of the petroleum coke at 55 °C (131 °F) or above must first be loaded into each hold, including those holds already containing a cooler layer of the petroleum coke; and

(3) Upon completion of the loading described in paragraph (e)(2) of this section, normal loading of the petroleum coke may be completed.

(f) The master of the vessel must warn members of a crew that petroleum coke is hot, and that injury due to burns is possible.

(g) During the voyage, the temperature of the petroleum coke must be monitored often enough to detect spontaneous heating.

§ 148.300 **Radioactive materials.**

(a) Radioactive materials that may be stowed or transported in bulk are limited to those radioactive materials defined in 49 CFR 173.403 as Low Specific Activity Material, LSA–1, or Surface Contaminated Object, SCO–1.

(b) Skin contact, inhalation or ingestion of dusts generated by Class 7 material listed in Table 148.10 of this part must be minimized.

(c) Each hold used for the transportation of Class 7 material (radioactive) listed in Table 148.10 of this part must be surveyed after the completion of offloading by a qualified person using appropriate radiation detection instruments. Such holds must not be used for the transportation of any other material until the non-fixed contamination on any surface, when averaged over an area of 300 cm², does not exceed the following levels:

(1) 4.0 Bq/cm² (10^{-4} uCi/cm²;) for beta and gamma emitters and low toxicity alpha emitters, natural uranium, natural thorium, uranium-235, uranium-238, thorium-232, thorium-228 and thorium-230 when contained in ores or physical or chemical concentrates, and radionuclides with a half-life of less than 10 days; and

(2) 0.4 Bq/cm² (10^{-5} uCi/cm²) for all other alpha emitters.

§ 148.310 Seed cake.

(a) This part does not apply to solvent-extracted rape seed meal, pellets, soya bean meal, cotton seed meal, or sunflower seed meal that—

(1) Contains a maximum of 4 percent vegetable oil and a maximum of 15 percent vegetable oil and moisture combined; and

(2) As far as practical, is free from flammable solvent.

(b) This part does not apply to mechanically expelled citrus pulp pellets containing not more than 2.5 percent oil and a maximum of 14 percent oil and moisture combined.

(c) Before loading, the seed cake must be aged per the instructions of the shipper.

(d) Before loading, the shipper must give the master or person in charge of a barge a certificate from a competent testing laboratory stating the oil and moisture content of the seed cake.

(e) The seed cake must be kept as dry as practical at all times.

(f) If the seed cake is solvent-extracted, it must be—

(1) As free as practical from flammable solvent; and

(2) Stowed in a mechanically ventilated hold.

(g) For a voyage with a planned duration greater than 5 days, the vessel must be equipped with facilities for introducing carbon dioxide or another inert gas into the hold.

(h) Temperature readings of the seed cake must be taken at least once in every 24-hour period. If the temperature exceeds 55 °C (131 °F) and continues to increase, ventilation to the cargo hold must be discontinued. If heating continues after ventilation has been discontinued, carbon dioxide or the inert gas required under paragraph (g) of this section must be introduced into the hold. If the seed cake is solvent-extracted, the use of inert gas must not be introduced until fire is apparent, to avoid the possibility of igniting the solvent vapors by the generation of static electricity.

(i) Seed cake must be carried under the terms of a Special Permit issued by the Commandant (CG–ENG–5) per subpart B of this part if—

(1) The oil was mechanically expelled; and

(2) It contains more than 10 percent vegetable oil or more than 20 percent vegetable oil and moisture combined.

§ 148.315 Sulfur.

(a) This part applies to lump or coarse grain powder sulfur only. Fine-grained powder ("flowers of sulfur") may not be transported in bulk.

(b) After the loading or unloading of lump or coarse grain powder sulfur has been completed, sulfur dust must be removed from the vessel's decks, bulkheads, and overheads. Cargo residues and deck sweepings must be disposed of pursuant to 33 CFR 151.55 through 151.77.

(c) A cargo space that contains sulfur or the residue of a sulfur cargo must be adequately ventilated, preferably by mechanical means. Each ventilator intake must be fitted with a spark-arresting screen.

§ 148.320 Tankage; garbage tankage; rough ammonia tankage; or tankage fertilizer.

(a) This part applies to rough ammonia tankage in bulk that contains 7 percent or more moisture by weight, and garbage tankage and tankage fertilizer that contains 8 percent or more moisture by weight.

(b) Tankage to which this part applies may not be loaded in bulk if its temperature exceeds 38 °C (100 °F).

§ 148.325

(c) During the voyage, the temperature of the tankage must be monitored often enough to detect spontaneous heating.

§ 148.325 Wood chips; wood pellets; wood pulp pellets.

(a) This part applies to wood chips and wood pulp pellets in bulk that may oxidize, leading to depletion of oxygen and an increase in carbon dioxide in the cargo hold.

(b) No person may enter a cargo hold containing wood chips, wood pellets, or wood pulp pellets, unless—

(1) The atmosphere in the cargo hold has been tested and contains enough oxygen to support life; or

(2) The person entering the cargo hold is wearing the appropriate self-contained breathing apparatus.

§ 148.330 Zinc ashes; zinc dross; zinc residues; zinc skimmings.

(a) The shipper must inform the cognizant Coast Guard Captain of the Port in advance of any cargo transfer operations involving zinc ashes, zinc dross, zinc residues, or zinc skimmings (collectively, "zinc material") in bulk.

(b) Zinc material must be aged by exposure to the elements for at least one year before shipment in bulk.

(c) Before loading in bulk, zinc material must be stored under cover for a period of time to ensure that it is as dry as practical. No zinc material that is wet may be accepted for shipment.

(d) Zinc material may not be loaded in bulk if its temperature is greater than 11.1 °C (52 °F) in excess of the ambient temperature.

(e) Paragraphs (e)(1) through (e)(5) of this section apply only when zinc materials are carried by a cargo vessel:

(1) Zinc material in bulk must be stowed in a mechanically ventilated hold that—

(i) Is designed for at least one complete air change every 30 minutes based on the empty hold;

(ii) Has explosion-proof motors approved for use in Class I, Division 1, Group B atmospheres or equivalent motors approved by the vessel's flag state administration for use in hydrogen atmospheres; and

(iii) Has nonsparking fans.

(2) Combustible gas detectors capable of measuring hydrogen concentrations of 0 to 4.1 percent by volume must be permanently installed in holds that will carry zinc material. If the concentration of hydrogen in the space above the cargo exceeds 1 percent by volume, the ventilation system must be run until the concentration drops below 1 percent by volume.

(3) Thermocouples must be installed approximately 6 inches below the surface of the zinc material or in the space immediately above the zinc material. If an increase in temperature is detected, the mechanical ventilation system required by paragraph (d) of this section must be used until the temperature of the zinc material is below 55 °C (131 °F).

(4) Except as provided in paragraph (e)(5) of this section, the cargo hatches of holds containing zinc material must remain sealed to prevent the entry of seawater.

(5) If the concentration of hydrogen is near 4.1 percent by volume and increasing, despite ventilation, or the temperature of the zinc material reaches 65 °C (150 °F), the cargo hatches should be opened provided that weather and sea conditions are favorable. When hatches are opened take care to prevent sparks and minimize the entry of water.

Subpart F—Additional Special Requirements

§ 148.400 Applicability.

Unless stated otherwise, the requirements of this subpart apply only to the shipment or loading of materials, listed in Table 148.10 of this part, for which Table 148.10 contains a reference to a section or paragraph of this subpart.

§ 148.405 Sources of ignition.

(a) Except in an emergency, no welding, burning, cutting, chipping, or other operations involving the use of fire, open flame, sparks, or arc-producing equipment, may be performed in a cargo hold containing a Table 148.10 material or in an adjacent space.

(b) A cargo hold or adjacent space must not have any flammable gas concentrations over 10 percent of the LFL before the master may approve operations involving the use of fire, open flame, or spark- or arc-producing equipment in that hold or adjacent space.

§ 148.407   Smoking.

When Table 148.10 of this part associates a material with a reference to this section, and that material is being loaded or unloaded, smoking is prohibited anywhere on the weatherdeck of the vessel. While such a material is on board the vessel, smoking is prohibited in spaces adjacent to the cargo hold and on the vessel's deck in the vicinity of cargo hatches, ventilator outlets, and other accesses to the hold containing the material. "NO SMOKING" signs must be displayed in conspicuous locations in the areas where smoking is prohibited.

§ 148.410   Fire hoses.

When Table 148.10 of this part associates a material with a reference to this section, a fire hose must be available at each hatch through which the material is being loaded.

§ 148.415   Toxic gas analyzers.

When Table 148.10 of this part associates a material with a reference to a paragraph in this section, each vessel transporting the material, other than an unmanned barge, must have on board a gas analyzer appropriate for the toxic gas listed in that paragraph. At least two members of the crew must be knowledgeable in the use of the equipment. The equipment must be maintained in a condition ready for use and calibrated according to the instructions of its manufacturer. The atmosphere in the cargo hold and adjacent spaces must be tested before a person is allowed to enter these spaces. If toxic gases are detected, the space must be ventilated and retested before entry. The toxic gases for which the requirements of this section must be met are:
   (a) Arsine;
   (b) Carbon monoxide;
   (c) Hydrogen cyanide;
   (d) Hydrogen sulfide;
   (e) Phosphine; and
   (f) Sulfur dioxide.

§ 148.420   Flammable gas analyzers.

When Table 148.10 of this part associates a material with a reference to a paragraph in this section, each vessel transporting the material, other than an unmanned barge, must have on board a gas analyzer appropriate for the flammable gas listed in that paragraph. At least two members of the crew must be knowledgeable in the use of the equipment. The equipment must be maintained in a condition ready for use, capable of measuring 0 to 100 percent LFL for the gas indicated, and calibrated in accordance with the instructions of its manufacturer. The atmosphere in the cargo hold must be tested before any person is allowed to enter. If flammable gases are detected, the space must be ventilated and retested before entry. The flammable gases for which the requirements of this section must be met are:
   (a) Carbon monoxide;
   (b) Hydrogen; and
   (c) Methane.

§ 148.435   Electrical circuits in cargo holds.

During transport of a material that Table 148.10 of this part associates with a reference to this section, each electrical circuit terminating in a cargo hold containing the material must be electrically disconnected from the power source at a point outside of the cargo hold. The point of disconnection must be marked to prevent the circuit from being reenergized while the material is on board.

§ 148.445   Adjacent spaces.

When transporting a material that Table 148.10 of this part associates with a reference to this section, the following requirements must be met:
   (a) Each space adjacent to a cargo hold must be ventilated by natural ventilation or by ventilation equipment safe for use in an explosive gas atmosphere.
   (b) Each space adjacent to a cargo hold containing the material must be regularly monitored for the presence of the flammable gas indicated by reference to § 148.420 of this part. If the level of flammable gas in any space reaches 30 percent of the LFL, all electrical equipment that is not certified

§ 148.450

safe for use in an explosive gas atmosphere must be de-energized at a location outside of that space. This location must be labeled to prohibit reenergizing until the atmosphere in the space is tested and found to be less than 30 percent of the LFL.

(c) Each person who enters any space adjacent to a cargo hold or compartment containing the material must wear a self-contained breathing apparatus unless—

(1) The space has been tested, or is routinely monitored, for the appropriate flammable gas and oxygen;

(2) The level of flammable gas is less than 10 percent of the LFL; and

(3) The level of toxic gas, if required to be tested, is less than the TLV.

(d) No person may enter an adjacent space if the level of flammable gas is greater than 30 percent of the LFL. If emergency entry is necessary, each person who enters the space must wear a self-contained breathing apparatus and caution must be exercised to ensure that no sparks are produced.

§ 148.450 Cargoes subject to liquefaction.

(a) This section applies only to cargoes identified in Table 148.10 of this part with a reference to this section and cargoes identified in the IMSBC Code (incorporated by reference, see § 148.8) as cargoes that may liquefy.

(b) This section does not apply to—

(1) Shipments by unmanned barge; or

(2) Cargoes of coal that have an average particle size of 10mm (.394 in.) or greater.

(c) Definitions as used in this section—

(1) *Cargo subject to liquefaction* means a material that is subject to moisture migration and subsequent liquefaction if shipped with moisture content in excess of the transportable moisture limit.

(2) *Moisture migration* is the movement of moisture by settling and consolidation of a material, which may result in the development of a flow state in the material.

(3) *Transportable moisture limit* or *TML* of a cargo that may liquefy is the maximum moisture content that is considered safe for carriage on vessels.

(d) Except on a vessel that is specially constructed or specially fitted for the purpose of carrying such cargoes (see also section 7 of the IMSBC Code, incorporated by reference, see § 148.8), a cargo subject to liquefaction may not be transported by vessel if its moisture content exceeds its TML.

(e) The shipper of a cargo subject to liquefaction must give the master the material's moisture content and TML.

(f) The master of a vessel shipping a cargo subject to liquefaction must ensure that—

(1) A cargo containing a liquid is not stowed in the same cargo space with a cargo subject to liquefaction; and

(2) Precautions are taken to prevent the entry of liquids into a cargo space containing a cargo subject to liquefaction.

(g) The moisture content and TML of a material may be determined by the tests described in Appendix 2, Section 1, of the IMSBC Code (incorporated by reference, see § 148.8).

PART 149 [RESERVED]

SUBCHAPTER O—CERTAIN BULK DANGEROUS CARGOES

PART 150—COMPATIBILITY OF CARGOES

Sec.
150.105 OMB control numbers assigned pursuant to the Paperwork Reduction Act.
150.110 Applicability.
150.115 Definitions.
150.120 Definition of incompatible cargoes.
150.130 Loading a cargo on vessels carrying cargoes with which it is incompatible.
150.140 Cargoes not listed in Table I or II.
150.150 Exceptions to the compatibility chart.
150.160 Carrying a cargo as an exception to the compatibility chart.
150.170 Right of appeal.
FIGURE I TO PART 150—COMPATIBILITY CHART
TABLE I TO PART 150—ALPHABETICAL LIST OF CARGOES
TABLE II TO PART 150—GROUPING OF CARGOES
APPENDIX I TO PART 150—EXCEPTIONS TO THE CHART
APPENDIX II TO PART 150—EXPLANATION OF FIGURE 1
APPENDIX III TO PART 150—TESTING PROCEDURES FOR DETERMINING EXCEPTIONS TO THE CHART
APPENDIX IV TO PART 150—DATA SHEET

AUTHORITY: 46 U.S.C. 3306, 3703; Department of Homeland Security Delegation No. 0170.1. Section 150.105 issued under 44 U.S.C. 3507; Department of Homeland Security Delegation No. 0170.1.

SOURCE: CGD 75–59, 45 FR 70263, Oct. 23, 1980, unless otherwise noted.

EDITORIAL NOTE: Nomenclature changes to part 150 appear at 77 FR 59783, Oct. 1, 2012.

§ 150.105 OMB control numbers assigned pursuant to the Paperwork Reduction Act.

(a) *Purpose.* This section collects and displays the control numbers assigned to information collection and recordkeeping requirements in this subchapter by the Office of Management and Budget (OMB) pursuant to the Paperwork Reduction Act of 1980 (44 U.S.C. 3501 *et seq.*). The Coast Guard intends that this section comply with the requirements of 44 U.S.C. 3507(f) which requires that agencies display a current control number assigned by the Director of the OMB for each approved agency information collection requirement.

(b) *Display.*

46 CFR part or section where identified or described	Current OMB control No.
§ 150.01–15	1625–0007
§ 153.5	1625–0007
§ 153.905	1625–0094
§ 153.910	1625–0094
§ 153.968	1625–0094
Part 154	1625–0029
§ 154.12	1625–0007

[49 FR 38121, Sept. 27, 1984, as amended by CGD 77–069, 52 FR 31626, Aug. 21, 1987; USCG–2004–18884, 69 FR 58349, Sept. 30, 2004]

§ 150.110 Applicability.

This subpart prescribes rules for identifying incompatible hazardous materials and rules for carrying these materials in bulk as cargo in permanently attached tanks or in tanks that are loaded or discharged while aboard the vessel. The rules apply to all vessels that carry liquid dangerous cargoes in bulk that are subject to 46 U.S.C. Chapter 37.

[CGD 95–028, 62 FR 51209, Sept. 30, 1997]

§ 150.115 Definitions.

As used in this subpart: *Hazardous material* means:

(a) A flammable liquid as defined in § 30.10–22 or a combustible liquid as defined in § 30.10–15 of this chapter;

(b) A material listed in Table 151.05, Table 1 of part 153, or Table 4 of part 154 of this chapter; or

(c) A liquid, liquefied gas, or compressed gas listed in 49 CFR 172.101.

Person in charge means the master of a self-propelled vessel, or the person in charge of a barge.

§ 150.120 Definition of incompatible cargoes.

Except as described in § 150.150, a cargo of hazardous material is incompatible with another cargo listed in Table I if the chemical groups of the two cargoes have an "X" where their columns intersect in Figure 1 and are not shown as exceptions in Appendix I. (See also § 150.140.)

[CGD 83–047, 50 FR 33038, Aug. 16, 1985]

§ 150.130 Loading a cargo on vessels carrying cargoes with which it is incompatible.

Except as described in § 150.160, the person in charge of a vessel shall ensure that the containment system for a cargo that is a hazardous material meets the following requirements:

(a) The containment system must separate the hazardous material or its residue from any cargo in table I with which it is incompatible by two barriers such as formed by a:

(1) Cofferdam;
(2) Empty tank;
(3) Void space;
(4) Cargo handling space;
(5) Tank containing a compatible cargo; or
(6) Piping tunnel.

(b) In this subpart, isolation across a cruciform joint is equivalent to isolation by two barriers.

(c) The containment system for the hazardous material must not have a piping or venting system that connects to a containment system carrying a cargo with which the hazardous material is incompatible. Any such piping or venting system must have been separated from the containment system carrying the incompatible cargo by:

(1) Removing a valve or spool piece and blanking off the exposed pipe ends, or
(2) Installing two spectacle flanges in series with a means of detecting leakage into the pipe between the spectacle flanges.

§ 150.140 Cargoes not listed in Table I or II.

A cargo of hazardous material not listed in Table I or II must be handled as if incompatible with all other cargoes until the Commandant CG–ENG–5) (Telephone 202–372–1420) assigns the hazardous material to a compatibility group. (Table I lists cargoes alphabetically while Table II lists cargoes by compatibility group).

[CGD 83–047, 50 FR 33038, Aug. 16, 1985, CGD 86–100, 52 FR 21037, June 4, 1987; CGD 95–072, 60 FR 50465, Sept. 29, 19955; CGD 96–041, 61 FR 50731, Sept. 27, 1996; USCG–2006–25697, 71 FR 55746, Sept. 25, 2006]

§ 150.150 Exceptions to the compatibility chart.

The Commandant (CG–ENG–5) authorizes, on a case by case basis, exceptions to the rules in this subpart under the following conditions:

(a) When two cargoes shown to be incompatible in Figure 1 meet the standards for a compatible pair in Appendix III, or

(b) When two cargoes shown to be compatible in Figure 1 meet the standards for an incompatible pair in Appendix III.

Appendix I contains cargoes which have been found to be exceptions to Figure 1, the Compatibility Chart.

[CGD 83–047, 50 FR 33038, Aug. 16, 1985, as amended at CGD 95–072, 60 FR 50465, Sept. 29, 1995; CGD 96–041, 61 FR 50731, Sept. 27, 1996]

§ 150.160 Carrying a cargo as an exception to the compatibility chart.

The Operator of a vessel having on board a cargo carried as an exception under § 150.150 but not listed in Appendix I, Exceptions to the Chart, shall make sure that:

(a) The Commandant (CG–ENG–5) has authorized by letter or message the cargo pair as an exception to the compatibility chart; and

(b) A copy of the letter or message is on the vessel.

[CGD 75–59, 45 FR 70263, Oct. 23, 1980, as amended by CGD 82–063b, 48 FR 4781, Feb. 3, 1983; CGD 83–047, 50 FR 33038, Aug. 16, 1985; CGD 95–072, 60 FR 50465, Sept. 29, 19955; CGD 96–041, 61 FR 50731, Sept. 27, 1996]

§ 150.170 Right of appeal.

Any person directly affected by a decision or action taken under this part, by or on behalf of the Coast Guard, may appeal therefrom in accordance with subpart 1.03 of this chapter.

[CGD 88–033, 54 FR 50381, Dec. 6, 1989]

Coast Guard, DHS — Pt. 150, Table I

FIGURE 1 TO PART 150—COMPATIBILITY CHART

Figure I - Compatibility chart

Reactive Groups:
1. Non-Oxidizing Mineral Acids
2. Sulfuric Acid
3. Nitric Acid
4. Organic Acids
5. Caustics
6. Ammonia
7. Aliphatic Amines
8. Alkanolamines
9. Aromatic Amines
10. Amides
11. Organic Anhydrides
12. Isocyanates
13. Vinyl Acetate
14. Acrylates
15. Substituted Allyls
16. Alkylene Oxides
17. Epichlorohydrin
18. Ketones
19. Aldehydes
20. Alcohols, Glycols
21. Phenols, Cresols
22. Caprolactam Solution

Cargo Group	1	2	3	4	5	6	7	8	9	10	11	12	13	14	15	16	17	18	19	20	21	22
1. Non-oxidizing mineral acids		X			X	X	X	X	X	X	X	X	X			X	X			X	X	X
2. Sulfuric acid	X		X	X	X	X	X	X	X	X	X	X	X	X	X	X	X	X	X	X	X	X
3. Nitric acid		X			X	X	X	X	X	X	X	X	X			X	X	X	X	X		
4. Organic acids		X			X	X	X	X	X			X				X	X			X	X	X
5. Caustics	X	X	X	X						X	X					X	X			X	X	X
6. Ammonia	X	X	X	X					X	X	X	X				X	X					
7. Aliphatic amines	X	X	X	X					X	X	X	X	X	X	X	X	X	X		X	X	
8. Alkanolamines	X	X	X	X					X	X	X	X	X	X	X	X	X			X		
9. Aromatic amines	X	X	X	X							X	X				X	X			X		
10. Amides	X	X	X			X						X								X		
11. Organic anhydrides	X	X	X	X	X	X	X	X														
12. Isocyanates	X	X	X	X	X	X	X	X	X											X		X
13. Vinyl acetate	X	X	X		X	X	X	X														
14. Acrylates		X	X				X	X														
15. Substituted allyls		X	X				X	X														
16. Alkylene oxides	X	X	X	X	X	X	X	X														
17. Epichlorohydrin	X	X	X	X	X	X	X	X														
18. Ketones			X				X															
19. Aldehydes			X		X	X	X	X														
20. Alcohols, glycols			X	X		X						X										
21. Phenols, cresols			X	X		X			X													
22. Caprolactam solution		X			X		X					X										
30. Olefins		X	X																			
31. Paraffins																						
32. Aromatic hydrocarbons			X																			
33. Miscellaneous hydrocarbon mixtures			X																			
34. Esters		X	X																			
35. Vinyl halides			X																		X	
36. Halogenated hydrocarbons																						
37. Nitriles		X																				
38. Carbon disulfide							X	X														
39. Sulfolane																						
40. Glycol ethers		X										X										
41. Ethers		X	X																			
42. Nitrocompounds					X	X	X	X														
43. Miscellaneous water solutions		X										X										

TABLE I TO PART 150—ALPHABETICAL LIST OF CARGOES

Chemical name	Group No.	Foot-note	CHRIS Code	Related CHRIS Codes
Acetaldehyde	19	....	AAD	
Acetic acid	4	2	AAC	
Acetic anhydride	11	....	ACA	
Acetochlor	10	....	ACG	
Acetone	18	2	ACT	
Acetone cyanohydrin	0	1, 2	ACY	
Acetonitrile	37	....	ATN	
Acetophenone	18	....	ACP	
Acrolein	19	2	ARL	
Acrylamide solution	10	....	AAM	
Acrylic acid	4	2	ACR	
Acrylonitrile	15	2	ACN	
Acrylonitrile-Styrene copolymer dispersion in Polyether polyol	20	....	ALE	
Adiponitrile	37	....	ADN	
Alachlor	33	....	ALH	
Alcohols (C13+)	20	....	ALY	
Including:				
Oleyl alcohol (octadecenol)				
Pentadecanol				
Tallow alcohol				
Tetradecanol				
Tridecanol				
Alcoholic beverages	20	....		
Alcohol polyethoxylates	20	....		APU/APV/APW/AET

Pt. 150, Table I

46 CFR Ch. I (10-1-13 Edition)

Chemical name	Group No.	Foot-note	CHRIS Code	Related CHRIS Codes
Alcohol polyethoxylates, secondary	20			AEA/AEB
Alkanes (C6-C9)	31	1	ALK	
Including:				
Heptanes				
Hexanes				
Nonanes				
Octanes				
n-Alkanes (C10+)	31	1	ALJ	
Including:				
Decanes				
Dodecanes				
Heptadecanes				
Tridecanes				
Undecanes				
iso- & cyclo-Alkanes (C10-C11)	31	1	AKI	
iso- & cyclo-Alkanes (C12+)	31	1	AKJ	
Alkane (C14-C17) sulfonic acid, sodium salt solution	34		AKA	
Alkaryl polyether (C9-C20)	41		AKP	
Alkenyl(C11+)amide	11		AKM	
Alkenyl(C16-C20)succinic anhydride	11		AAH	
Alkyl acrylate-Vinyl pyridine copolymer in Toluene	32		AAP	
Alkyl(C8+)amine, Alkenyl (C12+) acid ester mixture	34		AAA	
Alkylaryl phosphate mixtures (more than 40% Diphenyl tolyl phosphate, less than 0.02% ortho-isomer).	34		APD	
Alkyl(C3-C4)benzenes	32		AKC	
Including:				
Butylbenzenes				
Cumene				
Propylbenzenes				
Alkyl(C5-C8)benzenes	32		AKD	
Including:				
Amylbenzenes				
Heptylbenzenes				
Hexylbenzenes				
Octylbenzenes				
Alkyl(C9+)benzenes	32		AKB	
Including:				
Decylbenzenes				
Dodecylbenzenes				
Nonylbenzenes				
Tetradecylbenzenes				
Tetrapropylbenzenes				
Tridecylbenzenes				
Undecylbenzenes				
Alkylbenzene, Alkylindane, Alkylindene mixture (each C12-C17)	32		AIH	
Alkylbenzenesulfonic acid	0	1, 2		ABS/ABN
Alkylbenzenesulfonic acid, sodium salt solutions	33		ABT	
Alkyl dithiothiadiazole (C6-C24)	33		ADT	
Alkyl ester copolymer (C4-C20)	34		AES	
Alkyl(C7-C9) nitrates	34	2	AKN	ONE
Alkyl(C7-C11) phenol poly(4-12)ethoxylate	40		APN	
Alkyl(C8-C40) phenol sulfide	34		AKS	
Alkyl(C8-C9) phenylamine in aromatic solvents	9		ALP	
Alkyl(C9-C15) phenyl propoxylate	40			
Alkyl phthalates	34			
Alkyl(C10-C20, saturated and unsaturated) phosphite	34		AKL	
Alkyl polyglucoside solutions	43			AGL/AGN/AGO/AGP/AGM
Alkyl sulfonic acid ester of phenol	34			
Allyl alcohol	15	2	ALA	
Allyl chloride	15	1	ALC	
Aluminium chloride, Hydrochloric acid solution	0	1	AHS	
Aluminum sulfate solution	43	2	ASX	ALM
2-(2-Aminoethoxy)ethanol	8		AEX	
Aminoethyldiethanolamine, Aminoethylethanolamine solution	8			
Aminoethylethanolamine	8		AEE	
N-Aminoethylpiperazine	7		AEP	
2-Amino-2-hydroxymethyl-1,3-propanediol solution	43		AHL	
2-Amino-2-methyl-1-propanol	8		APQ	APR
Ammonia, anhydrous	6		AMA	
Ammonia, aqueous (28% or less Ammonia) (*IMO cargo name*), see Ammonium hydroxide.	6			AMH
Ammonium bisulfite solution	43	2	ABX	ASU

48

Coast Guard, DHS   Pt. 150, Table I

Chemical name	Group No.	Foot-note	CHRIS Code	Related CHRIS Codes
Ammonium hydrogen phosphate solution	0	1	AMI	
Ammonium hydroxide (28% or less Ammonia)	6		AMH	
Ammonium lignosulfonate solution, see also Lignin liquor	43			
Ammonium nitrate solution	0	1	ANR	AND/AMN
Ammonium nitrate, Urea solution (containing Ammonia)	6		UAS	
Ammonium nitrate, Urea solution (not containing Ammonia)	43		ANU	UAT
Ammonium polyphosphate solution	43		AMO	APP
Ammonium sulfate solution	43		AME	AMS
Ammonium sulfide solution	5		ASS	ASF
Ammonium thiocyanate, Ammonium thiosulfate solution	0	1	ACS	
Ammonium thiosulfate solution	43		ATV	ATF
Amyl acetate	34		AEC	IAT/AML/AAS/AYA
Amyl alcohol	20		AAI	IAA/AAN/ASE/APM
Amylene, see Pentene			AMZ	PTX
tert-Amyl methyl ether (see also, Methyl tert-pentyl ether)	41		AYE	
Amyl methyl ketone, see Methyl amyl ketone			AMK	MAK
Aniline	9		ANL	
Animal and Fish oils, n.o.s.	34		AFN	
Including:				
Cod liver oil				
Lanolin				
Neatsfoot oil				
Pilchard oil				
Sperm oil				
Animal and Fish acid oils and distillates, n.o.s.	34		AFA	
Including:				
Animal acid oil				
Fish acid oil				
Lard acid oil				
Mixed acid oil				
Mixed general acid oil				
Mixed hard acid oil				
Mixed soft acid oil				
Anthracene oil (Coal tar fraction), see Coal tar	33		AHO	COR
Apple juice	43			
Aryl polyolefin (C11-C50)	30		AYF	
Asphalt	33		ASP	ACU
Asphalt blending stocks, roofers flux	33		ARF	
Asphalt blending stocks, straight run residue	33		ASR	
Asphalt emulsion (ORIMULSION)	33		ASQ	
Aviation alkylates	33		AVA	GAV
Barium long chain alkaryl(C11-C50) sulfonate	34		BCA	
Barium long chain alkyl(C8-C14)phenate sulfide	34		BCH	
Behenyl alcohol	20			
Benzene	32		BNZ	
Benzene hydrocarbon mixtures (having 10% Benzene or more)	32		BHB	BHA
Benzenesulfonyl chloride	0	1, 2	BSC	
Benzene, Toluene, Xylene mixtures	32	2	BTX	
Benzene tricarboxylic acid, trioctyl ester	34			
Benzylacetate	34		BZE	
Benzyl alcohol	21		BAL	
Benzyl chloride	36		BCL	
Brake fluid base mixtures	20		BFX	
Bromochloromethane	36		BCM	
Butadiene	30		BDI	
Butadiene, Butylene mixtures (cont. Acetylenes)	30		BBM	
Butane	31	1	BMX	IBT/BUT
1,4-Butanediol, see Butylene glycol			BDO	BUG
2-Butanone, see Methyl ethyl ketone				
Butene, see Butylene				IBL/BTN
Butene oligomer	30		BOL	
Butyl acetate	34		BAX	IBA/BCN/BTA/BYA
Butyl acrylate	14	1	BAR	BAI/BTC
Butyl alcohol	20	2	BAY	IAL/BAN/BAS/BAT
Butylamine	7		BTY	IAM/BAM/BTL/BUA
Butylbenzene, see Alky(C3-C4)benzenes	32		BBE	AKC
Butyl benzyl phthalate	34		BPH	
Butyl butyrate	34		BBA	BUB/BIB
Butylene	30		BTN	IBL
Butylene glycol	20	2	BUG	BDO
1,3-Butylene glycol, see Butylene glycol				BUG
Butylene oxide	16	1	BTO	
Butyl ether	41		BTE	

49

Chemical name	Group No.	Foot-note	CHRIS Code	Related CHRIS Codes
Butyl formate	34			BFI/BFN
Butyl heptyl ketone	18		BHK	
Butyl methacrylate	14	1	BMH	BMI/BMN
Butyl methacrylate, Decyl methacrylate, Cetyl-Eicosyl methacrylate mixture.	14	1	DER	
Butyl methyl ketone, see Methyl butyl ketone				MBK
Butyl phenol, Formaldehyde resin in Xylene	32			
n-Butyl propionate	34		BPN	
Butyl stearate	34			
Butyl toluene	32		BUE	
Butyraldehyde	19		BAE	BAD/BTR
Butyric acid	4		BRA	IBR
gamma-Butyrolactone	0	1, 2	BLA	
C9 Resinfeed (DSM)	32	2	CNR	
Calcium alkyl(C9)phenol sulfide, polyolefin phosphorosulfide mixture	34		CPX	
Calcium alkyl salicylate, see Calcium long chain alkyl salicylate (C13+)				CAK
Calcium bromide solution, see Drilling brines				DRB
Calcium bromide, Zinc bromide solution, see Drilling brine (containing Zinc salts).				DZB
Calcium carbonate slurry	34			
Calcium chloride solution	43		CCS	CLC
Calcium hydroxide slurry	5		COH	
Calcium hypochlorite solutions	5			CHZ/CHU/CHY
Calcium lignosulfonate solution, see also Lignin liquor	43			
Calcium long chain alkaryl sulfonate (C11-C50)	34		CAY	
Calcium long chain alkyl phenates	34			CAN/CAW
Calcium long chain alkyl phenate sulfide (C8-C40)	34		CPI	
Calcium long chain alkyl salicylate (C13+)	34		CAK	
Calcium long chain alkyl phenolic amine (C8-C40)	9		CPQ	
Calcium nitrate solution	34		CNU	
Calcium nitrate, Magnesium nitrate, Potassium chloride solution	34			
Calcium sulfonate, Calcium carbonate, Hydrocarbon solvent mixture	33			
Camphor oil	18		CPO	
Canola oil, see rapeseed oil under "oils, edible."				
Caprolactam solution	22		CLS	
Caramel solutions	43			
Carbolic oil	21		CBO	
Carbon disulfide	38		CBB	
Carbon tetrachloride	36	2	CBT	
Cashew nut shell oil (untreated)	4		OCN	
Catoxid feedstock	36	2	CXF	
Caustic potash solution	5	2	CPS	
Caustic soda solution	5	2	CSS	
Cetyl alcohol (hexadecanol), see Alcohols (C13+)				ALY
Cetyl-Eicosyl methacrylate mixture	14	1	CEM	
Cetyl-Stearyl alcohol, see Alcohols (C13+)				ALY
Chlorinated paraffins (C10-C13)	36		CLH	
Chlorinated paraffins (C14-C17) (with 52% Chlorine)	36		CLJ	
Chlorine	0	1	CLX	
Chloroacetic acid solution	4		CHM	CHL/MCA
Chlorobenzene	36		CRB	
Chlorodifluoromethane (monochlorodifluoromethane)	36		MCF	
Chloroform	36		CRF	
Chlorohydrins	17	1	CHD	
4-Chloro-2-methylphenoxyacetic acid, Dimethylamine salt solution	9		CDM	
Chloronitrobenzene	42		CNO	
1-(4-Chlorophenyl)-4,4-dimethyl pentan-3-one	18	2	CDP	
Chloropropionic acid	4		CPM	CLA/CLP
Chlorosulfonic acid	0	1	CSA	
Chlorotoluene	36		CHI	CTM/CTO/CRN
Choline chloride solutions	20		CCO	
Citric acid	4		CIS	CIT
Clay slurry, see also Kaolin clay slurry	43			
Coal tar	33		COR	OCT
Coal tar distillate	33		CDL	
Coal tar, high temperature	33		CHH	
Coal tar pitch	33		CTP	
Cobalt naphthenate in solvent naphtha	34		CNS	
Coconut oil, fatty acid	34		CFA	
Copper salt of long chain (C17+) alkanoic acid	34		CUS	CFT
Corn syrup	43		CSY	
Cottonseed oil, fatty acid	34		CFY	
Creosote	21	2	CCT	CCW/CWD

Coast Guard, DHS

Pt. 150, Table I

Chemical name	Group No.	Foot-note	CHRIS Code	Related CHRIS Codes
Cresols	21	....	CRS	CRL/CSL/CSO
Cresylate spent caustic	5	....	CSC	
Cresylic acid	21	....	CRY	
Cresylic acid, dephenolized	21	....	CAD	
Cresylic acid, sodium salt solution (*IMO cargo name*), see Cresylate spent caustic.	5	....		CSC
Cresylic acid tar	21	....	CRX	
Crotonaldehyde	19	2	CTA	
Cumene (isopropyl benzene), see Propylbenzene	....	....	CUM	PBY
1,5,9-Cyclododecatriene	30	....	CYT	
Cycloheptane	31	1	CYE	
Cyclohexane	31	1	CHX	
Cyclohexanol	20	....	CHN	
Cyclohexanone	18	....	CCH	
Cyclohexanone, Cyclohexanol mixtures	18	2	CYX	
Cyclohexyl acetate	34	....	CYC	
Cyclohexylamine	7	....	CHA	
1,3-Cyclopentadiene dimer	30	....	CPD	DPT
Cyclopentadiene, Styrene, Benzene mixture	30	....	CSB	
Cyclopentane	31	1	CYP	
Cyclopentene	30	....	CPE	
Cymene	32	....	CMP	
Decahydronaphthalene	33	....	DHN	
Decaldehyde	19	....		IDA/DAL
Decane, see n-Alkanes (C10+)	....	....	DCC	ALJ
Decanoic acid	4	....	DCO	
Decene	30	....	DCE	
Decyl acetate	34	....	DYA	
Decyl acrylate	14	1	DAT	IAI/DAR
Decyl alcohol	20	2	DAX	ISA/DAN
Decylbenzene, see Alkyl(C9+) benzenes	32	....	DBZ	AKB
Decyloxytetrahydro-thiophene dioxide	0	1, 2	DHT	
Degummed C9 (DOW)	33	....	DGC	
Dextrose solution, see Glucose solution	43	....	DTS	GLU
Diacetone alcohol	20	2	DAA	
Dialkyl(C10-C14) benzenes, see Alkyl(C9+) benzenes	32	....	DAB	AKB
Dialkyl(C8-C9) diphenylamines	9	....	DAQ	
Dialkyl(C7-C13) phthalates	34	....	DAH	
Including:				
Diisodecyl phthalate				
Diisononyl phthalate				
Dinonyl phthalate				
Ditridecyl phthalate				
Diundecyl phthalate				
Dibromomethane	36	....	DBH	
Dibutylamine	7	....	DBA	
Dibutyl carbinol, see Nonyl alcohol	....	....		NNS
Dibutyl hydrogen phosphonate	34	....	DHD	
Dibutylphenols	21	....		DBT/DBV, DBW
Dibutyl phthalate	34	....	DPA	
Dichlorobenzene	36	....	DBX	DBM/DBO/DBP
3,4-Dichloro-1-butene	36	....	DCD	DCB
Dichlorodifluoromethane	36	....	DCF	
1,1-Dichloroethane	36	....	DCH	
2,2'-Dichloroethyl ether	41	....	DEE	
1,6-Dichlorohexane	36	....	DHX	
2,2'-Dichloroisopropyl ether	36	....	DCI	
Dichloromethane	36	....	DCM	
2,4-Dichlorophenol	21	....	DCP	
2,4-Dichlorophenoxyacetic acid, Diethanolamine salt solution	43	....	DDE	
2,4-Dichlorophenoxyacetic acid, Dimethylamine salt solution	0	1, 2	DAD	DDA/DSX
2,4-Dichlorophenoxyacetic acid, Triisopropano-lamine salt solution	43	2	DTI	
Dichloropropane	36	....	DPX	DPB/DPP/DPC/DPL
1,3-Dichloropropene	15	1	DPS	DPU/DPF
Dichloropropene, Dichloropropane mixtures	15	1	DMX	
2,2-Dichloropropionic acid	4	....	DCN	
Dicyclopentadiene, see also 1,3-Cyclopentadiene dimer	30	....	DPT	CPD
Diethanolamine	8	....	DEA	
Diethanolamine salt of 2,4-Dichlorophenoxyacetic acid solution, see 2,4-Dichlorophenoxyacetic acid, Diethanolamine salt solution.	....	....		DDE
Diethylamine	7	....	DEN	
Diethylaminoethanol (IMO cargo name), see Diethylethanolamine	8	....		DAE
2,6-Diethylaniline	9	....	DMN	

51

Chemical name	Group No.	Foot-note	CHRIS Code	Related CHRIS Codes
Diethylbenzene	32		DEB	
Diethylene glycol	40	2	DEG	
Diethylene glycol butyl ether, see Poly(2-8)alkylene glycol monoalkyl(C1-C6) ether.			DME	PAG
Diethylene glycol butyl ether acetate, see Poly(2-8)alkylene glycol monoalkyl(C1-C6) ether acetate.			DEM	PAF
Diethylene glycol dibenzoate	34		DGZ	
Diethylene glycol dibutyl ether	40		DIG	
Diethylene glycol diethyl ether	40			
Diethylene glycol ethyl ether, see Poly(2-8)alkylene glycol monoalkyl (C1-C6) ether.			DGE	PAG
Diethylene glycol ethyl ether acetate, see Poly(2-8)alkylene glycol monoalkyl(C1-C6) ether acetates.			DGA	PAF
Diethylene glycol n-hexyl ether, see Poly(2-8)alkylene glycol monoalkyl(C1-C6) ether.			DHE	PAG
Diethylene glycol methyl ether, see Poly(2-8)alkylene glycol monoalkyl(C1-C6) ether.			DGM	PAG
Diethylene glycol methyl ether acetate, see Poly(2-8)alkylene glycol monoalkyl(C1-C6) ether acetate.			DGR	PAF
Diethylene glycol phenyl ether	40		DGP	
Diethylene glycol phthalate	34		DGL	
Diethylene glycol propyl ether, see Poly(2-8)alkylene glycol monoalkyl(C1-C6) ether.			DGO	PAG
Diethylenetriamine	7	2	DET	
Diethylenetriamine pentaacetic acid, pentasodium salt solution	43			
Diethylethanolamine	8		DAE	
Diethyl ether (IMO cargo name), see Ethyl ether	41			EET
Diethyl hexanol, see Decyl alcohol				DAX
Di-(2-ethylhexyl)adipate	34		DEH	
Di-(2-ethylhexyl)phosphoric acid	1	1	DEP	
Di-(2-ethylhexyl)phthalate, see Dioctyl phthalate	34		DIE	DOP
Diethyl phthalate	34		DPH	
Diethyl sulfate	34		DSU	
Diglycidyl ether of Bisphenol A	41		BDE	BPA
Diglycidyl ether of Bisphenol F	41		DGF	
Diheptyl phthalate	34		DHP	
Di-n-hexyl adipate	34		DHA	
Dihexyl phthalate	34			
1,4-Dihydro-9,10-dihydroxy anthracene, disodium salt solution	5		DDH	
Diisobutylamine	7		DBU	
Diisobutyl carbinol (commercial cargo name), see Nonyl alcohol	20		DBC	NNS
Diisobutylene	30		DBL	
Diisobutyl ketone	18		DIK	
Diisobutyl phthalate	34		DIT	
Diisodecyl phthalate, see Dialkyl(C7-C13) phthalates			DID	DAH
Diisononyl adipate	34		DNY	
Diisononyl phthalate, see Dialkyl(C7-C13) phthalates			DIN	DAH
Diisooctyl phthalate	34		DIO	
Diisopropanolamine	8		DIP	
Diisopropylamine	7		DIA	
Diisopropylbenzene	32		DIX	
Diisopropyl naphthalene	32		DII	
N,N-Dimethylacetamide	10		DAC	
N,N-Dimethylacetamide solution	10		DLS	
Dimethyl adipate	34		DLA	
Dimethylamine	7		DMA	
Dimethylamine solution	7			DMG/DMY/DMC
Dimethylamine salt of 4-Chloro-2-methylphenoxyacetic acid solution, see 4-Chloro-2-methylphenoxyacetic acid, Dimethylamine salt solution.				CDM
Dimethylamine salt of 2,4-Dichlorophenoxyacetic acid solution, see 2,4-Dichlorophenoxyacetic acid, Dimethylamine salt solution.				DAD/(DDA/DSX)
2,6-Dimethylaniline	9		DMM	
Dimethylbenzene, see Xylenes				XLX
Dimethylcyclicsiloxane hydrolyzate	34			
N,N-Dimethylcyclohexylamine	7		DXN	
N,N-Dimethyldodecylamine (IMO cargo name), see Dodecyldimethylamine	7		DDY	
Dimethylethanolamine	8		DMB	
Dimethylformamide	10		DMF	
Dimethyl furan	41			
Dimethyl glutarate	34		DGT	
Dimethyl hydrogen phosphite	34	2	DPI	
Dimethyl naphthalene sulfonic acid, sodium salt solution	34	2	DNS	
Dimethyloctanoic acid	4		DMO	

Coast Guard, DHS

Pt. 150, Table I

Chemical name	Group No.	Foot-note	CHRIS Code	Related CHRIS Codes
Dimethyl phthalate	34		DTL	
Dimethylpolysiloxane, see Polydimethylsiloxane	34		DMP	
2,2-Dimethylpropane-1,3-diol	20		DDI	
Dimethyl succinate	34		DSE	
Dinitrotoluene	42		DNM	DTT/DNL/DNU
Dinonyl phthalate, see Dialkyl(C7-C13) phthalates			DIF	DAH
Dioctyl phthalate	34		DOP	DIE
1,4-Dioxane	41		DOX	
Dipentene	30		DPN	
Diphenyl	32		DIL	
Diphenylamine (molten)	9		DAG	DAM/LRM
Diphenylamines, alkylated	7		DAJ	
Diphenylamine, reaction product with 2,2,4-trimethylpentene	7		DAK	
Diphenyl, Diphenyl ether mixture	33		DDO	DTH
Diphenyl ether	41		DPE	
Diphenyl ether, Diphenyl phenyl ether mixture	41		DOB	
Diphenylmethane diisocyanate	12		DPM	
Diphenylol propane-Epichlorohydrin resins	0	1	DPR	
Diphenyl oxide, see as diphenyl ether				
Di-n-propylamine	7		DNA	
Dipropylene glycol	40		DPG	
Dipropylene glycol butyl ether, see Poly(2-8)alkylene glycol monoalkyl(C1-C6) ether.			DBG	PAG
Dipropylene glycol dibenzoate	34		DGY	
Dipropylene glycol methyl ether, see Poly (2-8)alkylene glycol monoalkyl(C1-C6) ether.			DPY	PAG
Distillates, flashed feed stocks	33		DFF	
Distillates, straight run	33		DSR	
Dithiocarbamate ester (C7-C35)	34		DHO	
Ditridecyl adipate	34			
Ditridecyl phthalate, see Dialkyl(C7-C13) phthalates			DTP	DAH
Diundecyl phthalate, see Dialkyl(C7-C13) phthalates			DUP	DAH
Dodecane	31	1	DOC	ALJ
tert-Dodecanethiol	0	2	DDL	
Dodecanol	20		DDN	LAL
Dodecene	30		DOZ	DDC/DOD
2-Dodecenylsuccinic acid, dipotassium salt solution	34			DSP
Dodecyl alcohol (IMO cargo name), see Dodecanol				DDN
Dodecylamine, Tetradecylamine mixture	7		DTA	
Dodecylbenzene, see Alkyl(C9+)benzenes	32	2	DDB	AKB
Dodecylbenzenesulfonic acid	0	1, 2	DSA	
Dodecyldimethylamine, Tetradecyldimethylamine mixture	7		DOT	
Dodecyl diphenyl ether disulfonate solution	43		DOS	
Dodecyl hydroxypropyl sulfide	0	1	DOH	
Dodecyl methacrylate	14	1	DDM	
Dodecyl-Octadecyl methacrylate mixture	14	1	DOM	
Dodecyl-Pentadecyl methacrylate mixtures	14	1	DDP	
Dodecyl phenol	21		DOL	
Dodecyl xylene	32	2	DXY	
Drilling brine (containing Calcium, Potassium or Sodium salts)	43			DRB
Drilling brine (containing Zinc salts)	43		DZB	
Drilling mud (low toxicity) (if flammable or combustible)	33			DRM
Drilling mud (low toxicity) (if non-flammable or non-combustible)	43			DRM
Epichlorohydrin	17	1	EPC	
Epoxy resin	18			
ETBE, see Ethyl tert-butyl ether				EBE
Ethane	31	1	ETH	
Ethanolamine (monoethanolamine)	8		MEA	
2-Ethoxyethanol, see Ethylene glycol monoalkyl ethers			EEO	EGC
2-Ethoxyethyl acetate	34		EEA	
Ethoxylated alcohols, C11-C15, see the alcohol poyletoxylates				
Ethoxylated long chain (C16+) alkyloxyalkanamine	8		ELA	
Ethoxy triglycol	40		ETG	
Ethyl acetate	34		ETA	
Ethyl acetoacetate	34		EAA	
Ethyl acrylate	14	1	EAC	
Ethyl alcohol	20	2	EAL	
Ethylamine	7	2	EAM	
Ethylamine solution	7		EAN	
Ethyl amyl ketone	18		EAK	ELK
Ethylbenzene	32		ETB	
Ethyl butanol	20		EBT	
N-Ethyl-n-butylamine	7		EBA	

53

Pt. 150, Table I 46 CFR Ch. I (10–1–13 Edition)

Chemical name	Group No.	Foot-note	CHRIS Code	Related CHRIS Codes
Ethyl tert-butyl ether	41	2	EBE	
Ethyl butyrate	34		EBR	
Ethyl chloride	36		ECL	
Ethyl cyclohexane	31	1	ECY	
N-Ethylcyclohexylamine	7		ECC	
Ethylene	30		ETL	
Ethyleneamine EA 1302	7	2	EMX	EDA
Ethylene carbonate	34			
Ethylene chlorohydrin	20		ECH	
Ethylene cyanohydrin	20		ETC	
Ethylenediamine	7	2	EDA	EMX
Ethylenediaminetetraacetic acid, tetrasodium salt solution	43		EDS	
Ethylene dibromide	36		EDB	
Ethylene dichloride	36	2	EDC	
Ethylene glycol	20	2	EGL	
Ethylene glycol acetate	34		EGO	
Ethylene glycol butyl ether, see Ethylene glycol monoalkyl ethers			EGM	EGC
Ethylene glycol tert-butyl ether, see Ethylene glycol monoalkyl ethers				EGC
Ethylene glycol butyl ether acetate	34		EMA	
Ethylene glycol diacetate	34		EGY	
Ethylene glycol dibutyl ether	40		EGB	
Ethylene glycol ethyl ether, see Ethyl glycol monoalkyl ethers			EGE	EGC/EEO
Ethylene glycol ethyl ether acetate, see 2-Ethoxyethyl acetate			EGA	EEA
Ethylene glycol hexyl ether	40		EGH	
Ethylene glycol isopropyl ether, see Ethylene glycol monoalkyl ethers			EGI	EGC
Ethylene glycol methyl butyl ether, see Ethylene glycol monoalkyl ethers	40		EMB	EGC
Ethylene glycol methyl ether, see Ethylene glycol monoalkyl ethers			EME	EGC
Ethylene glycol methyl ether acetate	34		EGT	
Ethylene glycol monoalkyl ethers	40		EGC	
Including:				
Ethylene glycol butyl ether				
Ethylene glycol isobutyl ether				
Ethylene glycol tert-butyl ether				
Ethylene glycol ethyl ether				
Ethylene glycol hexyl ether				
Ethylene glycol methyl ether				
Ethylene glycol propyl ether				
Ethylene glycol isopropyl ether				
Ethylene glycol phenyl ether	40		EPE	
Ethylene glycol phenyl ether, Diethylene glycol phenyl ether mixture	40		EDX	
Ethylene glycol propyl ether, see Ethylene glycol monoalkyl ethers			EGP	EGC
Ethylene glycol iso-propyl ether, see Ethylene glycol monoalkyl ethers			EGI	EGC
Ethylene oxide	0	1	EOX	
Ethylene oxide, Propylene oxide mixture	16	1	EPM	
Ethylene-Propylene copolymer	30			
Ethylene-Vinyl acetate copolymer emulsion	43			
Ethyl ether	41		EET	
Ethyl-3-ethoxypropionate	34		EEP	
2-Ethylhexaldehyde, see Octyl aldehydes			HA	OAL
2-Ethylhexanoic acid, see Octanoic acids			EHO	OAY
2-Ethylhexanol, see Octanol			EHX	OCX
2-Ethylhexyl acrylate	14	1	EAI	
2-Ethylhexylamine	7		EHM	
Ethyl hexyl phthalate	34		EHE	
Ethyl hexyl tallate	34		EHT	
2-Ethyl-1-(hydroxymethyl)propane-1,3-diol, C8-C10 ester	34		EHD	
Ethylidene norbornene	30	2	ENB	
Ethyl methacrylate	14	1	ETM	
N-Ethylmethylallylamine	7		EML	
2-Ethyl-6-methyl-N-(1′-methyl-2-methoxyethyl)aniline	9		EEM	
o-Ethyl phenol	21		EPL	
Ethyl propionate	34		EPR	
2-Ethyl-3-propylacrolein	19	2	EPA	
Ethyl toluene	32		ETE	
Fatty acids (saturated, C13+), see Fatty acids (saturated, C14+)				
Fatty acids (saturated, C14+)	34		FAD	SRA
Ferric chloride solution	1	1	FCS	FCL
Ferric hydroxyethylethylenediaminetriacetic acid, trisodium salt solution	43	2	FHX	STA
Ferric nitrate, Nitric acid solution	3		FNN	
Fish solubles (water based fish meal extracts)	43		FSO	
Fluorosilicic acid	1	1	FSJ	
Formaldehyde, Methanol mixtures	19	2	MTM	
Formaldehyde solution	19	2	FMS	

Coast Guard, DHS   Pt. 150, Table I

Chemical name	Group No.	Foot-note	CHRIS Code	Related CHRIS Codes
Formamide	10		FAM	
Formic acid	4	2	FMA	
Fructose solution	43		FAR	
Fumaric adduct of Rosin, water dispersion	43		FAR	
Furfural	19		FFA	
Furfuryl alcohol	20	2	FAL	
Gas oil, cracked	33		GOC	
Gasoline blending stock, alkylates	33		GAK	
Gasoline blending stock, reformates	33		GRF	
Gasolines:				
Automotive (*not over 4.23 grams lead per gal.*)	33		GAT	
Aviation (*not over 4.86 grams lead per gal*)	33		GAV	AVA
Casinghead (*natural*)	33		GCS	
Polymer	33		GPL	
Straight run	33		GSR	
Glucose solution	43		GLU	DTS
Glutaraldehyde solution	19		GTA	
Glycerine	20	2	GCR	
Glycerine, Dioxanedimethanol mixture	20		GDM	
Glycerol monooleate	20		GMO	
Glycerol polyalkoxylate	34			
Glyceryl triacetate	34			
Glycidyl ester of C10 trialkyl acetic acid (*IMO cargo name*), *see* Glycidyl ester of tridecyl acetic acid.	34			GLT
Glycidyl ester of tridecylacetic acid	34		GLT	
Glycidyl ester of Versatic acid, *see* Gylcidyl ester of tridecylacetic acid				GLT
Glycine, sodium salt solution	7			
Glycol diacetate, *see* Ethylene glycol diacetate				EGY
Glycolic acid solution	4		GLC	
Glyoxal solutions	19		GOS	
Glyoxylic acid	4		GAC	
Glyphosate solution (not containing surfactant) (See also ROUNDUP)	7		GIO	
Heptadecane, *see* n-Alkanes (C10+)				ALJ
Heptane	31	1	HMX	ALK (HPI/HPT)
n-Heptanoic acid	4		HEP	
Heptanol	20		HTX	HTN
Heptene	30		HPX	HTE
Heptyl acetate	34		HPE	
Herbicide (C15-H22-NO2-Cl), *see* Metolachlor				MCO
Hexadecanol (cetyl alcohol), *see* Alcohols (C13+)				ALY
1-Hexadecylnaphthalene, 1,4-bis(Hexadecyl)naphthalene mixture	32			
Hexaethylene glycol, *see* Polyethylene glycol				
Hexamethylene glycol	20			
Hexamethylenediamine	7		HME	HMD/HMC
Hexamethylenediamine solution	7		HMC	HMD/HME
Hexamethylenediamine adipate solution	43		HAM	
Hexamethylene diisocyanate	12		HDI	
Hexamethylenetetramine	7		HMT	
Hexamethylenetetramine solutions	7		HTS	
Hexamethylenimine	7		HMI	
Hexane	31	2	HXS	ALK (IHA/HXA)
Hexanoic acid	4		HXO	
Hexanol	20		HXN	
Hexene	30		HEX	HXE/HXT/MPN/MTN
Hexyl acetate	34		HAE	HSA
Hexylene glycol	20		HXG	
HiTec 321	7		HIT	
Hog grease, *see* Lard				
Hydrochloric acid	1	1	HCL	
Hydrofluorosilicic acid, *see* Fluorosilicic acid			HFS	FSJ
bis(Hydrogenated tallow alkyl)methyl amines	7		HTA	
Hydrogen peroxide solutions	0	1		HPN/HPS/HPO
2-Hydroxyethyl acrylate	14	2	HAI	
N-(Hydroxyethyl)ethylenediamine triacetic acid, trisodium salt solution	43		HET	FHX
N,N-bis(2-Hydroxyethyl) oleamide	10		HOO	
2-Hydroxy-4-(methylthio)butanoic acid	4		HBA	
Hydroxy terminated polybutadiene (*IMO cargo name*), *see* Polybutadiene, hydroxy terminated.	20			
alpha-hydro-omega-Hydroxytetradeca(oxytetramethylene), *see* Poly(tetramethylene ether) glycols (mw 950-1050).				HTO
Icosa(oxypropane-2,3-diyl)s	20		IOP	
Isophorone	18	2	IPH	
Isophorone diamine	7		IPI	

Chemical name	Group No.	Foot-note	CHRIS Code	Related CHRIS Codes
Isophorone diisocyanate	12		IPD	
Isoprene	30		IPR	
Isoprene concentrate (Shell)	30		ISC	
Isopropylbenzene (cumene), see Propylbenzene				PBY
Jet fuels:				
JP-4	33		JPF	
JP-5	33		JPV	
JP-8	33		JPE	
Kaolin clay slurry	43			
Kerosene	33		KRS	
Ketone residue	18		KTR	
Kraft black liquor	5			KPL
Kraft pulping liquors (*Black, Green, or White*)	5		KPL	
Lactic acid	0	1, 2	LTA	
Lactonitrile solution	37		LNI	
Lard	34			
Latex (ammonia inhibited)	30		LTX	
Latex, liquid synthetic	43		LLS	LTX
Lauric acid	34		LRA	
Lauryl polyglucose, see Alkyl(C12 -C14) polyglucoside solution (55% or less).			LAP	AGM
Lecithin	34		LEC	
Lignin liquor	43			
Lignin sulfonic acid, sodium salt solution, see Sodium lignosulfonate solution.				
d-Limonene, see Dipentene				
Liquid Streptomyces solubles	43			
Long chain alkaryl polyether (C11-C20)	41		LCP	
Long chain alkaryl sulfonic acid (C16-C60)	0	1, 2	LCS	
Long chain alkylphenate/Phenol sulfide mixture	21		LPS	
Long chain polyetheramine in alkyl(C2-C4)benzenes	7		LCE	
l-Lysine solution	43		LYS	
Magnesium chloride solution	0	1, 2		
Magnesium hydroxide slurry	5			
Magnesium long chain alkaryl sulfonate (C11-C50)	34		MAS	MSE
Magnesium long chain alkyl phenate sulfide (C8-C20)	34		MPS	
Magnesium long chain alkyl salicylate (C11+)	34		MLS	
Magnesium nonyl phenol sulfide, see Magnesium long chain alkyl phenate sulfide (C8-C20).				MPS
Magnesium sulfonate, see Magnesium long chain alkaryl sulfonate (C11-C50).			MSE	MAS
Maleic anhydride	11		MLA	
Mercaptobenzothiazol, sodium salt solution (*IMO cargo name*), *see* Sodium-2-mercaptobenzothiazol solution.	5			SMB
Mesityl oxide	18	2	MSO	
Metam sodium solution	7		MSS	SMD
Methacrylic acid	4		MAD	
Methacrylic resin in Ethylene dichloride	14	1	MRD	
Methacrylonitrile	15	2	MET	
Methane	31	1	MTH	
3-Methoxy-1-butanol	20			
3-Methoxybutyl acetate	34		MOA	
N-(2-Methoxy-1-methyl ethyl)-2-ethyl-6-methyl chloroacetanilide (*IMO cargo name*), *see* Metolachlor.	34			MCO
1-Methoxy-2-propyl acetate	34		MPO	
Methoxy triglycol	40		*MTG*	
Methyl acetate	34		MTT	
Methyl acetoacetate	34		MAE	
Methyl acetylene, Propadiene mixture	30		MAP	
Methyl acrylate	14	1	MAM	
Methyl alcohol	20	2	MAL	
Methylamine solutions	7		MSZ	
Methyl amyl acetate	34		MAC	
Methyl amyl alcohol	20		MAA	MIC
Methyl amyl ketone	18		MAK	
Methyl bromide	36		MTB	
Methyl butanol, see the amyl alcohols				AAI
Methyl butenol	20		MBL	
Methyl butenes (tert-amylenes), see Pentene				PTX
Methyl tert-butyl ether	41	2	MBE	
Methyl butyl ketone	18	2	MBK	
Methylbutynol, *see* 2-Methyl-2-hydroxy-3-butyne	20		MBY	MHB
3-Methyl butyraldehyde	19			

Coast Guard, DHS
Pt. 150, Table I

Chemical name	Group No.	Foot-note	CHRIS Code	Related CHRIS Codes
Methyl butyrate	34		MBU	
Methyl chloride	36		MTC	
Methylcyclohexane	31	1	MCY	
Methylcyclopentadiene dimer	30		MCK	
Methyl diethanolamine	8		MDE	MAB
Methylene chloride, see Dichloromethane				DCM
2-Methyl-6-ethylaniline	9		MEN	
Methyl ethyl ketone	18	2	MEK	
2-Methyl-5-ethylpyridine	9		MEP	
Methyl formate	34		MFM	
N-Methylglucamine solution	43		MGC	
Methyl heptyl ketone	18		MHK	
2-Methyl-2-hydroxy-3-butyne	20		MHB	
Methyl isoamyl ketone	18			MAK
Methyl isoamyl carbinol, see Methyl amyl alcohol			MIC	MAA
Methyl isobutyl ketone	18	2	MIK	
Methyl methacrylate	14	1	MMM	
3-Methyl-3-methoxybutanol	20			
3-Methyl-3-methoxybutyl acetate	34			
Methyl naphthalene	32		MNA	
Methylolureas	19		MUS	
2-Methyl pentane	31	1		IHA
2-Methyl-1-pentene, see Hexene			MPN	HEX
4-Methyl-1-pentene, see Hexene			MTN	HEX
Methyl tert-pentyl ether (*IMO cargo name*), *see* tert-Amyl methyl ether	41			AYE
2-Methyl-1,3-propanediol	20		MDL	
Methyl propyl ketone	18		MKE	
Methylpyridine	9			MPR/MPE/MPF
N-Methyl-2-pyrrolidone	9	2	MPY	
Methyl salicylate	34		MES	
alpha-Methylstyrene	30		MSR	
3-(Methylthio)propionaldehyde	19		MTP	
Metolachlor	34		MCO	
Milk	43			
Mineral spirits	33		MNS	
Molasses	20			
Molasses residue	0	1		
Monochlorodifluoromethane	36		MCF	
Monoethanolamine, see Ethanolamine				
Monoisopropanolamine, see Propanolamine				
Morpholine	7	2	MPL	
Motor fuel antiknock compounds containing lead alkyls	0	1	MFA	
MTBE, see Methyl tert-butyl ether				MBE
Myrcene	30		MRE	
Naphtha:				
Aromatic	33			
Coal tar solvent	33		NCT	
Heavy	33			
Paraffinic	33			
Petroleum	33		PTN	
Solvent	33		NSV	
Stoddard solvent	33		NSS	
Varnish Makers' and Painters'	33		NVM	
Naphthalene	32		NTM	
Naphthalene still residue	32	2	NSR	
Naphthalene sulfonic acid-formaldehyde copolymer, sodium salt solution	0	1	NFS	
Naphthalene sulfonic acid, sodium salt solution	34		NSA	
Naphthenic acid	4		NTI	
Naphthenic acid, sodium salt solution	43		NTS	
Neodecanoic acid	4		NEA	
NIAX POLYOL APP 240C	0	1, 2	NXP	
Nitrating acid	0	1	NIA	
Nitric acid (70% or less)	3		NCD	
Nitric acid (greater than 70%)	0	1		NAC
Nitrobenzene	42		NTB	
o-Nitrochlorobenzene, see Chloronitrobenzene				CNO
Nitroethane	42		NTE	
Nitroethane, 1-Nitropropane mixtures	42		NNO	
o-Nitrophenol	0	1, 2	NTP	NIP/NPH
Nitropropane	42		NPM	NPN/NPP
Nitropropane, Nitroethane mixture	42			NNO (NNM/NNL)
Nitrotoluene	42		NIT	NIE/NTT/NTR
Nonane	31	1	NAX	ALK (NAN)

57

Pt. 150, Table I

Chemical name	Group No.	Foot- note	CHRIS Code	Related CHRIS Codes
Nonanoic acid	4		NNA	NAI/NIN
Nonanoic, Tridecanoic acid mixture	4		NAT	
Nonene	30		NOO	NON/NNE
Nonyl acetate	34		NAE	
Nonyl alcohol	20	2	NNS	NNI/NNN/DBC
Nonylbenzene, see Alkyl(C9+)benzenes				AKB
Nonyl methacrylate	14	1	NMA	
Nonyl phenol	21		NNP	
Nonyl phenol poly(4+)ethoxylates	40		NPE	
Nonyl phenol sulfide solution, see Alkyl phenol sulfide (C8-C40)				AKS/NPS
Noxious Liquid Substance, n.o.s. (NLS's)	0	1		
1-Octadecene, see the olefin or alpha-olefin entries				
Octadecenoamide	10		ODD	
Octadecenol (oleyl alcohol), see Alcohols (C13+)				ALY
Octane	31	1	OAX	ALK (IOO/OAN)
Octanoic acid	4		OAY	OAA/EHO
Octanol	20	2	OCX	IOA/OTA/EHX
Octene	30		OTX	OTE
n-Octyl acetate	34		OAF	OAE
Octyl alcohol, see Octanol				OCX
Octyl aldehyde	19		OAL	IOC/OLX/EHA
Octyl decyl adipate	34		ODA	
Octyl nitrate, see Alkyl(C7-C9) nitrates			ONE	AKN
Octyl phenol	21			
Octyl phthalate, see Dioctyl phthalate				DOP
Oil, edible:				
Beechnut	34		OBN	VEO
Castor	34		OCA	VEO
Cocoa butter	34		OCB	VEO
Coconut	34	2	OCC	VEO
Cod liver	34		OCL	AFN
Corn	34		OCO	VEO
Cottonseed	34		OCS	VEO
Fish	34	2	OFS	AFN
Groundnut	34		OGN	VEO
Hazelnut	34		OHN	VEO
Lard	34		OLD	AFN
Maize	34			VEO (OCO)
Nutmeg butter	34		ONB	VEO
Olive	34		OOL	VEO
Palm	34	2	OPM	VEO
Palm kernel	34		OPO	VEO
Peanut	34		OPN	VEO
Poppy	34		OPY	VEO
Poppy seed	34			VEO
Raisin seed	34		ORA	VEO
Rapeseed	34		ORP	VEO
Rice bran	34		ORB	VEO
Safflower	34		OSF	VEO
Salad	34		OSL	VEO
Sesame	34		OSS	VEO
Soya bean	34		OSB	VEO
Sunflower seed	34		OSN	VEO
Tucum	34		OTC	VEO
Vegetable	34		OVG	VEO
Walnut	34		OWN	VEO
Oil, fuel:				
No. 1	33		OON	
No. 1-D	33		OOD	
No. 2	33		OTW	
No. 2-D	33		OTD	
No. 4	33		OFR	
No. 5	33		OFV	
No. 6	33		OSX	
Oil, misc:				
Aliphatic	33			
Animal	34		OMA	AFN
Aromatic	33			
Clarified	33		OCF	
Coal	33			
Coconut oil, fatty acid methyl ester	34		OCM	
Cotton seed oil, fatty acid	34		CFY	
Crude	33		OIL	

Coast Guard, DHS — Pt. 150, Table I

Chemical name	Group No.	Foot-note	CHRIS Code	Related CHRIS Codes
Diesel	33		ODS	
Gas, high pour	33			
Gas, low pour	33			
Gas, low sulfur	33			
Heartcut distillate	33			
Lanolin	34		OLL	AFN
Linseed	33		OLS	
Lubricating	33		OLB	
Mineral	33		OMN	
Mineral seal	33		OMS	
Motor	33		OMT	
Neatsfoot	33		ONF	AFN
Oiticica	34		OOI	
Palm oil, fatty acid methyl ester	34		OPE	
Penetrating	33		OPT	
Perilla	34		OPR	
Pilchard	34		OPL	AFN
Pine	33		OPI	PNL
Residual	33			
Road	33		ORD	
Rosin	33		ORN	
Seal	34			
Soapstock	34		OIS	
Soybean (epoxidized)	34			EVO
Sperm	33		OSP	AFN
Spindle	33		OSD	
Tall	34		OTL	
Tall, fatty acid	34	2	TOF	
Transformer	33		OTF	
Tung	34		OTG	
Turbine	33		OTB	
Wood	34			
Olefin/Alkyl ester copolymer (molecular weight 2000+)	34		OCP	
Olefin mixtures	30			OFX/OFY
alpha-Olefins (C6-C18) mixtures	30		OAM	
Olefins (C13+)	30			
Oleic acid	34		OLA	
Oleum	0	1, 2	OLM	
Oleyl alcohol (octadecenol), see Alcohols (C13+)				ALY
Oleylamine	7		OLY	
ORIMULSION, see Asphalt emulsion				ASQ
Oxyalkylated alkyl phenol formaldehyde	33			
Palm kernel acid oil	34		PNO	
Palm kernel acid oil, methyl ester	34		PNF	
Palm kernel oil, fatty acid, see Palm kernel acid oil				PNO
Palm kernel oil, fatty acid methyl ester, see Palm kernel acid oil, methyl ester.				PNF
Palm stearin	34		PMS	
n-Paraffins (C10-C20), see n-Alkanes (C10+)			PFN	ALJ
Paraldehyde	19		PDH	
Paraldehyde-Ammonia reaction product	9		PRB	
Pentachloroethane	36		PCE	
Pentacosa(oxypropane-2,3-diyl)s	20		POY	
Pentadecanol, see Alcohols (C13+)			PDC	ALY
1,3-Pentadiene	30		PDE	PDN
Pentaethylene glycol, see Polyethylene glycols				
Pentaethylene glycol methyl ether, see Poly(2-8)alkylene glycol monoalkyl(C1-C6) ether.				PAG
Pentaethylenehexamine	7		PEN	
Pentaethylenehexamine, Tetraethylenepentamine mixture	7		PEP	
Pentane	31	1	PTY	IPT/PTA
Pentanoic acid	4		POC	
n-Pentanoic acid, 2-Methyl butyric acid mixture	4		POJ	POC
Pentasodium salt of Diethylenetriamine pentaacetic acid solution, see Diethylenetriamine pentaacetic acid, pentasodium salt solution.				
Pentene	30		PTX	PTE
Pentyl aldehyde	19			
n-Pentyl propionate	34		PPE	
Perchloroethylene	36	2	PER	TTE
Petrolatum	33		PTL	
Phenol	21		PHN	
1-Phenyl-1-xylyl ethane	32		PXE	
Phosphate esters, alkyl(C12-C14)amine	7		PEA	

Pt. 150, Table I — 46 CFR Ch. I (10–1–13 Edition)

Chemical name	Group No.	Footnote	CHRIS Code	Related CHRIS Codes
Phosphoric acid	1	1	PAC	
Phosphorus	0	1	PPW	PPR/PPB
Phthalate based polyester polyol	0	1, 2	PBE	
Phthalic anhydride	11		PAN	
alpha-Pinene	30		PIO	PIN
beta-Pinene	30		PIP	PIN
Pine oil	33		PNL	OPI
Polyalkyl(C18-C22) acrylate in Xylene	14	1	PIX	
Polyalkylene glycol butyl ether, see Poly(2-8)alkylene glycol monoalkyl(C1-C6) ether.			PGB	PAG
Poly(2-8)alkylene glycol monoalkyl(C1-C6) ether	40		PAG	
Including:				
Diethylene glycol butyl ether				
Diethylene glycol ethyl ether				
Diethylene glycol n-hexyl ether				
Diethylene glycol methyl ether				
Diethylene glycol n-propyl ether				
Dipropylene glycol butyl ether				
Dipropylene glycol methyl ether				
Polyalkylene glycol butyl ether				
Polyethylene glycol monoalkyl ether				
Polypropylene glycol methyl ether				
Tetraethylene glycol methyl ether				
Triethylene glycol butyl ether				
Triethylene glycol ethyl ether				
Triethylene glycol methyl ether				
Tripropylene glycol methyl ether				
Poly(2-8)alkylene glycol monoalkyl(C1-C6) ether acetate	34		PAF	
Including:				
Diethylene glycol butyl ether acetate				
Diethylene glycol ethyl ether acetate				
Diethylene glycol methyl ether acetate				
Polyalkylene glycols, Polyalkylene glycol monoalkyl ethers mixtures	40		PPX	
Polyalkylene oxide polyol	20		PAO	
Polyalkyl methacrylate (C1-C20)				
Polyalkyl(C10-C20)methacrylate	14	1	PMT	
Polyalkyl(C10-C18)methacrylate/Ethylene propylene copolymer mixture	14	1	PEM	
Polyaluminum chloride solution	1	1		
Polybutadiene, hydroxyl terminated	20			
Polybutene	30		PLB	
Polybutenyl succinimide	10		PBS	
Poly(2+)cyclic aromatics	32		PCA	
Polydimethylsiloxane	34			
Polyether (molecular weight 2000+)	41		PYR	
Polyethylene glycol	40			
Polyethylene glycol dimethyl ether	40			
Polyethylene glycol monoalkyl ether, see Poly(2-8)alkylene glycol monoalkyl(C1-C6) ether.			PEE	PAG
Polyethylene polyamines	7	2	PEB	
Polyferric sulfate solution	34		PSS	
Polyglycerine, Sodium salts solution (containing less than 3% Sodium hydroxide).	20	2	PGT	
Polyglycerol	20			GCR
Polyisobutenamine in aliphatic (C10-C14) solvent	7		PIB	
Polyisobutenyl anhydride adduct	11			
Poly(4+)isobutylene	30			
Polymethylene polyphenyl isocyanate	12		PPI	
Polymethylsiloxane	34			
Polyolefin (molecular weight 300+)	30			
Polyolefin amide alkeneamine (C17+)	33		POH	
Polyolefin amide alkeneamine (C28+)	33		POD	
Polyolefin amide alkeneamine borate (C28-C250)	33		PAB	
Polyolefin amide alkeneamine/Molybdenum oxysulfide mixture	7			
Polyolefin amide alkeneamine polyol	20		PAP	
Poly(C17+)olefin amine	7		POG	
Polyolefinamine (C28-C250)	33		POM	
Polyolefinamine in alkyl(C2-C4)benzenes	32		POF	
Polyolefin aminoester salt	34		PAE	
Polyolefin anhydride	11		PAR	
Polyolefin ester (C28-C250)	34		POS	
Polyolefin phenolic amine (C28-C250)	7		PPH	
Polyolefin phosphorosulfide, barium derivative (C28-C250)	34		PPS	
Poly(20)oxyethylene sorbitan monooleate	34		PSM	

Chemical name	Group No.	Foot-note	CHRIS Code	Related CHRIS Codes
Poly(5+)propylene	30		PLQ	PLP
Polypropylene glycol	40		PGC	
Polypropylene glycol methyl ether, see Propylene glycol monoalkyl ether			PGM	PGE
Polysiloxane	34			DMP
Poly(tetramethylene ether) glycols (mw 950-1050) (*alpha-hydro-omega-Hydroxytetradeca(oxytetramethylene)*).	40		HTO	
Polytetramethylene ether glycol	40			
Potassium chloride solution	43		PCS	(DRB)
Potassium formate solution	34		PFR	
Potassium hydroxide solution (*IMO cargo name*), see Caustic potash solution.	5	2		CPS
Potassium oleate	34		POE	
Potassium salt of polyolefin acid	34			
Potassium thiosulfate solution	43		PTF	
Propane	31	1	PRP	
Propanolamine	8		PAX	MPA/PLA
Propionaldehyde	19		PAD	
Propionic acid	4		PNA	
Propionic anhydride	11		PAH	
Propionitrile	37		PCN	
n-Propoxypropanol, see Propylene glycol monoalkyl ether			PXP	PGE
Propyl acetate	34			IAC/PAT
Propyl alcohol	20	2		IPA/PAL
Propylamine	7			IPP/PRA
iso-Propylamine solution	7			IPO/IPQ
Propylbenzene	32	2	PBY	PBZ/CUM
n-Propyl chloride	36		PRC	
iso-Propylcyclohexane	31	1	IPX	
Propylene	30		PPL	
Propylene-butylene copolymer	30		PBP	
Propylene carbonate	34			
Propylene dimer	30		PDR	
Propylene glycol	20	2	PPG	
Propylene glycol n-butyl ether, see Propylene glycol monoalkyl ether			PGD	PGE
Propylene glycol ethyl ether, see Propylene glycol monoalkyl ether			PGY	PGE
Propylene glycol methyl ether, see Propylene glycol monoalkyl ether			PME	PGE
Propylene glycol methyl ether acetate	34		PGN	
Propylene glycol monoalkyl ether	40		PGE	
Including:				
n-Propoxypropanol				
Propylene glycol n-butyl ether				
Propylene glycol ethyl ether				
Propylene glycol methyl ether				
Propylene glycol propyl ether				
Propylene glycol phenyl ether	40		PGP	
Propylene glycol propyl ether, see Propylene glycol monoalkyl ether				PGE
Propylene oxide	16	1	POX	
Propylene, Propane, MAPP gas mixture	30	2	PPM	
Propylene tetramer	30		PTT	
Propylene trimer	30		PTR	
Propyl ether	41			IPE/PRE
Pseudocumene, see Trimethylbenzene				TME/TRE
Pyridine	9		PRD	
Pyridine bases, see Paraldehyde-Ammonia reaction product				PRB
Roehm monomer 6615	14	1	RMN	
Rosin oil	33		ORN	
Rosin soap (disproportionated) solution	43		RSP	
ROUNDUP (See also Glyphosate solution)	7		RUP	
Rum, see Alcoholic beverages				
SAP 7001	0	1	SON	
Sewage sludge	43			
Silica slurry	43			
Sludge, treated	43			
Sodium acetate, Glycol, Water mixture (not containing Sodium hydroxide)	34	2	SAO	SAP
Sodium acetate, Glycol, Water mixture (containing Sodium hydroxide)	5		SAP	SAO
Sodium acetate solution	34		SAN	AKP
Sodium alkyl sulfonate solution	43		SSU	
Sodium alkyl (C14-C17) sulfonates 60-65% solution (*IMO cargo name*), see Alkane (C14-C17) sulfonic acid, sodium salt solution.	34		AKA	
Sodium aluminate solution	5		SAU	
Sodium aluminosillicate slurry	34			
Sodium benzoate solution	34		SBN	
Sodium borohydride, Sodium hydroxide solution	5		SBX	SBH/SBI

Pt. 150, Table I   46 CFR Ch. I (10–1–13 Edition)

Chemical name	Group No.	Foot-note	CHRIS Code	Related CHRIS Codes
Sodium carbonate solutions	5		SCE	
Sodium chlorate solution	0	1, 2	SDD	SDC
Sodium cyanide solution	5		SCS	SCN
Sodium dichromate solution	0	1, 2	SDL	SCR
Sodium dimethyl naphthalene sulfonate solution, see Dimethyl naphthalene sulfonic acid, sodium salt solution.				DNS
Sodium hydrogen sulfide, Sodium carbonate solution	0	1, 2	SSS	
Sodium hydrogen sulfite solution	43		SHX	
Sodium hydrosulfide solution	5	2	SHR	
Sodium hydrosulfide, Ammonium sulfide solution	5	2	SSA	
Sodium hydroxide solution (*IMO cargo name*), see Caustic soda solution	5	2		CSS
Sodium hypochlorite solution	5			SHP/SHQ/(SHC)
Sodium lignosulfonate solution, see also Lignin liquor	43			
Sodium long chain alkyl salicylate (C13+)	34		SLS	
Sodium 2-mercaptobenzothiazol solution	5		SMB	
Sodium N-methyl dithio carbamate solution, see Metam sodium solution				MSS
Sodium naphthalene sulfonate solution, see Naphthalene sulfonic acid, sodium salt solution.			SNS	NSA
Sodium naphthenate solution, see Naphthenic acid, sodium salt solution				NTS
Sodium nitrite solution	5		SNI	SNT
Sodium petroleum sulfonate	33		SPS	
Sodium polyacrylate solution	43	2		
Sodium salt of Ferric hydroxyethylethylenediaminetriacetic acid solution, see Ferric hydroxyethylethylenediaminetriacetic acid, trisodium salt solution.			STA	FHX
Sodium silicate solution	43	2	SSN	SSC
Sodium sulfide, Hydrosulfide solution	0	1, 2		SSH/SSI/SSJ
Sodium sulfide solution	43		SDR	
Sodium sulfite solution	43		SUP	SUS
Sodium tartrates, Sodium succinates solution	43		STM	
Sodium thiocyanate solution	0	1, 2	STS	SCY
Sorbitol solutions	20			SBT
Soyabean oil (expoxidized)	34			OSC/EVO
Stearic acid, see Fatty acids (saturated, C14+)			SRA	FAD
Stearyl alcohol	20			
Styrene	30		STY	STX
Styrene monomer	30		STY	STX
Sulfohydrocarbon (C3-C88)	33		SFO	
Sulfohydrocarbon, long chain (C18+) alkylamine mixture	7		SFX	
Sulfolane	39		SFL	
Sulfonated polyacrylate solutions	43	2		
Sulfur	0	1	SXX	
Sulfuric acid	2	2	SFA	
Sulfuric acid, spent	2		SAC	
Sulfurized fat (C14-C20)	33		SFT	
Sulfurized polyolefinamide alkene(C28-C250) amine	33		SPO	
Tall oil	34		OTL	
Tall oil fatty acid (*Resin acids less than 20%*)	34	2	TOF	
Tall oil fatty acid, barium salt	0	1, 2	TOB	
Tall oil soap (disproportionated) solution	43		TOS	
Tallow	34	2	TLO	
Tallow fatty acid	34	2	TFD	
Tallow fatty alcohol, see Alcohols (C13+)			TFA	ALY
Tallow nitrile	37		TAN	
TAME, see tert-Amyl methyl ether				AYE
1,1,2,2-Tetrachloroethane	36		TEC	
Tetrachloroethylene, see Perchloroethylene			TTE	PER
Tetradecanol, see Alcohols (C13+)			TTN	ALY
Tetradecene, see the olefins entries			TTD	
Tetradecylbenzene, see Alkyl(C9+) benzenes	32		TDB	AKB
Tetraethylene glycol	40		TTG	
Tetraethylene glycol methyl ether, see Poly(2-8)alkylene glycol monoalkyl(C1-C6) ether.				PAG
Tetraethylenepentamine	7	2	TTP	
Tetrahydrofuran	41		THF	
Tetrahydronaphthalene	32		THN	
1,2,3,5-Tetramethylbenzene, see Tetramethylbenzene			TTB	TTC
Tetramethylbenzene	32		TTC	TTB
Tetrapropylbenzene, see Alkyl(C9+)benzenes				AKB
Tetrasodium salt of EDTA solution, see Ethylenediaminetetraacetic acid, tetrasodium salt solution.				EDS
Titanium dioxide slurry	43		TDS	
Titanium tetrachloride	2		TTT	

Coast Guard, DHS

Pt. 150, Table I

Chemical name	Group No.	Foot-note	CHRIS Code	Related CHRIS Codes
Toluene	32		TOL	
Toluenediamine	9		TDA	
Toluene diisocyanate	12		TDI	
o-Toluidine	9		TLI	
Triarylphosphate, see Triisopropylated phenyl phosphates			TRA	TPL
Tributyl phosphate	34		TBP	
1,2,4-Trichlorobenzene	36		TCB	
1,1,1-Trichloroethane	36	2	TCE	
1,1,2-Trichloroethane	36		TCM	
Trichloroethylene	36	2	TCL	
1,2,3-Trichloropropane	36	2	TCN	
1,1,2-Trichloro-1,2,2-trifluoroethane	36		TTF	
Tricresyl phosphate	34			TCO/TCP
Tridecane, see n-Alkanes (C10+)			TRD	ALJ
Tridecanoic acid	34		TDO	
Tridecanol, see Alcohols (C13+)			TDN	ALY
Tridecene, see Olefins (C13+)			TDC	
Tridecyl acetate	34		TAE	
Tridecylbenzene, see Alkyl(C9+) benzenes	32	2	TRB	AKB
Triethanolamine	8	2	TEA	
Triethylamine	7		TEN	
Triethylbenzene	32	2	TEB	
Triethylene glycol	40		TEG	
Triethylene glycol butyl ether, see Poly(2-8)alkylene glycol monoalkyl(C1-C6) ether.				PAG
Triethylene glycol butyl ether mixture	40			
Triethylene glycol dibenzoate	34		TGB	
Triethylene glycol di-(2-ethylbutyrate)	34		TGD	
Triethylene glycol ether mixture	40			
Triethylene glycol ethyl ether, see Poly(2-8)alkylene glycol monoalkyl(C1-C6) ether.			TGE	PAG
Triethylene glycol methyl ether, see Poly(2-8)alkylene glycol monoalkyl(C1-C6) ether.			TGY	PAG
Triethylenetetramine	7	2	TET	
Triethyl phosphate	34		TPS	
Triethyl phosphite	34	2	TPI	
Triisobutylene	30		TIB	
Triisooctyl trimellitate	34			
Triisopropanolamine	8		TIP	
Triisopropanolamine salt of 2,4-Dichlorophenoxyacetic acid solution, see 2,4-Dichlorophenoxyacetic acid, Triisopropanolamine salt solution.				DTI
Triisopropylated phenyl phosphates	34		TPL	
Trimethylacetic acid	4		TAA	
Trimethylamine solution	7		TMT	
Trimethylbenzene	32	2	TRE	TME/TMB/TMD
Trimethylhexamethylenediamine (2,2,4- and 2,4,4-)	7		THA	
Trimethylhexamethylene diisocyanate (2,2,4- and 2,4,4-)	12		THI	
Trimethyl nonanol, see Dodecanol				DDN
Trimethylol propane polyethoxylate	20		TPR	
2,2,4-Trimethyl-1,3-pentanediol diisobutyrate	34		TMQ	
2,2,4-Trimethyl-1,3-pentanediol-1-isobutyrate	34		TMP	
2,2,4-Trimethyl-3-pentanol-1-isobutyrate	34			
Trimethyl phosphite	34	2	TPP	
1,3,5-Trioxane	41	2	TRO	
Triphenylborane, Caustic soda solution	5		TPB	
Tripropylene, see Propylene trimer				PTR
Tripropylene glycol	40		TGC	
Tripropylene glycol methyl ether, see Poly(2-8)alkylene glycol monoalkyl(C1-C6) ether.			TGM	PAG
Trisodium nitrilotriacetate	34			
Trisodium phosphate solution	5		TSP	
Trisodium salt of N-(Hydroxyethyl)ethylenediaminetriacetic acid solution, see N-(Hydroxyethyl)ethylenediaminetriacetic acid, trisodium salt solution.				HET
Trixylyl phosphate (IMO cargo name), see Trixylenyl phosphate	34			TRP
Trixylenyl phosphate	34		TRP	
Turpentine	30		TPT	
Ucarsol CR Solvent 302 SG	8		UCS	
Undecanoic acid	4		UDA	
Undecanol, see Undecyl alcohol				UND
Undecene	30		UDC	
Undecyl alcohol	20		UND	
Undecylbenzene, see Alkyl(C9+) benzenes			UDB	AKB

63

Chemical name	Group No.	Foot-note	CHRIS Code	Related CHRIS Codes
Urea, Ammonium mono- and di-hydrogen phosphate, Potassium chloride solution.	0	1	UPX	
Urea, Ammonium nitrate solution (containing Ammonia)	6		UAS	
Urea, Ammonium nitrate solution (not containing Ammonia)	43		UAT	ANU
Urea, Ammonium phosphate solution	43		UAP	
Urea solution	43			URE
Valeraldehyde	19		VAK	IVA/VAL
Vanillin black liquor	5		VBL	
Vegetable oils, n.o.s.	34		VEO	
Including:				
Beechnut oil				
Castor oil				
Cocoa butter				
Coconut oil				
Corn oil				
Cottonseed oil				
Groundnut oil				
Hazelnut oil				
Linseed oil				
Nutmeg butter				
Oiticica oil				
Olive oil				
Palm kernel oil				
Palm oil				
Peel oil (oranges and lemons)				
Perilla oil				
Poppy oil				
Raisin seed oil				
Rapeseed oil				
Rice bran oil				
Safflower oil				
Salad oil				
Sesame oil				
Soya bean oil				
Sunflower seed oil				
Tucum oil				
Tung oil				
Walnut oil				
Vegetable acid oils and distillates, n.o.s.	34		VAO	
Including:				
Corn acid oil				
Cottonseed acid oil				
Dark mixed acid oil				
Groundnut acid oil				
Mixed acid oil				
Mixed general acid oil				
Mixed hard acid oil				
Mixed soft acid oil				
Rapeseed acid oil				
Safflower acid oil				
Soya acid oil				
Sunflower seed acid oil				
Vegetable protein solution	43			
Vinyl acetate	13	1	VAM	
Vinyl chloride	35		VCM	
Vinyl ethyl ether	13	1	VEE	
Vinylidene chloride	35		VCI	
Vinyl neodecanate	13	1	VND	
Vinyltoluene	13	1	VNT	
Water	43			
Waxes:			WAX	
Candelilla	34		WDC	
Carnauba	34		WCA	
Paraffin	31	1	WPF	
Petroleum	33			
Wine, see Alcoholic beverages				
White spirit (low (15-20%) aromatic)	33		WSL	WSP
Xylene	32		XLX	XLM/XLO/XLP
Xylenes, Ethylbenzene mixture	32		XEB	
Xylenols	21		XYL	
Zinc alkaryl dithiophosphate (C7-C16)	34		ZAD	
Zinc alkenyl carboxamide	10		ZAA	
Zinc alkyl dithiophosphate (C3-C14)	34		ZAP	

Coast Guard, DHS

Pt. 150, Table I, Nt.

Chemical name	Group No.	Foot-note	CHRIS Code	Related CHRIS Codes
Zinc bromide, Calcium bromide solution, *see* Drilling brine (containing Zinc salts).	....	....		DZB

1. Because of very high reactivity or unusual conditions of carriage or potential compatibility problems, this commodity is not assigned to a specific group in the Compatibility Chart. For additional compatibility information, contact Commandant (CG–ENG–5), Attn: Hazardous Materials Division, U.S. Coast Guard Stop 7509, 2703 Martin Luther King Jr. Avenue SE., Washington, DC 20593–7509. Telephone 202–372–1420 or email hazmatstandards@uscg.mil.
2. See Appendix I—Exceptions to the Chart.

[USCG 2000–7079, 65 FR 67162, Nov. 8, 2000, as amended by USCG–2006–25697, 71 FR 55746, Sept. 25, 2006; USCG–2008–0906, 73 FR 56510, Sept. 29, 2008; USCG–2009–0702, 74 FR 49236, Sept. 25, 2009; USCG–2010–0759, 75 FR 60003, Sept. 29, 2010; USCG–2012–0832, 77 FR 59783, Oct. 1, 2012; USCG–2013–0671, 78 FR 60155, Sept. 30, 2013]

EFFECTIVE DATE NOTE: By USCG–2013–0423, 78 FR 50162, Aug. 16, 2013, Table I to part 150 was revised, effective Sept. 16, 2013. At 78 FR 56837, Sept. 16, 2013, the effectiveness was delayed until Jan. 16, 2014. For the convenience of the user, the revised text is set forth as follows:

TABLE I TO PART 150—ALPHABETICAL LIST OF CARGOES

Chemical name	Group No.	Foot-note	CHRIS Code	Related CHRIS Codes
Acetaldehyde	19	....	AAD	
Acetic acid	4	2	AAC	
Acetic anhydride	11	2	ACA	
Acetochlor	10	....	ACG	
Acetone	18	2	ACT	
Acetone cyanohydrin	0	1, 2	ACY	
Acetonitrile	37	....	ATN	
Acetonitrile (low purity grade)*	37	3	AIL	
Acetophenone	18	....	ACP	
Acid oil mixture from soybean, corn (maize) and sunflower oil refining, see Oil, misc: Acid mixture from soybean, corn (maize) and sunflower oil refining*.	34	3		AOM.
Acrolein	19	2	ARL	
Acrylamide solution (50% or less)*	10	3	AAM	AAO.
Acrylic acid	4	2	ACR	
Acrylic acid/ethenesulfonic acid copolymer with phosphonate groups, sodium salt solution*.	30	3	APG	
Acrylonitrile	15	2	ACN	
Acrylonitrile-Styrene copolymer dispersion in Polyether polyol	20	....	ALE	
Adiponitrile	37	....	ADN	
Alachlor technical (90% or more)*	33	3	ALH	ALI.
Alcohol (C12-C13, branched and linear) poly (4-8) propoxy sulfates, sodium salt 25-30% solution*.	41	3	ABL	
Alcohol (C9-C11) poly (2.5-9) ethoxylates*	40	3	AET	ALY/APV/APW.
Alcohol (C6-C17) (secondary) poly (3-6) ethoxylates*	40	3	AEA	AEB.
Alcohol (C6-C17) (secondary) poly (7-12) ethoxylates*	40	3	AEB	AEA.
Alcohol (C12-C16) poly (1-6) ethoxylates*	40	3	AED	AET/ALY/APW.
Alcohol (C12-C16) poly (7-19) ethoxylates*	40	3	APV	AET/ALY/APV.
Alcohol (C12-C16) poly (20+) ethoxylates*	40	3	APW	AET/ALY.
Alcoholic beverages, n.o.s.*	20	3	ABV	
Alcohols (C13+)	20	....	ALY	ASY/AYK.
Including:				
Oleyl alcohol (octadecenol).				
Pentadecanol.				
Tallow alcohol.				
Tetradecanol.				
Tridecanol.				
Alcohol polyethoxylates	20	....		AEA/AEB/AED/AET/APV/APW.
Alcohol polyethoxylates, secondary	20	....		AEA/AEB.
Alcohol (C12-C15) poly (. . .) ethoxylate, see Alcohol (C12-C16) poly (. . .) ethoxylate.	20			
Alcohols (C12+), primary, linear*	20	3	ASY	ALR/AYK/AYL.
Alcohols (C8-C11), primary, linear and essentially linear	20	....	ALR	AYK/AYL.
Alcohols (C12-C13), primary, linear and essentially linear*	20	3	AYK	ALR/ASY/AYL.
Alcohols (C14-C18), primary, linear and essentially linear*	20	3	AYL	ALR/ASY/AYK.
Alkanes (C6-C9)	31	....	ALK	
Including:				
Heptanes.				
Hexanes.				

Pt. 150, Table I, Nt.   46 CFR Ch. I (10–1–13 Edition)

Chemical name	Group No.	Footnote	CHRIS Code	Related CHRIS Codes
Nonanes.				
Octanes.				
iso- & cyclo-Alkanes (C10-C11)	31	....	AKI	
iso- & cyclo-Alkanes (C12+)	31	....	AKJ	
Alkanes (C10-C26), linear and branched (flash point >60 °C)*	31	3	ABD	
n-Alkanes (C10+) (all isomers)	31	....	ALV	ALJ.
Including:				
Decanes.				
Dodecanes.				
Heptadecanes.				
Tridecanes.				
Undecanes.				
Alkane (C14-C17) sulfonic acid, sodium salt solutions, see Sodium alkyl (C14-C17) sulfonates (60-65% solution).	34	....	AKA	SAA (AKE/SSU).
Alkaryl polyethers (C9-C20)	41	....	AKP	
Alkenoic acid, polyhydroxy ester borated*	0	1, 3	AAY	
Alkenyl(C11+)amide	10	....	AKM	
Alkenyl (C8+) amine, Alkenyl (C12+) acid ester mixture.				
Alkenyl (C16-C20) succinic anhydride	11	....	AAH	
Alkyl acrylate-Vinyl pyridine copolymer in Toluene	32	....	AAP	
Alkyl amine (C17+)	7	....	AKY	
Alkylaryl phosphate mixtures (more than 40% Diphenyl tolyl phosphate, less than 0.02% ortho-isomers)	34	....	ADP	
Alkylated (C4-C9) hindered phenols*	21	3	AYO	
Alkyl(C3-C4)benzenes	32	....	AKC	
Including:				
Butylbenzenes.				
Cumene.				
Propylbenzenes.				
Alkyl(C5-C8)benzenes	32	....	AKD.	
Including:				
Amylbenzenes.				
Heptylbenzenes.				
Hexylbenzenes.				
Octylbenzenes.				
Alkyl(C9+)benzenes	32	....	AKB	
Including:				
Decylbenzenes.				
Dodecylbenzenes.				
Nonylbenzenes.				
Tetradecylbenzenes.				
Tetrapropylbenzenes.				
Tridecylbenzenes.				
Undecylbenzenes.				
Alkylbenzene, Alkylindane, Alkylindene mixture (each C12-C17)	32	....	AIH	
Alkyl benzene distillation bottoms*	0	1, 3	ABB	
Alkylbenzene mixtures (containing at least 50% of Toluene)*	32	3	AZT	
Alkyl (C11-C17) benzene sulfonic acid*	0	1, 3	ABN	ABS/ABQ.
Alkylbenzenesulfonic acid (less than 4%)	0	1, 2	ABQ	ABS/ABN.
Alkylbenzene sulfonic acid, sodium salt solution	33	....	ABT	
Alkyl (C12+) dimethylamine*	7	3	ADM	
Alkyl dithiocarbamate (C19-C35)*	34	3	ADB	
Alkyl dithiothiadiazole (C6-C24)	33	....	ADT	
Alkyl polyglucoside solution, see individual polyglucoside solution	43	....	AGD	AGL/AGM AGN/AGO/AGP.
Alkyl ester copolymer (C4-C20)	34	....	AES	AEQ.
Alkyl (C8-C10)/(C12-C14):(40% or less/60% or more) polyglucoside solution (55% or less)*.	43	3	AGN	AGD/AGL AGM/AGO/AGP.
Alkyl (C8-C10)/(C12-C14):(50%/50%) polyglucoside solution (55% or less)*.	43	3	AGO	AGD/AGL/AGN/AGP.
Alkyl (C8-C10)/(C12-C14):(60% or more/40% or less) polyglucoside solution (55% or less)*.	43	3	AGP	AGD/AGL/AGM/AGN/AGO.
Alkyl(C7-C9) nitrates	34	2	AKN	ONE.
Alkyl (C4-C9) phenols	21	....	AYI	BLT/BTP/NNP/OPH.
Alkyl(C7-C11) phenol poly(4-12)ethoxylate	40	....	APN	NPE.
Alkyl (C8-C40) phenol sulfide	34	....	AKS	
Alkyl phenol sulfide (C8-C40), see Alkyl (C8-C40) phenol sulfide	34	....	....	AKS.
Alkyl(C8-C9) phenylamine in aromatic solvents	9	....	ALP	
Alkyl(C9-C15) phenyl propoxylate	40	....	AXL	
Alkyl (C8-C10) polyglucoside solution (65% or less)*	43	3	AGL	AGD/AGM/AGN/AGO/AGP.
Alkyl (C12-C14) polyglucoside solution (55% or less)*	43	3	AGM	AGD/AGL/AGN/AGO/AGP.

Coast Guard, DHS

Pt. 150, Table I, Nt.

Chemical name	Group No.	Foot-note	CHRIS Code	Related CHRIS Codes
Alkyl (C12-C16) propoxyamine ethoxylate*	8	3	AXE	LPE.
Alkyl ester copolymer in mineral oil	34		AEQ	AES.
Alkyl phthalates, see individual phthalates	34		AYS	
Alkyl(C10-C20), saturated and unsaturated phosphite	34		AKL	
Alkyl succinic anhydride	11		AUA	
Alkyl sulfonic acid ester of phenol	34		AKH	
Alkyl (C18+) toluenes*	32	3	AUS	AYL.
Alkyl toluene	32		AYL	AUS.
Alkyl (C18-C28) toluenesulfonic acid*	0	1, 3	AUU	
Alkyl (C18-C28) toluenesulfonic acid, Calcium salts, borated*	34	3	AUB	
Alkyl (C18-C28) toluenesulfonic acid, Calcium salts, low overbase*	33	3	AUL	
Alkyl (C18-C28) toluenesulfonic acid, Calcium salts, high overbase*	33	3	AUC	
Allyl alcohol	15	2	ALA	
Allyl chloride	15		ALC	
Aluminum chloride, Hydrochloric acid solution, see "Aluminum chloride/Hydrogen chloride solution".	0	1	AHS	AHG.
Aluminum chloride/Hydrogen chloride solution*	0	1,3	AHG	AHS.
Aluminum hydroxide, sodium hydroxide, sodium carbonate solution (40% or less)*.	43	3	AHN	
Aluminum sulfate solution	43	2	ASX	ALM.
Amine C-6, morpholine process residue	9		AOI	
2-(2-Aminoethoxy)ethanol	8		AEX	
Aminoethyldiethanolamine/Aminoethylethanolamine solution	8		ADY	
Aminoethylethanolamine	8		AEE	
N-Aminoethylpiperazine	7		AEP	
2-Amino-2-hydroxymethyl-1,3-propanediol solution	43		AHL	
2-Amino-2-methyl-1-propanol	8		APZ	APQ/APR.
Ammonia, anhydrous	6		AMA	
Ammonia, aqueous (28% or less Ammonia), see Ammonium hydroxide	6			AMH.
Ammonium bisulfite solution (70% or less)	43	2	ABX	ASU.
Ammonium chloride solution (less than 25%)*	43	3	AIS	AMC.
Ammonium hydrogen phosphate solution	0	1	AMI	
Ammonium hydroxide (28% or less Ammonia)	6		AMH	
Ammonium lignosulfonate solution, see also Lignin liquor	43		ALG	LNL.
Ammonium nitrate solution (93% or less)	0	1	ANW	AMN/AND/ANR.
Ammonium nitrate solution (45% or less)	0	1	AND	AMN/ANR/ANW.
Ammonium nitrate/Urea solution (containing Ammonia), see Urea/Ammonium nitrate solution (containing more than 2% Ammonia).	6			UAS (ANU/UAT/UAU/UAV).
Ammonium nitrate/Urea solution (containing less than 2% free Ammonia), see Urea/Ammonium nitrate solution (containing less than 2% free Ammonia).	6			UAT (ANU/UAS/UAU/UAV).
Ammonium nitrate/Urea solution (not containing Ammonia), see Urea/Ammonium nitrate solution (containing less than 1% Ammonia).	6			UAU (ANU/UAS/UAT/UAV).
Ammonium phosphate/Urea solution, see Urea/Ammonium phosphate solution.	43			UAP (APP/URE).
Ammonium polyphosphate solution	43		AMO	
Ammonium sulfate solution	43		ASW	AME/AMS.
Ammonium sulfate solution (20% or less)	43		AME	AMS/ASW.
Ammonium sulfide solution (45% or less)*	5	3	ASS	ASF.
Ammonium thiocyanate/Ammonium thiosulfate solution	0	1	ACV	ACS.
Ammonium thiosulfate solution (60% or less*)	43	3	ATV	ATF.
Amyl acetate (all isomers*)	34	3	AEC	IAT/AML/AAS/AYA.
Amyl acid phosphate	34		AIA	
n*-Amyl alcohol	20	3	AAN	AAI/AAL/APM/ASE/IAA.
Amyl alcohol, primary*	20	3	APM	AAI/AAL/ANN/APM/IAA.
sec-Amyl alcohol*	20	3	ASE	AAI/AAL/ANN/APM/IAA.
tert-Amyl alcohol*	20	3	AAL	AAI/APM/ASE/IAA.
Amylene, see Pentene (all isomers)	30		AMW	PTX (AMX/AMZ/PTE).
tert-Amylenes, see Pentene	30		AMZ	PTX (AMW).
tert-Amyl methyl ether	41		AYE	
Amyl methyl ketone, see Methyl amyl ketone	18		AMJ	MAK (AMK).
Aniline	9		ANL	
Animal and Fish oils, n.o.s.	34		AFN	
Including: Cod liver oil. Lanolin. Neatsfoot oil. Pilchard oil. Sperm oil.				
Animal and Fish acid oils and distillates, n.o.s.	34		AFA	

67

Pt. 150, Table I, Nt.   46 CFR Ch. I (10-1-13 Edition)

Chemical name	Group No.	Foot-note	CHRIS Code	Related CHRIS Codes
Including:				
Animal acid oil.				
Fish acid oil.				
Lard acid oil.				
Mixed acid oil.				
Mixed general acid oil.				
Mixed hard acid oil.				
Mixed soft acid oil.				
Anthracene oil (Coal tar fraction), see Coal tar	33	....	AHO	COR.
Apple juice	43	....	APJ	
Argon, *liquefied*	0	1	ARG	
Aryl polyolefins (C11-C50)	32	....	AYF	
Asphalt	33	....	ASP	ACU.
Asphalt blending stocks, roofers flux	33	....	ARF	
Asphalt blending stocks, straight run residue	33	....	ASR	
Asphalt emulsion	33	....	ASQ	
Asphalt, Kerosene, and other components	33	....	AKO	
Aviation alkylates (C8 paraffins and iso-paraffins BPT 95-120 °C*)	31	3	AVA	GAK/GAV.
Barium long-chain (C11-C50) alkaryl sulfonate	34	....	BCA	
Barium long- chain alkyl(C8-C14)phenate sulfide	34	....	BCH	
Behenyl alcohol	20	....	BHY	
Benzene	32	2	BNZ	BHA/BHB/PYG.
Benzene and mixtures having 10% Benzene or more	32	....	BHB	BHA/BNZ/PYG.
Benzene hydrocarbon mixtures (containing Acetylenes) (having 10% Benzene or more).	32	....	BHA	BHB/BNZ/PYG.
Benzene sulfonyl chloride	0	1, 2	BSC	
Benzene/Toluene/Xylene mixtures (having 10% Benzene or more)	32	....	BTX	BHB/BNZ/PYG/TOL/XLX/XLM/XLO/XLP.
Benzenetricarboxylic acid, trioctyl ester	34	....	BCE	
Benzyl acetate	34	....	BZE	
Benzyl alcohol	21	....	BAL	
Benzyl chloride	36	....	BCL	
Bio-fuel blends of Diesel/gas oil and Alkanes (C10-C26), linear and branched with a flash point >60 °C (>25% but <99% by volume)*.	33	3	BIF	BIG/BIH/BII/BIJ/BIK.
Bio-fuel blends of Diesel/gas oil and Alkanes (C10-C26), linear and branched with a flash point >60 °C (>25% but <99% by volume)*.	33	3	BIG	BIF/BIH/BII/BIJ/BIK.
Bio-fuel blends of Diesel/gas oil and FAME (>25% but <99% by volume)*	34	3	BIH	BIF/BIG/BII/BIJ/BIK.
Bio-fuel blends of Diesel/gas oil and vegetable oil (>25% but <99% by volume)*.	34	3	BII	BIF/BIG/BIH/BIJ/BIK.
Bio-fuel blends of Gasoline and Ethyl alcohol (>25% but <99% by volume)*.	20	3	BIJ	BIF/BIG/BIH/BII/BIK.
Boronated Calcium sulfonate	34	....	BCU	
Brake fluid base mix: Poly(2-8)alkylene (C2-C3) glycols/Polyalkylene (C2-C10) glycols monoalkyl (C1-C4) ethers and their borate esters*.	20	3	BFY	
Brominated Epoxy Resin in Acetone	41	....	BER	
Bromochloromethane	36	....	BCM	
Butadiene (all isomers)	30	....	BDI	
Butadiene/Butylene mixtures (containing Acetylenes)	30	....	BBM	BBX/BDI/BTN/IBL.
Butane (all isomers)	31	....	BMX	IBT/BUT.
Butane/Propane mixture	31	....	BUP	LPG
1,4-Butanediol, see Butylene glycol	20	....	BDO	BUG.
2-Butanone, see Methyl ethyl ketone	18	....		MEK.
Butene, see Butylene	....	....		BUT/IBL.
Butene oligomer	30	....	BOL	
Butyl acetate (all isomers*)	34	3	BAX	BCN/BTA/BYA/IBA.
Butyl acrylate (all isomers*)	14	3	BAR	BAI/BTC.
Butyl alcohol (iso-, n-, sec-, tert-), see Butyl alcohol (all isomers)	20	2		BAN/BAS/BAT/BAY/IAL.
Butyl alcohol (all isomers*)	20	2, 3	BAY	BAN/BAS/BAT/IAL.
Butylamine (all isomers*)	7	3	BTY	BAM/BTL/BUA/IAM.
Butylbenzene (all isomers), see* Alkyl(C3-C4)benzenes	32	3	BBE	AKC.
Butyl benzyl phthalate	34	....	BPH	
Butyl butyrate (all isomers*)	34	3	BBA	BIB/BUB.
Butyl/Decyl/Cetyl/Eicosyl methacrylate mixture*	14	3	DER	BMH/BMI/BMN/CEM.
Butylenes (all isomers)	30	....	BTN	IBL.
n*-Butyl ether	41	....	BTE	
Butylene glycol	20	2	BUG	BDO.
1,2-Butylene oxide	16	....	BTO	
n-Butyl ether	41	3	BTE	
n-Butyl formate	34	....	BFN	BFI/BFO.
Butyl heptyl ketone	18	....	BHK	
Butyl methacrylate	14	....	BMH	BMI/BMN.
Butyl methacrylate, Decyl methacrylate, Cetyl-Eicosyl methacrylate mixture, see Butyl/Decyl/Cetyl/Eicosyl methacrylate.	34	....		DER (BMH/BMI/BMN/CEM).

68

Chemical name	Group No.	Foot-note	CHRIS Code	Related CHRIS Codes
Butyl methyl ketone, see Methyl butyl ketone	18			MBJ (MBK/MIK).
n-Butyl propionate	34		BPN	
Butyl stearate	34		BST	
Butyl toluene	32		BUE	
Butyraldehyde (all isomers*)	19	3	BAE	BAD/BTR.
Butyric acid	4		BRA	IBR.
gamma-Butyrolactone	0	1, 2	BLA	
Calcium alkaryl sulfonate (C11-C50), see Calcium long-chain alkaryl sulfonate (C11-C50)*.	34	3	CAE	CAY.
Calcium alkyl(C9)phenol sulfide, polyolefin phosphorosulfide mixture	34		CPX	
Calcium alkyl (C10-C28) salicylate*	34	3	CAJ	
Calcium alkyl salicylate, see Calcium long-chain alkyl salicylate (C13+), Calcium long-chain alkyl (C18-C28) salicylate, or Calcium alkyl (C10-C28) salicylate.	34			CAJ/CAK/CAZ.
Calcium bromide solution, see Drilling brines	43		CBI	DRS.
Calcium bromide/Zinc bromide solution, see Drilling brine (containing Zinc salts).	43			DZB.
Calcium carbonate slurry	34		CSR	
Calcium chloride solution	43		CCS	CLC.
Calcium hydroxide slurry	5		COH	CAH.
Calcium hypochlorite solution (15% or less*)	5	3	CHU	CHY/CHZ.
Calcium hypochlorite solution (more than 15%*)	5	3	CHZ	CHU/CHY.
Calcium lignosulfonate solution, see also Lignin liquor	43		CLL	LNL.
Calcium long-chain alkaryl sulfonate (C11-C50)	34		CAY	
Calcium long-chain alkyl (C5-C10*) phenate	34	3	CAU	CAN/CAQ/CAV/CAW.
Calcium long-chain alkyl (C5-C20) phenate	34		CAV	CAN/CAQ/CAU/CAW.
Calcium long-chain alkyl (C11-C40) phenate*	34	3	CAW	CAN/CAQ/CAU/CAV.
Calcium long-chain alkyl (C8-C40) phenate, see Calcium long-chain alkyl (C5-C10) phenate or Calcium long-chain alkyl (C11-C40) phenate.	34		CAQ	CAU/CAV (CAN/CAW).
Calcium long-chain alkyl phenate sulfide (C8-C40)	34		CPI	
Calcium long-chain alkyl phenolic amine (C8-C40)	9		CPQ	
Calcium long-chain alkyl salicylate (C13+)	34		CAK	CAJ/CAZ.
Calcium long-chain alkyl (C18-C28) salicylate*	34	3	CAJ	
Calcium nitrate solutions (50% or less*)	34	3	CNU	CNT.
Calcium nitrate/Magnesium nitrate/Potassium chloride solution	34		CLM	CNT/CNU/MGN/MGO/PCS/PCU/PSD.
Calcium salts of fatty acids	34		CFF	
Calcium stearate	34		CSE	
Calcium sulfonate/Calcium carbonate/Hydrocarbon solvent mixture	33		CSH	
Camelina oil*	34	3	CEL	
Camphor oil (light)	18		CPO	
Canola oil, see Oil, edible: Repeseed, (low erucic acid containing less than 4% free fatty acids).	34			ORO (ORP).
epsilon-Caprolactam (molten or aqueous solutions)*	22	3	CLU	CLS.
Caramel solution	43		CML	
Carbolic oil	21		CBO	
Carbon dioxide, *liquefied*	0	1	CDO	CDH/CDQ.
Carbon dioxide (high purity)	0	1	CDH	CDO/CDQ.
Carbon dioxide (reclaimed quality)	0	1	CDQ	CDH/CDO.
Carbon disulfide	38		CBB	
Carbon tetrachloride	36	2	CBT	CBU.
Cashew nut shell oil (untreated), see Oil, misc: Cashew nut shell (untreated).	4			OCN.
Castor oil, see Oil, edible: Castor	34			OCA (VEO).
Catoxid feedstock	36	2	CXF	
Caustic potash solution	5	2	CPS	
Caustic soda solution	5	2	CSS	
Cesium formate solution*	34	3	CSM	
Cetyl alcohol, see Alcohols (C13+)	20			ALY (ASY/AYL).
Cetyl/Eicosyl methacrylate mixture	14	1	CEM	
Cetyl/Stearyl alcohol, see Alcohols (C13+)	20			ALY (ASY/AYL).
Chlorinated paraffins (C10-C13)	36		CLH	CLG/CLJ/CLQ.
Chlorinated paraffins (C14-C17) (with 50% Chlorine or more, and less than 1% C13 or shorter chains*).	36	3	CLJ	CLG/CLH/CLQ.
Chlorinated paraffins (C14-C17) (with 52% Chlorine)	36		CLQ	CLG/CLH/CLJ.
Chlorinated paraffins (C18+) with any level of chlorine	36		CLG	CLH/CLJ.
Chlorine	0	1	CLX	
Chloroacetic acid (80% or less*)	4	3	CHM	CHL/MCA.
Chlorobenzene	36		CRB	
Chlorodifluoromethane (*monochlorodifluoromethane*)	36		MCF	
2-Chloro-4-ethylamino-6-isopropylamino-5-triazine solution	0	1	CET	
Chloroform	36		CRF	
Chlorohydrins (crude*)	17	3	CHD	

Pt. 150, Table I, Nt. 46 CFR Ch. I (10–1–13 Edition)

Chemical name	Group No.	Foot-note	CHRIS Code	Related CHRIS Codes
4-Chloro-2-methylphenoxyacetic acid, dimethylamine salt solution	9	....	CDM	
o-Chloronitrobenzene	42	....	CNO	CNP.
1-(4-Chlorophenyl)-4,4-dimethyl pentan-3-one	18	2	CDP	
2- or 3-Chloropropionic acid	4	....	CPM	CLA/CLP.
Chlorosulfonic acid	0	1	CSA	
m-Chlorotoluene*	36	3	CTM	CHI/CRN/CTO.
o-Chlorotoluene*	36	3	CTO	CHI/CRN/CTM.
p-Chlorotoluene*	36	3	CRN	CHI/CTM/CTO.
Chlorotoluenes (mixed isomers)*	36	3	CHI	CRN/CTM/CTO.
Choline chloride solution	20	....	CCO	
Citric acid (70% or less*)	4	3	CIS	CIT.
Clay slurry	43	....	CLY	
Coal slurry	43	....	COG	COA.
Coal tar	33	....	COR	OCT.
Coal tar crude bases	33	....	CTB	
Coal tar distillate, see Naphtha: Coal tar solvent	33	....	CDL	NCT (CTU).
Coal tar naphtha solvent, see Naphtha: Coal tar solvent	33	....		NCT (CDL/CTU).
Coal tar pitch (molten*)	33	3	CTP	
Cocoa butter, see Oil, edible: Cocoa butter	34	....		OCB (VEO).
Coconut oil, see Oil, edible: Coconut	34	....		OCC (VEO).
Coconut oil, fatty acid, see Oil, misc: Coconut fatty acid	34	2		CFA.
Coconut oil, fatty acid methyl ester, see Oil, misc: Coconut fatty acid methyl ester*	34	3		OCM.
Copper salt of long-chain (C17+) alkanoic acid	34	....	CUS	CFT.
Copper salt of long-chain (C3-C16) fatty acid	34	....	CFT	CUS.
Corn oil, see Oil, edible: Corn	34	....		OCO (VEO).
Cotton seed oil, see Oil, edible: Cotton seed	34	....		OCS (VEO).
Cottonseed oil, fatty acid	34	....	CFY	
Creosote	21	2	CCW	CCT/CWD.
Creosote (coal tar*)	21	2, 3	CCT	CCW.
Creosote (wood tar*)	21	2, 3	CWD	CCT/CCW.
Cresols (all isomers*)	21	3	CRS	CFO/CFP/CRL/CRO/CSC/CSO.
Cresols with less than 5% Phenol, see Cresols (all isomers)	21	....	CFO	CRS (CFP/CRL/CRO/CSO).
Cresols with 5% or more Phenol, see Phenol	21	....	CFP	PHN (CFO/CRL/CRO/CRS/CSO).
Cresylate spent caustic, see Cresylic acid, sodium salt solution	5	....	CSC	CYD.
Cresylic acid, dephenolized	21	....	CAD	CRY/CYN.
Cresylic acid, sodium salt solution	5	....	CYD	CSC.
Cresylic acid with 5% or more phenol	21	....	CYN	CAD/CRY.
Cresylic acid tar	21	....	CRX	
Crotonaldehyde	19	2	CTA	
Crude isononylaldehyde, see Isononyldehyde (crude)	19	....		INC.
Crude isopropanol, see Isoproyl alcohol, crude	20	....		IPB (IPA/PAL).
Crude piperazine, see Piperazine, crude	7	....		PZC (PPZ/PIZ).
Cumene, see Propylbenzene (all isomers)	32	....	CUM	AKD (PBY/PBZ).
1,5,9-Cyclododecatriene	30	....	CYT	
Cycloheptane	31	....	CYE	
Cyclohexane	31	....	CHX	
Cyclohexanol	20	....	CHN	
Cyclohexanone	18	2	CCH	
Cyclohexanone/Cyclohexanol mixture	18	2	CYX	
Cyclohexyl acetate	34	....	CYC	
Cyclohexylamine	7	....	CHA	
1,3-Cyclopentadiene dimer (molten*)	30	3	CPD	DPT/DPV.
Cyclopentadiene/Styrene/Benzene mixture	30	....	CSB	
Cyclopentane	31	....	CYP	
Cyclopentene	30	....	CPE	
p*-Cymene	32	....	CMP	
Decahydronaphthalene	33	....	DHN	
Decaldehyde	19	....	DAY	IDA/DAL.
Decane (all isomers), see n-Alkanes (C10+) (all isomers)	31	....	DCC	ALV (ALJ).
Decanoic acid	4	....	DCO	NEA.
Decene	30	....	DCE	
Decyl acetate	34	....	DYA	
Decyl acrylate	14	....	DAT	IAI/DAR.
Decyl alcohol (all isomers*)	20	2, 3	DAX	ISA/DAN.
Decyl/Dodecyl/Tetradecyl alcohol mixture*	20	3	DYO	DAN/DAX/DDN/ISA.
Decylbenzene, see Alkyl(C9+) benzenes	32	....	DBZ	AKB.
Decyloxytetrahydrothiophene dioxide	0	1	DHT	
Detergent alkylate	32	....	DKY	AKB/DBZ/DDB/TDB/TRB/UDB.

Coast Guard, DHS — Pt. 150, Table I, Nt.

Chemical name	Group No.	Foot-note	CHRIS Code	Related CHRIS Codes
Dextrose solution, see Glucose solution	43	....	DTS	GLU.
Diacetone alcohol	20	2	DAA	
Dialkyl(C10-C14) benzenes, see Alkyl(C9+) benzenes	32	....	DAB	AKB.
Dialkyl(C8-C9) diphenylamines	9	....	DAQ	
Dialkyl(C7-C13) phthalates	34	....	DAH	
Including:				
Di-(2-ethylhexyl) phthalate.				
Diheptyl phthalate.				
Dihexyl phthalate.				
Diisooctyl phthalate.				
Diisodecyl phthalate.				
Diisononyl phthalate.				
Dinonyl phthalate.				
Dioctyl phthalate.				
Ditridecyl phthalate.				
Diundecyl phthalate.				
Dialkyl (C9-C10) phthalates, see Dialkyl (C7-C13) phthalates	34	....	DLK	DLH (DAP/DHL/DHP/ DID/DIE/DIF/DIN/ DIO/DIT/DOP/DPA/ DTP/DUP).
Dialkyl thiophosphates sodium salts solution*	34	3	DYH	
Dibromomethane	36	....	DBH	
Dibutylamine	7	....	DBA	
Dibutyl carbinol, see Nonyl alcohol (all isomers)	20	....		NNS (DBC/NNI/NNN).
Dibutyl hydrogen phosphonate	34	....	DHD	
Dibutylphenols	21	....	DBT	DBV/DBW.
2,6-Di-tert-butylphenol*	21	3	DBW	DBF/DBT/DBV.
Dibutyl phthalate	34	....	DPA	DIT.
Dibutyl terephthalate*	34	3	DYE	
Dichlorobenzene (all isomers*)	36	3	DBX	DBM/DBO/DBP.
3,4-Dichloro-1-butene	36	....	DCD	DCB.
Dichlorodifluoromethane	36	....	DCF	
1,1-Dichloroethane	36	2	DCH	
Dichloroethyl ether*	41	3	DYR	DEE.
1,6-Dichlorohexane	36	....	DHX	
2,2′-Dichloroisopropyl ether	41	....	DCI	
Dichloromethane	36	2	DCM	
2,4-Dichlorophenol	21	....	DCP	
2,4-Dichlorophenoxyacetic acid/Diethanolamine salt solution	43	....	DDE	
2,4-Dichlorophenoxyacetic acid/Dimethylamine salt solution (70% or less)*	0	1, 2, 3	DDA	DAD/DSX.
2,4-Dichlorophenoxyacetic acid/Triisopropanolamine salt solution	43	2	DTI	
1,1-Dichloropropane	36	....	DPB	DPC/DPL/DPP/DPX.
1,2-Dichloropropane*	36	3	DPP	DPB/DPC/DPL/DPX.
1,3-Dichlorpropane	36	....	DPC	DPB/DPL/DPP/DPX.
Dichloropropene (all isomers)	15	....	DCW	DPF/DPU.
1,3-Dichloropropene	15	....		DCW/DPF.
Dichloropropene/Dichloropropane mixtures	15	....	DMX	DCW/DPB/DPC/DPL/ DPP/DPU/DPX.
2,2-Dichloropropionic acid	4	....	DCN	
Dicyclopentadiene, see 1,3-Cyclopentadiene dimer (molten)	30	....	DPT	CPD (DPV).
Dicyclopentadiene, Resin Grade, 81-89%*	30	3	DPV	CPD/DPT.
Diethanolamine	8	....	DEA	
Diethanolamine salt of 2,4-Dichlorophenoxyacetic acid solution, see 2,4-Dichlorophenoxyacetic acid, Diethanolamine salt solution.	43	....	DZZ	DDE.
Diethylamine	7	....	DEN	
Diethylaminoethanol	8	....	DAE	
2,6-Diethylaniline	9	....	DMN	DIY.
Diethylbenzene	32	....	DEB	
Diethylene glycol	40	2	DEG	
Diethylene glycol butyl ether, see Poly(2-8) alkylene glycol monoalkyl(C1-C6) ether.	40	....	DME	PAG.
Diethylene glycol butyl ether acetate, see Poly(2-8)alkylene glycol monoalkyl(C1-C6) ether acetate.	34	....	DEM	PAF.
Diethylene glycol dibutyl ether	40	....	DIG	
Diethylene glycol diethyl ether	40	....	DGS	
Diethylene glycol ethyl ether, see Poly(2-8)alkylene glycol monoalkyl (C1-C6) ether.	40	....	DGE	PAG.
Diethylene glycol ethyl ether acetate, see Poly(2-8)alkylene glycol monoalkyl(C1-C6) ether acetates.	34	....	DGA	PAF.
Diethylene glycol n-hexyl ether, see Poly(2-8)alkylene glycol monoalkyl(C1-C6) ether.	40	....	DHE	PAG.
Diethylene glycol methyl ether, see Poly(2-8)alkylene glycol monoalkyl(C1-C6) ether.	40	....	DGM	PAG.

Chemical name	Group No.	Footnote	CHRIS Code	Related CHRIS Codes
Diethylene glycol methyl ether acetate, see Poly(2-8)alkylene glycol monoalkyl(C1-C6) ether acetate.	34	....	DGR	PAF.
Diethylene glycol phenyl ether	40	....	DGP	
Diethylene glycol phthalate	34	....	DGL	
Diethylene glycol propyl ether, see Poly(2-8)alkylene glycol monoalkyl(C1-C6) ether.	40	....	DGO	PAG.
Diethylenetriamine	7	2	DET	
Diethylenetriaminepentaacetic acid, pentasodium salt solution	43	....	DYS	
Diethylethanolamine, see Diethylaminoethanol	8	....		DAE.
Diethyl ether	8	....	EET	
Diethyl hexanol, see Decyl alcohol (all isomers)	20	....		DAX.
Di-(2-ethylhexyl) adipate	34	....	DEH	
Di-(2-ethylhexyl) phosphoric acid	1	....	DEP	
Di-(2-ethylhexyl) phthalate, see Dialkyl (C7-C13) phthalate	34	....	DIE	DAH.
Di-(2-ethylhexyl) terephthalate	34	....	DHH	
Diethyl phthalate	34	....	DPH	
Diethyl sulfate	34	....	DSU	
Diglycidyl ether of Bisphenol A	41	....	BDE	
Diglycidyl ether of Bisphenol F	41	....	DGF	
Diheptyl phthalate, see Dialkyl (C7-C13) phthalate	34	....	DHP	DAH.
Di-n-hexyl adipate	34	....	DHA	
Dihexyl phthalate	34	....	DHL	
1,4-Dihydro-9,10-dihydroxy anthracene, disodium salt solution	5	....	DDH	
Diisobutylamine	7	....	DBU	
Diisobutyl carbinol, see Nonyl alcohol (all isomers)	20	....	DBC	NNS.
Diisobutylene	30	....	DBL	
Diisobutyl ketone	18	....	DIK	
Diisobutyl phthalate	34	....	DIT	DPA.
Diisodecyl phthalate, see Dialkyl (C7-C13) phthalates	34	....	DID	DAH.
Diisononyl adipate	34	....	DNY	
Diisononyl phthalate, see Dialkyl (C7-C13) phthalates	34	2	DIN	DAH.
Diisooctyl phthalate, see Dialkyl (C7-C13) phthalate	34	....	DIO	DAH/(DIE/DOP).
Diisopropanolamine	8	....	DIP	
Diisopropylamine	7	....	DIA	DNA.
Diisopropylbenzene (all isomers)	32	....	DIX	
Diisopropylnaphthalene	32	....	DII	
N,N-Dimethylacetamide	10	....	DAC	DLS.
N,N-Dimethylacetamide solution (40% or less *)	10	3	DLS	DAL.
Dimethyl adipate	34	....	DLA	
Dimethylamine	7	....	DMA	DMC/DMG/DMY.
Dimethylamine solution (45% or less *)	7	3	DMG	DMA/DMC/DMY.
Dimethylamine solution (greater than 45% but not greater than 55%) *	7	3	DMY	DMA/DMC/DMG.
Dimethylamine solution (greater than 55% but not greater than 65%) *	7	3	DMC	DMA/DMG/DMY.
Dimethylamine salt of 4-Chloro-2-methylphenoxyacetic acid solution, see 4-Chloro-2-methylphenoxyacetic acid, Dimethylamine salt solution.	9	....		CDM.
Dimethylamine salt of 2,4-Dichlorophenoxyacetic acid solution, see 2,4-Dichlorophenoxyacetic acid, Dimethylamine salt solution (70% or less).	9	....	DAD	DDA (DSX).
2,6-Dimethylaniline	9	....	DMM	DDL.
Dimethylbenzene, see Xylenes	32	....		XLX/XLM/XLO/XLP.
N,N-Dimethylcyclohexylamine	7	....	DXN	
Dimethyl disulfide *	0	1, 2, 3	DSK	
Dimethyldodecylamine, see N,N-Dimethyldodecylamine	7	....		DDY.
N,N-Dimethyldodecylamine	7	....	DDY	
Dimethylethanolamine	8	....	DMB	
Dimethyl ether	41	....	DIM	
Dimethylformamide	10	....	DMF	
Dimethyl glutarate	34	....	DGT	
Dimethyl hydrogen phosphite	34	2	DPI	
Dimethyl octanoic acid	4	....	DMO	
Dimethyl phthalate	34	....	DTL	
Dimethylpolysiloxane	34	....	DMP	
2,2-Dimethylpropane-1,3-diol (molten or solution *)	20	3	DDI	
Dimethyl succinate	34	....	DSE	
Dinitrotoluene	42	3	DNM	DNL/DNU/DTT.
Dinonyl phthalate, see Dialkyl (C7-C13) phthalates	34	....	DIF	DAH.
Dioctyl phthalate, see Dialkyl (C7-C13) phthalates	34	....	DOP	DAH (DIE/DIO).
1,4-Dioxane	41	....	DOX	
Dipentene	30	....	DPN	
Diphenyl	32	....	DIL	
Diphenylamine (molten)	9	....	DAG	DAM.
Diphenylamine, reaction product with 2,2,4-trimethylpentene	9	....	DAK	
Diphenylamines, alkylated	9	....	DAJ	
Diphenyl/Diphenyl ether mixtures	33	....	DDO	

Coast Guard, DHS

Pt. 150, Table I, Nt.

Chemical name	Group No.	Foot-note	CHRIS Code	Related CHRIS Codes
Diphenyl ether	41		DPE	
Diphenyl ether/Biphenyl ether mixture, see Diphenyl/Diphenyl ether mixture.	41			DDO.
Diphenyl ether/Diphenyl phenyl ether mixture	41		DOB	
Diphenylmethane diisocyanate	12		DPM	
Diphenylol propane-Epichlorohydrin resins	0	1	DPR	
Diphenyl oxide, see Diphenyl ether	40			DPE.
Di-n-propylamine	7		DNA	DIA.
Dipropylene glycol	40		DPG	
Dipropylene glycol butyl ether, see Poly(2-8)alkylene glycol monoalkyl(C1-C6) ether.	40		DBG	PAG.
Dipropylene glycol dibenzoate	34		DGY	
Dipropylene glycol methyl ether, see Poly (2-8)alkylene glycol monoalkyl(C1-C6) ether.	40		DPY	PAG.
Distillates, flashed feed stocks	33		DFF	
Distillates, straight run	33		DSR	
Di-tert-butyl phenol	21		DBF	DBT/DBV/DBW.
2,4-Di-tert-butyl phenol	21		DBV	DBF/DBT/DBW.
2,6-Di-tert-butyl phenol	21		DBW	DBF/DBT/DBV.
Dithiocarbamate ester (C7-C35)	34		DHO	
Ditridecyl adipate	34		DTY	
Ditridecyl phthalate, see Dialkyl (C7-C13) phthalate	34		DTP	DAH.
Diundecyl phthalate, see Dialkyl (C7-C13) phthalates	34		DUP	DAH.
Dodecane (all isomers), see Alkanes (C10+) (all isomers)	31		DOF	ALV (ALJ/DOC).
tert-Dodecanethiol	0	1, 2	DDL	LRM.
Dodecene (all isomers*)	30	3	DOZ	DDC/DOD.
Dodecanol (all isomers), see Dodecyl alcohol (all isomers)	20	2	DDN	LAL.
2-Dodecenylsuccinic acid, dipotassium salt solution	34		DSP	
Dodecyl alcohol (all isomers)	20		DDN	ASK/ASY/LAL.
Dodecylamine/Tetradecylamine mixture	7		DTA	
Dodecylbenzene, see Alkyl (C9+) benzenes	32		DDB	AKB.
Dodecyldimethylamine/Tetradecyldimethylamine mixture	7		DOT	
Dodecyl diphenyl ether disulfonate solution	43		DTA	
Dodecyl hydroxypropyl sulfide	0	1	DOH	
Dodecyl methacrylate	14		DDM	
Dodecyl/Octadecyl methacrylate mixture	14		DOM	DDM.
Dodecyl/Pentadecyl methacrylate mixture	14		DDP	
Dodecyl phenol	21		DOL	
Dodecyl xylene	32		DXY	
Drilling brines (containing Calcium, Potassium or Sodium salts)	43		DRL	DRB/DRS.
Drilling brines (containing Zinc salts)	43		DZB	DRB.
Drilling brines, including: Calcium bromide solution, Calcium chloride solution and Sodium chloride solution*.	43	3		DRS/DRL.
Drilling mud (low toxicity) (if flammable or combustible)	33		DRO	DRM/DRN/DRP.
Drilling mud (low toxicity) (if non-flammable or non-combustible)	43		DRP	DRM/DRN/DRO.
Epichlorohydrin	17		EPC	
Epoxy resin	18		EPN	
ETBE, see Ethyl tert-butyl ether	40			EBE.
Ethane	31		ETH	
Ethanolamine	8		MEA	
2-Ethoxyethanol, see Ethylene glycol monoalkyl ethers	40		EEO	EGC (EGE).
2-Ethoxyethyl acetate	34	2	EEA	EGA.
Ethoxylated alkyloxy alkyl amine	8		ELM	
Ethoxylated alcohols, C11-C15, see the alcohol poylethoxylates	40			AEA/AEB/AED/AET/ APV/APW/APX.
Ethoxylated long-chain (C16+) alkyloxyalkylamine	8		ELA	
Ethoxylated tallow alkyl amine	7		TAY	TAG/TAR.
Ethoxylated tallow alkyl amine (>95%)*	7	3	TAR	TAG/TAY.
Ethoxylated tallow alkyl amine, glycol mixture	7		TAG	TAR/TAY.
Ethoxy triglycol, see Poly (2-8) alkylene glycol monoalkyl (C1-C6) ether	40		ETG	PAG (ETR/TGE).
Ethoxy triglycol (crude)	40		ETR	
Ethyl acetate	34	2	ETA	
Ethyl acetoacetate	34		EAA	
Ethyl acrylate	14	2	EAC	
Ethyl alcohol	20	2	EAL	
Ethylamine	7	2	EAM	EAN/EAO.
Ethylamine solution (72% or less*)	7	3	EAN	EAM/EAO.
Ethyl amyl ketone	18		EAK	ELK.
Ethylbenzene	32		ETB	
Ethyl butanol	20		EBT	
N-Ethyl-butylamine	7		EBA	
Ethyl tert-butyl ether	41	2	EBE	
Ethyl butyrate	34		EBR	

Chemical name	Group No.	Foot-note	CHRIS Code	Related CHRIS Codes
Ethyl chloride	36		ECL	
Ethyl cyclohexane	31		ECY	
N-Ethylcyclohexylamine	7		ECC	
2-Ethyl-2-(2,4-dichlorophenoxy) acetate	34		EDY	
2-Ethyl-2-(2,4-dichlorophenoxy) propionate	34		EDP	
S-Ethyl dipropylthiocarbamate*	34	3	ECB	
Ethylene	30		ETL	
Ethylene carbonate	34		ECR	
Ethylene chlorohydrin	20		ECH	
Ethylene cyanohydrin	20	2	ETC	
Ethylenediamine	7	2	EDA	EMX.
Ethylenediaminetetraacetic acid/tetrasodium salt solution	43		EDS	
Ethylene dibromide	36		EDB	
Ethylene dichloride	36	2	EDC	
Ethylene glycol	20	2	EGL	EAG.
Ethylene glycol acetate	34		EGO	
Ethylene glycol butyl ether, see Ethylene glycol monoalkyl ethers	40		EGM	EGC.
Ethylene glycol tert-butyl ether, see Ethylene glycol monoalkyl ethers	40		EGG	EGC.
Ethylene glycol butyl ether acetate	34		EMA	
Ethylene glycol diacetate	34		EGY	
Ethylene glycol dibutyl ether	40		EGB	
Ethylene glycol ethyl ether, see Ethyl glycol monoalkyl ethers	40		EGE	EGC/EEO.
Ethylene glycol ethyl ether acetate, see 2-Ethoxyethyl acetate	34	2	EGA	EEA.
Ethylene glycol hexyl ether, see Ethylene glycol monoalkyl ethers	40		EGH	EGC.
Ethylene glycol isobutyl ether, see Ethylene glycol monoalkyl ethers	40			EGC (EGG/EGM).
Ethylene glycol isopropyl ether, see Ethylene glycol monoalkyl ethers	40		EGI	EGN/EGP.
Ethylene glycol methyl butyl ether, see Ethylene glycol monoalkyl ethers	40		EMB	EGC.
Ethylene glycol methyl ether, see Ethylene glycol monoalkyl ethers	40		EME	EGC.
Ethylene glycol methyl ether acetate	34		EGT	
Ethylene glycol monoalkyl ethers	40	2	EGC	
Including:				
Ethylene glycol butyl ether.				
Ethylene glycol isobutyl ether.				
Ethylene glycol methyl butyl ether.				
Ethylene glycol tert-butyl ether.				
Ethylene glycol ethyl ether.				
Ethylene glycol hexyl ether.				
Ethylene glycol methyl ether.				
Ethylene glycol propyl ether.				
Ethylene glycol iso-propyl ether.				
Ethylene glycol phenyl ether	40		EPE	
Ethylene glycol phenyl ether/Diethylene glycol phenyl ether mixture	40		EDX	
Ethylene glycol propyl ether, see Ethylene glycol monoalkyl ethers	40		EGP	EGC/EGI/EGN.
Ethylene glycol iso-propyl ether, see Ethylene glycol monoalkyl ethers	40		EGI	EGC/EGN/EGP.
Ethylene glycol n-propyl ether, see Ethylene glycol monoalkyl ethers	40		EGN	EGC (EGI/EGP).
Ethylene oxide	0	1	EOX	
Ethylene oxide/Propylene oxide mixture	16		EPF	EPM.
Ethylene oxide/Propylene oxide mixture with an Ethylene oxide content not more than 30% by mass*	16	3	EPM	EPF.
Ethylene-Propylene copolymer (in liquid mixtures)	31		EPY	
Ethylene-Vinyl acetate copolymer (emulsion)	43		ECV	
Ethyl ether, see Diethyl ether	41			EET.
Ethyl-3-ethoxypropionate	34		EEP	
2-Ethylhexaldehyde, see Octyl aldehydes	19		EHA	OAL (OLX).
2-Ethylhexanoic acid, see Octanoic acid	4		EHO	OAY (OAA).
2-Ethylhexanol, see Octanol	20		EHX	OCA (OTA).
2-Ethylhexyl acrylate	14		EAI	
2-Ethylhexylamine	7		EHM	
Ethyl hexyl phthalate	34		EHE	
Ethyl hexyl tallate	34		EHT	
2-Ethyl-2-(hydroxymethyl) propane-1,3-diol, (C8-C10) ester	34		EHD	
Ethyl lactate	34		ELT	
Ethylidene norbornene	30	2	ENB	
Ethyl methacrylate	14		ETM	
N-Ethylmethylallylamine	7		EML	
Ethyl propionate	34		EPR	
2-Ethyl-3-propylacrolein	19	2	EPA	
Ethyl toluene	32		ETE	
Fatty acids (saturated, C13+)	34		FAB	FAD.
Fatty acids (saturated, C14+), see Fatty acids (saturated, C13+)	34		FAD	FAB.
Fatty acid methyl esters*	4	3	FME	
Fatty acids, (C8-C10)*	4	3	FDS	
Fatty acids, (C12+)*	4	3	FDT	FAB/FAD/FAI/FDI.

Coast Guard, DHS

Pt. 150, Table I, Nt.

Chemical name	Group No.	Foot-note	CHRIS Code	Related CHRIS Codes
Fatty acids, (C16+)*	4	3	FDI	
Fatty acids, essentially linear (C6-C18) 2-ethylhexyl ester*	4	2, 3	FAE	
Ferric chloride solution	1		FCS	FCL.
Ferric hydroxyethylethylenediaminetriacetic acid, trisodium salt solution	43	2	FHX	STA.
Ferric nitrate/Nitric acid solution	3	2	FNN	
Fish oil, see Oil, edible: Fish	34	2		OFS (AFN).
Fish solubles (water based fish meal extracts)	43		FSO	
Fluorosilicic acid (20-30%) in water solution*	1	3	FSK	FSJ/FSL/HFS.
Fluorosilicic acid (30% or less)	1		FSJ	FSK/FSL/HFS.
Formaldehyde (50% or more), Methanol mixtures	19	2	MTM	
Formaldehyde solutions (37%–50%)	19	2	FMS	FMG/FMR.
Formaldehyde solutions (45% or less*)	19	2, 3	FMR	FMG/FMS.
Formamide	10		FAM	
Formic acid	4	2	FMA	FMB.
Formic acid (85% or less)	19	2	FMB	FMA.
Formic acid (over 85%)*	4	2, 3	FMD	
Formic acid mixture (containing up to 18% Propionic acid and up to 25% Sodium formate)*.	4	2, 3	FMC	FMA/FMB.
Fructose solution	43		FTS	FRT.
Fumaric adduct of Rosin, water dispersion	43		FAR	
Furfural	19		FFA	
Furfuryl alcohol	20	2	FAL	
Gas oil, cracked, see Oil, misc: Gas, cracked	33			GOC.
Gasoline blending stock, alkylates	33		GAK	
Gasoline blending stock, reformates	33		GRF	
Gasolines:				
Automotive (containing not over 4.23 grams lead per gal.)	33		GAT	
Aviation (containing not over 4.86 grams lead per gal.)	33		GAV	AVA.
Casinghead (natural)	33		GCS	
Polymer	33		GPL	
Straight run	33		GSR	
Gasolines: Pyrolysis (containing Benzene), see Pyrolysis gasoline (containing Benzene).	33		GPY	PYG.
Glucitol/Glycerol blend propoxylated (containing less than 10% amines)*	40	3	GGA	
Glucose solution	43		GLS	DTS.
Glutaraldehyde solutions (50% or less)	19		GTA	
Glycerine	20	2	GCR	
Glycerine (83%)/Dioxanedimethanol (17%) mixture	20		GDN	GDM.
Glycerol, see Glycerine	20			GCR.
Glycerol ethoxylated	40		GXA	
Glycerol monooleate	20		GMO	
Glycerol polyalkoxylate	40		GPA	
Glycerol propoxylated*	40	3	GXP	
Glycerol, propoxylated and ethoxylated*	40	3	GXE	
Glycerol/Sucrose blend propoxylated and ethoxylated*	40	3	GSB	
Glyceryl triacetate	34		GCT	
Glycidyl ester of tertiary carboxylic acid, see Glycidyl ester of C10 trialkyl acetic acid.	34		GLT	GLU.
Gylcidyl ester of tridecyl acetic acid, see Glycidyl ester of C10 trialkyl acetic acid.	34		GLT	GLU.
Glycidyl ester of C10 trialkyl acetic acid	34		GLU	GLT.
Glycidyl ester of Versatic acid, see Gylcidyl ester of C10 trialkyl acetic acid.	34		GLT	GLU.
Glycine, sodium salt solution	7		GSS	
Glycol mixture, crude	20		GMC	
Glycol diacetate, see Ethylene glycol diacetate	34			EGY.
Glycolic acid solution (70% or less*)	4	3	GLC	
Glycol triacetate, see Glyceryl triacetate	34			GCT.
Glyoxal solution (40% or less*)	19	3	GOS	
Glyoxylic acid solution (50% or less*)	4	3	GAC	
Glyphosate solution (not containing surfactant)	7		GIO	RUP.
Groundnut oil, see Oil, edible: Groundnut	34			OGN (VEO).
Heptadecane (all isomers), see Alkanes (C10+) (all isomers)	31			ALV (ALJ).
Heptane (all isomers), see Alkanes (C6-C9)	31		HMX	ALK(HPI/HPT).
n-Heptanoic acid	4		HEN	HEP.
Heptanol (all isomers*)	20	3	HTX	HTN.
Heptene (all isomers*)	30	3	HPX	THE.
Heptyl acetate	34		HPE	
Heptylbenzenes, see Alkyl (C3-C4) benzenes	32			AKD.
Herbicide (C15–H22–NO2-Cl), see Metolachlor	34			MCO.
Hexadecanol, see Alcohols (C13+)	20			ALY (ASY/AYL).
1-Hexadecylnaphthalene/1,4-bis(Hexadecyl)naphthalene mixture	32		HNH	HNI.
1-n-Hexadecylnaphthalene (90%)/1,4-di-n-(Hexadecyl)naphthalene (10%)	32		HNI	HNH.

75

Chemical name	Group No.	Foot-note	CHRIS Code	Related CHRIS Codes
Hexaethylene glycol, see Polyethylene glycol	20		HMG	PEG.
Hexamethylenediamine adipate solution	43		HAN	HAM.
Hexamethylenediamine adipate (50% in water)	43		HAM	HAN.
Hexamethylenediamine (molten*)	7	3	HME	HMD/HMC.
Hexamethylenediamine solution	7		HMC	HMD/HME.
Hexamethylene diisocyanate	12		HMS	HDI.
Hexamethylene glycol	20		HMG	HXG.
Hexamethyleneimine	7		HMI	
Hexamethylenetetramine solutions	7		HTS	HMT.
1,6-Hexanediol, distillation overheads*	4	2, 3	HDO	
Hexanoic acid	4		HXO	
Hexanol	20		HXM	HEW/HEZ/HXN.
Hexene (all isomers*)	30	3	HEX	HXE/HXT/HXU/HXV/ MPN/MTN.
Hexyl acetate	34		HAE	
Hexylbenzenes, see Alkyl (C3-C4) benzenes	32			AKD.
Hexylene glycol, see Hexamethylene glycol	20		HXG	HMG.
Hog grease, see Lard	34			LRD.
Hydrochloric acid	1		HCL	
Hydrofluorosilicic acid (25% or less), see Fluorosilicic acid (30% or less)	1			FSJ(FSK/FSL/HFS).
Hydrogenated starch hydrolysate*	0	1, 3	HSH	
bis(Hydrogenated tallow alkyl)methyl amines	7		HTA	
Hydrogen peroxide solutions (over 8% but not over 60% by mass)*	0	1,3	HPN	HPO/HPS.
Hydrogen peroxide solutions (over 60% but not over 70% by mass*)	0	1, 3	HPS	HPN/HPO.
alpha-Hydro-omega-hydroxytetradeca(oxytetramethylene)	40		HTO	PYS/PYT.
2-Hydroxyethyl acrylate	14	2	HAI	
N-(Hydroxyethyl)ethylenediamine triacetic acid, trisodium salt solution	43		HET	
2-Hydroxy-4-(methylthio)butanoic acid	4		HBA	
Hydroxy terminated polybutadiene, see Polybutadiene, hydroxy terminated	31			PHT.
Illipe oil, see Oil, edible: Illipe	34			ILO (VEO).
Isoamyl alcohol*	20	3	IAA	AAI/AAL/AAN/APM/ ASE.
Isobutyl alcohol*	20	2, 3	IAL	BAN/BAS/BAT/BAY.
Isobutyl formate*	34	3	BFI	BFN/BFO.
Isobutyl methacrylate*	14	3	BMI	BMH/BMN.
Isononylaldehyde (crude)	19		INC	
Isophorone	18	2	IPH	
Isophoronediamine	7		IPI	
Isophorone diisocyanate	12		IPD	
Isoprene (all isomers)	30		IPR	
Isoprene (part refined)	30		IPS	IPR/ISC.
Isoprene concentrate (Shell)	30		ISC	
Isopropanolamine*	8	3	MPA	IPF/PAX/PLA.
Isopropanolamine solution*	8	3	PAI	MPA/PAY/PLA/PRG.
Isopropyl acetate*	34	3	IAC	PAT.
Isopropyl alcohol*	20	2, 3	IPA	IPB/PAL.
Isopropylamine*	7	3	IPP	IPO/IPQ/PRA.
Isopropylamine (70% or less) solution*	7	3	IPQ	IPO/IPP/PRA.
Isopropylbenzenes, see Alkyl (C3-C4) benzenes	32			AKC(CUM/PBY/PBZ).
Isopropylcyclohexane*	31	3	IPX	
Isopropyl ether*	41	3	IPE	PRL/PRN.
Jatropha oil, see Oil, misc: Jatropha	34			JTO.
Jet fuels:				
JP–4	33		JPF	
JP–5	33		JPV	
JP–8	33		JPE	
Kaolin clay solution	43		KLC	KLS.
Kaolin slurry	43		KLS	KLC.
Kerosene	33		KRS	
Kraft black liquor	5		KBL	KPL.
Kraft pulping liquors (free alkali content 3% or more) (*Black, Green, or White*)	5		KPL	KBL.
Lactic acid	0	1	LTA	
Lactonitrile solution (80% or less*)	37	3	LNI	
Lard	34		LRD	OLD.
Latex, ammonia (1% or less*)-inhibited	30	3	LTX	
Latex: Carboxylated Styrene-Butadiene copolymer; Styrene-Butadiene rubber*.	43	3	LCC	LCB/LSB.
Latex, liquid synthetic	43		LLS	LCB/LCC/LSB.
Lauric acid	34		LRA	
Lauric acid methyl ester/Myristic acid methyl ester mixture	34		LMM	
Lauryl polyglucose, see Alkyl(C12-C14) polyglucoside solution (55% or less)	43			AGM/LAP.

Coast Guard, DHS
Pt. 150, Table I, Nt.

Chemical name	Group No.	Footnote	CHRIS Code	Related CHRIS Codes
Lauryl polyglucose (50% or less), see Alkyl (C12-C14) polyglucoside solution (55% or less).	43	....	LAP	AMG.
Lecithin	34	....	LEC	
Lignin liquor	43	....	LNL	ALG/CLL/LGA/LGM/ LSL/SHC/SHP/ SHQ/SLP.
Ligninsulfonic acid, magnesium salt solution *	43	3	LGM	LGA/LNL/LSL.
Ligninsulfonic acid, sodium salt solution, see Lignin liquor or Sodium lignosulfonate solution.	43	....	LGA	LNL or SLG.
d-Limonene, see Dipentene	30	....		DPN.
Linear alkyl (C12-C16) propoxyamine ethoxylate	8	....	LPE	
Linseed oil, see Oil, misc: Linseed	34	....		OLS.
Liquefied Natural Gas, see Methane	34	....	LNG	MTH.
Liquid chemical wastes *	0	1, 3	LCW	
Long-chain alkaryl polyether (C11-C20)	41	....	LCP	
Long-chain alkaryl sulfonic acid (C16-C60)	0	1	LCS	
Long-chain alkyl amine	7	....	LAA	
Long-chain alkylphenate/Phenol sulfide mixture	21	....	LPS	
Long-chain alkyl (C13+) salicylic acid	4	....	LAS	
L-Lysine solution (60% or less *)	43	3	LYS	
Magnesium chloride solution	0	1, 2	MGL	
Magnesium hydroxide slurry	5	....	MHS	
Magnesium long-chain alkaryl sulfonate (C11-C50)	34	....	MAS	MSE.
Magnesium long-chain alkyl phenate sulfide (C8-C20)	34	....	MPS	
Magnesium long-chain alkyl salicylate (C11+)	34	....	MLS	
Magnesium nitrate solution (66.7%)	43	....	MGP	MGN/MGO.
Magnesium nonyl phenol sulfide, see Magnesium long-chain alkyl phenate sulfide (C8-C20).	34	....		MPS.
Magnesium sulfonate, see Magnesium long-chain alkaryl sulfonate (C11-C50).	34	....	MSE	MAS.
Maleic anhydride	11	....	MLA	
Maltitol solution *	0	1, 3	MTI	
Mango kernel oil, see Oil, edible: Mango kernel	34	....		MKO (VEO).
2-Mercaptobenzothiazol (in liquid mixture)	5	....	BTM	SMD.
Mercaptobenzothiazol, sodium salt solution	5	....	SMB	MBT.
Mesityl oxide	18	2	MSO	
Metam sodium solution	7	....	MSS	SMD.
Methacrylic acid	4	....	MAD	
Methacrylic acid—Alkoxypoly(alkylene oxide) methacrylate copolymer, sodium salt aqueous solution (45% or less) *.	20	3	MAQ	
Methacrylic resin in ethylene dichloride	14	....	MRD	
Methacrylonitrile	15	2	MET	
Methane	31	....	MTH	LNG.
3-Methoxy-1-butanol	20	....	MTX	
3-Methoxybutyl acetate	34	....	MOA	
N-(2-Methoxy-1-methyl ethyl)-2-ethyl-6-methyl chloroacetanilide, *see* Metolachlor.	34	....		MCO.
1-Methoxy-2-propyl acetate	34	....	MXP	
Methoxy triglycol, see Poly (2-8) alkylene glycol monoalkyl (C1-C6) ether	40	....	MTG	PAG (TGY).
Methyl acetate	34	....	MTT	
Methyl acetoacetate	34	....	MAE	
Methyl acetylene/Propadiene mixture	30	....	MAP	
Methyl acrylate	14	....	MAM	
Methyl alcohol	20	2	MAL	
Methylamine solutions (42% or less *)	7	3	MSZ	
Methylamyl acetate	34	....	MAC	
Methylamyl alcohol	20	....	MAA	MIC.
Methyl amyl ketone	18	....	MAK	
N-Methylaniline *	9	3	MAN	
alpha-Methylbenzyl alcohol with Acetophenone (15% or less) *	20	3	MBA	
Methyl bromide	36	....	MTB	
Methyl butanol, see the amyl alcohols	20	....		AAI/AAL/AAN/APM/ ASE/IAA.
Methyl butenol	20	....	MBL	
Methyl butenes, see Pentene	30	....		PTX (AMW/AMZ/ PTE).
Methyl tert-butyl ether	41	2	MBE	
Methyl butyl ketone	18	2	MBB	MBK/MIK.
Methyl 3-(3,5 di-tert-butyl-4-hydroxyphenyl) propionate crude melt	20	....	MYP	
Methylbutynol	20	....	MBY	MHB.
Methyl butyrate	34	....	MBU	
Methyl chloride	36	....	MTC	
Methylcyclohexane	31	....	MCY	

77

Chemical name	Group No.	Foot-note	CHRIS Code	Related CHRIS Codes
Methylcyclohexanemethanol (crude)	20		MYH	
Methylcyclopentadiene dimer	30		MCK	
Methylcyclopentadienyl manganese tricarbonyl*	0	1, 3	MCT	MCW.
Methylcyclopentadienyl manganese tricarbonyl (60–70%) in mineral oil	0	1	MCW	MCT.
Methyl diethanolamine	8		MDE	MAB.
Methylene bridged isobtylenated phenols	21		MBP	
Methylene chloride, see Dichloromethane	21			DCM.
2-Methyl-6-ethyl aniline	9		MEN	
Methyl ethyl ketone	18	2	MEK	
2-Methyl-5-ethyl pyridine	9		MEP	
Methyl formate	34		MFM	
N-Methylglucamine solution (70% or less*)	43	3	MGC	
2-Methylglutaronitrile	37		MLN	MGN.
2-Methylglutaronitrile with 2-Ethylsuccinonitrile (12% or less)*	37	3	MGE	MLN.
Methyl heptyl ketone	18		MHK	
2-Methyl-2-hydroxy-3-butyne	20		MHB	MBY.
Methyl isoamyl ketone, see Methyl amyl ketone	18		MAJ	MAK.
Methyl isobutyl carbinol, see Methyl amyl alcohol	20		MIC	MAA.
Methyl isobutyl ketone	18		MIK	MBB/MBK.
Methyl methacrylate	14		MMM	
3-Methyl-3-methoxybutanol	20		MXB	
3-Methyl-3-methoxybutyl acetate	34		MMB	
Methyl naphthalene (molten*)	32	3	MNA	
Methylourea	19		MUT	
2-Methyl pentane, see Hexane (all isomers)	31			HXS (ALK/HXA/IHA/NHX).
2-Methyl-1,5-pentanediamine	7		MPM	
2-Methyl-1-pentene, see Hexene (all isomers)	30		MPN	HEX (HXE/HXT/HXU/HXV/MTN).
4-Methyl-1-pentene, see Hexene (all isomers)	30		MTN	HEX (HXE/HXT/HXU/HXV/MPN).
*Methyl tert-pentyl ether, see tert-*Amyl methyl ether	41			AYE.
2-Methyl-1,3-propanediol	20		MDL	
Methyl propyl ketone	18		MKE	
Methylpyridine, see the Methylpyridines	9		MPQ	MPE/MPF/MPR.
2-Methylpyridine*	9	3	MPR	MPE/MPF/MPQ.
3-Methylpyridine*	9	3	MPE	MPF/MPQ/MPR.
4-Methylpyridine*	9	3	MPF	MPE/MPQ/MPR.
N-Methyl-2-pyrrolidone	9	2	MPY	
Methyl salicylate	34		MES	
alpha-Methylstyrene	30		MSR	
3-(Methylthio)propionaldehyde	19		MTP	
Metolachlor	34		MCO	
Microsillica slurry	4		MOS	
Milk	43		MLK	
Mineral spirits	33		MNS	
Mixed C4 Cargoes	30		MIX	
Molasses	20		MOL	MON.
Molasses residue (from fermentation)	0	1	MON	MOL.
Molybdenum polysulfide long-chain alkyl dithiocarbamide complex*	0	1, 3	MOP	
Monochlorodifluoromethane	36		MCF	
Monoethanolamine, see Ethanolamine	8		MEA	
Monoisopropanolamine, see Isopropanolamine	8			MPA (PLA/PLX).
Monoethylamine, see Methylamine	7			EAM (EAN/EAO).
Morpholine	7	2	MPL	
Motor fuel anti-knock compound (containing lead alkyls)	0	1	MFA	
MTBE, see Methyl tert-butyl ether	41			MBE.
Myrcene	30		MRE	
Naphtha:				
Aromatic	33		NAR	
Coal tar solvent	33		NCT	
Heavy	33		NAG	
Paraffinic	33		NPF	
Petroleum	33		PTN	
Solvent	33		NSV	
Stoddard solvent	33		NSS	
Varnish Makers' and Painters'	33		NVM	
Naphthalene (molten*)	32	3	NTM	
Naphthalene sulfonic acid-Formaldehyde copolymer, sodium salt solution	0	1	NFS	
Naphthalene sulfonic acid, sodium salt solution	34		NSB	NSA.
Naphthenic acid	4		NTI	
Naphthenic acid, sodium salt solution	43		NTS	
Neodecanoic acid	4		NEA	DCO/NAT.

Coast Guard, DHS Pt. 150, Table I, Nt.

Chemical name	Group No.	Foot-note	CHRIS Code	Related CHRIS Codes
Nitrating acid (mixture of Sulfuric and Nitric acids)	0	1	NIA	
Nitric acid (70% and over)*	3	2, 3	NCE	NAC/NCD.
Nitric acid (less than 70%)	3	2	NCD	NAC/NCE.
Nitrilotriacetic acid, trisodium salt solution*	34	3	NCA	
Nitrobenzene	42		NTB	
o-Nitrochlorobenzene, see o-Chloronitrobenzene	42			CNO (CNP).
Nitroethane	42		NTE	
Nitroethane(80%)/Nitropropane (20%)*	42	2, 3	NNL	NNM/NNO/NPM/NPN/NPP/NTE.
Nitroethane/1-Nitropropane (each 15% or more) mixture	42	2	NNO	NNL/NNM/NPM/NPN/NPP/NTE.
Nitrogen	0	1	NXX	
Nitrophenol (mixed isomers)	42		NPX	NIP/NPH/NPX.
o-Nitrophenol (molten)	0	1, 2	NTP	NIP/NPH/NPX.
1-or 2-Nitropropane	42		NPM	NPN/NPP.
Nitropropane (60%)/Nitroethane (40%) mixture	42		NNM	NNL/NNO/NPM/NPN/NPP/NTE.
o- or p-Nitrotoluenes*	42	3	NIT	NIE/NTR/NTT.
Nonane (all isomers), see Alkanes (C6-C9)	31		NAX	ALK (NAN).
Nonanoic acid (all isomers)	4		NNA	NAI/NIN.
Nonanoic/Tridecanoic acid mixture	4		NAT	NAI/NIN/NNA.
Non-edible industrial grade palm oil, see Oil, misc: Palm, non-edible industrial grade.	34			OPB.
Nonene (all isomers)	30		NOO	NNE/NON/OAM/OFX/OFY.
Nonyl acetate	34		NAE	
Non-noxious Liquid Substance, (12) n.o.s. Cat OS	0	1	NOL	
Nonyl alcohol (all isomers)	20	2	NNS	ALR/DBC/NNI/NNN.
Nonylbenzene, see Alkyl(C9+)benzenes	32			AKB.
Nonyl methacrylate monomer	14		NMA	
Nonyl phenol	21		NNP	
Nonylphenol (48–62%)/Phenol (42–48%)/Dinonylphenol (1–10%) mixture	21		NYL	
Nonyl phenol poly(4+)ethoxylate, see Alkyl (C7-C11) phenol poly (4–12) ethoxylate.	40		NPE	APN.
Nonyl phenol sulfide (90% or less) solution, see Alkyl phenol sulfide (C8-C40).	34			AKS (NPS).
Noxious Liquid Substance, n.o.s. (NLS')	0	1		
1-Octadecanol, see Stearyl alcohol	20			SYL (ALY/ASY).
1-Octadecene, see the olefin or alpha-olefin entries	30			OAM/OFZ.
Octadecenoamide solution	10		ODD	
Octadecenol, see Alcohols (C13+)	20			ALY (AYL/ASY/OYL).
Octamethylcyclotetrasiloxane*	34	3	OSA	
Octane (all isomers), see Alkanes (C6-C9)	31		OAX	ALK (IOO/OAN).
Octanoic acid (all isomers)	4		OAY	EHO/OAA.
Octanol (all isomers)	20	2	OCX	EHX/OPA/OTA.
Octene (all isomers)	30	2	OTX	OAM/OFC/OFY/OFW/OTE.
n-Octyl acetate	34		OAF	OAE.
Octyl alcohol, see Octanol (all isomers)	20	2		OCX (EHX/IOA/OTA).
Octyl aldehydes	19		OAL	EHA/IOC//OLX.
Octylbenzenes, see Alkyl (C3-C4) benzenes	32			AKD.
Octyl decyl adipate	34		ODA	
n-Octyl Mercaptan	34		OME	
Octyl nitrates (all isomers), see Alkyl(C7-C9) nitrates	34	2	ONE	AKN.
Octyl phenol	21		OPH	
Octyl phthalate, see Dialkyl (C7-C13) phthalates	34			DAH (DIE/DIO/DLK/DOP).
Oil, edible:				
Beechnut	34		OBN	VEO.
Castor	34		OCA	VEO.
Cocoa butter	34		OCB	VEO.
Coconut	34	2	OCC	VEO.
Cod liver	34		OCL	AFN.
Corn	34		OCO	VEO.
Cotton seed	34		OCS	VEO.
Fish	34	2	OFS	AFN.
Groundnut	34		OGN	VEO.
Hazelnut	34		OHN	VEO.
Illipe	34		ILO	VEO.
Lard	34		OLD	AFN.
Maize, see Oil, edible: Corn	34			OCO (VEO).
Mango kernel*	34	3	MKO	
Nutmeg butter	34		ONB	VEO.

Chemical name	Group No.	Foot-note	CHRIS Code	Related CHRIS Codes
Olive	34		OOL	VEO.
Palm	34	2	OPM	VEO.
Palm kernel	34		OPO	VEO.
Palm kernel olein	34		PKO	VEO.
Palm kernel stearin	34		PKS	VEO.
Palm mid fraction	34		PFM	VEO.
Palm olein	34		PON	VEO.
Palm stearin	34		PMS	VEO.
Peanut	34		OPN	VEO.
Poppy	34		OPY	VEO.
Poppy seed	34		OPS	VEO.
Raisin seed	34		ORA	VEO.
Rapeseed (low erucic acid containing less than 4% free fatty acids).	34		ORO	ORP/VEO.
Rice bran	34		ORB	VEO.
Safflower	34		OSF	VEO.
Salad	34		OSL	VEO.
Sesame	34		OSS	VEO.
Shea butter	34		OSH	VEO.
Soya bean	34		OSB	VEO.
Sunflower, see Oil, edible Sunflower seed	34			OSN (VEO).
Sunflower seed	34		OSN	VEO.
Tucum	34		OTC	VEO.
Vegetable	34		OVG	VEO.
Walnut	34		OWN	VEO.
Oil, fuel:				
No. 1	33		OON	
No. 1–D	33		OOD	
No. 2	33		OTW	
No. 2–D	33		OTD	
No. 4	33		OFR	
No. 5	33		OFV	
No. 6	33		OSX	
Oil, misc:				
Acid mixture from soybean, corn (maize) and sunflower oil refining.	34		AOM	
Aliphatic	33		OML	
Animal	34		OMA	AFN.
Aromatic	33		OMR	
Camelina	34		OCI	
Cashew nut shell (untreated)	4		OCN	
Clarified	33		OCF	
Coal	33		OMC	
Coconut fatty acid	34	2	CFA	
Coconut oil, fatty acid methyl ester	34		OCM	
Cotton seed oil, fatty acid	34		CFY	
Crude	33		OFA	
Diesel	33		ODS	
Disulfide	0	1	ODI	
Gas, cracked	33		GOC	
Gas, high pour	33		OGP	
Gas, low pour	33		OGL	
Gas, low sulfur	33		OGS	
Heartcut distillate	33		OHD	
Jatropha	34		JTO	
Lanolin	34		OLL	AFN.
Linseed	33		OLS	
Lubricating	33		OLB	
Mineral	33		OMN	
Mineral seal	33		OMS	
Motor	33		OMT	
Neatsfoot	33		ONF	AFN.
Oiticica	34		OOI	
Palm acid	34		PLM	
Palm fatty acid distillate	34		PFD	
Palm oil fatty acid methyl ester	34		OPE	
Palm kernel acid	34		OPK	
Palm kernel fatty acid distillate	34		PNG	
Palm, non-edible industrial grade	34		OPB	
Penetrating	33		OPT	
Perilla	34		OPR	
Pilchard	34		OPL	AFN.
Pine	33		OPI	PNL.

Coast Guard, DHS   Pt. 150, Table I, Nt.

Chemical name	Group No.	Foot-note	CHRIS Code	Related CHRIS Codes
Rape seed fatty acid methyl esters*	34	3	ORP	
Residual	33		ORL	
Resin, distilled	34		ORR	
Road	33		ORD	
Rosin	33		ORN	
Seal	34		OSE	
Soapstock	34		OIS	
Soyabean (epoxidized)	34		OSC	
Soyabean fatty acid methyl ester	34			OST.
Spindle	33		OSD	
Tall	34		OTL	OTI/OTJ.
Tall, crude	34	2	OTI	OTJ/OTL.
Tall, distilled	34	2	OTJ	OTI/OTL.
Tall, fatty acid	34	2	OTT	
Tall fatty acid (resin acids less than 20%)	34	2	OTK	OTT.
Tall pitch	34		OTP	
Transformer	33		OTF	
Tung	34		OTG	
Turbine	33		OTB	
Vacuum gas oil	32		OVC	
Oleamide solution, see Octadecenoamide solution	10			ODD.
Olefin-Alkyl ester copolymer (molecular weight 2000+)	34		OCP	
Olefin mixture (C7-C9) C8 rich, stabilized*	30	3	OFC	OFW/OFY/OFX.
Olefin mixtures (C5-C7)*	30	3	OFX	OAM/OFC/OFW/OFX/OFZ.
Olefin mixtures (C5-C15)*	30	3	OFY	OAM/OFC/OFW/OFX/OFZ.
Olefins (C13+, all isomers)	30		OFZ	OAM/OFW.
alpha-Olefins (C6-C18) mixtures	30		OAM	OFC/OFW/OFX/OFY/OFZ.
Oleic acid	34		OLA	
Oleum	0	1, 2	OLM	SAC/SFX.
Oleyl alcohol, see Alcohols (C13+)	20		OYL	ALY (ASY).
Oleylamine	7		OLY	
Olive oil, see Oil, edible: Olive	34			OOL (VEO).
Orange juice (concentrated)*	0	1, 3	OJC	OJN.
Orange juice (not concentrated)*	0	1, 3	OJN	OJC.
Organomolybdenum amide	10		OGA	
ORIMULSION, see Asphalt emulsion	33			ASQ.
Oxyalkylated alkyl phenol formaldehyde	33		OPF	
Oxygenated aliphatic hydrocarbon mixture*	0	1, 3	OAH	
Palm acid oil, see Oil, misc: Palm acid*	34	3		PLM.
Palm fatty acid distillate, see Oil, misc: Palm fatty acid distillate*	34	3		PFD.
Palm kernel acid oil, see Oil, misc: Palm kernel acid	34			PNO.
Palm kernel acid oil, methyl ester, see Oil, misc: Palm kernel acid, methyl ester.	34			PNF.
Palm kernel oil fatty acid distillate, see Oil, misc: Palm kernel fatty acid distillate.	34			PNG.
Palm kernel oil, see Oil, edible: Palm kernel	34			OPO (VEO).
Palm kernel olein, see Oil, edible: Palm kernel olein*	34	3		PKO (VEO).
Palm kernel stearin, see Oil, edible: Palm kernel stearin*	34	3		PKS (VEO).
Palm mid fraction, see Oil, edible: Palm mid fraction*	34	3		PFM (VEO).
Palm oil, see Oil, edible: Palm*	34	3		OPM (VEO).
Palm oil fatty acid methyl ester, see Oil, misc: Palm fatty acid methyl ester*.	34	3		OPE.
Palm olein, see Oil, edible: Palm Olein*	34	3		PON (VEO).
Palm stearin, see Oil, edible: Palm stearin	34			PMS (VEO).
Parachlorobenzotrifluoride	32		PBF	
n-Paraffins (C10-C20), see n-Alkanes (C10+)	31		PFN	ALJ.
Paraffin wax, see Waxes: Paraffin*	31	3		WPF.
Paraldehyde	19		PDH	
Paraldehyde-Ammonia reaction product	9		PRB	
Pentachloroethane	36		PCE	
Pentadecanol, see Alcohols (C13+)	20		PDC	ALY.
1,3-Pentadiene	30		PDE	PDN.
1,3-Pentadiene (greater than 50%), Cyclopentene and isomers, mixtures*	30	3	PMM	
Pentaethylene glycol, see Polyethylene glycols	20			PEG.
Pentaethylene glycol methyl ether, see Poly(2-8)alkylene glycol monoalkyl (C1-C6) ether.	40			PAG.
Pentaethylenehexamine	7		PEN	
Pentaethylenehexamine/Tetraethylenepentamine mixture	7		PEP	
Pentane (all isomers)	31		PTY	IPT/PTA.
Pentanoic acid	4		POC	

81

Chemical name	Group No.	Foot-note	CHRIS Code	Related CHRIS Codes
n-Pentanoic acid (64%)/2-Methyl butryic acid (36%) mixture	4		POJ	POC.
Pentasodium salt of Diethylenetriamine pentaacetic acid solution, see Diethylenetriamine pentaacetic acid, pentasodium salt solution.	43			DYS.
Pentene (all isomers)	30		PTX	PTE.
n-Pentyl propionate	34		PPE	
Perchloroethylene	36	2	PER	TTE.
Petrolatum	33		PTL	
Phenol	21	2	PHN	PNS.
Phenol solutions (2% or less)	43		PNS	PHN.
1-Phenyl-1-xylyl ethane	32		PXE	
Phosphate esters	34		PZE	
Phosphate esters, alkyl (C12-C14) amine	7		PEA	
Phosphoric acid	1		PAC	
Phosphorus, yellow or white	0	1	PPW	PPB/PPR.
Phosphosulfurized bicycle terpene	0	1	PBT	
Phthalate based polyester polyol	0	1, 2	PBE	
Phthalic anhydride (molten)	11		PAN	
alpha-Pinene	30		PIO	PIB/PIN.
beta-Pinene	30		PIP	PIN/PIO.
Pine oil, see Oil, misc: Pine	33		PNL	OPI.
Piperazine (crude)	34		PZC	PPZ/PIZ.
Piperazine (70% or less)	30		PIZ	PPB/PPZ.
Piperylene concentrate	30		PIC	PDE/PDN.
Polyacrylic acid solution (40% or less)	43		PYA	
Polyalkenyl succinic anhydride amine	7		PSN	
Polyalkyl acrylate	14		PAY	
Polyalky (C18-C22) acrylate in Xylene	14		PIX	
Polyalkyl alkenamine succinimide, molybdenum oxysulfide	7		PSO	
Polyalkylene glycols/Polyalkylene glycol monoalkyl ether mixtures	40		PPX	
Polyalkylene glycol butyl ether, see Poly(2-8)alkylene glycol monoalkyl(C1-C6) ether.	40		PGB	PAG.
Poly(2-8)alkylene glycol monoalkyl(C1-C6) ether	40		PAG	
Including: Diethylene glycol butyl ether. Diethylene glycol ethyl ether. Diethylene glycol n-hexyl ether. Diethylene glycol methyl ether. Diethylene glycol propyl ether. Dipropylene glycol butyl ether. Dipropylene glycol methyl ether. Polyalkylene glycol butyl ether. Polyethylene glycol monoalkyl ether. Polypropylene glycol methyl ether. Triethylene glycol butyl ether. Triethylene glycol ethyl ether. Triethylene glycol methyl ether. Tripropylene glycol methyl ether.				
Poly(2-8)alkylene glycol monoalkyl(C1-C6) ether acetate	34		PAF	
Including: Diethylene glycol butyl ether acetate. Diethylene glycol ethyl ether acetate. Diethylene glycol methyl ether acetate.				
Polyalkylene glycols/Polyalkylene glycol monoalkyl ethers mixtures	40		PPX	
Polyalkylene oxide polyol	20		PAO	
Polyalkyl (C10-C20) methacrylate	14		PMT	PYY.
Polyalkyl methacrylate in mineral oil	14		PYY	PMT.
Polyalkyl(C10-C18) methacrylate/Ethylene-Propylene copolymer mixture	14		PEM	
Polyalpha olefins	31		PYO	
Polyaluminum chloride solution	1		PLS	
Polybutadiene, hydroxyl terminated	20		PHT	
Polybutene	33		PLB	
Polybutenyl succinimide	10		PBS	
Polycarboxylic ester (C9+), see Ditridecyl adipate	34			DTY.
Poly(2+)cyclic aromatics	32		PCA	
Polydimethylsiloxane, see Dimethylpolysiloxane	34			DMP.
Polyether, borated	41		PED	
Polyether (molecular weight 1350+)	41		PYR	
Polyether polyols	41		PEO	
Polyethylene glycol	40		PEG	
Polyethylene glycol dimethyl ether	40		PEF	
Poly (ethylene glycol) methylbutenyl ether (MW >1000)	40		PBN	
Polyethylene glycol monoalkyl ether, see Poly(2-8)alkylene glycol monoalkyl(C1-C6) ether.	40		PEE	PAG.

Coast Guard, DHS   Pt. 150, Table I, Nt.

Chemical name	Group No.	Foot-note	CHRIS Code	Related CHRIS Codes
Polyethylene polyamines	7	2	PEB	PEY.
Polyethylene polyamines (more than 50% C5-C20 Paraffin oil)*	7	2,3	PEY	PEB.
Polyferric sulfate solution	34		PSS	
Polyglycerine/Sodium salts solution (containing less than 3% Sodium hydroxide).	20	2	PGT	PGS.
Polyglycerol	20		PGL	
Poly(iminoethylene)-graft-N-poly(ethyleneoxy) solution (90% or less)*	7	3	PIG	PIM.
Polyisobutenamine in aliphatic (C10-C14) solvent	7		PIB	PIA.
Polyisobutenyl anhydride adduct	11		PBA	
Polyisobutenyl succinimide	10		PIS	
Poly(4+)isobutylene	30		PIL	
Polyisobutylene succinic anhydride	11		PYS	
Polymerized esters	34		PYM	
Polymethylene polyphenyl isocyanate	12		PPI	
Polyolefin (molecular weight 300+)	31		PMW	PLF.
Polyolefin amide alkeneamine (C17+)	33		POH	POD.
Polyolefin amide alkeneamine (C28+), see Polyolefin amide alkeneamine (C17+).	33		POD	POH.
Polyolefin amide alkeneamine borate (C28-C250)	34		PAB	
Polyolefin amide alkeneamine in mineral oil	33		PLK	
Polyolefin amide alkeneamine/Molybdenum oxysulfide mixture	7		PMO	
Polyolefin amide alkeneamine polyol	20		PAP	
Polyolefinamine (C28-C250)	33		POM	
Polyolefinamine in alkyl(C2-C4) benzenes	32		POF	POR.
Polyolefinamine in aromatic solvent*	32	3	POR	POF.
Polyolefin aminoester salts (molecular weight 2000+)	34		PAE	
Polyolefin anhydride	11		PAR	
Polyolefin ester (C28-C250)	34		POS	
Polyolefin in mineral oil	30		PLF	PMW.
Polyolefin phenolic amine (C28-C250)	9		PPH	
Polyolefin phosphorosulfide, barium derivative (C28-C250)	34		PPS	
Poly (oxyalkylene) alkenyl ether (MW>1000)	41		PXY	
Polyoxybutylene alcohol	41		PXA	
Poly(20)oxyethylene sorbitan monooleate	34		PSM	
Polyoxypropylenediamine (MW 2000)	7		PYD	
Poly(5+)propylene	30		PLQ	PLP.
Polypropylene glycol	40		PGC	
Polypropylene glycol methyl ether, see Poly(2-8)alkylene glycol monoalkyl (C1-C6) ether.	40		PGM	PAG.
Polysiloxane	34		PSX	
Polysiloxane/White spirit, low (15–20%) aromatic	34		PWS	
Potassium chloride solution	43		PCU	PCD/PSD.
Potassium chloride solution (10% or more)	43		PCS	PCD/PCU.
Potassium chloride solution (less than 26%)	43		PSD	CLM/DRL/PCS/PCU.
Potassium formate solutions	34		PFR	
Potassium hydroxide solution, see Caustic potash solution	5	2		CPS/PTH.
Potassium oleate	34		POE	
Potassium polysulfide/Potassium thiosulfide solution (41% or less)	0	1	PYP	PSF/PTF.
Potassium salt of polyolefin acid	34		PSP	
Potassium thiosulfate (50% or less)	43		PTF	
Propane	31		PRP	LPG.
iso-Propanolamine, see Isopropanolamine	8			MPA (PAX/PLA).
n-Propanolamine	8		PLA	MPA/PAX.
2-Propene-1-aminium, N,N-dimethyl-N-2-propenyl-, chloride, homopolymer solution*.	0	1, 3	PLN	
beta-Propiolactone*	18	3	PLT	
Propionaldehyde	19		PAD	
Propionic acid	4		PNA	
Propionic anhydride	11		PAH	
Propionitrile	37		PCN	
n-Propoxypropanol, see Propylene glycol monoalkyl ether	40		PXP	PGE.
n-Propyl acetate	34		PAT	IAC.
n-Propyl alcohol	20	2	PAL	IPA.
n-Propylamine	7		PRA	IPO/IPP/IPQ.
iso-Propylamine solution, see Isopropylamine (70% or less) solution	7			IPQ (IPO/IPP/PRA).
Propylbenzenes, see Alkyl (C3-C4) benzens	32		PBY	AKC (CUM/PBZ).
iso-Propyl cyclohexane, see Isopropylcyclohexane	34			IPX.
Propylene	30		PPL	
Propylene-Butylene copolymer	30		PBP	
Propylene carbonate	34		PLC	
Propylene dimer	30		PDR	
Propylene glycol	20	2	PPG	
Propylene glycol n-butyl ether, see Propylene glycol monoalkyl ether	40		PGD	PGE.

Chemical name	Group No.	Foot-note	CHRIS Code	Related CHRIS Codes
Propylene glycol ethyl ether, see Propylene glycol monoalkyl ether	40		PGY	PGE.
Propylene glycol methyl ether, see Propylene glycol monoalkyl ether	40		PME	PGE.
Propylene glycol methyl ether acetate	34		PGN	
Propylene glycol monoalkyl ether	40		PGE	
Including:				
n-Propoxypropanol.				
Propylene glycol n-butyl ether.				
Propylene glycol ethyl ether.				
Propylene glycol methyl ether.				
Propylene glycol propyl ether.				
Propylene glycol phenyl ether	40		PGP	
Propylene glycol propyl ether, see Propylene glycol monoalkyl ether				PGE.
Propylene oxide	16		POX	
Propylene tetramer	30		PTT	
Propylene trimer	30		PTR	
Pseudocumene, see Trimethylbenzene (all isomers)	32			TMB/TMD/TME/TRE.
Pyridine	9		PRD	
Pyridine bases, see Paraldehyde-Ammonia reaction product	9			PRB.
Pyrolysis gasoline (containing Benzene)*	32	3	PYG	GPY.
Rapeseed oil, see Oil, edible: Rapeseed	34			ORO (VEO).
Rapeseed oil (low erucic acid containing less than 4% free fatty acids), see Oil, edible: Rapeseed, (low erucic acid containing less than 4% free fatty acids)*.	34	3		ORO (VEO).
Rapeseed oil fatty acid methyl esters, see Oil, misc: Rapeseed fatty acid methyl esters*.	34	3		RSO.
Refrigerant gases	0	1	RFG	
Resin oil, distilled, see Oil, misc: Resin, distilled*	33	3		ORR (ORS).
Rice bran oil, see Oil, misc: Rice bran	34			ORB.
Rosin, see Oil, misc: Rosin	33			ORN.
ROUNDUP	7		RUP	GIO.
Rum, see Alcoholic beverages	20			ABV.
Safflower oil, see Oil, edible: Safflower	34			OSF (VEO)
Sewage sludge	43		SWS	
Shea butter, see Oil, edible: Shea butter*	34	3		OSH (VEO).
Silica slurry	43		SLC	
Siloxanes	34		SLX	
Sludge, treated	43		SWA	
Sodium acetate, Glycol, Water mixture (not containing Sodium hydroxide)	34	2	SAW	SAO/SAP/SAQ/SAY.
Sodium acetate, Glycol, Water mixture (containing Sodium hydroxide)	5		SAQ	SAO/SAP/SAW/SAY.
Sodium acetate, Glycol, Water mixture (1% or less Sodium hydroxide) (if non-flammable or non-combustible).	5	2	SAY	SAO/SAP/SAQ/SAY.
Sodium acetate solutions	34		SAN	
Sodium alkyl (C14-C17) sulfonates (60–65% solution)	34		SSA	AKA/AKE/SSU.
Sodium aluminate solution	5		SAV	SAU.
Sodium aluminate solution (45% or less)	5		SAU	SAV.
Sodium aluminosilicate slurry	34		SLR	
Sodium benzoate solution	34		SBN	SBM.
Sodium bicarbonate solution (less than 10%)	34		SBC	
Sodium borohydride (15% or less)/Sodium hydroxide solution	5		SBX	CSS/SBH/SBI/SHD.
Sodium bromide solution (less than 50%)*	43	3	SBL	SBR.
Sodium carbonate solution	5		SCE	
Sodium chlorate solution (50% or less)	0	1, 2	SDD	SDC.
Sodium cyanide solution	5		SCO	SCN/SCS.
Sodium dichromate solution (70% or less)	0	1, 2	SDL	SCR.
Sodium hydrogen sulfide (6% or less)/Sodium carbonate (3% or less) solution.	0	1, 2	SSS	SCE/SHW.
Sodium hydrogen sulfite solution (45% or less)	43		SHY	SHX.
Sodium hydrosulfide/Ammonium sulfide solution	5	2	SSA	ASF/ASS.
Sodium hydrosulfide solution (45% or less)	5	2	SHR	
Sodium hydroxide solution, see Caustic soda solution	5	2		CSS (SHD).
Sodium hypochlorite solution (15% or less)	5		SHP	SHC/SHQ.
Sodium hypochlorite solution (20% or less)	5		SHQ	SHC/SHP.
Sodium lignosulfonate solution	43		SLG	LNL.
Sodium long-chain alkyl salicylate (C13+)	34		SLS	
Sodium-2-mercaptobenzothiazol solution, see Mercaptobenzothiazol, sodium salt solution.	5			SMB.
Sodium methoxide (25% in methanol)	5		SMO	
Sodium methylate 21–30% in methanol*	20	3	SMT	SMS.
Sodium naphthalene sulfonate solution, see Naphthalene sulfonic acid (40% or less), sodium salt solution (40% or less).	34		SNS	NSA (NSB).
Sodium naphthenate solution, see Naphthenic acid, sodium salt solution	34			NTS.
Sodium nitrite solution	5		SNI	SNT.
Sodium petroleum sulfonate	34		SPS	

Coast Guard, DHS — Pt. 150, Table I, Nt.

Chemical name	Group No.	Foot-note	CHRIS Code	Related CHRIS Codes
Sodium polyacrylate solution	43		SOO	SOP.
Sodium poly(4+)acrylate solution	43	2	SOP	SOO.
Sodium salt of Ferric hydroxyethylethylenediaminetriacetic acid solution, see Ferric hydroxyethylethylenediaminetriacetic acid, trisodium salt solution.	34		STA	FHX.
Sodium silicate solution	43	2	SSN	SSC.
Sodium sulfate solution*	34	3	SST	SSO.
Sodium sulfide/Hydrosulfide solution (H_2S 15 ppm or less)	0	1, 2	SSH	SDS/SHR/SSI/SSJ.
Sodium sulfide/Hydrosulfide solution (H_2S greater than 15 ppm but less than 200 ppm)	0	1, 2	SSI	SDS/SHR/SSH/SSJ.
Sodium sulfide/Hydrosulfide solution (H_2S greater than 200 ppm)	0	1, 2	SSJ	SDS/SHR/SSH/SSI.
Sodium sulfide solution (15% or less)	43		SDR	SDS.
Sodium sulfite solution (25% or less)	43		SUP	SSF/SUS.
Sodium thiocyanate solution (56% or less)	0	1, 2	STS	SCY.
Sorbitol solution	20		SBU	SBT.
Soyabean fatty acid methyl ester, see Oil, misc: Soyabean fatty acid methyl ester.	34			OST.
Soyabean oil, see Oil, edible: Soyabean	34			OSB (VEO).
Stearic acid, see Fatty acids (saturated, C14+)	34		SRA	FAD (FAB/FAE/FDI/FDT).
Stearyl alcohol	20		SYL	ALY/ASY.
Stoddard solvent, see Naphtha: Stoddard solvent	33			NSS.
Styrene monomer	30		STY	
Sulfohydrocarbon (C3-C88)	33		SFO	
Sulfohydrocarbon, long-chain (C18+) alkylamine mixture	7		SFX	
Sulfolane	39		SFL	
Sulfonated polyacrylate solutions	43	2	SPA	
Sulfur (molten)	0	1, 2	SXX	
Sulfur dioxide	0	1	SFD	
Sulfuric acid	2	2	SFA	SAC.
Sulfuric acid, spent	2	2	SAC	SFA.
Sulfurized fat (C14-C20)	33		SFT	
Sulfurized polyolefinamide	7		SPY	
Sulfurized polyolefinamide alkene(C28-C250) amine	7		SPO	
Sunflower seed oil, see Oil, edible: Sunflower seed	34			OSN (VEO).
Tall oil, see Oil, misc: Tall	34			OTL (OTI/OTJ).
Tall oil, crude, see Oil, misc: Tall, crude*	34	2, 3		OTI (OTJ/OTL).
Tall oil, distilled, see Oil, misc: Tall, distilled*	34	3		OTJ (OTI/OTL).
Tall oil, fatty acid, see Oil, misc: Tall fatty acid	34			OTT.
Tall oil fatty acid (resin acids less than 20%), see Oil, misc: Tall oil fatty acid (resin less than 20%).	34	2		OTK (OTT).
Tall oil soap (crude)	4		TOR	TOS.
Tall oil, pitch, see Oil, misc: Tall pitch*	34	3		OTP (OTI/OTJ/OTL).
Tallow	34	2	TLO	
Tallow alcohol, see Alcohols (C13+)	20	2	TFA	ALY (ASY).
Tallow alkyl nitrile	37		TAN	
Tallow fatty acid	34	2	TFD	
Tallow fatty alcohol, see Alcohols (C13+)	20		TFA	ALY.
TAME, see tert-Amyl methyl ether	40			AYE.
Tertiary butyl phenols	21		BLT	BTP.
1,1,2,2-Tetrachloroethane	36		TEC	TEE.
Tetradecanol, see Alcohols (C13+)	20		TTN	ALY.
Tetradecene, see the olefins or alpha-olefin entries	30			OAM/OFY/OFW/OFZ/TDD.
Tetradecylbenzene, see Alkyl(C9+) benzenes	32		TDB	AKB.
Tetraethylene glycol	40		TTG	
Tetraethylene glycol methyl ether, see Poly(2-8)alkylene glycol monoalkyl(C1-C6) ether.	40			PAG.
Tetraethylene pentamine	7	2	TTP	
Tetraethyl silicate monomer/oligomer (20% in ethanol)*	0	1, 3	TSM	
Tetrahydrofuran	41		THF	
Tetrahydronaphthalene	32		THN	
Tetramethylbenzene (all isomers)	32		TTC	TTB.
Tetrapropylbenzene, see Alkyl(C9+)benzenes	32			AKB.
Tetrasodium salt of ethylenediaminetetraacetic acid solution, see Ethylenediaminetetraacetic acid, tetrasodium salt solution.	43.			EDS.
Titanium dioxide slurry	43		TDS	
Titanium tetrachloride	2		TTT	
Toluene	32		TOL	
Toluenediamine	9		TDA	
Toluene diisocyanate	12		TDJ	TDI/TDJ.
o-Toluidine	9		TLI	TOD/TOI.
Triarylphosphate, see Triisopropylated phenyl phosphates	34		TRA	TPL.

85

Chemical name	Group No.	Foot-note	CHRIS Code	Related CHRIS Codes
Tributyl phosphate	34		TBP	
1,2,3-Trichlorobenzene (molten)*	36	3	TBZ	TCB.
1,2,4-Trichlorobenzene	36		TCB	TBZ.
1,1,1-Trichloroethane	36	2	TCE	TCM.
1,1,2-Trichloroethane	36		TCM	TCE.
Trichloroethylene	36	2	TCL	
1,2,3-Trichloropropane	36	2	TCN	
1,1,2-Trichloro-1,2,2-trifluoroethane	36		TTF	
Tricresyl phosphate (containing 1% or more ortho-isomer)*	34	3	TCO	TCP/TCQ.
Tricresyl phosphate (containing less than 1% ortho-isomer)*	34	3	TCP	TCO/TCQ.
Tridecane (all isomers), see Alkanes (C10+) (all isomers)	31		TRD	ALV (ALJ).
Tridecanoic acid	34		TDO	
Tridecanol, see Alcohols (C13+)	20		TDN	ALY (ASK/ASY/AYK/LAL).
Tridecene, see Olefins (C13+)	30		TRD	OAM/OFY/OFW/OFZ/TDC.
Tridecyl acetate	34		TAE	
Tridecylbenzene, see Alkyl(C9+) benzenes	32		TRB	AKB.
Triethanolamine	8	2	TEA	
Triethylamine	7		TEN	
Triethylbenzene	32		TEB	
Triethylene glycol	40		TEG	
Triethylene glycol butyl ether, see Poly(2-8)alkylene glycol monoalkyl (C1-C6) ether.	40		TBE	PAG.
Triethylene glycol butyl ether mixture	40		TBD	
Triethylene glycol di-(2-ethylbutyrate)	34		TGD	
Triethylene glycol ether mixture	40		TYM	
Triethylene glycol ethyl ether, see Poly(2-8)alkylene glycol monoalkyl(C1-C6) ether.	40		TGE	PAG.
Triethylene glycol methyl ether, see Poly(2-8)alkylene glycol monoalkyl(C1-C6) ether.	40		TGY	PAG.
Triethylenetetramine	7	2	TET	
Triethyl phosphate	34		TPS	
Triethyl phosphite	34	2	TPI	
Triisobutylene	30		TIB	
Triisooctyl trimellitate	34		TIS	
Triisopropanolamine	8		TIP	
Triisopropanolamine salt of 2,4-Dichlorophenoxyacetic acid solution, see 2,4-Dichlorophenoxyacetic acid, Triisopropanolamine salt solution.	43			DTI.
Triisopropylated phenyl phosphates	34		TPL	
Trimethylacetic acid	4		TAA	
Trimethylamine solution (30% or less)	7		TMT	TMA.
Trimethylbenzene (all isomers)	32		TRE	TMB/TMD/TME.
Trimethyl nonanol, see Dodecanol	20			DDN (ASK/ASY/LAL).
Trimethylol propane polyethoxylated	40		TPR	
2,2,4-Trimethyl-1,3-pentanediol diisobutyrate	34		TMQ	
2,2,4-Trimethyl-1,3-pentanediol-1-isobutyrate	34		TMP	
2,2,4-Trimethyl-3-pentanol-1-isobutyrate	34		TMR	
1,3,5-Trioxane	41	2	TRO	
Triphenylborane (10% or less)/Caustic soda solution	5		TPB	
Tripropylene, see Propylene trimer	30			PTR.
Tripropylene glycol	40		TGC	
Tripropylene glycol methyl ether, see Poly(2-8)alkylene glycol monoalkyl(C1-C6) ether.	40		TGM	PAG.
Trisodium nitrilotriacetate solution, see Nitrilotriacetic acid, trisodium salt solution.	34		TSO	NCA (TSN).
Trisodium phosphate solution	5		TSP	
Trisodium salt of N-(Hydroxyethyl)ethylenediaminetriacetic acid solution, see N-(Hydroxyethyl)ethylenediaminetriacetic acid, trisodium salt solution.	43			HET.
Trixylenyl phosphate, see Trixylyl phosphate	34			TRP.
Trixylyl phosphate	34			TRP.
Tung oil, see Oil, misc: Tung	34			OTG
Turpentine	30		TPT	
Turpentine substitute, see White spirit (low (15–20%) aromatic)	33			WSL (WSP).
Ucarsol CR Solvent 302 SG	8		UCS	
Undecane (all isomers), see Alkanes (C10+) (all isomers)	31		UDN	ALV (ALJ).
Undecanoic acid	4		UDA	
Undecanol, see Undecyl alcohol	20			UND (ALR).
Undecene	30		UDD	UDC.
1-Undecene	30		UDC	UDD.
Undecyl alcohol	20		UND	ALR.
Undecylbenzene, see Alkyl(C9+) benzenes			UDB	AKB.

Coast Guard, DHS — Pt. 150, Table I, Nt.

Chemical name	Group No.	Foot-note	CHRIS Code	Related CHRIS Codes
Urea, Ammonium mono- and di-hydrogen phosphate/Potassium chloride solution.	0	1	UPX	
Urea/Ammonium nitrate solution *	34	3	UAV	ANU/UAS/UAT/UAU.
Urea/Ammonium nitrate solution (containing less than 1% free Ammonia)	43	....	UAU	ANU/UAS/UAT/UAV.
Urea/Ammonium nitrate solution (containing less than 2% free Ammonia)	6	....	UAT	ANU/UAS/UAU/UAV.
Urea/Ammonium phosphate solution	43	....	UAP	
Urea solution	43	....	USL	URE.
Valeraldehyde (all isomers)	19	....	VAK	IVA/VAL.
Vanillin black liquor (free alkali content 3% or more)	5	....	VBL	
Vegetable oils, n.o.s	34	....	VEO	
Including:				
Beechnut oil.				
Camelina oil.				
Cashew nut shell.				
Castor oil.				
Cocoa butter.				
Coconut oil.				
Corn oil.				
Cottonseed oil.				
Croton oil.				
Groundnut oil.				
Hazelnut oil.				
Illipe oil.				
Jatropha oil.				
Linseed oil.				
Mango kernel oil.				
Nutmeg butter.				
Oiticica oil.				
Olive oil.				
Palm kernel oil.				
Palm kernel olein.				
Palm kernel stearin.				
Palm mid fraction.				
Palm, non-edible industrial grade.				
Palm oil.				
Palm olein.				
Palm stearin.				
Peanut oil.				
Peel oil (oranges and lemons).				
Perilla oil.				
Pine oil.				
Poppy seed oil.				
Poppy oil.				
Raisin seed oil.				
Rapeseed oil.				
Rapeseed (low erucic acid containing less than 4% free fatty acids).				
Resin, distilled.				
Resin oil.				
Rice bran oil.				
Rosin oil.				
Safflower oil.				
Salad oil.				
Sesame oil.				
Shea butter.				
Soyabean oil.				
Sunflower seed oil.				
Tall.				
Tall, crude.				
Tall, distilled.				
Tall, pitch.				
Tucum oil.				
Tung oil.				
Walnut oil.				
Vegetable acid oils, n.o.s.	34	....	VAD	
Including:				
Corn acid oil.				
Cottonseed acid oil.				
Dark mixed acid oil.				
Groundnut acid oil.				
Mixed acid oil.				
Mixed general acid oil.				
Mixed hard acid oil.				

Chemical name	Group No.	Footnote	CHRIS Code	Related CHRIS Codes
Mixed soft acid oil.				
Rapeseed acid oil.				
Safflower acid oil.				
Soya acid oil.				
Sunflower seed acid oil.				
Vegetable fatty acid distillates*	34	3	VFD	
Including:				
Palm kernel fatty acid distillate.				
Palm oil fatty acid distillate.				
Tall fatty acid distillate.				
Tall oil fatty acid distillate.				
Vegetable protein solution (hydrolyzed)	43		VPS	
Vinyl acetate	13	2	VAM	
Vinyl chloride	35		VCM	
Vinyl ethyl ether	13		VEE	
Vinylidene chloride	35		VCI	
Vinyl neodecanoate	13	2	VND	
Vinyltoluene	13		VNT	
Water	43		WTR	
Waxes			WAX	
Candelilla	34		WCD	
Carnauba	34		WCA	
Paraffin	31		WPF	
Petroleum	33		WPT	
White spirit, see White spirit (low (15–20%) aromatic)	33		WSP	WSL.
White spirit (low (15–20%) aromatic)	33		WSL	WSP.
Wine, see Alcoholic beverages	20		ABV	
Wood lignin with Sodium acetate/oxalate*	0	1, 3	WOL	
Xylenes	32		XLX	XLM/XLO/XLP.
Xylenes/Ethylbenzene (10% or more) mixture	32		XEB	
Xylenol	21		XYL	
Zinc alkaryl dithiophosphate (C7-C16)	34		ZAD	
Zinc alkenyl carboxamide	10		ZAA	
Zinc alkyl dithiophosphate (C3-C14)	34		ZAP	
Zinc bromide/Calcium bromide solution, see Drilling brine (containing Zinc salts).	43			DZB.

Notes:
1. Because of very high reactivity or unusual conditions of carriage or potential compatibility problems, this commodity is not assigned to a specific group in Figure 1 to 46 CFR part 150 (Compatibility Chart).
2. See Appendix I to 46 CFR part 150 (Exceptions to the Chart).
3. "*" From the March 2012 Annex to the 2007 edition of the IBC Code.
4. Italicized words are not part of the cargo name but may be used in addition to the cargo name.

TABLE II TO PART 150—GROUPING OF CARGOES

0. UNASSIGNED CARGOES

Acetone cyanohydrin [1,2]
Alkylbenzenesulfonic acid [1,2]
Aluminium chloride, Hydrochloric acid solution [1]
Ammonium hydrogen phosphate solution [1]
Ammonium nitrate solution [1]
Ammonium thiocyanate, Ammonium thiosulfate solution [1]
Benzenesulfonyl chloride [1,2]
gamma-Butyrolactone [1,2]
Chlorine [1]
Chlorosulfonic acid [1]
Decyloxytetrahydro-thiophene dioxide [2]
tert-Dodecanethiol [2]
2,4-Dichlorophenoxyacetic acid, Dimethylamine salt solution [1,2]
Dimethylamine salt of 2,4-Dichlorophenoxyacetic acid solution [1,2]
Diphenylol propane-Epichlorohydrin resins [1]
Dodecylbenzenesulfonic acid [1,2]
Dodecyl hydroxypropyl sulfide [2]
Ethylene oxide [1]
Hydrogen peroxide solutions [1]
Lactic acid [2]
Long chain alkaryl sulfonic acid (C16–C60) [2]
Magnesium chloride solution [1,2]
Molasses residue [1]
Motor fuel antiknock compounds containing Lead alkyls [1]
Naphthalene sulfonic acid-formaldehyde copolymer, sodium salt solution [1]
NIAX POLYOL APP 240C [1,2]
Nitrating acid [1]
Nitric acid (greater than 70%) [1]
o-Nitrophenol [1,2]
Noxious Liquid Substance, n.o.s. (NLS's) [1]
Oleum [1,2]
Phosphorus [1]
Phthalate based polyester polyol [2]
SAP 7001 [1]
Sodium chlorate solution [1,2]
Sodium dichromate solution [1,2]
Sodium hydrogen sulfide, Sodium carbonate solution [1,2]

Sodium sulfide, Hydrosulfide solution [1] [2]
Sodium thiocyanate solution [1] [2]
Sulfur [1]
Tall oil fatty acid, barium salt [2]
Urea, Ammonium mono- and di-hydrogen phosphate, Potassium chloride solution

1. Non-Oxidizing Mineral Acids

Di-(2-ethylhexyl)phosphoric acid
Ferric chloride solution
Fluorosilicic acid
Hydrochloric acid
Phosphoric acid
Polyaluminum chloride solution

2. Sulfuric Acids

Sulfuric acid [2]
Sulfuric acid, spent
Titanium tetrachloride

3. Nitric Acid

Ferric nitrate, Nitric acid solution
Nitric acid (70% or less)

4. Organic Acids

Acetic acid [2]
Acrylic acid [2]
Butyric acid
Cashew nut shell oil (untreated)
Citric acid
Chloroacetic acid solution
Chloropropionic acid
Decanoic acid
2,2-Dichloropropionic acid
2,2-Dimethyloctanoic acid
2-Ethylhexanoic acid
Formic acid [2]
Glycolic acid
Glyoxylic acid
n-Heptanoic acid
Hexanoic acid
2-Hydroxy-4-(methylthio)butanoic acid
Methacrylic acid
Naphthenic acid
Neodecanoic acid
Nonanoic acid
Nonanoic, Tridecanoic acid mixture
Octanoic acid
n-Pentanoic acid, 2-Methyl butryic acid mixture
Pentanoic acid
Propionic acid
Trimethylacetic acid
Undecanoic acid

5. Caustics

Ammonium sulfide solution
Calcium hypochlorite solutions
Caustic potash solution [2]
Caustic soda solution [2]
Cresylate spent caustic
Cresylic acid, sodium salt solution
Kraft black liquor
Kraft pulping liquors
Mercaptobenzothiazol, sodium salt solution
Potassium hydroxide solution [2]
Sodium acetate, Glycol, Water mixture (containing Sodium hydroxide)
Sodium aluminate solution
Sodium borohydride, Sodium hydroxide solution
Sodium carbonate solutions
Sodium cyanide solution
Sodium hydrosulfide solution [2]
Sodium hydrosulfide, Ammonium sulfide solution [2]
Sodium hydroxide solution [2]
Sodium hypochlorite solution
Sodium 2-mercaptobenzothiazol solution
Sodium naphthenate solution
Sodium nitrite solution
Triphenylborane, Caustic soda solution
Trisodium phosphate solution
Vanillin black liquor

6. Ammonia

Ammonia, anhydrous
Ammonia, aqueous
Ammonium hydroxide (28% or less Ammonia)
Ammonium nitrate, Urea solution (containing Ammonia)
Urea, Ammonium nitrate solution (containing Ammonia)

7. Aliphatic Amines

N-Aminoethylpiperazine
Butylamine
Cyclohexylamine
Dibutylamine
Diethylamine [2]
Diethylenetriamine [2]
Diisobutylamine
Diisopropylamine
Dimethylamine
Dimethylamine solution
N,N-Dimethylcyclohexylamine
N,N-Dimethyldodecylamine
Di-n-propylamine
Diphenylamine, reaction product with 2,2,4-Trimethylpentene
Diphenylamines, alkylated
Dodecylamine, Tetradecylamine mixture [2]
Dodecyldimethylamine, Tetradecyldimethylamine mixture
Ethylamine [2]
Ethylamine solution
Ethyleneamine EA 1302 [2]
N-Ethyl-n-butylamine
N-Ethyl cyclohexylamine
Ethylenediamine [2]
2-Ethyl hexylamine
N-Ethylmethylallylamine
Glyphosate solution (not containing surfactant)
Hexamethylenediamine
Hexamethylenediamine solution
Hexamethylenetetramine
Hexamethylenetetramine solutions
Hexamethylenimine
HiTec 321

bis-(Hydrogenated tallow alkyl)methyl amines
Isophorone diamine
Long chain polyetheramine in alkyl(C2–C4)benzenes
Metam sodium solution
Methylamine solutions
Morpholine [2]
Oleylamine
Pentaethylenehexamine
Pentaethylenehexamine, Tetraethylenepentamine mixture
Phosphate esters, alkyl (C12–C14) amine
Polyethylene polyamines [2]
Polyolefin amide alkeneamine (C28+)
Polyisobutenamine in aliphatic (C10–C14) solvent
Poly (C17+) olefin amine
Polyolefin amide alkeneamine/Molybdenum oxysulfide mixture
Propanil, Mesityl oxide, Isophorone mixture
Propylamine
iso-Propylamine solution
Roundup
Sulfohydrocarbon, long chain (C18+) alkylamine mixture
Tetraethylenepentamine [2]
Triethylamine
Triethylenetetramine [2]
Trimethylamine solution
Trimethylhexamethylene diamine (2,2,4- and 2,4,4-)

8. ALKANOLAMINES

2-(2-Aminoethoxy)ethanol
Aminoethyldiethanolamine, Aminoethylethanolamine solution
Aminoethylethanolamine
2-Amino-2-methyl-1-propanol
Diethanolamine
Diethylaminoethanol
Diethylethanolamine
Diisopropanolamine
Dimethylethanolamine
Ethanolamine
Ethoxylated long chain (C16+) alkyloxyalkanamine
Methyl diethanolamine
Propanolamine
Triethanolamine [2]
Triisopropanolamine
Ucarsol CR Solvent 302 SG

9. AROMATIC AMINES

Alkyl (C8–C9) phenylamine in aromatic solvents
Aniline
Calcium long chain alkyl phenolic amine (C8–C40)
4-Chloro-2-methylphenoxyacetic acid, Dimethylamine salt solution
Dialkyl (C8–C9) diphenylamines
2,6-Diethylaniline
Dimethylamine salt of 4-Chloro-2-methylphenoxyacetic acid solution
2,6-Dimethylaniline
Diphenylamine
2-Ethyl-6-methyl-N-(1′-methyl-2-methoxyethyl)aniline
2-Methyl-6-ethyl aniline
2-Methyl-5-ethyl pyridine
Methyl pyridine
3-Methylpyridine
N-Methyl-2-pyrrolidone [2]
Paraldehyde-Ammonia reaction product
Pyridine
Pyridine bases
Toluenediamine
p-Toluidine

10. AMIDES

Acetochlor
Acrylamide solution
Alkenyl(C11+)amide
N,N-Dimethylacetamide
N,N-Dimethylacetamide solution
Dimethylformamide
Formamide
N,N-bis(2-Hydroxyethyl) oleamide
Octadecenoamide
Zinc alkenyl carboxamide

11. ORGANIC ANHYDRIDES

Acetic anhydride
Alkenylsuccinic anhydride
Maleic anhydride
Phthalic anhydride
Polyisobutenyl anhydride adduct
Polyolefin anhydride
Propionic anhydride

12. ISOCYANATES

Diphenylmethane diisocyanate
Hexamethylene diisocyanate
Isophorone diisocyanate
Polymethylene polyphenyl isocyanate
Toluene diisocyanate
Trimethylhexamethylene diisocyanate (2,2,4- and 2,4,4-)

13. VINYL ACETATE

Vinyl acetate
Vinyl ethyl ether
Vinyl neodecanate
Vinyl toluene

14. ACRYLATES

Butyl acrylate
Butyl methacrylate
Butyl methacrylate, Decyl methacrylate, Cetyl-Eicosyl methacrylate mixture
Cetyl-Eicosyl methacrylate mixture
Decyl acrylate
Dodecyl methacrylate
Dodecyl-Octadecyl methacrylate mixture
Dodecyl-Pentadecyl methacrylate mixture
Ethyl acrylate
2-Ethylhexyl acrylate
Ethyl methacrylate
2-Hydroxyethyl acrylate [2]
Methacrylic resin in Ethylene dichloride

Methyl acrylate
Methyl methacrylate
Nonyl methacrylate
Polyalkyl(C18 - C22) acrylate in Xylene
Polyalkyl (C10–C18) methacrylate/Ethylene
Polyalkyl (C10–C20) methacrylate
Propylene copolymer mixture
Roehm monomer 6615

15. SUBSTITUTED ALLYLS

Acrylonitrile [2]
Allyl alcohol [2]
Allyl chloride
1,3-Dichloropropene
Dichloropropene, Dichloropropane mixtures
Methacrylonitrile

16. ALKYLENE OXIDES

Butylene oxide
Ethylene oxide, Propylene oxide mixtures
Propylene oxide

17. EPICHLOROHYDRIN

Chlorohydrins
Epichlorohydrin

18. KETONES

Acetone [2]
Acetophenone
Amyl methyl ketone
Butyl heptyl ketone
Camphor oil
1-(4-Chlorophenyl)-4,4-dimethyl pentan-3-one [2]
Cyclohexanone
Cyclohexanone, Cyclohexanol mixtures [2]
Diisobutyl ketone
Ethyl amyl ketone
Epoxy resin
Ketone residue
Isophorone [2]
Mesityl oxide [2]
Methyl amyl ketone
Methyl butyl ketone
Methyl butyl ketone
Methyl ethyl ketone [2]
Methyl heptyl ketone
Methyl isoamyl ketone
Methyl isobutyl ketone [2]
Methyl propyl ketone
Trifluralin in Xylene

19. ALDEHYDES

Acetaldehyde
Acrolein [2]
Butyraldehyde
Crotonaldehyde [2]
Decaldehyde
Ethylhexaldehyde
2-Ethyl-3-propylacrolein [2]
Formaldehyde, Methanol mixtures [2]
Formaldehyde solution [2]
Furfural
Glutaraldehyde solution
Glyoxal solutions
3-Methyl butyraldehyde
Methylolureas
3-(Methylthio)propionaldehyde
Octyl aldehyde
Paraldehyde
Pentyl aldehyde
Propionaldehyde
Valeraldehyde

20. ALCOHOLS, GLYCOLS

Acrylonitrile-Styrene copolymer dispersion in Polyether polyol
Alcoholic beverages
Alcohol polyethoxylates
Alcohol polyethoxylates, secondary
Alcohols (C13+)
Amyl alcohol
Behenyl alcohol
Brake fluid base mixtures
1,4-Butanediol
Butyl alcohol [2]
Butylene glycol [2]
Cetyl-Stearyl alcohol
Choline chloride solutions
Cyclohexanol
Decyl alcohol [2]
Diacetone alcohol [2]
Diethyl hexanol
Diisobutyl carbinol
2,2-Dimethylpropane-1,3-diol
Dodecanol
Dodecyl alcohol
Ethoxylated alcohols, C11-C15
2-Ethoxyethanol
Ethyl alcohol [2]
Ethyl butanol
Ethylene chlorohydrin
Ethylene cyanohydrin
Ethylene glycol [2]
2-Ethylhexanol
Furfuryl alcohol [2]
Glycerine [2]
Glycerine, Dioxanedimethanol mixture
Glycerol monooleate
Heptanol
Hexamethylene glycol
Hexanol
Hexylene glycol
Hydroxy terminated polybutadiene
Icosa(oxypropane-2,3-diyl)s
Lauryl polyglucose (50% or less)
3-Methoxy-1-butanol
Methyl alcohol [2]
Methyl amyl alcohol
Methyl butenol
Methylbutynol
2-Methyl-2-hydroxy-3-butyne
Methyl isobutyl carbinol
3-Methyl-3-methoxybutanol
2-Methyl-1,3-propanediol
Molasses
Nonyl alcohol [2]
Octanol [2]
Octyl alcohol [2]
Penacosa(oxypropane-2,3-diyl)s
Pentadecanol
Polyalkylene oxide polyol

Polybutadiene, hydroxy terminated
Polyglycerol
Polyglycerine, Sodium salts solution (containing less than 3% Sodium hydroxide)[2]
Polyolefin amide alkeneamine polyol
Propyl alcohol[2]
Propylene glycol[2]
Rum
Sorbitol solutions
Stearyl alcohol
Tallow fatty alcohol
Tetradecanol
Tridecanol
Trimethyl nonanol
Trimethylol propane polyethoxylate
Undecanol
Undecyl alcohol

21. PHENOLS, CRESOLS

Benzyl alcohol
Carbolic oil
Creosote[2]
Cresols
Cresylic acid
Cresylic acid dephenolized
Cresylic acid, tar
Dibutylphenols
2,4-Dichlorophenol
Dodecyl phenol
o-Ethylphenol
Long chain alkylphenate/phenol sulfide mixture
Nonyl phenol
Octyl phenol
Phenol
Xylenols

22. CAPROLACTAM SOLUTIONS

Caprolactam solution

23–29. UNASSIGNED

30. OLEFINS

Amylene
Aryl polyolefin (C11–C50)
Butadiene
Butadiene, Butylene mixtures (cont. Acetylenes)
Butene
Butene oligomer
Butylene
1,5,9-Cyclododecatriene
1,3-Cyclopentadiene dimer
Cyclopentadiene, Styrene, Benzene mixture
Cyclopentene
Decene
Dicyclopentadiene
Diisobutylene
Dipentene
Dodecene
Ethylene
Ethylene-Propylene copolymer
Ethylidene norbornene[2]
1-Heptene
Hexene
Isoprene
Isoprene concentrate (Shell)
Latex (ammonia (1% or less) inhibited)
Methyl acetylene, Propadiene mixture
Methyl butene
Methylcyclopentadiene dimer
2-Methyl-1-pentene
4-Methyl-1-pentene
alpha-Methyl styrene
Myrcene
Nonene
1-Octadecene
Octene
Olefin mixtures
alpha-Olefins (C6 - C18) mixtures
alpha-Olefins (C13+)
1,3-Pentadiene
Pentene
alpha-Pinene
beta-Pinene
Polybutene
Poly(4+)isobutylene
Polyolefin (molecular weight 300+)
Polypropylene
Poly(5+)propylene
Propylene
Propylene-butylene copolymer
Propylene dimer
Propylene, Propane, MAPP gas mixture
Propylene tetramer
Propylene trimer
Styrene monomer
Tetradecene
Tridecene
Triisobutylene
Tripropylene
Turpentine
Undecene

31. PARAFFINS

Alkanes (C6–C9)
n-Alkanes (C10+)
iso- & cyclo-Alkanes (C10–C11)
iso- & cyclo-Alkanes (C12+)
Butane
Cycloheptane
Cyclohexane
Cyclopentane
Decane
Dodecane
Ethane
Ethyl cyclohexane
Heptane
Hexane[2]
Methane
Methylcyclohexane
2-Methyl pentane
Nonane
Octane
Pentane
Propane
iso-Propylcyclohexane
Tridecane
Waxes:
    Paraffin

32. AROMATIC HYDROCARBONS

Alkyl(C3–C4)benzenes
Alkyl(C5–C8)benzenes
Alkyl(C9+)benzenes
Alkyl acrylate-Vinyl pyridine copolymer in Toluene
Alkylbenzene, Alkylindane, Alkylindene mixture (each C12–C17)
Benzene
Benzene hydrocarbon mixtures (having 10% Benzene or more)
Benzene, Toluene, Xylene mixtures
Butylbenzene
Butyl phenol, Formaldehyde resin in Xylene
Butyl toluene
Cumene
Cymene
Decylbenzene
Dialkyl(C10 - C14) benzenes
Diethylbenzene
Diisopropylbenzene
Diisopropyl naphthalene
Diphenyl
Dodecylbenzene
Dodecyl xylene
Ethylbenzene
Ethyl toluene
1-Hexadecylnaphthalene, 1,4-bis(Hexadecyl)
Isopropylbenzene
Methyl naphthalene
Naphthalene
Naphthalene mixture
Naphthalene still residue
1-Phenyl-1-xylyl ethane
Poly(2+)cyclic aromatics
Polyolefin amine in alkylbenzenes (C2–C4)
Propylbenzene
Pseudocumene
C9 Resinfeed (DSM)[2]
Tetradecylbenzene
Tetrahydronaphthalene
1,2,3,5-Tetramethylbenzene
Toluene
Tridecylbenzene
Triethylbenzene
Trimethylbenzene
Undecylbenzene
Xylene
Xylenes, Ethylbenzene mixture

33. MISCELLANEOUS HYDROCARBON MIXTURES

Alachlor
Alkylbenzenesulfonic acid, sodium salt solutions
Alkyl dithiothiadiazole (C6–C24)
Asphalt blending stocks, roofers flux
Asphalt blending stocks, straight run residue
Asphalt emulsion
Aviation alkylates
Calcium sulfonate, Calcium carbonate, Hydrocarbon solvent mixture
Coal tar
Coal tar distillate
Coal tar, high temperature
Coal tar pitch
Decahydronaphthalene
Degummed C9 (DOW)
Diphenyl, Diphenyl ether
Distillates, flashed feed stocks
Distillates, straight run
Drilling mud (low toxicity) (*if flammable or combustible*)
Gas oil, cracked
Gasoline blending stock, alkylates
Gasoline blending stock, reformates
Gasolines:
  Automotive (*not over 4.23 grams lead per gal.*)
  Aviation (*not over 4.86 grams lead per gal.*)
  Casinghead (*natural*)
  Polymer
  Straight run
Jet Fuels:
  JP-4
  JP-5
  JP-8
Kerosene
Mineral spirits
Naphtha:
  Coal tar solvent
  Petroleum
  Solvent
  Stoddard solvent
  Varnish Makers' and Painters'
Oil, fuel:
  No. 1
  No. 1-D
  No. 2
  No. 2-D
  No. 4
  No. 5
  No. 6
Oil, misc:
  Aliphatic
  Aromatic
  Clarified
  Coal
  Crude
  Diesel
  Gas, high pour
  Heartcut distillate
  Linseed
  Lubricating
  Mineral
  Mineral seal
  Motor
  Neatsfoot
  Penetrating
  Pine
  Rosin
  Sperm
  Spindle
  Turbine
  Residual
  Road
  Transformer
Oxyalkylated alkyl phenol formaldehyde
Petrolatum
Pine oil
Polyolefin amine (C28–C250)
Polyolefin amide alkeneamine (C17+)

Polyolefin amide alkeneamine borate (C28–C250)
Sodium petroleum sulfonate
Sulfohydrocarbon (C3–C88)
Waxes:
  Petroleum
Sulfurized fat (C14–C20)
Sulfurized polyolefinamide alkeneamines (C28–C250)
White spirit (low (15-20%) aromatic)

34. Esters

Alkane (C14–C17) sulfonic acid, sodium salt solution
Alkyl(C8+)amine, Alkenyl (C12+) acid ester mixture
Alkyl ester copolymer (C6–C18)
Alkyl(C7–C9) nitrates [2]
Alkyl (C8–C40) phenol sulfide
Alkyl (C10–C20, saturated and unsaturated) phosphite
Alkyl sulfonic acid ester of phenol
Alkylaryl phosphate mixtures (more than 40%)
Amyl acetate
Animal and Fish oils, n.o.s.
Animal and Fish acid oils and distillates, n.o.s.
Barium long chain alkaryl (C11–C50) sulfonate
Barium long chain alkyl(C8–C14)phenate sulfide
Benzene tricarboxylic acid trioctyl ester
Benzyl acetate
Butyl acetate
Butyl benzyl phthalate
n-Butyl butyrate
Butyl formate
iso-Butyl isobutyrate
n-Butyl propionate
Calcium alkyl(C9)phenol sulfide, polyolefin phosphorosulfide mixture
Calcium long chain alkaryl sulfonate (C11–C50)
Calcium long chain alkyl phenate sulfide (C8–C40)
Calcium long chain alkyl phenates
Calcium long chain alkyl salicylate (C13+)
Calcium nitrate, Magnesium nitrate, Potassium chloride solution
Calcium nitrate solution
Cobalt naphthenate in solvent naphtha
Coconut oil, fatty acid
Copper salt of long chain alkanoic acids
Cottonseed oil, fatty acid
Cyclohexyl acetate
Decyl acetate
Dialkyl(C7 - C13) phthalates
Dibutyl hydrogen phosphonate
Dibutyl phthalate
Diethylene glycol butyl ether acetate
Diethylene glycol dibenzoate
Diethylene glycol ethyl ether acetate
Diethylene glycol methyl ether acetate
Diethylene glycol phthalate
Di-(2-ethylhexyl)adipate
Di-(2-ethylhexyl)phthalate
Diethyl phthalate
Diethyl sulfate
Diheptyl phthalate
Dihexyl phthalate
Di-n-hexyl adipate
Diisobutyl phthalate
Diisodecyl phthalate
Diisononyl adipate
Diisononyl phthalate
Diisooctyl phthalate
Dimethyl adipate
Dimethylcyclicsiloxane hydrolyzate
Dimethyl glutarate
Dimethyl hydrogen phosphite [2]
Dimethyl naphthalene sulfonic acid, sodium salt solution [2]
Dimethyl phthalate
Dimethyl polysiloxane
Dimethyl succinate
Dinonyl phthalate
Dioctyl phthalate
Diphenyl tolyl phosphate, less than 0.02% ortho-isomer)
Dipropylene glycol dibenzoate
Dithiocarbamate ester (C7–C35)
Ditridecyl adipate
Ditridecyl phthalate
2-Dodecenylsuccinic acid, dipotassium salt solution
Diundecyl phthalate
2-Ethoxyethyl acetate
Ethyl acetate
Ethyl acetoacetate
Ethyl butyrate
Ethylene carbonate
Ethylene glycol acetate
Ethylene glycol butyl ether acetate
Ethylene glycol diacetate
Ethylene glycol ethyl ether acetate
Ethylene glycol methyl ether acetate
Ethyl-3-ethoxypropionate
Ethyl hexyl phthalate
Ethyl propionate
Ethyl propionate
Fatty acids (saturated, C14+)
Glycerol polyalkoxylate
Glyceryl triacetate
Glycidyl ester of C10 trialkyl acetic acid
Gylcidyl ester of tridecylacetic acid
Heptyl acetate
Hexyl acetate
Lauric acid
Lecithin
Magnesium long chain alkaryl sulfonate (C11–C50)
Magnesium long chain alkyl phenate sulfide (C8–C20)
Magnesium long chain alkyl salicylate (C11+)
3-Methoxybutyl acetate
1-Methoxy-2-propyl acetate
Methyl acetate
Methyl acetoacetate
Methyl amyl acetate
Methyl butyrate
Methyl formate
3-Methyl-3-methoxybutyl acetate

Methyl salicylate
Metolachlor
Naphthalene sulfonic acid, sodium salt solution (40% or less)
Nonyl acetate
n-Octyl acetate
Octyl decyl adipate
Oil, edible:
  Beechnut
  Castor
  Cocoa butter
  Coconut [2]
  Cod liver
  Corn
  Cotton seed
  Fish [2]
  Groundnut
  Hazelnut
  Lard
  Lanolin
  Nutmeg butter
  Olive
  Palm [2]
  Palm kernel
  Peanut
  Poppy
  Poppy seed
  Raisin seed
  Rapeseed
  Rice bran
  Safflower
  Salad
  Sesame
  Soya bean
  Sunflower
  Sunflower seed
  Tucum
  Vegetable
  Walnut
Oil, misc:
  Animal
  Coconut oil, fatty actid methyl ester
  Cotton seed oil, fatty acid
  Lanolin
  Palm kernel oil, fatty acid methyl ester
  Palm oil, methyl ester
  Pilchard
  Perilla
  Soapstock
  Soyabean (epoxidized)
  Tall
  Tall, fatty acid [2]
  Tung
Olefin/Alkyl ester copolymer (molecular weight 2000+)
Oleic acid
Palm kernel acid oil
Palm kernel acid oil, methyl ester
Palm stearin
n-Pentyl propionate
Poly(2-8)alkylene glycol monoalkyl(C1–C6) ether acetate
Polydimethylsiloxane
Polyferric sulfate solution
Polymethylsiloxane
Poly(20)oxyethylene sorbitan monooleate
Polysiloxane
Polyolefin aminoester salt
Polyolefin ester (C28–C250)
Polyolefin phosphorosulfide, barium derivative (C28–C250)
Potassium formate solution
Potassium oleate
Potassium salt of polyolefin acid
Propyl acetate
Propylene carbonate
Propylene glycol methyl ether acetate
Sodium acetate, Glycol, Water mixture (not containing Sodium hydroxide) [2]
Sodium acetate solution
Sodium benzoate solution
Sodium dimethyl naphthalene sulfonate solution [2]
Sodium long chain alkyl salicylate (C13+)
Sodium naphthalene sulfonate solution
Soyabean oil (epoxidized)
Stearic acid
Tall oil
Tall oil fatty acid (*Resin acids less than 20%*) [2]
Tallow [2]
Tallow fatty acid [2]
Tributyl phosphate
Tricresyl phosphate
Tridecanoic acid
Tridecyl acetate
Triethylene glycol dibenzoate
Triethylene glycol di-(2-ethylbutyrate)
Triethyl phosphate
Triethyl phosphite [2]
Triisooctyl trimellitate [2]
Triisopropylated phenyl phosphates
2,2,4-Trimethyl-1,3-pentanediol diisobutyrate
2,2,4-Trimethyl-1,3-pentanediol-1-isobutyrate
2,2,4-Trimethyl-3-pentanol-1-isobutyrate
Trimethyl phosphite [2]
Trisodium nitrilotriacetate
Trixylyl phosphate
Trixylenyl phosphate
Vegetable acid oils and distillates, n.o.s.
Vegetable oils, n.o.s.
Waxes:
  Carnauba
Zinc alkaryl dithiophosphate (C7–C16)
Zinc alkyl dithiophosphate (C3–C14)

35. Vinyl Halides

Vinyl chloride
Vinylidene chloride

36. Halogenated Hydrocarbons

Benzyl chloride
Bromochloromethane
Carbon tetrachloride [2]
Catoxid feedstock [2]
Chlorinated paraffins (C10 - C13)
Chlorinated paraffins (C14 - C17)
Chlorobenzene
Chlorodifluoromethane
Chloroform
Chlorotoluene

Dibromomethane
Dibutylphenols
3,4-Dichloro-1-butene
Dichlorobenzene
Dichlorodifluoromethane
1,1-Dichloroethane
1,6-Dichlorohexane
2,2′-Dichloroisopropyl ether
Dichloromethane
Dichloropropane
Ethyl chloride
Ethylene dibromide
Ethylene dichloride [2]
Methyl bromide
Methyl chloride
Monochlorodifluoromethane
n-Propyl chloride
Pentachloroethane
Perchloroethylene
1,1,2,2-Tetrachloroethane
1,2,3-Trichlorobenzene
1,2,4-Trichlorobenzene
1,1,1-Trichloroethane [2]
1,1,2-Trichloroethane
Trichloroethylene [2]
1,2,3-Trichloropropane
1,1,2-Trichloro-1,2,2-trifluoroethane

37. Nitriles

Acetonitrile
Adiponitrile
Lactonitrile solution
Propionitrile
Tallow nitrile

38. Carbon Disulfide

Carbon disulfide

39. Sulfolane

Sulfolane

40. Glycol Ethers

Alkyl (C7-C11) phenol poly(4-12)ethoxylate
Alkyl (C9-C15) phenyl propoxylate
Diethylene glycol [2]
Diethylene glycol butyl ether
Diethylene glycol dibutyl ether
Diethylene glycol diethyl ether
Diethylene glycol ethyl ether
Diethylene glycol methyl ether
Diethylene glycol n-hexyl ether
Diethylene glycol phenyl ether
Diethylene glycol propyl ether
Dipropylene glycol
Dipropylene glycol butyl ether
Dipropylene glycol methyl ether
Ethoxy triglycol
Ethylene glycol hexyl ether
Ethylene glycol methyl butyl ether
Ethylene glycol monoalkyl ethers
Ethylene glycol tert-butyl ether
Ethylene glycol butyl ether
Ethylene glycol dibutyl ether
Ethylene glycol ethyl ether
Ethylene glycol isopropyl ether
Ethylene glycol methyl ether
Ethylene glycol phenyl ether
Ethylene glycol phenyl ether, Diethylene glycol phenyl ether mixture
Ethylene glycol propyl ether
Hexaethylene glycol
Methoxy triglycol
Nonyl phenol poly(4+)ethoxylates
Pentaethylene glycol methyl ether
Polyalkylene glycol butyl ether
Polyalkylene glycols, Polyalkylene glycol monoalkyl ethers mixtures
Polyethylene glycols
Polyethylene glycol dimethyl ether
Poly(2-8)alkylene glycol monoalkyl(C1–C6) ether
Polyethylene glycol monoalkyl ether
Polypropylene glycol methyl ether
Polypropylene glycols
Poly(tetramethylene ether) glycols (mw 950–1050)
Polytetramethylene ether glycol
n-Propoxypropanol
Propylene glycol monoalkyl ether
Propylene glycol ethyl ether
Propylene glycol methyl ether
Propylene glycol n-butyl ether
Propylene glycol phenyl ether
Propylene glycol propyl ether
Tetraethylene glycol
Tetraethylene glycol methyl ether
Triethylene glycol
Triethylene glycol butyl ether
Triethylene glycol butyl ether mixture
Triethylene glycol ether mixture
Triethylene glycol ethyl ether
Triethylene glycol methyl ether
Tripropylene glycol
Tripropylene glycol methyl ether

41. Ethers

Alkaryl polyether (C9–C20)
tert-Amyl methyl ether
Butyl ether
2,2′-Dichloroethyl ether
Diethyl ether
Diglycidyl ether of Bisphenol A
Diglycidyl ether of Bisphenol F
Dimethyl furan
1,4-Dioxane
Diphenyl ether
Diphenyl ether, Diphenyl phenyl ether mixture
Ethyl tert-butyl ether [2]
Ethyl ether
Long chain alkaryl polyether (C11–C20)
Methyl-tert-butyl ether [2]
Methyl tert-pentyl ether
Propyl ether
Tetrahydrofuran
1,3, 5-Trioxane
Polyether (molecular weight 2000+)

42. Nitrocompounds

o-Chloronitrobenzene
Dinitrotoluene
Nitrobenzene

Nitroethane
Nitroethane, 1-Nitropropane mixture
Nitropropane
Nitropropane, Nitroethane mixtures
Nitrotoluene

43. MISCELLANEOUS WATER SOLUTIONS

Alkyl polyglucoside solutions
Aluminum sulfate solution [2]
2-Amino-2-hydroxymethyl-1,3-propanediol solution
Ammonium bisulfite solution [2]
Ammonium lignosulfonate solution
Ammonium nitrate, Urea solution (not containing Ammonia)
Ammonium polyphosphate solution
Ammonium sulfate solution
Ammonium thiosulfate solution
Sulfonated polyacrylate solutions [2]
Calcium bromide solution
Calcium chloride solution
Calcium lignosulfonate solution
Caramel solutions
Clay slurry
Corn syrup
Dextrose solution
2,4-Dichlorophenoxyacetic acid, Diethanolamine salt solution
2,4-Dichlorophenoxyacetic acid, Triisopropanolamine salt solution [2]
Diethanolamine salt of 2,4-Dichlorophenoxyacetic acid solution
Diethylenetriamine pentaacetic acid, pentasodium salt solution
Dodecyl diphenyl ether disulfonate solution
Drilling brine (containing Calcium, Potassium, or Sodium salts)
Drilling brine (containing Zinc salts)
Drilling mud (low toxicity) (*if non-flammable or non-combustible*)
Ethylenediaminetetracetic acid, tetrasodium salt solution
Ethylene-Vinyl acetate copolymer emulsion
Ferric hydroxyethylethylenediamine triacetic acid, trisodium salt solution [2]
Fish solubles (*water based fish meal extracts*)
Fructose solution
Fumaric adduct of Rosin, water dispersion
Hexamethylenediamine adipate solution
N-(Hydroxyethyl)ethylene diamine triacetic acid, trisodium salt solution
Kaolin clay slurry
Latex, liquid synthetic
Lignin liquor
Liquid Streptomyces solubles
l-Lysine solution
N-Methylglucamine solution
Naphthenic acid, sodium salt solution
Potassium chloride solution
Potassium thiosulfate solution
Rosin soap (disproportionated) solution
Sewage sludge, treated
Sodium alkyl sulfonate solution
Sodium hydrogen sulfite solution
Sodium lignosulfonate solution
Sodium polyacrylate solution [2]
Sodium salt of Ferric hydroxyethylethylenediamine triacetic acid solution
Sodium silicate solution [2]
Sodium sulfide solution
Sodium sulfite solution
Sodium tartrates, Sodium succinates solution
Sulfonated polyacrylate solutions [2]
Tall oil soap (disproportionated) solution
Tetrasodium salt of EDTA solution
Titanium dioxide slurry
Triisopropanolamine salt of 2,4-Dichlorophenoxyacetic acid solution
Urea, Ammonium nitrate solution (not containing Ammonia)
Urea, Ammonium phosphate solution
Urea solution
Vegetable protein solution (hydrolysed)
Water

FOOTNOTES TO TABLE II

[1] Because of very high reactivity or unusual conditions of carriage or potential compatibility problems, this product is not assigned to a specific group in the Compatibility Chart. For additional compatibility information, contact Commandant (CG–ENG–5), Attn: Hazardous Materials Division, U.S. Coast Guard Stop 7509, 2703 Martin Luther King Jr. Avenue SE., Washington, DC 20593–7509. Telephone 202–372–1420 or email *hazmatstandards@uscg.mil*.

[2] See Appendix I—Exceptions to the Chart.

[CGD 88–100, 54 FR 40012, Sept. 29, 1989]

EDITORIAL NOTE: For FEDERAL REGISTER citations affecting Table II to part 150, see the List of CFR Sections Affected, which appears in the Finding Aids section of the printed volume and at *www.fdsys.gov*.

EFFECTIVE DATE NOTE: By USCG–2013–0423, 78 FR 50187, Aug. 16, 2013, Table II to Part 150 was revised, effective Sept. 16, 2013. At 78 FR 56837, Sept. 16, 2013, the effectiveness was delayed until Jan. 16, 2014. For the convenience of the user, the revised text is set forth as follows:

TABLE II TO PART 150—GROUPING OF CARGOES

Group	Cargo
0. Unassigned	Acetone cyanohydrin [1] [2]

Group	Cargo
	Alkenoic acid, polyhydroxy ester borated [1]
	Alkyl (C8-C10)/(C12-C14) : (60% or more/40% or less) [1]
	Alkyl (C18-C28) toluenesulfonic acid [1]
	Alkyl (C11-C17) benzene sulfonic acid polyglucoside solution (55% or less) [1]
	Alkylbenzenesulfonic acid [1] [2]
	Alkyl benzene distillation bottoms [1]
	Aluminium chloride, Hydrochloric acid solution [1]
	Aluminum chloride/Hydrogen chloride solution [1]
	Ammonium hydrogen phosphate solution [1]
	Ammonium nitrate solution [1]
	Ammonium thiocyanate, Ammonium thiosulfate solution [1]
	Benzenesulfonyl chloride [1] [2]
	gamma-Butyrolactone [1] [2]
	Chlorine [1]
	Chlorosulfonic acid [1]
	Decyloxytetrahydro-thiophene dioxide [1]
	tert-Dodecanethiol [1]
	2,4-Dichlorophenoxyacetic acid, Dimethylamine salt solution (70% or less) [1] [2]
	Dimethylamine salt of 2,4-Dichlorophenoxyacetic acid solution [1] [2]
	Dimethyl disulfide [1]
	Diphenylol propane-Epichlorohydrin resins [1]
	Dodecylbenzenesulfonic acid [1] [2]
	Dodecyl hydroxypropyl sulfide [1] [2]
	Ethylene oxide [1]
	Hydrogen peroxide solutions [1]
	Hydrogenated starch hydrolysate [1]
	Lactic acid [1] [2]
	Ligninsulfonic acid, sodium salt solution [1]
	Liquid chemical wastes [1]
	Long chain alkaryl sulfonic acid (C16-C60) [1] [2]
	Magnesium chloride solution [1] [2]
	Malitol solution [1]
	Methyl cyclopentadienyl manganese tricarbonyl [1]
	Methyl cyclopentadienyl manganese tricarbonyl (60–70%) in mineral oil [1]
	Molybdenum polysulfide long chain alkyl dithiocarbamide complex [1]
	Molasses residue [1]
	Motor fuel antiknock compounds containing Lead alkyls [1]
	Naphthalene sulfonic acid-formaldehyde copolymer, sodium salt solution [1]
	NIAX POLYOL APP 240C [1] [2]
	Nitrating acid [1]
	Nitric acid (greater than 70%) [1]
	o-Nitrophenol [1] [2]
	Noxious Liquid Substance, n.o.s. (NLS's) [1]
	Oleum [1] [2]
	Orange juice (concentrated) [1]
	Orange juice (not concentrated) [1]
	Oxygenated aliphatic hydrocarbon mixture [1]
	Phosphorus [1]
	Phthalate based polyester polyol [1] [2]
	Potassium polysulfide, Potassium thiosulfide solution (41% or less) [1]
	2-Propene-1-aminium, N,N-dimethyl-N-2-propenyl-, chloride, homopolymer solution [1]
	SAP 7001 [1]
	Sodium chlorate solution [1] [2]
	Sodium dichromate solution [1] [2]
	Sodium hydrogen sulfide, Sodium carbonate solution [1] [2]
	Sodium sulfide, Hydrosulfide solution [1] [2]
	Sodium thiocyanate solution [1] [2]
	Sulfur [1]
	Tall oil fatty acid, barium salt [1] [2]
	Tetraethyl silicate monomer/oligomer (20% in ethanol) [1]
	Urea, Ammonium mono- and di-hydrogen phosphate, Potassium chloride solution [1]
	Wood lignin with Sodium acetate/oxalate [1]
1. Non-Oxidizing Mineral Acids	Di-(2-ethylhexyl)phosphoric acid
	Ferric chloride solution
	Fluorosilicic acid (20–30%) in water solution
	Fluorosilicic acid (30% or less)
	Hydrochloric acid
	Phosphoric acid
	Polyaluminum chloride solution
2. Sulfuric Acids	Sulfuric acid [2]
	Sulfuric acid, spent
	Titanium tetrachloride
3. Nitric Acids	Ferric nitrate, Nitric acid solution

Group	Cargo
4. Organic Acids	Nitric acid (70% or less) Nitric acid (70% and over) Acetic acid [2] Acid oil mixture from soya bean, corn (maize) and sunflower oil refining Acrylic acid [2] Butyric acid i-Butyric acid Cashew nut shell oil (untreated) Citric acid (70% or less) Chloroacetic acid solution Chloroacetic acid (80% or less) Chloropropionic acid Decanoic acid 2,2-Dichloropropionic acid 2,2-Dimethyloctanoic acid 2-Ethylhexanoic acid Fatty acids, (C8-C10) Fatty acids, (C12+) Fatty acids, (C16+) Fatty acids, essentially linear (C6-C18) 2-ethylhexyl ester Fatty acid methyl esters Formic acid [2] Formic acid (over 85%) [2] Formic acid mixture (containing up to 18% Propionic acid and up to 25% Sodium formate) [2] Glycolic acid Glyoxylic acid n-Heptanoic acid 1,6-Hexanediol distillation overheads Hexanoic acid 2-Hydroxy-4-(methylthio)butanoic acid Jatropha oil Long chain alkyl (C13+) salicylic acid Metal fatty acid salt Metal long chain alkyl salt Methacrylic acid Microsilica slurry Naphthenic acid Neodecanoic acid Nonanoic acid Nonanoic, Tridecanoic acid mixture Octanoic acid (all isomers) n-Pentanoic acid, 2-Methyl butyric acid mixture Pentanoic acid Propionic acid Trimethylacetic acid Undecanoic acid
5. Caustics	Ammonium sulfide solution (45% or less) Calcium hypochlorite solutions Calcium hypochlorite solution (15% or less) Calcium hypochlorite solution (more than 15%) Caustic potash solution [2] Caustic soda solution [2] Cresylate spent caustic Cresylic acid, sodium salt solution Kraft black liquor Kraft pulping liquors Mercaptobenzothiazol, sodium salt solution Potassium hydroxide solution [2] Sodium acetate, Glycol, Water mixture (containing Sodium hydroxide) Sodium aluminate solution Sodium borohydride, Sodium hydroxide solution Sodium carbonate solutions Sodium cyanide solution Sodium hydrosulfide solution [2] Sodium hydrosulfide, Ammonium sulfide solution [2] Sodium hydroxide solution [2] Sodium hypochlorite solution Sodium 2-mercaptobenzothiazol solution Sodium naphthenate solution Sodium nitrite solution Triphenylborane, Caustic soda solution Trisodium phosphate solution Vanillin black liquor
6. Ammonia	Ammonia, anhydrous

Group	Cargo
7. Aliphatic Amines	Ammonia, aqueous Ammonium hydroxide (28% or less Ammonia) Ammonium nitrate, Urea solution (containing Ammonia) Urea, Ammonium nitrate solution (containing Ammonia) Alkenylamine mixtures Alkyl (greater than C8) amine, Alkenyl (greater than C12) acid ester in mineral oil Alkyl amine (C17 or greater) Alkyl (C12+) dimethylamine N-Aminoethylpiperazine Butylamine (all isomers) Calcium long chain alkyl phenolic amine (C8-C40) Crude piperazine Cyclohexylamine Dibutylamine Diethylamine Diethylenetriamine [2] Diisobutylamine Diisopropylamine Dimethylamine Dimethylamine solution (45% or less) Dimethylamine solution (greater than 45% but not greater than 55%) Dimethylamine solution (greater than 55% but not greater than 65%) N,N-Dimethylcyclohexylamine N,N-Dimethyldodecylamine Di-n-propylamine Diphenylamine, reaction product with 2,2,4-Trimethylpentene Diphenylamines, alkylated Dodecylamine, Tetradecylamine mixture [2] Dodecyldimethylamine, Tetradecyldimethylamine mixture Ethoxylated tallow alkyl amine Ethoxylated tallow amine (>95%) Ethoxylated tallow alkyl amine, glycol mixture Ethylamine [2] Ethylamine solution (72% or less) Ethyleneamine EA 1302 [2] N-Ethyl-n-butylamine N-Ethyl cyclohexylamine Ethylenediamine [2] 2-Ethyl hexylamine N-Ethylmethylallylamine Glyphosate solution (not containing surfactant) Hexamethylenediamine Hexamethylenediamine (molten) Hexamethylenediamine solution Hexamethylenetetramine Hexamethylenetetramine solutions Hexamethylenimine HiTec 321 bis-(Hydrogenated tallow alkyl)methyl amines Isophorone diamine Isopropylamine Isopropylamine (70% or less) solution Long chain alkyl amine Long chain polyetheramine in alkyl(C2-C4)benzenes Metam sodium solution Methylamine solutions (42% or less) Morpholine [2] Oleylamine Pentaethylenehexamine Pentaethylenehexamine, Tetraethylenepentamine mixture Phosphate esters, alkyl (C12-C14) amine Polyalkenyl succinic anhydride amine Polyalkyl alkeneamine succinimide, molybdenum oxysulfide Polyethylene polyamines [2] Polyethylene polyamines (more than 50% C5-C20 paraffin oil) Poly(iminoethylene)-graft-N-poly (ethyleneoxy) solution (90% or less) Polyisobutenamine in aliphatic (C10-C14) solvent Polyolefin amide alkeneamine (C28+) Polyolefin amide alkeneamine polyol Poly olefin amine Poly (C17+) olefin amine Polyolefin amide alkeneamine/Molybdenum oxysulfide mixture Polyoxypropylenediamine (MW 2000) Propanil, Mesityl oxide, Isophorone mixture

Group	Cargo
	Propylamine
	iso-Propylamine solution
	Roundup
	Sulfohydrocarbon, long chain (C18+) alkylamine mixture
	Tetraethylenepentamine [2]
	Triethylamine
	Triethylenetetramine [2]
	Trimethylamine solution
	Trimethylhexamethylene diamine (2,2,4- and 2,4,4-)
8. Alkanolamines	Alkyl (C12-C16) propoxyamine ethoxylate
	2-(2-Aminoethoxy)ethanol
	Aminoethyldiethanolamine, Aminoethylethanolamine solution
	Aminoethylethanolamine
	2-Amino-2-methyl-1-propanol
	Diethanolamine
	Diethylaminoethanol
	Diethylethanolamine
	Diisopropanolamine
	Dimethylethanolamine
	Ethanolamine
	Ethoxylated alkyloxy alkyl amine
	Ethoxylated long chain (C16+) alkyloxyalkanamine
	Isopropanolamine
	Isopropanolamine solution
	N,N-bis (2-Hydroxyethyl) oleamide
	Linear alkyl (C12-C16) propoxyamine ethoxylate
	Methyl diethanolamine
	Propanolamine
	Triethanolamine [2]
	Triisopropanolamine
	Ucarsol CR Solvent 302 SG
9. Aromatic Amines	Alkyl (C8-C9) phenylamine in aromatic solvents
	Amine C-6, morpholine process residue
	Aniline
	Calcium long chain alkyl phenolic amine (C8-C40)
	4-Chloro-2-methylphenoxyacetic acid, Dimethylamine salt solution
	Dialkyl (C8-C9) diphenylamines
	2,6-Diethylaniline
	Dimethylamine salt of 4-Chloro-2-methylphenoxyacetic acid solution
	2,6-Dimethylaniline
	Diphenylamine
	Diphenylamine (molten)
	Diphenylamine, reaction product with 2,2,4-trimethylpentene
	Diphenylamines, alkylated
	2-Ethyl-6-methyl-N-(1′-methyl-2-methoxyethyl)aniline
	N-Methylaniline
	2-Methyl-6-ethyl aniline
	2-Methyl-5-ethyl pyridine
	Methyl pyridine
	2-Methylpyridine
	3-Methylpyridine
	4-Methylpyridine
	N-Methyl-2-pyrrolidone [2]
	Paraldehyde-Ammonia reaction product
	Polyolefin phenolic amine (C28-C250)
	Pyridine
	Pyridine bases
	Toluenediamine
	p-Toluidine
10. Amides	Acetochlor
	Acrylamide solution (50% or less)
	Alkenyl(C11+)amide
	N,N-Dimethylacetamide
	N,N-Dimethylacetamide solution
	N,N-Dimethylacetamide solution (40% or less)
	Dimethylformamide
	Formamide
	N,N-bis(2-Hydroxyethyl) oleamide
	Octadecenoamide
	Organomolybdenum amide
	Polybutenyl succinimide
	Polyisobutenyl succinimide
	Zinc alkenyl carboxamide
11. Organic Anhydrides	Acetic anhydride

Pt. 150, Table II, Nt. 46 CFR Ch. I (10–1–13 Edition)

Group	Cargo
	Alkenylsuccinic anhydride
	Alkyl succinic anhydride
	Maleic anhydride
	Phthalate based polyester polyol
	Phthalic anhydride
	Polyisobutenyl anhydride adduct
	Polyisobutylene succinic anhydride
	Polyolefin anhydride
	Propionic anhydride
12. Isocyanates	Diphenylmethane diisocyanate
	Hexamethylene diisocyanate
	Isophorone diisocyanate
	Polymethylene polyphenyl isocyanate
	Toluene diisocyanate
	Trimethylhexamethylene diisocyanate (2,2,4- and 2,4,4-)
13. Vinyl Acetates	Vinyl acetate
	Vinyl ethyl ether
	Vinyl neodecanate
	Vinyl toluene
14. Acrylates	Butyl acrylate (all isomers)
	Butyl/Decyl/Cetyl/Eicosyl methacrylate mixture
	Butyl methacrylate
	i-Butyl methacrylate
	Butyl methacrylate, Decyl methacrylate, Cetyl-Eicosyl methacrylate mixture
	Cetyl-Eicosyl methacrylate mixture
	Decyl acrylate
	Dodecyl methacrylate
	Dodecyl-Octadecyl methacrylate mixture
	Dodecyl-Pentadecyl methacrylate mixture
	Ethyl acrylate
	2-Ethylhexyl acrylate
	Ethyl methacrylate
	2-Hydroxyethyl acrylate [2]
	Isobutyl methacrylate
	Methacrylic resin in Ethylene dichloride
	Methyl acrylate
	Methyl methacrylate
	Nonyl methacrylate
	Polyalkyl acrylate
	Polyalkyl(C18-C22) acrylate in Xylene
	Polyalkyl (C10-C18) methacrylate/Ethylene
	Polyalkyl methacrylate
	Polyalkyl methacrylate in mineral oil
	Polyalkyl (C10-C20) methacrylate
	Polyalkyl methacrylate solution (containing max 40% active material)
	Propylene copolymer mixture
	Roehm monomer 6645
15. Substituted Allyls	Acrylonitrile [2]
	Allyl alcohol [2]
	Allyl chloride
	1,3-Dichloropropene
	Dichloropropene
	Dichloropropene, Dichloropropane mixtures
	Methacrylonitrile
16. Alkylene Oxides	Butylene oxide
	Ethylene oxide, Propylene oxide mixtures
	Ethylene oxide/Propylene oxide mixture with an Ethylene oxide content not more than 30% by mass)
	Propylene oxide
17. Epichlorohydrins	Chlorohydrins (crude)
	Epichlorohydrin
18. Ketones	Acetone [2]
	Acetophenone
	Amyl methyl ketone
	Butyl heptyl ketone
	Camphor oil
	1-(4-Chlorophenyl)-4,4-dimethyl pentan-3-one [2]
	Cyclohexanone
	Cyclohexanone, Cyclohexanol mixtures [2]
	Diisobutyl ketone
	Ethyl amyl ketone
	Epoxy resin
	Ketone residue
	Isophorone [2]

Coast Guard, DHS　　　　　　　　　　　　　　　　　　　　　　　　　Pt. 150, Table II, Nt.

Group	Cargo
	Mesityl oxide [2]
	Methyl amyl ketone
	Methyl butyl ketone
	Methyl ethyl ketone [2]
	Methyl heptyl ketone
	Methyl isoamyl ketone
	Methyl isobutyl ketone [2]
	Methyl propyl ketone
	beta-Propriolactone
	Trifluralin in Xylene
19. Aldehydes	Acetaldehyde
	Acrolein [2]
	Butyraldehyde (all isomers)
	Crotonaldehyde [2]
	Decaldehyde
	Ethylhexaldehyde
	2-Ethyl-3-propylacrolein [2]
	Formaldehyde, Methanol mixtures [2]
	Formaldehyde solutions [2]
	Furfural
	Glutaraldehyde solution
	Glyoxal solutions
	3-Methyl butyraldehyde
	Methylolureas
	3-(Methylthio)propionaldehyde
	Octyl aldehyde
	Paraldehyde
	Pentyl aldehyde
	Propionaldehyde
	Valeraldehyde
20. Alcohols, Glycols	Acrylonitrile-Styrene copolymer dispersion in Polyether polyol
	Alcoholic beverages
	Alcohol polyethoxylates
	Alcohol polyethoxylates, secondary
	Alcohols (C13+)
	Alcohols (C12+), primary, linear
	Alcohols (C12-C13), primary, linear and essentially linear
	Alcohols (C14-C18), primary, linear and essentially linearAlkyl (C4-C9) phenols
	n-Amyl alcohol
	Amyl alcohol, primary
	sec—Amyl alcohol
	tert- Amyl alcohol
	Behenyl alcohol
	Bio-fuel blends of Gasoline and Ethyl alcohol (>25% but <99% by volume)
	Brake fluid base mixtures
	Brake fluid base mix: Poly(2-8)alkylene (C2-C3) glycols/Polyalkylene (C2-C10) glycols monoalkyl (C1-C4) ethers and their borate esters1,4-Butanediol
	Butyl alcohol [2] (all isomers)
	n-Butyl alcohol
	iso-Butyl alcohol
	t-Butyl alcohols
	Butylene glycol [2]
	Cetyl-Stearyl alcohol
	Choline chloride solutions
	Cyclohexanol
	Cyclopentanol
	Decyl alcohol (all isomers) [2]
	Decyl/Dodecyl/Tetradecyl alcohol mixture
	Diacetone alcohol [2]
	Diethyl hexanol
	Diethylene glycol
	Diethylene glycol dibenzoate
	Diisobutyl carbinol
	2,2-Dimethylpropane-1,3-diol
	Dodecanol
	Dodecyl alcohol
	Dodecyl hydroxypropyl sulfide
	Ethoxylated alcohols, C11-C15
	2-Ethoxyethanol
	Ethyl alcohol [2]
	Ethyl butanol
	Ethylene chlorohydrin
	Ethylene cyanohydrin
	Ethylene glycol [2]

103

Group	Cargo
	2-Ethylhexanol
	Furfuryl alcohol [2]
	Glycerine [2]
	Glycerine, Dioxanedimethanol mixture
	Glycerol monooleate
	Glycol
	Glycol mixture, crude
	Heptanol
	Hexamethylene glycol
	Hexanol
	Hexylene glycol
	Hydroxy terminated polybutadiene
	Icosa(oxypropane-2,3-diyl)s
	Isoamyl alcohol
	Isobutyl alcohol
	Isopropyl alcohol
	Lauryl polyglucose (50% or less)
	Methacrylic acid-alkyloxypoly (alkylene oxide) methacrylate copolymer sodium salt aqueous solution (45% or less)
	3-Methoxy-1-butanol
	Methyl alcohol [2]
	Methyl amyl alcohol
	alpha-Methylbenzyl alcohol with acetophenone (15% or less)
	Methyl butenol
	Methylbutynol
	2-Methyl-2-hydroxy-3-butyne
	Methyl isobutyl carbinol
	3-Methyl-3-methoxybutanol
	2-Methyl-1,3-propanediol
	Molasses
	Nonyl alcohol [2]
	Octanol (all isomers) [2]
	Octyl alcohol [2]
	Penacosa(oxypropane-2,3-diyl)s
	Pentadecanol
	Polyalkylene oxide polyol
	Polybutadiene, hydroxy terminated
	Polyglycerol
	Polyglycerine, Sodium salts solution (containing less than 3% Sodium hydroxide) [2]
	Polyolefin amide alkeneamine polyol
	Propyl alcohol [2]
	Propylene glycol [2]
	Rum
	Sodium methylate solution (21–30% in Methanol)
	Sorbitol solutions
	Stearyl alcohol
	Tallow fatty alcohol
	Tetradecanol
	Tridecanol
	Trimethyl nonanol
	Trimethylol propane polyethoxylate
	Undecanol
	Undecyl alcohol
21. Phenols, Cresols	Alkylated (C4-C9) hindered phenols
	Benzyl alcohol
	Carbolic oil
	Creosote [2]
	Creosote (coal tar) [2]
	Creosote (wood tar) [2]
	Cresols (all isomers)
	Cresylic acid
	Cresylic acid dephenolized
	Cresylic acid, tar
	Dibutylphenols
	2,4-Dichlorophenol
	Di-tert-butyl phenols
	2,4-Di-tert-butyl phenols
	2,6-Di-tert-butyl phenols
	Dodecyl phenol
	o-Ethylphenol
	Long chain alkylphenate/phenol sulfide mixture
	Methylene bridged isobutylenated phanols
	Nonyl phenol
	Nonyl phenol (48–62%)/Phenol (42–48%)/Dinonyl phenol (1–10%) mixture

Group	Cargo
	Octyl phenol
	Phenol
	Xylenols
22. Caprolactam Solutions	Caprolactam solution
	epsilon-Caprolactam (molten or aqueous solutions)
23-29. Unassigned.	
30. Olefins	Acrylic acid/ethenesulfonic acid copolymer with phosphonate groups, sodium salt solution
	Amylene
	Aryl polyolefin (C11-C50)
	Butadiene
	Butadiene, Butylene mixtures (cont. Acetylenes)
	Butadiene Feedstock [Kirby]
	Butene
	Butene oligomer
	Butylene
	1,5,9-Cyclododecatriene
	1,3-Cyclopentadiene dimer (molten)
	Cyclopentadiene, Styrene, Benzene mixture
	Cyclopentene
	Decene
	Dichloropropene
	Dicyclopentadiene
	Dicyclopentadiene, Resin Grade, 81–89%
	Diisobutylene
	Dipentene
	Dodecene
	Ethylene
	Ethylene-Propylene copolymer
	Ethylidene norbornene [2]
	1-Heptene
	Hexene (all isomers)
	Isoprene
	Isoprene concentrate (Shell)
	Latex (ammonia (1% or less) inhibited
	Methyl acetylene, Propadiene mixture
	Methyl butene
	Methylcyclopentadiene dimer
	2-Methyl-1-pentene
	4-Methyl-1-pentene
	alpha-Methyl styrene
	Myrcene
	Nonene
	1-Octadecene
	Octene
	Olefin mixtures
	Olefin mixture (C7-C9) C8 rich, stabilized
	Olefin mixtures (C5-C7)
	Olefin mixtures (C5-C15)
	alpha-Olefins (C6-C18) mixtures
	alpha-Olefins (C13+)
	1,3-Pentadiene
	1,3-Pentadiene (greater than 50%), Cyclopentene and isomers, mixtures
	Pentene
	alpha-Pinene
	beta-Pinene
	Polybutene
	Poly(4+)isobutylene
	Polyolefin in mineral oil
	Polyolefin (molecular weight 300+)
	Polypropylene
	Poly(5+)propylene
	Propylene
	Propylene-butylene copolymer
	Propylene dimer
	Propylene, Propane, MAPP gas mixture
	Propylene tetramer
	Propylene trimer
	Styrene monomer
	Tetradecene
	Tridecene
	Triisobutylene
	Tripropylene
	Turpentine
	Undecene

Group	Cargo
31. Paraffins	Alkanes (C6-C9)
	Alkanes (C10-C26) linear and branched
	Alkanes (C10-C26) linear and branched (flash point >60 °C)n-Alkanes (C10+)
	iso- & cyclo-Alkanes (C10-C11)
	iso- & cyclo-Alkanes (C12+)
	Aviation alkylates (C8 paraffins and iso-paraffins BPT 95-120 °C)
	Butane
	Cycloheptane
	Cyclohexane
	Cyclopentane
	Decane
	Dodecane
	Ethane
	Ethyl cyclohexane
	Heptane
	Hexane [2]
	Isopropylcyclohexane
	Methane
	Methylcyclohexane
	2-Methyl pentane
	Mineral oil
	Nonane
	Octane
	Paraffin wax
	Pentane
	Polyalpha olefins
	Polyolefin (molecular weight 300+)
	Propane
	iso-Propylcyclohexane
	Tridecane
	Waxes:
	Paraffin
32. Aromatic Hydrocarbons	Alkyl(C3-C4)benzenes
	Alkyl(C5-C8)benzenes
	Alkyl(C9+)benzenes
	Alkyl acrylate-Vinyl pyridine copolymer in Toluene
	Alkylbenzene, Alkylindane, Alkylidene mixture (each C12-C17)
	Alkylbenzene mixtures (containing at least 50% of Toluene)
	Alkyl toluene
	Alkyl (C18+) toluene
	Aryl polyolefin (C11-C50)
	Benzene
	Benzene hydrocarbon mixtures (having 10% Benzene or more)
	Benzene, Toluene, Xylene mixtures
	Butylbenzene (all isomers)
	Butyl phenol, Formaldehyde resin in Xylene
	Butyl toluene
	Cumene
	Cymene
	Decylbenzene
	Dialkyl(C10-C14) benzenes
	Diethylbenzene
	Diisopropylbenzene (all isomers)
	Diisopropyl naphthalene
	Diphenyl
	Dodecylbenzene
	Dodecyl xylene
	Ethylbenzene
	Ethyl toluene
	1-Hexadecylnaphthalene, 1, 4-bis(Hexadecyl)
	1,1-Hexadecylnaphthalene/1,4-bis (hexadecyl) naphthalene mixture
	1,n-Hexadecylnaphthalene (90%), 1,4-Di-n-(hexadecyl-naphthalene (10%)
	Isopropylbenzene
	Methyl naphthalene (molten)
	Naphthalene (molten)
	Naphthalene mixture
	Naphthalene still residue
	1-Phenyl-1-xylyl ethane
	Parachlorobenzotrifluoride
	Poly(2+)cyclic aromatics
	Polyolefin amine in alkylbenzenes (C2-C4)
	Polyolefin amine in aromatic solvent
	Propylbenzene
	Pseudocumene

Group	Cargo

33. Miscellaneous Hydrocarbon Mixtures.	Pyrolysis gasoline (containing Benzene)
	C9 Resinfeed (DSM) [2]
	Tetradecylbenzene
	Tetrahydronaphthalene
	1,2,3,5-Tetramethylbenzene
	Toluene
	Tridecylbenzene
	Triethylbenzene
	Trimethylbenzene
	Undecylbenzene
	Xylene
	Xylenes, Ethylbenzene mixture
	Alachlor
	Alachlor technical (90% or more)
	Alkylbenzenesulfonic acid, sodium salt solutions
	Alkyl dithiothiadiazole (C6-C24)
	Alkyl toluene sulfonic acid, calcium salts
	Alkyl (C18-C28) toluene sulfonic acid, Calcium salts, high overbase
	Alkyl (C18-C28) toluene sulfonic acid, Calcium salts, low overbaseAsphalt blending stocks, roofers flux
	Asphalt blending stocks, straight run residue
	Asphalt emulsion
	Asphalt, kerosene, and other components
	Bio-fuel blends of Diesel/gas oil and Alkanes (C10-C26), linear and branched with a flash point >60 °C (>25% but <99% by volume)
	Bio-fuel blends of Diesel/gas oil and Alkanes (C10-C26), linear and branched with a flash point <60 °C (>25% but <99% by volume)
	Calcuim sulfonate, Calcium carbonate, Hydrocarbon solvent mixture
	Coal tar
	Coal tar distillate
	Coal tar, high temperature
	Coal tar pitch (molten)
	Decahydronaphthalene
	Degummed C9 (DOW)
	Diphenyl, Diphenyl ether
	Distillates
	Distillates, flashed feed stocks
	Distillates, straight run
	Drilling mud (low toxicity) (*if flammable or combustible*)
	Gas oil, cracked
	Gasoline blending stock, alkylates
	Gasoline blending stock, reformates
	Gasolines:
	   Automotive (*not over 4.23 grams lead per gal.*)
	   Aviation (*not over 4.86 grams lead per gal.*)
	   Casinghead (*natural*)
	   Polymer
	   Straight run
	Jet Fuels:
	   JP–4
	   JP–5
	   JP–8
	Kerosene
	Maleated ethylene-propylene copolymer reaction product [synthetic rubber]
	Mineral spirits
	Naphtha:
	   Coal tar solvent
	   Petroleum
	   Solvent
	   Stoddard solvent
	   Varnish Makers' and Painters'
	Oil, fuel:
	   No. 1
	   No. 1–D
	   No. 2
	   No. 2–D
	   No. 4
	   No. 5
	   No. 6
	Oil, misc:
	   Aliphatic
	   Aromatic
	   Clarified
	   Coal

Group	Cargo
	Crude
	Diesel
	Gas, high pour
	Heartcut distillate
	Linseed
	Lubricating
	Mineral
	Mineral seal
	Motor
	Neatsfoot
	Penetrating
	Pine
	Rosin
	Sperm
	Spindle
	Turbine
	Residual
	Road
	Transformer
	Oxyalkylated alkyl phenol formaldehyde
	Petrolatum
	Pine oil
	Polybutene
	Polyolefin amine (C28-C250)
	Polyolefin amide alkeneamine (C17+)
	Polyolefin amide alkeneamine (C28+)
	Polyolefin amide alkeneamine borate (C28-C250)
	Polyolefin amide alkeneamine in mineral oil
	Resin oil, distilled
	Sodium petroleum sulfonate
	Sulfohydrocarbon (C3-C88)
	Waxes:
	Petroleum
	Sulfurized fat (C14-C20)
	Sulfurized polyolefinamide alkeneamines (C28-C250)
	White spirit (low (15–20%) aromatic)
34. Esters	Acid oil mixture from soybean, corn (maize) and sunflower oil refining
	Alkane (C14-C17) sulfonic acid, sodium salt solution
	Alkyl(C8+)amine, Alkenyl (C12+) acid ester mixture
	Alkylaryl phosphate mixtures, (more than 40% Diphenyl tolyl phosphate. Less than 0.02% ortho-isomer)
	Alkyl dithiocarbamate (C19-C35)
	Alkyl ester copolymer (C4-C20)
	Alkyl ester copolymer (C6-C18)
	Alkyl ester copolymer in mineral oil
	Alkyl(C7-C9) nitrates [2]
	Alkyl (C8-C40) phenol sulfide
	Alkyl (C10-C20, saturated and unsaturated) phosphite
	Alkyl sulfonic acid ester of phenol
	Alkyl (C18-C28) toluene sulfonic acid, Calcium salts, borated
	Alkylaryl phosphate mixtures (more than 40%)
	Amyl acetate (all isomers)
	Amyl acid phosphate
	t-Amyl formate
	Animal and Fish oils, n.o.s.
	Animal and Fish acid oils and distillates, n.o.s.
	Barium long chain alkaryl (C11-C50) sulfonate
	Barium long chain alkyl(C8-C14)phenate sulfide
	Benzene tricarboxylic acid trioctyl ester
	Benzyl acetate
	Bio-fuel blends of Diesel/gas oil and FAME (>25% but <99% by volume)
	Bio-fuel blends of Diesel/gas oil and vegetable oil (>25% but <99% by volume)
	Boronated calcium sulfonate
	Butyl acetate (all isomers)
	Butyl benzyl phthalate
	Butyl butyrate (all isomers)
	Butyl formate
	iso-Butyl isobutyrate
	n-Butyl propionate
	Butyl stearate
	Calcium alkaryl sulfonate (C11-C50) Calcium alkyl(C9)phenol sulfide, polyolefin phosphorosulfide mixture
	Calcium alkyl (C10-C28) salicylateCalcium carbonate slurry
	Calcium long chain alkaryl sulfonate (C11-C50)

Group	Cargo
	Calcium long chain alkyl (C5-C10) phenate
	Calcium long chain alkyl (C5-C20) phenate
	Calcium long chain alkyl (C11-C40) phenate
	Calcium long chain alkyl phenate sulfide (C8-C40)
	Calcium long chain alkyl phenates
	Calcium long chain alkyl salicylate (C13+)
	Calcium long chain alkyl (C18-C28) salicylate
	Calcium nitrate, Magnesium nitrate, Potassium chloride solution
	Calcium nitrate
	Calcium nitrate solutions (50% or less)
	Calcium salts of fatty acids
	Calcium stearate
	Camelina oil
	Cesium formate solution
	Cobalt naphthenate in solvent naphtha
	Coconut oil, fatty acid
	Coconut oil, fatty acid methyl ester
	Copper salt of long chain (C3-C16) fatty acid
	Copper salt of long chain (C17+) fatty acid
	Copper salt of long chain alkanoic acids
	Cottonseed oil, fatty acid
	Cyclohexyl acetate
	Decyl acetate
	Dialkyl(C7-C13) phthalates
	Dialkyl(C7-C17) phthalates
	Dialkyl thiophosphates sodium salts solution
	Dibutyl hydrogen phosphonate
	Dibutyl phthalate
	Dibutyl terephthalate
	Diethylene glycol butyl ether acetate
	Diethylene glycol dibenzoate
	Diethylene glycol ethyl ether acetate
	Diethylene glycol methyl ether acetate
	Diethylene glycol phthalate
	Di-(2-ethylhexyl)adipate
	Di-(2-ethylhexyl)phthalate
	Diethyl phthalate
	Diethyl sulfate
	Diheptyl phthalate
	Dihexyl phthalate
	Di-n-hexyl adipate
	Diisobutyl phthalate
	Diisodecyl phthalate
	Diisononyl adipate
	Diisononyl phthalate
	Diisooctyl phthalate
	Dimethyl adipate
	Dimethylcyclicsiloxane hydrolyzate
	Dimethyl glutarate
	Dimethyl hydrogen phosphite [2]
	Dimethyl naphthalene sulfonic acid, sodium salt solution [2]
	Dimethyl phthalate
	Dimethyl polysiloxane
	Dimethyl succinate
	Dinonyl phthalate
	Dioctyl phthalate
	Diphenyl tolyl phosphate, less than 0.02% ortho-isomer)
	Dipropylene glycol dibenzoate
	Dithiocarbamate ester (C7-C35)
	Ditridecyl adipate
	Ditridecyl phthalate
	2-Dodecenylsuccinic acid, dipotassium salt solution
	Diundecyl phthalate
	2-Ethoxyethyl acetate
	Ethyl acetate
	Ethyl acetoacetate
	Ethyl butyrate
	2-Ethyl-2-(2,4-dichlorophenoxy) acetate
	2-Ethyl-2-(2,4-dichlorophenoxy) propionate
	s-Ethyl dipropylthiocarbamate
	Ethylene carbonate
	Ethylene glycol
	Ethylene glycol acetate
	Ethylene glycol butyl ether acetate

Group	Cargo
	Ethylene glycol diacetate
	Ethylene glycol ethyl ether acetate
	Ethylene glycol methyl ether acetate
	Ethyl-3-ethoxypropionate
	Ethyl hexyl phthalate
	2-Ethyl-2-(hydroxymethyl) propane-1,3-diol, C8-C10 ester
	Ethyl propionate
	Ethyl propionate
	Fatty acids (saturated, C14+)
	Glycerol polyalkoxylate
	Glyceryl triacetate
	Glycidyl ester of C10 trialkyl acetic acid
	Gylcidyl ester of tridecylacetic acid
	Heptyl acetate
	Hexyl acetate
	Isobutyl formate
	Isopropyl acetate
	Lard
	Lauric acid
	Lecithin
	Magnesium long chain alkaryl sulfonate (C11-C50)
	Magnesium long chain alkyl phenate sulfide (C8-C20)
	Magnesium long chain alkyl phenate sulfide (C8-C40)
	Magnesium long chain alkyl salicylate (C11+)
	Magnesium long chain alkyl salicylate (C13+)
	Mango kernel
	3-Methoxybutyl acetate
	1-Methoxy-2-propyl acetate
	Methyl acetate
	Methyl acetoacetate
	Methyl amyl acetate
	Methyl butyrate
	Methyl formate
	3-Methyl-3-methoxybutyl acetate
	Methyl salicylate
	Metolachlor
	Naphthalene sulfonic acid, sodium salt solution (40% or less)
	Nitrilotriacetic acid, trisodium salt solution
	Nonyl acetate
	Octamethylcyclotetrasiloxane
	n-Octyl acetate
	Octyl decyl adipate
	Oil, edible:
	Beechnut
	Castor
	Cocoa butter
	Coconut [2]
	Cod liver
	Corn
	Cotton seed
	Fish [2]
	Groundnut
	Hazelnut
	Lard
	Lanolin
	Nutmeg butter
	Olive
	Palm [2]
	Palm kernel
	Peanut
	Poppy
	Poppy seed
	Raisin seed
	Rapeseed
	Rice bran
	Safflower
	Salad
	Sesame
	Soya bean
	Sunflower
	Sunflower seed
	Tucum
	Vegetable
	Walnut

Coast Guard, DHS   **Pt. 150, Table II, Nt.**

Group	Cargo
	Oil, misc:
	Animal
	Coconut oil, fatty actid methyl ester
	Cotton seed oil, fatty acid
	Lanolin
	Palm kernel oil, fatty acid methyl ester
	Palm oil, methyl ester
	Pilchard
	Perilla
	Soapstock
	Soyabean (epoxidized)
	Tall
	Tall, fatty acid [2]
	Tung
	Olefin/Alkyl ester copolymer (molecular weight 2000+)
	Oleic acid
	Palm acid oil
	Palm fatty acid distillate
	Palm kernel acid oil
	Palm kernel acid oil, methyl esterPalm kernel oil fatty acid
	Palm mid fraction
	Palm oil
	Palm oil fatty acid
	Palm oil fatty acid methyl ester
	Palm kernel olein
	Palm kernel stearin
	Palm olein
	Palm stearin
	n-Pentyl propionate
	Phosphate esters
	Poly(2-8)alkylene glycol monoalkyl(C1-C6) ether acetate
	Polydimethylsiloxane
	Polyferric sulfate solution
	Polymethylsiloxane
	Polyolefin amide alkeneamine borate (C28-C250)
	Poly(20)oxyethylene sorbitan monooleate
	Polysiloxane
	Polysiloxane/White spirit, low (15–20%) aromatic
	Polyolefin aminoester salt
	Polyolefin ester (C28-C250)
	Polyolefin phosphorosulfide, barium derivative (C28-C250)
	Potassium formate solution
	Potassium formate solution (75% or more)
	Potassium oleate
	Potassium salt of polyolefin acid
	Propyl acetate
	Propylene carbonate
	Propylene glycol methyl ether acetate
	Rapeseed oil fatty acid methyl esters
	Rapeseed oil (low erucic acid containing less than 4% free fatty acids)
	Shea butter
	Siloxanes
	Sodium acetate, Glycol, Water mixture (not containing Sodium hydroxide) [2]
	Sodium acetate solution
	Sodium alkyl (C14-C17) sulfonates 60–65% solution
	Sodium benzoate solution
	Sodium bicarbonate solution (less than 10%)
	Sodium bromide solution (less than 50%)
	Sodium dimethyl naphthalene sulfonate solution [2]
	Sodium long chain alkyl salicylate (C13+)
	Sodium naphthalene sulfonate solution
	Sodium petroleum sulfonate
	Sodium sulfate solutions
	Soyabean oil (epoxidized)
	Stearic acid
	Tall oil
	Tall oil, crude
	Tall oil, distilled
	Tall oil fatty acid (*Resin acids less than 20%*) [2]
	Tall oil, pitch
	Tall oil soap, crude
	Tallow [2]
	Tallow fatty acid [2]
	Tributyl phosphate

Pt. 150, Table II, Nt. 46 CFR Ch. I (10–1–13 Edition)

Group	Cargo
	Tricresyl phosphate
	Tricresyl phosphate (containing 1% or more ortho-isomer)
	Tricresyl phosphate (containing less than 1% ortho-isomer)
	Tridecanoic acid
	Tridecyl acetate
	Triethylene glycol dibenzoate
	Triethylene glycol di-(2-ethylbutyrate)
	Triethyl phosphate
	Triethyl phosphite [2]
	Triisooctyl trimellitate
	Triisopropylated phenyl phosphates
	2,2,4-Trimethyl-1,3-pentanediol diisobutyrate
	2,2,4-Trimethyl-1,3-pentanediol-1-isobutyrate
	2,2,4-Trimethyl-3-pentanol-1-isobutyrate
	Trimethyl phosphite [2]
	Trisodium nitrilotriacetate
	Trixylyl phosphate
	Trixylenyl phosphate
	Urea/Ammonium nitrate solution
	Vegetable acid oils and distillates, n.o.s.
	Vegetable fatty acid distillates
	Vegetable oils, n.o.s.
	Waxes:
	Carnauba
	Zinc alkaryl dithiophosphate (C7-C16)
	Zinc alkyl dithiophosphate (C3-C14)
35. Vinyl Halides	Vinyl chloride
	Vinylidene chloride
36. Halogenated Hydrocarbons	Benzyl chloride
	Bromochloromethane
	Carbon tetrachloride [2]
	Catoxid feedstock [2]
	Chlorinated paraffins (C10-C13)
	Chlorinated paraffins (C14-C17) (with 50% Chlorine or more, and less than 1% C13 or shorter chains)
	Chlorinated paraffins (C14-C17) (with 52% chlorine)
	Chlorinated paraffins (C18+) with any level of chlorine
	Chlorobenzene
	Chlorodifluoromethane
	Chloroform
	Chlorotoluene
	m-Chlorotoluene
	o-Chlorotoluene
	p-Chlorotoluene
	Chlorotoluenes (mixed isomers)
	Dibromomethane
	Dibutylphenols
	3,4-Dichloro-1-butene
	Dichlorobenzene (all isomers)
	Dichlorodifluoromethane
	1,1-Dichloroethane
	1,6-Dichlorohexane
	Dichloromethane
	Dichloropropane
	Ethyl chloride
	Ethylene dibromide
	Ethylene dichloride [2]
	Methyl bromide
	Methyl chloride
	Monochlorodifluoromethane
	n-Propyl chloride
	Pentachloroethane
	Perchloroethylene
	1,1,2,2-Tetrachloroethane
	1,2,3-Trichlorobenzene
	1,2,3-Trichlorobenzene (molten)
	1,2,4-Trichlorobenzene
	1,1,1-Trichloroethane [2]
	1,1,2-Trichloroethane
	Trichloroethylene [2]
	1,2,3-Trichloropropane
	1,1,2-Trichloro-1,2,2-trifluoroethane
37. Nitriles	Acetonitrile
	Acetonitrile (low purity grade)

Coast Guard, DHS
Pt. 150, Table II, Nt.

Group	Cargo
	Adiponitrile
	Lactonitrile solution (80% or less)
	2-Methylglutaronitrile
	2-Methylglutaronitrile with 2-Ethylsuccinonitrile (12% or less)
	Propionitrile
	Tallow nitrile
38. Carbon Disulfide	Carbon disulfide
39. Sulfolane	Sulfolane
40. Glycol Ethers	Alcohol (C9-C11) poly (2.5-9) ethoxylates
	Alcohol (C6-C17) (secondary) poly (3-6) ethoxylates
	Alcohol (C6-C17) (secondary) poly (7-12) ethoxylates
	Alcohol (C12-C16) poly (1-6) ethoxylates
	Alcohol (C12-C16) poly (7-19) ethoxylates
	Alcohol (C12-C16) poly (20+) ethoxylates
	Alkyl (C7-C11) phenol poly(4-12)ethoxylate
	Alkyl (C9-C15) phenyl propoxylate
	Diethylene glycol [2]
	Diethylene glycol butyl ether
	Diethylene glycol dibutyl ether
	Diethylene glycol diethyl ether
	Diethylene glycol ethyl ether
	Diethylene glycol methyl ether
	Diethylene glycol n-hexyl ether
	Diethylene glycol phenyl ether
	Diethylene glycol propyl ether
	Dipropylene glycol
	Dipropylene glycol butyl ether
	Dipropylene glycol methyl ether
	Ethoxy triglycol
	Ethylene glycol hexyl ether
	Ethylene glycol methyl butyl ether
	Ethylene glycol monoalkyl ethers
	Ethylene glycol tert-butyl ether
	Ethylene glycol butyl ether
	Ethylene glycol dibutyl ether
	Ethylene glycol ethyl ether
	Ethylene glycol isopropyl ether
	Ethylene glycol methyl ether
	Ethylene glycol phenyl ether
	Ethylene glycol phenyl ether, Diethylene glycol phenyl ether mixture
	Ethylene glycol propyl ether
	Glucitol/glycerol blend propoxylated (containing less than 10% amines)
	Glycerol, ethoxylated
	Glycerol, propoxylated
	Glycerol, propoxylated and ethoxylated
	Glycerol/Sucrose blend propoxylated and ethoxylated
	Hexaethylene glycol
	alpha-Hydro-omega-hydroxytetradeca (oxytetramethylene)
	Methoxy triglycol
	Nonyl phenol poly(4+)ethoxylates
	Pentaethylene glycol methyl ether
	Polyalkylene glycol butyl ether
	Polyalkylene glycols, Polyalkylene glycol monoalkyl ethers mixtures
	Polyether glycol (MW 600-700) (TETRAETHANE 650)
	Polyether glycol (MW 950-1050) (TETRAETHANE 1000)
	Polyether glycol (MW 1350-1450) (TETRAETHANE 1400)
	Polyether glycol (MW 1900-2100) (TETRAETHANE 2000)
	Polyether glycol (MW 2825-2975) (TETRAETHANE 2900)
	Polyethylene glycols
	Polyethylene glycol dimethyl ether
	Poly(ethylene glycol) methylbutenyl ether (MW>1000)
	Poly(2-8)alkylene glycol monoalkyl(C1-C6) ether
	Poly(2-8)alkylene glycol monoalkyl(C1-C6) ether acetate
	Polyethylene glycol monoalkyl ether
	Polypropylene glycol methyl ether
	Polypropylene glycols
	Poly(tetramethylene ether) glycols (MW 950-1050)
	Polytetramethylene ether glycol
	n-Propoxypropanol
	Propylene glycol monoalkyl ether
	Propylene glycol ethyl ether
	Propylene glycol methyl ether
	Propylene glycol n-butyl ether
	Propylene glycol phenyl ether

Group	Cargo
41. Ethers	Propylene glycol propyl ether Tetraethylene glycol Tetraethylene glycol methyl ether Triethylene glycol Triethylene glycol butyl ether Triethylene glycol butyl ether mixture Triethylene glycol ether mixture Triethylene glycol ethyl ether Triethylene glycol methyl ether Tripropylene glycol Tripropylene glycol methyl ether Alcohol (C12-C13, branched and linear) poly (4-8) propoxy sulfates, sodium salt 25–30% solution Alkaryl polyether (C9-C20) tert-Amyl methyl ether Brominated Epoxy Resin in Acetone Butyl ether n-Butyl ether-Dichloroethyl ether 2,2′-Dichloroisopropyl etherDiethyl ether Diethylene glycol propyl ether Diglycidyl ether of Bisphenol A Diglycidyl ether of Bisphenol F Dimethyl furan 1,4-Dioxane Diphenyl ether Diphenyl ether, Diphenyl phenyl ether mixture Ethyl tert-butyl ether Ethyl ether Isopropyl ether Long chain alkaryl polyether (C11-C20) Methyl-tert-butyl ether [2] Methyl tert-pentyl ether Polyether (molecular weight 2000+) Polyether, borated Polyether polyols Poly(oxyalkylene)alkenyl ether (MW>1000) Polyoxybutylene alcohol Propyl ether Tetrahydrofuran 1,3, 5-Trioxane
42. Nitrocompounds	o-Chloronitrobenzene Dinitrotoluene Nitrobenzene Nitroethane Nitroethane (80%)/Nitropropane (20%) Nitroethane, 1-Nitropropane mixture Nitropropane Nitropropane, Nitroethane mixtures Nitrophenol (mixed isomers) o- or p-Nitrotoluenes
43. Miscellaneous Water Solutions.	Alkyl (C8-C10)/(C12-C14):(40% or less/60% or more) polyglucoside solution (55% or less) Alkyl (C8-C10)/(C12-C14):(50%/50%) polyglucoside solution (55% or less) Alkyl (C8-C10)/(C12-C14):(60% or more/40% or less) polyglucoside solution (55% or less) Alkyl (C8-C10) polyglucoside solution (65% or less) Alkyl (C12-C14) polyglucoside solution (55% or less) Alkyl polyglucoside solutions Aluminum hydroxide, sodium hydroxide, sodium carbonate solution (40% or less) Aluminum sulfate solution [2] 2-Amino-2-hydroxymethyl-1,3-propanediol solution Ammonium bisulfite solution [2] Ammonium chloride solution (less than 25%) drilling brines Ammonium chloride solution (less than 25%) Ammonium lignosulfonate solution Ammonium nitrate, Urea solution (not containing Ammonia) Ammonium polyphosphate solution Ammonium sulfate solution Ammonium thiosulfate solution (60% or less) Barium sulfate slurry Calcium bromide solution Calcium chloride solution Calcium formate solution Calcium lignosulfonate solution Calcium lignosulfonate solution (free alkali content 1% or less)

Coast Guard, DHS   Pt. 150, Table II, Nt.

Group	Cargo
	Caramel solutions
	Clay slurry
	Coal slurry
	Corn syrup
	Dextrose solution
	2,4-Dichlorophenoxyacetic acid, Diethanolamine salt solution
	2,4-Dichlorophenoxyacetic acid, Triisopropanolamine salt solution [2]
	Diethanolamine salt of 2,4-Dichlorophenoxyacetic acid solution
	Diethylenetriamine pentaacetic acid, pentasodium salt solution
	Dodecyl diphenyl ether disulfonate solution
	Drilling brine (containing Calcium, Potassium, or Sodium salts)
	Drilling brine (containing Zinc salts)
	Drilling brines, including: Calcium bromide solution, Calcium chloride solution and Sodium chloride solution
	Drilling mud (low toxicity) (*if non-flammable or non-combustible*)
	Ethylenediaminetetracetic acid, tetrasodium salt solution
	Ethylene-Vinyl acetate copolymer emulsion
	Ferric hydroxyethylethylenediamine triacetic acid, trisodium salt solution [2]
	Ferrous chloride solution (less than 40%, containing less than 10% Manganese and Aluminum chlorides)
	Fish solubles (*water based fish meal extracts*)
	Fructose solution
	Fumaric adduct of Rosin, water dispersion
	Hexamethylenediamine adipate solution
	N-(Hydroxyethyl)ethylene diamine triacetic acid, trisodium salt solution
	Kaolin clay slurry
	Latex: Carboxylated Styrene-Butadiene copolymer; Styrene-butadiene rubber
	Latex, liquid synthetic
	Lignin liquor
	Ligninsulfonic acid, magnesium salt solution
	Liquid Streptomyces solubles
	L-Lysine solution (60% or less)
	Magnesium nitrate solution (66.7%)
	N-Methylglucamine solution
	N-Methylglucamine solution (70% or less)
	Naphthenic acid, sodium salt solution
	Polyacrylic acid solution (40% or less)
	Potassium chloride solution
	Potassium chloride solution (less than 26%)
	Potassium thiosulfate solution
	Potassium thiosulfate solution (50% or less)
	Rosin soap (disproportionated) solution
	Sewage sludge, treated
	Sodium alkyl sulfonate solution
	Sodium bromide solution (less than 50%)
	Sodium hydrogen sulfite solution
	Sodium lignosulfonate solution
	Sodium polyacrylate solution [2]
	Sodium salt of Ferric hydroxyethylethylenediamine triacetic acid solution
	Sodium silicate solution [2]
	Sodium sulfide solution
	Sodium sulfite solution
	Sodium sulfite solution (25% or less)
	Sodium tartrates, Sodium succinates solution
	Sulfonated polyacrylate solutions [2]
	Tall oil soap (disproportionated) solution
	Tetrasodium salt of EDTA solution
	Titanium dioxide slurry
	Triisopropanolamine salt of 2,4-Dichlorophenoxyacetic acid solution
	Urea, Ammonium nitrate solution (not containing Ammonia)
	Urea, Ammonium phosphate solution
	Urea solution
	Vegetable protein solution (hydrolysed)
	Water

Notes:
[1] Because of very high reactivity or unusual conditions of carriage or potential compatibility problems, this commodity is not assigned to a specific group in Figure 1 to 46 CFR part 150 (Compatibility Chart).
[2] See Appendix I to 46 CFR part 150 (Exceptions to the Chart).

APPENDIX I TO PART 150—EXCEPTIONS TO THE CHART

(a) The binary combinations listed below have been tested as prescribed in Appendix III and found not to be dangerously reactive. These combinations are exceptions to the Compatibility Chart (Figure 1) and may be stowed in adjacent tanks.

Member of reactive group	Compatible with
Acetone (18)	Diethylenetriamine (7)
Acetone cyanohydrin (0)	Acetic acid (4)
Acrylonitrile (15)	Triethanolamine (8)
1,3-Butylene glycol (20)	Morpholine (7)
1,4-Butylene glycol (20)	Ethylamine (7)
	Triethanolamine (8)
gamma-Butyrolactone (0)	N-Methyl-2-pyrrolidone (9)
Caustic potash, 50% or less (5).	Isobutyl alcohol (20)
	Ethyl alcohol (20)
	Ethylene glycol (20)
	Isopropyl alcohol (20)
	Methyl alcohol (20)
	iso-Octyl alcohol (20)
Caustic soda, 50% or less (5)	Butyl alcohol (20)
	tert-Butyl alcohol, Methanol mixtures
	Decyl alcohol (20)
	iso-Decyl alcohol (20)
	Diacetone alcohol (20)
	Diethylene glycol (40)
	Dodecyl alcohol (20)
	Ethyl alcohol (20)
	Ethyl alcohol (40%, whiskey) (20)
	Ethylene glycol (20)
	Ethylene glycol, Diethylene glycol mixture (20)
	Ethyl hexanol (Octyl alcohol) (20)
	Methyl alcohol (20)
	Nonyl alcohol (20)
	iso-Nonyl alcohol (20)
	Propyl alcohol (20)
	iso-Propyl alcohol (20)
	Propylene glycol (20)
	Sodium chlorate solution (0)
	iso-Tridecanol (20)
tert-Dodecanethiol (0)	Acrylonitrile (15)
	Diisodecyl phthalate (34)
	Methyl ethyl ketone (18)
	iso-Nonyl alcohol (20)
	Perchloroethylene (36)
	iso-Propyl alcohol (20)
	Tall oil, crude
Dodecyl and Tetradecylamine mixture (7).	Tall oil, fatty acid (34)
Ethylenediamine (7)	Butyl alcohol (20)
	tert-Butyl alcohol (20)
	Butylene glycol (20)
	Creosote (21)
	Diethylene glycol (40)
	Ethyl alcohol (20)
	Ethylene glycol (20)
	Ethyl hexanol (20)
	Glycerine (20)
	Isononyl alcohol (20)
	Isophorone (18)
	Methyl butyl ketone (18)
	Methyl iso-butyl ketone (18)
	Methyl ethyl ketone (18)
	Propyl alcohol (20)

Member of reactive group	Compatible with
Oleum (0)	Propylene glycol (20)
	Hexane (31)
	Dichloromethane (36)
	Perchloroethylene (36)
1,2-Propylene glycol (20)	Diethylenetriamine (7)
	Polyethylene polyamines (7)
	Triethylenetetramine (7)
Sodium dichromate, 70% (0)	Methyl alcohol (20)
Sodium hydrosulfide solution (5).	Methyl alcohol (20)
Sulfuric acid (2)	Iso-Propyl alcohol (20)
	Coconut oil (34)
	Coconut oil acid (34)
	Palm oil (34)
	Tallow (34)
Sulfuric acid, 98% or less (2)	Choice white grease tallow (34)

(b) The binary combinations listed below have been determined to be dangerously reactive, based on either data obtained in the literature or on laboratory testing which has been carried out in accordance with procedures prescribed in Appendix III. These combinations are exceptions to the Compatibility Chart (Figure 1) and may not be stowed in adjacent tanks.

Acetone cyanohydrin (0) is not compatible with Groups 1-12, 16, 17 and 22.

Acrolein (19) is not compatible with Group 1, Non-Oxidizing Mineral Acids.

Acrylic acid (4) is not compatible with Group 9, Aromatic Amines.

Acrylonitrile (15) is not compatible with Group 5 (Caustics).

Alkylbenzenesulfonic acid (0) is not compatible with Groups 1-3, 5-9, 15, 16, 18, 19, 30, 34, 37, and strong oxidizers.

Allyl alcohol (15) is not compatible with Group 12, Isocyanates.

Alkyl(C7–C9) nitrates (34) is not compatible with Group 1, Non-oxidizing Mineral Acids.

Aluminum sulfate solution (43) is not compatible with Groups 5-11.

Ammonium bisulfite solution (43) is not compatible with Groups 1, 3, 4, and 5.

Benzenesulfonyl chloride (0) is not compatible with Groups 5-7, and 43.

1,4-Butylene glycol (20) is not compatible with Caustic soda solution, 50% or less (5).

gamma-Butyrolactone (0) is not compatible with Groups 1-9.

C9 Resinfeed (DSM) (32) is not compatible with Group 2, Sulfuric acid.

Carbon tetrachloride (36) is not compatible with Tetraethylenepentamine or Triethylenetetramine, both Group 7, Aliphatic amines.

Catoxid feedstock (36) is not compatible with Group 1, 2, 3, 4, 5, or 12.

Caustic soda solution, 50% or less (5) is not compatible with 1,4-Butylene glycol (20).

1-(4-Chlorophenyl)-4,4-dimethyl pentan-3-one (18) is not compatible with Group 5 (Caustics) or 10 (Amides).

Crotonaldehyde (19) is not compatible with Group 1, Non-Oxidizing Mineral Acids.

Cyclohexanone, Cyclohexanol mixture (18) is not compatible with Group 12, Isocyanates.

2,4-Dichlorophenoxyacetic acid, Triisopropanolamine salt solution (43) is not compatible with Group 3, Nitric Acid.

2,4-Dichlorophenoxyacetic acid, Dimethylamine salt solution (0) is not compatible with Groups 1-5, 11, 12, and 16.

Diethylenetriamine (7) is not compatible with 1,2,3-Trichloropropane, Group 36, Halogenated hydrocarbons.

Dimethyl hydrogen phosphite (34) is not compatible with Groups 1 and 4.

Dimethyl naphthalene sulfonic acid, sodium salt solution (34) is not compatible with Group 12, Formaldehyde, and strong oxidizing agents.

Dodecylbenzenesulfonic acid (0) is not compatible with oxidizing agents and Groups 1, 2, 3, 5, 6, 7, 8, 9, 15, 16, 18, 19, 30, 34, and 37.

Ethylenediamine (7) and Ethyleneamine EA 1302 (7) are not compatible with either Ethylene dichloride (36) or 1,2,3-Trichloropropane (36).

Ethylene dichloride (36) is not compatible with Ethylenediamine (7) or Ethyleneamine EA 1302 (7).

Ethylidene norbornene (30) is not compatible with Groups 1-3 and 5-8.

2-Ethyl-3-propylacrolein (19) is not compatible with Group 1, Non-Oxidizing Mineral Acids.

Ethyl tert-butyl ether (41) is not compatible with Group 1, Non-oxidizing mineral acids.

Ferric hydroxyethylethylenediamine triacetic acid, Sodium salt solution (43) is not compatible with Group 3, Nitric acid.

Fish oil (34) is not compatible with Sulfuric acid (2).

Formaldehyde (over 50%) in Methyl alcohol (over 30%) (19) is not compatible with Group 12, Isocyanates.

Formic acid (4) is not compatible with Furfural alcohol (20).

Furfuryl alcohol (20) is not compatible with Group 1, Non-Oxidizing Mineral Acids and Formic acid (4).

2-Hydroxyethyl acrylate (14) is not compatible with Group 5, 6, or 12.

Isophorone (18) is not compatible with Group 8, Alkanolamines.

Magnesium chloride solution (0) is not compatible with Groups 2, 3, 5, 6 and 12.

Mesityl oxide (18) is not compatible with Group 8, Alkanolamines.

Methacrylonitrile (15) is not compatible with Group 5 (Caustics).

Methyl tert-butyl ether (41) is not compatible with Group 1, Non-oxidizing Mineral Acids.

NIAX POLYOL APP 240C (0) is not compatible with Group 2, 3, 5, 7, or 12.

o-Nitrophenol (0) is not compatible with Groups 2, 3, and 5-10.

Octyl nitrates (all isomers), see Alkyl(C7–C9) nitrates.

Oleum (0) is not compatible with Sulfuric acid (2) and 1,1,1-Trichloroethane (36).

Phthalate based polyester polyol (0) is not compatible with group 2, 3, 5, 7 and 12.

Polyglycerine, Sodium salts solution (20) is not compatible with Groups 1, 4, 11, 16, 17, 19, 21 and 22.

Propylene, Propane, MAPP gas mixture (containing 12% or less MAPP gas) (30) is not compatible with Group 1 (Non-oxidizing mineral acids), Group 36 (Halogenated hydrocarbons), nitrogen dioxide, oxidizing materials, or molten sulfur.

Sodium acetate, Glycol, Water mixture (1% or less Sodium hydroxide) (34) is not compatible with Group 12 (Isocyanates).

Sodium chlorate solution (50% or less) (0) is not compatible with Groups 1-3, 5, 7, 8, 10, 12, 13, 17 and 20.

Sodium dichromate solution (70% or less) (0) is not compatible with Groups 1-3, 5, 7, 8, 10, 12, 13, 17 and 20.

Sodium dimethyl naphthalene sulfonate solution (34) is not compatible with Group 12, Formaldehyde and strong oxidizing agents.

Sodium hydrogen sulfide, Sodium carbonate solution (0) is not compatible with Groups 6 (Ammonia) and 7 (Aliphatic amines).

Sodium hydrosulfide (5) is not compatible with Groups 6 (Ammonia) and 7 (Aliphatic amines).

Sodium hydrosulfide, Ammonium sulfide solution (5) is not compatible with Groups 6 (Ammonia) and 7 (Aliphatic amines).

Sodium polyacrylate solution (43) is not compatible with Group 3, Nitric Acid.

Sodium silicate solution (43) is not compatible with Group 3, Nitric Acid.

Sodium sulfide, hydrosulfide solution (0) is not compatible with Groups 6 (Ammonia) and 7 (Aliphatic amines).

Sodium thiocyanate (56% or less) (0) is not compatible with Groups 1-4.

Sulfonated polyacrylate solution (43) is not compatible with Group 5 (Caustics).

Sulfuric acid (2) is not compatible with Fish oil (34), or Oleum (0).

Tall oil fatty acid (Resin acids less than 20%) (34) is not compatible with Group 5, Caustics.

Tallow fatty acid (34) is not compatible with Group 5, Caustics.

Tetraethylenepentamine (7) is not compatible with Carbon tetrachloride, Group 36, Halogenated hydrocarbons.

1,2,3-Trichloropropane (36) is not compatible with Diethylenetriamine, Ethylenediamine, Ethyleaneamine EA 1302, or Triethylenetetramine, all Group 7, Aliphatic amines.

1,1,1-Trichloroethane (36) is not compatible with Oleum (0).

Trichloroethylene (36) is not compatible with Group 5, Caustics.

Triethylenetetramine (7) is not compatible with Carbon tetrachloride, or 1,2,3-Trichloropropane, both Group 36, Halogenated hydrocarbons.

Triethyl phosphite (34) is not compatible with Groups 1, and 4.

Trimethyl phosphite (34) is not compatible with Groups 1 and 4.

1,3,5-Trioxane (41) is not compatible with Group 1 (non-oxidizing mineral acids) and Group 4 (Organic acids).

[CGD 88–100, 54 FR 40012, Sept. 29, 1989 as amended by CGD 88–100, 55 FR 17277, Apr. 24, 1990; CDG 92–100, 59 FR 17026, Apr. 11, 1994; CGD 94–902, 60 FR 34043, June 29, 1995; CGD 95–900, 60 FR 34050, June 29, 1995; USCG 2000–7079, 65 FR 67182, Nov. 8, 2000]

EFFECTIVE DATE NOTE: By USCG–2013–0423, 78 FR 50205, Aug. 16, 2013, appendix I to part 150 was revised, effective Sept. 16, 2013. At 78 FR 56837, Sept. 16, 2013, the effectiveness was delayed until Jan. 16, 2014. For the convenience of the user, the revised text is set forth as follows:

APPENDIX I TO PART 150—EXCEPTIONS TO THE CHART

(a) The binary combinations listed below have been tested as prescribed in Appendix III to part 150 and found not to be dangerously reactive. These combinations are exceptions to Figure 1 of part 150 (Compatibility Chart) and may be stowed in adjacent tanks.

Member of reactive group	Compatible with
Acetone (18)	Diethylenetriamine (7).
Acetone cyanohydrin (0)	Acetic acid (4).
Acrylonitrile (15)	Triethanolamine (8).
n-Butyl alcohol (20)	Caustic Potash (50% or less).
1,3-Butylene glycol (20)	Morpholine (7).
1,4-Butylene glycol (20)	Ethylamine (7).
	Triethanolamine (8).
gamma-Butyrolactone (0)	N-Methyl-2-pyrrolidone (9).
Caustic potash, 50% or less (5)	Isobutyl alcohol (20).
	Ethyl alcohol (20).
	n-Butyl alcohol (20).
	Ethylene glycol (20).
	Isopropyl alcohol (20).
	Methyl alcohol (20).
	iso-Octyl alcohol (20).
	Propylene glycol (20).
Caustic soda, 50% or less (5)	Acrylonitrile/Styrene copolymer dispersion in Polyether polyol (20).
	iso-Butyl alcohol (20).
	Butyl alcohol (20).
	tert-Butyl alcohol, Methanol mixtures.
	Decyl alcohol (20).
	Cetyl alcohol (20).
	Alcohol (C12-C16) poly(1-6)ethoxylates) (20).
	iso-Decyl alcohol (20).
	Diacetone alcohol (20).
	Diethylene glycol (40).
	Dodecyl alcohol (20).
	Ethyl alcohol (20).
	Ethyl alcohol (40%, whiskey) (20).
	Ethylene glycol (20).
	Ethylene glycol, Diethylene glycol mixture (20).
	Ethyl hexanol (Octyl alcohol) (20).
	Methyl alcohol (20).
	Nonyl alcohol (20).
	iso-Decyl alcohol (20).
	iso-Nonyl alcohol (20).
	Propyl alcohol (20).
	iso-Propyl alcohol (20).
	Propylene glycol (20).
	Sodium chlorate solution (0).
	iso-Tridecanol (20).

Coast Guard, DHS   Pt. 150, App. I, Nt.

Member of reactive group	Compatible with
1,1-Dichloroethane (36) .... Dimethyl disulfide (0)	Dimethyl disulfide (0). Acetic acid (4). Acetic anhydride (11). Acetone (18). Acrylates (14). Acrylic acid (4). Alcohols, Glycols (20). Aromatic hydrocarbons (32). Benzene (32). Cyclohexanone (18). Diisononyl phthalate (34). Esters (34). Ethyl acetate (34). Ethyl acrylate (14). Ethyl dichloride (36) [1,1-Dichloroethane]. Ethylene cyanohydrin (20). Ethylene glycol ethyl ether acetate (34) [2-Ethoxyethyl acetate]. Formic acid (4). Halogenated hydrocarbons (36). Ketones (18). Mesityl oxide, Methyl ethyl ketone (18). Octene, Olefins (30). Organic acids (4). Organic anhydrides (11). Paraffins (31). Phenol (21). Phenols, Cresols (21). Trichloroethylene (36).
Diphenylmethane diisocyanate (12)	Perchloroethylene (36). Dichloromethane (36). 2,2-Dimethylpropane-1,3-diol (20). Polypropylene glycol (40). Trichloroethylene (36).
tert-Dodecanethiol (0)	Acetone (18). Acrylonitrile (15). 2-Butoxyethanol (20). n-Butyl acrylate (14). Caustic soda solution (50%) (5). Chloroform (36). iso-Decyl alcohol (20). Dichloromethane (36). Diglycidyl ether of Bisphenol A (41). Diisodecyl phthalate (34). Diglycidyl ether of Bisphenol A (41). Dichloromethane (36). Diisodecyl phthalate (DIDP) (34). Dipropylene glycol (40). Epichlorohydrin (17). Ethyl acrylate (14). Methanol (20). Methyl ethyl ketone (18). Naphtha, Solvent (33). iso-Nonyl alcohol (20). Perchloroethylene (36). iso-Propyl alcohol (20). iso-Propylamine solution (70%) (7). Propylene glycol methyl ether (40). Propylene glycol methyl ether acetate (34). Tall oil, crude (34). Toluene (32). Toluene diisocyanate (TDI) (12). White mineral oil (Carnation oil) (33).
Dodecyl and Tetradecylamine mixture (7) .... Ethylenediamine (7)	Tall oil, fatty acid (34). Butyl alcohol (20). tert-Butyl alcohol (20). Butylene glycol (20). Creosote (21). Diethylene glycol (40). Ethyl alcohol (20). Ethylene glycol (20). Ethyl hexanol (20). Fatty alcohols (C12-C14). Glycerine (20). Isononyl alcohol (20).

Member of reactive group	Compatible with
Lactic acid (0)	Isophorone (18). Methyl butyl ketone (18). Methyl iso-butyl ketone (18). Methyl ethyl ketone (18). Propyl alcohol (20). Propylene glycol (20). Acetic acid (4). Benzene (32). Ethanol (20). Polypropylene glycol (40). Vinyl acetate (13).
Oleum (0)	Hexane (31). Dichloromethane (36). Perchloroethylene (36).
1,2-Propylene glycol (20)	Diethylenetriamine (7). Polyethylene polyamines (7). Triethylenetetramine (7).
Sodium cresylate as Cresylate spent caustic (5)	Methyl alcohol (20).
Sodium dichromate, 70% (0)	Methyl alcohol (20).
Sodium dichromate, 69% (0)	1-Hexene (30).
Sodium hydrogen sulfide solution (5)	iso-Propyl alcohol (20).
Sodium hydrosulfide solution (5)	Methyl alcohol (20). Iso-Propyl alcohol (20).
Sulfuric acid (2)	Coconut oil (34). Coconut oil acid (34). Palm oil (34). Tallow (34).
Sulfuric acid, 98% or less (2)	Choice white grease tallow (34).

(b) The binary combinations listed below have been determined to be dangerously reactive, based on either data obtained in the literature or on laboratory testing which has been carried out in accordance with procedures prescribed in Appendix III. These combinations are exceptions to the Compatibility Chart (Figure 1) and may not be stowed in adjacent tanks.

Acetone cyanohydrin (0) is not compatible with Groups 1-12, 16, 17 and 22.

Acrolein (19) is not compatible with Group 1, Non-Oxidizing Mineral Acids.

Acrylic acid (4) is not compatible with Group 9, Aromatic Amines.

Acrylonitrile (15) is not compatible with Group 5 (Caustics).

Alkylbenzenesulfonic acid (0) is not compatible with Groups 1–3, 5–9, 15, 16, 18, 19, 30, 34, 37, and strong oxidizers.

Allyl alcohol (15) is not compatible with Group 12, Isocyanates.

Alkyl (C7-C9) nitrates (34) is not compatible with Group 1, Non-oxidizing Mineral Acids.

Aluminum sulfate solution (43) is not compatible with Groups 5–11.

Ammonium bisulfite solution (43) is not compatible with Groups 1, 3, 4, and 5.

Benzenesulfonyl chloride (0) is not compatible with Groups 5–7, and 43.

1,4-Butylene glycol (20) is not compatible with Caustic soda solution, 50% or less (5).

gamma-Butyrolactone (0) is not compatible with Groups 1–9.

C9 Resinfeed (DSM) (32) is not compatible with Group 2, Sulfuric acid.

Carbon tetrachloride (36) is not compatible with Tetraethylenepentamine or Triethylenetetramine, both Group 7, Aliphatic amines.

Catoxid feedstock (36) is not compatible with Group 1, 2, 3, 4, 5, or 12.

Caustic soda solution, 50% or less (5) is not compatible with 1,4-Butylene glycol (20).

1-(4-Chlorophenyl)-4,4-dimethyl pentan-3-one (18) is not compatible with Group 5 (Caustics) or 10 (Amides).

Crotonaldehyde (19) is not compatible with Group 1, Non-Oxidizing Mineral Acids.

Cyclohexanone, Cyclohexanol mixture (18) is not compatible with Group 12, Isocyanates.

2,4-Dichlorophenoxyacetic acid, Triisopropanolamine salt solution (43) is not compatible with Group 3, Nitric Acid.

2,4-Dichlorophenoxyacetic acid, Dimethylamine salt solution (0) is not compatible with Groups 1–5, 11, 12, and 16.

Diethylenetriamine (7) is not compatible with 1,2,3-Trichloropropane, Group 36, Halogenated hydrocarbons.

Dimethyl hydrogen phosphite (34) is not compatible with Groups 1 and 4.

Dimethyl naphthalene sulfonic acid, sodium salt solution (34) is not compatible with Group 12, Formaldehyde, and strong oxidizing agents.

Dodecylbenzenesulfonic acid (0) is not compatible with oxidizing agents and Groups 1, 2, 3, 5, 6, 7, 8, 9, 15, 16, 18, 19, 30, 34, and 37.

Ethylenediamine (7) and Ethyleneamine EA 1302 (7) are not compatible with either

Ethylene dichloride (36) or 1,2,3-Trichloropropane (36).

Ethylene dichloride (36) is not compatible with Ethylenediamine (7) or Ethyleneamine EA 1302 (7).

Ethylidene norbornene (30) is not compatible with Groups 1–3 and 5–8.

2-Ethyl-3-propylacrolein (19) is not compatible with Group 1, Non-Oxidizing Mineral Acids.

Ethyl tert-butyl ether (41) is not compatible with Group 1, Non-oxidizing mineral acids.

Fatty acids, essentially linear, C6-C18, 2-ethylhexyl ester (4) is not compatible with Group 3, Nitric acid.

Ferric hydroxyethylethylenediamine triacetic acid, Sodium salt solution (43) is not compatible with Group 3, Nitric acid.

Fish oil (34) is not compatible with Sulfuric acid (2).

Formaldehyde (over 50%) in Methyl alcohol (over 30%) (19) is not compatible with Group 12, Isocyanates.

Formic acid (4) is not compatible with Furfural alcohol (20).

Furfuryl alcohol (20) is not compatible with Group 1, Non-Oxidizing Mineral Acids and Formic acid (4).

1,6-Hexanediol distillation overheads (4) is not compatible with Group 3, Nitric acid, and Group 9, Aromatic amines.

2-Hydroxyethyl acrylate (14) is not compatible with Group 5, 6, or 12.

Isophorone (18) is not compatible with Group 8, Alkanolamines.

Lactic acid (0) is not compatible with Caustic soda solution.

Magnesium chloride solution (0) is not compatible with Groups 2, 3, 5, 6 and 12.

Mesityl oxide (18) is not compatible with Group 8, Alkanolamines.

Methacrylonitrile (15) is not compatible with Group 5 (Caustics).

Methyl tert-butyl ether (41) is not compatible with Group 1, Non-oxidizing Mineral Acids.

Nitroethane, 1-Nitropropane (each 15% or more) mixture (42) is not compatible with Group 7, Aliphatic amines, Group 8, Alkanol amines, and Group 9, Aromatic amines.

Nitropropane (20%), nitroethane (80%) mixture (42) is not compatible with Group 7 (Aliphatic amines), Group 8 (Alkanol amines), and Group 9 (Aromatic amines).

NIAX POLYOL APP 240C (0) is not compatible with Groups 2, 3, 5, 7, or 12.

o-Nitrophenol (0) is not compatible with Groups 2, 3, and 5–10.

Octyl nitrates (all isomers), see Alkyl(C7-C9) nitrates.

Oleum (0) is not compatible with Sulfuric acid (2) and 1,1,1-Trichloroethane (36).

Phthalate based polyester polyol (0) is not compatible with Groups 2, 3, 5, 7 and 12.

Polyglycerine, Sodium salts solution (20) is not compatible with Groups 1, 4, 11, 16, 17, 19, 21 and 22.

Propylene, Propane, MAPP gas mixture (containing 12% or less MAPP gas) (30) is not compatible with Group 1 (Non-oxidizing mineral acids), Group 36 (Halogenated hydrocarbons), nitrogen dioxide, oxidizing materials, or molten sulfur.

Sodium acetate, Glycol, Water mixture (1% or less Sodium hydroxide) (34) is not compatible with Group 12 (Isocyanates).

Sodium chlorate solution (50% or less) (0) is not compatible with Groups 1–3, 5, 7, 8, 10, 12, 13, 17 and 20.

Sodium dichromate solution (70% or less) (0) is not compatible with Groups 1–3, 5, 7, 8, 10, 12, 13, 17 and 20.

Sodium dimethyl naphthalene sulfonate solution (34) is not compatible with Group 12, Formaldehyde and strong oxidizing agents.

Sodium hydrogen sulfide, Sodium carbonate solution (0) is not compatible with Groups 6 (Ammonia) and 7 (Aliphatic amines).

Sodium hydrosulfide (5) is not compatible with Groups 6 (Ammonia) and 7 (Aliphatic amines).

Sodium hydrosulfide, Ammonium sulfide solution (5) is not compatible with Groups 6 (Ammonia) and 7 (Aliphatic amines).

Sodium polyacrylate solution (43) is not compatible with Group 3, Nitric Acid.

Sodium silicate solution (43) is not compatible with Group 3, Nitric Acid.

Sodium sulfide, hydrosulfide solution (0) is not compatible with Groups 6 (Ammonia) and 7 (Aliphatic amines).

Sodium thiocyanate (56% or less) (0) is not compatible with Groups 1–4.

Sulfonated polyacrylate solution (43) is not compatible with Group 5 (Caustics).

Sulfuric acid (2) is not compatible with Fish oil (34), or Oleum (0).

Tall oil fatty acid (Resin acids less than 20%) (34) is not compatible with Group 5, Caustics.

Tallow fatty acid (34) is not compatible with Group 5, Caustics.

Tetraethylenepentamine (7) is not compatible with Carbon tetrachloride, Group 36, Halogenated hydrocarbons.

1,2,3-Trichloropropane (36) is not compatible with Diethylenetriamine, Ethylenediamine, Ethyleaneamine EA 1302, or Triethylenetetramine, all Group 7, Aliphatic amines.

1,1,1-Trichloroethane (36) is not compatible with Oleum (0).

Trichloroethylene (36) is not compatible with Group 5, Caustics.

Triethylenetetramine (7) is not compatible with Carbon tetrachloride, or 1,2,3-Trichloropropane, both Group 36, Halogenated hydrocarbons.

Triethyl phosphite (34) is not compatible with Groups 1, and 4.

Trimethyl phosphite (34) is not compatible with Groups 1 and 4.

1,3,5-Trioxane (41) is not compatible with Group 1 (non-oxidizing mineral acids) and Group 4 (Organic acids).

Vinyl neodecanoate (13) is not compatible with Group 5, Caustics.

APPENDIX II TO PART 150—EXPLANATION OF FIGURE 1

Definition of a hazardous reaction— As a first approximation, a mixture of two cargoes is considered hazardous when, under specified condition, the temperature rise of the mixture exceeds 25 °C or a gas is evolved. It is possible for the reaction of two cargoes to produce a product that is significantly more flammable or toxic than the original cargoes even though the reaction is non-hazardous from temperature or pressure considerations, although no examples of such a reaction are known at this time.

Chart format— There are different degrees of reactivity among the various cargoes. Many of them are relatively non-reactive: For example, aromatic hydrocarbons or paraffins. Others will form hazardous combinations with many groups: For example, the inorganic acids.

The cargo groups in the compatibility chart are separated into two categories: 1 through 22 are "Reactive Groups" and 30 through 43 are "Cargo Groups". Left unassigned and available for future expansion are groups 23 through 29 and those past 43. Reactive Groups contain products which are chemically the most reactive; dangerous combinations may result between members of different Reactive Groups and between members of Reactive Groups and Cargo Groups. Products assigned to Cargo Groups, however, are much less reactive; dangerous combinations involving these can be formed only with members of certain Reactive Groups. Cargo Groups do not react hazardously with one another.

Using the Compatibility Chart— The following procedure explains how the compatibility chart should be used to find compatibility information:

(1) Determine the group numbers of the two cargoes by referring to the alphabetical listing of cargoes and the corresponding groups (Table I). Many cargoes are listed under their parent names; unless otherwise indicated, isomers or mixtures of isomers of a particular cargo are assigned to the same group. For example, to find the group number for Isobutyl Alcohol, look under the parent name Butyl Alcohol. Similarly, the group number for para-Xylene is found under the entry Xylene. If a cargo cannot be found in this listing, contact the Coast Guard for a group determination (see § 150.140).

(2) If both group numbers are between 30 and 43 inclusive, the products are compatible and the chart need not be used.

(3) If both group numbers do not fall between 30 and 43 inclusive, locate one of the numbers on the left of the chart (Cargo Groups) and the other across the top (Reactive Groups). (Note that if a group number is between 30 and 43, it can only be found on the left side of the chart.) The box formed by the intersection of the column and row containing the two numbers will contain one of the following:

(a) Blank—The two cargoes are compatible.

(b) "X"—The two cargoes are not compatible.

(Note that reactivity may vary among the group members. Refer to Table I or Table II to find whether the products in question are referenced by a footnote which indicates that exceptions exist and are listed in Appendix I. Unless the combination is specifically mentioned in Appendix I, it is compatible.)

EXAMPLES

Combination	Groups	Compatible
Butyraldehyde/Acetic Acid	19/4	Yes.
Allyl Alcohol/Toluene Diisocyanate ...	15/12	No.
Decene/Ethyl Benzene	30/32	Yes.
Ethanolamine/Acetone	8/18	Yes.
Ammonia/Dimethylformamide	6/10	No.

[CGD 75–59, 45 FR 70263, Oct. 23, 1980, as amended by CGD 83–047, 50 FR 33046, Aug. 16, 1985]

APPENDIX III TO PART 150—TESTING PROCEDURES FOR DETERMINING EXCEPTIONS TO THE CHART

EXPERIMENTAL PROCEDURE FOR EVALUATING BINARY CHEMICAL REACTIVITY

General safety precautions—Chemical reactivity tests have, by their nature, serious potential for injuring the experimenter or destroying equipment. The experimenter should 1) have knowledge of the magnitude of the reactivity to be expected, 2) use adequate facilities and protective equipment to prevent injury from splatter of materials or release of fumes, and 3) start on a small scale so that unexpected reactions can be safely contained. All tests should be performed in a well-ventilated laboratory hood provided with shields.

Testing chemicals other than liquids—The procedure outlined below was developed for chemicals which are liquids at ambient temperatures. If one or both chemicals are normally shipped at elevated temperatures, the same procedure may be followed except the chemicals are tested at their respective shipping temperatures and the oil bath in Step 3 is maintained at a level 25 °C above the higher temperature. This information is then indicated on the data sheet. If one of the chemicals is a gas at ambient temperatures, consult the Coast Guard for additional instructions before proceeding with the compatibility test.

Step 1

Objective—To determine if the test chemicals react violently and present a safety hazard in further tests.

Procedure—Place 0.5ml of one (A) of the test chemicals in a 25×150mm test tube. Clamp the test tube to a stand behind a safety shield (in a hood). Carefully add from a dropper 0.5ml of the other substance (B). Shake to induce mixing. If no immediate reaction occurs, retain the mixture for at least 10 minutes to check for a delayed reaction.

Results—If a violent reaction occurs, such as sputtering, boiling of reactants or release of fumes, record the results on the Data Sheet (appendix IV) and do not proceed to Step 2. If no reaction or a minor reaction occurs, proceed to Step 2.

Step 2

Objective—To determine the heat of reaction of two chemicals on mixing under specified conditions.

Procedure—These separate mixes of the proposed binary combination will be tested. These are 2 ml : 18 ml, 10 ml : 10 ml, and 18 ml : 2 ml, respectively, to result in a final mixture of about 20 ml in each case.

A reference-junctioned thermocouple is prepared by inserting two lengths of 20 gauge or finer iron-constantan or chromelalumel duplex thermocouple wire into glass capilary sheaths. The common wire of each probe is joined, while the other wire of each is connected to a strip-chart recorder. The thermocouple probe which produces a negative pen deflection upon warming is the reference junction and is placed in a test tube of water at ambient laboratory temperature. The other probe is placed near the bottom of a Dewar flask of about 300ml capacity, such that the thermocouple will be below the surface of the test mixture. The Dewar flask is equipped with a magnetic stirrer having a stirring bar coated with an inert material such as a flourinated hydrocarbon.

Start the temperature recorder and stirrer. Deliver the test chemicals to the Dewar Flask simultaneously from separate graduated syringes. If an exothermic reaction occurs, continue the test until the maximum temperature is reached and begins to subside. If no apparent reaction occurs, continue the test for at least 30 minutes to check for a delayed reaction. Stop agitation and observe the mixture at five-minute intervals to determine if the mixture is miscible, if gases are evolved, or if other visible changes occur. In the interest of safety, a mirror can be used for these observations. Repeat the above test for the other mixture combinations.

Results—Record the results in the appropriate places on the Data Sheet. If no reaction occurs or if the temperature rise is less than 25 °C, proceed to Step 3. If the observed temperature rise exceeds 25 °C or gases are evolved, do not proceed to Step 3.

Step 3

Objective—To determine if exothermic reactions occur at temperatures up to 50 °C.

Procedure—If a non-hazardous reaction occurred in Step 2, the ratio of chemicals which resulted in the greatest temperature rise will be tested. Fresh chemicals will be used with a total volume for this test of about 10ml (a ratio of 1ml:9ml, 5ml:5ml, or 9ml:1ml). If no reaction was observed in Step 2, use a ratio of 5ml:5ml. Using the thermocouple prepared for Step 2, insert the reference probe into a 25×150mm test tube containing 10ml of water. Place the other probe into an empty test tube. Start the temperature recorder and add the two chemicals of the combination, one at a time, to the empty test tube. Lower the two test tubes into an oil bath maintained at 50 ±2 °C. Hold the samples in the oil bath until the maximum temperature differential is recorded, and in all cases at least 15 minutes. Observe the test mixture to determine if gases are evolved or if other visible changes occur. Follow prescribed safety precautions.

Results—Record the maximum differential temperature measured, the time required to reach this temperature, and any other observations in the proper space on the Data Sheet.

Send a copy of the Data Sheet for each binary chemical mixture tested to: Commandant (CG-ENG-5), Attn: Hazardous Materials Division, U.S. Coast Guard Stop 7509, 2703 Martin Luther King Jr. Avenue SE., Washington, DC 20593-7509.

[CGD 75-59, 45 FR 70263, Oct. 23, 1980, as amended by CGD 82-063b, 48 FR 4782, Feb. 3, 1983; CGD 83-047, 50 FR 33046, Aug. 16, 1985; CGD 88-070, 53 FR 34535, Sept. 7, 19885; CGD 96-041, 61 FR 50731, Sept. 27, 1996; USCG-2012-0832, 77 FR 59783, Oct. 1, 2012; USCG-2013-0671, 78 FR 60155, Sept. 30, 2013]

Pt. 150, App. IV

APPENDIX IV TO PART 150—DATA SHEET

CHEMICAL REACTIVITY TEST DATA

Chemicals: A _____ B _____

Synonyms: _____ _____

Formula: _____ _____

	A	B
Description of Products:		
Manufacturer		
Sample Source		
Composition (by weight %)		
Inhibitors or Stabilizers		

Deviations from Prescribed Method (including special equipment)

Step Number 1

Products miscible? _____ Gases evolved? _____

Other Observations:

124

Coast Guard, DHS   **Pt. 151**

Step Number 2

A/B Ratio:	2/18	10/10	18/2
Initial Temperature			
Maximum ΔT			
Time to reach Max. Temp.			
Products miscible?			
Gases evolved?			
Other Observations			

Size of Dewar Flask (inside measurements): Width _____ mm   Height _____ mm

Step Number 3

A/B Ratio	
Oil Bath Temperature	
Maximum ΔT	
Time to reach Max. Temp.	
Gases evolved?	
Other Observations	

Date of Test: _____

Submitting Organization: _____

Test Data Approved By: _____

PART 151—BARGES CARRYING BULK LIQUID HAZARDOUS MATERIAL CARGOES

Subpart 151.01—General

Sec.
151.01-1 Applicability.
151.01-2 Incorporation by reference.
151.01-3 [Reserved]
151.01-5 [Reserved]
151.01-10 Application of vessel inspection regulations.
151.01-15 Dangerous cargoes not specifically named.
151.01-20 Use of minimum requirements.
151.01-25 Existing barges.
151.01-30 Effective date.
151.01-35 Right of appeal.

Subpart 151.02—Equivalents

151.02-1 Conditions under which equivalents may be used.
151.02-5 Design of unmanned barges.

Subpart 151.03—Definitions

151.03-1 Definitions of terms.
151.03-3 Angle of downflooding.
151.03-5 Approved.
151.03-7 Barge.
151.03-9 Cargo.
151.03-11 Coastwise.
151.03-13 Cofferdam.
151.03-15 Commandant.
151.03-17 Compatible.
151.03-19 Environment.
151.03-21 Filling density.
151.03-23 Flame arrestor.
151.03-25 Flame screen.

151.03-27 Gas free.
151.03-29 Great Lakes.
151.03-30 Hazardous material.
151.03-31 Headquarters.
151.03-33 Lakes, bays, and sounds.
151.03-35 Limiting draft.
151.03-36 Liquid.
151.03-37 Maximum allowable working pressure.
151.03-38 Nondestructive testing.
151.03-39 Ocean.
151.03-41 Officer in Charge, Marine Inspection (OCMI).
151.03-43 Pressure.
151.03-45 Rivers.
151.03-47 Service.
151.03-49 Sounding tube.
151.03-51 Tank barge.
151.03-53 Tankerman.
151.03-55 [Reserved]

Subpart 151.04—Inspection and Certification

151.04-1 Certificate of inspection.
151.04-2 Inspection required.
151.04-3 Initial inspection.
151.04-5 Inspection for certification.
151.04-7 Nondestructive testing.

Subpart 151.05—Summary of Minimum Requirements for Specific Cargoes

151.05-1 Explanation of column headings in Table 151.05.
151.05-2 Compliance with requirements for tank barges carrying benzene and benzene containing cargoes, or butyl acrylate cargoes.
TABLE 151.05 TO SUBPART 151.05 OF PART 151—SUMMARY OF MINIMUM REQUIREMENTS

Subpart 151.10—Barge Hull Construction Requirements

151.10-1 Barge hull classifications.
151.10-5 Subdivision and stability.
151.10-15 Certificate endorsement.
151.10-20 Hull construction.

Subpart 151.12—Equipment and Operating Requirements for Control of Pollution From Category D NLS Cargoes

151.12-5 Equipment for Category D NLS.
151.12-10 Operation of oceangoing non-self-propelled ships carrying Category D NLS.

Subpart 151.13—Cargo Segregation

151.13-1 General.
151.13-5 Cargo segregation—tanks.

Subpart 151.15—Tanks

151.15-1 Tank types.
151.15-3 Construction.
151.15-5 Venting.
151.15-6 Venting piping.
151.15-10 Cargo gauging devices.

Subpart 151.20—Cargo Transfer

151.20-1 Piping—general.
151.20-5 Cargo system valving requirements.
151.20-10 Cargo system instrumentation.
151.20-15 Cargo hose if carried on the barge.
151.20-20 Cargo transfer methods.

Subpart 151.25—Environmental Control

151.25-1 Cargo tank.
151.25-2 Cargo handling space.

Subpart 151.30—Portable Fire Extinguishers

151.30-1 Type.

Subpart 151.40—Temperature or Pressure Control Installations

151.40-1 Definitions.
151.40-2 Materials.
151.40-5 Construction.
151.40-10 Operational requirements.
151.40-11 Refrigeration systems.

Subpart 151.45—Operations

151.45-1 General.
151.45-2 Special operating requirements.
151.45-3 Manning.
151.45-4 Cargo-handling.
151.45-5 Open hopper barges.
151.45-6 Maximum amount of cargo.
151.45-7 Shipping papers.
151.45-8 Illness, alcohol, drugs.
151.45-9 Signals.

Subpart 151.50—Special Requirements

151.50-1 General.
151.50-5 Cargoes having toxic properties.
151.50-6 Motor fuel antiknock compounds.
151.50-10 Alkylene oxides.
151.50-12 Ethylene oxide.
151.50-13 Propylene oxide.
151.50-20 Inorganic acids.
151.50-21 Sulfuric acid.
151.50-22 Hydrochloric acid.
151.50-23 Phosphoric acid.
151.50-30 Compressed gases.
151.50-31 Chlorine.
151.50-32 Ammonia, anhydrous.
151.50-34 Vinyl chloride (vinyl chloride monomer).
151.50-36 Argon or nitrogen.
151.50-40 Additional requirements for carbon disulfide (carbon bisulfide) and ethyl ether.
151.50-41 Carbon disulfide (carbon bisulfide).
151.50-42 Ethyl ether.
151.50-50 Elemental phosphorus in water.
151.50-55 Sulfur (molten).

Coast Guard, DHS § 151.01-2

151.50-60 Benzene.
151.50-70 Cargoes requiring inhibition or stabilization.
151.50-73 Chemical protective clothing.
151.50-74 Ethylidene norbornene.
151.50-75 Ferric chloride solution.
151.50-76 Hydrochloric acid, spent (NTE 15%).
151.50-77 Fluorosilicic acid (30% or less) (hydrofluorosilicic acid).
151.50-79 Methyl acetylene-propadiene mixture.
151.50-80 Nitric acid (70% or less).
151.50-81 Special operating requirements for heat sensitive cargoes.
151.50-84 Sulfur dioxide.
151.50-86 Alkyl (C7–C9) nitrates.

Subpart 151.55—Special Requirements for Materials of Construction

151.55-1 General.

Subpart 151.56—Prohibited Materials of Construction

151.56-1 Prohibited materials.

Subpart 151.58—Required Materials of Construction

151.58-1 Required materials.

AUTHORITY: 33 U.S.C. 1903; 46 U.S.C. 3703; Department of Homeland Security Delegation No. 0170.1.

SOURCE: CGFR 70-10, 35 FR 3714, Feb. 25, 1970, unless otherwise noted.

EDITORIAL NOTE: Nomenclature changes to part 151 appear by USCG–2009–0702, 74 FR 49236, Sept. 25, 2009, and USCG–2012–0832, 77 FR 59784, Oct. 1, 2012.

Subpart 151.01—General

§ 151.01-1 Applicability.

This part applies to the following:
(a) Oceangoing, as defined in 33 CFR 151.05(j), non-self-propelled United States ships and non-self-propelled foreign ships operating in United States waters that carry a bulk cargo that is—
(1) Listed in Table 151.05;
(2) Not being carried in a portable tank regulated under subpart 98.30 or 98.33 of this chapter; and
(3) Not an NLS or is an NLS cargo that is a Category D listed in § 151.12-5 of this part.
(b) All non-self-propelled United States ships that are not oceangoing that carry a bulk cargo that is—
(1) Listed in Table 151.05, and
(2) Not being carried in a portable tank regulated under subpart 98.30 or 98.33 of this chapter.

[CGD 81-101, 52 FR 7776, Mar. 12, 1987, as amended by CGD 84-043, 55 FR 37413, Sept. 11, 1990]

§ 151.01-2 Incorporation by reference.

(a) Certain standards and specifications are incorporated by reference into this part with the approval of the Director of the Federal Register in accordance with 5 U.S.C. 552(a). To enforce any edition other than the ones listed in paragraph (b) of this section, notice of change must be published in the FEDERAL REGISTER and the material made available to the public. All approved material is on file at the National Archives and Records Administration (NARA), and is available from the sources indicated in paragraph (b) of this section. For information on the availability of this material at NARA, call 202–741–6030, or go to: *http://www.archives.gov/federal_register/code_of_federal_regulations/ibr_locations.html.*

(b) The standards and specifications approved for incorporation by reference in this part and the sections affected, are:

American Society for Nondestructive Testing (ASNT)

4153 Arlingate Road, Caller #28518, Columbus, OH 43228–0518

ASNT "Recommended Practice No. SNT-TC-1A (1988), Personnel Qualification and Certification in Nondestructive Testing" ....151.04–7(c)(2)

American Society of Mechanical Engineers (ASME) International

Three Park Avenue, New York, NY 10016–5990

ASME Boiler and Pressure Vessel Code Section V, Nondestructive Examination (1986) ....151.04–7(a)(1)

American Society for Testing and Materials (ASTM)

100 Barr Harbor Drive, West Conshohocken, PA 19428–2959.

ASTM D 4986–98, Standard Test Method for Horizontal Burning Characteristics of Cellular Polymeric Materials..151.15–3
ASTM E 84–98, Standard Test Method

§ 151.01-3

for Surface Burning Characteristics of Building Materials—151.15-3

[CGD 85-061, 54 FR 50965, Dec. 11, 1989, as amended by USCG-1999-6216, 64 FR 53227, Oct. 1, 1999; USCG-1999-5151, 64 FR 67183, Dec. 1, 1999; 69 FR 18803, Apr. 9, 2004]

§ 151.01-3 [Reserved]

§ 151.01-5 [Reserved]

§ 151.01-10 Application of vessel inspection regulations.

(a) The regulations in this part are requirements which may be in addition to, supplement, or modify requirements in other subchapters in this chapter. When a specific requirement in another part or section in another subchapter in this chapter is in conflict with or contrary to requirement or intent expressed in this part, the regulations in this part shall take precedence.

(b) Every unmanned tank barge which carries or is intended to carry in bulk any liquid or liquefied gas listed in Table 151.05 and has flammability or combustibility characteristics as indicated by a fire protection requirement in Table 151.05 shall be inspected and certified under the provisions in subchapter D (Tank Vessels) of this chapter and the regulations in this part.

(c) Every unmanned tank barge prior to the carriage in bulk of any liquid or liquefied gas listed in Table 151.05 which does not have the flammability or combustibility characteristics as indicated by the fire protection requirement in Table 151.05 shall be inspected and certified under the applicable provisions of subchapter D or subchapter I of this chapter, at the option of the barge owner, in addition to the regulations in this part. However, unless the barge owner notifies the Officer in Charge, Marine Inspection of his option to have the barge inspected and certified under subchapter I at the time he submits the application for inspection (Form CG-3752), the unmanned tank barge shall be inspected and certified under the provisions of subchapter D of this chapter and the regulations in this part.

(c-1) Each unmanned tank barge constructed on or after September 6, 1977, that carries in bulk a cargo listed in Table 151.05 and that is certificated under subchapter I of this chapter must meet the loading information requirements in § 31.10-32 of this chapter.

(d) The provisions of subchapter D of this chapter shall apply to all unmanned tank barges which carry in bulk any of the liquids or liquefied gases listed in Table 30.25-1 of this chapter. The provisions of this part shall not apply to such barges unless it is also desired to carry one or more of the liquids or liquefied gases listed in Table 151.05.

(e) Manned barges which carry or intend to carry in bulk the cargoes specified in Table 151.05 will be considered individually by the Commandant and may be required to meet the requirements of this subchapter and of subchapter D (Tank Vessels) or I (Cargo and Miscellaneous Vessels) of this chapter as applicable.

[CGFR 70-10, 35 FR 3714, Feb. 25, 1970]

EDITORIAL NOTE: For FEDERAL REGISTER citations affecting § 151.01-10, see the List of CFR Sections Affected, which appears in the Finding Aids section of the printed volume and at *www.fdsys.gov*.

§ 151.01-15 Dangerous cargoes not specifically named.

(a) Any liquid or liquefied gas, which meets the definitions referred to in § 151.01-1 and is not named in Table 151.05 or Table 30.25-1 of this chapter shall not be transported in bulk in a manned or unmanned tank barge without the prior specific approval of the Commandant.

(b) Mixtures or blends of two or more cargoes, one or more of which appears in Table 151.05, will be treated as though they were new products and specific approval of the Commandant must be obtained prior to undertaking their transportation.

[CGFR-70-10, 35 FR 3714, Feb. 25, 1970, as amended by CGD 81-101, 52 FR 7777, Mar. 12, 1987; CGD 81-101, 53 FR 28974, Aug. 1, 1988 and 54 FR 12629, Mar. 28, 1989; CGD 88-100, 54 FR 40029, Sept. 29, 1989]

§ 151.01-20 Use of minimum requirements.

(a) The minimum requirements governing transportation of any liquid or liquefied gas listed in Table 151.05 are set forth in this part when such substances are carried in bulk in unmanned tank barges.

(b) Before any liquid or liquefied gas listed in Table 151.05 may be carried in an unmanned tank barge, the certificate of inspection issued to such barge shall be appropriately endorsed to show approval to transport such cargo.

[CFGR 70–10, 35 FR 3714, Feb. 25, 1970, as amended by CGD 88–100, 54 FR 40029, Sept. 29, 1989]

§ 151.01–25 Existing barges.

(a) Except as provided in paragraph (c) of this section, barges certified for, or used within the previous 2 years prior to the effective date of this regulation, or barges equivalent to such barges, for the transportation of any cargo regulated by this subchapter which do not meet the specific requirements herein, may be continued in service subject to the following conditions:

(1) Venting, gauging, and all operating requirements shall be met within a 1–year period subsequent to the effective date.

(2) All other requirements shall be met within a 2–year period subsequent to the effective date.

(b) If an existing barge, which has been designed to carry or has regularly been carrying one or more of the cargoes regulated by this subchapter, is found to be so arranged, or outfitted that conversion to bring it into compliance with any or all of the requirements of this subchapter is impractical or impossible, the Commandant, upon application, may review the plans of the barge to determine if it is suitable and safe for the cargoes to be transported.

(c) Except for operating and vinyl chloride requirements, barges constructed and certificated for the transportation of any cargo for which specific regulations existed, in parts 36, 38, 39, 40, and 98 of this chapter at the time of their construction or conversion, may continue and will be certificated to operate without the requirement that they comply with the provisions of subchapter O of this chapter.

[CFGR 70–10, 35 FR 3714, Feb. 25, 1970, as amended by CGD 74–167k, 40 FR 17026, Apr. 16, 1975]

§ 151.01–30 Effective date.

(a) The regulations in this subchapter are effective on and after June 1, 1970. However, amendments, revisions, or additions shall become effective ninety (90) days after the date of publication in the FEDERAL REGISTER unless the Commandant shall fix a different time.

(b) The regulations in this subchapter are not retroactive in effect unless specifically made so at the time the regulations are issued. Changes in specification requirements of articles of equipment, or materials used in construction of tank barges, shall not apply to such items which have been passed as satisfactory until replacement shall become necessary, unless a specific finding is made that such equipment or materials used is unsafe or hazardous and has to be removed from tank barges.

§ 151.01–35 Right of appeal.

Any person directly affected by a decision or action taken under this part, by or on behalf of the Coast Guard, may appeal therefrom in accordance with subpart 1.03 of this chapter.

[CGD 88–033, 54 FR 50381, Dec. 6, 1989]

Subpart 151.02—Equivalents

§ 151.02–1 Conditions under which equivalents may be used.

(a) Where in this part it is provided that a particular fitting, material, appliance, apparatus, or equipment, or type thereof, shall be fitted or carried in a vessel, or that any particular provision shall be made or arrangement including cargo segregation shall be adopted, the Commandant may accept in substitution therefor any other fitting, material, apparatus or equipment, or type thereof, or any other provision or arrangement. However, the Commandant shall be satisfied by suitable evidence that the fitting, material, appliance, apparatus, or equipment, or the type thereof, or the provision or arrangement shall be at least as effective as that specified in this part.

(b) In any case where it is shown to the satisfaction of the Commandant that the use of any particular equipment, apparatus, or arrangement not

§ 151.02-5

specifically required by law is unreasonable or impracticable, the Commandant may permit the use of alternate equipment apparatus, or arrangement to such an extent and upon such conditions as will insure, to his satisfaction, a degree of safety consistent with the minimum standards set forth in this part.

§ 151.02-5 Design of unmanned barges.

(a) In order not to inhibit design and application, the Commandant may approve vessels of novel design, both new and for conversion, after it is shown to his satisfaction that such a vessel is at least as safe as any vessel which meets the standards required by this part.

(b) [Reserved]

Subpart 151.03—Definitions

§ 151.03-1 Definitions of terms.

Certain terms used in the regulations in this subchapter are defined in this subpart.

§ 151.03-3 Angle of downflooding.

The angle of heel of the vessel at which any opening in the hull not provided with a water tight closure would be immersed.

§ 151.03-5 Approved.

This term means approved by the Commandant unless otherwise stated.

§ 151.03-7 Barge.

This term means any non-self-propelled vessel designed to carry cargo.

§ 151.03-9 Cargo.

This term means any liquid, gas or solid having one or more of the dangerous properties defined in this subchapter.

§ 151.03-11 Coastwise.

This designation refers to all vessels normally navigating the waters of any ocean or the Gulf of Mexico 20 nautical miles or less offshore.

§ 151.03-13 Cofferdam.

This term means a void or empty space separating two or more compartments for the purpose of isolation or to prevent the contents of one compartment from entering another in the event of the failure of the walls of one to retain their tightness.

§ 151.03-15 Commandant.

This term means Commandant of the U.S. Coast Guard.

§ 151.03-17 Compatible.

Compatible means that a cargo will not react in an unsafe manner with other cargo or materials used in construction of the barge. The prime considerations are the chemical, physical, or thermal properties of the reaction including heat, pressure, toxicity, stability, and explosive nature of the reaction and its end products.

§ 151.03-19 Environment.

This term refers to the atmosphere within a cargo tank and the spaces adjacent to the tank or spaces in which cargo is handled.

§ 151.03-21 Filling density.

The ratio, expressed as a percentage, of the weight of cargo that may be loaded into a tank compared to the weight of water that the tank will hold at 60 °F. The weight of a gallon of water at 60 °F in air shall be 8.32828 pounds.

§ 151.03-23 Flame arrestor.

Any device or assembly of cellular, tubular, pressure or other type used for preventing the passage of flames into enclosed spaces.

§ 151.03-25 Flame screen.

A fitted single screen of corrosion-resistant wire of at least 30 by 30 mesh or two fitted screens, both of corrosion-resistant wire, of at least 20 by 20 mesh spaced not less than one-half inch or more than 1½ inches apart.

§ 151.03-27 Gas free.

Free from dangerous concentrations of flammable or toxic gases.

§ 151.03-29 Great Lakes.

A designation for all vessels in Great Lakes service.

§ 151.03-30   Hazardous material.

In this part *hazardous material* means a liquid material or substance that is—
(a) Flammable or combustible;
(b) Designated a hazardous substance under section 311(b) of the Federal Water Pollution Control Act (33 U.S.C. 1321); or
(c) Designated a hazardous material under 49 U.S.C. 5103.

NOTE: The Environmental Protection Agency designates hazardous substances in 40 CFR Table 116.4A. The Coast Guard designates hazardous materials that are transported as bulk liquids by water in § 153.40.

[CGD 81–101, 52 FR 7777, Mar. 12, 1987, as amended by CGD 95–028, 62 FR 51209, Sept. 30, 1997]

§ 151.03-31   Headquarters.

Commandant (CG–5P), Attn: Assistant Commandant for Prevention, U.S. Coast Guard Stop 7501, 2703 Martin Luther King Jr. Avenue SE., Washington, DC 20593–7501

[CGFR 70–10, 35 FR 3714, Feb. 25, 1970, as amended by CGD 88–070, 53 FR 34535, Sept. 7, 1988; USCG–2013–0671, 78 FR 60155, Sept. 30, 2013]

§ 151.03-33   Lakes, bays, and sounds.

A designation for all vessels navigating the waters of any of the lakes, bays, or sounds other than the waters of the Great Lakes.

§ 151.03-35   Limiting draft.

Maximum allowable draft to which a barge may be loaded. Limiting draft is a function of hull type and cargo specific gravity. A barge may be assigned different limiting drafts for different hull types or within one hull type for different specific gravities.

§ 151.03-36   Liquid.

In this part *liquid* includes liquefied and compressed gases.

[CGD 81–101, 52 FR 7777, Mar. 12, 1987]

§ 151.03-37   Maximum allowable working pressure.

The maximum allowable working pressure shall be as defined in section VIII of the ASME Boiler and Pressure Vessel Code.

[CGFR 70–10, 35 FR 3714, Feb. 25, 1970, as amended by CGD 85–061, 54 FR 50965, Dec. 11, 1989]

§ 151.03-38   Nondestructive testing.

Nondestructive testing includes ultrasonic examination, liquid penetrant examination, magnetic particle examination, radiographic examination, eddy current, and acoustic emission.

[CGD 85–061, 54 FR 50965, Dec. 11, 1989]

§ 151.03-39   Ocean.

A designation for all vessels normally navigating the waters of any ocean or the Gulf of Mexico more than 20 nautical miles offshore.

§ 151.03-41   Officer in Charge, Marine Inspection (OCMI).

This term means any person from the civilian or military branch of the Coast Guard designated as such by the Commandant and who, under the superintendence and direction of the Coast Guard District Commander, is in charge of an inspection zone for the performance of duties with respect to the enforcement and administration of Subtitle II of Title 46, U.S. Code, Title 46 and Title 33 U.S. Code, and regulations issued under these statutes.

[CGD 95–028, 62 FR 51209, Sept. 30, 1997]

§ 151.03-43   Pressure.

Terminology used in this part are: pounds per square inch gauge (p.s.i.g.) or pounds per square inch absolute (p.s.i.a.). 14.7 p.s.i.a. is equal to 0 p.s.i.g. P.s.i.g. is normally used in reference to design or operating requirements.

§ 151.03-45   Rivers.

A designation for all vessels whose navigation is restricted to rivers and/or canals, exclusively.

§ 151.03-47   Service.

The waters upon which a vessel may be operated as endorsed upon the certificate of inspection.

§ 151.03-49 Sounding tube.

This is an unperforated tube fitted to an ullage hole, secured so as to be vapor tight to the underside of the tank top open at the bottom, and extending to within 18 inches or less of the bottom of the tank.

§ 151.03-51 Tank barge.

A non-self-propelled vessel especially constructed or converted to carry bulk liquid cargo in tanks.

§ 151.03-53 Tankerman.

The following ratings are established in part 13 of this chapter. The terms for the ratings identify persons holding valid merchant mariner credentials or merchant mariners' documents for service in the ratings issued under that part:

(a) Tankerman-PIC.
(b) Tankerman-PIC (Barge).
(c) Restricted Tankerman-PIC.
(d) Restricted Tankerman-PIC (Barge).
(e) Tankerman-Assistant.
(f) Tankerman-Engineer.

[CGD 79–116, 60 FR 17157, Apr. 4, 1995, as amended by USCG–2006–24371, 74 FR 11266, Mar. 16, 2009]

§§ 151.03-55 [Reserved]

Subpart 151.04—Inspection and Certification

§ 151.04-1 Certificate of inspection.

(a) A certificate of inspection is required for every unmanned tank barge subject to the requirements in this subchapter. A certificate of inspection shall be issued to the barge or to its owners by the Officer in Charge, Marine Inspection, if the barge is found to comply with applicable inspection laws and the regulations in this chapter.

(b) The certificate of inspection shall be endorsed with respect to the waters over which the barge may be operated.

(c) The certificate shall be endorsed describing the cargoes by name as given in Table 151.05 or as specifically approved by the Commandant. No other dangerous cargo as defined in Subpart 151.01-1 shall be carried. Certificates shall specify maximum cargo weight (short tons), maximum density (pounds per gallon) and any operating limitations and a limiting draft.

[CFGR 70–10, 35 FR 3714, Feb. 25, 1970, as amended by CGD 88–100, 54 FR 40029, Sept. 29, 1989]

§ 151.04-2 Inspection required.

(a) Every unmanned tank barge subject to the regulations in this subchapter shall be inspected every five years. More frequent inspections may be required, if necessary, by the Officer in Charge, Marine Inspection, to see that the hull, equipment and appliances of the vessel comply with the marine inspection laws, and the regulations of this subchapter and other subchapters where applicable.

(b) [Reserved]

[CGFR 70–10, 35 FR 3714, Feb. 25, 1970, as amended by USCG–2007–29018, 72 FR 53967, Sept. 21, 2007]

§ 151.04-3 Initial inspection.

(a) The initial inspection which may consist of a series of inspections during the construction of an unmanned barge shall include a complete inspection of the structure, auxiliary machinery, and equipment. The inspection shall be such as to insure that the arrangement, materials, and scantlings of the hull structure, tanks and pressure vessels and their appurtenances comply with applicable regulations of this chapter and with the requirements of this part.

(b) [Reserved]

§ 151.04-5 Inspection for certification.

(a) An inspection for certification is a prerequisite of the reissuance of a Certificate of Inspection as provided for in applicable regulations of this chapter.

(b) Unless otherwise specified in table 151.05, cargo tanks are internally examined as follows:

(1) Where the cargo tank is of the gravity type and the structural framing is on the internal tank surface, the tank shall be inspected internally at the time of inspection for certification.

(2) Where the cargo tank is of the gravity type and the structural framing is on the external tank surface accessible for examination from voids, cofferdams, double bottoms, and other

similar spaces, tanks shall be inspected internally at 4-year intervals.

(3) If the tank is a pressure-vessel type cargo tank, an internal inspection of the tank is conducted within—

(i) Ten years after the last internal inspection on an unmanned barge carrying cargo at temperatures of $-67\ °F$ ($-55\ °C$) or warmer; or

(ii) Eight years after the last internal inspection if the tank is a pressure type cargo tank carrying cargo at temperatures colder than $-67\ °F$ ($-55\ °C$).

(4) Internal inspection may be required at more frequent intervals as deemed necessary by the Officer in Charge, Marine Inspection.

(c) An external examination of unlagged tanks and the visible parts of lagged tanks is made at each biennial inspection. If the vessel has single skin construction, the underwater portion of the tank need not be examined unless deemed necessary by the Officer in Charge, Marine Inspection. If an external examination of the tank is not possible because of insulation, the owner shall ensure that—

(1) The amount of insulation deemed necessary by the marine inspector is removed during each cargo tank internal inspection to allow spot external examination of the tanks and insulation; or

(2) The thickness of the tanks is gauged by a nondestructive means accepted by the marine inspector without the removal of insulation.

(d) If required by the Officer in Charge, Marine Inspection the owner shall conduct nondestructive testing of each tank designated by the Officer in Charge, Marine Inspection in accordance with §151.04–7.

(e) If the Officer in Charge, Marine Inspection considers a hydrostatic test necessary to determine the condition of the tanks, the owner shall perform the test at a pressure of 1½ times the tank's—

(1) Maximum allowable pressure, as determined by the safety relief valve setting; or

(2) Design pressure, when cargo tanks operate at maximum allowable pressures reduced below the design pressure in order to satisfy special mechanical stress relief requirements.

NOTE: See the ASME Code, Section VIII, Appendix 3 for information on design pressure.

(f) Quick closing valves shall be tested by operating the emergency shutoff system from each operating point at the time of each vessel's inspection for certification.

(g) Excess flow valves shall be inspected at the time of inspection for certification. The Officer in Charge, Marine Inspection, shall satisfy himself that the valve is in working condition by visual inspection, and if this is impossible, by one of the following means:

(1) Removing the valve and bench testing ashore; the valve shall close at or below its rated closing flow.

(2) By any other means acceptable to the Officer in Charge, Marine Inspection, which will demonstrate that the valve is operable.

(h) Pressure vaccum relief valves shall be examined to determine that the operating mechanism is free and capable of activation.

(i) Safety relief valves shall be tested by bench testing or other suitable means. The valves shall relieve and reseat within the design tolerances of the set pressure, or it shall be removed and reset prior to being returned to service. This test shall be conducted at the time of the inspection for certification.

(j) Cargo hose stored on board the vessel which is used in transferring cargoes listed in Table 151.05 shall be inspected every 2 years. This inspection shall consist of a visual examination and a hydrostatic test of 1½ times the maximum pressure to which the hose will be subjected in service. The date of the most recent inspection and the test pressure shall be stenciled or otherwise marked on the hose.

(k) Cargo piping shall be inspected and tested at the same time as the cargo tanks.

(l) If the tank is a pressure vessel type cargo tank with an internal inspection interval of 10 years, and is 30 years old or older, determined from the date it was built, the owner shall conduct nondestructive testing of each

§ 151.04-7

tank in accordance with § 151.04-7, during each internal inspection.

[CFGR 70-10, 35 FR 3714, Feb. 25, 1970, as amended by CGD 88-100, 54 FR 40029, Sept. 29, 1989; CGD 85-061, 54 FR 50965, Dec. 11, 1989]

§ 151.04-7 Nondestructive testing.

(a) Before nondestructive testing may be conducted to meet § 151.04-5 (d) and (l), the owner shall submit a proposal to the Officer in Charge, Marine Inspection that includes—

(1) The test methods and procedures to be used all of which must meet section V of the ASME Boiler and Pressure Vessel Code (1986);

(2) Each location on the tank to be tested; and

(3) The test method and procedure to be conducted at each location on the tank.

(b) If the Officer in Charge, Marine Inspection rejects the proposal, the Officer in Charge, Marine Inspection informs the owner of the reasons why the proposal is rejected.

(c) If the Officer in Charge, Marine Inspection accepts the proposal, then the owner shall ensure that—

(1) The proposal is followed; and

(2) Nondestructive testing is performed by personnel meeting ASNT "Recommended Practice No. SNT-TC-1A (1988), Personnel Qualification and Certification in Nondestructive Testing."

(d) Within 30 days after completing the nondestructive test, the owner shall submit a written report of the results to the Officer in Charge, Marine Inspection.

[CGD 85-061, 54 FR 50966, Dec. 11, 1989]

Subpart 151.05—Summary of Minimum Requirements for Specific Cargoes

§ 151.05-1 Explanation of column headings in Table 151.05.

(a) *Cargo identification/name.* This column identifies cargoes by name. Words in italics are not part of the cargo name but may be used in addition to the cargo name. When one entry references another entry by use of the word "see" and both names are in roman type, either name may be used as the cargo name (e.g., "Diethyl ether *see* Ethyl ether"). However, the referenced entry is preferred.

(b) *Cargo identification/pressure.* This column identifies cargo in terms of pressure within the tank. Terms used are:

(1) *Pressurized.* Cargo carried at a pressure in excess of 10 pounds per square inch gauge as measured at the top of the tank (i.e., exclusive of static head).

(2) *Atmospheric pressure.* Cargo carried at not more than 10 pounds per square inch gauge, exclusive of static head.

(c) *Cargo identification/temperature.* This column identifies the cargo by the temperature of the cargo during transit.

(1) *Ambient temperature.* Cargo which is carried at naturally occurring temperatures.

(2) *Low temperature.* Cargo carried below ambient temperatures when the product temperature is below 0 °F.

(3) *Elevated temperature.* Cargo carried above ambient temperatures.

(d) *Hull type.* This column refers to the flotation features of the barge. Terms used are explained and defined in Subpart 151.10 of this part.

(e) *Cargo segregation/tanks.* This column refers to the separation of the cargo from its surroundings. Terms are explained in § 151.13-5 and in footnotes to Table 151.05 of this part.

(f) *Tanks/type.* This column refers to the design requirements for cargo tanks and their placement within the hull of the vessel. Terms are explained in § 151.15-1.

(g) *Tanks/venting.* This column refers to arrangements for preventing excess pressure or vacuum within the cargo tank. Terms used are explained and defined in § 151.15-5.

(h) *Tanks/gauging devices.* This column refers to arrangements provided for determining the amount of cargo present in cargo tanks. Terms used are explained and defined in § 151.15-10.

(i) *Cargo transfer/piping.* This column refers to the classification of piping in accordance with Subchapter F of this chapter as discussed in § 151.20-1.

(j) *Cargo transfer/control.* This column refers to the valving requirements for the cargo piping system. These requirements are defined in § 151.20-5.

(k) *Environmental control/cargo tanks.* This column refers to control of the composition of the environment within cargo tanks. Definitions and detailed requirements are given in § 151.25–1.

(l) *Environmental control/cargo handling space.* This column refers to control of the environment in the cargo handling spaces. Definitions and detailed requirements are found in § 151.25–2.

(m) *Fire protection.* This column specifies whether portable fire extinguishers are required on barges carrying the cargo named. Requirements for cargoes requiring extinguishers are given in Subpart 151.30 of this part.

(n) *Special requirements.* This column refers to requirements in subparts 151.40, 151.50, 151.55, 151.56, and 151.58 of this part which apply to specific cargoes. The section numbers listed omit the preceding part designation, "151".

(o) *Electrical hazard class—group.* This column lists the electrical hazard class and group used for the cargo when determining requirements for electrical equipment under subchapter J (Electrical engineering) of this chapter.

(p) *Temperature control installations.* This column refers to systems which are used to control the temperature of the cargo. Definitions and requirements which are applicable if such systems are used are given in Subpart 151.40 of this part.

(q) *Tank inspection period.* This column refers to the maximum period in years between internal cargo tank inspections. Applicable requirements are given in § 151.04–5.

[CGFR 70–10, 35 FR 3714, Feb. 25, 1970; 35 FR 6431, Apr. 22, 1970, as amended by CGD 74–275, 40 FR 21958, May 20, 1975; CGD 88–100, 54 FR 40029, Sept. 29, 19895; CGD 96–041, 61 FR 50731, Sept. 27, 1996; USCG 2000–7079, 65 FR 67183, Nov. 8, 2000]

§ 151.05–2 Compliance with requirements for tank barges carrying benzene and benzene containing cargoes, or butyl acrylate cargoes.

A tank barge certificated to carry benzene and benzene containing cargoes or butyl acrylate cargoes must comply with the gauging requirement of Table 151.05 of this part by August 15, 1998. Until that date, a tank barge certificated to carry benzene and benzene containing cargoes must meet either the gauging requirement of Table 151.05 or the restricted or closed gauging requirements in effect on September 29, 1994; and a tank barge certificated to carry butyl acrylate cargoes must meet either the gauging requirements of Table 151.05 or comply with the open, restricted, or closed gauging requirements in effect on September 29, 1994.

[CGD 95–900, 60 FR 34050, June 29, 1995]

TABLE 151.05 TO SUBPART 151.05 OF PART 151—SUMMARY OF MINIMUM REQUIREMENTS

Cargo identification[1]					Tanks			Cargo transfer		Environmental control		Fire protection required	Special requirements in 46 CFR Part 151	Electrical hazard class and group	Temp. control install.	Tank internal inspect. period—years
Cargo name	Pressure	Temp.	Hull type	Cargo segregation tank	Type	Vent	Gauging device	Piping class	Control	Cargo tanks	Cargo handling space					
a.	b.	c.	d.	e.	f.	g.	h.	i.	j.	k.	l.	m.	n.	o.	p.	q.
Acetaldehyde	Press.	Amb.	II	1NA 2 i i	Ind. Pressure.	SR	Restr.	II	P-1	Inert	Vent F	Yes	.55-1(h)	I-C	NA	G
Acetic acid	Atmos.	Amb.	III	1 i i 2 i i	Integral Gravity.	Open	Open	II	G-1	NR	Vent N	Yes	.50-73 .55-1(g)	I-D	NA	G
Acetic anhydride	Atmos.	Amb.	III	1 i i 2 i i	Integral Gravity.	PV	Restr.	II	G-1	NR	Vent F	Yes	.50-73 .55-1(g)	I-D	NA	G
Acetone cyanohydrin	Atmos.	Amb.	I	1 i i i 2 i i	Integral Gravity.	PV	Closed	I	G-1	NR	Vent F	Yes	.50-5 .50-70(b) .50-73 .50-81	I-D	NA	G
Acetonitrile	Atmos.	Amb.	III	1 i i 2 i i	Integral Gravity.	PV	Restr.	II	G-1	NR	Vent F	Yes	No	I-D	NA	G
Acrylic acid	Atmos.	Amb.	III	1 i i i 2 i i	Integral Gravity.	PV	Restr.	II	G-1	NR	Vent F	Yes	.50-70(a) .50-73 .50-81 .58-1(a)	I-D	NA	G
Acrylonitrile	Atmos.	Amb.	II	1 i i 2 i i	Integral Gravity.	PV	Closed	II	G-1	NR	Vent F	Yes	.55-1(e) .50-70(a)	I-D	NA	G
Adiponitrile	Atmos.	Amb.	II	1 i i 2 i i	Integral Gravity.	PV	Open	II	G-1	NR	Vent N	Yes	No	I-D	NA	G
Alkylbenzenesulfonic acid (greater than 4%)	Atmos.	Elev.	III	1 i i i 2 i i	Integral Gravity.	Open	Open	II	G-1	NR	Vent N	Yes	.50-73 .58-1(e)	I-B	NA	G
Alkyl(C7–C9) nitrates	Atmos.	Amb.	III	1 i i 2 i i	Integral Gravity.	Open	Open	II	G-1	NR	Vent F	Yes	.50-81 .50-86	NA	NA	G
Allyl alcohol	Atmos.	Amb.	I	1 i i i 2 i i	Integral Gravity.	PV	Closed	I	G-1	NR	Vent F	Yes	.50-5 .50-73	I-C	NA	G

Coast Guard, DHS — Pt. 151, Subpt. 151.05, Table 151.05

Name																
Allyl chloride	Atmos.	Amb.	I	1 i ii / 2 i i	Integral Gravity.	PV	Closed	I	G-1	NR	Vent F	Yes	.50-5	I-D	NA	G
Aluminum sulfate solution.	Atmos.	Amb.	III	1 i / 2 i	Integral Gravity.	Open	Open	II	G-1	NR	Vent N	Yes	.58-1(e)	NA	NA	G
Aminoethylethanolamine.	Atmos.	Amb.	III	1 i / 2 i	Integral Gravity.	Open	Open	II	G-1	NR	Vent N	Yes	.55-1(b)	NA	NA	G
Ammonia, anhydrous	Press.	Amb.	II	1NA 2 i i	Ind. Pressure.	SR250 p.s.i.	Restr.	II	P-2	NR	Vent F	No	.50-30 / .50-32	I-D	NA	G
Ammonia, anhydrous	Atmos.	Low	II	1NA 2 i i	Ind. Gravity	PV	Restr.	II-L	G-2	NR	Vent F	No	.50-30 / .50-32	I-D	.40-1(b)(1)	8
Ammonium bisulfite solution (70% or less).	Atmos.	Amb.	III	1 i / 2 i	Integral Gravity.	Open	Open	II	G-1	NR	Vent N	No	.50-73 / .56-1(a), (b), (c).	NA	NA	G
Ammonium hydroxide (28% or less NH$_3$).	Atmos.	Amb.	III	1 i / 2 i	Integral Gravity.	PV	Restr.	II	G-1	NR	Vent F	No	.56-1(a), (b), (c), (f), (g).	I-D	NA	G
Aniline	Atmos.	Amb.	I	1 i ii / 2 i i	Integral Gravity.	PV	Closed	I	G-1	NR	Vent F	Yes	.50-5 / .50-73	I-D	NA	G
Anthracene oil (Coal tar fraction).	Atmos.	Amb. Elev.	II	1 i ii / 2 i i	Integral Gravity.	Open	Open	II	G-1	NR	Vent N	Yes	No	I-D	NA	G
Argon, *liquefied*	Press.	Low	III	1NA 2 i	Ind. Pressure.	SR	Restr.	II-L	P-1	NR	Vent F	No	.40-1(a) / .50-30 / .50-36	NA	.40-1(a)	G
Benzene	Atmos.	Amb.	III	1 i ii / 2 i i	Integral Gravity.	PV	Closed	II	G-1	NR	Vent F	Yes	.50-60	I-D	NA	G
Benzene hydrocarbon mixtures (containing Acetylenes) (*having 10% Benzene or more*).	Atmos.	Amb.	III	1 i / 2 i	Integral Gravity.	PV	Closed	II	G-1	NR	Vent F	Yes	.50-60 / .56-1(b), (d), (f), (g)..	I-D	NA	G
Benzene hydrocarbon mixtures (*having 10% Benzene or more*).	Atmos.	Amb.	III	1 i ii / 2 i i	Integral Gravity.	PV	Closed	II	G-1	NR	Vent F	Yes	.50-60	I-D	NA	G

Pt. 151, Subpt. 151.05, Table 151.05   46 CFR Ch. I (10–1–13 Edition)

Cargo identification[1]					Tanks				Cargo transfer		Environmental control		Fire protection required	Special requirements in 46 CFR Part 151	Electrical hazard class and group	Temp. control install.	Tank internal inspect. period—years
Cargo name	Pressure	Temp.	Hull type	Cargo segregation tank	Type	Vent	Gauging device	Piping class	Control		Cargo tanks	Cargo handling space					
a.	b.	c.	d.	e.	f.	g.	h.	i.	j.		k.	l.	m.	n.	o.	p.	q.
Benzene, Toluene, Xylene mixtures (having 10% Benzene or more).	Atmos.	Amb.	III	1 i 2 i i	Integral Gravity.	PV	Closed	II	G-1		NR	Vent F	Yes	50-60	I-D	NA	G
Butadiene	Press.	Amb.	II	1NA 2 i i	Ind. Pressure.	SR	Restr.	II	P-2		NR	Vent F	Yes	50-70(a) 50-73	I-B	NA	G
Butadiene, Butylene mixtures (containing Acetylenes).	Press.	Amb.	II	1NA 2 i i	Ind. Pressure.	SR	Restr.	II	P-1		NR	Vent F	Yes	50-30 50-70(a) 50-73 56-1(b), (d), (f), (g).	I-B	NA	G
Butyl acrylate (all isomers).	Atmos.	Amb.	III	1 i 2 i i	Integral Gravity.	PV	Restr.	II	G-1		NR	Vent F	Yes	50-70(a) 50-81(a), (b).	I-D	NA	G
Butylamine (all isomers).	Atmos.	Amb.	II	1 i i 2 i i	Ind. Gravity	PV	Closed	II	G-1		NR	Vent F	Yes	55-1(c)	I-D	NA	G
Butyl methacrylate	Atmos.	Amb.	III	1 i 2 i i	Integral Gravity.	PV	Restr.	II	G-1		NR	Vent F	Yes	50-70(a) 50-81(a), (b).	I-D	NA	G
Butyraldehyde (all isomers).	Atmos.	Amb.	III	1 i 2 i i	Integral Gravity.	PV	Open	II	G-1		NR	Vent F	Yes	55-1(h)	I-C	NA	G
Camphor oil (light)	Atmos.	Amb.	II	1 i i 2 i i	Integral Gravity.	Open	Open	II	G-1		NR	Vent N	Yes	No	I-D	NA	G
Carbolic oil	Atmos.	Amb.	I	1 i i 2 i i	Integral Gravity.	PV	Closed	I	G-1		NR	Vent F	Yes	50-5 50-73	NA	NA	G
Carbon dioxide, liquefied.	Press.	Low	III	1NA 2 i	Ind. Pressure.	SR	Restr.	I-L	P-1		NR	Vent F	No	50-30	NA	40-1(b)(1)	G
Carbon disulfide	Atmos.	Amb.	II	1NA 2 i i	Ind. Gravity	PV	Restr.	II	G-1		Inert	Vent F	Yes	50-40 50-41	I-A	NA	G

Coast Guard, DHS — Pt. 151, Subpt. 151.05, Table 151.05

Carbon tetrachloride	Atmos.	Amb.	III	1 i 2 i	Integral Gravity.	PV	Open	II	G-1	NR	Vent N	No	No	NA	NA	G
Cashew nut shell oil (untreated).	Atmos.	Amb.	III	1 i i 2 i	Integral Gravity.	PV	Restr.	II	G-2	NR	Vent N	Yes	.50-73	NA	NA	G
Caustic potash solution.	Atmos.	Amb. Elev.	III	1 i 2 i	Integral Gravity.	Open	Open	II	G-1	NR	NR	No	.50-73 .55-1(j)	NA	NA	G
Caustic soda solution	Atmos.	Amb. Elev.	III	1 i 2 i	Integral Gravity.	Open	Open	II	G-1	NR	NR	No	.50-73 .55-1(j)	NA	NA	G
Chlorine	Press.	Amb.	I	1NA 2 i i	Ind. Pressure.	SR300 p.s.i.	Indirect	I	P-2	NR	Vent F	No	.50-30 .50-31	NA	NA	3
Chlorobenzene	Atmos.	Amb.	III	1 i 2 i	Integral Gravity.	PV	Open	II	G-1	NR	Vent N	Yes	No	I-D	NA	G
Chloroform	Atmos.	Amb.	III	1 i 2 i	Integral Gravity.	Open	Open	II	G-1	NR	Vent F	No	No	NA	NA	G
Chlorohydrins (crude)	Atmos.	Amb.	I	1 i i 2 i i	Integral Gravity.	PV	Closed	I	G-1	NR	Vent F	Yes	.50-5	I-D	NA	G
o-Chloronitrobenzene	Atmos.	Amb.	I	1 i i 2 i i	Integral Gravity.	PV	Closed	I	G-1	NR	Vent F	Yes	.50-5 .50-73	NA	NA	G
Chlorosulfonic acid	Atmos.	Amb.	III	1 i i 2 i i	Integral Gravity.	PV	Open	II	G-1	NR	Vent N	No	.50-20 .50-21 .50-73	I-B	NA	G
Coal tar naphtha solvent.	Atmos.	Amb.	III	1 i 2 i	Integral Gravity.	PV	Restr.	II	G-1	NR	Vent F	Yes	.50-73	I-D	NA	G
Coal tar pitch (molten)	Atmos.	Elev.	III	1 i i 2 i	Integral Gravity.	PV	Restr.	II	G-1	NR	Vent F	Yes	.50-73	I-D	NA	G
Creosote	Atmos.	Amb.	III	1 i 2 i	Integral Gravity.	Open	Open	II	G-1	NR	Vent N	Yes	No	NA	NA	G
Cresols (all isomers)	Atmos.	Amb.	III	1 i 2 i	Integral Gravity.	Open	Open	II	G-1	NR	Vent N	Yes	No	NA	NA	G
Cresols with less than 5% Phenol, see Cresols (all isomers).													
Cresols with 5% or more Phenol, see Phenol.													

Pt. 151, Subpt. 151.05, Table 151.05   46 CFR Ch. I (10–1–13 Edition)

Cargo identification[1]					Tanks			Cargo transfer		Environmental control		Fire protection required	Special requirements in 46 CFR Part 151	Electrical hazard class and group	Temp. control install.	Tank internal inspect. period—years
Cargo name	Pressure	Temp.	Hull type	Cargo segregation tank	Type	Vent	Gauging device	Piping class	Control	Cargo tanks	Cargo handling space					
a.	b.	c.	d.	e.	f.	g.	h.	i.	j.	k.	l.	m.	n.	o.	p.	q.
Cresylate spent caustic.	Atmos.	Amb.	III	1 i i / 2 i	Integral Gravity.	Open	Open	II	G-1	NR	Vent N	No	.50-73 .... .55-1(b)	NA	NA	G
Cresylic acid, sodium salt solution, see Cresylate spent caustic.																
Crotonaldehyde	Atmos.	Amb.	II	1 i i / 2 i	Integral Gravity.	PV	Restr.	II	G-1	NR	Vent F	Yes	.55-1(h)	I-C	NA	G
Cyclohexanone	Atmos.	Amb.	III	1 i i / 2 i	Integral Gravity.	PV	Restr.	II	G-1	NR	Vent F	Yes	.56-1(a), (b).	I-D	NA	G
Cyclohexanone, Cyclohexanol mixture.	Atmos.	Amb.	III	1 i i / 2 i	Integral Gravity.	PV	Restr.	II	G-1	NR	Vent F	Yes	.56-1(b)	I-D	NA	G
Cyclohexylamine	Atmos.	Amb.	III	1 i i / 2 i	Integral Gravity.	PV	Restr.	II	G-1	NR	Vent F	Yes	.56-1(a), (b), (c), (g).	I-D	NA	G
Cyclopentadiene, Styrene, Benzene mixture.	Atmos.	Amb.	III	1 i i / 2 i	Integral Gravity.	Open	Open	II	G-1	NR	Vent F	Yes	.50-60 .... .56-1(b)	I-D	NA	G
iso-Decyl acrylate	Atmos.	Amb.	III	1 i i / 2 i	Integral Gravity.	Open	Open	II	G-1	NR	Vent N	Yes	.50-70(a) .. .50-81(a), (b). .55-1(c)	NA	NA	G
Dichlorobenzene (all isomers).	Atmos.	Amb.	III	1 i i / 2 i	Integral Gravity.	PV	Restr.	II	G-1	NR	Vent F	Yes	.56-1(a), (b).	I-D	NA	G
Dichlorodifluoromethane.	Press.	Amb.	III	1 NA / 2 i	Ind. Pressure.	SR	Restr.	II	P-1	NR	NR	No	No	NA	NA	G
1,1-Dichloroethane	Atmos.	Amb.	III	1 i i / 2 i	Integral Gravity.	PV	Restr.	II	G-1	NR	Vent F	Yes	No	I-D	NA	G

Coast Guard, DHS
Pt. 151, Subpt. 151.05, Table 151.05

2,2'-Dichloroethyl ether.	Atmos.	Amb.	II	1 i ii 2 i	Integral Gravity.	PV	Restr.	=	G-1	NR	Vent F	Yes	.55-1(f)	I-C	NA	G
Dichloromethane	Atmos.	Amb.	III	1 i 2 i	Integral Gravity.	PV	Restr.	=	G-1	NR	Vent F	No	No	I-D	NA	G
2,4-Dichlorophenoxy acetic acid, diethanolamine salt solution.	Atmos.	Amb.	III	1 i 2 i	Integral Gravity.	Open	Open	=	G-1	NR	Vent N	No	.56-1(a), (b), (c), (g).	NA	NA	G
2,4-Dichlorophenoxyac-etic acid, dimethyl-amine salt solution.	Atmos.	Amb. Elev.	III	1 i 2 i	Integral Gravity.	PV	Restr.	=	G-1	NR	Vent F	No	.56-1(a), (b), (c), (g).	NA	NA	G
2,4-Dichlorophenoxyac-etic acid, triisopropanolamine salt solution.	Atmos.	Amb.	III	1 i 2 i	Integral Gravity.	Open	Open	=	G-1	NR	Vent N	No	.56-1(a), (b), (c), (g).	NA	NA	G
1,1-Dichloropropane	Atmos.	Amb.	III	1 i 2 i	Integral Gravity.	PV	Restr.	=	G-1	NR	Vent F	Yes	No	I-D	NA	G
1,2-Dichloropropane	Atmos.	Amb.	III	1 i 2 i	Integral Gravity.	PV	Restr.	=	G-1	NR	Vent F	Yes	No	I-D	NA	G
1,3-Dichloropropane	Atmos.	Amb.	III	1 i 2 i	Integral Gravity.	PV	Restr.	=	G-1	NR	Vent F	Yes	No	I-D	NA	G
1,3-Dichloropropene	Atmos.	Amb.	II	1 i 2 i	Integral Gravity.	PV	Restr.	=	G-1	NR	Vent F	Yes	No	I-D	NA	G
Dichloropropene, Dichloropropane mixtures.	Atmos.	Amb.	II	1 i ii 2 i	Integral Gravity.	PV	Closed	=	G-1	NR	Vent F	Yes	No	I-D	NA	G
2,2-Dichloropropionic acid.	Atmos.	Amb.	II	1 i 2 i	Integral Gravity.	PV	Restr.	=	G-1	Dry	Vent F	Yes	.50-73 .58-1(e)	NA	NA	G
Diethanolamine	Atmos.	Amb.	III	1 i 2 i	Integral Gravity.	Open	Open	=	G-1	NR	Vent N	Yes	.55-1(c)	NA	NA	G
Diethylamine	Atmos.	Amb.	III	1 i ii 2 i	Integral Gravity.	PV	Restr.	=	G-1	NR	Vent F	Yes	.55-1(c)	I-C	NA	G
Diethylenetriamine	Atmos.	Amb.	III	1 i 2 i	Integral Gravity.	Open	Open	=	G-1	NR	Vent N	Yes	.55-1(c)	NA	NA	G

Pt. 151, Subpt. 151.05, Table 151.05   46 CFR Ch. I (10–1–13 Edition)

Cargo identification[1]					Tanks				Cargo transfer		Environmental control		Fire protection required	Special requirements in 46 CFR Part 151	Electrical hazard class and group	Temp. control install.	Tank internal inspect. period—years
Cargo name	Pressure	Temp.	Hull type	Cargo segregation tank	Type	Vent	Gauging device	Piping class	Control		Cargo tanks	Cargo handling space					
a.	b.	c.	d.	e.	f.	g.	h.	i.	j.		k.	l.	m.	n.	o.	p.	q.
Diethyl ether, see Ethyl ether.																	
Diisobutylamine	Atmos.	Amb.	III	1 i i i 2 i i	Integral Gravity.	PV	Restr.	II	G–1		NR	Vent F	Yes	.55–1(c)	I–C	NA	G
Diisopropanolamine	Atmos.	Amb.	III	1 i i 2 i	Integral Gravity.	Open	Open	II	G–1		NR	Vent N	Yes	.55–1(c)	NA	NA	G
Diisopropylamine	Atmos.	Amb.	II	1 i i i 2 i i	Integral Gravity.	PV	Closed	II	G–1		NR	Vent F	Yes	.55–1(c)	I–C	NA	G
N,N-Dimethylacetamide.	Atmos.	Amb.	III	1 i i i 2 i i	Integral Gravity.	PV	Restr.	II	G–1		NR	Vent F	Yes	.56–1(b)	I–D	NA	G
Dimethylamine	Press.	Amb.	II	1NA 2 i i	Ind. Pressure.	SR	Restr.	II	P–2		NR	Vent F	Yes	.55–1(c)	I–C	NA	G
Dimethylethanolamine	Atmos.	Amb.	III	1 i i 2 i	Integral Gravity.	PV	Restr.	II	G–1		NR	Vent F	Yes	.56–1(b), (c).	I–C	NA	G
Dimethylformamide	Atmos.	Amb.	III	1 i i i 2 i i	Integral Gravity.	PV	Restr.	II	G–1		NR	Vent F	Yes	.55–1(e)	I–D	NA	G
1,4-Dioxane	Atmos.	Amb.	II	1 i i i 2 i i	Integral Gravity.	PV	Closed	II	G–1		Inert	Vent F	Yes	No	I–C	NA	G
Diphenylmethane diisocyanate.	Atmos.	Elev.	II	1 i i i 2 i i	Integral Gravity.	PV	Closed	I	G–1		Inert Dry	Vent F	Yes	.50-5 .56–1(a), (b).	NA	Yes	G
Di-n-propylamine	Atmos.	Amb.	II	1 i i i 2 i i	Integral Gravity.	PV	Restr.	II	G–1		NR	Vent F	Yes	.55–1(c)	I–C	NA	G
Dodecyl- dimethyl-amine, Tetradecyldimethyl-amine mixture.	Atmos.	Amb.	III	1 i i 2 i	Integral Gravity.	Open	Open	II	G–1		NR	Vent N	Yes	.56–1(b)	NA	NA	G
Dodecyl phenol	Atmos.	Amb.	I	1 i i 2 i	Integral Gravity.	Open	Open	II	G–1		NR	Vent N	Yes	.50–73	I–D	NA	2

142

Pt. 151, Subpt. 151.05, Table 151.05

Name	Pressure	Temp.	Grade	Subdivision	Tank type	Gauging	Vapor rec.	Type	Materials	Protection	Ventilation	Fire prot.	Special req.	Cargo	Pollution	Class
Epichlorohydrin	Atmos.	Amb.	I	1 i; 2 i i	Integral Gravity	PV	Closed	I	G-1	NR	Vent F	Yes	.50-5	I-C	NA	G
Ethanolamine	Atmos.	Amb.	III	1 i; 2	Integral Gravity	Open	Open	II	G-1	NR	Vent N	Yes	.55-1(c)	I-D	NA	G
Ethyl acrylate	Atmos.	Amb.	III	1 i; 2 i i	Integral Gravity	PV	Restr.	II	G-1	NR	Vent F	Yes	.50-70(a); .50-81(a),(b).	I-D	NA	G
Ethylamine solution (72% or less)	Atmos.	Amb.	II	1 i i; 2 i i	Integral Gravity	PV	Closed	II	G-1	NR	Vent F	Yes	.55-1(b)	I-D	NA	G
N-Ethylbutylamine	Atmos.	Amb.	III	1 i; 2 i i	Integral Gravity	PV	Restr.	II	G-1	NR	Vent F	Yes	.55-1(b)	I-C	NA	G
Ethyl chloride	Press.	Amb.	II	1NA; 2 i i	Ind. Pressure	SR	Restr.	II	P-2	NR	Vent F	Yes	No	I-D	NA	8
N-Ethylcyclohexylamine	Atmos.	Amb.	III	1 i; 2 i i	Integral Gravity	PV	Restr.	II	G-1	NR	Vent F	Yes	.55-1(b)	I-C	NA	G
Ethylene chlorohydrin	Atmos.	Amb.	I	1 i; 2 i i	Integral Gravity	PV	Closed	I	G-1	NR	Vent F	Yes	.50-5; .50-73	I-D	NA	G
Ethylene cyanohydrin	Atmos.	Amb.	III	1 i; 2 i i	Integral Gravity	Open	Open	II	G-1	NR	Vent N	Yes	No	NA	NA	G
Ethylenediamine	Atmos.	Amb.	III	1 i; 2 i i	Integral Gravity	PV	Restr.	II	G-1	NR	Vent F	Yes	.55-1(c)	I-D	NA	G
Ethylene dibromide	Atmos.	Amb.	II	1 i; 2	Integral Gravity	PV	Closed	II	G-1	NR	Vent F	No	No	NA	NA	G
Ethylene dichloride	Atmos.	Amb.	III	1 i; 2 i i	Integral Gravity	PV	Restr.	II	G-1	NR	Vent F	Yes	No	I-D	NA	G

Cargo identification[1]					Tanks				Cargo transfer			Environmental control		Fire protection required	Special requirements in 46 CFR Part 151	Electrical hazard class and group	Temp. control install.	Tank internal inspect. period—years
Cargo name	Pressure	Temp.	Hull type	Cargo segregation tank	Type	Vent	Gauging device		Piping class	Control		Cargo tanks	Cargo handling space					
a.	b.	c.	d.	e.	f.	g.	h.		i.	j.		k.	l.	m.	n.	o.	p.	q.
Ethylene glycol monoalkyl ethers. Including: 2-Ethoxyethanol Ethylene glycol butyl ether Ethylene glycol tert-butyl ether Ethylene glycol ethyl ether Ethylene glycol methyl ether Ethylene glycol n-propyl ether Ethylene glycol iso-propyl ether	Atmos.	Amb.	III	1 i 2 i	Integral Gravity.	PV	Restr.		II	G-1		NR	Vent F	Yes	No	I-C	NA	G
Ethylene glycol hexyl ether.	Atmos.	Amb.	III	1 i 2 i	Integral Gravity.	Open	Open		II	G-1		NR	Vent N	Yes	No	NA	NA	G
Ethylene glycol propyl ether.	Atmos.	Amb.	III	1 i 2 i	Integral Gravity.	Open	Open		II	G-1		NR	Vent N	Yes	No	NA	NA	G
Ethylene oxide	Press.	Amb.	I	1NA 2 i	Ind. Pressure.	SR	Restr.		II	P-2		Inert	Vent F	Yes	.50-10 .50-12	I-B	.40-1(c)	4
Ethyl ether	Atmos.	Amb.	II	1NA 2 i	Ind. Gravity	PV	Closed		II	G-1		Inert	Vent F	Yes	.50-40 .50-42	I-C	NA	G
2-Ethylhexyl acrylate	Atmos.	Amb.	III	1 i 2 i	Integral Gravity.	Open	Open		II	G-1		NR	Vent N	Yes	.50-70(a) .50-81(a), (b).	I-D	NA	G
Ethylidene norbornene	Atmos.	Amb.	II	1 i 2 i	Integral Gravity.	PV	Closed		II	G-1		NR	Vent F	Yes	.50-5 .50-74	NA	NA	G
Ethyl methacrylate	Atmos.	Amb.	III	1 i 2 i	Integral Gravity.	PV	Restr.		II	G-1		NR	Vent F	Yes	.50-70(a)	I-D	NA	G

Pt. 151, Subpt. 151.05, Table 151.05

Cargo	Pressure	Temp	Type	Subs	Tank	Venting	Gauging	Class	Electrical	NR	Vent	Inert	Special Requirements	Cargo Transfer		Firefighting
2-Ethyl-3-propylacrolein.	Atmos.	Amb.	III	1 i i / 2 i	Integral Gravity.	PV	Restr.	II	G-1	NR	Vent F	Yes	No	I-C	NA	G
Ferric chloride solutions.	Atmos.	Amb.	III	1 i i / 2 i i	Integral Gravity.	Open	Open	II	G-1	NR	Vent N	No	.50-20, .50-75	I-B	NA	G
Fluorosilicic acid (30% or less).	Atmos.	Amb.	=	1 i i / 2 i i	Ind. Gravity.	PV	Closed	II	G-1	NR	Vent F	No	.50-20, .50-22, .50-73, .50-77	I-B	NA	4
Formaldehyde solution (37% to 50%).	Atmos.	Amb.	III	1 i i / 2 i i	Integral Gravity.	PV	Restr.	II	G-1	NR	Vent F	No	.55-1(h)	I-B	NA	G
Formic acid.	Atmos.	Amb.	III	1 i i / 2 i i	Integral Gravity.	PV	Restr.	II	G-1	NR	Vent F	Yes	.50-73, .55-1(i)	I-D	NA	G
Furfural.	Atmos.	Amb.	III	1 i i / 2 i i	Integral Gravity.	PV	Restr.	II	G-1	NR	Vent F	Yes	.55-1(h)	I-C	NA	G
Glutaraldehyde solution (50% or less).	Atmos.	Amb.	III	1 i i / 2 i i	Integral Gravity.	Open	Open	II	G-1	NR	Vent N	No	No	NA	NA	G
Glyoxylic acid solution (50% or less).	Atmos.	Amb.	III	1 i i / 2 i i	Integral Gravity.	Open	Open	II	G-1	NR	Vent N	Yes	.50-73, .50-81, .58-1(e)	NA	NA	G
Hexamethylenediamine solution.	Atmos.	Amb.	III	1 i i / 2 i i	Integral Gravity.	PV	Restr.	II	G-1	NR	Vent F	Yes	.55-1(c)	I-D	NA	G
Hexamethyleneimine.	Atmos.	Amb.	III	1 i i / 2 i i	Integral Gravity.	PV	Restr.	II	G-1	NR	Vent F	Yes	.56-1(b), (c).	I-C	NA	G
Hydrochloric acid.	Atmos.	Amb.	III	1 NA / 2 i i	Ind. Gravity.	Open	Open	II	G-1	NR	Vent F	No	.50-20, .50-22, .50-73	I-B	NA	4
Hydrofluorosilicic acid (25% or less), see Fluorosilicic acid (30% or less).																
2-Hydroxyethyl acrylate.	Atmos.	Amb.	I	1 i i / 2 i i	Integral Gravity.	PV	Closed	I	G-1	NR	Vent F	Yes	.50-5, .50-70(a), .50-73, .50-81(a), (b).	NA	NA	G

Cargo identification[1]					Tanks				Cargo transfer		Environmental control		Fire protection required	Special requirements in 46 CFR Part 151	Electrical hazard class and group	Temp. control install.	Tank internal inspect. period—years
Cargo name	Pressure	Temp.	Hull type	Cargo segregation tank	Type	Vent	Gauging device	Piping class	Control		Cargo tanks	Cargo handling space					
a.	b.	c.	d.	e.	f.	g.	h.	i.	j.		k.	l.	m.	n.	o.	p.	q.
Isoprene	Atmos.	Amb.	III	1 i i 2 i i	Integral Gravity.	PV	Open	II	G-1		NR	Vent F	Yes	.50-70(a) .50-81(a), (b).	I-D	NA	G
Kraft pulping liquors (free alkali content 3% or more) (including: Black, Green, or White liquor).	Atmos.	Amb.	III	1 i i 2 i	Integral Gravity.	Open	Open	II	G-1		NR	NR	No	.50-73 .56-1(a), (c), (g).	NA	NA	G
Mesityl oxide	Atmos.	Amb.	III	1 i i 2 i i	Integral Gravity.	PV	Restr.	II	G-1		NR	Vent F	Yes	No	I-D	NA	G
Methylacetylene, Propadiene mixture.	Press.	Amb.	III	1 NA 2 i i	Ind. Pressure.	SR	Restr.	II	P-2		NR	Vent F	Yes	.50-79	I-C	NA	G
Methyl acrylate	Atmos.	Amb.	III	1 i i 2 i	Integral Gravity.	PV	Restr.	II	G-1		NR	Vent F	Yes	.50-70(a) .50-81(a), (b).	I-D	NA	G
Methylamine solution (42% or less).	Atmos.	Amb.	II	1NA 2 i i	Ind. Gravity	PV	Closed	II	G-1		NR	Vent F	Yes	.56-1(a), (b), (c), (g).	I-D	NA	G
Methyl bromide	Press.	Amb.	I	1NA 2 i i i	Ind. Pressure.	SR	Closed	I	P-2		NR	Vent F	Yes	.50-5	I-D	NA	2
Methyl chloride	Press.	Amb.	II	1NA 2 i i	Ind. Pressure.	SR	Restr.	II	P-2		NR	Vent F	Yes	.55-1(c)	I-D	NA	8
Methylcyclopentadiene dimer.	Atmos.	Amb.	III	1 i 2 i	Integral Gravity.	PV	Restr.	II	G-1		NR	Vent F	Yes	No	I-B	NA	G
Methyl diethanolamine	Atmos.	Amb.	III	1 i 2 i	Integral Gravity.	Open	Open	II	G-1		NR	Vent N	Yes	.56-1(b), (c).	I-C	NA	G
2-Methyl-5-ethylpyridine.	Atmos.	Amb.	III	1 i 2 i	Integral Gravity.	Open	Open	II	G-1		NR	Vent N	Yes	.55-1(e)	I-D	NA	G

Pt. 151, Subpt. 151.05, Table 151.05

Chemical																
Methyl methacrylate	Atmos.	Amb.	III	1 i 2 i	Integral Gravity.	PV	Restr.	II	G-1	NR	Vent F	Yes	.50-70(a) .50-81(a), (b).	I-D	NA	G
2-Methylpyridine	Atmos.	Amb.	III	1 i 2 i i	Integral Gravity.	PV	Restr.	II	G-1	NR	Vent F	Yes	.55-1(c)	I-D	NA	G
alpha-Methylstyrene	Atmos.	Amb.	III	1 i 2 i i	Integral Gravity.	PV	Restr.	II	G-1	NR	Vent F	Yes	.50-70(a) .50-81(a), (b).	I-D	NA	G
Monochloro-difluoromethane.	Press.	Amb.	III	1NA 2 i	Ind. Pressure.	SR	Restr.	I	P-1	NR	NR	No		NA	NA	G
Morpholine	Atmos.	Amb.	III	1 i 2 i i	Integral Gravity.	Open	Open	II	G-1	NR	Vent N	Yes	.55-1(c)	I-C	NA	G
Motor fuel anti-knock compounds (containing lead alkyls).	Atmos.	Amb.	I	1 i 2 i i	Ind. Gravity	PV	Closed	I	G-1	NR	Vent F	Yes	.50-70(a) .50-81(a), (b).	I-D	NA	.50-6
Nitric acid (70% or less).	Atmos.	Amb.	II	1 i i 2 i i	Integral Gravity.	PV	Restr.	II	G-1	NR	Vent F	No	.50-20 .50-73 .50-80	I-B	NA	4
Nitrobenzene	Atmos.	Amb.	I	1 i 2 i i	Integral Gravity.	PV	Closed	I	G-1	NR	Vent F	Yes	.50-5 .50-73	I-D	NA	G
Nitrogen, *liquefied*	Press.	Low	III	1NA 2 i	Ind. Pressure.	SR	Restr.	II-L	P-1	NR	Vent F	No	.40-1(a) .50-30 .50-36	NA	.40-1(a)	G
1- or 2-Nitropropane	Atmos.	Amb.	III	1 i 2 i i	Integral Gravity.	PV	Restr.	II	G-1	NR	Vent F	Yes	.50-81	I-C	NA	G
o-Nitrotoluene	Atmos.	Amb.	I	1 i 2 i i	Integral Gravity.	PV	Closed	I	G-1	NR	Vent F	Yes	.50-5 .50-73	I-D	NA	G
Octyl nitrates (all isomers), see Alkyl(C7–C9) nitrates.																
Oleum	Atmos.	Amb.	III	1 i i 2 i i	Integral Gravity.	Open	Open	II	G-1	NR	Vent N	No	.50-20 .50-21 .50-73	I-B	NA	4
Pentachloroethane	Atmos.	Amb.	III	1 i 2 i i	Integral Gravity.	PV	Restr.	II	G-1	NR	Vent F	No	No	NA	NA	G

Cargo identification[1]					Tanks			Cargo transfer		Environmental control		Fire protection required	Special requirements in 46 CFR Part 151	Electrical hazard class and group	Temp. control install.	Tank internal inspect. period—years
Cargo name	Pressure	Temp.	Hull type	Cargo segregation tank	Type	Vent	Gauging device	Piping class	Control	Cargo tanks	Cargo handling space					
a.	b.	c.	d.	e.	f.	g.	h.	i.	j.	k.	l.	m.	n.	o.	p.	q.
1,3-Pentadiene	Atmos.	Amb.	III	1 i i 2 i i	Integral Gravity.	PV	Restr.	II	G-1	NR	Vent F	Yes	.50-70(a).. .50-81	I-D	NA	G
Perchloroethylene	Atmos.	Amb.	III	1 i i 2 i i	Integral Gravity.	PV	Restr.	II	G-1	NR	Vent F	No	No	NA	NA	G
Phenol	Atmos.	Amb.	I	1 i i 2 i i	Integral Gravity.	PV	Closed	I	G-1	NR	Vent F	Yes	.50-5 .... .50-73	I-D	NA	2
Phosphoric acid	Atmos.	Amb.	III	1 i i 2 i i	Integral Gravity.	Open	Open	II	G-1	NR	Vent N	No	.50-20 ...... .50-23 ...... .50-73	I-B	NA	4
Phosphorus, white (elemental).	Atmos.	Elev.	I	1 i i 2 i i	Integral Gravity.	PV	Closed	I	G-1	Water Pad	Vent F	Yes	.50-50	NA	NA	4-8
Phthalic anhydride (molten).	Atmos.	Elev.	III	1 i i 2 i i	Integral Gravity.	PV	Restr.	II	G-1	NR	Vent F	Yes	No	I-D	NA	G
Polyethylene polyamines.	Atmos.	Amb.	III	1 i i 2 i i	Integral Gravity.	Open	Open	II	G-1	NR	Vent N	Yes	.55-1(e) ...	NA	NA	G
Polymethylene polyphenyl isocyanate.	Atmos.	Amb.	II	1 i i 2 i i	Integral Gravity.	PV	Closed	II	G-1	Dry	Vent F	Yes	.55-1(e) ...	NA	NA	G
Potassium hydroxide solution, see Caustic potash solution.																
iso-Propanolamine	Atmos.	Amb.	III	1 i i 2 i i	Integral Gravity.	Open	Open	II	G-1	NR	Vent N	Yes	.55-1(c) ...	I-D	NA	G
Propanolamine (iso-, n-).	Atmos.	Amb.	III	1 i i 2 i i	Integral Gravity.	Open	Open	II	G-1	NR	Vent N	Yes	.56-1(b), (c).	I-D	NA	G
Propionic acid	Atmos.	Amb.	III	1 i i 2 i i	Integral Gravity.	Open	Open	II	G-1	NR	Vent N	Yes	.50-73 ...... .55-1(g) ...	I-D	NA	G
iso-Propylamine	Atmos.	Amb.	II	1 i i 2 i i	Integral Gravity.	PV	Closed	II	G-1	NR	Vent F	Yes	.55-1(c) ...	I-D	NA	G

Coast Guard, DHS — Pt. 151, Subpt. 151.05, Table 151.05

Name	Press.	Amb.		1NA 2 i i	Ind. Pressure	SR			Inert	Vent	Yes/No	Refs			
Propylene oxide	Press.	Amb.	II	1NA 2 i i	Ind. Pressure	SR	=	P-1	Inert	Vent F	Yes	.50-10 .50-13	I-B	NA	G
iso-Propyl ether	Atmos.	Amb.	III	1 i i 2 i i	Integral Gravity	PV	=	G-1	Inert	Vent F	Yes	.50-70(a)	I-D	NA	G
Pyridine	Atmos.	Amb.	III	1 i i 2 i i	Integral Gravity	PV	=	G-1	NR	Vent F	Yes	.55-1(e)	I-D	NA	G
Sodium aluminate solution (45% or less)	Atmos.	Amb. Elev.	III	1 i 2 i	Integral Gravity	Open	=	G-1	NR	NR	No	.50-73 .56-1(a), (b), (c)	NA	NA	G
Sodium chlorate solution (50% or less)	Atmos.	Amb.	III	1 i i 2 i	Integral Gravity	Open	=	G-1	NR	Vent N	No	.50-73	NA	NA	G
Sodium dichromate solution (70% or less)	Atmos.	Amb.	II	1 i i 2 i i	Integral Gravity	Open	=	G-1	NR	Vent N	No	.50-5(d) .50-73 .56-1(b), (c)	NA	NA	G
Sodium hydroxide solution, see Caustic soda solution.															
Sodium hypochlorite solution (20% or less)	Atmos.	Amb.	III	1 i i 2 i	Integral Gravity	PV	=	G-1	NR	Vent F	No	.50-73 .56-1(a), (b)	NA	NA	G
Sodium sulfide, hydrosulfide solutions (H_2S 15ppm or less)	Atmos.	Amb.	III	1 i i 2 i	Integral Gravity	Open	=	G-1	NR	Vent N	No	.50-73 .55-1(b)	NA	NA	G
Sodium sulfide, hydrosulfide solutions (H_2S greater than 15ppm but less than 200ppm)	Atmos.	Amb.	III	1 i i 2 i	Integral Gravity	PV	=	G-1	NR	Vent F	No	.50-73 .55-1(b)	NA	NA	G
Sodium sulfide, hydrosulfide solutions (H_2S greater than 200ppm)	Atmos.	Amb.	II	1 i i 2 i	Integral Gravity	PV	=	G-1	NR	Vent F	No	.50-73 .55-1(b)	NA	NA	G
Sodium thiocyanate solution (56% or less)	Atmos.	Amb.	III	1 i i 2 i	Integral Gravity	Open	=	G-1	NR	Vent N	Yes	.58-1(a)	NA	NA	G

149

Pt. 151, Subpt. 151.05, Table 151.05   46 CFR Ch. I (10–1–13 Edition)

Cargo identification[1]					Tanks				Cargo transfer		Environmental control		Fire protection required	Special requirements in 46 CFR Part 151	Electrical hazard class and group	Temp. control install.	Tank internal inspect. period—years
Cargo name	Pressure	Temp.	Hull type	Cargo segregation tank	Type	Vent	Gauging device	Piping class	Control		Cargo tanks	Cargo handling space					
a.	b.	c.	d.	e.	f.	g.	h.	i.	j.		k.	l.	m.	n.	o.	p.	q.
Styrene *monomer*	Atmos.	Amb.	III	1 i i 2 i i	Integral Gravity.	Open	Open	II	G-1		NR	Vent N	Yes	.50-70(a) .50-81(a), (b).	I-D	NA	G
Sulfur (molten)	Atmos.	Elev.	III	1 i i 2 i i	Integral Gravity.	Open	Open	II	G-1		Vent N	Vent N	Yes	.50-55	I-C	.40-1(f)(1)	G
Sulfur dioxide	Press.	Amb.	I	1NA 2 i i	Ind. Pressure.	SR	Closed		P-2		NR	Vent F	No	.50-30 .50-84 .55-1(j)	NA	NA	2
Sulfuric acid	Atmos.	Amb.	III	1 i i i 2 i i	Integral Gravity.	Open	Open	II	G-1		NR	Vent N	No	.50-20 .50-21 .50-73	I-B	NA	4
Sulfuric acid, spent	Atmos.	Amb.	III	1 i i i 2 i i	Integral Gravity.	Open	Open	II	G-1		NR	Vent N	No	.50-20 .50-21 .50-73	I-B	NA	4
1,1,2,2-Tetrachloroethane.	Atmos.	Amb.	III	1 i i 2 i i	Integral Gravity.	PV	Restr.	II	G-1		NR	Vent F	No	No	NA	NA	G
Tetraethylenepentamine.	Atmos.	Amb.	III	1 i i 2 i i	Integral Gravity.	Open	Open	II	G-1		NR	Vent N	Yes	.55-1(c)	I-C	NA	G
Tetrahydrofuran	Atmos.	Amb.	III	1 i i 2 i i	Integral Gravity.	PV	Restr.	II	G-1		NR	Vent F	Yes	.50-70(b)	I-C	NA	G
Toluenediamine	Atmos.	Elev.	II	1 i i 2 i	Integral Gravity.	PV	Closed	II	G-1		NR	Vent F	Yes	.50-73 .56-1(a), (b), (c), (g).	NA	NA	G
Toluene diisocyanate	Atmos.	Amb.	I	1 i i 2 i i	Integral Gravity.	PV	Closed	I	G-1		Dry N₂	Vent F	Yes	.50-5 .55-1(e)	I-D	NA	G
o-Toluidine	Atmos.	Amb.	II	1 i i 2 i i	Integral Gravity.	PV	Closed	II	G-1		NR	Vent F	Yes	.50-5 .50-73	I-D	NA	G
1,2,4-Trichlorobenzene	Atmos.	Amb.	III	1 i i i 2 i i	Integral Gravity.	PV	Restr.	II	G-1		NR	Vent F	Yes	No	I-D	NA	G

Coast Guard, DHS — Pt. 151, Subpt. 151.05, Table 151.05

1,1,2-Trichloroethane	Atmos.	Amb.	III	1 i 2 i	Integral Gravity.	PV	Restr.	II	G-1	NR	Vent F	No	.50-73 .56-1(a)	I-D	NA	G
Trichloroethylene	Atmos.	Amb.	III	1 i 2 i	Integral Gravity.	PV	Restr.	II	G-1	NR	Vent F	No	No	I-D	NA	G
1,2,3-Trichloropropane	Atmos.	Amb.	II	1 i 2 i	Integral Gravity.	PV	Restr.	II	G-1	NR	Vent F	Yes	.50-73 .56-1(a)	I-D	NA	G
Triethanolamine	Atmos.	Amb.	III	1 i 2 i	Integral Gravity.	Open	Open	II	G-1	NR	Vent N	Yes	.55-1(b)	I-C	NA	G
Triethylamine	Atmos.	Amb.	II	1 i 2 i	Integral Gravity.	PV	Restr.	II	G-1	NR	Vent F	Yes	.55-1(e)	I-C	NA	G
Triethylenetetramine	Atmos.	Amb.	III	1 i 2 i	Integral Gravity.	Open	Open	II	G-1	NR	Vent N	Yes	.55-1(b)	I-C	NA	G
Triphenylborane (10% or less), Caustic soda solution.	Atmos.	Amb.	III	1 i 2 i	Integral Gravity.	Open	Open	II	G-1	NR	NR	No	.56-1(a), (b), (c).	NA	NA	G
Trisodium phosphate solution.	Atmos.	Amb. Elev.	III	1 i 2 i	Integral Gravity.	Open	Open	II	G-1	NR	NR	No	.50-73 .56-1(a), (c).	NA	NA	G
Urea, Ammonium nitrate solution (containing more than 2% NH 3).	Atmos.	Amb.	III	1 i 2 i	Integral Gravity.	PV	Restr.	II	G-1	Inert	Vent F	No	.56-1(b)	I-D	NA	G
Valeraldehyde (all Isomers).	Atmos.	Amb.	III	1 i 2 ii	Integral Gravity.	PV	Restr.	II	G-1	NR	NR	Yes	No	I-C	NA	G
Vanillan black liquor (free alkali content 3% or more).	Atmos.	Amb.	III	1 i 2 i	Integral Gravity.	Open	Open	II	G-1	NR	Vent F	No	.50-73 .56-1(a), (c), (g).	NA	NA	G
Vinyl acetate	Atmos.	Amb.	II	1 i 2 ii	Integral Gravity.	PV	Open	II	G-1	NR	Vent F	Yes	.50-70(a) .50-81(a), (b).	I-D	NA	8
Vinyl chloride	Press.	Amb.	II	1NA 2 ii	Ind. Pressure.	SR	Closed	II	P-2	NR	Vent F	Yes	.50-30 .50-34	I-D	NA	8
Vinyl chloride	Atmos.	Low	II	1NA 2 ii	Ind. Gravity	PV	Closed	II-L	G-2	NR	Vent F	Yes	.50-30 .50-34	I-D	.40-1(b)(1)	8

151

Cargo identification[1]					Tanks				Cargo transfer			Environmental control		Fire protection required	Special requirements in 46 CFR Part 151	Electrical hazard class and group	Temp. control install.	Tank internal inspect. period—years
Cargo name	Pressure	Temp.	Hull type	Cargo segregation tank	Type	Vent	Gauging device		Piping class	Control		Cargo tanks	Cargo handling space					
a.	b.	c.	d.	e.	f.	g.	h.		i.	j.		k.	l.	m.	n.	o.	p.	q.
Vinylidene chloride	Atmos.	Amb.	II	1NA 2 i i	Ind. Gravity	PV	Closed		II	P-2		Padded	Vent F	Yes	.55-1(f) .50-70(a) .50-81(a), (b).	I-D	NA	G
Vinyltoluene	Atmos.	Amb.	III	1 i i 2 i i	Integral Gravity.	PV	Restr.		II	G-1		NR	Vent F	Yes	.50-70(a) .50-81 .56-1(a), (b), (c), (g).	I-D	NA	G
For requirements see these sections in Part 151:			.10-1	.13-5	.15-1	.15-5	.15-10		.20-1	.20-5		.25-1	.25-2	.30		111.105 (Subchapter J)	.40	.04-5

See Table 2 of Part 153 for additional cargoes permitted to be carried by tankbarge.
Terms and symbols:
Segregation—Tank—
  Line 1—Segregation of cargo from surrounding waters:
    i = Skin of vessel (single skin) only required. Cargo tank wall can be vessel's hull.
    i i = Double skin required. Cargo tank wall cannot be vessel's hull.
  Line 2—Segregation of cargo space from machinery spaces and other spaces which have or could have a source of ignition:
    i = Single bulkhead only required. Tank wall can be sole separating medium.
    i i = Double bulkhead required. Cofferdam, empty tank, pumproom, tank with Grade E Liquid (if compatible with cargo) is satisfactory.
Internal tank inspection—
  G—Indicates cargo is subject to general provisions of 151.04-5(b).
  Specific numbers in this column are changes from the general provisions.
Abbreviations used:
Tank type: Ind = Independent.
Vent:
  PV = Pressure vacuum valve.
  SR = Safety relief.
Gauging device: Restr. = Restricted.
General usage:
  NR = No requirement.
  NA = Not applicable.
1. The provisions contained in 46 CFR Part 197, subpart C, apply to liquid cargoes containing 0.5% or more benzene by volume.

[USCG 2000–7079, 65 FR 67183, Nov. 8, 2000]

Subpart 151.10—Barge Hull Construction Requirements

§ 151.10-1 Barge hull classifications.

(a) Each barge constructed or converted in conformance with this subpart shall be assigned a hull type number.

(1) Effective dates for certain requirements:

(i) Barges constructed or converted between July 1, 1964, and June 1, 1970, in accordance with the construction requirements of §§ 32.63 and 98.03 of this chapter are considered to comply with the basic provisions of this subpart and will retain the hull type classification for the service for which they were originally approved. Changes in product endorsement will not be considered a change in service, except when a change to a product of higher specific gravity necessitates a reevaluation of the intact and damage stability requirements in subpart E of part 172 of this chapter.

(2) [Reserved]

(b) For this purpose the barge hull types shall be defined as follows:

(1) *Type I barge hull.* Barge hulls classed as Type I are those designed to carry products which require the maximum preventive measures to preclude the uncontrolled release of the cargo. These barges are required to meet:

(i) Standards of intact stability and a modified two compartment standard of subdivision and damage stability, as specified in subpart E of part 172 of this chapter; and

(ii) Hull structural requirements, including an assumed grounding condition.

(2) *Type I-S (special) barge hulls.* Type I-S (special) barge hulls are those constructed or converted for the carriage of chlorine in bulk prior to July 1, 1964, and modified to higher stability standards prior to July 1, 1968, but not meeting the requirements for full Type I classification.

(3) *Type II barge hull.* Barge hulls classed as Type II are those designed to carry products which require significant preventive measures to preclude the uncontrolled release of the cargo. These barges are required to meet:

(i) Standards of intact stability and a modified one compartment standard of subdivision and damage stability, as specified in subpart E of part 172 of this chapter; and

(ii) Hull structural requirements, including an assumed grounding condition.

(4) *Type III barge hull.* Barge hulls classed as Type III are those designed to carry products of sufficient hazard to require a moderate degree of control. These barges are required to meet:

(i) Standards of intact stability as specified in subpart E of part 172 of this chapter; and

(ii) Hull structural requirements.

[CGFR 70–10, 35 FR 3714, Feb. 25, 1970, as amended by CGD 79–023, 48 FR 51008, Nov. 4, 1983; CGD 88–100, 54 FR 40040, Sept. 29, 1989]

§ 151.10-5 Subdivision and stability.

Each barge must meet the applicable requirements in subchapter S of this chapter.

[CGD 70–023, 48 FR 51009, Nov. 4, 1983]

§ 151.10-15 Certificate endorsement.

(a)–(b) [Reserved]

(c) *Certificate endorsement.* The following information shall be submitted, and upon approval of calculations shall form part of the endorsement on the Certificate of Inspection:

(1) Limiting draft for each hull type service for which approval is requested.

(2) Maximum density (lb./gal.) and maximum cargo weight (tons) for each tank for which approval is requested. Their weights will normally reflect uniform loading except that for trim purposes the individual tank cargo weight may exceed the uniform loading tank cargo weight, corresponding to the barge fresh water deadweight at the limiting draft, by 5 percent. Where a greater degree of nonuniform loading is desired, longitudinal strength calculations shall be submitted.

[CGFR 70–10, 35 FR 3714, Feb. 25, 1970, as amended by CGD 79–023, 48 FR 51009, Nov. 4, 1983]

§ 151.10-20 Hull construction.

(a) *Construction features.* (1) Each barge hull shall be constructed with a suitable bow form (length, shape, and height of headlog) to protect against diving at the maximum speed at which the barge is designed to be towed. In

§ 151.10-20

any integrated tow, only the lead barge need comply with this requirement.

(2) All "open hopper" type barges shall be provided with coamings around the hopper space and a 36-inch minimum height plowshare breakwater on the forward rake. The plowshare breakwater may be omitted, if it is demonstrated to the satisfaction of the Commandant that sufficient protection is achieved without it. Coamings shall have a minimum height of 36 inches forward and may be graduated to a minimum height of 24 inches at midlength and 18 inches thereafter. All hopper barges constructed with a weathertight rain shield over the hopper space are exempt from these requirements, except that they shall be provided with an 18-inch minimum coaming all around the hopper.

(3) All "open hopper" type barges modified for the carriage of chlorine in bulk shall be provided with 36-inch minimum height coamings around the hopper.

(4) All barges in ocean or coastwise service shall be provided with a structural deck and hatches in accordance with the applicable provisions of subchapter E of this chapter and the scantling requirements of the American Bureau of Shipping.

(b) *Hull structural requirements.* (1) All Types I, II, and III barges shall comply with the basic structural requirements of the American Bureau of Shipping for barges of the ordinary types and the applicable supplementary requirements of this section.

(2) Types I and II barges in inland service: A grounding condition shall be assumed where the forward rake bulkhead rests upon a pinnacle at the water surface. The maximum hull and tank bending moment and tank saddle reactions (if applicable) shall be determined. The hull bending stress shall not exceed the applicable limits of paragraphs (b)(2) (i), (ii), or (iii) of this section. The maximum tank bending moment and saddle reaction shall be used in the tank design calculations required by § 151.15-2(b)(3).

(i) Independent tanks supported by only two saddles do not contribute to the strength and stiffness of the barge hull. In such case, the hull stress shall not exceed either 50 percent of the minimum ultimate tensile strength of the material or 70 percent of the yield strength when specified, whichever is greater.

(ii) Independent tanks supported by three or more saddles contribute to the strength and stiffness of the hull. In such case, the hull stress shall not exceed the percentage stress values prescribed in § 151.10-20(b)(2)(i), multiplied by the quantity

$(1.5 - SWT/UTS)$,

where SWT is the stress calculated without including the effect of the tanks, and UTS is the minimum ultimate tensile strength of the material. The value SWT, however, shall in no case be more than 75 percent of UTS.

(iii) Integral tanks may be considered as contributing to the strength and stiffness of the barge hull. The hull stresses for integral tank barges shall not exceed the percentage stress values prescribed in paragraph (b)(2)(i), of this section.

(3) Types I and II barges in ocean service:

(i) Independent tank barges with tanks supported by three or more saddles shall be subjected to a $0.6L^{0.6}$ trochoidal wave hogsag analysis to determine the maximum hull and tank bending moments and tank saddle reactions.

(ii) All independent tank barges, regardless of the number of saddle supports shall be subject to a still water bending analysis to determine the hull bending moment. For those barges with independent tanks supported by three or more saddles, this analysis shall consider tank-hull interaction so as to determine tank bending moments and saddle reactions.

(iii) The still water tank bending moments and saddle reactions shall be superimposed upon those obtained by simultaneous application of the following dynamic loadings:

(*a*) Rolling 30° each side (120° full cycle) in 10 seconds.

(*b*) Pitching 6° half amplitude (24° full cycle) in 7 seconds.

(*c*) Heaving $L/80$ half amplitude ($L/20$ full cycle) in 8 seconds.

(iv) The hull structure and saddle support system shall be analyzed, using the maximum hull bending moments and saddle reactions obtained from the foregoing. Bending stress shall not exceed 60 percent of the yield strength or 42 percent of the minimum tensile strength of the material, whichever is less. Critical buckling strength shall be at least 75 percent greater than calculated buckling stresses. The maximum tank bending moments and saddle reactions shall be used in the tank design calculations required by § 151.15–3(b)(8).

Subpart 151.12—Equipment and Operating Requirements for Control of Pollution From Category D NLS Cargoes

SOURCE: CGD 81–101, 52 FR 7777, Mar. 12, 1987, unless otherwise noted.

§ 151.12–5 Equipment for Category D NLS.

The Coast Guard endorses the Certificate of Inspection and for ships making foreign voyages issues the endorsed NLS Certificate required by § 151.12–10 for an oceangoing non-self-propelled ship to carry as bulk cargo the following Category D NLSs if the ship meets the requirements of this part and the requirements applying to ships that carry Category D NLS cargoes in §§ 153.470, 153.486, and 153.490 of this chapter:

Acetic acid
Acrylic acid
Adiponitrile
Aminoethylethanolamine
Ammonium bisulfite solution
Butyl methacrylate
Caustic soda solution
Coal tar pitch
Cyclohexanone
Cyclohexanone, Cychexanol mixture
Dichloromethane
2,2-Dichloropropionic acid
Diethylenetriamine
N,N-Dimethylacetamide
Dimethylethanolamine
Dimethylformamide
1,4-Dioxane
Ethanolamine
N-Ethylcyclohexylamine
Ethylene cyanohydrin
Ethylene glycol monoalkyl ethers
Ethyl methacrylate
Formic acid
Glutaraldehyde solution
Glyoxylic acid solution (50% or less)
Hydrochloric acid
Mesityl oxide
Methyl methacrylate
Morpholine
1- or 2-Nitropropane
Phosphoric acid
Polyethylene polyamines
Polymethylene polyphenyl isocyanate
Propionic acid
iso-Propyl ether
Pyridine
Tetraethylenepentamine
Tetrahydrofuran
Triethanolamine
Triethylenetetramine

[CGD 81–101, 52 FR 7777, Mar. 12, 1989, as amended by CGD 88–100, 54 FR 40040, Sept. 29, 1989; CGD 92–100, 59 FR 17028, Apr. 11, 1994; CGD 94–900, 59 FR 45139, Aug. 31, 1994; CGD 94–902, 60 FR 34043, June 29, 1995; USCG 2000–7079, 65 FR 67196, Nov. 8, 2000]

§ 151.12–10 Operation of oceangoing non-self-propelled ships Carrying Category D NLS.

(a) An oceangoing non-self-propelled ship may not carry in a cargo tank a Category D NLS cargo listed under § 151.12–5 unless the ship has on board a Certificate of Inspection and for ships making foreign voyages an NLS Certificate endorsed under that section to allow the cargo tank to carry the NLS cargo.

(b) The person in charge of an oceangoing non-self-propelled ship that carries a Category D NLS listed under § 151.12–5 shall ensure that the ship is operated as prescribed for the operation of oceangoing ships carrying Category D NLSs in §§ 153.901, 153.909, 153.1100, 153.1102, 153.1104, 153.1106, 153.1124, 153.1126, 153.1128, 153.1130 and 153.1132 of this chapter.

[CGD 81–101, 52 FR 7777, Mar. 12, 1987, as amended by CGD 81–101, 53 FR 28974, Aug. 1, 1988 and 54 FR 12629, Mar. 28, 1989]

Subpart 151.13—Cargo Segregation

§ 151.13–1 General.

This subpart prescribes the requirements for cargo segregation for cargo tanks. These requirements are based on considerations of cargo reactivity, stability, and contamination of the surroundings and other cargoes.

[CGD 88–100. 54 FR 40029, Sept. 29, 1989, as amended by CGD 96–041, 61 FR 50731, Sept. 27, 1996]

§ 151.13-5 Cargo segregation—tanks.

(a) The configurations listed in this paragraph refer to the separation of the cargo from its surroundings and list the various degrees of segregation required. Paragraphs and (2) of this section explain the symbols used in lines 1 and 2, in order, under the tank segregation column of Table 151.05.

(1) Segregation of cargo from surrounding waters (Line 1 of Table 151.05).

- i = Skin of vessel (single skin) only required. Cargo tank wall can be vessel's hull.
- ii = Double skin required. Cargo tank wall cannot be vessel's hull.
- NA = Nonapplicable for this case. Independent tanks already have such segregation built in through design.

(2) Segregation of cargo space from machinery spaces and other spaces which have or could have a source of ignition (Line 2 of Table 151.05).

- i = Single bulkhead only required. Tank wall can be sole separating medium.
- ii = Double bulkhead, required. Cofferdam, empty tank, pumproom, tank with Grade E Liquid (if compatible with cargo) is satisfactory.

(b) [Reserved]

(c) If a cofferdam is required for segregation purposes and a secondary barrier is required for low temperature protection by § 151.15-3(d)(4), the void space between the primary and secondary barriers shall not be acceptable in lieu of the required cofferdam.

[CGFR 70-10, 35 FR 3714, Feb. 25, 1970, as amended by CGD 75-59, 45 FR 70273, Oct. 23, 19805; CGD 96-041, 61 FR 50731, Sept. 27, 1996]

Subpart 151.15—Tanks

§ 151.15-1 Tank types.

This section lists the definitions of the various tank types required for cargo containment by Table 151.05.

(a) *Integral.* A cargo containment envelope which forms a part of the vessel's hull in which it is built, and may be stressed in the same manner and by the same loads which stress the contiguous hull structure. An integral tank is essential to the structural completeness of its vessel's hull.

(b) *Independent.* A cargo containment envelope which is not a contiguous part of the hull structure. An independent tank is built and installed so as to eliminate, wherever possible (or, in any event, to minimize) its stressing as a result of stressing or motion of the adjacent hull structure. In general, therefore, motion of parts of the tank relative to the adjacent hull structure is possible. An independent tank is not essential to the structural completeness of its carrying vessel's hull.

(c) *Gravity.* Tanks having a design pressure (as described in Part 54 of this chapter) not greater than 10 pounds per square inch gauge and of prismatic shape or other geometry where stress analysis is neither readily nor completely determinate. (Integral tanks are of the gravity type.)

(d) *Pressure.* Independent tanks whose design pressure (as described in Part 54 of this chapter) is above 10 pounds per square inch gauge and fabricated in accordance with part 54, of this chapter. Independent gravity tanks which are of normal pressure vessel configuration (i.e., bodies of revolution, in which the stresses are readily determinate) shall be classed as pressure vessel type tanks even though their maximum allowable working pressure is less than 10 pounds per square inch gauge. Pressure vessel tanks shall be of Classes I, I-L, II, II-L, or III, as defined in subchapter F of this chapter.

§ 151.15-3 Construction.

This section lists the requirements for construction of the types of cargo tanks defined in § 151.15-1.

(a) *Gravity type tanks.* Gravity type cargo tanks vented at a pressure of 4 pounds per square inch gauge or less shall be constructed and tested as required by standards established by the American Bureau of Shipping or other recognized classification society. Gravity type tanks vented at a pressure exceeding 4 but not exceeding 10 pounds per square inch gauge will be given special consideration by the Commandant.

(b) *Pressure vessel type tanks.* Pressure vessel type tanks shall be designed and tested in accordance with the requirements of Part 54 of this chapter.

Coast Guard, DHS § 151.15–3

(1) Uninsulated cargo tanks, where the cargo is transported, at or near ambient temperatures, shall be designed for a pressure not less than the vapor pressure of the cargo at 115 °F. The design shall also be based on the minimum internal pressure (maximum vacuum), plus the maximum external static head to which the tank may be subjected.

(2) When cargo tanks, in which the cargo is transported at or near ambient temperature, are insulated with an insulation material of a thickness to provide a thermal conductance of not more than 0.075 B.t.u. per square foot per degree Fahrenheit differential in temperature per hour, the tanks shall be designed for a pressure of not less than the vapor pressure of the cargo at 105 °F. The insulation shall also meet the requirements of paragraph (f) of this section.

(3) Cargo tanks in which the temperature is maintained below the normal atmospheric temperature by refrigeration or other acceptable means shall be designed for a pressure of not less than 110 percent of the vapor pressure corresponding to the temperature of the liquid at which the system is maintained, or the pressure corresponding to the greatest dynamic and static loads expected to be encountered in service. For mechanically stressed relieved cargo tanks, additional factors relating design pressure and maximum allowable pressure shall be as specified by the Commandant. The material of the tank shall meet the material requirements specified in part 54 of this chapter for the service temperature, and this temperature shall be permanently marked on the tank as prescribed in § 54.10–20 of this chapter.

(4) The maximum allowable temperature of the cargo is defined as the boiling temperature of the liquid at a pressure equal to the setting of the relief valve.

(5) The service temperature is the minimum temperature of a product at which it may be contained, loaded and/or transported. However, the service temperature shall in no case be taken higher than given by the following formula:

$t_z = t_w - 0.25(t_w - t_B)$

where:
t_z=Service temperature.
t_w=Boiling temperature of gas at normal working pressure of container but not higher than +32 °F.
t_B=Boiling temperature of gas at atmospheric pressure.

Under normal circumstances, only temperatures due to refrigerated service will be considered in determining the service temperature. Refrigerated service for purposes of this paragraph is defined as service where the temperature is controlled in the process rather than being caused by atmospheric conditions.

(6) Heat transmission studies, where required, shall assume the minimum ambient temperatures of 0 °F still air and 32 °F still water, and maximum ambient temperatures of 115 °F still air and 90 °F still water.

(7) Where applicable, the design of the cargo tanks shall investigate the thermal stresses induced in the tanks at the service temperature.

(8) Calculations showing the stress level in the tanks under dynamic loading conditions for ocean service barges (see § 151.10–20(b)(4)) and grounding conditions for inland service barges (see § 151.10–20–(b)(2)) shall be submitted to the Commandant for approval. These calculations shall take into account the local stresses due to the interaction between the barge hull and the tanks.

(c) *High density cargo.* Cargoes with a specific gravity greater than that for which the scantlings of the tank are designed may be carried provided that:

(1) The maximum cargo weight (tons) in a specific tank does not exceed the maximum cargo weight (tons) endorsed on the certificate of inspection.

(2) The scantlings of the tank are sufficient to prevent rupture under a full head of the higher density cargo. Scantlings meeting ordinary bulkhead requirements for the full head will satisfy this requirement.

(d) *Arrangements*—(1) *Collision protection.* (i) Tanks containing cargoes which are required to be carried in Type I hulls by Table 151.05 shall be located a minimum of 4 feet inboard from the side shell and box end of the vessel. Tanks containing cargoes which are required to be carried in Type II

§ 151.15-3

hulls by Table 151.05 shall be located a minimum of 3 feet inboard from the side shell and box end of the vessel.

(ii) All independent cargo tanks installed on Type I or Type II barge hulls shall be protected with suitable collision chocks or collision straps. A longitudinal collision load of one and one half times the combined weight of the tank and the cargo shall be assumed. All other independent cargo tanks shall be provided with suitable collision chocks or collision straps assuming a longitudinal collision load equal to the combined weight of the tank and the cargo. The design bearing stress shall not exceed 2 times the yield strength or 1.5 times the minimum ultimate strength, whichever is less.

(iii) Tanks containing cargoes, which are required to be carried in Type I or Type II hulls by Table 151.05, shall be located a minimum of 25 feet from the head log at the bow. Box barges and trail barges need not comply with this requirement.

(2) *Inspection clearances.* The distance between tanks or between a tank and the vessel's structure shall be such as to provide adequate access for inspection and maintenance of all tank surfaces and hull structure; but shall not normally be less than 15 inches except in way of web frames or similar major structural members where the minimum clearance shall be equal to the flange or faceplate width.

(3) *Access openings.* Each tank shall be provided with at least a 15″×18″ diameter manhole, fitted with a cover located above the maximum liquid level as close as possible to the top of the tank. Where access trunks are fitted to tanks, the diameter of the trunks shall be at least 30 inches.

(4) *Low temperature protection.* (i) When low temperature cargoes are to be carried in gravity type tanks at a temperature lower than that for which the hull steel is adequate, a secondary barrier designed to contain leaked cargo temporarily shall be provided. The design of the cargo containment system shall be such that under normal service conditions, or upon failure of the primary tank, the hull structure shall not be cooled down to a temperature which is unsafe for the materials involved. The secondary barrier and structural components of the hull which may be exposed to low temperatures shall meet the material requirements (i.e., chemistry and physical properties) specified in part 54 of this chapter for the service temperature involved. Heat transmission studies and tests may be required to demonstrate that the structural material temperatures in the hull are acceptable.

(ii) The design shall take into consideration the thermal stresses induced in the cargo tank at the service temperature during loading.

(iii) Where necessary, devices for spray loading or other methods of precooling or cooling during loading shall be included in the design.

(iv) Pressure-vessel type tanks shall be radiographed in accordance with the requirements of part 54 of this chapter. For gravity type tanks, all weld intersections or crossings in joints of primary tank shells shall be radiographed for a distance of 10 thicknesses from the intersection. All other welding in the primary tank and in the secondary barrier, shall be spot radiographed in accordance with the requirements specified in part 54 of this chapter for Class II-L pressure vessels.

(v) For nonpressure vessel type containment systems, access shall be arranged to permit inspection one side each of the primary tank and secondary barrier, under normal shipyard conditions. Containment systems which, because of their peculiar design, cannot be visually inspected to this degree, may be specially considered provided an equivalent degree of safety is attained.

(e) *Installation of cargo tanks.* (1) Cargo tanks shall be supported on foundations of steel or other suitable material and securely anchored in place to prevent the tanks from shifting when subjected to external forces. Each tank shall be supported so as to prevent the concentration of excessive loads on the supporting portions of the shell or head.

(2) Foundations, and stays where required, shall be designed for support and constraint of the weight of the full tank, and the dynamic loads imposed thereon. Thermal movement shall also be considered.

Coast Guard, DHS § 151.15-3

(3) Foundations and stays shall be suitable for the temperatures they will experience at design conditions.

(4) Cargo tanks may be installed "on deck," "under deck," or with the tanks protruding through the deck. All tanks shall be installed with the manhole openings located in the open above the weather deck. Provided an equivalent degree of safety is attained, the Commandant may approve cargo tanks installed with manhole openings located below the weather deck. Where a portion of the tank extends above the weather deck, provision shall be made to maintain the weathertightness of the deck, except that the weathertightness of the upper deck need not be maintained on:

(i) Vessels operating on restricted routes which are sufficiently protected; or,

(ii) Open hopper type barges of acceptable design.

(5) No welding shall be performed on tanks which require and have been stress relieved unless authorized by the Commandant.

(f) *Materials.* (1) Materials used in the construction of cargo tanks shall be suitable for the intended application and shall be in accordance with the applicable requirements of part 54 of this chapter. For cargoes carried at low temperatures, the tank supports and foundations, and portions of the hull which may be exposed to low temperature, shall also meet the applicable requirements of that part.

(2) When required, cargo tanks shall be lined with rubber or other material acceptable to the Commandant. The interior surfaces of the cargo tanks shall be made smooth, welds chipped or ground smooth, and the surfaces thoroughly cleaned before the lining is applied. The lining material shall be resistive to attack by the cargo, not less elastic than the metal of the tank proper, and nonporous when tested after application. It shall be of substantially uniform thickness. The lining shall be directly bonded to the tank plating, or attached by other satisfactory means acceptable to the Commandant.

(g) *Insulation.* (1) Insulation, when provided, shall be compatible with the cargo and the tank materials.

(2) Insulation in a location exposed to possible high temperature or source of ignition shall be one of the following:

(i) Incombustible, complying with the requirements of Subpart 164.009 of Part 164 of this chapter; or

(ii) Fire retardant, having a flame spread rating of 50 or less as determined by ASTM Specification E 84 (incorporated by reference, see § 151.01-2) (Tunnel Test); or,

(iii) Nonburning or "self-extinguishing" as determined by ASTM Specification D 4986, "Horizontal Burning Characteristics of Cellular Polymeric Materials" (incorporated by reference, see § 151.01-2) and covered by a steel jacket having a minimum thickness of 18 gauge (0.0428 inches) (U.S. Standard Gauge) or an equivalent means of protection acceptable to the Commandant.

(3) Insulation in a location protected against high temperature or source of ignition need satisfy no requirement for combustibility.

(4) Insulation shall be impervious to water vapor, or have a vapor-proof coating of a fire-retardant material acceptable to the Commandant. Unless the vapor barrier is inherently weather resistant, tanks exposed to the weather shall be fitted with a removable sheet metal jacket of not less than 18 gauge over the vapor-proof coating and flashed around all openings so as to be weathertight. Insulation which is not exposed to the weather when installed on tanks carrying cargoes above ambient temperatures need not be impervious to water vapor nor be covered with a vapor-proof coating.

(5) Insulation shall be adequately protected in areas of possible mechanical damage.

(h) *Fire exposure protection.* Tanks which are provided with fire exposure protection of one of the following categories may be allowed a reduction in the size of relief valves.

(1) Approved incombustible insulation meeting the requirements of subpart 164.007 of part 164 of this chapter which is secured to the tank with steel bands.

(2) Located in a hold or protected by a self-supporting steel jacket or cover (such as a hopper cover) of at least 10 gauge (0.1345) for insulation.

§ 151.15-5

(i) Tanks not protected against fire exposure as described in this paragraph shall not be permitted a reduction in size of relief valves.

[CFGR 70–10, 35 FR 3714, Feb. 25, 1970, as amended by CGD 88–100, 54 FR 40040, Sept. 29, 1989; USCG–1999–5151, 64 FR 67183, Dec. 1, 1999; USCG–2000–7790, 65 FR 58363, Sept. 29, 2000]

§ 151.15-5 Venting.

This section contains definitions and requirements for the various methods of venting specified in Table 151.05. In addition to the requirement that all vents must penetrate into tanks at the top of the vapor space, the following methods of venting and the applicable restrictions are listed:

(a) *Open venting.* A venting system which offers no restriction (except pipe losses and flame screen, where used) to the movement of liquid or vapor to or from the cargo tank (via the vent) under normal operating conditions. The total cross-sectional area of the vents shall not be less than the total cross-sectional area of the filling pipe or pipes. Ullage openings may be counted as part of the required cross-sectional area: *Provided,* That each cargo tank has at least one permanent vent. The minimum size of a cargo tank vent shall be not less than 2½ inches. The outlet end of the vent shall terminate in a gooseneck bend and shall be located at a reasonable height above the weather deck, clear of all obstructions. No shut-off valve or frangible disk shall be fitted in the vent lines except that a float check valve may be installed so as to exclude the entry of water into the tank (i.e., to prevent downflooding). An open venting system may be fitted with a flame screen.

(b) *Pressure-vacuum venting.* A normally closed venting system fitted with a device to automatically limit the pressure or vacuum in the tank to design limits. Pressure-vacuum relief valves shall comply with the requirements of subpart 162.017 of this chapter. The required capacity of the venting system shall be in accordance with part 54 of this chapter.

(c) *Safety relief venting.* A closed venting system fitted with a device to automatically limit the pressure in the tank to below its maximum allowable working pressure. The maximum safety relief valve setting shall not exceed the maximum allowable working pressure of the tank. For cargoes carried at ambient temperatures, the minimum safety relief valve setting shall correspond to the saturated vapor pressure of the cargo at 105 °F if carried in an insulated tank, or 115 °F if carried in an uninsulated tank. For cargoes carried below ambient temperature, the safety relief valve setting shall be selected to provide a suitable margin between normal operating pressure of the tank and the opening pressure of the valve but in no case shall it exceed the maximum allowable working pressure of the tank. The safety relief valves shall be of a type approved under subparts 162.001 or 162.018 of subchapter Q of this chapter. The required capacity of the safety relief valves shall be in accordance with the requirements of part 54 of this chapter.

(d) *Rupture disks.* (1) When required by the nature of the cargo, rupture disks may be installed in lieu of or in addition to other pressure limiting devices in accordance with the requirements of § 54.15–13 of this chapter.

(2) When a pressure-vacuum relief valve or safety relief valve normally protected by a rupture disk or breaking pin device is exposed to the cargo due to breakage of the disk, the valve shall be reinspected before being returned to service.

§ 151.15-6 Venting piping.

(a) The back pressure in the relief valve discharge lines shall be taken into account when determining the flow capacity of the relief valve to be used. The back pressure in the discharge line shall be limited to 10 percent of the valve operating pressure or a compensating-type valve shall be used. Suitable provision shall be made for draining condensate which may accumulate in the vent piping.

(b) [Reserved]

§ 151.15-10 Cargo gauging devices.

This section contains definitions and requirements for types of gauging devices specified in Table 151.05.

(a) *Open gauging.* A gauging method which uses an opening in the cargo tank and which may expose the gauge user to the cargo and its vapors. Examples of this type are gauge hatch, ullage hole.

(b) *Restricted.* A gauging device which penetrates the cargo tank and which, in operation, causes or permits the release to the atmosphere of small quantities of cargo vapor or liquid. The amount of cargo released is controlled by the small diameter of the tank penetration opening and by a locally operated valve or similar closure device in that opening. When not in use, this type gauging device is closed to maintain the complete integrity of cargo containment. Examples of this type are rotary tube, fixed tube, slip tube, sounding tube. (See §§ 151.03–49 and 151.15–10(g).)

(c) *Closed.* A gauging device which penetrates the cargo tank, but which is part of a closed system maintaining the complete integrity of cargo containment. This device is designed and installed so as not to release cargo liquid or vapor in any amount to the atmosphere. Examples of this type are automatic float, continuous tape (magnetic coupled), sight glass (protected), electronic probe, magnetic, differential pressure cell.

(d) *Isolated or indirect.* A gauging method or device which is isolated from the tank (no penetration of the tank shell) and which may employ an indirect measurement to obtain the desired quantity. Examples of this type are weighing of cargo, sonic depth gauge (without penetration of tank shell), pipe flow meter.

(e) All gauging devices and related fixtures which form a part of the cargo containment barrier shall be of suitable material and shall be designed for the pressure and temperature of the cargo in accordance with the requirements of Subchapter F of this chapter.

(f) *Use of restricted gauging devices.* (1) When required in Table 151.05, cargoes carried under pressure shall have restricted gauging devices designed so that the maximum bleed valve opening is not larger than 0.055;inch; diameter, unless provided with an excess flow valve. Sounding tubes are prohibited for use with cargoes having a vapor pressure in excess of 14.7 p.s.i.a. at 115 °F, if carried in an uninsulated tank, or at 105 °F, if carried in an insulated tank.

(2) When utilizing a sounding tube, the cargo tank vent system shall be designed to prevent the discharge of cargo through the sounding tube due to pressure build up in the cargo tank vapor space. (See § 151.03–43) When cargoes carried at atmospheric pressure are required to have a restricted gauging device, open gauges may be provided in addition to restricted gauges for this type of cargo. However, open gauges may not be used while cargo transfer operations are actually being performed.

(g) Fixed tube gauges are not acceptable as primary means of gauging. They may be used as a check on the calibration of other gauging devices.

(h) For pressure-vessel type tanks, each automatic float, continuous reading tape or similar type gauge not mounted directly on the tank or dome shall be fitted with a shutoff device located as close to the tank as practicable. When an automatic float gauging device, which gauges the entire height of the tank, is used, a fixed tube gauge set in the range of 85 percent to 90 percent of the water capacity of the tank shall be provided in addition as a means of checking the accuracy of the automatic float gauge, or other alternate means acceptable to the Commandant may be used.

(i) Gauge glasses of the columnar type are prohibited.

(j) Flat sight glasses may be used in the design of automatic float continuous reading tape gauges. However such glasses shall be made of high strength material, suitable for the operating temperatures, of not less than one-half inch in thickness and adequately protected by a metal cover.

[CGFR 70–10, 35 FR 3714, Feb. 25, 1970, as amended by USCG–2005–22329, 70 FR 57183, Sept. 30, 2005]

Subpart 151.20—Cargo Transfer

§ 151.20–1 Piping—general.

(a) Cargo piping systems shall be arranged and fabricated in accordance with this section and Subchapter F. The class of piping system required for a specific cargo shall be as listed in Table 151.05 as a minimum; however, a

§ 151.20-1

higher class may be required when the actual service temperature or pressure so dictates. See Table 56.04-2 of this chapter.

(b) Piping system components shall be suitable for use with the cargoes for which the barge is certificated, and shall be of materials listed in Subchapter F of this chapter, or such other material as the Commandant may specifically approve. All piping materials shall be tested in accordance with the requirements of Subchapter F of this chapter. The valve seat material, packing, gaskets, and all other material which comes into contact with the cargo shall be resistant to the chemical action of the cargoes for which the barge is certificated.

(c) Cargo piping systems, when subject to corrosive attack of the cargo, and when serving cargo tanks which are required by this subchapter to be lined or coated, shall be constructed of, lined or coated with corrosion-resistant material. Vent systems shall be similarly constructed, lined, or coated up to and including the vent control device.

(d) All piping systems components shall have a pressure rating at operating temperature (according to the applicable American National Standards Institute, Inc., pressure/temperature relations) not less than the maximum pressure to which the system may be subjected. Piping which is not protected by a relief valve, or which can be isolated from its relief valve, shall be designed for the greatest of:

(1) The cargo vapor pressure at 115 °F.

(2) The maximum allowable working pressure of the cargo tank.

(3) The pressure of the associated pump or compressor relief valve.

(4) The total discharge head of the associated pump or compressor where a discharge relief valve is not used.

The escape from cargo piping system relief valves shall be run to venting system or to a suitable recovery system. Provisions shall be made for pressure relief of all piping, valves, fittings, etc., in which excessive pressure build-up may occur because of an increase in product temperature.

(e) Provisions shall be made by the use of offsets, loops, bends, expansion joints, etc., to protect the piping and tank from excessive stress due to thermal movement and/or movements of the tank and hull structure. Expansion joints shall be held to a minimum and where used shall be subject to individual approval by the Commandant.

(f) Low temperature piping shall be isolated from the hull structure. Where necessary, arrangements to provide for the protection of the hull structure from leaks in low temperature systems in way of pumps, flanges, etc., shall be provided.

(g) Connections to tanks shall be protected against mechanical damage and tampering. Underdeck cargo piping shall not be installed between the outboard side of cargo containment spaces and the skin of the barge, unless provision is made to maintain the minimum inspection and collision protection clearances (where required) between the piping and the skin. Cargo piping which is external to tanks, and is installed below the weather deck shall be joined by welding, except for flanged connections to shutoff valves and expansion joints.

(h) Piping shall enter independent cargo tanks above the weatherdeck, either through or as close to the tank dome as possible.

(i) Horizontal runs of cargo piping on integral tank barges may be run above or below the weatherdeck. When run below the weatherdeck, the following are applicable:

(1) Horizontal runs located entirely within integral cargo tanks shall be fitted with a stop valve, located inside the tank that is being serviced and operable from the weatherdeck. There shall be cargo compatibility in the event of a piping failure.

(2) Horizontal runs of cargo piping installed in pipe tunnels may penetrate gravity type tanks below the weatherdeck: *Provided,* That each penetration is fitted with a stop valve operable from the weatherdeck. If the tunnel is directly accessible from the weatherdeck without penetrating the cargo tank, the stop valve shall be located on the tunnel side. If the tunnel is not accessible from the weatherdeck, the valve shall be located on the tank side of the penetration.

(3) The tunnel shall comply with all tank requirements for construction, location, ventilation, and electrical hazard. There shall be cargo compatibility in the event of a piping failure.

(4) The tunnel shall have no other openings except to the weatherdeck or a cargo pumproom.

§ 151.20-5 Cargo system valving requirements.

For the purpose of adequately controlling the cargo, both under normal operating and casualty conditions, every cargo piping system shall be provided with one of the following sets of control valves and meet the requirements listed below. Cargo tanks, whether gravity or pressure vessel type, for cargoes having a saturated vapor pressure of 10 pounds per square inch gauge or less at 115 °F (105 °F if the tank is insulated) shall be provided with a valving system designated as Gravity-1. Cargo tanks, whether gravity or pressure vessel type, for cargoes which are carried below ambient temperature and whose vapor pressure is maintained at 10 pounds per square inch gauge or below shall be provided with a valving system designated as Gravity-2. Cargo tanks for cargoes which have vapor pressures above 10 p.s.i.g. at 115 °F (105 °F if tank is insulated) shall be provided with a valving system designated as Pressure-1. Cargo tanks for cargoes which have vapor pressures above 10 pounds per square inch gauge at 115 °F (105 °F if tank is insulated) and which require greater protection due to their hazardous characteristics shall be provided with a valving system designated as Pressure-2. The requirements of paragraphs (a) through (d) of this section for stop valves or excess flow valves to be fitted at tank penetrations are not applicable to nozzles at which pressure vacuum or safety relief valves are fitted.

(a) *Gravity-1 (G-1)*. (1) One manually operated stop valve shall be installed on each tank filling and discharge line, located near the tank penetration.

(2) One stop valve or blind flange shall be installed at each cargo hose connection. When a cargo hose connection is in use, it shall be provided with a stop valve; which may be part of the vessel's equipment or may be part of the shore facility and attached to the barge end of the loading hose. When a cargo hose connection is not in use, it may be secured with a blind flange.

(3) If individual deepwell pumps are used to discharge the contents of each cargo tank, and the pumps are provided with a remote shutdown device, a stop valve at the tank is not required on the tank discharge line.

(b) *Gravity-2 (G-2)*. (1) One manually operated stop valve shall be installed on each tank penetration, located as close as possible to the tank.

(2) One remote operated, quick closing shut-off valve shall be installed at each cargo hose connection.

(3) A remote shutdown device shall be installed for all cargo handling machinery.

(c) *Pressure-1 (P-1)*. (1) One manually operated stop valve and one excess flow valve shall be installed on each tank penetration, located as close as possible to the tank.

(2) One manually operated stop valve shall be installed at each cargo hose connection, when in use.

(d) *Pressure-2 (P-2)*. (1) One manually operated stop valve and one excess flow valve shall be installed at each tank penetration, located as close as possible to the tank.

(2) One remote operated quick closing shutoff valve shall be installed at each cargo hose connection when in use.

(3) No tank penetration shall be less than 1 inch diameter.

(e) Cargo tank penetrations which are connections for gauging or measuring devices need not be equipped with excess flow or remote operated quick closing valves provided that the opening is constructed so that the outward flow of tank contents shall not exceed that passed by a No. 54 drill size (0.055-inch diameter).

(f) The control system for any required quick closing shutoff valves shall be such that the valves may be operated from at least two remote locations on the vessel; if means of fire protection is required by Table 151.05, the control system shall also be provided with fusible elements designed to melt between 208 °F and 220 °F, which will cause the quick closing shutoff valves to close in case of fire. Quick closing shutoff valves shall be of the fail-closed (closed on loss of power) type and be capable of local manual operation. Quick closing shutoff valves shall operate from full open to full closed under all service conditions in not more than 10 seconds, without causing excessive pressure surges.

(g) Excess flow valves, where required, shall close automatically at the rated closing flow of vapor or liquid as tested and specified by the manufacturer. The piping, including fittings, valves, and appurtenances protected by an excess flow valve, shall have a greater capacity than the rated closing flow of the excess flow valve. Excess flow valves may be designed with a bypass not to exceed 0.040–inch diameter opening to allow equalization of pressure, after an operating shutdown.

(h) Suitable means shall be provided to relieve the pressure and remove liquid contents from cargo lines and hoses to the cargo tank or other safe location prior to effecting disconnections.

§ 151.20-10 Cargo system instrumentation.

(a) Each tank operated at other than ambient temperature shall be provided with at least one remote reading temperature sensor located in the liquid phase of the cargo. The temperature gauge shall be located at the cargo handling control station or another approved location.

(b) Where required, each tank equipped with safety relief valves shall be fitted with a pressure gauge which shall be located at the cargo handling control station or at another approved location.

§ 151.20-15 Cargo hose if carried on the barge.

(a) Liquid and vapor line hose used for cargo transfer shall be of suitable material resistant to the action of the cargo. Hose shall be suitable for the temperatures to which it may be subjected and shall be acceptable to the Commandant.

(b) Hose subject to tank pressure, or the discharge pressure of pumps or vapor compressors, shall be designed for a bursting pressure of not less than 5 times the maximum safety relief valve setting of the tank, pump, or compressor, whichever determines the maximum pressure to which the hose may be subjected in service.

(c) Each new type of cargo hose, complete with end fittings, shall be prototype tested to a pressure not less than five times its specified maximum working pressure. The hose temperature during this prototype test shall duplicate the intended extreme service temperature. Thereafter, each new length of cargo hose produced shall be hydrostatically tested at ambient temperature to a pressure not less than twice its maximum working pressure nor more than two-fifths its bursting pressure. The hose shall be marked with its maximum working pressure, and if used in other than ambient temperature service, its maximum or minimum temperature.

§ 151.20-20 Cargo transfer methods.

(a) Cargo transfer may be accomplished by means of gravity, pumping, vapor or gas pressurization, or fluid displacement unless otherwise provided in Subpart 151.50 of this part.

(b) Vapor or gas pressurization may be used only in transferring cargo from pressure vessel type cargo tanks. The pressurizing vapor or gas lines shall be provided with safety relief device in the lines set to open at a pressure no greater than 90 percent of the set pressure of the cargo tank safety relief valve. The pressurizing line shall be fitted with a stop valve at the tank, and a check valve to prevent the accidental release of cargo through the pressure line.

(c) Fluid displacement is permitted with either gravity or pressure vessel type cargo tanks. The displacing fluid shall enter the tank under low relative pressure. The fluid entry line shall be fitted with a safety relief valve set to lift at a pressure no higher than 80 percent of the cargo tank safety relief valve setting.

(d) When cargo vapors are flammable, combustible or toxic, cargo filling lines entering the top of the tank shall lead to a point at or near the bottom. Spray filling lines, discharging near the top of the tank, may be fitted in lieu of, or in addition to, the above cargo filling lines.

Subpart 151.25—Environmental Control

§ 151.25-1 Cargo tank.

When carrying certain commodities regulated by this subchapter, one of the following types of cargo protection may be required, within the main cargo tank, and in some cases, in the space between the primary and secondary barriers.

(a) *Inerted.* All vapor spaces within the cargo tank are filled and maintained with a gas or vapor which will not support combustion and which will not react with the cargo.

(b) *Padded.* All vapor spaces within the cargo tanks are filled and maintained with a liquid, gas (other than air), or vapor which will not react with the cargo.

(c) *Ventilated (forced).* Vapor space above the liquid surface in the tank is continuously swept with air by means of blowers or other mechanical devices requiring power.

(d) *Ventilated (natural).* Vapor space above the liquid surface in the tank is continuously swept with atmospheric air without the use of blowers or other mechanical devices requiring power (e.g., "chimney-effect" ventilation).

(e) *Dry.* All vapor space within the cargo tank is filled and maintained with a gas or vapor containing no more than 100 ppm water.

[CFGR 70–10, 35 FR 3714, Feb. 25, 1970, as amended by CGD 88–100, 54 FR 40340, Sept. 29, 1989]

§ 151.25-2 Cargo handling space.

Pump rooms, compressor rooms, refrigeration rooms, heating rooms, instrument rooms or other closed spaces regularly entered by operating personnel, in which work is performed on the cargo or in which the cargo movement is locally controlled, may be required to be fitted with one of the following types of ventilation:

(a) *Forced ventilation.* The forced ventilation system shall be designed to insure sufficient air movement through these spaces to avoid the accumulation of toxic or flammable vapors and to insure sufficient oxygen to support life, and, in any event, the ventilation system shall have a minimum capacity sufficient to permit a change of air every 3 minutes.

(b) *Natural ventilation.* The natural ventilation system shall be designed to insure sufficient air movement to avoid the accumulation of toxic or flammable vapors and to insure sufficient oxygen to support life.

Subpart 151.30—Portable Fire Extinguishers

§ 151.30-1 Type.

When required by Table 151.05, approved portable fire extinguishers shall be installed in accordance with Subpart 34.50 of this chapter. The fire extinguishing media shall be dry chemical or other suitable agent for all locations.

Subpart 151.40—Temperature or Pressure Control Installations

§ 151.40-1 Definitions.

This section defines the various methods by which the cargo may be heated or cooled.

(a) *Boiloff.* Cargo pressure and temperatures are maintained by permitting the cargo to boil naturally and the cargo vapor thus generated removed from the tank by venting.

(b) *External cargo cooling*—(1) *Cargo vapor compression.* A refrigeration system in which the cargo vapors generated within the tank are withdrawn, compressed, and the lower energy vapor or its condensate returned to the tank.

(2) *External heat exchange.* A refrigeration system in which the cargo vapor or liquid is cooled outside the cargo tanks by being passed through a heat exchanger. Refrigeration is not accomplished by direct compression of the cargo.

(c) *Internal heat exchange.* A refrigeration system in which a cooling fluid is passed through heat transfer coils immersed in the cargo tank liquid or vapor phases.

(d) *Tank refrigeration.* A refrigeration system in which the cooling fluid is passed around the cargo tank exterior in order to remove heat from the tank or its surroundings.

§ 151.40-2

(e) *No refrigeration.* A system that allows the liquefied gas to warm up and increase in pressure. The insulation and tank design pressure shall be adequate to provide for a suitable margin for the operating time and temperatures involved.

(f) *Tank heating.* (1) A system in which the cargo is heated by means of steam or other heat transfer fluid running through coils within or around the tank. The cargo itself does not leave the tank.

(2) A recirculating system in which the cargo leaves the tank, is pumped through a heater and then returned to the tank.

§ 151.40-2 Materials.

Materials used in the construction of temperature or pressure control systems shall be suitable for the intended application and meet the requirements of Subchapter F and the Special Requirements section of this subchapter.

§ 151.40-5 Construction.

Construction of machinery or equipment, such as heat exchangers, condensers, piping, etc., associated with temperature or pressure control systems shall meet the requirements of Subchapter F of this chapter. The electrical portions of these installations shall meet the requirements of Subchapter J of this chapter.

§ 151.40-10 Operational requirements.

Control systems, required by Table 151.05 shall be provided with an audible or visual high cargo temperature or high cargo pressure alarm which is discernible at the towboat. The alarm shall operate when either the pressure or the temperature exceeds the operating limits of the system. The alarm may monitor either pressure or temperature, but must be independent of the control system.

§ 151.40-11 Refrigeration systems.

(a) *Boiloff systems.* The venting of cargo boiloff to atmosphere shall not be used as a primary means of temperature or pressure control unless specifically authorized by the Commandant.

(b) Vapor compression, tank refrigeration, and secondary refrigeration systems: The required cooling capacity of refrigeration systems shall be sufficient to maintain the cargo at design operating conditions with ambient temperature of 115 °F still air and 90 °F still water. The number and arrangement of compressors shall be such that the required cooling capacity of the system is maintained with one compressor inoperative. Portions of the system other than the compressors need not have standby capacity.

Subpart 151.45—Operations

§ 151.45-1 General.

(a) Barges certificated as tank barges (Subchapter D of this chapter) or cargo barges (Subchapter I of this chapter) for the carriage of cargoes regulated by this subchapter shall meet all applicable requirements for operations in the appropriate subchapter; in addition, requirements prescribed in this subpart shall apply to either type of certification.

(b) [Reserved]

§ 151.45-2 Special operating requirements.

(a) The requirements of this section shall apply to all barges carrying in bulk any cargoes regulated by this subchapter; however, the provisions of this section are not applicable to such barges when empty and gas-freed.

(b) When it is necessary to operate box or square-end barges as lead barges of tows, the person in charge of the towing vessel shall control the speed to insure protection against diving and swamping of such barges, having due regard to their design and freeboard, and to the operating conditions.

(c) No cargo tank hatch, ullage hole, or tank cleaning openings shall be opened or remain open except under the supervision of the person in charge, except when the tank is gas free.

(d) Barges, when tendered to the carrier for transportation, shall have all bilges and void spaces (except those used for ballasting) substantially free of water. Periodic inspections and necessary pumping shall be carried out to insure maintenance of such water-free condition in order to minimize the free surface effects, both in longitudinal and transverse directions. Except when otherwise considered necessary for inspection or pumping, all hatch covers and other hull closure devices for void spaces and hull compartments other than cargo spaces shall be closed and secured at all times.

(e) *Cargo signs and cards.* (1) Warning signs shall be displayed on the vessel, port and starboard, facing outboard without obstructions, at all times except when the vessel is gas free. The warning sign shall be rectangular and a minimum of 3 feet wide and 2 feet high. It shall be of sufficient size to accommodate the required alerting information, which shall be shown in black block style letters and numerals (characters) at least 3 inches high on a white background. The minimum spacing between adjacent words and lines of characters shall be 2 inches. The minimum spacing between adjacent characters shall be one-half inch. All characters shall have a minimum stroke width of one-half inch and shall be a minimum of 2 inches wide, except for the letters "M" and "W", which shall be a minimum of 3 inches wide, and except for the letter "I" and the Numeral "1", which may be ½-inch wide. The signs shall have a 2-inch minimum white border clear of characters. The signs shall be maintained legible. The alerting information shall include the following:

WARNING

DANGEROUS CARGO

(This sign may be covered or removed when Subchapter O commodities are not being carried.)

NO VISITORS

NO SMOKING

(This sign may be removed or covered when the commodity is not flammable or combustible.)

NO OPEN LIGHTS

(This sign may be removed or covered when the commodity is not flammable or combustible.)

(2)(i) Names and locations of all cargoes will be displayed in a readily discernible manner on all barges carrying one or more commodities regulated by this subchapter. This may be an individual sign at or on each tank or by a single sign similar to the following example:

Tank No.	Cargo
1P	/xxxx/
1S	/xxxx/
2P	/xxxx/
2S	/xxxx/

These signs may be printed, handwritten, permanent or changeable, but be visible and readable at all times. These signs should be as readable, as those specified in paragraph (e)(1) of this section. Cargoes regulated by other subchapters will be included whenever carried simultaneously with commodities regulated by this subchapter.

(ii) When the dangerous cargo barge is carrying only a single product, the Warning Sign required by paragraph (e)(1) of this section can be considered as meeting the requirements for the cargo location sign. The name of the commodity shall be added to the Warning Sign.

(3) A cargo information card for each cargo regulated by this subchapter shall be carried on the bridge or in the pilot house of the towing vessel, readily available for use by the person in charge of the watch. This information card shall also be carried aboard the barge, mounted near the Warning Sign required by paragraph (e)(1) of this section, in such position as to be easily read by a man standing on the deck of the barge. The minimum card size shall be 7"×9½". The card shall have legible printing on one side only. The card shall be laminated in clear plastic or otherwise made weatherproof. The following data shall be listed:

(i) *Cargo identification and characteristics.* Identification of the cargo, as listed in Table 151.05, its appearance and odor. A statement of the hazards involved and instructions for the safe handling of the cargo and, as applicable, the need for special cargo environments.

(ii) *Emergency procedures.* Precautions to be observed in the event of spills, leaks, or equipment or machinery breakdown and/or uncontrolled release of the cargo into the waterway or atmosphere. Precautions to be observed in the event of exposure of personnel to toxic cargoes.

(iii) *Firefighting procedures.* Precautions to be observed in the event of a fire occurring on or adjacent to the barge, and enumeration of firefighting media suitable for use in case of a cargo fire.

(f) *Surveillance.* During the time the cargo tanks contain any amount of liquid or gaseous dangerous cargoes requiring Type I or Type II barge hulls, the barge shall be under surveillance, as set forth in this paragraph:

(1) The licensed operator, person in command, and mate of a vessel towing a tank barge that need not be manned, and each of them, shall be responsible for monitoring the security and integrity of the tank barge and for ensuring adherence to proper safety precautions. These responsibilities include, but are not limited to—

(i) Ensuring that every tank barge added to the tow has all tank openings properly secured; has its freeing-ports and scuppers, if any, unobstructed; meets any loadline or freeboard requirements; and neither leaks cargo into the water, voids, or cofferdams nor leaks water into the tanks, voids, or cofferdams;

(ii) Ensuring that every tank barge in the tow is properly secured within the tow;

(iii) Ensuring that periodic checks are made of every tank barge in the tow for leakage of cargo into the water, voids, or cofferdams and for leakage of water into the tanks, voids, or cofferdams;

(iv) Knowing the cargo of every tank barge in the tow, all hazards associated with the cargo, and what to do on discovery of a leak;

(v) Ensuring that the crew of the vessel know the cargo of every tank barge in the tow, all hazards associated with the cargo, and what to do on discovery of a leak;

(vi) Reporting to the Coast Guard any leaks from a tank barge in the tow into the water, as required by 33 CFR 151.15; and

(vii) Ensuring that the crew of the vessel and other personnel in the vicinity of the tank barges in the tow follow the proper safety precautions for tank vessels, and that no activity takes place in the vicinity of the barges that could create a hazard.

(2) A towing vessel engaged in transporting such unmanned barges shall not leave them unattended. When a barge is moored, but not gas free, it shall be under the care of a watchman who may be a member of the complement of the towing vessel, or a terminal employee, or other person. This person shall be responsible for the security of the barge and for keeping unauthorized persons off the barge. Such person shall be provided with, read, and have in his possession for ready reference the information cards required by paragraph (e) of this section.

(g) All cargo hatches shall be closed, dogged down, or otherwise tightly secured.

[CFGR 70–10, 35 FR 3714, Feb. 25, 1970, as amended by CGD 88–100, 54 FR 40040, Sept. 29, 1989; CGD 79–116, 60 FR 17158, Apr. 4, 1995]

§ 151.45–3 Manning.

Except as provided for in this section, barges need not be manned unless in the judgment of the Officer in Charge, Marine Inspection, such manning is necessary for the protection of life and property and for safe operation of the vessel. Vessels requiring manning for safe operation shall be subject to additional requirements as determined by the Commandant. Towing vessels, while towing barges which are not required to be manned, shall be provided with and have on board the information card required by § 151.45–2(e)(3). This card shall be in the possession of the master or person in charge.

§ 151.45–4 Cargo-handling.

(a) On a United States tank barge subject to inspection—

(1) The owner and operator of the vessel, and his or her agent, and each of them, shall ensure that no transfer of liquid cargo in bulk or cleaning of a cargo tank takes place unless under the supervision of a qualified person designated as the person in charge of the transfer or the cleaning under Subpart C of 33 CFR part 155.

(2) The person in charge of the transfer shall ensure that enough qualified personnel are on duty to safely transfer liquid cargo in bulk or to safely clean cargo tanks.

(b) *Closing of sea and ballast valves.* All sea and ballast valves are to be

Coast Guard, DHS § 151.45-4

properly aligned and lashed, or sealed in their correct position prior to beginning cargo transfer operations. Under no circumstances shall such valves be secured by locks.

(c) *Connecting for cargo transfer.* (1) Movement of the vessel shall be considered when making the cargo connections to insure safe cargo transfer. Suitable material shall be used in joints and in couplings when making connections to insure that they are tight. Under no circumstances shall less than three bolts be used in a bolted flanged coupling.

(2) When cargo connections are supported by the vessel's tackle, the person in charge of the transfer operations shall inspect the vessel to insure that sufficient tackles are used.

(3) Pans or buckets shall be placed under cargo hose connections.

(4) Cargo transfer operations for any cargo requiring a PV or safety relief venting device in Table 151.05 shall be performed with cargo hatch covers closed.

(d) *Inspection prior to transfer of cargo.* Prior to the transfer of cargo, the person in charge of the transfer operation shall inspect the barge and other cargo equipment to assure himself that the following conditions exist:

(1) The Certificate of Inspection is endorsed for the products to be loaded. Loading restrictions, if any, should be noted.

(2) Warning signs are displayed as required.

(3) Cargo information cards for the product are aboard.

(4) No repair work in way of cargo space is being carried out.

(5) Cargo connections and hatch covers conform with the provisions of paragraph (c) of this section and cargo valves are properly set.

(6) All connections for cargo transfer have been made to the vessel's fixed pipeline system.

(7) In transferring flammable or combustible cargoes, there are no fires or open flames present on the deck, or in any compartment which is located on, facing, open or adjacent to the part of the deck on which cargo connections have been made.

(8) The shore terminal or other tank vessel concerned has reported itself in readiness for transfer of cargo.

(9) All sea valves are properly set and those connected to the cargo piping are closed.

(10) When transferring flammable or combustible cargoes that a determination was made as to whether or not boiler and/or galley fires can be maintained with reasonable safety.

(e) *Duties of the person in charge during transfer operations.* The person in charge of the transfer operations shall control the operations as follows:

(1) Supervise the operation of the cargo system valves.

(2) Start transfer of cargo slowly.

(3) Observe cargo connections and hose for leakage.

(4) Observe operating pressure on cargo systems.

(5) Comply with loading limitations placed on the vessel by the Certificate of Inspection, if, any, for the purpose of not overloading individual tanks or the vessel.

(6) Observe the loading rate for the purpose of avoiding overflow of the tanks.

(f) Cargo transfer operations shall not be started or, if started, shall be discontinued under the following conditions:

(1) During severe electrical storms.

(2) If a fire occurs on the barge, the wharf or in the immediate vicinity.

(3) If potentially dangerous leakage occurs.

(g) No vessel shall come alongside or remain alongside a barge in way of its cargo tanks while it is transferring cargo unless the conditions then prevailing are mutually acceptable to the persons in charge of cargo handling.

(h) *Auxiliary steam, air, fuel, or electric current.* When discharging cargo from one or more barges, the towing vessel may furnish steam, air, fuel, or electric current for pumps on barges or dock, but in no case shall the cargo pass through or over the towing vessel.

(i) *Termination of transfer operations.* When transfer operations are completed, the valves on cargo connections on the vessel shall be closed. The cargo connections shall be drained of cargo.

(j) *Transfer of other cargo or stores on a barge.* (1) Packaged goods, freight, and ship's stores shall not be loaded or discharged during the loading of flammable cargoes except by permission of the person in charge of the transfer operation. Explosives shall not be loaded or carried on any barge containing products regulated by this subchapter.

(2) Where package and general cargo is carried directly over bulk cargo tanks, it shall be properly dunnaged to prevent chafing of metal parts and securely lashed or stowed.

(k) *Transportation of other cargo or stores on barges.* Barges may be permitted to transport deck cargoes directly over bulk cargo spaces when the nature of such deck cargoes and the methods of loading and unloading same do not create an undue hazard. Such barges shall have their decks properly dunnaged to prevent chafing between the steel parts of the vessel and the deck cargo.

(l) Deck construction must be adequate to support the intended load. Provisions for carrying deck cargo shall be endorsed on the Certificate of Inspection by the Officer in Charge, Marine Inspection.

(m) *Emergencies.* In case of emergencies, nothing in the regulations in this subchapter shall be construed as preventing the person in charge of transfer operations from pursuing the most effective action in his judgment for rectifying the conditions causing the emergency.

[CGFR 70–10, 35 FR 3714, Feb. 25, 1970; 35 FR 6431, Apr. 22, 1970, as amended by CGD 75–59, 45 FR 70375, Oct. 23, 1980; CGD 81–059, 54 FR 151, Jan. 4, 1989; CGD 79–116, 60 FR 17158, Apr. 4, 1995]

§ 151.45–5 **Open hopper barges.**

(a) All open hopper barges not constructed or modified in conformance with the provisions of Subpart 151.10 of this part when carrying in bulk any cargoes regulated by this subchapter shall meet the provisions of this section. However, the provisions of this section are not applicable to such barges when empty (not necessarily cleaned or gas-freed).

(1) Except as otherwise provided in this section, no such open hopper type barge shall be placed as lead barge in any tow. These barges shall be placed in protected positions within the tow so that the danger from diving or swamping will be minimized. Where, due to operating conditions, compliance with this paragraph is impossible, the provisions of paragraph (a)(3) of this section apply. The person in charge of the towing vessel shall be responsible for compliance with this paragraph.

(2) No such open hopper type barge shall be moved from a loading facility unless all void spaces and bilges are substantially free of water. Periodic inspections and necessary pumping shall be carried out to insure the maintenance of such water-free conditions, in order to minimize the free surface effect in both the longitudinal and transverse directions. Except when considered necessary for inspection or pumping, all hatch covers and other hull closure devices for void spaces and hull compartments shall be closed and secured at all times. In the case of unmanned barges, the person in charge of the towing vessel shall be deemed to be in charge of the barge, and all requirements to be carried out on the barge shall be carried out by or under the direction of this person.

(3) When an open hopper type barge is in an exposed position, such that protection from swamping provided by adjoining barges cannot be obtained from the location within the tow, it shall be the responsibility of the person in charge of the towing vessel to control speed so as to insure protection against diving and swamping of the barge, having regard to its design and freeboard, and other operating conditions.

(b) To show that special operating requirements apply to a specific open hopper type barge, additional placards or signs shall be displayed in at least four different locations on the barge when the cargoes subject to this part are carried in any form in the cargo tanks. The placards or signs shall be posted on the barge approximately amidships on each side and near the centerline fore and aft facing outboard. Racks, or other suitable means for mounting such placards or signs, shall be so arranged as to provide clear visibility and shall be protected from becoming readily damaged or obscured. The placards or signs shall be at least equal in dimensions to the DOT standard tank car "Dangerous" placard (10¾ inches square or larger) and shall display a circle (10 inches in diameter or larger) with alternating quadrants of white and red, and so mounted that the red quadrants are centered on the vertical axis. The shipper and/or owner of the barge shall be responsible for the installation of the required placards or signs, including maintenance of them while such barge is in temporary storage with cargo aboard. The person in charge of the towing vessel shall be responsible for the continued maintenance of the placards or signs while such barge is in transit.

§ 151.45-6 Maximum amount of cargo.

(a) Tanks carrying liquids or liquefied gases at ambient temperatures regulated by this subchapter shall be limited in the amount of cargo loaded to that which will avoid the tank being liquid full at 105 °F if insulated, or 115 °F if uninsulated. If specific filling densities are designated in Subpart 151.50 of this part, they shall take precedence over that noted above.

(b) Refrigerated and semirefrigerated tanks shall be filled so that there is an outage of at least 2 percent of the volume of the tank at the temperature corresponding to the vapor pressure of the cargo at the safety relief valve setting. A reduction in the required outage may be permitted by the Commandant when warranted by special design considerations. Normally, then, the maximum volume to which a tank may be loaded is:

$V_L = 0.98 d_r V \div d_L$

where:

V_L = Maximum volume to which tank may be loaded.
V = Volume of tank.
d_r = Density of cargo at the temperature required for a cargo vapor pressure equal to the relief valve setting.
d_L = Density of cargo at the loading temperature and pressure.

§ 151.45-7 Shipping papers.

Each barge carrying dangerous cargo shall have on board a bill of lading, manifest, or shipping document giving the name of shipper, location of the loading point, and the kind, grade, and approximate quantity by compartment of each cargo in the barge. Such manifest or bills of lading may be made out by the shipper, master of the towing vessel, owner, or agent of the owner. However, in the case of unmanned barges the master of the towing vessel shall either have a copy of the shipping papers for each barge in his tow or he shall make an entry in the towing vessel's log book giving the name of the shipper, location where the barge was loaded, and the kind, grade, and quantity of cargo by compartment in the barge. The barge shall not be delayed in order to secure the exact quantities of cargo.

§ 151.45-8 Illness, alcohol, drugs.

A person who is under the influence of liquor or other stimulants, or is so ill as to render him unfit to perform service shall not be permitted to perform any duties on the barge.

§ 151.45-9 Signals.

While fast to a dock, a vessel during transfer of bulk cargo shall display a red flag by day or a red light by night, which signal shall be so placed that it will be visible on all sides. When at anchor, a vessel during transfer of bulk cargo shall display a red flag by day, placed so that it will be visible on all sides. This flag may be metallic.

Subpart 151.50—Special Requirements

EDITORIAL NOTE: Nomenclature changes to subpart 151.50 of part 151 appear at 60 FR 50465, Sept. 29, 1995, and 61 FR 50732, Sept. 27, 1996.

§ 151.50-1 General.

Special requirements found in this subpart pertain to specific cargoes and to similar groups of cargoes. These requirements are in addition to and take precedence over any other requirements found in these regulations.

§ 151.50-5 Cargoes having toxic properties.

When table 151.05 refers to this section, the following apply:

(a) [Reserved]

(b) Independent tanks shall be designed and tested for a head of at least 8 feet above the top of the tank using the specific gravity of the product to be carried. In addition, tank design calculations shall demonstrate that the tank can withstand, without rupture, a single loading to the highest level to which the product may rise, if that exceeds 8 feet. In general, plate less than five-sixteenths inch in thickness shall not be used in the fabrication of independent tanks unless otherwise approved.

(c)(1) Cargo tanks transporting liquids having a Reid vapor pressure exceeding 14 pounds per square inch absolute or vented at a gauge pressure exceeding 4 pounds per square inch, or where air or water pressure is used to discharge the cargo, shall be fabricated as arc-welded unfired pressure vessels.

(2) Unfired pressure vessel cargo tanks shall be designed for a pressure not less than the vapor pressure, in pounds per square inch gauge, of the lading at 115 °F, or the maximum air or water pressure used to discharge the cargo, whichever is greater, but in no case shall the design pressure of such tanks be less than 30 pounds per square inch gauge.

(d) *Piping.* (1) The pumps and piping used for cargo transfer shall be independent of all other piping.

(2) Where multiple cargoes are carried, and the cargo piping conveying cargoes covered under this section are led through cargo tanks containing other products, the piping shall be encased in a tunnel.

(3) Where cargo lines handling other products, or bilge and ballast piping are led through tanks containing cargoes covered by this section, the piping shall be enclosed in a tunnel.

(e) Gravity type cargo tanks shall be fitted with an approved pressure-vacuum relief valve of not less than 2½-inch size, which shall be set at a pressure of not less than 3 pounds per square inch gauge, but not in excess of the design pressure of the tank.

(f) The discharge fittings from each safety relief or pressure vacuum relief valve shall be directed in such a manner as to not impinge on another tank, piping or any other equipment which would increase the fire hazard should burning products be discharged from the safety or pressure vacuum relief valve as a result of a fire or other casualty. In addition, the discharges shall be directed away from areas where it is likely that persons might be working and as remote as practicable from ventilation inlets and ignition sources. A common discharge header may be employed if desired. The area near the discharge fittings shall be clearly marked as a hazardous area.

(g) A means shall be provided for either the reclamation or safe venting of vapors during the loading and unloading operations. For this purpose the safety relief or pressure vacuum relief valve shall be provided with a valved bypass to a vapor return line shore connection which shall be used whenever vapor return shore facilities are available. In the event vapors must be vented to the atmosphere, a vent riser shall extend at least 12 feet above the highest level accessible to personnel. The vent riser may be collapsible for ease of stowage when not in use. Vapor return lines or vent risers for tanks carrying the same class product may be connected to a common header system if desired. Tanks carrying cargoes covered by this section shall be vented independent of tanks carrying other products.

(h) The pump room ventilation outlet duct exhausts shall terminate at a distance of at least 6 feet above the enclosed space or pump room and at least 6 feet from any entrance to the interior part of the vessel. The discharge end of the exhaust ducts shall be located so as to preclude the possibility of recirculating contaminated air through the pump room, or other spaces where personnel may be present.

[CGFR 70–10, 35 FR 3714, Feb. 25, 1970, as amended by CGD 88–100, 54 FR 40040, Sept. 29, 1989]

§ 151.50–6 Motor fuel antiknock compounds.

When transporting motor fuel antiknock compounds containing tetraethyl lead and tetramethyl lead the requirements listed in this section shall be observed.

(a) Tanks used for these cargoes shall not be used for the transportation of any other cargo except those commodities to be used in the manufacture of tetraethyl lead and tetramethyl lead.

(b) Pump rooms shall be equipped with forced ventilation with complete air change every 2 minutes. Air analysis shall be run for lead content to determine if the atmosphere is satisfactory prior to personnel entering the pump room.

(c) Entry into cargo tanks used for the transportation of these cargoes is not permitted.

(d) No internal tank inspection is required. If it is desired to internally inspect tanks used for these cargoes, the Commandant must be notified in advance before such inspection is made.

(e) The provisions of § 151.50-5 shall also be met as a requirement for shipping antiknock compounds containing tetraethyl lead and tetramethyl lead.

§ 151.50-10 Alkylene oxides.

(a) For the purpose of this part, alkylene oxides are considered to be ethylene oxide and propylene oxide.

(b) Alkylene oxides transported under the provisions of this part shall be acetylene free.

(c)(1) No other product may be transported in tanks certified for an alkylene oxide except that the Commandant may approve subsequent transportation of other products and return to alkylene oxide service if tanks, piping and auxiliary equipment are adequately cleaned to the satisfaction of the Marine Inspector.

(2) Unless authorized by the Commandant, no other kind of cargo except methane, ethane, propane, butane and pentane shall be on board a tank vessel certificated for the carriage of an alkylene oxide at the same time an alkylene oxide in either the liquid or vapor state is present in any cargo tank. Alkylene oxide tanks shall not be installed in tanks intended for any other cargo.

(d) All valves, flanges, fittings, and accessory equipment shall be of a type suitable for use with the alkylene oxides and shall be made of steel or stainless steel, or other materials acceptable to the Commandant. Impurities of copper, magnesium and other acetylide-forming metals shall be kept to a minimum. The chemical composition of all material used shall be submitted to the Commandant for approval prior to fabrication. Disks or disk faces, seats and other wearing parts of valves shall be made of stainless steel containing not less than 11 percent chromium. Mercury, silver, aluminum, magnesium, copper, and their alloys shall not be used for any valves, gauges, thermometers, or any similar devices. Gaskets shall be constructed of spirally wound stainless steel with "Teflon" or other suitable material. All packing and gaskets shall be constructed of materials which do not react spontaneously with or lower the autoignition temperature of the alkylene oxides.

(e) The pressure rating of valves, fittings, and accessories shall be not less than the maximum pressure for which the cargo tank is designed, or the shutoff head of the cargo pump, whichever is greater, but in no case less than 150 pounds per square inch. Welded fittings manufactured in accordance with A.N.S.I. Standards shall be used wherever possible, and the number of pipe joints shall be held to a minimum. Threaded joints in the cargo liquid and vapor lines are prohibited.

(f) The thermometer shall terminate in the liquid space and shall be attached to the shell by welding with the end of the fitting being provided with a gastight screwed plug or bolted cover.

(g) Automatic float continuous reading tape gauge, and similar types, shall be fitted with a shutoff valve located as close to the tank as practicable, which shall be designed to close automatically in the event of fracture of the external gauge piping. An auxiliary gauging device shall always be used in conjunction with an automatic gauging device.

(h) Filling and discharge piping shall extend to within 4 inches of the bottom of the tank or sump pit if one is provided.

(i) *Venting.* (1) The discharge fittings from each safety relief or pressure vacuum relief valve shall be directed in such a manner as to not impinge on another tank, piping or any other equipment which would increase the fire hazard should burning products be discharged from the safety or pressure vacuum relief valve as a result of a fire or other casualty. In addition, the discharges shall be directed away from areas where it is likely that persons

§ 151.50–10

might be working and as remote as practicable from ventilation inlets and ignition sources. A common discharge header may be employed if desired. The area near the discharge fittings shall be clearly marked as a hazardous area.

(2) A means shall be provided for either the reclamation or safe venting of vapors during the loading and unloading operations. For this purpose, the safety relief or pressure vacuum relief valve shall be provided with a valved bypass to a vapor return line shore connection which shall be used whenever vapor return shore facilities are available. In the event vapors must be vented to the atmosphere, a vent riser shall be connected to the vapor return line and extend at least 12 feet above the highest level accessible to personnel. The vent riser may be collapsible for ease of stowage when not in use. The vent riser shall not be connected to a safety relief or pressure vacuum valve. Vapor return lines or vent risers for tanks carrying the same class product may be connected to a common header system if desired. Tanks carrying alkylene oxides shall be vented independent of tanks carrying other products.

(3) The outlet of each vent riser shall be fitted with acceptable corrosion-resistant flame screen of suitable material or a flame arrester suitable for use with alkylene oxide.

(j) *Ventilation.* (1) All enclosed spaces within the hull shall be vented or ventilated in accordance with the provisions of this subchapter except as otherwise provided for in this subpart.

(2) The enclosed spaces in which the cargo tanks are located shall be inerted by injection of a suitable inert gas or shall be well ventilated.

(3) The enclosed spaces in which the cargo tanks are located, if an inerting system is not installed, shall be fitted with forced ventilation of such capacity to provide a complete change of air every three minutes and arranged in such a manner that any vapors lost into the space will be removed. The ventilation system shall be in operation at all times cargo is being loaded or discharged. No electrical equipment shall be fitted within the spaces or within ten feet of the ventilation exhaust from these spaces.

(4) All ventilation machinery shall be of nonsparking construction and shall not provide a source of vapor ignition.

(5) Each vent shall be fitted with a flame screen of corrosion resistant wire which is suitable for use with the alkylene oxide.

(k)(1) Flexible metal hose fabricated of stainless steel or other acceptable material, resistant to the action of the alkylene oxide, shall be fitted to the liquid and vapor lines during cargo transfer.

(2) The hose shall be marked with the maximum pressure guaranteed by the manufacturer, and with his certification with the words "Certified for _____ Oxide."

(3) Cargo hose intended for alkylene oxide service shall not be used for any other products except those which are compatible with the alkylene oxide.

(l) Vessel shall be electrically bonded to the shore piping prior to connecting the cargo hose. This electrical bonding shall be maintained until after the cargo hose has been disconnected and any spillage has been removed.

(m) Cargo shall be discharged by pumping or by displacement with nitrogen or other acceptable inert gas. In no case shall air be allowed to enter the system. During loading and unloading operations, the vapor shall not be discharged to the atmosphere. Provisions shall be made to return all displaced vapor to the loading facility. The loading rate and the pressure applied to the tank to discharge the cargo shall be so limited to prevent opening the safety relief valves.

(n) During cargo transfer, a water hose with pressure to the nozzle, when atmospheric temperatures permit, shall be connected to a water supply for immediate use during filling and discharge operations and any spillage of alkylene oxide shall be immediately washed away. This requirement can be met by facilities provided from shore.

(o) Prior to disconnecting shore lines, the pressure in the liquid and vapor lines shall be relieved through suitable valves installed at the loading header. The liquid and vapor discharged from these lines shall not be discharged to atmosphere.

(p) The safety relief valves shall be tested by liquid, gas, or vapor pressure at least once every 2 years to determine the accuracy of adjustment and, if necessary, shall be reset. Alkylene oxides shall not be used as the testing medium.

(q) The special requirements for ethylene oxide contained in § 151.50–12 and for propylene oxide contained in § 151.50–13 shall also be observed.

[CGFR 70–10, 35 FR 3714, Feb. 25, 1970, as amended by CGD 85–061, 54 FR 50966, Dec. 11, 1989]

§ 151.50–12 Ethylene oxide.

(a)(1) Ethylene oxide shall be carried in fixed, independent, pressure vessel type cargo tanks, designed, constructed, arranged and, if necessary, equipped with machinery to maintain the cargo temperature below 90 °F except as otherwise provided for in paragraph (a)(3) of this section.

(2) Ethylene oxide shall be loaded at a temperature below 70 °F.

(3) When ethylene oxide is to be transported at or near atmospheric pressure, the Commandant may permit the use of alternate methods of storage which are consistent with the minimum requirements of this subpart.

(b)(1) All cargo tanks shall be constructed of a carbon steel or stainless steel acceptable to the Commandant. Impurities of copper, magnesium and other acetylide-forming metals shall be kept to a minimum. The chemical composition of all steel used shall be submitted to the Commandant for approval prior to fabrication. Aluminum, copper and other acetylide-forming metals, such as silver, mercury, magnesium, and their alloys shall not be used as materials of construction for tanks or equipment used in handling ethylene oxide.

(2) Cargo tanks shall meet the requirements of Class I pressure vessels.

(3) Cargo tanks shall be designed for the maximum pressure of vapor or gas used in discharging the cargo but in no case shall the design pressure of such tanks be less than 75 pounds per square inch gauge. The tank shell and heads shall not be less than $5/16$-inch thick.

(c)(1) Cargo tanks shall be located below deck in holds or enclosed spaces with the domes or trunks extended above the weather deck and terminating in the open. Provisions shall be made to maintain the watertightness of the deck by means of watertight seals around such domes or trunks. The holds or enclosed spaces, in which the ethylene oxide tanks are located, shall not be used for any other purpose. However, in open hopper type barges of a suitable design approved for such service, the weatherdeck may not be required to be watertight.

(2) All cargo tanks shall be installed with the manhole openings and all tank connections located above the weatherdeck in the open.

(3) Tanks shall be electrically bonded to the hull.

(4) No welding of any kind shall be done on cargo tanks or supporting structure unless authorized by the Commandant.

(d) All cargo tanks, piping, valves, fittings, and similar equipment which may contain ethylene oxide in either the liquid or vapor phase, including the vent risers, shall be insulated. Flanges need not be covered, but if covered, a small opening shall be left at the bottom of the flange cover to detect leaks. Insulation shall be of an approved incombustible material suitable for use with ethylene oxide, which does not significantly lower the autoignition temperature and which does not react spontaneously with ethylene oxide. The insulation shall be of such thickness as to provide a thermal conductance of not more than 0.075 B.t.u. per square foot per degree Fahrenheit differential in temperature per hour.

(e)(1) When cooling systems are installed to maintain the temperature of the liquid below 90 °F, at least two complete cooling plants, automatically regulated by temperature variations within the tanks shall be provided; each to be complete with the necessary auxiliaries for proper operation. The control system shall also be capable of being manually operated. An alarm shall be provided to indicate malfunctioning of the temperature controls. The capacity of each cooling system shall be sufficient to maintain the temperature of the liquid cargo at or below the design temperature of the system.

(2) An alternate arrangement may consist of three cooling plants, any two of which shall be sufficient to maintain the temperature of the liquid cargo at

§ 151.50-13

or below the design temperature of the system.

(3) Cooling systems requiring compression of ethylene oxide are prohibited.

(f) In addition to the shutoff valve required, all tank connections larger than one-half inch inside pipe size, except safety relief valves and liquid level gauging devices, shall be fitted with either internal back pressure check valves or internal excess flow valves in conjunction with a quick closing stop valve operable from at least two remote locations. The quick closing stop valve shall be of the "fail safe" type acceptable to the Commandant and shall be equipped with a fusible plug designed to melt between 208 °F and 220 °F, which will cause the quick closing valve to close automatically in case of fire. The quick closing valve shall be located as close to the tank as possible.

(g) Piping systems intended for ethylene oxide service shall not be used for any other product and shall be completely separate from all other systems. The piping system shall be designed so that no cross connections may be made either through accident or design.

(h) Each safety relief valve shall be set to start to discharge at not less than 75 pounds per square inch gauge, nor more than the design pressure of the tank.

(i) The filling density shall not exceed 83 percent.

(j)(1) The cargo shall be shipped under a suitable protective inerting gas system, such as nitrogen. When nitrogen gas is used, the gas inerting system shall be so designed that the vapor space above the liquid cargo will be filled and maintained with a gas mixture of not less than 45 percent nitrogen. Other gases proposed for inerting use may be given consideration by the Commandant. Original charging only of protective inerting gas at the loading facility is not considered adequate. A sufficient amount of spare inerting gas as approved by the Commandant shall be provided on the vessel in order to maintain the proper concentration of the gas in the event of normal leakage or other losses.

(2) Any inerting gas selected should be at least 98 percent pure and free of reactive materials, such as ammonia, hydrogen sulfide, sulfur compounds, and acetylene.

(k) Prior to loading, a sample from the cargo tank will be taken to insure that the pad gas will meet the requirements of paragraph (j) of this section and that the oxygen content of the vapor space will be not more than 2 percent maximum. If necessary, a sample will be taken after loading to insure the vapor space meets this requirement.

(l) The cargo piping shall be inspected and tested at least once in each 2 calendar years.

(m) In those cases where the cargo transfer hose used is not part of the barge's equipment, the person in charge of the transfer operation shall determine that the provisions of § 151.50-10(k) have been met before using this hose. A certificate of test, supplied by the transfer facility, will be considered as adequate for this determination.

(n) The provisions of § 151.50-10 shall be complied with as a requirement for shipping ethylene oxide.

(o) A hydrostatic test of 1½ times the design pressure shall be made on the cargo tanks at least once in each 4 years at the time the internal examination is made and at such other times as considered necessary by the Officer in Charge, Marine Inspection.

[CGFR 70-10, 35 FR 3714, Feb. 25, 1970, as amended by CGD 85-061, 54 FR 50966, Dec. 11, 1989]

§ 151.50-13 Propylene oxide.

(a)(1) Pressure vessel cargo tanks shall meet the requirements of Class II pressure vessels.

(2) Cargo tanks shall be designed for the maximum pressure expected to be encountered during loading, storing and discharging the cargo but in no case shall the design pressure of pressure vessel tanks be less than thirty (30) pounds per square inch gauge. The tank shell and heads shall not be less than ⁵⁄₁₆-inch thick.

(b) When propylene oxide is carried on board a vessel, piping systems in propylene oxide service shall not be used for any other product and shall be completely separate from all other systems. The piping system shall be designed so that no cross connection may be made through inadvertence.

(c) Each safety relief valve shall be set to start to discharge at not less than 30 pounds per square inch gauge, nor more than the design pressure of the tank.

(d) Filling density shall not exceed 80 percent.

(e)(1) The cargo shall be shipped under a suitable protective padding, such as nitrogen gas. Other gases proposed for use as padding may be given consideration by the Commandant. Original charging only of protective gas padding at the loading facility is not considered adequate. A sufficient amount of spare padding gas as approved by the Commandant shall be provided on the vessel in order to maintain the proper concentration of the gas in the event of normal leakage or other losses.

(2) Any padding gas selected should be at least 98 percent pure and free of reactive materials.

(f) Prior to loading, a sample from the cargo tank will be taken to insure that the pad gas will meet the requirements of paragraph (e) of this section and that the oxygen content of the vapor space will be not more than 2 percent maximum. If necessary, a sample will be taken after loading to insure the vapor space meets this requirement.

(g) The cargo piping shall be subjected to a hydrostatic test of 1½ times the maximum pressure to which they may be subjected in service.

(h) The Commandant may permit the transportation of propylene oxide in other than pressure vessel type tanks if it is shown to his satisfaction that a degree of safety is obtained consistent with the minimum requirements of this subpart.

(i) The provisions of § 151.50-10 shall be complied with as a requirement for shipping propylene oxide.

§ 151.50-20   Inorganic acids.

(a)(1) Gravity type cargo tanks shall be designed and tested to meet the rules of the American Bureau of Shipping for a head of water at least 8 feet above the tank top or the highest level the lading may rise, whichever is the greater. The plate thickness of any part of the tank shall not be less than three-eighths inch.

(2) Gravity tank vents. (i) The outlet end of the gravity tank vent shall terminate above the weatherdeck, clear of all obstructions and away from any source of ignition.

(ii) The gravity tank vent shall terminate in a gooseneck bend and shall be fitted with a single flame screen or two fitted flame screens as described in § 151.03–25. No shutoff valve or frangible disk shall be fitted in the vent lines.

(b)(1) Pressure vessel type cargo tanks shall be independent of the vessel's structure and shall be designed for the maximum pressure to which they may be subjected when compressed air is used to discharge the cargo, but in no case shall the design pressure be less than that indicated as follows:

Fluorosilicic Acid—50 pounds per square inch gauge.
Hydrochloric Acid—50 pounds per square inch gauge.
Hydrofluorosilicic Acid, see Fluorosilicic Acid.
Phosphoric Acid—30 pounds per square inch gauge.
Sulfuric Acid—50 pounds per square inch gauge.

(2) Pressure vessel type cargo tanks shall be of welded construction meeting the requirements for Class II or Class III given in Part 54 of this chapter.

(3) When compressed air is used to discharge the cargo, the tank shall be fitted with a vent led to the atmosphere in which a rupture disk shall be installed. The rupture disk shall be designed to burst at a pressure not exceeding the design pressure of the tank. An auxiliary vent to relieve the pressure or vacuum in the tank during the cargo transfer operation may be led from the vent line between the tank and the rupture disk. A shutoff valve may be fitted in the auxiliary vent.

(c) Openings in tanks are prohibited below deck, except for access openings used for inspection and maintenance of tanks, or unless otherwise specifically approved by the Commandant. Openings shall be fitted with bolted cover plates and acid-resistant gaskets.

§ 151.50-21

(d) Where special arrangements are approved by the Commandant to permit a pump suction to be led from the bottom of the tank, the filling and discharge lines shall be fitted with shutoff valves located above the weatherdeck or operable therefrom.

(e) The outage shall not be less than 1 percent.

(f) All enclosed compartments containing cargo tanks and all machinery spaces containing cargo pumps shall be fitted with effective means of ventilation.

(g) A separator shall be fitted in compressed air lines to the tank when air pressure is used to discharge the cargo.

(h) Only installed electric or portable battery lights shall be used during the cargo transfer operations. Smoking is prohibited and the person in charge of cargo transfer shall post No Smoking signs during cargo transfer operations.

(i) Tanks approved for the transportation of acid cargoes subject to this section shall not be used for the transportation of any other commodity, except upon authorization by the Commandant (CG–ENG).

(j) Each cargo tank shall be subjected to an internal examination at least once in every 4 years. If cargo tank lining is required and the lining of the cargo tank has deteriorated in service or is not in place, the Marine Inspector may require the tank to be tested by such nondestructive means as he may consider necessary to determine its condition.

(k) The special requirements for fluorosilicic acid in § 151.50-77, for hydrochloric acid in § 151.50-22, for *hydrofluorosilicic acid, see* fluorosilicic acid, for phosphoric acid in § 151.50-23, and for sulfuric acid in § 151.50-21 also apply to the carriage of those acids.

[CGFR 70–10, 35 FR 3714, Feb. 25, 1970, as amended by GGD 80–001, 46 FR 63279, Dec. 31, 1981; CGD 82–063b, 48 FR 4781, Feb. 3, 1983; CGD 88–100, 54 FR 40040, Sept. 29, 1989; CGD 92–100, 59 FR 17028, Apr. 11, 1994]

§ 151.50-21 Sulfuric acid.

(a) *How sulfuric acid may be carried.* (1) Sulfuric acid of concentration of 77.5 percent (1.7019 specific gravity) (59.8° Baumé) or greater concentrations with or without an inhibitor, provided the corrosive effect on steel measured at 100 °F is not greater than that of 66° Baumé commercial sulfuric acid, may be transported in unlined gravity type cargo tanks or unlined pressure vessel type cargo tanks.

(2) Sulfuric acid of concentration of 65.25 percent (1.559 specific gravity) (52° Baumé) or greater concentrations, provided the corrosive effect on steel measured at 100 °F is not greater than that of 52° Baumé commercial sulfuric acid, may be transported in unlined pressure vessel type cargo tanks independent of the vessel's structure.

(3) Sulfuric acid of concentration not to exceed 65.25 percent (1.559 specific gravity) (52° Baumé) may be transported in gravity type cargo tanks or pressure-vessel type cargo tanks which are lined with lead or other equally suitable acid-resistant material acceptable to the Commandant.

(4) Sulfuric acid of concentration not to exceed 51 percent (1.408 specific gravity) (42° Baumé) and spent sulfuric acid resulting from the use of sulfuric acid in industrial processes may be transported in gravity type cargo tanks which are lined with rubber or other equally suitable acid-resistant material acceptable to the Commandant. See § 151.15-3(f)(2).

(5) Spent or sludge sulfuric acid resulting from the use of sulfuric acid in industrial processes may be transported in unlined gravity type cargo tanks or unlined pressure vessel type cargo tanks, provided the corrosive effect on steel is not greater than that of commercial sulfuric acid as prescribed in paragraph (a)(1) of this section.

(b) Heating coils will be the only acceptable means of liquefying frozen or congealed sulfuric acid.

(c) During cargo transfer, a water hose shall be connected to a water supply ready for immediate use and any leakage or spillage of acid shall be immediately washed down. This requirement can be met by facilities provided from shore.

(d) The requirements of § 151.50-20 are also applicable to the shipment of sulfuric acid.

§ 151.50-22 Hydrochloric acid.

(a) Hydrochloric acid shall be carried in gravity or pressure type cargo tanks which are independent of the vessel's structure provided such tanks are lined with rubber or other equally suitable material acceptable to the Commandant. See § 151.15–3(f)(2).

(b) Notwithstanding the provisions of § 151.50–20(b)(3), compressed air may be used to discharge hydrochloric acid from gravity type cargo tanks only if the tanks are of cylindrical shape with dished heads, provided the air pressure does not exceed the design pressure of the tank but in no case shall it exceed 10 pounds per square inch gauge. Such tanks shall be fitted with pressure relief devices and need not be vented to the atmosphere as required by § 151.50–20(b)(3).

(c) During cargo transfer, a water hose shall be connected to a water supply and be ready for immediate use. Any leakage or spillage of acid shall be immediately washed down. This requirement can be met by facilities provided from shore.

(d) Spent hydrochloric acid or hydrochloric acid adulterated by other chemicals, inhibitors, oils, solvents, water, etc., shall not be transported in bulk except upon authorization by the Commandant (CG–ENG).

(e) The requirements of § 151.50–20 are also applicable to the shipment of hydrochloric acid.

[CFGR 70–10, 35 FR 3714, Feb. 25, 1970, as amended by CGD 88–100, 54 FR 40040, Sept. 29, 1989]

§ 151.50–23 Phosphoric acid.

(a) The term *phosphoric acid* as used in this subpart shall include, in addition to phosphoric acid, aqueous solutions of phosphoric acid, and super phosphoric acid.

(b) Phosphoric acid may be carried in either gravity or pressure type cargo tanks. The tanks shall be rubber-lined, or lined or clad with other suitable material acceptable to the Commandant, or shall be fabricated of a phosphoric acid resistant stainless steel. See § 151.15–3(f)(2).

(c) The vessel's shell plating shall not be used as any part of the boundaries of gravity type cargo tanks.

(d) Cargo piping, including valves, fittings, and flanges where exposed to the acid, shall be rubber-lined, or lined, coated or clad with other corrosion-resistant material, or shall be fabricated of a phosphoric acid resistant stainless steel. Vent piping, including flanges and fittings, shall be similarly protected at least to the height of the flangible disk if such is installed.

(e) Phosphoric acid adulterated by other chemicals, inhibitors, oils, solvents, etc., shall not be transported in bulk cargo tanks except upon authorization by the Commandant (CG–ENG).

(f) The requirements of § 151.50–20 are also applicable to the shipment of phosphoric acid.

[CGFR 70–10, 35 FR 3714, Feb. 25, 1970, as amended by CGD 82–063b, 48 FR 4781, Feb. 3, 1983]

§ 151.50–30 Compressed gases.

(a) All tank inlet and outlet connections, except safety relief valves, liquid level gauging devices, and pressure gauges shall be marked to designate whether they terminate in the vapor or liquid space. Labels, when used, shall be of corrosion-resistant materials and may be attached to valves.

(b) *Venting.* (1) Except as provided in paragraph (b)(2) of this section each safety relief valve installed on a cargo tank shall be connected to a branch vent of a venting system which shall be constructed so that the discharge of gas will be directed vertically upward to a point at least 10 feet above the weatherdeck or the top of any tank or house located above the weatherdeck.

(2) Safety valves on cargo tanks in barges may be connected to individual or common risers which shall extend to a reasonable height above the deck. Where the escape of vapors from the venting system may interfere with towing operations, the installation shall be acceptable to the Commandant, and the arrangement shall be such as to minimize the hazard of escaping vapors. Arrangements specially provided for venting cargo tanks forming part of the hull on unmanned barges will be given special consideration by the Commandant.

(3) The capacity of branch vents or vent headers shall depend upon the number of cargo tanks connected to such branch or header as provided in Table 151.50–30(b)(3).

§ 151.50-30

TABLE 151.50-30(b)(3)—CAPACITY OF BRANCH VENTS OR VENT HEADERS

Number of cargo tanks	Percent of total valve discharge
1 or 2	100
3	90
4	80
5	70
6 or more	60

(4) Return bends and restrictive pipe fittings are prohibited. Vents and headers shall be so installed as to minimize stresses on safety relief valves and their mounting nozzles.

(5) When vent discharge risers are installed, they shall be so located as to protect against physical damage and be fitted with loose raincaps.

(6) When vent discharge risers are installed and their installation in accordance with the provisions of this paragraph results in restrictions in the operation of the barge due to navigation clearances, the vents may be designed so as to be collapsible when passing under such low clearance obstacles.

(c) *Repairs involving welding or burning.* (1) Repairs involving welding or burning shall not be undertaken on the cargo tanks or piping while cargo in either the liquid or vapor state is present therein.

(2) Repairs involving welding or burning on parts of the barge other than cargo tanks or piping may be undertaken provided positive pressure is maintained in the tanks or the tanks have been vented or washed internally.

(d) *Respiratory equipment.* (1) At least one approved self-contained breathing apparatus shall be available in a readily accessible location off the barge at all times during the cargo transfer operations. This equipment shall not be considered to be part of the barge equipment, and the barge shall not be required to carry this equipment en route.

(2) The approved self-contained breathing apparatus, masks, and all respiratory protective devices shall be of types suitable for starting and operating at the temperatures encountered, and shall be maintained in good operating condition.

(3) Personnel involved in the cargo transfer operations shall be adequately trained in the use of the respiratory equipment.

(e) *Filling densities and container design pressure.* For compressed gases transported at or near ambient temperatures, the maximum filling densities and minimum design pressure of container as indicated in Table 151.50-30(e) shall apply. Deviations from the tabulated values shall be submitted to the Commandant for approval. Where cargo is to be carried at temperatures below ambient, the tank shall be designed in accordance with § 151.15-3(b)(3) and the maximum amount of cargo shall be in accordance with § 151.45-6(b).

TABLE 151.50-30(e)—FILLING DENSITIES AND CONTAINER DESIGN PRESSURES

Kind of gas	Maximum permitted filling density (percent by weight, see § 151.03-21)		Minimum design pressure of tank (pounds per square inch gauge)	
	Uninsulated tanks	Insulated tanks	Uninsulated tanks	Insulated tanks
Ammonia, anhydrous	57	58	250	215
Chlorine	125	125	300	300
Dichlorodifluoromethane	123	125	147	127
Dimethylamine	61	62	46	36
Methyl chloride	85	87	131	112
Monochlorodi-fluoromethane	110	113	243	211
Vinyl chloride	86	87	81	67

(f) The shell and head thickness of liquefied compressed cargo tanks shall not be less than five-sixteenths inch.

(g) The special requirements for ammonia (anhydrous) in § 151.50-32, for argon in § 151.50-36, for chlorine in § 151.50-31, for nitrogen in § 151.50-36, and for vinyl chloride in § 151.50-34 also apply to the carriage of those gases.

[CFGR 70-10, 35 FR 3714, Feb. 25, 1970, as amended by CGD 88-100, 54 FR 40040, Sept. 29, 1989]

§ 151.50-31 Chlorine.

(a) *Chlorine barges.* Subparts 98.03 and 98.20 of Part 98 of this chapter have been revoked. However, chlorine barges that were certified in accordance with the requirements of subpart 98.20 of part 98 of this chapter and having hulls modified, if necessary, to comply with §§ 98.03-5(c) and 98.03-25(c) of this chapter, shall be considered as complying with this part.

(b) *Design and construction of cargo tanks.* (1) The cargo tanks shall meet the requirements of Class I pressure vessels.

(2) Tanks shall be designed for a pressure of not less than 300 pounds per square inch gauge. For the maximum allowable working pressure of tanks in service, see paragraph (q) of this section.

(3) Each tank shall be provided with one or more 24-inch inside diameter manhole, fitted with a cover located above the maximum liquid level and as close as possible to the top of the tank. There shall be no other openings in the tank.

(c) Tanks may be installed "on deck" or "under deck" with the tank protruding above deck. If a portion of the tank extends above the weatherdeck, provision shall be made to maintain the weathertightness on the deck. All tanks shall be installed with the manhole opening located above the weatherdeck. Hopper type barges operating on protected inland waters may have tanks located in the hopper space.

(d) All valves, flanges, fittings and accessary equipment shall be of a type suitable for use with chlorine and shall be made of metal, corrosion-resistant to chlorine in either the gas or liquid phase. Cast or malleable iron shall not be used. Valves, flanges, and flanged joints shall be 300 pounds A.N.S.I. standard minimum with tongue and groove or raised face. Joints shall be fitted with sheet lead or other suitable gasket material. Welded fittings shall be used wherever possible and the number of pipe joints held to a minimum. Threaded joints in cargo lines and vapor lines shall not be used in sizes above 1 inch internal diameter. Welded "hammerlock" unions or other unions approved by the Commandant may be used at terminal points of fixed barge piping.

(e) Each tank shall be provided with liquid and vapor connections fitted with manually operated shutoff valves and with safety relief valves. All valves shall be bolted to the cover or covers specified in paragraph (b)(3) of this section and shall be protected against mechanical damage by a suitable protective metal housing. A drain connection shall be provided from the protective housing.

(f) All liquid and vapor connections, except safety relief valves, shall be fitted with automatic excess flow valves, which shall be located on the inside of the tank. Bypass openings are not permitted in excess flow valves.

(g) Chlorine barge cargo piping shall not be fitted with the nonreturn valves specified by § 151.20-20(b).

(h) Liquid level gauging devices of any type are prohibited on chlorine tanks.

(i) A pressure gauge shall be attached to the vapor shutoff valve or vapor line so as to indicate the pressure in the tank at all times during loading and unloading.

(j) Piping including connections between tank valves and fixed barge piping, shall be of a thickness of not less than Schedule 80.

(k) In multiple tank installations the tanks shall not be interconnected by piping or manifolds which may contain liquid chlorine. Manifolding of vapor lines of individual tanks into a common header for connection to shore is permitted. More than one cargo tank may be filled or discharged at a time, provided each tank is filled from or discharged to shore tanks through separate lines.

(l) Connections between fixed barge piping and shore piping shall be fabricated from one of the following:

(1) Schedule 80 seamless pipe, having flexible metallic joints.

(2) Corrosion-resistant metallic pipe (equivalent to Schedule 80) not subject to deterioration by chlorine, having flexible metallic joints.

§ 151.50-31

(3) Flexible metallic hose acceptable to the Commandant. If paragraphs (k)(1) or (2) of this section are used, the flexible metallic joints shall meet the requirements for cargo hose. See § 151.04-5(h).

(m) Safety relief valves shall discharge into the protective housing surrounding the valves. Suitable provisions shall be made to vent the housing. The arrangement shall be such as to minimize the hazard of escaping vapors.

(n) *Cargo transfer operations.* (1) The amount of chlorine loaded into each cargo tank shall be determined by weight. Draft marks shall not be used as a means of weighing. Any chlorine vapors vented during the filling operation shall be disregarded when calculating the maximum amount of chlorine to be loaded into the cargo tanks.

(2) Prior to the start of filling operations, care shall be exercised to insure that the cargo tanks are empty, dry, and free from foreign matter.

(3) After the filling operation is completed, the vapor in each cargo tank shall be analyzed to determine the percentage of gaseous chlorine in the vapor space. If it should contain less than 80 percent chlorine by volume, vapors shall be withdrawn through the vent or vapor line until the vapor in the cargo tanks contains at least 80 percent chlorine by volume.

(4) After filling connections are removed, upon completion of the loading of a cargo tank, all connections at the tank shall be tested for leakage of chlorine by the aqua ammonia method.

(5) The chlorine in the cargo tanks shall be discharged by the pressure differential method. If the vapor pressure of the chlorine is not sufficient to force the liquid out of the tank, compressed air, or other nonreactive gas, may be used to secure the desired rate of discharge, provided the air or gas is oil-free and thoroughly dried by passing it over activated aluminum oxide, silica gel, or other acceptable drying agent, and provided the supply pressure is limited to 75 percent of maximum allowable pressure of chlorine tanks.

(6) After completion of cargo transfer, any liquid chlorine in the cargo piping shall be removed and cargo transfer piping shall be disconnected at the cargo tanks. After disconnecting the cargo piping, both ends of the line shall be closed and all inlet and outlet valves on the tank shall be plugged or fitted with blind flanges.

(o) During cargo transfer, every person on the barge shall carry on his person a respiratory protective device which will protect the wearer against chlorine vapors and will provide respiratory protection for emergency escape from a contaminated area resulting from cargo leakage. This respiratory protective equipment shall be of such size and weight that the person wearing it will not be restricted in movement or in the wearing of a life-saving device.

(p) During each internal inspection, each cargo tank must be tested hydrostatically to 1½ times the maximum allowable pressure as determined by the safety relief valve setting.

(q) During each internal inspection, each cargo tank excess flow valve and safety relief valve must be inspected and tested in accordance with paragraphs (g) and (i) of § 151.04-5 of this chapter.

(r) When periodic inspection indicates that a cargo tank has deteriorated in service, the maximum allowable pressure shall be recalculated, using the minimum thickness found by actual measurement. The recalculated maximum allowable pressure shall be not less than 275 pounds per square inch gauge. If the recalculated maximum allowable pressure is less than 275 pounds per square inch gauge, the cargo tanks shall be withdrawn from service.

(s) The following substances shall not be carried as stores on board barges transporting chlorine in bulk: hydrogen, methane, liquefied petroleum gases, coal gas, acetylene, ammonia, turpentine, compounds containing metallic powders, finely divided metals or finely divided organic materials.

(t) The requirements of § 151.50-30 for compressed gases are also applicable to the shipment of chlorine.

[CGFR 70-10, 35 FR 3714, Feb. 25, 1970, as amended by CGD 85-061, 54 FR 50966, Dec. 11, 1989; CGD 85-061, 55 FR 41918, Oct. 16, 1990]

§ 151.50-32 Ammonia, anhydrous.

(a) The anhydrous ammonia tanks may be installed in the bulk liquid cargo tanks provided the liquid surrounding the enclosed anhydrous ammonia tanks complies with the following chemical and physical properties:

(1) Boiling point above 125 °F atmospheric pressure.

(2) Inert to ammonia at 100 °F at atmospheric pressure.

(3) Noncorrosive in the liquid and vapor phase to the ammonia tanks and piping.

(b) Copper, copper alloys, and copper bearing alloys shall not be used as materials of construction for tanks, pipelines, valves, fittings, and other items of equipment that may come in contact with anhydrous ammonia liquid or vapor.

(c) Valves, flanges and pipe fittings shall be of the tongue and groove or raised-face type, fitted with suitable gasket material. Welded fittings shall be used wherever possible and the number of pipe joints shall be held to a minimum. Threaded joints are not permitted for pipe diameters exceeding 2 inches. Brazed joints are prohibited.

(d) All enclosed spaces containing cargo tanks fitted with bottom outlet connections shall be provided with mechanical ventilation of sufficient capacity to assure a change of air every 3 minutes.

(e) Each cargo tank shall be electrically grounded to the hull.

(f) When transferring cargo, a hose shall be connected to a water supply so that if leakage of anhydrous ammonia occurs the vapor may be dispersed by the use of water fog. This requirement can be met by facilities provided from shore.

(g) During cargo transfer operations, every person on the vessel shall carry on his person or have close at hand at all times a canister mask approved for ammonia or each person shall carry on his person a respiratory protective device which will protect the wearer against ammonia vapors and will provide respiratory protection for emergency escape from a contaminated area resulting from cargo leakage. This respiratory protective equipment shall be of such size and weight that the person wearing it will not be restricted in movement or in the wearing of a life-saving device.

(h) [Reserved]

(i) The requirements of § 151.50-30 for compressed gases are also applicable to the shipment of anhydrous ammonia.

[CGFR 70-10, 35 FR 3714, Feb. 25, 1970, as amended by CGD 85-061, 54 FR 50966, Dec. 11, 1989]

§ 151.50-34 Vinyl chloride (vinyl chloride monomer).

(a) Copper, aluminum, magnesium, mercury, silver, and their alloys shall not be used as materials of construction for tanks, pipelines, valves, fittings, and other items of equipment that may come in contact with vinyl chloride liquid or vapor.

(b) Valves, flanges, and pipe fittings shall be of the tongue and groove or raised-face type, fitted with suitable gasket material. Welded fittings shall be used wherever possible and the number of pipe joints shall be held to a minimum. Threaded joints are not permitted for pipe diameters exceeding 2 inches. Brazed joints are prohibited.

(c) Each cargo tank shall be electrically grounded to the hull.

(d) The vessel shall be electrically bonded to the shore piping prior to connecting the cargo hose. This electrical bonding shall be maintained until after the cargo hose has been disconnected and any spillage has been removed.

(e) To the extent he deems it necessary, the Officer in Charge, Marine Inspection, may require that sufficient insulation shall be removed from insulated tanks at least once in each 8 calendar years to permit spot external examination of the tanks and insulation in accordance with § 151.04-5(c).

(f) The requirements of § 151.50-30 for compressed gases are also applicable to the shipment of vinyl chloride.

(g) The person in charge of cargo transfer shall ensure that:

(1) Cargo vapors are returned to the cargo tank or shore disposition for reclamation or destruction during cargo transfer operations;

(2) Continuous monitoring for vinyl chloride vapor leaks is conducted aboard a tank barge undergoing vinyl chloride transfer operations. Fixed or

portable instrumentation may be utilized to ensure that personnel are not exposed to vinyl chloride vapor concentrations in excess of 1 ppm averaged over any eight hour period of 5 ppm averaged over any period not exceeding 15 minutes. The method of monitoring and measurement shall have an accuracy (with a confidence level of 95 percent) of not less than plus or minus 50 percent from 0.25 through 0.5 ppm, plus or minus 35 percent from over 0.5 ppm through 1.0 ppm, and plus or minus 25 percent over 1.0 ppm;

(3) Cargo transfer operation is discontinued or corrective action is initiated by the person in charge to minimize exposure to personnel whenever a vinyl chloride vapor concentration in excess of 1 ppm is detected. If the vinyl chloride vapor concentration exceeds 5 ppm for over 15 minutes, action to reduce the leak can be continued only if the respiratory protection requirements of 29 CFR 1910.1017 are met by all personnel in the area of the leak;

(4) Those portions of cargo lines which will be open to the atmosphere after piping is disconnected are free of vinyl chloride liquid and that the vinyl chloride vapor concentration in the area of the cargo piping disconnect points is not greater than 5 ppm;

(5) Any restricted gauge fitted on a tank containing vinyl chloride is effectively out of service by locking or sealing the device so that it cannot be used; and

(6) A restricted gauge is not to be used as a "check" on the required closed gauge, nor as a means or sampling.

(h) The words "CANCER—SUSPECT AGENT" must be added to the warning signs required by 46 CFR 151.45–2(e).

(i) Signs bearing the legend:

CANCER—SUSPECT AGENT IN THIS AREA

PROTECTIVE EQUIPMENT REQUIRED

AUTHORIZED PERSONNEL ONLY

must be posted whenever hazardous operations, such as tank cleaning, are in progress.

(j) A tank barge undergoing cargo transfer operations must be designated a "regulated area" having access limited to authorized persons and requiring a daily roster of authorized persons who may board the barge.

(k) Employees engaged in hazardous operations, such as tank cleaning, must be provided, and be required to wear and use respiratory protection in accordance with the provisions of 29 CFR 1910.1017 and protective garments, provided clean and dry for each use, to prevent skin contact with liquid vinyl chloride.

[CGFR 70–10, 35 FR 3714, Feb. 25, 1970, as amended by CGD 74–167R, 40 FR 17026, Apr. 16, 1975; CGD 88–100, 54 FR 40040, Sept. 29, 1989]

§ 151.50–36 Argon or nitrogen.

(a) A cargo tank that contains argon or nitrogen and that has a maximum allowable working pressure of 172 kPa (25 psig) or greater must have one of the following arrangements:

(1) A refrigeration system that keeps the tank pressure below the safety relief valve operating pressure when ambient temperatures are 46 °C (115 °F) air and 32 °C (90 °F) water.

(2) A relief valve or pressure control valve that maintains the tank pressure below the setting of the tank's required safety relief valve in ambient temperatures of 46 °C (115 °F) air and 32 °C (90 °F) water.

(b) A cargo tank with a maximum allowable working pressure of less than 172 kPa (25 psig) is approved by the Commandant (CG–ENG) on a case by case basis.

(c) Section 151.50–30 also applies to the carriage of argon or nitrogen.

[CGD 88–100, 54 FR 40040, Sept. 29, 1989]

§ 151.50–40 Additional requirements for carbon disulfide (carbon bisulfide) and ethyl ether.

(a) The provisions of this section are applicable if specifically referenced in the Special Requirements column of Table 151.05.

(b) Cargo tanks shall be electrically bonded to the hull of the vessel. A vessel shall be electrically bonded to the shore piping prior to connecting the cargo hose. This electrical bonding shall be maintained until after the cargo hose has been disconnected and any spillage has been removed.

(c) Pumps may be used for discharging cargo: *Provided*, That they are the vertical submerged type designed to avoid liquid pressure against the shaft gland and are suitable for use with the cargo.

(d) Provisions shall be made to maintain an inert gas padding in the cargo tank during loading, unloading and during transit.

(e) Provisions shall be made to prevent any leakage being washed into the waterways at the loading and unloading points.

(f) The special requirements of §151.50–41 for carbon disulfide (*carbon bisulfide*) and §151.50–42 for ethyl ether shall also be observed.

[CFGR 70–10, 35 FR 3714, Feb. 25, 1970, as amended by CGD 88–100, 54 FR 40029, Sept. 29, 1989]

§ 151.50–41   Carbon disulfide (carbon bisulfide).

(a) All openings shall be in the top of the tank.

(b) Loading lines shall terminate near the bottom of the tank.

(c) A standard ullage opening shall be provided for secondary and emergency sounding.

(d) If a cargo discharge pump is used, it shall be inserted through a cylindrical well extending from the tank top to a point near the tank bottom. A blanket of water shall be formed in this well before attempting pump removal.

(e) Water or inert gas displacement may be used for discharging cargo provided the cargo system is designed for the expected pressure and temperature. This method for discharging may be used with pressure type tanks only.

(f) Adequate natural ventilation shall be provided for the voids around the cargo tanks while the vessel is under way. During loading and unloading, forced ventilation shall be used. The forced ventilation shall be of sufficient capacity to provide a complete change of air within each void space every 5 minutes. The ventilating fan shall be of nonsparking construction.

(g) Because of its low ignition temperature and the close clearances required to arrest its flame propagation, carbon disulfide (*carbon bisulfide*) requires safeguards beyond those required for any electrical hazard groups.

(h) The requirements of §151.50–40 are also applicable to the shipment of carbon disulfide (*carbon bisulfide*).

[CFGR 70–10, 35 FR 3714, Feb. 25, 1970, as amended by CGD 88–100, 54 FR 40040, Sept. 29, 1989]

§ 151.50–42   Ethyl ether.

(a)(1) Gravity tanks shall be designed and tested to meet the rules of the American Bureau of Shipping for a head of water at least 8 feet above the tank top or the highest level the lading may rise, whichever is greater. All openings shall be in the top of the tank.

(2) Pressure vessel type tanks shall be designed for the maximum pressure to which they may be subjected when pressure is used to discharge the cargo, but in no case shall the design pressure be less than 50 pounds per square inch gauge. All openings shall be in the top of the tank.

(b) Adequate natural ventilation shall be provided for the voids around the cargo tanks while the vessel is underway. If a power ventilation system is installed, all blowers shall be of nonsparking construction. Power driven ventilation equipment shall not be located in the void spaces surrounding the cargo tanks.

(c) Pressure relief valve settings shall not be less than 3 pounds per square inch gauge for gravity tanks. For pressure vessels, the relief valve setting shall not exceed the design pressure of the tank.

(d) Inert gas displacement may be used for discharging cargo from pressure vessel tanks provided the cargo system is designed for the expected pressure and the discharge pressure does not exceed 50 pounds per square inch gauge or the design pressure of the tank, whichever is less.

(e) No electrical equipment except for approved lighting fixtures shall be installed in enclosed spaces adjacent to the cargo tanks. Lighting fixtures must be approved for use in Class I, Group C, hazardous locations. The installation of electrical equipment on the weather deck shall comply with the requirements of part 111, subpart 111.105 of this chapter.

(f) Copper, silver, mercury and magnesium or other acetylide forming metals and their alloys shall not be used as materials of construction for tanks, pipelines, valves, fittings and other items of equipment that may come in contact with the cargo vapor or liquid.

(g) Precautions shall be taken to prevent the contamination of ethyl ether by strong oxidizing agents.

(h) The requirements of § 151.50–40 are also applicable to the shipment of ethyl ether.

[CFGR 70–10, 35 FR 3714, Feb. 25, 1970, as amended by CGD 88–100, 54 FR 40040, Sept. 29, 1989]

§ 151.50–50 Elemental phosphorus in water.

(a) Tanks shall be designed and tested for a head equivalent to the design lading of phosphorus and its water blanket extended to 8 feet above the tank top. In addition, tank design calculations shall demonstrate that the tank can withstand, without rupture, a single loading to the highest level to which the water blanket may rise, if that exceeds 8 feet. Tanks shall not be less than 5/16-inch thick.

(b) When a water displacement method of discharge is used, pressure vessel type cargo tanks, designed and tested in accordance with Subchapter F of this chapter shall be employed. Such tanks shall be designed for the maximum pressure to which they may be subjected when water pressure is used to discharge the cargo.

(c) Each cargo tank shall be fitted with an approved pressure vacuum relief valve set to discharge at a pressure not exceeding 2 pounds per square inch. When transferring cargo, the vent discharge shall lead overboard above the waterline. When pressure vessel type tanks are used, each tank shall be fitted with a relief valve of suitable size.

(d) Sufficient outage shall be provided to prevent the tank from being liquid full at any time, but in no case shall the outage be less than 1 percent. When pressure vessel type tanks are used, outage need not be provided.

(e) The use of compressed air to discharge cargo is prohibited.

(f) Cargo shall be loaded at a temperature not exceeding 140 °F, and then cooled until the water above the cargo has a temperature not exceeding 105 °F prior to the movement of the vessel. Upon presentation of satisfactory proof that procedures followed will provide adequate safety in transportation and handling, the Commandant may authorize movement of the vessel following cooling of the water above the cargo to a temperature exceeding 105 °F.

(g) Coils in which steam or hot water is circulated to heat the cargo so that it may be pumped shall be located outside the cargo tanks.

(h) A fixed ballast piping system (including a power driven pump of ample capacity), or other means acceptable to the Commandant shall be installed so that any void space surrounding the tanks may be flooded.

(i) All openings shall be in the top of the tank and shall be fitted with bolted cover plates and gaskets resistant to the attack of phosphorus pentoxide.

(j) All enclosed compartments containing cargo tanks shall be provided with effective means of ventilation.

(k) Cargo lines shall be traced with steam piping and secured thereto by lagging to prevent solidification of cargo during transfer operations.

(l) During cargo transfer, a water hose shall be connected to a water supply ready for immediate use, and any spillage of phosphorus shall be immediately washed down. This requirement can be met by facilities provided from shore.

(m) At least two fresh air masks or self-contained breathing apparatus shall be stowed on board the vessel at all times for use of personnel entering the tanks or adjacent spaces.

(n) Authorization from the Commandant (CG–ENG) shall be obtained to transport lading other than phosphorus in the cargo tanks or to have on board any other cargo when phosphorus is laden in the tanks.

(o) Mechanical ventilation of sufficient capacity to insure a change of air within the cargo tanks every 3 minutes shall be provided during the inspection and maintenance of the cargo tanks.

(p) Cargo tanks shall be electrically bonded to the hull of the barge. A vessel shall be electrically bonded to the shore piping prior to connecting the cargo hose. This electrical bonding shall be maintained until after the cargo hose has been disconnected.

[CGFR 70–10, 35 FR 3714, Feb. 24, 1970, as amended by CGD 82–063b, 48 FR 4781, Feb. 3, 1983]

§ 151.50–55 Sulfur (molten).

(a) Ventilation (cargo tank):

(1) Cargo tank ventilation shall be provided to maintain the concentration of H_2S below one-half of its lower explosive limit throughout the cargo tank vapor space for all conditions of carriage; i.e., below 1.85 percent by volume.

(2) Where mechanical ventilation systems are used for maintaining low gas concentrations in cargo tanks, an alarm system shall be provided to give warning if the system fails.

(3) Connections shall be provided to enable sampling of the atmosphere over the cargo in each cargo tank for analysis.

(4) The ventilation system shall be designed and arranged to preclude the depositing of sulfur within the system.

(b) Void spaces:

(1) Openings to void spaces adjacent to cargo tanks shall be designed and fitted to prevent the entry of water, sulfur or cargo vapors.

(2) Connections shall be provided to enable sampling and analyzing vapors in void spaces.

(c) Temperature controls shall be provided in accordance with § 151.20–10 and applicable sections of Subpart 151.40 of this part. Heat transfer media shall be steam, and alternate media will require specific approval of the Commandant.

[CGFR 70–10, 35 FR 3714, Feb. 25, 1970]

§ 151.50–60 Benzene.

The person in charge of a Coast Guard inspected barge must ensure that the provisions of part 197, subpart C, of this chapter are applied.

[CGD 88–040, 56 FR 65006, Dec. 13, 1991]

§ 151.50–70 Cargoes requiring inhibition or stabilization.

When table 151.05 refers to this section, that cargo must be—

(a) Inhibited; or

(b) Stabilized.

[CGD 88–100, 54 FR 40040, Sept. 29, 1989]

§ 151.50–73 Chemical protective clothing.

When table 151.05 refers to this section, the following apply:

(a) The person in charge of cargo handling operations shall ensure that the following chemical protective clothing constructed of materials resistant to permeation by the cargo being handled is worn by all personnel engaged in an operation listed in paragraph (b) of this section:

(1) Splash protective eyewear.

(2) Long-sleeved gloves.

(3) Boots or shoe covers.

(4) Coveralls or lab aprons.

NOTE: "Guidelines for the Selection of Chemical Protective Clothing", Third Edition, 1987, available from the American Conference of Governmental Industrial Hygienists, 1330 Kemper Meadow Drive, Cincinnati, OH 45240–1634, provides information on the proper clothing for the cargo being handled.

(b) The section applies during the following operations:

(1) Sampling cargo.

(2) Transferring cargo.

(3) Making or breaking cargo hose connections.

(4) Gauging a cargo tank, unless gauging is by closed system.

(5) Opening cargo tanks.

(c) Coveralls or lab aprons may be replaced by splash suits or aprons constructed of light weight or disposable materials if, in the judgment of the person in charge of cargo handling operations,

(1) Contact with the cargo is likely to occur only infrequently and accidentally; and

(2) The splash suit or apron is disposed of immediately after contamination.

(d) Splash protective eyewear must be tight-fitting chemical-splash goggles, face shields, or similar items intended specifically for eye protection from chemical splashing or spraying.

(e) The person in charge of cargo handling operations shall ensure that each person in the vicinity of an operation listed in the paragraph (b) of this section or in the vicinity of tanks, piping, or pumps being used to transfer the

§ 151.50-74

cargo wears splash protective eyewear under paragraph (d) of this section.

[CGD 88–100, 54 FR 40040, Sept. 29, 1989, as amended by USCG–1999–6216, 64 FR 53227, Oct. 1, 1999]

§ 151.50-74 Ethylidene norbornene.

When Table 151.05 refers to this section, the following apply:

(a) 151.50–5 (g) and (h)

(b) Rubber hoses or fittings may not be used in transfer operations.

[CGD 80–001, 46 FR 63279, Dec. 31, 1981]

§ 151.50-75 Ferric chloride solution.

A containment system (cargo tank piping system, venting system, and gauging system) carrying this solution must be lined with rubber, corrosion resistant plastic, or a material approved by the Commandant (CG–ENG).

[CGD 80–001, 46 FR 63279, Dec. 31, 1981, as amended by CGD 82–063b, 48 FR 4781, Feb. 3, 1983; CGD 88–100, 54 FR 40041, Sept. 29, 1989; 55 FR 17276, Apr. 24, 1990]

§ 151.50-76 Hydrochloric acid, spent (NTE 15%).

(a)(1) Gravity type cargo tanks must be designed and tested to meet the rules of the American Bureau of Shipping for a head of water at least 8 feet above the tank top or the highest level the lading may rise, whichever is greater. The plate thickness of any part of the tank may not be less than three-eighths inch. A shell plating of a barge may not be on the boundary of any part of the cargo tank.

(2) Gravity tank vents must:

(i) Terminate above the weatherdeck, clear of all obstructions and away from any from any source of ignition; and

(ii) Be fitted with a single flame screen or two fitted flame screens as described in § 151.03–25. Neither a shutoff valve nor a frangible disk may be fitted in the vent lines.

(b) Openings in the tanks are prohibited below deck, except for access openings used for inspection and maintenance of tanks, or unless otherwise specifically approved by the Commandant (CG–ENG). Openings must be fitted with bolted cover plates and acid-resistant gaskets.

(c) Where special arrangements are approved by the Commandant (CG–ENG) to permit a pump suction to be led from the bottom of the tank, the filling and discharge lines must be fitted with shutoff valves located above the weatherdeck or operable from it.

(d) The outage may not be less than 1 percent.

(e) An enclosed compartment containing, or a compartment adjacent to, a cargo tank:

(1) May have no electrical equipment that does not meet or exceed class I-B electrical requirements; and

(2) Must have at least one gooseneck vent of 2.5 inch diameter or greater. The structural arrangement of the compartment must provide for the free passage of air and gases to the vent or vents.

(f) No lights may be used during the cargo transfer operations, except installed electric or portable battery lights. Smoking is prohibited and the person in charge of cargo transfer shall ensure that "No Smoking" signs are displayed during cargo transfer operations.

(g) Tanks approved for the transportation of acid cargoes subject to this section may not be used for the transportation of any other commodity, except upon authorization by the Commandant (CG–ENG).

(h) Each cargo tank must be examined internally at least once in every 4 years. If the lining of the cargo tank has deteriorated in service or is not in place, the Marine Inspector may require the tank to be tested by such nondestructive means as he may consider necessary to determine its condition.

[CGD 80–001, 46 FR 63279, Dec. 31, 1981, as amended by CGD 82–063b, 48 FR 4781, Feb. 3, 1983]

§ 151.50-77 Fluorosilicic acid (30% or less) (hydrofluorosilicic acid).

(a) Hydrofluorosilicic acid must be carried in gravity or pressure type cargo tanks independent of the vessel's structure. The tanks must be lined with rubber or other equally suitable material approved by the Commandant (CG–ENG). See § 151.15–3(f)(2).

(b) Notwithstanding the provisions of § 151.50–20(b)(3), no compressed air may be used to discharge hydrofluorosilicic acid from gravity type cargo tanks unless:

(1) The tanks are of cylindrical shape with dished heads, and

(2) The air pressure does not exceed:

(i) The design pressure of the tank, and

(ii) 10 pounds per square inch gauge. The tanks must be fitted with pressure relief devices.

(c) During cargo transfer, a water hose must be connected to a water supply and be ready for immediate use. Any leakage or spillage of acid must be immediately washed down. This requirement can be met by facilities provided from shore.

[CGD 80–001, 46 FR 63279, Dec. 31, 1981, as amended by CGD 82–063b, 48 FR 4781, Feb. 3, 1983; CGD 92–100, 59 FR 17028, Apr. 11, 1994]

§ 151.50–79 Methyl acetylene-propadiene mixture.

(a) The composition of the methyl acetylene-propadiene mixture at loading must be within one of the following sets of composition limits:

(1) Composition 1 is:

(i) Maximum methyl acetylene to propadiene molar ratio of 3 to 1;

(ii) Maximum combined concentration of methyl acetylene and propadiene of 65 mole percent;

(iii) Minimum combined concentration of propane, butane, and isobutane of 24 mole percent, of which at least one-third (on a molar basis) must be butanes and one-third propane; and

(iv) Maximum combined concentration of propylene and butadiene of 10 mole percent.

(2) Composition 2 is:

(i) Maximum methyl acetylene and propadiene combined concentration of 30 mole percent;

(ii) Maximum methyl acetylene concentration of 20 mole percent;

(iii) Maximum propadiene concentration of 20 mole percent;

(iv) Maximum propylene concentration of 45 mole percent;

(v) Maximum butadiene and butylenes combined concentration of 2 mole percent;

(vi) Minimum saturated C_4 hydrocarbon concentration of 4 mole percent; and

(vii) Minimum propane concentration of 25 mole percent.

(b) A barge carrying a methyl acetylene-propadiene mixture must have a refrigeration system that does not compress the cargo vapor or have a refrigeration system with the following features:

(1) A vapor compressor that does not raise the temperature and pressure of the vapor above 60 °C (140 °F) and 1.72 MPa guage (250 psig) during its operations, and that does not allow vapor to stagnate in the compressor while it continues to run.

(2) At the discharge piping from each compressor stage or each cylinder in the same stage of a reciprocating compressor:

(i) Two temperature actuated shutdown switches set to operate at 60 °C (140 °F) or less;

(ii) A pressure actuated shutdown switch set to operate at 1.72 MPa gauge (250 psig) or less; and

(iii) A safety relief valve set to relieve at 1.77 MPa gauge (256 psig) or less anywhere except into the compressor suction line.

(c) The piping system, including the cargo refrigeration system, for tanks to be loaded with methyl acetylene-propadiene mixture must be completely separate from piping and refrigeration systems for other tanks. If the piping system for the tanks to be loaded with methyl acetylene-propadiene mixture is not independent, the required piping separation must be accomplished by the removal of spool pieces, valves or other pipe sections and the installation of blank flanges at these locations. The required separation applies to all liquid and vapor piping, liquid and vapor vent lines and any other possible connections, such as common inert gas supply lines.

[CGD 80–001, 46 FR 63279, Dec. 31, 1981]

§ 151.50–80 Nitric acid (70% or less).

(a) Tanks, cargo piping, valves, fittings, and flanges (where exposed to the acid) must be lined with nitric acid resistant rubber or fabricated from nitric acid resistant stainless steel. See § 151.15–3(f)(2).

(b) During cargo transfer, a water hose must be connected to a water supply, ready for immediate use. Any leakage or spillage of acid must be immediately washed down. This requirement can be met by facilities provided from shore.

(c) Nitric acid contaminated by other chemicals, oils, solvents, etc. may not be transported in bulk without an authorization from the Commandant (CG–ENG).

[CGD 80–001, 46 FR 63280, Dec. 31, 1981, as amended by CGD 82–063b, 48 FR 4781, Feb. 3, 1983; CGD 88–100, 54 FR 40041, Sept. 29, 1989]

§ 151.50–81 Special operating requirements for heat sensitive cargoes.

When table 151.05 refers to this section, the following apply to the cargo:

(a) Must not be carried in a tank equipped with heating coils unless the heating supply to the coils is disconnected.

(b) Must not be carried in a tank adjacent to another tank containing an elevated temperature cargo.

(c) Must not be carried in a deck tank.

[CGD 80–001, 46 FR 63280, Dec. 31, 1981, as amended by CGD 88–100, 54 FR 40041, Sept. 29, 1989]

§ 151.50–84 Sulfur dioxide.

(a) Sulfur dioxide that is transported under the provisions of this part may not contain more than 100 ppm of water.

(b) Cargo piping must be at least Schedule 40 pipe.

(c) Flanges must be 150 lb. A.N.S.I. Standard minimum with tongue and groove or raised face.

(d) A cargo tank must:

(1) Meet the requirements of a Class I welded pressure vessel;

(2) Be designed for a maximum allowable working pressure of at least 125 psig;

(3) Be hydrostatically tested every two years to at least 188 psig;

(4) Be provided with one or more manholes that are fitted with a cover sized not less than 15 inches by 23 inches or 13 inches nominal diameter, located above the maximum liquid level, and as close as possible to the top of the tank;

(5) Have no openings other than those required in paragraph (d)(4) of this section;

(6) Have no liquid level gauges other than closed or indirect gauges;

(7) Have all valves and the closed gauge that is required by Table 151.05 bolted to the cover or covers that are required in paragraph (d)(4) of this section;

(8) Have a metal housing that is fitted with a drain and vent connection protecting all valves and the closed gauge within this housing against mechanical damage;

(9) Have all safety relief valves discharging into the protective housing;

(10) Not be interconnected with another cargo tank by piping or manifold that carriers cargo liquid, except vapor lines connected to a common header, and

(11) Have an excess flow valve that is located on the inside of the tank for every liquid and vapor connection, except the safety relief valve;

(12) Have no bypass opening on any excess flow valve.

(e) Cargo transfer operations:

(1) May not be conducted with more than one cargo tank at a time unles each tank is filled from or discharged to shore tanks through separate lines;

(2) Must be conducted with connections between fixed barge piping and shore piping of either Schedule 40 pipe having flexible metallic joints that meet § 151.04–5(h) or of flexible metallic hose that is acceptable to the Commandant (CG–ENG);

(3) From barge to shore must be by pressurization with an oil free, non-reactive gas that has a maximum of 100 ppm moisture;

(4) Must be conducted with vapor return to shore connections that ensure that all vapor is returned to shore; and

(5) Must be conducted with every person on the barge carrying a respiratory protective device that protects the wearer against sulfur dioxide vapors and provides respiratory protection for emergency escape from a contaminated area that results from cargo leakage.

(f) Respiratory protective equipment must be of a size and weight that allows unrestricted movement and wearing of a lifesaving device.

(g) After the completion of cargo transfer, all liquid sulfur dioxide in the cargo piping must be removed and

Coast Guard, DHS § 151.56-1

cargo transfer piping must be disconnected at the cargo tanks. After the cargo piping is disconnected, both ends of the line must be plugged or fitted with blind flanges.

[CGD 80–001, 46 FR 63280, Dec. 31, 1981, as amended by CGD 82–063b, 48 FR 4781, Feb. 3, 1983; CGD 88–100, 54 FR 40041, Sept. 29, 1989; 55 FR 17276, Apr. 24, 1990]

§ 151.50–86 Alkyl (C7–C9) nitrates.

(a) The carriage temperature of octyl nitrates must be maintained below 100 °C (212 °F) in order to prevent the occurrence of a self-sustaining exothermic decomposition reaction.

(b) Octyl nitrates may not be carried in a deck tank unless the tank has a combination of insulation and a water deluge system sufficient to maintain the tank's cargo temperature below 100 °C (212 °F) and the cargo temperature rise at or below 1.5 °C(2.7 °F)/hour, for a fire of 650 °C (1200 °F).

[CGD 88–100, 54 FR 40040, Sept. 29, 1989; CGD 92–100, 59 FR 17028, Apr. 11, 1994]

Subpart 151.55—Special Requirements for Materials of Construction

§ 151.55–1 General.

(a) This section provides special requirements for the materials of construction of equipment that may come into contact with various cargoes. Table 151.05 contains specific requirements for various cargoes.

(b) Copper, copper alloys, zinc, and aluminum shall not be used as materials of construction for tanks, pipelines, valves, fittings, and other items of equipment that may come in contact with the cargo liquid or vapor. (Equivalent to § 151.56–1(a),(b), and (c).)

(c) Copper, copper alloys, zinc, galvanized steel, and mercury shall not be used as materials of construction for tanks, pipelines, valves, fittings, and other items of equipment that may come in contact with the cargo liquid or vapor. (Equivalent to § 151.56–1(b),(c), and (g).)

(d) Aluminum, magnesium, zinc, and lithium shall not be used as materials of construction for tanks, pipelines, valves, fittings, and other items of equipment that may come in contact with the cargo liquid or vapor. (Equivalent to § 151.56–1(a),(c), and (d).)

(e) Copper and copper bearing alloys shall not be used as materials of construction for tanks, pipelines, valves, fittings, and other items of equipment that may come in contact with the cargo liquid or vapor. (Equivalent to § 151.56–1(b).)

(f) Aluminum or copper or alloys of either shall not be used as materials of construction for tanks, pipelines, valves, fittings, and other items of equipment that may come in contact with the cargo vapor or liquid. (Equivalent to § 151.56–1(a) and (b).)

(g) Aluminum, stainless steel, or steel covered with a suitable protective lining or coating shall be used as materials of construction for tanks, pipelines, valves fittings, and other items of equipment that may come in contact with the cargo liquid or vapor. (Equivalent to § 151.58–1(a).)

(h) Alkaline or acidic materials, such as caustic soda or sulfuric acid, should not be allowed to contaminate this cargo.

(i) For concentrations of 98 percent or greater, aluminum or stainless steel shall be used as materials of construction. For concentrations of less than 98 percent, 304L or 316 stainless steel shall be used as materials of construction.

(j) Zinc, alloys that have more than 10 percent zinc by weight, and aluminum may not be used as materials of construction for tanks, pipelines, valves, fittings, and other items of equipment that may come in contact with cargo liquid or vapor. (Equivalent to § 151.56–1(a) and (c).)

[CGFR 70–10, 35 FR 3714, Feb. 25, 1970, as amended by CGD 73–275R, 41 FR 3087, Jan. 21, 1976; CGD 75–223, 42 FR 8378, Feb. 10, 1977; CGD 88–100, 54 FR 40041, Sept. 29, 1989]

Subpart 151.56—Prohibited Materials of Construction

§ 151.56–1 Prohibited materials.

When one of the following paragraphs of this section is referenced in table 151.05, the materials listed in that paragraph may not be used in components that contact the cargo or its vapor:

(a) Aluminum or aluminum alloys.
(b) Copper or copper alloys.

§ 151.58-1

(c) Zinc, galvanized steel, or alloys having more than 10 percent zinc by weight.
(d) Magnesium.
(e) Lead.
(f) Silver or silver alloys.
(g) Mercury.

[CGD 88-100, 54 FR 40041, Sept. 29, 1989]

Subpart 151.58—Required Materials of Construction

§ 151.58-1 Required materials.

When one of the following paragraphs of this section is referenced in table 151.05, only those materials listed in that paragraph may be used in components that contact the cargo or its vapor:

(a) Aluminum, stainless steel, or steel covered with a protective lining or coating. (See § 151.15-3(f)(2).)
(b)-(c) [Reserved]
(d) Solid austenitic stainless steel.
(e) Stainless steel or steel covered with a suitable protective lining or coating. (See § 151.15-3(f)(2).)

[CGD 88-100, 54 FR 40041, Sept. 29, 1989]

PART 152 [RESERVED]

PART 153—SHIPS CARRYING BULK LIQUID, LIQUEFIED GAS, OR COMPRESSED GAS HAZARDOUS MATERIALS

Subpart A—General

Sec.
153.0 Availability of materials.
153.1 Applicability.
153.2 Definitions and acronyms.
153.3 Right of appeal.
153.4 Incorporation by reference.
153.7 Ships built before December 27, 1977 and non-self-propelled ships built before July 1, 1983: Application.
153.8 Procedures for requesting an endorsed Certificate of Inspection.
153.9 Foreign flag vessel endorsement application.
153.10 Procedures for requesting alternatives and waivers; termination of waivers.
153.12 IMO Certificates for United States Ships.
153.15 Conditions under which the Coast Guard issues a Certificate of Inspection or Certificate of Compliance.
153.16 Requirements for foreign flag vessel permits.
153.30 Special area endorsement.
153.40 Determination of materials that are hazardous.

Subpart B—Design and Equipment

GENERAL VESSEL REQUIREMENTS

153.190 Stability requirements.
153.201 Openings to accommodation, service or control spaces.
153.208 Ballast equipment.
153.209 Bilge pumping systems.
153.214 Personnel emergency and safety equipment.
153.215 Safety equipment lockers.
153.216 Shower and eyewash fountains.
153.217 Access to enclosed spaces and dedicated ballast tanks.
153.219 Access to double bottom tanks serving as dedicated ballast tanks.

CARGO CONTAINMENT SYSTEMS

153.230 Type I system.
153.231 Type II system.
153.232 Type III system.
153.233 Separation of tanks from machinery, service and other spaces.
153.234 Fore and aft location.
153.235 Exceptions to cargo piping location restrictions.
153.236 Prohibited materials.
153.238 Required materials.
153.239 Use of cast iron.
153.240 Insulation.

CARGO TANKS

153.250 Double-bottom and deep tanks as cargo tanks.
153.251 Independent cargo tanks.
153.252 Special requirement for an independent cargo tank.
153.254 Cargo tank access.
153.256 Trunks, domes, and openings of cargo tanks.
153.266 Tank linings.

PIPING SYSTEMS AND CARGO HANDLING EQUIPMENT

153.280 Piping system design.
153.281 Piping to independent tanks.
153.282 Cargo filling lines.
153.283 Valving for cargo piping.
153.284 Characteristics of required quick closing valves.
153.285 Valving for cargo pump manifolds.
153.292 Separation of piping systems.
153.294 Marking of piping systems.
153.296 Emergency shutdown stations.
153.297 Emergency actuators at the point of cargo control.

CARGO HANDLING SPACE VENTILATION

153.310 Ventilation system type.
153.312 Ventilation system standards.

153.314 Ventilation of spaces not usually occupied.
153.316 Special cargo pumproom ventilation rate.

Cargo Pumprooms

153.330 Access.
153.332 Hoisting arrangement.
153.333 Cargo pump discharge pressure gauge.
153.334 Bilge pumping systems.
153.336 Special cargo pump or pumproom requirements.

Cargo Venting Systems

153.350 Location of B/3 vent discharges.
153.351 Location of 4 m vent discharges.
153.352 B/3 and 4 m venting system outlets.
153.353 High velocity vents.
153.354 Venting system inlet.
153.355 PV venting systems.
153.358 Venting system flow capacity.
153.360 Venting system restriction.
153.361 Arrangements for removal of valves from venting systems having multiple relief valves.
153.362 Venting system drain.
153.364 Venting system supports.
153.365 Liquid overpressurization protection.
153.368 Pressure-vacuum valves.
153.370 Minimum relief valve setting for ambient temperature cargo tanks.
153.371 Minimum relief valve setting for refrigerated cargo tanks.
153.372 Gauges and vapor return for cargo vapor pressures exceeding 100 kPa (approx. 14.7 psia).

Cargo Gauging Systems

153.400 General requirements for gauges.
153.404 Standards for containment systems having required closed gauges.
153.406 Standards for containment systems having required restricted gauges.
153.407 Special requirements for sounding tube gauges.
153.408 Tank overflow control.
153.409 High level alarms.

Cargo Temperature Control Systems

153.430 Heat transfer systems; general.
153.432 Cooling systems.
153.434 Heat transfer coils within a tank.
153.436 Heat transfer fluids: compatibility with cargo.
153.438 Cargo pressure or temperature alarms required.
153.440 Cargo temperature sensors.

Special Requirements for Flammable or Combustible Cargoes

153.460 Fire protection systems.
153.461 Electrical bonding of independent tanks.
153.462 Static discharges from inert gas systems.
153.463 Vent system discharges.
153.465 Flammable vapor detector.
153.466 Electrical equipment.

Design and Equipment for Pollution Control

153.470 System for discharge of NLS residue to the sea: Categories A, B, C, and D.
153.480 Stripping quantity for Category B and C NLS tanks on ships built after June 30, 1986: Categories B and C.
153.481 Stripping quantities and interim standards for Category B NLS tanks on ships built before July 1, 1986: Category B.
153.482 Stripping quantities and interim standards for Category C NLS tanks on ships built before July 1, 1986: Category C.
153.483 Restricted voyage waiver for Category B and C NLS tanks on ships built before July 1, 1986: Category B and C.
153.484 Prewash equipment.
153.486 Design and equipment for removing NLS residue by ventilation: Categories A, B, C, and D.
153.488 Design and equipment for tanks carrying high melting point NLSs: Category B.
153.490 Cargo Record Book and Approved Procedures and Arrangements Manual: Categories A, B, C, and D.
153.491 Waiver of certain equipment for dedicated cargo tanks.

Special Requirements

153.500 Inert gas systems.
153.501 Requirement for dry inert gas.
153.515 Special requirements for extremely flammable cargoes.
153.520 Special requirements for carbon disulfide.
153.525 Special requirements for unusually toxic cargoes.
153.526 Toxic vapor detectors.
153.527 Toxic vapor protection.
153.530 Special requirements for alkylene oxides.
153.545 Special requirements for liquid sulfur.
153.554 Special requirements for acids.
153.555 Special requirements for inorganic acids.
153.556 Special requirements for sulfuric acid and oleum.
153.557 Special requirements for hydrochloric acid.
153.558 Special requirements for phosphoric acid.
153.559 Special requirements for nitric acid (less than 70 percent).
153.560 Special requirements for Alkyl (C7–C9) nitrates.
153.565 Special requirements for temperature sensors.

153.602 Special requirements for cargoes reactive with water.

TESTING AND INSPECTION

153.806 Loading information.
153.808 Examination required for a Certificate of Compliance.
153.809 Procedures for having the Coast Guard examine a vessel for a Certificate of Compliance.
153.812 Inspection for Certificate of Inspection.

Subpart C—Operations

DOCUMENTS AND CARGO INFORMATION

153.900 Certificates and authorization to carry a bulk liquid hazardous material.
153.901 Documents: Posting, availability, and alteration.
153.902 Expiration and invalidation of the Certificates of Compliance.
153.903 Operating a United States ship in special areas: Categories A, B, and C.
153.904 Limitations in the endorsement.
153.905 Regulations required to be on board.
153.907 Cargo information.
153.908 Cargo viscosity and melting point information; measuring cargo temperature during discharge: Categories A, B, and C.
153.909 Completing the Cargo Record Book and record retention: Categories A, B, C, and D.
153.910 Cargo piping plan.
153.912 Certficate of inhibition or stabilization.

GENERAL CARGO OPERATIONAL REQUIREMENTS

153.920 Cargo quantity limitations.
153.921 Explosives.
153.923 Inerting systems.

GENERAL VESSEL SAFETY

153.930 Cargo antidotes.
153.931 Obstruction of pumproom ladderways.
153.932 Goggles and protective clothing.
153.933 Chemical protective clothing.
153.934 Entry into spaces containing cargo vapor.
153.935 Opening of tanks and cargo sampling.
153.935a Storage of cargo samples.
153.936 Illness, alcohol, drugs.

MARKING OF CARGO TRANSFER HOSE

153.940 Standards for marking of cargo hose.

CARGO TRANSFER PROCEDURES

153.953 Signals during cargo transfer.
153.955 Warning signs during cargo transfer.
153.957 Persons in charge of transferring liquid cargo in bulk or cleaning cargo tanks.
153.959 Approval to begin transfer operations required.
153.964 Discharge by gas pressurization.
153.966 Discharge by liquid displacement.
153.968 Cargo transfer conference.
153.970 Cargo transfer piping.
153.972 Connecting a cargo hose.
153.975 Preparation for cargo transfer.
153.976 Transfer of packaged cargo or ship's stores.
153.977 Supervision of cargo transfer.
153.979 Gauging with a sounding tube.
153.980 Isolation of automatic closing valves.
153.981 Leaving room in tank for cargo expansion.
153.983 Termination procedures.

SPECIAL CARGO PROCEDURES

153.1000 Special operating requirements for cargoes reactive with water.
153.1002 Special operating requirements for heat sensitive cargoes.
153.1003 Prohibited carriage in deck tanks.
153.1004 Inhibited and stabilized cargoes.
153.1010 Alkylene oxides.
153.1011 Changing containment systems and hoses to and from alkylene oxide service.
153.1020 Unusually toxic cargoes.
153.1025 Motor fuel antiknock compounds.
153.1035 Acetone cyanohydrin or lactonitrile solutions.
153.1040 Carbon disulfide.
153.1045 Inorganic acids.
153.1046 Sulfuric acid.
153.1052 Carriage of other cargoes in acid tanks.
153.1060 Benzene.
153.1065 Sodium chlorate solutions.

APPROVAL OF SURVEYORS AND HANDLING OF CATEGORIES A, B, C, AND D CARGO AND NLS RESIDUE

153.1100 Responsibility of the person in charge.
153.1101 Procedures for getting a Surveyor: Approval of Surveyors.
153.1102 Handling and disposal of NLS residue: Categories A, B, C, and D.
153.1104 Draining of cargo hose: Categories A, B, C, and D.
153.1106 Cleaning agents.
153.1108 Heated prewash for solidifying NLS, high viscosity NLS and required prewashes of NLS whose viscosity exceeds 25 mPa sec at 20 °C: Categories A, B, and C.
153.1112 Prewash for tanks containing Category A NILS residue.
153.1114 Conditions under which a prewash may be omitted: Categories A, B, and C.
153.1116 Prewash for tanks unloaded without following the approved Procedures and Arrangements Manual: Category B and C.

Coast Guard, DHS § 153.1

153.1118 Prewash of Categories B and C cargo tanks not meeting stripping standards: Categories B and C.
153.1119 When to prewash and discharge NLS residues from a prewash; unloading an NLS cargo in a country whose Administration is not signatory to MARPOL 73/78: Categories A, B, and C.
153.1120 Procedures for tank prewash: Categories A, B, and C.
153.1122 Discharges of NLS residue from tank washing other than a prewash: Categories A, B, and C.
153.1124 Discharges of Category D NLS residue.
153.1126 Discharge of NLS residue from a slop tank to the sea: Categories A, B, C, and D.
153.1128 Discharge of NLS residue from a cargo tank to the sea: Categories A, B, C, and D.
153.1130 Failure of slops discharge recording equipment; operating with, reporting failures, and replacing pollution equipment: Category A, B, C, D.
153.1132 Reporting spills and non-complying discharges: Category A, B, C, and D.

MAINTENANCE

153.1500 Venting system rupture disks.
153.1502 Fixed ballast relocation.
153.1504 Inspection of personnel emergency and safety equipment.

Subpart D—Test and Calculation Procedures for Determining Stripping Quantity, Clingage NLS Residue, and Total NLS Residue

153.1600 Equipment required for conducting the stripping quantity test.
153.1602 Test procedure for determining the stripping quantity.
153.1604 Determining the stripping quantity from the test results.
153.1608 Calculation of total NLS residue and clingage NLS residue.
TABLE 1 TO PART 153—SUMMARY OF MINIMUM REQUIREMENTS
TABLE 2 TO PART 153—CARGOES NOT REGULATED UNDER SUBCHAPTERS D OR O OF THIS CHAPTER WHEN CARRIED IN BULK ON NON-OCEANGOING BARGES
APPENDIX I TO PART 153 [RESERVED]
APPENDIX II TO PART 153—METRIC UNITS USED IN PART 153

AUTHORITY: 46 U.S.C. 3703; Department of Homeland Security Delegation No. 0170.1. Section 153.40 issued under 49 U.S.C. 5103. Sections 153.470 through 153.491, 153.1100 through 153.1132, and 153.1600 through 153.1608 also issued under 33 U.S.C. 1903 (b).

SOURCE: CGD 73-96, 42 FR 49027, Sept. 26, 1977, unless otherwise noted.

EDITORIAL NOTE: Nomenclature changes to part 153 appear at 60 FR 50465, Sept. 29, 1995, 61 FR 50732, Sept. 27, 1996, 74 FR 49235, Sept. 25, 2009, and at 77 FR 59784, Oct. 1, 2012.

Subpart A—General

§ 153.0 Availability of materials.

(a) Various sections in this part refer to the following documents which are incorporated in Annex II of MARPOL 73/78.

(1) IMO *Standards for Procedures and Arrangements for the Discharge of Noxious Liquid Substances,* Resolution MEPC 18(22), 1985 in effect on April 6, 1987.

(2) IMO *International Code for the Construction and Equipment of Ships Carrying Dangerous Chemicals in Bulk,* Resolution MEPC 19(22), 1985 in effect on April 6, 1987.

(3) IMO *Code for the Construction and Equipment of Ships Carrying Dangerous Chemicals in Bulk,* Resolution MEPC 20(22), 1985 in effect on April 6, 1987.

(b) The IMO documents listed in this section are available from the following:

(1) IMO Secretariat, Publications section, 4 Albert Embankment, London SE1 7SR, United Kingdom, Telex 23588;

(2) New York Nautical Instrument and Service Company, 140 West Broadway, New York, NY 10013;

(3) Baker, Lyman & Company, 3220 South I-10 Service Road, Metairie, LA 70001.

(4) UNZ & Company, 190 Baldwin Avenue, Jersey City, NJ 07306.

(5) Southwest Instrument Company, 235 West 7th Street, San Pedro, CA 90731.

(6) Marine Education Textbooks, 124 North Van Avenue, Houma, LA 70363-5895.

[CGD 81-101, 52 FR 7777, Mar. 12, 1987, as amended by CGD 92-100, 59 FR 17028, Apr. 11, 1994]

§ 153.1 Applicability.

This part applies to the following:

(a) All United States self-propelled ships and those foreign self-propelled ships operating in United States waters that carry in bulk a cargo listed in Table 1 or allowed in a written permission under § 153.900(d), unless—

§ 153.2

(1) The ship is carrying the cargo under 33 CFR part 151;

(2) The ship is carrying the cargo in a portable tank under subpart 98.30 or 98.33 of this chapter; or

(3) The ship is an offshore supply vessel carrying the cargo under subpart 98.31 of the chapter; or

(b) All United States oceangoing non-self-propelled ships and those foreign non-self-propelled ships operating in United States waters that carry in bulk a Category A, B, or C NLS cargo listed in Table 1 or allowed in a written permission under § 153.900(d), unless—

(1) The ship is carrying the cargo under 33 CFR part 151;

(2) The ship is carrying the cargo in a portable tank under subpart 98.30 or 98.33 of this chapter;

(3) The ship is an offshore supply vessel carrying the cargo under subpart 98.31 of this chapter; or

(4) The ship's Certificate of Inspection is endorsed for a limited short protected coastwise route and the ship is constructed and certificated primarily for service on an inland route.

(c) All ships that carry a bulk liquid, liquefied gas, or compressed gas cargo that is not—

(1) Listed in Table 1 of this part;

(2) Listed in Table 2 of this part;

(3) Carried under a written permission granted under § 153.900(d);

(4) Carried under part 30 through 35, 98, 151, or 154 of this chapter; or

(5) Carried as an NLS under 33 CFR part 151.

[CGD 81–101, 52 FR 7777, Mar. 12, 1987, as amended by CGD 84–025, 53 FR 15844, May 4, 1988; CGD 81–101, 53 FR 28974, Aug. 1, 1988 and 54 FR 12629, Mar. 28, 1989; CGD 84–043, 55 FR 37413, Sept. 11, 19905; CGD 96–041, 61 FR 50732, Sept. 27, 1996]

§ 153.2 Definitions and acronyms.

As used in this part:

Accommodation spaces means halls, dining rooms, lounges, lavatories, cabins, staterooms, offices, hospitals, cinemas, game and hobby rooms, pantries containing no cooking appliances, and similar permanently enclosed spaces.

Adequate reception facility means each facility certified as adequate under 33 CFR 158.160 and each facility provided by a Administration signatory to MARPOL 73/78 under Regulation 7 of Annex II.

Annex II means Annex II to MARPOL 73/78 and is the Annex to MARPOL 73/78 regulating the discharge of noxious liquid substances to the sea.

B means the breadth of the vessel and is defined in § 42.13–15(d) of this chapter.

Built means that a ship's construction has reached any of the following stages:

(1) The keel is laid.

(2) The mass of the partially assembled ship is 50,000 kg.

(3) The mass of the partially assembled ship is one percent of the estimated mass of the completed ship.

Cargo area means that part of a vessel that includes the cargo tanks, spaces adjacent to the cargo tanks and the part of the deck over the cargo tanks and adjacent spaces.

Cargo containment system means a cargo tank, its cargo piping system, its venting system, and its gauging system.

Cargo handling space means an enclosed space that must be entered during a routine loading, carriage, or discharge of cargo and that contains an element of the cargo containment system having a seal or packing to prevent the escape of cargo, such as a valve, cargo pump, or cargo vapor compressor.

Cargo piping system means a tankship's permanently installed piping arrangement, including any valves and pumps, that carries cargo to or from a cargo tank.

Cargo tank means a tank that:

(1) Is part of or permanently affixed to a tankship; and

(2) Carries a cargo described in part 153, table 1—SUMMARY OF MINIMUM REQUIREMENTS in any quantity, including residual liquid or vapor.

Certificate of Compliance means a certificate issued by the Coast Guard that a foreign flag vessel had been examined and found to comply with the regulations in this chapter.

Closed gauging system means an arrangement for gauging the amount of cargo in a tank, such as a float and tape or a magnetically coupled float and indicator, that does not have any opening through which cargo vapor or liquid can escape.

Combustible is defined in §30.10–15 of this chapter.

Commandant means Commandant (staff symbol), Attn: (Staff title), U.S. Coast Guard Stop (mailing code) 2703 Martin Luther King Jr. Avenue SE., Washington, DC 20593–(mailing code). The term is often followed by a mailing code in parentheses. The mailing address should include any mailing code and should be written as follows:

Commandant (mailing code), U.S. Coast Guard, 2100 2nd Street SW., Stop 7126, Washington, DC 20593–7126.

Control space is defined in §30.10–19a of this chapter.

Cycle, means that the tank washing machine progresses through complete rotations until it reaches an orientation identical to its starting orientation.

NOTE: For a typical one or two nozzle tank washing machine that rotates in both the horizontal and vertical planes though more slowly in one than the other, a cycle would be at least one rotation in each plane of rotation.

Dedicated ballast tank means a tank that is used only for ballast.

Emergency shutdown station means a part of the tankship where the required emergency shutdown controls are clustered.

Flammable is defined in §30.10–22 of this chapter.

Forward perpendicular is defined in §42.13–15(b) of this chapter.

Hazardous material means a liquid material or substance that is—

(1) Flammable or combustible;

(2) Designated a hazardous substance under section 311(b) of the Federal Water Pollution Control Act (33 U.S.C. 1321); or

(3) Designated a hazardous material under 49 U.S.C. 5103.

NOTE: The Environmental Protection Agency designates hazardous substances in 40 CFR Table 116.A. The Coast Guard designates hazardous materials that are transported as bulk liquids by water in §153.40.

High viscosity NLS includes high viscosity Category B NLS and high viscosity Category C NLS.

High viscosity Category B NLS means any Category B NLS having a viscosity of at least 25 mPa.s at 20 °C and at least 25 mPa.s at the time it is unloaded.

High viscosity Category C NLS means any Category C NLS having a viscosity of at least 60 mPa.s at 20 °C and at least 60 mPa.s at the time it is unloaded.

IMO means the International Maritime Organization (IMO, formerly Inter-Governmental Maritime Consultative Organization or IMCO).

IMO Bulk Chemical Code includes the IMO *International Code for the Construction and Equipment of Ships Carrying Dangerous Chemicals in Bulk*, Resolution MEPC 19(22), 1985 and the IMO *Code for the Construction and Equipment of Ships Carrying Dangerous Chemicals in Bulk*, Resolution MEPC 20(22), 1985.

IMO Certificate includes a Certificate of Fitness for the Carriage of Dangerous Chemicals in Bulk issued under the IMO *Code for the Construction and Equipment of Ships Carrying Dangerous Chemicals in Bulk*, Resolution MEPC 20(22), 1985 and an International Certificate of Fitness for the Carriage of Dangerous Chemicals in Bulk issued under the IMO *International Code for the Construction and Equipment of Ships Carrying Dangerous Chemicals in Bulk*, Resolution MEPC 19(22), 1985.

Independent, as applied to a cargo piping, venting, heating or cooling system means that the system is connected to no other system, and has no means available for connection to another system.

Independent tank means a cargo tank that is permanently affixed to the vessel, that is self-supporting, that incorporates no part of the vessel's hull and that is not essential to the integrity of the hull.

Intank cargo pump means a pump:

(1) Located within the cargo tank it serves; and

(2) Whose piping passes through only the top of the cargo tank.

Integral tank means a cargo tank that also is part of or is formed in part by the vessel's hull structure so that the tank and the hull may be stressed by the same loads.

IOPP Certificate means an International Oil Pollution Prevention Certificate required under 33 CFR 151.19.

§ 153.2

L means the length of the vessel and is defined in § 42.13–15(a) of this chapter.

Liquid means each substance having a vapor pressure of 172 kPa or less at 37.8 °C.

Marine Inspector is defined in § 30.10–43 of this chapter.

MARPOL 73/78 means the International Convention for Prevention of Pollution from Ships, 1973 (done at London, November 2, 1973), modified by the Protocol of 1978 relating to the International Convention for Prevention of Pollution from Ships, 1973 (done at London, on February 17, 1978).

Master means the person-in-charge of a self-propelled or non-self-propelled ship.

Mixture means a mixture containing only the substances described in conjunction with the term.

Nearest land has the same meaning as in 33 CFR 151.05(h).

Noxious liquid substance (NLS) means—

(1) Each substance listed in 33 CFR 151.47 or 33 CFR 151.49;

(2) Each substance having an "A," "B," "C," or "D" beside its name in the column headed "Pollution Category" in Table 1; and

(3) Each substance that is identified as an NLS in a written permission issued under § 153.900(c).

NLS Certificate means an International Pollution Prevention Certificate for the Carriage of Noxious Liquid Substances in Bulk issued under Annex II of MARPOL 73/78.

Oceangoing ship has the same meaning as in 33 CFR 151.05(j).

Officer in Charge, Marine Inspection, is defined in § 1.05(b) of this chapter.

Open gauging means an arrangement for gauging the amount of cargo in a tank through a large opening, such as a tank hatch or ullage opening.

Open venting system means a venting system that always allows vapor to flow freely to and from the tank.

Phosphoric acid means phosphoric acid, superphosphoric acid, and aqueous solutions of phosphoric acid.

Pressure-vacuum (PV) valve means a valve that is normally closed and which opens under a preset positive pressure or a vacuum.

Prewash means a tank washing operation that meets the procedure in § 153.1120.

Pumproom means any enclosed space containing a pump that is part of a cargo containment system.

Reception facility means anything capable of receiving NLS residues in a country whose Administration is not signatory to MARPOL 73/78 and each adequate reception facility.

Refrigerated tank means a cargo tank that is equipped to carry a cargo that must be cooled in order to keep the cargo's vapor pressure from exceeding the tank's pressure-vacuum or safety relief valve setting under ambient conditions of 32 °C (approx. 90 °F) still water and 46 °C (approx. 115 °F) still air.

Relief valve setting means the inlet line pressure at which a vent system's pressure-vacuum or safety relief valve fully opens.

Residues and mixtures containing NLSs (NLS residue) means—

(1) Any Category A, B, C, or D NLS cargo retained on the ship because it fails to meet consignee specifications;

(2) Any part of a Category A, B, C, or D NLS cargo remaining on the ship after NLS is discharged to the consignee, including but not limited to puddles on the tank bottom and in sumps, clingage in the tanks, and substance remaining in the pipes; or

(3) Any material contaminated with a Category A, B, C, or D NLS cargo, including but not limited to bilge slops, ballast, hose drip pan contents, and tank wash water.

Restricted gauging system means a method of gauging the amount of cargo in a tank through an opening of limited size that restricts or prevents the release of cargo vapors from the tank vapor space.

Safety relief (SR) valve means a normally closed valve that opens under a preset positive pressure.

Separate and *separated*, as applied to a cargo piping, venting, heating or cooling system, means either an independent system or one that may be disconnected from all other systems by:

(a) Removing spool pieces or valves and blanking the open pipe ends; or

(b) Blocking each system interconnection with two blind flanges in series and providing a means of detecting leakage into the pipe section between the flanges.

Service spaces means spaces outside the cargo area used for galleys, pantries containing cooking appliances, lockers, store rooms, workshops other than those forming part of machinery spaces, and trunks to such spaces.

Ship means a vessel of any type whatsoever, including hydrofoils, air-cushion vehicles, submersibles, floating craft whether self-propelled or not, and fixed or floating platforms.

Slop tanks include slop tanks and cargo tanks used as slop tanks.

Solidifying NLS means a Category A, B, or C NLS that has a melting point—

(1) Greater than 0 °C but less than 15 °C and a temperature, measured under the procedure in § 153.908(d), that is less than 5 °C above its melting point at the time it is unloaded; or

(2) 15 °C or greater and has a temperature, measured under the procedure in § 153.908(d), that is less than 10 °C above its melting point at the time it is unloaded.

Solution means a water solution.

Special area means the Baltic Sea Area as defined in 33 CFR 151.13(a)(2) and the Black Sea Area as defined in 33 CFR 151.13(a)(3).

SR venting system means a venting system in which an SR valve controls vapor flow from the cargo tank.

Tankship has the same meaning as "ship".

Venting system means a permanent piping arrangement leading from a cargo tank and used to control the flow of vapor to and from the tank.

[CGD 73–96, 42 FR 49027, Sept. 26, 1977]

EDITORIAL NOTE: For FEDERAL REGISTER citations affecting § 153.2, see the List of CFR Sections Affected, which appears in the Finding Aids section of the printed volume and at *www.fdsys.gov*.

§ 153.3 Right of appeal.

Any person directly affected by a decision or action taken under this part, by or on behalf of the Coast Guard, may appeal therefrom in accordance with subpart 1.03 of this chapter.

[CGD 88–033, 54 FR 50381, Dec. 6, 1989]

§ 153.4 Incorporation by reference.

(a) Certain material is incorporated by reference into this part with the approval of the Director of the Federal Register in accordance with 5 U.S.C. 552(a). To enforce any edition other than that specified in paragraph (b) of this section, the Coast Guard must publish notice of change in the FEDERAL REGISTER and make the material available to the public. All approved material is on file at Coast Guard Headquarters. Contact Commandant (CG–ENG), Attn: Office of Design and Engineering Systems, U.S. Coast Guard Stop 7509, 2703 Martin Luther King Jr. Avenue SE., Washington, DC 20593–7509; or contact the National Archives and Records Administration (NARA). For information on the availability of this material at NARA, call 202–741–6030, or go to: *http://www.archives.gov/federal_register/code_of_federal_regulations/ibr_locations.html*. All material is available from the sources indicated in paragraph (b) of this section.

(b) American National Standards Institute (ANSI), 25 West 43rd Street, 4th Floor, New York, NY 10036, *http://www.ansi.org*.

(1) ANSI B16.5, Pipe Flanges and Flanged Fittings, 1988, incorporation by reference approved for § 153.940.

(2) ANSI B16.24, Bronze Pipe Flanges and Flanged Fittings, 1979, incorporation by reference approved for § 153.940.

(3) ANSI B16.31, Non-Ferrous Flanges, 1971, incorporation by reference approved for § 153.940.

(c) American Society for Testing and Materials (ASTM), 100 Barr Harbor Drive, West Conshohocken, PA 19428–2959, 877–909–2786, *http://www.astm.org*.

(1) ASTM F 1122–87 (1992), Standard Specification for Quick Disconnect Couplings, incorporation by reference approved for § 153.940.

(2) ASTM F1271–90 (Reapproved 2012), Standard Specification for Spill Valves

§ 153.7

for Use in Marine Tank Liquid Overpressure Protections Applications (approved May 1, 2012), incorporation by reference approved for § 153.365.

[CGD 88–032, 56 FR 35826, July 29, 1991, as amended by CGD 96–041, 61 FR 50732, Sept. 27, 1996; CGD 97–057, 62 FR 51048, Sept. 30, 1997; USCG–1999–5151, 64 FR 67183, Dec. 1, 1999; 69 FR 18803, Apr. 9, 2004; USCG–2012–0832, 77 FR 59784, Oct. 1, 2012; USCG–2012–0866, 78 FR 13251, Feb. 27, 2013; USCG–2013–0671, 78 FR 60155, Sept. 30, 2013]

§ 153.7 Ships built before December 27, 1977 and non-self-propelled ships built before July 1, 1983: Application.

(a) *Definitions.* (1) *Permit* means a Certificate of Inspection, Letter of Compliance, or Certificate of Compliance.

(2) *Existing tankship* means a tankship for which a contract was let on or before December 27, 1977.

(3) *Letter of Compliance* in this section means a letter issued by the Coast Guard before 27 December 1977 which permitted a foreign flag tankship to carry a bulk cargo regulated under this part.

(b) *Endorsements for existing tankships.* (1) The Coast Guard endorses the permit of an existing tankship to carry a cargo listed in Table 1 if:

(i) The tankship held a permit on December 27, 1977, endorsed for the cargo in question;

(ii) The tankship meets the construction standards under which the Coast Guard issued the permit; and

(iii) The tankship meets the standards in paragraph (c) of this section.

(2) The Coast Guard endorses the permit of an existing tankship to carry a cargo listed in Table 1 if:

(i) The tankship held a permit on December 27, 1977;

(ii) The Coast Guard did not require the permit to be endorsed with the name of the cargo at any time before December 27, 1977;

(iii) The tankship meets the construction standards under which the Coast Guard issued the permit;

(iv) The tankship carried the cargo in question; and

(v) The tankship meets the standards in paragraph (c) of this section.

(3) The Coast Guard endorses the permit of an existing tankship to carry a cargo listed in Table 1 if:

(i) The tankship held a permit on December 27, 1977 endorsed to carry class B or C poisons under 46 CFR part 39;

(ii) The cargo in question is a class B or C poison;

(iii) The tankship meets the construction standards in 46 CFR part 39; and

(iv) The tankship meets the standards in paragraph (c) of this section.

(4) The Commandant (CG–ENG) considers on a case by case basis endorsing the permit of an existing tankship to carry a cargo listed in Table 1 if:

(i) The tankship does not come within the categories described in paragraphs (b) (1) through (3) of this section;

(ii) The tankship meets paragraph (c) of this section; and

(iii) The tankship meets any additional requirements the Commandant (CG–ENG) may prescribe.

(c) An existing tankship must meet all the requirements of this part except as provided in paragraphs (c) (3), (4), (5) and (6) of this section.

(1)–(2) [Reserved]

(3) The Commandant (CG–ENG) considers on a case by case basis endorsing as a type II containment system one that fails to meet §§ 153.231(b), 153.234, 172.130 and 172.133 of this chapter if the tankship and containment system meet the following minimum conditions:

(i) The tankship has a loadline certificate.

(ii) The cargo tank is not part of the tankship's shell plating.

(iii) The distance between the bottom plating of the cargo tank and the bottom shell plating of the tankship is at least 76 cm measured parallel to the vertical axis of the tankship.

(4) The Commandant (CG–ENG) considers on a case by case basis endorsing a containment system as a type II containment system if:

(i) The containment system is modified to meet § 153.231(b) by adding double bottoms or wing tanks; and

(ii) The tankship can survive the damage described in §§ 172.135 and 172.150 of this chapter to those parts of the tankship other than machinery spaces.

(5) The Commandant (CG–ENG) considers on a case by case basis endorsing

as a type III containment system one that does not meet §§ 153.234, 172.130 and 172.133 of this chapter if the tankship has a load line certificate.

(6) The Commandant (CG–ENG) considers on a case by case basis endorsing the tankship to carry cargoes listed in Table 1 of this part if the tankship does not meet §§ 153.217, 153.219 and 153.254.

(d) Except as required by this paragraph, subpart B of this part does not apply to a non-self-propelled ship that carries an NLS cargo under this part if—

(1) The ship was built before July 1, 1983;

(2) The ship carries no NLS cargo or NLS residue at any time it is in waters of another Administration signatory to MARPOL 73/78;

(3) The NLS does not require a type I containment system;

(4) The ship meets all requirements in parts 30 through 34 and part 151 of this chapter that apply to the cargo;

(5) The ship meets the provisions in § 153.216 and §§ 153.470 through 153.491 applying to the NLS category of that cargo;

(6) When the "Special Requirements" column of Table 1 contains an entry for § 153.408 or § 153.409 beside the cargo name, the ship meets the section, except the system prescribed by the section need be capable of operation only during loading;

(7) [Reserved]

(8) No part of the ship's hull plating is a component of a cargo tank if the cargo tank is endorsed to carry a cargo having a type II containment system in Table 1.

[CGD 73–96, 42 FR 49027, Sept. 26, 1977, as amended by CGD 78–128, 47 FR 21204, May 17, 1982; CGD 82–063b, 48 FR 4781, Feb. 3, 1983; CGD 79–023, 48 FR 51009, Nov. 4, 1983; CGD 81–052, 50 FR 8733, Mar. 5, 1985; CGD 81–101, 52 FR 7779, Mar. 12, 1987; CGD 81–101, 53 FR 28974, Aug. 1, 1988 and 54 FR 12629, Mar. 28, 1989; CGD 95–072, 60 FR 54106, Oct. 19, 1995]

§ 153.8 Procedures for requesting an endorsed Certificate of Inspection.

(a) When applying for the endorsed Certificate of Inspection that § 153.900 requires for a ship to carry a cargo listed in Table 1, the applicant must proceed as follows:

(1) Send a letter to one of the Coast Guard offices listed in § 91.55–15 of this chapter that includes—

(i) A request for the endorsed Certificate of Inspection;

(ii) The name of the ship; and

(iii) A list of the cargoes from Table 1 the applicant wishes the endorsement to allow.

(2) Supply to the Coast Guard when requested—

(i) Hull type calculations;

(ii) The plans and information listed in §§ 54.01–18, 56.01–10, 91.55–5 (a), (b), (d), (g), and (h), and 110.25–1 of this chapter;

(iii) A copy of the Procedures and Arrangements Manual required by § 153.490; and

(iv) Any other ship information, including plans, design calculations, test results, certificates, and manufacturer's data, that the Coast Guard needs to determine if the ship meets this part.

(b) The Coast Guard notifies the applicant in writing—

(1) Whether any further information is necessary to evaluate the request for the endorsed Certificate of Inspection; and

(2) Of the outcome of the request for the endorsed Certificate of Inspection.

(c) The Coast Guard returns the Procedures and Arrangements Manual stamped "Approved" or indicating what corrections are necessary.

NOTE: The procedures for requesting an IOPP Certificate are found in 33 CFR Part 151.

[CGD 81–101, 52 FR 7779, Mar. 12, 1987]

§ 153.9 Foreign flag vessel endorsement application.

(a) *Application for a vessel whose flag administration is signatory to MARPOL 73/78 and issues IMO Certificates.* A person who desires a Certificate of Compliance endorsed to carry a cargo in table 1 of this part, as described in § 153.900 of this part, must request the endorsement from the cognizant Officer in Charge, Marine Inspection and have aboard the vessel copies of IMO Certificates issued by the vessel's administration and—

(1) An additional classification society statement that the vessel complies with § 153.530 (b), (d), and (p)(1) if a person desires a Certificate of Compliance

§ 153.10

endorsed with the name of an alkylene oxide; and

(2) An additional classification society statement that the vessel complies with §§ 153.370, 153.371, and 153.438 if a person desires a Certificate of Compliance endorsed with the name of a cargo whose vapor pressure exceeds 100 kPa absolute at 37.8 °C (approximately 14.7 psia at 100 °F).

(b) *Application for a vessel whose flag administration does not issue IMO Certificates.* A person who desires a Certificate of Compliance endorsed with the name of a cargo in Table 1 of this part, as described in § 153.900, must submit an application, in a written or electronic format, to Commanding Officer (MSC), Attn: Marine Safety Center, U.S. Coast Guard Stop 7410, 4200 Wilson Boulevard Suite 400, Arlington, VA 20598–7410, that includes the following information:

(1) A copy of the vessel's Cargo Ship Safety Construction Certificate and Cargo Ship Safety Equipment Certificate issued under the International Convention for Safety of Life at Sea, 1974.

(2) A list of those cargoes for which the Letter of Compliance is to be endorsed.

(3) The specific tanks that are to be endorsed for each cargo.

(4) The names of the U.S. ports in which the person anticipates operating the vessel.

(5) The name of the vessel's flag administration.

(6) The name of the society that classes the vessel.

(7) A brief description of the vessel's cargo containment systems.

(8) Hull type calculations.

(9) The plans and information listed in §§ 54.01–18, 56.01–10, 91.55–5 (a), (b), (d), (g), and (h), and 111.05–5(d) of this chapter.

(c) *Conditions applying to all Certificate of Compliance applications.* (1) If requested by the Commanding Officer, U.S. Coast Guard Marine Safety Center, a person desiring a Certificate of Compliance for a vessel must furnish any other vessel information such as plans, design calculations, test results, certificates, and manufacturer's data, that the Coast Guard needs to determine that the vessel meets the standards of this part.

(2) Correspondence with the Coast Guard and vessel information submitted under this part must be in English except IMO Certificates which may be in French.

[CGD 73–96, 42 FR 49027, Sept. 26, 1977]

EDITORIAL NOTE: For FEDERAL REGISTER citations affecting § 153.9, see the List of CFR Sections Affected, which appears in the Finding Aids section of the printed volume and at www.fdsys.gov.

§ 153.10 Procedures for requesting alternatives and waivers; termination of waivers.

(a) The Coast Guard considers allowing the use of an alternative in place of a requirement in this part if—

(1) The person wishing to use the alternative sends a written application to the Commandant (CG–ENG) explaining—

(i) The requirement in this part that would not be met and the reason why;

(ii) The alternative the person proposes to be substituted; and

(iii) How the alternative would ensure a level of safety and pollution protection at least equal to that of the requirement for which the alternative would substitute;

(2) The alternative does not substitute an operational standard for a design or equipment standard; and

(3) The Commandant (CG–ENG) determines that the alternative provides a level of protection for purposes of safety and pollution at least equal to the requirement in this part.

(b) The Coast Guard considers granting a waiver of a requirement for which this part allows a waiver if the person wishing the waiver sends a written application to the Commandant (CG–ENG) that includes—

(1) A citation of the regulation that allows the waiver; and

(2) Any information and pledges that the regulation requires to be submitted with the application for the waiver.

(c) The Commandant notifies the applicant in writing—

(1) Whether any further information is necessary to evaluate the request for an alternative or waiver; and

(2) Of the outcome of the request for an alternative or waiver.

(d) A waiver issued under this part terminates if any—

(1) Information required to be supplied with the application for the waiver changes;

(2) Pledges required to be supplied with the application for the waiver are repudiated;

(3) Restrictions or procedures applying to operations under the waiver are violated; or

(4) Requirements in the section of this part authorizing the waiver are violated.

[CGD 81–101, 52 FR 7780, Mar. 12, 1987]

§ 153.12 IMO Certificates for United States Ships.

Either a classification society authorized under 46 CFR part 8, or the Officer in Charge, Marine Inspection, issues a United States ship an IMO Certificate endorsed to allow the carriage of a hazardous material or NLS cargo in table 1 of this part if the following requirements are met:

(a) The ship's owner must make a request to the OCMI for the IMO Certificate.

(b) The ship must meet this part.

(c) Self-propelled ships contracted for after November 1, 1973 but built before December 28, 1977 must meet requirements in this part that apply to a self-propelled ship built on December 28, 1977.

(d) Non-self-propelled ships contracted for after November 1, 1973 but built before July 1, 1983 must meet the requirements in this part applying to non-self-propelled ships built on July 1, 1983.

[CGD 81–101, 52 FR 7780, Mar. 12, 1987, as amended by CGD 95–010, 62 FR 67537, Dec. 24, 1997]

§ 153.15 Conditions under which the Coast Guard issues a Certificate of Inspection or Certificate of Compliance.

(a) The Coast Guard issues the endorsed Certificate of Inspection required under § 153.900 for a United States ship to carry a hazardous material or NLS listed in Table 1 if—

(1) The person wishing the Certificate of Inspection applies following the procedures under § 153.8; and

(2) The ship meets the design and equipment requirements of this part and—

(i) Subchapter D of this chapter if the hazardous material or NLS is flammable or combustible; or

(ii) Either Subchapter D or I of this chapter, at the option of the ship owner, if the hazardous material or NLS is non-flammable or non-combustible.

(b) The Coast Guard issues the endorsed Certificate of Compliance required under § 153.900 for a foreign ship to carry a hazardous material or NLS listed in Table 1 if—

(1) The person wishing the Certificate of Compliance follows the procedures under § 153.9;

(2) The ship has an IMO Certificate issued by its Administration and endorsed with the name of the hazardous material or NLS if the ship's Administration is signatory to MARPOL 73/78;

(3) The ship meets the requirements of this part applying to United States ships and § 30.01–5(e) of this chapter if the ship's Administration is not signatory to MARPOL 73/78; and

(4) The ship meets any additional design and equipment requirements specified by the Commandant (CG–ENG).

[CGD 81–101, 52 FR 7780, Mar. 12, 1987]

§ 153.16 Requirements for foreign flag vessel permits.

To have its Certificate of Compliance endorsed to carry a cargo listed in Table 1, a foreign flag vessel must:

(a) Have an IMO Certificate, if the flag administration issues IMO Certificates, endorsed with the name of the cargo and meet any specific requirements in this subpart that the Commandant (CG–ENG) may prescribe; or

(b) Meet the requirements of this subpart and § 30.01–5(e) of this chapter.

[CGD 73–96, 42 FR 49027, Sept. 26, 1977, as amended by CGD 82–063b, 48 FR 4781, Feb. 3, 1983; CGD 81–052, 50 FR 8733, Mar. 5, 1985; CGD 81–101, 52 FR 7780, Mar. 12, 1987; CGD 95–027, 61 FR 26008, May 23, 1996]

§ 153.30 Special area endorsement.

The Coast Guard endorses the Certificate of Inspection of a United States ship allowing it to operate in special areas if the ship owner—

§ 153.40

(a) Requests the endorsement following the procedures in § 153.8;

(b) Shows that the ship meets the design and equipment requirements applying to ships operating in special areas contained in Regulations 5, 5A, and 8 of Annex II and the Standards for Procedures and Arrangements.

[CGD 81–101, 52 FR 7780, Mar. 12, 1987]

§ 153.40 Determination of materials that are hazardous.

Under the authority delegated by the Secretary of Transportation in 49 CFR 1.46(t) to carry out the functions under 49 U.S.C. 1803, the Coast Guard has found the following materials to be hazardous when transported in bulk:

(a) Materials listed in Table 30.25–1 of this chapter.

(b) Materials listed in Table 151.05.

(c) Materials listed in Table 1.[1]

(d) Materials listed in Table 4 of Part 154.

(e) Materials that are NLSs under MARPOL Annex II.

(f) Liquids, liquefied gases, and compressed gases, that are—

(1) Listed in 49 CFR 172.101;

(2) Listed in 49 CFR 172.102; or

(3) Listed or within any of the definitions in subparts C through O of 49 CFR part 173.

(g) Those liquid, liquefied gas, and compressed gas materials designated as hazardous in the permissions granted under § 153.900(c).[2]

[CGD 81–101, 52 FR 7780, Mar. 12, 1987]

---

[1] Those hazardous material cargoes designated Category A, B, C, or D in Table 1 are also Noxious Liquid Substances under Annex II and the Act to Prevent Pollution from Ships, 33 U.S.C. 1901 *et seq.*

[2] The Coast Guard continues to propose in the FEDERAL REGISTER any addition of these designated hazardous materials to one of the tables referred to in paragraphs (a) through (d).

Subpart B—Design and Equipment

GENERAL VESSEL REQUIREMENTS

§ 153.190 Stability requirements.

Each vessel must meet the applicable requirements in Subchapter S of this chapter.

[CGD 79–023, 48 FR 51009, Nov. 4, 1983. Redesignated by CGD 81–101, 52 FR 7780, Mar. 12, 1987]

§ 153.201 Openings to accommodation, service or control spaces.

(a) Except as allowed in paragraph (b) of this section, entrances, ventilation intakes and exhausts, and other openings to accommodation, service, or control spaces must be located aft of the house bulkhead facing the cargo area a distance at least equal to the following:

(1) 3 m (approx. 10 ft) if the vessel length is less than 75 meters (approx. 246 ft).

(2) L/25 if the vessel length is between 75 and 125 meters (approx. 246 ft and 410 ft).

(3) 5 m (approx. 16.5 ft) if the vessel length is more than 125 meters (approx. 410 ft).

(b) Fixed port lights, wheelhouse doors, and windows need not meet the location requirements specified in paragraph (a) of this section if they do not leak when tested with a fire hose at 207 kPa gauge (30 psig).

[CGD 81–078, 50 FR 21173, May 22, 1985]

§ 153.208 Ballast equipment.

(a) Except for the arrangement described in paragraph (b) of this section no piping that serves a dedicated ballast tank that is adjacent to a cargo tank may enter an engine room or accommodation space.

(b) Piping used only to fill a dedicated ballast tank adjacent to a cargo tank may enter an engine room or accommodation space if the piping has a valve or valving arrangement:

(1) Within the part of the tankship where a containment system may be located under § 153.234;

(2) That allows liquid to flow only towards that ballast tank (such as a check valve); and

(3) That enables a person to shut off the fill line from the weatherdeck (such as a stop valve).

(c) Except as prescribed in paragraph (d) of this section, pumps, piping, vent lines, overflow tubes and sounding tubes serving dedicated ballast tanks must not be located within a cargo containment system.

(d) Each vent line, overflow tube and sounding tube that serves a dedicated ballast tank and that is located within a cargo containment system must meet § 32.60–10(e)(2) of this chapter.

[CGD 73–96, 42 FR 49027, Sept. 26, 1977, as amended by CGD 78–128, 47 FR 21207, May 17, 1982]

§ 153.209 Bilge pumping systems.

Bilge pumping systems for cargo pumprooms, slop tanks, and void spaces separated from cargo tanks by only a single bulkhead must be entirely within the locations allowed containment systems in § 153.234.

§ 153.214 Personnel emergency and safety equipment.

Each self-propelled ship must have the following:

(a) Two stretchers or wire baskets complete with equipment for lifting an injured person from a pumproom or a cargo tank.

(b) In addition to any similar equipment required by Subchapter D of this chapter, three each of the following:

(1) A 30 minute self-contained breathing apparatus of the pressure demand type, approved by the Mining Safety and Health Administration (formerly the Mining Enforcement and Safety Administration) and the National Institute for Occupational Safety and Health, or the tankship's flag administration with five refill tanks or cartridges of 30 minutes capacity each.

(2) A set of overalls or large apron, boots, long sleeved gloves, and goggles, each made of materials resistant to the cargoes in Table 1 that are endorsed on the Certificate of Inspection or Certificate of Compliance.

(3) A steel-cored lifeline with harness.

(4) An explosion-proof lamp.

(c) First aid equipment.

[GCD 73–96, 42 FR 49027, Sept. 26, 1977, as amended by CGD 77–222, 43 FR 57256, Dec. 7, 1978; CGD 78–128, 47 FR 21207, May 17, 1982; CGD 81–052, 50 FR 8733, Mar. 5, 1985; CGD 81–101, 52 FR 7781, Mar. 12, 1987]

§ 153.215 Safety equipment lockers.

Each self-propelled ship must have the following:

(a) Each tankship must have at least two safety equipment lockers.

(b) One safety equipment locker must be adjacent to the emergency shutdown station required by § 153.296(b). This locker must contain one set of the equipment required by § 153.214(a) and two sets of that required by § 153.214(b).

(c) The second safety equipment locker must be adjacent to the second emergency shutdown station required by § 153.296. This locker must contain the remaining equipment required by § 153.214 (a) and (b).

(d) Each safety equipment locker must be marked as described in § 153.955 (c), (d), and (e) with the legend "SAFETY EQUIPMENT."

[CGD 73–96, 42 FR 49027, Sept. 26, 1977, as amended by CGD 78–128, 47 FR 21207, May 17, 1982; CGD 81–101, 52 FR 7781, Mar. 12, 1987]

§ 153.216 Shower and eyewash fountains.

(a) Each non-self-propelled ship must have a fixed or portable shower and eyewash fountain that operates during cargo transfer and meets paragraph (c) of this section.

(b) Each self-propelled ship must have a shower and eyewash fountain that operates at all times and meets paragraph (c) of this section.

(c) The shower and eyewash fountains required by paragraphs (a) and (b) of this section must—

(1) Operate in any ambient temperature;

(2) Dispense water at a temperature between 0 °C and 40 °C (approx. 32 °F and 104 °F);

(3) Be located on the weatherdeck; and

(4) Be marked "EMERGENCY SHOWER" as described in § 153.955 (c), (d), and (e), so that the marking is visible from work areas in the part of the deck

§ 153.217

where the cargo containment systems are located.

[CGD 81–101, 52 FR 7781, Mar. 12, 1987]

§ 153.217 Access to enclosed spaces and dedicated ballast tanks.

An access opening to an enclosed space or a dedicated ballast tank must meet the requirements for a cargo tank access in § 153.254 (b), (c), and (d) if:

(a) The enclosed space or dedicated ballast tank is located within the cargo area of the vessel; or

(b) A part of a cargo containment system lies within the enclosed space or dedicated ballast tank.

[CGD 78–128, 47 FR 21207, May 17, 1982]

§ 153.219 Access to double bottom tanks serving as dedicated ballast tanks.

(a) Except as prescribed in paragraph (b) of this section, access openings to double bottom tanks serving as dedicated ballast tanks must not be located within a cargo containment system.

(b) Each access opening to a double bottom tank that is a dedicated ballast tank and that is located within a cargo containment system must be:

(1) Enclosed in an access trunk extending to the weatherdeck;

(2) Separated from the cargo containment system by two manhole coverings; or

(3) Approved by the Commandant (CG–ENG).

[CGD 78–128, 47 FR 21207, May 17, 1982, as amended by CGD 82–063b, 48 FR 4782, Feb. 3, 1983]

CARGO CONTAINMENT SYSTEMS

§ 153.230 Type I system.

A type I containment system must meet the following requirements:

(a) The vessel must meet the requirements in subpart F of part 172 of this chapter for a type I hull.

(b) Except as described in § 153.235:

(1) It may be no closer to the tankship's shell than 76 cm (approx. 29.9 in.); and

(2) It may not be located in any part of the tankship subject to the damage described in Table 172.135 of this chapter for:

(i) COLLISION PENETRATION, Transverse extent; and

(ii) GROUNDING PENETRATION, Vertical extents from the baseline upward.

[CGD 73–96, 42 FR 49027, Sept. 26, 1977, as amended by CGD 79–023, 48 FR 51009, Nov. 4, 1983]

§ 153.231 Type II system.

A type II containment system must meet the following requirements:

(a) The vessel must meet the requirements in subpart F of part 172 of this chapter for a type I or II hull.

(b) Except as allowed in §§ 153.7 and 153.235—

(1) It may be no closer to the tankship's shell than 76 cm (approx. 29.9 in.); and

(2) It may not be located in any part of the tankship subject to the damage described in Table 172.135 of this chapter for GROUNDING PENETRATION, Vertical extent from the baseline upward.

[CGD 73–96, 42 FR 49027, Sept. 26, 1977, as amended by CGD 79–023, 48 FR 51009, Nov. 4, 1983; CGD 81–101, 52 FR 7781, Mar. 12, 1987]

§ 153.232 Type III system.

A type III containment system must be in either a type I, II, or III hull. The requirements for type I, II, and III hulls are in subpart F of part 172 of this chapter.

[CGD 79–023, 48 FR 51009, Nov. 4, 1983]

§ 153.233 Separation of tanks from machinery, service and other spaces.

(a) To prevent leakage through a single weld failure, the following spaces must be separated from a cargo by two walls, two bulkheads, or a bulkhead and a deck not meeting in a cruciform joint:

(1) Machinery spaces.
(2) Service spaces.
(3) Accommodation spaces.
(4) Spaces for storing potable domestic, or feed water.
(5) Spaces for storing edibles.

(b) Some examples of arrangements that may separate cargo from the spaces listed in paragraph (a) of this section are the following:

(1) Dedicated ballast tanks.
(2) Cargo pumprooms.

Coast Guard, DHS §153.240

(3) Ballast pumprooms.

(4) Tanks not carrying a cargo listed in this part.[3]

(5) A cofferdam aft of the cargo containment systems and whose forward bulkhead is forward of any joint common to an accommodations space and the deck.

(6) Double walled piping or a piping tunnel.

§153.234 Fore and aft location.

Except as allowed in §153.7, each ship must meet the following:

(a) Each cargo containment system and any compartments within which a containment system is located must be forward of a tankship's accommodation spaces.

(b) Except as described in §153.235, each cargo containment system must be located at least 0.05L aft of the forward perpendicular, but in no case forward of a collision bulkhead.

[CGD 73-96, 42 FR 49027, Sept. 26, 1977, as amended by CGD 81-101, 52 FR 7781, Mar. 12, 1987]

§153.235 Exceptions to cargo piping location restrictions.

Cargo piping must not be located in those areas from which a containment system is excluded by §§153.230(b), 153.231(b), and 153.234(b) unless the cargo piping:

(a) Drains back to the cargo tank under any heel or trim resulting from the damage specified in §172.135 of this chapter; and

(b) Enters the cargo tank above the liquid level for a full tank in any condition of heel or trim resulting from the damage specified in §172.135 of this chapter.

[CGD 73-96, 42 FR 49027, Sept. 26, 1977, as amended by CGD 79-023, 48 FR 51009, Nov. 4, 1983]

§153.236 Prohibited materials.

When one of the following paragraphs of this section is referenced in Table 1, the materials listed in that paragraph may not be used in components that contact the cargo liquid or vapor:

(a) Aluminum or aluminum alloys.

(b) Copper or copper alloys.

(c) Zinc, galvanized steel or alloys having more than 10 percent zinc by weight.

(d) Magnesium.

(e) Lead.

(f) Silver or silver alloys.

(g) Mercury.

§153.238 Required materials.

When one of the following paragraphs of this section is referenced in Table 1, only those materials listed in that paragraph may be used in components that contact the cargo liquid or vapor:

(a) Aluminum, stainless steel, or steel covered with a protective lining or coating.

(b) With cargo concentrations of 98 percent or greater, aluminum or stainless steel.

(c) With cargo concentrations of less than 98 percent, 304L or 316 stainless steel.

(d) Solid austenitic stainless steel.

(e) Stainless steel or steel covered with a suitable protective lining or coating. (See §153.266.)

[CGD 73-96, 42 FR 49027, Sept. 26, 1977, as amended by CGD 88-100, 54 FR 40041, Sept. 29, 1989]

§153.239 Use of cast iron.

(a) Cast iron used in a cargo containment system must meet the requirements of §56.60-10(b) of this chapter.

(b) For purposes of this section, the term "lethal products" in §56.60-10(b) means those cargoes that Table 1 references to §153.525 or §153.527.

[CGD 78-128, 47 FR 21207, May 17, 1982]

§153.240 Insulation.

Cargo containment system insulation made necessary by the requirements of this part must meet the requirements in §38.05-20 of this chapter. However, the vapor barrier required by §38.05-20(b) is unnecessary if the insulation is:

(a) Protected from the weather, and attached to a containment system maintained at a temperature in excess of 46 °C (approx. 115 °F); or

(b) In an atmosphere whose dewpoint is less than the temperature of any surface in contact with the insulation.

---

[3] See also §§32.56-5 and 32.60-10 of this chapter for limitations on the stowage of combustible liquids adjacent to ignition sources.

Cargo Tanks

§ 153.250 Double-bottom and deep tanks as cargo tanks.

Except in those cases in which Commandant (CG–ENG) specifically approves another arrangement, such as a double-bottom or deep tank as a cargo tank, an integral cargo tank or the hold within which an independent cargo tank is located must extend to the weatherdeck.

[CGD 73–96, 42 FR 49027, Sept. 26, 1977, as amended by CGD 82–063b, 48 FR 4781, Feb. 3, 1983]

§ 153.251 Independent cargo tanks.

All independent cargo tank must meet § 38.05–10 (a)(1), (b), (d), and (e)(1) of this chapter.

[CGD 78–128, 47 FR 21208, May 17, 1982]

§ 153.252 Special requirement for an independent cargo tank.

When Table 1 refers to this section, the cargo tank must be an independent tank that meets §§ 38.05–2(d) and 38.05–4(g) of this chapter. (See also § 153.256(b)).

[CGD 78–128, 47 FR 21208, May 17, 1982]

§ 153.254 Cargo tank access.

(a) A cargo tank must have at least one covered manhole opening into the vapor space described in § 153.354.

(b) An access through a vertical cargo tank surface must be at least 60 cm by 80 cm (approx. 23.6 × 31.5 in.) and no more than 60 cm above a foothold grating, or surface on both sides of the access way.

(c) An access through a horizontal cargo tank surface must be at least 60 cm by 60 cm (approx. 23.6 × 23.6 in.).

(d) An access trunk must be no less than 76 cm (approx. 29.9 in.) in diameter.

§ 153.256 Trunks, domes, and openings of cargo tanks.

(a) The hatch of a cargo tank must:
(1) Be at the highest point of the tank; and
(2) Open on or above the weatherdeck.

(b) To be endorsed to carry a cargo requiring an independent cargo tank, a tank must have:

(1) A trunk or dome at the uppermost part of the tank, extending above the weatherdeck;
(2) Its hatch at the top of the trunk or dome; and
(3) No openings below the weatherdeck.

§ 153.266 Tank linings.

A tank lining must be:
(a) At least as elastic as the tank material; and
(b) Applied or attached to the tank as recommended by the lining manufacturer.

Piping Systems and Cargo Handling Equipment

§ 153.280 Piping system design.

(a) Each cargo piping system must meet the standards of Part 56 and §§ 38.10–1(b), 38.10–1(e), and 38.10–10(a) of this chapter.

(b) Piping carrying cargo or cargo residue may not enter any machinery space except a cargo pumproom.

§ 153.281 Piping to independent tanks.

Piping for an independent cargo tank must penetrate the tank only through that part of the tank or dome extending above the weatherdeck.

[CGD 78–128, 47 FR 21208, May 17, 1982]

§ 153.282 Cargo filling lines.

The discharge point of a cargo tank filling line must be no higher above the bottom of the cargo tank or sump than 10 cm (approx. 4 in.) or the radius of the filling line, whichever is greater.

§ 153.283 Valving for cargo piping.

(a) Except as described in this section, a cargo line must have a deck operable, manual stop valve:
(1) In each tank which the line serves; and
(2) At each cargo hose connection point.

(b) The valve required by paragraph (a)(1) of this section may be in a cargo pumproom at the pumproom bulkhead if the cargo tank the cargo line serves is adjacent to the pumproom.

(c) The valve required by paragraph (a)(1) of this section may be on the weatherdeck if:

(1) The weatherdeck is the top of the tank;
(2) The line goes through the weatherdeck into the tank; and
(3) The valve is at the point where the line penetrates the weatherdeck.

(d) The valve required by paragraph (a)(1) of this section may be outside the tank if:
(1) The tank is an independent tank; and
(2) The valve is at the point where the line penetrates the tank.

(e) The discharge line of an intank cargo pump need not have the valve required by paragraph (a)(1) of this section.

(f) If the cargo exerts a gravity head pressure on a valve required by this section, the valve must be a positive shutoff valve that meets § 56.50–60(d) of this chapter.

[CGD 73–96, 42 FR 49027, Sept. 26, 1977, as amended by CGD 78–128, 47 FR 21208, May 17, 1982]

§ 153.284 Characteristics of required quick closing valves.

A remotely actuated quick closing shutoff valve required by § 153.530(n) must:
(a) Be a positive shutoff valve;
(b) Be of the fail-closed type that closes on loss of power;
(c) Be capable of local manual closing;
(d) Close from the time of actuation in 30 seconds or less; and
(e) Be equipped with a fusible element that melts at less than 104 °C (approx. 220 °F) and closes the valve.

[CGD 78–128, 47 FR 21208, May 17, 1982; 47 FR 27293, June 24, 1982]

§ 153.285 Valving for cargo pump manifolds.

(a) When cargo lines serving different tanks enter a pumproom and connect to the same pump:
(1) Each cargo line must have a stop valve within the line;
(2) The valve must be before the cargo line joins the other lines or pump; and
(3) The valve must be within the pumproom.

(b) The valve in paragraph (a) of this section is required in addition to any valve required under § 153.283(b).

§ 153.292 Separation of piping systems.

Cargo piping systems must be arranged so that operations necessary to provide separate systems can be accomplished in a cargo handling space or on the weatherdeck.

[CGD 78–128, 47 FR 21208, May 17, 1982]

§ 153.294 Marking of piping systems.

(a) Each cargo piping system must be marked with the designation number of the cargo tank it serves at each hose connection, valve, and blind in the piping system. The markings must be in characters at least 5 cm (approx. 2 in.) high.

(b) Every hose connection of a cargo piping system must be marked with the cargo piping system's working pressure required by § 38.10–10(a) of this chapter.[4]

§ 153.296 Emergency shutdown stations.

(a) Each tankship must have at least two emergency shutdown stations.

(b) One emergency shutdown station must be located forward of the deckhouse, in the after part of the weatherdeck in which the cargo tanks are located.

(c) A second emergency shutdown station must be located so that one of the two stations is accessible from any part of the weatherdeck if a break in a cargo piping system or hose causes spraying or leaking.

(d) Each emergency shutdown station must contain a single remote actuator for all quick closing shutoff valves required by this part.

(e) Each emergency shutdown station must have the controls necessary to stop all cargo pumps on the tankship.

(f) Any remote emergency actuator, such as that for a quick closing shutoff valve, a cargo pump, or a water spray system, must be of a type that will not defeat the operation of other remote emergency actuators. The emergency action must occur whether one or several actuators are operated.

(g) Each emergency shutdown station must be marked as described in § 153.955 (c), (d), and (e) with the legend

---
[4] See § 153.280 of the part.

"EMERGENCY SHUTDOWN STATION" so that the legend is visible from work areas in the part of the deck where the cargo containment systems are located.

[CGD 73–96, 42 FR 49027, Sept. 26, 1977, as amended by CGD 78–128, 47 FR 21208, May 17, 1982]

§ 153.297 Emergency actuators at the point of cargo control.

(a) The point from which cargo transfer is controlled must have the same actuators an emergency shutdown station must have under § 153.296 and an actuator for any deck water spray systems required by this part.

(b) The point from which cargo transfer is controlled may be one of the emergency shutdown stations required under § 153.296 if it meets the requirements of that section.

CARGO HANDLING SPACE VENTILATION

§ 153.310 Ventilation system type.

A cargo handling space must have a permanent forced ventilation system of the exhaust type.

§ 153.312 Ventilation system standards.

A cargo handling space ventilation system must meet the following:

(a) A ventilation system exhaust duct must discharge no less than 10 m (approx. 32.8 ft) from openings into or ventilation intakes for, accommodation or service spaces.

(b) A ventilation system must not recycle vapors from ventilation discharges.

(c) Except for the space served by the ventilation duct, a ventilation duct must not pass through a machinery room, an accommodation space, or working spaces.

(d) A ventilation system must be operable from outside the space it ventilates.

(e) A ventilation system must be sized to change the air in the ventilated space at least 30 times per hour.

(f) A ventilation system must not allow air to stagnate in any part of a ventilated space.

(g) A ventilation system must be able to exhaust air from both above and below the deck plates of a ventilated space.

§ 153.314 Ventilation of spaces not usually occupied.

(a) Each tankship must have portable ventilation equipment that fits the mount required in paragraph (b)(1) of this section.

(b) Each enclosed space within the cargo area that does not have a permanent ventilation system meeting § 153.312 must have:

(1) A mount for the portable mechanical ventilation equipment required by this section; and

(2) Either permanent ventilation ductwork connected to the mount and arranged to supply air to the extremities of the space; or

(3) An attachment for temporary ductwork at the mount with enough ductway in the ventilated space and temporary ductwork stowed aboard the vessel to supply air to the extremities of the space.

[CGD 73–96, 42 FR 49027, Sept. 26, 1977, as amended by CGD 78–128, 47 FR 21208, May 17, 1982]

§ 153.316 Special cargo pumproom ventilation rate.

When Table 1 refers to this section, the cargo pumproom ventilation system must change the air in the cargo pumproom 45 times per hour and discharge no less than 4 m (approx. 13.1 ft) above the deck.

CARGO PUMPROOMS

§ 153.330 Access.

(a) The access door to a cargo pumproom must open on the weatheredeck.

(b) The access way to a cargo pumproom and its valving must allow passage of a man wearing the breathing apparatus required by § 153.214(b)(1).

(c) Each ladderway in a cargo pumproom must be free from obstructions by piping, framework, or other equipment.

(d) Cargo pumproom ladders and platforms must have guard railings.

(e) Each ladder to a cargo pump-room must have an incline from the horizontal of less than 60°.

§ 153.332 Hoisting arrangement.

(a) A cargo pumproom located below the weatherdeck must have a permanent hoisting arrangement with a lifting capacity of 2500 N (approx. 562 lbs), operable from the weatherdeck, for the removal of an unconscious person.

(b) The cargo pumproom must have a 60 cm by 60 cm (approx. 2 ft by 2 ft) cross-sectional clearance through the hoistway.

§ 153.333 Cargo pump discharge pressure gauge.

Each cargo pump within a pumproom must have a discharge pressure gauge outside the pumproom.

§ 153.334 Bilge pumping systems.

(a) A cargo pumproom must have a bilge pumping system.

(b) The bilge pumping system must have:

(1) Complete remote operating controls outside the cargo pumproom; and

(2) An alarm that operates when the depth of liquid in the bilges exceeds 50 cm (approx. 19.7 in.).

§ 153.336 Special cargo pump or pumproom requirements.

(a) When Table 1 refers to this section:

(1) The cargo pump must be an intank cargo pump;

(2) The cargo pumproom must be on or above the weatherdeck; or

(3) The cargo pumproom must have the specific approval of the Commandant (CG–ENG).

(b) For a cargo pumproom described in paragraph (a)(2) or (a)(3) the tankship must:

(1) Have a low pressure breathing quality air supply system for use with the breathing apparatus in the pumproom; or

(2) Meet any requirements specified by the Commandant (CG–522).

(c) A low pressure air supply system described in paragraph (b)(1) of this section must:

(1) Run from fixed air bottles to the pumproom;

(2) Have an air compressor to recharge the fixed air bottles; and

(3) have hose connections in the pumproom suitable for use with the breathing apparatus required in § 153.214(b)(1); and

(4) have the air capacity to enable two men to work in the pumproom for at least one hour each without using the cartridges for the breathing apparatus required in § 153.214(b)(1).

[CGD 78–128, 47 FR 21208, May 17, 1982, as amended by CGD 82–063b, 48 FR 4781, Feb. 3, 1983]

CARGO VENTING SYSTEMS

§ 153.350 Location of B/3 vent discharges.

Except as prescribed in § 153.353, a B/3 venting system must discharge:

(a) At the highest of the following points:

(1) 6m (approx. 19.7 ft) above the weatherdeck.

(2) B/3 above the weatherdeck.

(3) 6m (approx. 19.7 ft) above a walkway, if the walkway is within a 6m (approx. 19.7 ft) horizontal radius from the vent discharge.

(b) At least 15m (approx. 49.2 ft) from air intakes for, or openings into, accommodation and service spaces.

[CGD 78–128, 47 FR 21208, May 17, 1982; 47 FR 27293, June 24, 1982]

§ 153.351 Location of 4m vent discharges.

Except as prescribed in § 153.353, a 4m venting system must discharge:

(a) At least 4m (approx. 13.1 ft) above the higher of:

(1) the weatherdeck; or

(2) any walkway that is within a 4m (approx. 13.1 ft) horizontal radius from the vent discharge.

(b) At least 10m (approx. 32.8 ft) from air intakes for, or openings into, accommodation or service spaces.

[CGD 78–128, 47 FR 21208, May 17, 1982]

§ 153.352 B/3 and 4 m venting system outlets.

A B/3 or 4 m venting system outlet must:

(a) Discharge vertically upwards; and

(b) Prevent precipitation from entering the vent system.

§ 153.353 High velocity vents.

The discharge point of a B/3 or 4m venting system must be located at

least 3m (approx. 10 ft) above the weatherdeck or walkway if:
(a) The discharge is a vertical, unimpeded jet;
(b) The jet has a minimum exit velocity of 30 m/sec (approx. 98.4 ft/sec); and
(c) The high velocity vent has been approved by Commandant (CG–ENG).

[CGD 78–128, 47 FR 21208, May 17, 1982, as amended by CGD 82–063b, 48 FR 4782, Feb. 3, 1983]

§ 153.354 Venting system inlet.

A venting system must terminate in the vapor space above the cargo when the tank is filled to a 2 percent ullage and the tankship has no heel or trim.

§ 153.355 PV venting systems.

When Table 1 requires a PV venting system, the cargo tank must have a PV valve in its vent line. The PV valve must be located between the tank and any connection to another tank's vent line (such as a vent riser common to two or more tanks).

§ 153.358 Venting system flow capacity.

(a) The cross-sectional flow area of any vent system segment, including any PV or SR valve, must at no point be less than that of a pipe whose inside diameter is 6.4 cm (approx. 2.5 in.).

(b) When Table 1 requires a closed or restricted gauging system, calculations must show that, under conditions in which a saturated cargo vapor is discharged through the venting system at the maximum anticipated loading rate, the pressure differential between the cargo tank vapor space and the atmosphere does not exceed 28 kPa gauge (approx. 4 psig), or, for independent tanks, the maximum working pressure of the tank.

§ 153.360 Venting system restriction.

A venting system must have no assembly that could reduce its cross-sectional flow area or flow capacity to less than that required in § 153.358.

§ 153.361 Arrangements for removal of valves from venting systems having multiple relief valves.

A venting system having multiple relief valves may be arranged to allow the removal of a valve (for repair, as an example) provided the venting system:

(a) Has valves that are interlocked, so that the removal of a valve does not reduce the venting system relieving capacity below the minimum relieving capacity required by § 153.358; and

(b) Is arranged so that cargo vapor will not escape through the opening left after a valve has been removed.

[CGD 78–128, 47 FR 21208, May 17, 1982; 47 FR 27293, June 24, 1982]

§ 153.362 Venting system drain.

Unless a cargo vent system at every point is level or slopes back to the cargo tank under all conditions of heel and trim allowed under § 153.806, the cargo vent system must have a drain valve at each low point (trap) in the vent line.

§ 153.364 Venting system supports.

Supports for a vent system must meet § 38.10–10(c) of this chapter.

§ 153.365 Liquid overpressurization protection.

(a) Except as noted in paragraph (b) of this section, a containment system requiring closed or restricted gauging must:

(1) Be designed to withstand the maximum pressure that develops during an overfill of the densest cargo endorsed for the containment system; or

(2) Have an overflow control system that meets § 153.408; or

(3) Meet the requirements specified by the Commandant (CG–ENG).

(b) A containment system requiring restricted gauging, except for those cargoes that reference §§ 153.525 or 153.527, may be equipped with a spill valve that:

(1) Meets ASTM F 1271 (incorporated by reference, see § 153.4); and

(2) Limits the maximum pressure during liquid overfill at a specified cargo loading rate to that which the containment system is able to withstand (see §§ 153.294(b) and 152.977(b)).

[CGD 78–128, 47 FR 21208, May 17, 1982, as amended by CGD 82–063b, 48 FR 4782, Feb. 3, 1983; CGD 88–032, 56 FR 35827, July 29, 1991; USCG–2000–7790, 65 FR 58463, Sept. 29, 2000]

§ 153.368 Pressure-vacuum valves.

(a) The pressure side of a required pressure-vacuum relief valve must begin to open only at a pressure exceeding 3.5 kPa gauge (approx. 0.5 psig).

(b) A pressure-vacuum relief valve must meet the requirements of Subpart 162.017 of this chapter.

§ 153.370 Minimum relief valve setting for ambient temperature cargo tanks.

The relief valve setting for a containment system that carries a cargo at ambient temperature must at least equal the cargo's vapor pressure at 46 °C (approx. 115 °F).

[CGD 81–078, 50 FR 21173, May 22, 1985]

§ 153.371 Minimum relief valve setting for refrigerated cargo tanks.

The relief valve setting for a containment system that carries a refrigerated cargo must at least equal the lesser of:

(a) That in § 153.370; or

(b) 110 percent of the cargo's vapor pressure at the steady state temperature obtained by a full tank of cargo with the refrigeration system operating under ambient conditions described within the definition of a refrigerated tank in § 153.2.

§ 153.372 Gauges and vapor return for cargo vapor pressures exceeding 100 kPa (approx. 14.7 psia).

When table 1 references this section, the containment system must have a:

(a) Tank pressure gauge at the point where cargo flow is controlled during transfer; and

(b) Vapor return connection.

[CGD 73–96, 42 FR 49027, Sept. 26, 1977; 42 FR 57126, Nov. 1, 1977, as amended by CGD 81–078, 50 FR 21173, May 22, 1985]

CARGO GAUGING SYSTEMS

§ 153.400 General requirements for gauges.

(a) Columnar gauge glasses must not be installed on a cargo containment system.

(b) Flat sight glasses must meet § 38.10–20(h) of this chapter.

§ 153.404 Standards for containment systems having required closed gauges.

When Table 1 requires a cargo's containment system to have a closed gauge, the containment system must have the following:

(a) A permanently installed closed gauging system.

(b) A vapor return connection.

(c) The high level alarm described in § 153.409.

(d) Either a closed cargo sampling system or a cargo sampling arrangement allowing the retrieval of a sample through an orifice not exceeding:

(1) 0.635 cm (approx. 0.25 in.) diameter when the cargo's vapor pressure is 28 kPa gauge (approx. 4 psig) or less; or

(2) 0.140 cm (approx. 0.055 in.) diameter when the cargo's vapor pressure exceeds 28 kPa (approx. 4 psig).

§ 153.406 Standards for containment systems having required restricted gauges.

When Table 1 requires a cargo's containment system to have a restricted gauge, the containment system must have:

(a) A closed gauging system; or

(b) A system that has:

(1) A restricted gauge (e.g., a sounding tube) with an orifice diameter not exceeding 20 cm (approx. 7.8 in.);

(2) A permanently attached gauge cover that is vapor tight when in place; and

(3) A venting system that has either:

(i) Lock open PV valves; or

(ii) Valved bypasses around the PV valves.

§ 153.407 Special requirements for sounding tube gauges.

(a) A sounding tube installed as a restricted gauge must extend to within one meter (approx. 39.4 in.) of the bottom of the tank.

(b) A sounding tube must not be installed on a tank whose relief valve setting exceeds 28 kPa (approx. 4 psig) unless it is specifically permitted by the Commandant (CG–ENG).

(c) A sounding tube must have no perforations in the tube wall.

[CGD 73–96, 42 FR 49027, Sept. 26, 1977, as amended by CGD 82–063b, 48 FR 4782, Feb. 3, 1983]

§ 153.408 Tank overflow control.

(a) When table 1 references this section, a cargo containment system must have a cargo high level alarm meeting

§ 153.409

§ 153.409 and one of the following additional systems:

(1) A second high level (cargo overflow) alarm.

(2) A system that automatically stops cargo flow to the tank (automatic shutdown system).

(b) The high level alarm and the cargo overflow alarm or automatic shutdown system must:

(1) Be independent of one-another; and

(2) Operate on loss of power.

(c) The cargo overflow alarm or the automatic shutdown system must operate early enough to:

(1) Stop the loading operation before the cargo tank overflows; and

(2) Avoid surge pressures that exceed the working pressure specified in § 153.294(b).

(d) A tank overflow must be identified with the legend "TANK OVERFLOW ALARM" in lettering as specified for the warning sign in § 153.955.

(e) A tank overflow alarm must be audible and visible in that part of the deck where the containment systems are located and at the point where cargo loading is controlled on the tankship.

(f) The automatic shutdown system or tank overflow alarm must be able to be checked at the tank for proper operation (for example, by electrically simulating an overfill at the tank gauge connection).

(g) In this section, "independent" as applied to two systems means that one system will operate with a failure of any part of the other system except high level power sources and electrical feeder panels. Conduit need not be independent; the control wiring for several independent systems may be carried in a single conduit.

[CGD 81–078, 50 FR 21173, May 22, 1985]

§ 153.409 High level alarms.

When Table 1 refers to this section or requires a cargo to have a closed gauging system, the cargo's containment system must have a high level alarm:

(a) That gives an audible and visual alarm before the tank fills to 97 percent of its capacity;

(b) That can be seen and heard where cargo transfer is controlled and on the open deck;

(c) Whose operation can be checked prior to each loading; and

(d) That must be marked as described in § 153.408(c)(6) with the legend "HIGH LEVEL ALARM."

[CGD 78–128, 47 FR 21209, May 17, 1982; 47 FR 27293, June 24, 1982]

CARGO TEMPERATURE CONTROL SYSTEMS

§ 153.430 Heat transfer systems; general.

Each cargo cooling system required by this part and each cargo heating system must:

(a) Meet the standards of Subchapters F (Marine Engineering) and J (Electrical Engineering) of this chapter;

(b) Have valving that enables the system to be separated from all other cooling and heating systems; and

(c) Allow manual regulation of the system's heat transfer rate.

[CGD 73–96, 42 FR 49027, Sept. 26, 1977, as amended by CGD 78–128, 47 FR 21209, May 17, 1982; CGD 81–078, 50 FR 21174, May 22, 1985]

§ 153.432 Cooling systems.

(a) Each cargo cooling system must have an equivalent standby unit that is installed and that can be placed in operation immediately after failure of the primary cooling system.

(b) Each tankship that has a cargo tank with a required cooling system must have a manual that contains:

(1) A piping diagram for the cooling system; and

(2) Instructions for changing over to the standby system described in paragraph (a) of this section.

[CGD 73–96, 42 FR 49027, Sept. 26, 1977, as amended by CGD 78–128, 47 FR 21209, May 17, 1982]

§ 153.434 Heat transfer coils within a tank.

When a cargo tank contains any quantity of cargo, a cargo cooling or heating system having coils within the tank must keep the heat transfer fluid at a pressure greater than the pressure exerted on the heating or cooling system by the cargo.

[CGD 78–128, 47 FR 21209, May 17, 1982]

§ 153.436 Heat transfer fluids: compatibility with cargo.

A heat transfer fluid separated from the cargo by only one wall (for example, the heat transfer fluid in a coil within a tank) must be compatible with the cargo under the standards prescribed for compatibility between two cargoes in Part 150 of this chapter.

[CGD 81–078, 50 FR 21174, May 22, 1985]

§ 153.438 Cargo pressure or temperature alarms required.

(a) Each refrigerated tank must have:

(1) An alarm that operates when the cargo's pressure exceeds the vapor pressure described in § 153.371(b); or

(2) An alarm that operates when the cargo's temperature exceeds the steady state temperature described in § 153.371(b).

(b) The alarm must give an audible and visual signal on the bridge and at the cargo control station.

(c) The cargo pressure or temperature alarm must be independent of other cargo pressure or temperature sensing arrangements.

§ 153.440 Cargo temperature sensors.

(a) Except as prescribed in paragraph (c) of this section, when Table 1 refers to this section, the containment system must meet the following requirements:

(1) A heated or refrigerated cargo tank must have a remote reading thermometer sensing the temperature of the cargo at the bottom of the tank.

(2) A refrigerated tank must have a remote reading second thermometer near the top of the tank and below the maximum liquid level allowed by § 153.981.

(3) Unless waived under § 153.491(a), a cargo tank endorsed to carry a Category A, B, or C NLS cargo must have a thermometer whose temperature reading is no greater than the temperature of the cargo at a level above the tank bottom at least one-eighth but no more than one-half the height of the tank if the cargo is—

(i) A Category A NLS or a Category B NLS having a viscosity of at least 25 mPa.s at 20 °C;

(ii) A Category C NLS having a viscosity of at least 60 mPa.s at 20 °C; or

(iii) A Category A, B, or C NLS that has a melting point greater than 0 °C.

(b) A readout for each remote thermometer required by this section must be at the point where cargo transfer is controlled.

(c) A portable thermometer may be substituted for the equipment required in paragraphs (a) and (b) of this section if—

(1) Table 1 allows open gauging with the cargo; or

(2) Table 1 allows restricted gauging with the cargo, and the portable thermometer is designed to be used through the containment system's restricted gauging system.

[CGD 78–128, 47 FR 21209, May 17, 1982, as amended by CGD 81–101, 52 FR 7781, Mar. 12, 1987; CGD 81–101, 53 FR 28974, Aug. 1, 1988 and 54 FR 12629, Mar. 28, 1989]

SPECIAL REQUIREMENTS FOR FLAMMABLE OR COMBUSTIBLE CARGOES

§ 153.460 Fire protection systems.

Each self-propelled ship and each manned non-self-propelled ship must meet the following:

(a) With the exception of the vent riser, each part of a cargo containment system exposed on the weatherdeck must be covered by the fire protection system listed beside the cargo in Table 1 and described in the footnotes to Table 1.

(b) The Commandant (CG–ENG) approves the substitution of a dry chemical (D) type fire protection system for an A or B type on a case by case basis.

(c) A fire protection system required by this part must meet part 34 of this chapter or be specifically approved by the Commandant (CG–ENG).

[CGD 73–96, 42 FR 49027, Sept. 26, 1977, as amended by CGD 82–063b, 48 FR 4782, Feb. 3, 1983; CGD 81–101, 52 FR 7781, Mar. 12, 1987]

§ 153.461 Electrical bonding of independent tanks.

An independent metallic cargo tank that carries a flammable or combustible cargo must be electrically bonded to the tankship's hull.

§ 153.462 Static discharges from inert gas systems.

An inert gas system on a tank that carries a flammable or combustible

§ 153.463

cargo must not create static arcing as the inert gas is injected into the tank.

§ 153.463 Vent system discharges.

The discharge of a venting system must be at least 10 m (approx. 32.8 ft) from an ignition source if:

(a) The cargo tank is endorsed to carry a flammable or combustible cargo; and

(b) Table 1 requires the cargo to have a PV venting system.

§ 153.465 Flammable vapor detector.

(a) A tankship that carries a flammable cargo must have two vapor detectors that meet § 35.30–15(b) of this chapter.

(b) At least one of the vapor detectors in paragraph (a) of this section must be portable.

§ 153.466 Electrical equipment.

A tankship carrying a flammable or combustible cargo under this part must meet subchapter J of this chapter.

DESIGN AND EQUIPMENT FOR POLLUTION CONTROL

SOURCE: Sections 153.470 through 153.491 appear at CGD 81–101, 52 FR 7781, Mar. 12, 1987, unless otherwise noted.

§ 153.470 System for discharge of NLS residue to the sea: Categories A, B, C, and D.

Unless waived under § 153.491, each ship that discharges Category A, B, or C NLS residue, or Category D NLS residue not diluted to ¹/₁₀th of its original concentration, into the sea under §§ 153.1126 and 153.1128 must have an NLS residue discharge system meeting the following:

(a) *Minimum diameter of an NLS residue discharge outlet.* The outlet of each NLS residue discharge system must have a diameter at least as great as that given by the following formula:

$$D = \frac{(Q_d)(\cosine \phi)}{5L}$$

where:

D=Minimum diameter of the discharge outlet in meters.

Q_d=Maximum rate in cubic meters per hour at which the ship operator wishes to discharge slops (note: Q_d affects the discharge rate allowed under § 153.1126(b)(2)).

L=Distance from the forward perpendicular to the discharge outlet in meters.

φ=The acute angle between a perpendicular to the shell plating at the discharge location and the direction of the average velocity of the discharged liquid.

(b) *Location of an NLS residue discharge outlet.* Each NLS residue discharge outlet must be located—

(1) At the turn of the bilge beneath the cargo area; and

(2) Where the discharge from the outlet is not drawn into the ship's seawater intakes.

(c) *Location of dual NLS residue discharge outlets.* If the value of 6.45 for K is used in § 153.1126(b)(2), the NLS residue discharge system must have two outlets located on opposite sides of the ship.

[CGD 81–101, 52 FR 7781, Mar. 12, 1987, as amended by CGD 81–101, 53 FR 28974, Aug. 1, 1988 and 54 FR 12629, Mar. 28, 1989; CGD 95–028, 62 FR 51209, Sept. 30, 1997]

§ 153.480 Stripping quantity for Category B and C NLS tanks on ships built after June 30, 1986: Categories B and C.

Unless waived under § 153.491, Category B and C NLS cargo tanks on each ship built after June 30, 1986 must have stripping quantities determined under § 153.1604 that are less than—

(a) 0.15 m³ if Category B; and

(b) 0.35 m³ if Category C.

§ 153.481 Stripping quantities and interim standards for Category B NLS tanks on ships built before July 1, 1986: Category B.

Unless waived under § 153.483 or § 153.491, each Category B NLS cargo tank on ships built before July 1, 1986 must meet the following:

(a) Unless the tank meets the interim standard provided by paragraph (b) of this section and is prewashed in accordance with § 153.1118, the tank must have a stripping quantity determined under § 153.1604 that is less than 0.35m³.

(b) Before October 3, 1994, the tank may have a total NLS residue determined under § 153.1608 that is less than 1.0 m³ or ¹/₃₀₀₀th of the tank's capacity and an NLS residue discharge system meeting the following:

(1) The system must be capable of discharging at a rate equal to or less than Q in the following formula:

$$Q = K\ U^{1.4}\ L^{1.6} \times 10^{-5}\ m^3/hr$$

where:

K=4.3, except K=6.45 if the discharge is equally distributed between two NLS residue discharge outlets on opposite sides of the ship (see §§ 153.470(c) and 153.1126(b)).

L=ship's length in meters.

U=for a ship that is self-propelled, the minimum speed in knots specified in the approved Procedures and Arrangements Manual for discharging Category B NLS residue, but at least 7;

U=for a ship that is not self-propelled, the minimum speed in knots specified in the approved Procedures and Arrangements Manual for discharging Category B NLS residue, but at least 4.

(2) The system must have equipment capable of automatically recording—

(i) The time of day that discharge of NLS residue through the residue discharge system starts and ends; and

(ii) The dates on which discharge begins and ends unless the equipment allows a person to enter these dates on the record manually.

(3) Each system that has the capacity to exceed Q calculated in paragraph (b)(1) of this section must have equipment that—

(i) Records the NLS residue flow through the system; and

(ii) Is sufficiently accurate that its recorded values averaged over any 30 second period differ no more than 15% from the actual flow averaged over the same 30 second period.

(4) Each system that has the capacity to exceed Q calculated under paragraph (b)(1) of this section and does not automatically control the flow rate must have—

(i) Manual controls that enable the flow to be adjusted to the value of Q calculated in paragraph (b)(1) of this section and that must be moved through at least 25% of their total range of movement for the discharge rate to change from 0.5Q to 1.5Q; and

(ii) A flow rate meter located where the flow is manually controlled.

[CGD 81-101, 52 FR 7781, Mar. 12, 1987, as amended by CGD 81-101, 53 FR 28974, Aug. 1, 1988 and 54 FR 12629, Mar. 28, 1989]

§ 153.482 Stripping quantities and interim standards for Category C NLS tanks on ships built before July 1, 1986: Category C.

Unless waived under § 153.483 or § 153.491, each Category C NLS cargo tank on ships built before July 1, 1986 must meet the following:

(a) Unless the tank meets the interim standard provided by paragraph (b) of this section, the tank must have a stripping quantity determined under 153.1604 that is less than 0.95 m³.

(b) Before October 3, 1994, the tank may have a total NLS residue determined under § 153.1608 that is less than 3.0 m³ or 1/1000th of the tank's capacity.

§ 153.483 Restricted voyage waiver for Category B and C NLS tanks on ships built before July 1, 1986: Category B and C.

At its discretion the Coast Guard waives §§ 153.481 and 153.482 under this section and allows a ship to carry Category B and C NLS cargoes between ports or terminals in one or more countries signatory to MARPOL 73/78 if the ship's owner requests a waiver following the procedures in § 153.10 and includes—

(a) A written pledge to—

(1) Limit the loading and discharge of Category B and C NLS cargoes in a foreign port to those ports and terminals in countries signatory to MARPOL 73/78 and listed in accordance with paragraph (b) of this section; and

(2) Prewash the cargo tank as required under § 153.1118 after each Category B or C NLS is unloaded unless the prewash is allowed to be omitted under § 153.1114;

(b) A list of—

(1) All foreign ports or terminals at which the ship is expected to load or discharge Category B or C NLS cargo, and

(2) All foreign ports or terminals at which the ship is expected to discharge Category B or C NLS residue from the tank;

(c) An estimate of the quantity of NLS residue to be discharged to each foreign port or terminal listed under paragraph (b)(2) of this section;

(d) Written statements from the owners of adequate reception facilities in

§ 153.484

the ports and terminals listed in accordance with paragraph (b)(2) of this section who have agreed to take NLS residue from the ship, showing the amount of NLS residue each agrees to take; and

(e) A written attestation from the person in charge of each port or terminal listed in accordance with paragraph (b)(1) of this section that the administration has determined the port or terminal to have adequate reception facilities for the NLS residue.

NOTE TO § 153.483: Certificates of Inspection and any IMO Certificates issued to ships on restricted voyage waivers indicate that while the ship carries an NLS cargo or NLS residue, it is limited to voyages between the ports or terminals listed on the certificate.

[CGD 81–101, 52 FR 7781, Mar. 12, 1987, as amended by CGD 81–101, 53 FR 28975, Aug. 1, 1988 and 54 FR 12629, Mar. 28, 1989]

§ 153.484 Prewash equipment.

Unless the ship operator shows that the prewash equipment specified in this section will be available at discharge or prewash facilities or the equipment is waived under § 153.491, to have its Certificate of Inspection or Certificate of Compliance endorsed to carry a Category A NLS or a Category B or C NLS requiring viscosity or melting point information under § 153.908 (a) and (b), a ship must have the following:

(a) For the tanks that carry the NLS, a tank washing system capable of washing all interior tank surfaces except those shielded from the washing system spray by ship's structure, and consisting of a wash water supply system and—

(1) A fixed tank washing machine in each tank; or

(2) A portable tank washing machine and, if required by the Coast Guard, equipment to move it during washing and when storing.

(b) Piping, valving, and crossovers needed to arrange the cargo piping so that the wash water passes through the cargo pump and cargo piping during tank washing or discharge of tank wash water.

(c) If the approved Procedures and Arrangements Manual specifies the hot water prewash required under 153.1108, a means of supplying water to the tank washing machine under paragraph (a) of this section at—

(1) A temperature of at least 60 °C (140 °F) when it leaves the washing machine; and

(2) The flow rate needed for the washing machine jets to meet paragraph (a) of this section.

§ 153.486 Design and equipment for removing NLS residue by ventilation: Categories A, B, C, and D.

(a) If NLS residue is to be removed from a cargo tank by ventilation, in addition to the equipment required under paragraph (b) of this section the ship must have—

(1) Openings in the tank deck near the sump or suction point;

(2) If the openings required by paragraph (a)(1) of this section are insufficient, an access opening for visually determining whether liquid remains in the sump area of the cargo tank after ventilation or some other means for making this determination; and

(3) An approved Procedures and Arrangements Manual with instructions that meet § 153.490(b)(3).

(b) Unless the ship operator shows that the ventilation equipment specified in this paragraph will be available from shore when needed, if NLS residue is to be removed from a cargo tank by ventilation, in addition to the equipment required under paragraph (a) of this section the ship must have—

(1) Portable forced air ventilating equipment fitting the ventilation openings required in paragraph (a) of this section and able to ventilate the extremities of the tank to the extent prescribed in Appendix C of the IMO *Standards for Procedures and Arrangements for the Discharge of Noxious Liquid Substances,* Resolution MEPC 18(22), 1985; and

(2) A connector that allows a fan or air supply to be connected to the hose connections for the tank at the manifold.

NOTE: The Clean Air Act (42 U.S.C. 7401 *et seq.*) allows states to regulate emissions from tank ventilation. There may be other regulations, both local and Federal, that affect the use of tank ventilation for safety or environmental purposes.

§ 153.488 Design and equipment for tanks carrying high melting point NLSs: Category B.

Unless waived under § 153.491, for a ship to have its Certificate of Inspection or Certificate of Compliance endorsed allowing a tank to carry a Category B NLS with a melting point of 15 °C or more, the cargo tank must have—

(a) An arrangement enabling the cargo to be heated before cargo transfer, using heat supplied by the ship or by another source; and

(b) Sides and bottom separate from the ship's side or bottom shell plating.

§ 153.490 Cargo Record Book and Approved Procedures and Arrangements Manual: Categories A, B, C, and D.

(a) Unless waived under § 153.491, to have a Certificate of Inspection or Certificate of Compliance endorsed to carry NLS cargo, a ship must have—

(1) If U.S., a Cargo Record Book published by the Coast Guard (OMB App. No. 1625–0094), or, if foreign, a Cargo Record Book having the same entries and format as Appendix 4 of Annex II; and

(2) A Procedures and Arrangements Manual meeting paragraph (b) of this section and approved by—

(i) The Coast Guard, if the ship is a United States ship or one whose Administration is not signatory to MARPOL 73/78; or

(ii) The Administration, if the ship is one whose Administration is signatory to MARPOL 73/78.

(b) Each Procedures and Arrangements Manual under paragraph (a)(2) of this section must include the following:

(1) The standard format and content prescribed in Chapter 2 and Appendix D of the IMO *Standards for Procedures and Arrangements for the Discharge of Noxious Liquid Substances,* Resolution MEPC 18(22), 1985, or, for ships for which the only NLS carried is a Category D NLS and ships having a waiver under § 153.483 or § 153.491, the format and content prescribed by the Commandant (CG–ENG).

(2) If the ship has a tank that carries a cargo under a waiver issued under § 153.483, procedures ensuring that—

(i) Category B and C NLSs are discharged from the tank only in the ports or terminals listed in accordance with § 153.483(b); and

(ii) The tank is prewashed after discharging each Category B or C NLS unless § 153.1114 allows the prewash to be omitted.

(3) If ventilation is used to clean a tank under § 153.1102(b)(2), ventilation procedures that meet those in Appendix C of the IMO *Standards for Procedures and Arrangements for the Discharge of Noxious Liquid Substances,* Resolution MEPC 18(22), 1985.

(4) If tank cleaning agents are used, quantities to use and instructions for using the cleaning agents.

(5) If the tank has the discharge recording equipment required in § 153.481(b), procedures to ensure that no NLS residue is discharged from the tank when the recording equipment is incapacitated unless the concentration and total quantity limits for the NLS in Annex II are not exceeded.

[CGD 81–101, 52 FR 7781, Mar. 12, 1987, as amended by CGD 81–101, 53 FR 28975, Aug. 1, 1988 and 54 FR 12629, Mar. 28, 1989; USCG–2006–25697, 71 FR 55747, Sept. 25, 2006]

§ 153.491 Waiver of certain equipment for dedicated cargo tanks.

(a) The Coast Guard waives §§ 153.440(a)(3), 153.480, 153.481, 153.482, and 153.488 and endorses a ship's Certificate of Inspection or Certificate of Compliance allowing a cargo tank to carry a single, specific NLS cargo and no other cargo if the ship's owner—

(1) Requests a waiver following the procedures in § 153.10; and

(2) Pledges in writing that while any waiver is in effect the cargo tank will—

(i) Carry only the NLS cargo listed on the Certificate of Inspection or Certificate of Compliance;

(ii) Carry no cargo other than the NLS; and

(iii) Not be washed or ballasted unless the wash water or ballast water is discharged to a reception facility.

(b) The Coast Guard waives §§ 153.470 and 153.490(a)(2) if—

(1) The ship's owner requests a waiver following the procedures in § 153.10;

(2) The Coast Guard has issued a waiver to each of the ship's NLS cargo

§ 153.500

tanks under paragraph (a) of this section; and

(3) The ship's owner adds to the ship's operational manual any provisions for preventing NLS discharge specified by the Commandant (CG–ENG) as a condition for issuing the waiver.

[CGD 81–101, 52 FR 7781, Mar. 12, 1987, as amended by CGD 81–101, 53 FR 28975, Aug. 1, 1988 and 54 FR 12629, Mar. 28, 1989]

SPECIAL REQUIREMENTS

§ 153.500 Inert gas systems.

When Table 1 refers to this section, a cargo containment system must have a permanent inert gas system that:

(a) Maintains the vapor space of the containment system in an inert state by filling the vapor space with a gas that is neither reactive with the cargo nor flammable;

(b) Has a pressure control system that:

(1) Prevents the inert gas system from raising the cargo tank pressure to more than the relief valve setting; and

(2) Maintains at least a 3.5 kPa gauge (approx. 0.5 psig) pressure within the containment system at all times, including cargo discharge;

(c) Has storage for enough inerting gas to replace that normally lost while the tank's atmosphere is maintained in an inert condition (e.g. through tank breathing and relief valve leakage), but in no case an amount less than 5 percent of the tank's capacity when measured with the gas at −18 °C (approx. 0 °F) and a pressure equal to the cargo tank's relief valve setting; and

(d) Has connections for any supplemental gas supply necessary to maintain the inert gas pressure described in paragraph (b) of this section during cargo discharge.

§ 153.501 Requirement for dry inert gas.

When Table 1 refers to this section, an inert gas system for the containment system must supply inert gas containing no more than 100 ppm water.

§ 153.515 Special requirements for extremely flammable cargoes.

When Table 1 refers to this section:

(a) An enclosed space containing a cargo tank must have an inerting system that meets the requirements in § 153.500 applying to the inert gas system of a containment system;

(b) Cargo discharge pumps must be of a type that does not subject the shaft gland to the cargo under pressure or that is submerged; and

(c) The cargo tank's relief valve setting must be no less than 21 kPa gauge (approx. 3 psig).

§ 153.520 Special requirements for carbon disulfide.

A containment system carrying carbon disulfide must meet the following:

(a) Each cargo pump must be of the intank type and encased within a cylindrical well that extends from the top of the tank to a point no more than 10 cm (approx. 4 in.) above the bottom of the tank.

(b) [Reserved]

(c) The cargo piping and venting systems must be completely independent of those for other cargo.

(d) Pressure relief valves must be made of type 304 or 316 stainless steel.

[CGD 73–96, 42 FR 49027, Sept. 26, 1977, as amended by CGD 78–128, 47 FR 21209, May 17, 1982]

§ 153.525 Special requirements for unusually toxic cargoes.

When Table 1 refers to this section a containment system must meet the following:

(a) Cargo piping and venting systems must be designed so that they can be separated from any containment system endorsed for a cargo not covered by this section.

(b) A cargo tank's relief valve setting must be not less than 21 kPa gauge (approx. 3 psig).

(c) All cargo pumps and valves located below the weatherdeck must be operable from the weatherdeck.

(d) A heat transfer system for the cargo must:

(1) Be independent of other ship service systems, except for other cargo heat transfer systems, and not enter the engine room;

(2) Be totally external to the cargo containment system; or

(3) Be approved by the Commandant (CG–ENG) for use with toxic cargoes.

(e) The cargo must be separated from any bunkers by at least two bulkheads.

(f) A cargo containment system must have a vapor return connection.

[CGD 73-96, 42 FR 49027, Sept. 26, 1977, as amended by CGD 78-128, 47 FR 21209, May 17, 1982; CGD 82-063b, 48 FR 4782, Feb. 3, 1983]

§ 153.526 Toxic vapor detectors.

(a) When Table 1 refers to this section, a tankship must have two toxic vapor detectors, at least one of which must be portable, each able to measure vapor concentrations in the range of the time weighted average (TWA) for the cargo. The portable detector may be a direct reading detector tube instrument. These vapor detectors may be combined with those required by § 153.465.

(b) When the toxic vapor detectors required by paragraph (a) of this section are not available and the cargo referenced to this section is transferred through a cargo pumproom, the tankship must meet § 153.336(b).

[CGD 78-128, 47 FR 21210, May 17, 1982]

§ 153.527 Toxic vapor protection.

When Table 1 refers to this section, a tankship must have on board for each crew member:

(a) An emergency escape breathing apparatus (EEBA) approved by the Mining Safety and Health Administration (formerly the Mining Enforcement and Safety Administration) and the National Institute for Occupational Safety and Health, or the tankship's flag administration.

(b) Where the emergency escape breathing apparatus does not protect the eyes from vapors, a set of goggles that either:

(1) Meet the specifications of ANSI Practice for Occupational and Educational Eye and Face Protection, Z-87.1(1979); or

(2) Are approved by the tankship's flag administration.

[CGD 78-128, 47 FR 21210, May 17, 1982]

§ 153.530 Special requirements for alkylene oxides.

When Table 1 refers to this section, a containment system must meet the following:

(a) Except as provided in paragraphs (b) and (c) of this section, a cargo containment system must be made of:

(1) Stainless steel other than types 416 and 442; and

(2) Steel.

(b) Except as provided in paragraph (c) of this section, gaskets must be composites of spirally wound stainless steel and Teflon or similar flourinated polymer.

(c) The Commandant (CG-ENG) approves a cargo containment system using materials other than those described in this section for alkylene oxides on a case by case basis if:

(1) The person wishing to have the containment system approved completes any tests prescribed by the Commandant (CG-ENG); and

(2) The Commandant (CG-ENG) approves the results of the tests and the material for use with alkylene oxides.

(d) The following materials are generally found unsatisfactory for gaskets, packing, insulation, and similar uses in alkylene oxide containment systems and would require extensive testing as described in paragraph (c) of this section before being approved:

(1) Neoprene or natural rubber if it might be in contact with the alkylene oxide.

(2) Asbestos or asbestos mixed with other materials such as with many common insulations, packing materials, and gasket materials.

(3) Materials containing oxides of magnesium, such as mineral wools.

(e) The tank's relief valve setting must not be less than 21 kPa gauge (approx. 3 psig).

(f) If the containment system is equipped with a cooling system, the cooling system must:

(1) Not compress the cargo; and

(2) Regulate the cargo temperature automatically and allow manual regulation.

(g) The cargo piping system must:

(1) Comply with Part 38 of this chapter;

(2) Be completely separate from all other systems;

(3) Be assembled from valves, fittings, and accessories having a pressure rating of not less than 1030 kPa gauge (approx. 150 psig) (American National Standards Institute); and

§ 153.545

(4) Have no threaded joints.

(h) The cargo containment system vapor space and each space listed in paragraphs (k) and (l) of this section must have continuous monitoring of oxygen concentration or have an arrangement to enable sampling with a portable oxygen analyzer.

(i) Valve disks or disk faces, seats, and other wearing valve parts must be made of stainless steel containing no less than 11 percent chromium.

(j) The venting system must be independent of other containment or tankship systems.

(k) When a cargo tank is in an enclosed space, the space must have:

(1) An inert gas system meeting the requirements that apply to the inert gas system of a containment system in § 153.500, or

(2) A forced ventilation system meeting the requirements that apply to a cargo handling space ventilation system in § 153.312.

(l) Cofferdams, cargo tanks, double bottom spaces, void spaces and other enclosed spaces adjacent to an integral cargo tank must have an inert gas system meeting the requirements that apply to the inert gas system of a containment system in § 153.500.

(m) An intank pump or inert gas displacement must be used to discharge cargo.

(n) The cargo discharge piping system must have a remotely actuated quick closing shutoff valve that meets § 153.284 at the cargo transfer hose connection.

(o) Cargo hose must:

(1) Have the specific approval of the Commandant (CG–ENG) for use in alkylene oxide transfer; and

(2) Be marked "For Alkylene Oxide Transfer Only".

(p) All exposed parts of the cargo containment system above or on the deck, such as tank domes, cargo piping, and loading manifolds, must be covered by a water spray system that:

(1) Operates automatically in a fire involving the cargo containment system;

(2) Has at least two remote manual actuators, one in each emergency shutdown station required by § 153.296; and

(3) Covers the area of application with a uniform spray of 0.175 l/m^2 sec (0.0043 gal/ft^2 sec).

[CGD 73–96, 42 FR 49027, Sept. 26, 1977, as amended by CGD 78–128, 47 FR 21210, May 17, 1982; CGD 82–063b, 48 FR 4782, Feb. 3, 1983; CGD 82–063b, 48 FR 39629, Sept. 1, 1983; CGD 81–078, 50 FR 21174, May 22, 1985]

§ 153.545 Special requirements for liquid sulfur.

(a) A containment system carrying liquid sulfur must have:

(1) A cargo tank ventilation system that:

(i) Maintains the H_2S vapor concentration below 1.85 percent by volume; and

(ii) Prevents sulfur buildup within itself; and

(2) An alarm system designed to operate when the ventilation system blower fails.

(b) The void spaces around a cargo tank that carries liquid sulfur must be oil tight.

(c) A cargo tank that carries liquid sulfur and the void spaces surrounding the tank must have connections for sampling vapor.

§ 153.554 Special requirements for acids.

When Table 1 refers to this section:

(a) Each containment system loading and discharge connection must have a spray shield;

(b) Each cargo containment system must be separated from bunkers by double walls, such as a cofferdam and piping tunnels; and

(c) Each vessel must have on board a means to determine whether cargo has leaked into the spaces adjacent to a cargo containment system.

§ 153.555 Special requirements for inorganic acids.

When Table 1 refers to this section, a tankship's shell plating must not be a part of the cargo tank.

[CGD 78–128, 47 FR 21210, May 17, 1982]

§ 153.556 Special requirements for sulfuric acid and oleum.

(a) Except as prescribed in paragraphs (b) and (c) of this section, containment systems carrying sulfuric acid, oleum, or contaminated sulfuric acid are approved by the Commandant (CG–ENG) on a case by case basis.

(b) A containment system carrying sulfuric acid may be:

(1) Made of unlined steel if the cargo composition is between 70 and 80 or between 90 and 100 percent acid by weight;

(2) Lined with lead if the cargo composition does not exceed 96 percent acid by weight; or

(3) Lined with natural rubber or neoprene if the cargo composition does not exceed 51 percent acid by weight.

(c) A containment system for oleum may be of unlined steel if the concentration of free sulfur trioxide in the oleum exceeds 20 percent by weight.

[CGD 73–96, 42 FR 49027, Sept. 26, 1977, as amended by CGD 82–063b, 48 FR 4782, Feb. 3, 1983]

§ 153.557 Special requirements for hydrochloric acid.

(a) A containment system that carries hydrochloric acid must be lined with:

(1) Natural rubber;

(2) Neoprene; or

(3) A material approved for hydrochloric acid tanks by the Commandant (CG–ENG).

(b) Containment systems for contaminated hydrochloric acid are approved by the Commandant (CG–ENG) on a case by case basis.

[CGD 73–96, 42 FR 49027, Sept. 26, 1977, as amended by CGD 82–063b, 48 FR 4781, Feb. 3, 1983]

§ 153.558 Special requirements for phosphoric acid.

A phosphoric acid containment system must be:

(a) Lined with natural rubber or neoprene;

(b) Lined with a material approved for phosphoric acid tanks by the Commandant (CG–ENG); or

(c) Made of a stainless steel that resists corrosion by phosphoric acid.

NOTE: "Phosphoric acid", as defined in § 153.2, includes phosphoric acid, superphosphoric acid, and aqueous solutions of phosphoric acid.

[CGD 73–96, 42 FR 49027, Sept. 26, 1977, as amended by CGD 82–063b, 48 FR 4782, Feb. 3, 1983; CGD 88–100, 54 FR 40042, Sept. 29, 1989]

§ 153.559 Special requirements for nitric acid (less than 70 percent).

A containment system that carries nitric acid (less than 70 percent) must be of stainless steel that resists corrosion by nitric acid.

§ 153.560 Special requirements for Alkyl (C7–C9) nitrates.

(a) The carriage temperature of octyl nitrates must be maintained below 100 °C (212 °F) in order to prevent the occurrence of a self-sustaining exothermic decomposition reaction.

(b) Octyl nitrates may not be carried in a deck tank unless the tank has a combination of insulation and a water deluge system sufficient to maintain the tank's cargo temperature below 100 °C (212 °F) and the cargo temperature rise at below 1.5 °C(2.7 °F)/hour, for a fire of 650 °C (1200 °F).

[CGD 88–100, 54 FR 40042, Sept. 29, 1989, as amended by CGD 92–100, 59 FR 17028, Apr. 11, 1994; CGD 94–900, 59 FR 45139, Aug. 31, 1994]

§ 153.565 Special requirement for temperature sensors.

If a cargo listed in table 1 of this part refers to this section, temperature sensors must be used to monitor the cargo pump temperature to detect overheating due to pump failures, when carrying that cargo.

[CGD 94–900, 59 FR 45139, Aug. 31, 1994]

§ 153.602 Special requirements for cargoes reactive with water.

When Table 1 refers to this section, the air inlet to the pressure-vacuum valve for the cargo tank must be located at least 2m (approx. 6.6 ft) above the weatherdeck.

[CGD 78–128, 47 FR 21210, May 17, 1982]

TESTING AND INSPECTION

§ 153.806 Loading information.

Each tankship must have a manual containing information that enables the master to load and ballast the tankship while keeping structural stresses within design limits.

[CGD 79–023, 48 FR 51009, Nov. 4, 1983]

§ 153.808 Examination required for a Certificate of Compliance.

Before a vessel receives either an initial or a reissued Certificate of Compliance endorsed to carry a cargo from Table 1 of this part, the vessel must call at a U.S. port for an examination during which the Officer in Charge, Marine Inspection, determines whether or not the vessel meets the requirements of this chapter.

[CGD 81–052, 50 FR 8733, Mar. 5, 1985, as amended by CGD 95–027, 61 FR 26009, May 23, 1996]

§ 153.809 Procedures for having the Coast Guard examine a vessel for a Certificate of Compliance.

The owner of a foreign flag vessel wishing to have the Coast Guard conduct a Certificate of Compliance examination, as required by § 153.808, must proceed as follows:

(a) Notify the Officer in Charge, Marine Inspection of the port where the vessel is to be inspected at least 7 days before the vessel arrives and arrange the exact time and other details of the examination. This notification is in addition to any other pre-arrival notice to the Coast Guard required by other regulations, but may be concurrent with the endorsement application in § 153.9, and must include—

(1) The name of the vessel's first U.S. port of call;

(2) The date that the vessel is scheduled to arrive;

(3) The name and telephone number of the owner's local agent; and

(4) The names of all cargoes listed in table 1 of this part that are on board the vessel.

(b) Before the examination required by § 153.808 is begun, make certain that the following plans are on board the vessel and available to the Marine Inspector. These plans include—

(1) A general arrangement (including the location of fire fighting, safety, and lifesaving gear);

(2) A capacity plan;

(3) A schematic diagram of cargo piping on deck and in tanks (including the location of all valves and pumps); and

(4) A schematic diagram of cargo tank vent piping (including the location of relief valves and flame screens).

[CGD 95–027, 61 FR 26009, May 23, 1996]

§ 153.812 Inspection for Certificate of Inspection.

The rules governing the issuance of Certificates of Inspection are contained in part 31 of this chapter.

Subpart C—Operations

DOCUMENTS AND CARGO INFORMATION

§ 153.900 Certificates and authorization to carry a bulk liquid hazardous material.

(a) Except as allowed in 33 CFR 151.33(a), no ship may carry a cargo of bulk liquid hazardous material or an NLS residue if the bulk liquid hazardous material or NLS is listed in Table 1 or carried under a written permission under paragraph (d) of this section unless the ship meets the following:

(1) The cargo must be carried in a cargo tank.

(2) If a United States ship, the ship must have a Subchapter D or I Certificate of Inspection that is endorsed to allow the cargo tank to carry the cargo.

(3) If a foreign ship, the ship must have a Certificate of Compliance that is endorsed to allow the cargo tank to carry the cargo.

(4) The ship must have an IMO Certificate of Fitness issued under § 153.12 that is endorsed to allow the cargo tank to carry the cargo if it is—

(i) A United States self-propelled ship in foreign waters; or

(ii) A United States non-self-propelled ship in the waters of another Administration signatory to MARPOL 73/78 and the cargo is a Category A, B, or C NLS.

(b) [Reserved]

(c) No ship may carry any bulk liquid cargo not listed in § 30.25–1 of this chapter, Table 151.05 of Part 151 of this chapter, Table 1 or Table 2 of this part, Table 4 of Part 154 of this chapter, 33 CFR 151.47, or 33 CFR 151.49 unless the cargo name is endorsed on the Certificate of Inspection or contained in a letter issued under paragraph (d) of this section.

(d) The Coast Guard at its discretion endorses the Certificate of Inspection with the name of or issues a letter allowing the carriage of an unlisted cargo described under paragraph (c) of this section if—

(1) The shipowner—

(i) Requests the Coast Guard to add the cargo; and

(ii) Supplies any information the Coast Guard needs to develop carriage requirements for the bulk liquid cargo; and

(2) The ship—

(i) Has a Certificate of Inspection, Certificate of Compliance, or IOPP Certificate as specified in this part;

(ii) Meets the design and equipment requirements of this part specified by the Coast Guard; and

(iii) Meets any additional requirements made by the Coast Guard.

[CGD 81–101, 52 FR 7783, Mar. 12, 1987, as amended by CGD 81–101, 53 FR 28975, Aug. 1, 1988 and 54 FR 12629, Mar. 28, 1989]

§ 153.901 Documents: Posting, availability, and alteration.

(a) No person may operate a United States ship unless the endorsed Certificate of Inspection is readily available on the ship.

(b) No person may operate a foreign ship unless the endorsed Certificate of Compliance or Certificate of Inspection is readily available on the ship.

(c) No person may operate a ship under an alternative or waiver granted under this part unless the document granting the alternative or waiver is attached to the ship's Certificate of Inspection or Certificate of Compliance.

(d) Except as allowed in paragraph (e) of this section, the Coast Guard does not accept the following if altered:

(1) Certificates of Inspection.

(2) Certificates of Compliance.

(3) Certificates of Fitness, unless the alteration is by the issuing authority.

(4) Approved Procedures and Arrangements Manuals, unless the alteration is approved by the issuing authority.

(5) NLS Certificates.

(e) A person wishing to change a Procedures and Arrangements Manual approved by the Coast Guard must submit a copy to the Coast Guard following the procedures for requesting an endorsed Certificate of Inspection in § 153.8.

[CGD 81–101, 52 FR 7783, Mar. 12, 1987]

§ 153.902 Expiration and invalidation of the Certificate of Compliance.

(a) The Certificate of Compliance shows its expiration date.

(b) The endorsement of a Certificate of Compliance under this part is invalid if the vessel does not have a valid IMO Certificate of Fitness.

(c) The endorsement on a Certificate of Compliance invalidated under paragraph (b) of this section, becomes valid again once the ship has the IMO Certificate of Fitness revalidated or reissued.

NOTE: See § 153.809 for procedures for having a Certificate of Compliance reissued.

[CGD 81–101, 52 FR 7784, Mar. 12, 1987; CGD 95–072, 60 FR 50465, Sept. 29, 1995; 60 FR 54906, Oct. 19, 1995; CGD 95–027, 61 FR 26009, May 23, 1996]

§ 153.903 Operating a United States ship in special areas: Categories A, B, and C.

No person may operate a United States ship that carries an NLS or NLS residue in a special area unless—

(a) The ship's Certificate of Inspection is endorsed in accordance with § 153.30; and

(b) The ship meets the operating requirements applying to special areas in Regulations 5, 5A, 8 and the Standards for Procedures and Arrangements of Annex II.

[CGD 81–101, 52 FR 7784, Mar. 12, 1987]

§ 153.904 Limitations in the endorsement.

No person may operate a tankship unless that person complies with all limitations in the endorsement on the tankship's Certificate of Inspection or Certificate of Compliance.

[CGD 81–052, 50 FR 8734, Mar. 5, 1985]

§ 153.905 Regulations required to be on board.

No person may operate a tankship unless the most recent editions of this part, and parts 35 and 150 of this chapter are on board.

[CGD 78-128, 47 FR 21210, May 17, 1982]

§ 153.907 Cargo information.

(a) The master shall ensure that the following information for each cargo carried under this part is readily available to those on the tankship engaged in cargo operations:

(1) The name of the cargo as listed in table 1.
(2) A description of the cargo's appearance and color.
(3) Hazards in handling the cargo.
(4) Any special handling procedures for the cargo, such as inerting.
(5) Procedures to follow if the cargo spills or leaks.
(6) Procedures for treating a person exposed to the cargo.
(7) A list of fire fighting procedures and extinguishing agents effective with cargo fires.
(8) Shipper's name.
(9) Loading point.
(10) Approximate quantity of cargo.
(11) Tank in which the cargo is located.
(12) The name of an agent in the United States authorized to accept service of legal process for the vessel.

(b) The master shall make sure that the following information for cargoes other than those carried under this part is readily available on the tankship:

(1) The name of the cargo as listed in Table 4 of Part 154 of this chapter or § 30.25-1 of this chapter if the cargo is listed in one of these two tables.
(2) The name of the cargo prescribed in the letter authorizing carriage of the cargo under § 153.900(d) if the cargo is a hazardous or flammable cargo authorized for carriage under that section.
(3) The shipper's name for the cargo and the name of the shipper if the cargo is neither a hazardous nor flammable cargo.

[CGD 81-078, 50 FR 21174, May 22, 1985; as amended by CGD 88-100, 54 FR 40042, Sept. 29, 1989]

§ 153.908 Cargo viscosity and melting point information; measuring cargo temperature during discharge: Categories A, B, and C.

(a) The person in charge of the ship may not accept a shipment of a Category A, B, or C NLS cargo having a reference to this paragraph in the "Special Requirements" column of Table 1 unless the person has, from the cargo's manufacturer or the person listed as the shipper on the bill of lading, a written statement of the following:

(1) For Category A or B NLS, the cargo's viscosity at 20 °C in mPa.s and, if the cargo's viscosity exceeds 25 mPa.s at 20 °C, the temperature at which the viscosity is 25 mPa.s.

(2) For Category C NLS, the cargo's viscosity at 20 °C in mPa.s and, if the cargo's viscosity exceeds 60 mPa.s at 20 °C, the temperature at which the viscosity is 60 mPa.s. If the cargo's viscosity varies from shipment to shipment, the maximum viscosity and maximum temperature values may be supplied.

(b) The person in charge of the ship may not accept a shipment of a Category A, B, or C cargo having a reference to this paragraph in the "Special Requirements" column of Table 1 unless the person has a written statement of the cargo's melting point in °C from the cargo's manufacturer or the person listed as the shipper on the bill of lading. If the cargo's melting point varies from shipment to shipment, the highest melting point may be supplied.

(c) The person in charge of the ship shall ensure that the cargo temperature is read and recorded in the Cargo Record Book following the procedures in paragraph (d) of this section when a cargo having a reference to paragraph (a) or (b) of this section in the "Special Requirements" column of Table 1 is unloaded.

(d) The cargo temperature measured in paragraph (c) of this section must be made using the following procedure:

(1) Each reading must be made with the sensor or thermometer required by § 153.440(a)(3) or (c). If a portable thermometer is used, it must be located as prescribed for the temperature sensor in § 153.440(a)(3).

(2) A total of 2 readings must be made, the first reading to be made no more than 30 minutes after cargo transfer begins and the second reading no more than 30 minutes before the main cargo pump is shut down.

(3) The cargo's temperature is the average of the 2 readings made under paragraph (d)(2) of this section.

[CGD 81–101, 52 FR 7784, Mar. 12, 1987]

§ 153.909 Completing the Cargo Record Book and record retention: Categories A, B, C, and D.

(a) The person in charge of a ship shall ensure that the Cargo Record Book required under § 153.490 is completed immediately after any of the following occurs:

(1) An NLS cargo is loaded.

(2) An NLS cargo is transferred between tanks on a ship.

(3) An NLS cargo is unloaded from a tank.

(4) A tank that last carried an NLS cargo is prewashed under this part.

(5) A tank that last carried an NLS cargo is washed, except as reported under paragraph (a)(4) of this section, cleaned, or ventilated.

(6) Washings from a tank that last carried an NLS cargo are discharged to the sea.

(7) Tanks that last carried an NLS cargo are ballasted.

(8) Ballast water is discharged to the sea from a cargo tank that last carried an NLS.

(9) An NLS cargo or NLS residue is discharged to the sea by accident or except as allowed by this part.

(10) A Surveyor is present during an operation that this part requires the presence of a Surveyor.

(11) NLS residue or NLS cargo is transferred from cargo pumproom bilges or transferred to an incinerator.

(12) A waiver is issued to the ship, ship owner, ship operator, or person in charge of the ship under this part.

(13) The concentration of a Category A NLS residue is measured under § 153.1120(a).

(14) Any discharge recording equipment required by § 153.481(b)(2) fails.

(b) The person in charge of the ship shall ensure that the Cargo Record Book is on board and readily available for inspection and copying by the Coast Guard and when the ship is a U.S. ship in the waters of a foreign country whose Administration is signatory to MARPOL 73/78, the authorities of that country.

(c) Each officer in charge of an operation listed under paragraph (a) of this section, and each Surveyor observing an operation that this part requires the presence of a Surveyor, shall attest to the accuracy and completeness of each Cargo Record Book entry concerning those operations by signing after each entry.

(d) After all the entries on a page of the Cargo Record Book are completed, and if the person in charge of the ship agrees with the entries, the person in charge of the ship shall sign the bottom of that page.

(e) The ship owner or operator shall ensure that—

(1) Each Cargo Record Book is retained on board the ship for at least 3 years after the last entry; and

(2) Each discharge recording required by § 153.1126(b)(1) is retained on board the ship for at least three years.

[CGD 81–101, 52 FR 7784, Mar. 12, 1987]

§ 153.910 Cargo piping plan.

No person may operate a tankship unless the tankship has a cargo piping plan that:

(a) Shows all cargo piping on the tankship;

(b) Shows all cargo valving, pumps, and other equipment that is used during cargo transfer;

(c) Shows the cargo tanks;

(d) Shows any modifications necessary to a containment system that is to be separated as prescribed under Part 150 of this subchapter, or §§ 153.525 and 153.1020;

(e) Emphasizes the piping and equipment described in paragraphs (a), (b) and (d) of this section by using contrasting colors, line widths, or similar methods; and

(f) Shows the cargo loading rates chosen under § 153.365(b) for all applicable cargo lines.

[CGD 73–96, 42 FR 49027, Sept. 26, 1977, as amended by CGD 78–128, 47 FR 21210, May 17, 1982]

§ 153.912 Certificate of inhibition or stabilization.

(a) When a cargo in Table 1 is referred to this section, no person may operate a tankship carrying the cargo without a written certification, carried on the bridge of the tankship, from the shipper that the cargo is:

(1) Inhibited; or

(2) Stabilized.

(b) The certification required by this section must contain the following information:

(1) Whether the cargo is inhibited or stabilized.

(2) The name and concentration of the inhibitor or stabilizer.

(3) The date the inhibitor or stabilizer was added.

(4) The length of time the inhibitor or stabilizer is effective.

(5) Any temperature limitations qualifying the inhibitor's or stabilizer's effective lifetime.

(6) The action to be taken should the duration of the voyage exceed the inhibitor's or stabilizer's useful life.

GENERAL CARGO OPERATIONAL REQUIREMENTS

§ 153.920 Cargo quantity limitations.

(a) No person may load a cargo tank or operate a tankship that carries a cargo tank containing in excess of 1250 m^3 (approx. 44,138 ft^3) of cargo requiring a type I containment system.

(b) No person may load a cargo tank or operate a tankship that carries a cargo tank containing in excess of 3000 m^3 (approx. 105,932 ft^3) of a cargo requiring a type II containment system.

§ 153.921 Explosives.

No person may load, off-load, or carry a cargo listed in this part on board a vessel that carries explosives unless he has the prior written permission of the Commandant (CG–ENG).

[CGD 73–96, 42 FR 49027, Sept. 26, 1977, as amended by CGD 82–063b, 48 FR 4782, Feb. 3, 1983]

§ 153.923 Inerting systems.

The master shall ensure that the inert gas systems for any cargo that this part requires to be inerted are operating correctly.

GENERAL VESSEL SAFETY

§ 153.930 Cargo antidotes.

No person may operate a tankship that carries a cargo listed in Table 1 unless the tankship has on board the antidotes described for the cargo in the *Medical First Aid Guide for Use in Accidents Involving Dangerous Goods*, published by IMO.

§ 153.931 Obstruction of pumproom ladderways.

The master shall ensure that all cargo pumproom ladderways are unobstructed at all times.

§ 153.932 Goggles and protective clothing.

(a) The master shall ensure that each person wear a face mask or tight-fitting goggles for eye protection against splashing or spraying liquids if that person is:

(1) Sampling cargo;

(2) Transferring cargo;

(3) Making or breaking a cargo hose connection;

(4) Gauging a cargo tank; or

(5) Opening a cargo tank by opening a Butterworth hatch, ullage hatch, cargo tank hatch, or similar opening.

(b) The master shall ensure that each person wear a face mask or tight-fitting goggles for eye protection against splashing or spraying liquids if the person is:

(1) In the area of the deck where the cargo tanks, cargo piping, and cargo pumprooms are located while a cargo transfer is taking place; or

(2) In a cargo pumproom, an enclosed space adjacent to a cargo tank, or a space containing part of a cargo containment system.

(c) The master shall ensure that each person in paragraphs (a) and (b) of this section wear any additional protective clothing the master believes necessary to protect the person from the cargo's hazards.

[CGD 73–96, 42 FR 49027, Sept. 26, 1977, as amended by CGD 78–128, 47 FR 21210, May 17, 1982]

§ 153.933 Chemical protective clothing.

When table 1 refers to this section, the following apply:

Coast Guard, DHS § 153.935a

(a) The master shall ensure that the following chemical protective clothing constructed of materials resistant to permeation by the cargo being handled is worn by all personnel engaged in an operation listed in paragraph (b) of this section:

(1) Splash protective eyewear.
(2) Long-sleeved gloves.
(3) Boots or shoe covers.
(4) Coveralls or lab aprons.

NOTE: "Guidelines for the Selection of Chemical Protective Clothing", Third Edition, 1987, available from the American Conference of Governmental Industrial Hygienists, 1330 Kemper Meadow Drive, Cincinnati, OH 45240–1634, provides information on the proper clothing for the cargo being handled.

(b) This section applies during the following operations:

(1) Sampling cargo.
(2) Transferring cargo.
(3) Making or breaking cargo hose connections.
(4) Gauging a cargo tank, unless gauging is by closed system.
(5) Opening cargo tanks.

(c) Coveralls or lab aprons may be replaced by splash suits or aprons constructed of light weight or disposable materials if, in the judgment of the master—

(1) Contact with the cargo being handled is likely to occur only infrequently and accidentally; and
(2) The splash suit or apron is disposed of immediately after contamination.

(d) Splash protective eyewear must be tight-fitting chemical-splash goggles, face shields, or similar items intended specifically for eye protection from chemical splashing or spraying.

(e) The master shall ensure that each person in the vicinity of an operation listed in paragraph (b) of this section or in the vicinity of tanks, piping, or pumps being used to transfer the cargo wears splash protective eyewear under paragraph (d) of this section.

[CGD 88–100, 54 FR 40042, Sept. 29, 1989; as amended by USCG–1999–6216, 64 FR 53227, Oct. 1, 1999]

§ 153.934 Entry into spaces containing cargo vapor.

(a) No person may enter a cargo tank, cargo handling space, pumproom or enclosed space in the cargo area without the permission of the master.

(b) Before permitting anyone to enter a cargo tank, cargo handling space, pumproom or other enclosed space in the cargo area, the master shall make sure that:

(1) The space is free of toxic vapors and has sufficient oxygen to support life; or
(2) Those entering the space wear protective equipment with self-contained breathing apparatus as described in § 153.214(b) and an officer closely supervises the entire operation.

[CGD 73–96, 42 FR 49027, Sept. 26, 1977, as amended by CGD 78–128, 47 FR 21210, May 17, 1982]

§ 153.935 Opening of tanks and cargo sampling.

(a) Except as provided in paragraph (b) of this section, the master shall ensure that all cargo tank hatches, ullage openings, and tank cleaning openings are tightly closed at all times.

(b) The master may not authorize the opening of a cargo tank, except:

(1) To clean a tank;
(2) To transfer a cargo that Table 1 allows in a containment system having an open gauging system;
(3) To sample a cargo that Table 1 allows in a containment system having an open gauging system; or
(4) To sample a cargo that Table 1 allows in a containment system having a restricted gauging system if:
   (i) The tank is not being filled during sampling;
   (ii) The vent system has relieved any pressure in the tank;
   (iii) The person sampling the cargo wears the protective clothing required during cargo transfer; and
   (iv) The tank is closed tightly following sampling.

(c) The master shall make sure that cargoes requiring closed gauging are sampled only through the controlled sampling arrangement required by § 153.404(d).

[CGD 73–96, 42 FR 49027, Sept. 26, 1977, as amended by CGD 78–128, 47 FR 21210, May 17, 1982]

§ 153.935a Storage of cargo samples.

(a) The master shall make sure that any cargo samples are stored in:

§ 153.936

(1) A designated and ventilated space in the cargo area of the vessel; or

(2) An area approved by the Commandant (CG–ENG) or the tankship's flag administration for the stowage of cargo samples.

(b) The master shall make sure that cargo sample bottles are stored:

(1) In a way that prevents shifting of the sample bottles when the vessel is at sea;

(2) In bins or containers constructed of materials that are resistant to the cargo samples; and

(3) Apart from other sample bottles containing incompatible liquids (See part 150, subpart A).

[CGD 78–128, 47 FR 21211, May 17, 1982, as amended by CGD 82–063b, 48 FR 4782, Feb. 3, 1983]

§ 153.936 Illness, alcohol, drugs.

The master shall ensure that no person participates in cargo related operations who appears to be intoxicated by alcohol or drugs or to be so ill as to be unfit for the particular operation.

MARKING OF CARGO TRANSFER HOSE

§ 153.940 Standards for marking of cargo hose.

No person may mark a hose assembly as meeting the standards of this section unless the hose assembly meets the following requirements:

(a) Each hose assembly must have:

(1) Fully threaded connections;

(2) Flanges that meet ANSI B16.5, B16.24, or B16.31; or

(3) Class 1 quick-disconnect couplings that comply with ASTM F 1122 (incorporated by reference, see § 153.4), and are marked "C1–1."

(b) Each hose assembly must be marked with the:

(1) Date of manufacture;

(2) Working pressure discribed in paragraph (d) of this section;

(3) Date of the last test made as prescribed in paragraph (e) of this section; and

(4) Manufacturer's recommended maximum and minimum temperatures.

(c) A cargo hose assembly must have a minimum bursting pressure as stated by the manufacturer of at least 5152 kPa gauge (approx. 750 psig).

(d) The working pressure marked on a hose must meet the following:

(1) Be at least 1030 kPa gauge (approx. 150 psig).

(2) Not exceeded 20 per cent (one-fifth) of the manufacturer's stated bursting pressure.

(3) Not exceed the manufacturer's recommended working pressure.

(4) Not exceed the test pressure used in the latest test under paragraph (e)(3) of this section.

(e) A cargo hose assembly must be inspected and tested by placing it in a straight, horizontal position so that its entire external surface is accessible. It must be ascertained that the hose assembly:

(1) Has no loose covers, kinks, bulges, soft spots, and no gouges, cuts, or slashes that penetrate any hose reinforcement;

(2) Has no external and, to the extent internal inspection is possible with both ends of the hose open, no internal deterioration; and

(3) Does not burst, bulge, leak, or abnormally distort under static liquid pressure at least as great as the recommended working pressure.

[CGD 73–96, 42 FR 49027, Sept. 26, 1977, as amended by CGD 78–128, 47 FR 21211, May 17, 1982; CGD 88–032, 56 FR 35827, July 29, 1991; USCG–2000–7790, 65 FR 58463, Sept. 29, 2000]

CARGO TRANSFER PROCEDURES

§ 153.953 Signals during cargo transfer.

The master shall ensure that:

(a) The tankship displays a red flag in the day and a red light at night when transferring cargo while fast to a dock;

(b) The tankship displays a red flag when transferring cargo while at anchor; and

(c) The red flag or the red light is visible from all sides of the tankship.

§ 153.955 Warning signs during cargo transfer.

(a) When transferring cargo while fast to a dock or at anchor in port, the master shall ensure that the tankship displays a warning sign at the gangway facing the shore so that it may be seen from the shore and another warning sign facing outboard toward the water

Coast Guard, DHS § 153.957

so that it may be seen from the water. (See figure 1).

(b) Except as provided in paragraph (f) of this section, each warning sign must have the following legends:
(1) Warning.
(2) Dangerous Cargo.
(3) No Visitors.
(4) No Smoking.
(5) No Open Lights.

(c) Each letter must be block style, black on a white background.

(d) Each letter must:
(1) Be 7.5 cm (approx. 3 in.) high;
(2) Be 5 cm (approx. 2 in.) wide except for "M" and "W" which must be 7.5 cm (approx. 3 in.) wide and the letter "I" which may be 1.3 cm (approx. ½ in.) wide; and

Figure 1 - Minimum Dimensions for Warning Sign

(3) Have 1.3 cm (approx. ½ in.) stroke width.

(e) The spacing must be:
(1) 1.3 cm (approx. ½ in.) between letters of the same word;
(2) 5 cm (approx. 2 in.) between words;
(3) 5 cm (approx. 2 in.) between lines; and
(4) 5 cm (approx. 2 in.) at the borders of the sign.

(f) Except as described in § 153.1045, the legends "No Smoking" and "No Open Lights" are not required when the cargoes on board the tankship are neither flammable nor combustible.

§ 153.957 Persons in charge of transferring liquid cargo in bulk or cleaning cargo tanks.

(a) The owner and operator of the vessel, and his or her agent, and each of them, shall ensure that—
(1) Enough "Tankerman-PICs" or restricted "Tankerman-PICs", and "Tankerman-Assistants", authorized for the classification of cargo carried, are on duty to safely transfer liquid cargo in bulk or to safely clean cargo tanks;

(2) Each transfer of liquid cargo in bulk and each cleaning of a cargo tank is supervised by a qualified person designated as a person in charge of the transfer or the cleaning under Subpart C of 33 CFR part 155;

(3) When cargo regulated under this part is due for transfer, the person in charge of the transfer has received special training in the particular hazards associated with the cargo and in all special procedures for its handling; and

(4) On each foreign vessel, the person in charge understands his or her responsibilities as described in this subchapter.

(b) Upon request by the Officer in Charge, Marine Inspection, in whose zone the transfer will take place, the owner and operator of the vessel, and his or her agent, and each of them, shall provide documentary evidence that the person in charge has received the training specified by paragraph (a)(3) of this section and is capable of competently performing the procedures necessary for the cargo.

[CGD 79–116, 60 FR 17158, Apr. 4, 1995]

§ 153.959 Approval to begin transfer operations required.

No person may make connections for cargo transfer or transfer cargo unless he has authorization from the person in charge of cargo transfer.

§ 153.964 Discharge by gas pressurization.

The person in charge of cargo transfer may not authorize cargo discharge by gas pressurization unless:

(a) The tank to be offloaded has an SR or PV venting system;

(b) The pressurization medium is either the cargo vapor or a nonflammable, nontoxic gas inert to the cargo; and

(c) The pressurizing line has:

(1) A pressure reducing valve whose setting does not exceed 90% of the tank's relief valve setting and a manual control valve between the pressure reducing valve and the tank; or

(2) For an inert gas medium:

(i) A safety relief valve with a cross sectional flow area at least equal to that of the pressurizing line and whose relieving pressure does not exceed 90 percent of the tank's relief valve setting;

(ii) A manual control valve between the safety relief valve and the tank; and

(iii) A check valve between the manual control valve and the tank.

§ 153.966 Discharge by liquid displacement.

The person in charge of cargo transfer may not authorize cargo discharge by liquid displacement unless the liquid supply line to the tank has:

(a) A safety relief or pressure reducing valve set to operate at no more than 80 percent of the tank's relief valve setting; and

(b) A manual control valve between the tank and the supply line's safety relief valve or pressure reducing valve.

§ 153.968 Cargo transfer conference.

(a) Before he may begin making connections for cargo transfer, the person in charge of cargo transfer shall confer with the person supervising the cargo transfer at the facility.

(b) The person in charge of cargo transfer shall discuss the important aspects of the transfer operation, such as the following, with the supervisor at the facility:

(1) The products to be transferred.

(2) The cargo loading rates marked on the cargo piping plan or the maximum safe transfer rates.

(3) The critical or hazardous stages of the transfer operation.

(4) The emergency procedures in case of a spill.

(5) If the vessel is equipped with the tank overflow alarm prescribed in § 153.408(c), a procedure for shutdown of shore pumps, shore valves, and ship's valves that prevents piping system pressures from exceeding those for which the piping system is designed.

[CGD 73–96, 42 FR 49027, Sept. 26, 1977, as amended by CGD 78–128, 47 FR 21211, May 17, 1982; CGD 81–078, 50 FR 21174, May 22, 1985]

§ 153.970 Cargo transfer piping.

The person in charge of cargo transfer shall ensure that:

(a) Cargo is transferred to or from a cargo tank only through the tankship's cargo piping system;

(b) Vapor not returned to shore through the tankship's vapor return system is discharged at the height required for the cargo's vent riser in Table 1, and

(c) All cargo vapor is returned to shore through the valved connection on the venting system if:

(1) The cargo requires closed gauging, is referenced to § 153.372 or is referenced to § 153.525;

(2) The transfer terminal has vapor return equipment; and

(3) In his estimation the vapor return equipment is adequate to handle the vapor expected from the tank.

§ 153.972 Connecting a cargo hose.

The person in charge of cargo transfer may not authorize the connection of a hose to a cargo containment system unless:

(a) He has ensured himself that the cargo will not weaken or damage the hose;

(b) The hose is marked as meeting the standards of § 153.940;

(c) The date of the hose's last pressure test is within one year of the date on which the hose is used to transfer cargo;

(d) The recommended working pressure marked on a hose used for discharge meets or exceeds the working pressure marked on the cargo piping at the hose connection; and

(e) The cargo's temperature is within the manufacturer's recommended maximum and minimum hose temperatures.

§ 153.975 Preparation for cargo transfer.

The person in charge of cargo transfer may not approve or continue cargo transfer unless the following conditions are met:

(a) No fires or open flames are on deck or in compartments near the hose connections when Table 1 requires the cargo's containment system to have a fire protection system.

(b) Any electrical bonding of the tankship to the transfer facility is made before the cargo transfer piping is joined.

(c) Any supplemental inert gas supply necessary to maintain the 3.5 kPa gauge (approx. 0.5 psig) pressure in the tank during offloading (see § 153.500) is connected to the inert gas pressure control system.

(d) The transfer connections have enough slack to allow for vessel movement.

(e) The transfer connections are supported by tackles.

(f) The cargo high level alarms, tank overflow alarms and overflow control systems are functioning correctly when the cargo is loaded.

(g) Joints and couplings are gasketed and mated tightly.

(h) Flanges are bolted tightly.

(i) No repair work is underway in areas where cargo or cargo vapors may collect.

(j) Cargo and sea valves are properly set, with those sea valves connected to cargo piping lashed or sealed shut.

(k) Venting system bypass valves are set for cargo transfer and are operating properly.

(l) All scuppers are plugged.

(m) Smoking is limited to safe places.

(n) Fire fighting and safety equipment is ready.

(o) He is in effective communication with the transfer terminal.

(p) The person in charge of the transfer terminal has acknowledged that he is ready to transfer.

(q) Pressures within the cargo transfer and containment systems do not exceed the pressure ranges for which the transfer hose and containment systems are designed.

(r) No vessels that would hazard cargo transfer are alongside the tankship.

[CGD 73–96, 42 FR 49027, Sept. 26, 1977, as amended by CGD 78–128, 47 FR 21211, May 17, 1982]

§ 153.976 Transfer of packaged cargo or ship's stores.

The person in charge of cargo transfer may neither begin nor continue the transfer of a flammable or combustible cargo while packaged cargo or ship's stores are transferred unless transfer of the packaged cargo or ship's stores does not hazard transfer of the flammable or combustible cargo.

§ 153.977 Supervision of cargo transfer.

The person in charge of cargo transfer shall:

(a) Supervise the operation of cargo system valves;

(b) Monitor the cargo loading rate to ensure it does not exceed that stated on the cargo piping plan; and

(c) Monitor the cargo level in the tanks to make sure they do not overflow.

[CGD 78–128, 47 FR 21211, May 17, 1982]

§ 153.979 Gauging with a sounding tube.

(a) No person may remove the cover of a sounding tube unless he has authorization from the person in charge of cargo transfer.

(b) The person in charge of cargo transfer may not authorize removal of the cover from a sounding tube gauge

§ 153.980

unless all tank pressure has been relieved through the tank's venting system.

§ 153.980 Isolation of automatic closing valves.

The person in charge of cargo transfer may isolate automatic closing valves described in § 153.408(b) from a cargo containment system if the following conditions are met:

(a) The containment system carries products to which § 153.408 does not apply.

(b) The valves are isolated by:

(1) Removing the valves; or

(2) Installing removable pipes and blind flanges to by-pass the valves.

[CGD 78–128, 47 FR 21211, May 17, 1982]

§ 153.981 Leaving room in tank for cargo expansion.

The person in charge of cargo transfer shall ensure that the amount of cargo in a tank does not exceed the tank's capacity at any ambient temperature between −18 °C (approx. 0 °F) and 46 °C (approx. 115 °F).

§ 153.983 Termination procedures.

Upon completion of the transfer operation, the person in charge of cargo transfer shall ensure that:

(a) The cargo transfer connections are closed off;

(b) The transfer lines and hoses are drained of cargo, either into the tank or back to the transfer terminal;

(c) Any electrical bonding between the vessel and the shore facility is broken only after the cargo hose is disconnected and all spills removed; and

(d) Each vent system is returned to its nonloading configuration.

SPECIAL CARGO PROCEDURES

§ 153.1000 Special operating requirements for cargoes reactive with water.

When Table 1 refers to this section, the master must ensure that the cargo:

(a) Is carried only in a containment system completely isolated from any systems containing water, such as slop tanks, ballast tanks, cargo tanks containing slops or ballast, their vent lines or piping; and

(b) Is separated by double walls, such as cofferdams and piping tunnels, from any system containing water, as for example those described in paragraph (a) of this section.

§ 153.1002 Special operating requirements for heat sensitive cargoes.

When Table 1 refers to this section, the master shall make sure that:

(a) The cargo temperature is maintained below the temperature that would induce polymerization, decomposition, thermal instability, evolution of gas or reaction of the cargo;

(b) Any heating coils in the cargo tank are blanked off; and

(c) The cargo is not carried in uninsulated deck tanks.

[CGD 78–128, 47 FR 21211, May 17, 1982]

§ 153.1003 Prohibited carriage in deck tanks.

When Table 1 refers to this section, cargoes may not be carried in deck tanks.

[CGD 95–900, 60 FR 34050, June 29, 1995]

§ 153.1004 Inhibited and stabilized cargoes.

(a) Before loading a cargo containment system with a cargo referenced to this section in Table 1, the person in charge of cargo transfer shall make sure that the cargo containment system is free of contaminants that could:

(1) Catalyze the polymerization or decomposition of the cargo; or

(2) Degrade the effectiveness of the inhibitor or stabilizer.

(b) The master shall make sure that the cargo is maintained at a temperature which will prevent crystallization or solidification of the cargo.

[CGD 78–128, 47 FR 21211, May 17, 1982]

§ 153.1010 Alkylene oxides.

(a) Before each loading of a cargo containment system with a cargo referenced to this section in Table 1, the person in charge of cargo transfer shall:

(1) Unless the tankship is equipped with independent cargo piping that meets paragraph (d) of this section:

(i) Obtain verification from a Coast Guard Marine Inspector or from a representative of the tankship's flag administration that separation of the alkylene oxide piping system complies with alkylene oxide handling plans approved by the Coast Guard or the tankship's flag administration; and

(ii) Make sure that each spectacle flange and blank flange connection that is required to separate alkylene oxide piping systems from other systems has a wire and seal attached by a Coast Guard Marine Inspector or a representative of the tankship's flag administration.

(2) Purge the containment system until the oxygen content of the cargo tank is less than 2% by volume.

(b) The person in charge of an alkylene oxide cargo transfer shall ensure that:

(1) No alkylene oxide vapor or liquid is released to the atmosphere during cargo transfer;

(2) No vapor return system connected to an alkylene oxide containment system is at the same time connected to another containment system;

(3) Alkylene oxide is discharged only by an intank cargo pump or inert gas displacement;

(4) Transfer hose is approved by the Commandant (CG–ENG) under §153.530(o) for alkylene oxide transfer and is marked "For Alkylene Oxide Transfer Only"; and

(5) A water hose is laid out on deck with water pressure to the nozzle, and all alkylene oxide spillages are washed away immediately.

(c) While alkylene oxides are onboard the vessel, the master shall make sure that the oxygen content of the vapor space above the alkylene oxide and those spaces specified in § 153.530 (k) and (l) is maintained below 2% by volume.

(d) Tankships with independent piping for alkylene oxides must have onboard:

(1) Alkylene oxide handling plans approved by the Coast Guard or the tankship's flag administration; and

(2) Certification from the Coast Guard or the tankship's flag administration that the cargo piping for alkylene oxides is independent.

[CGD 73–96, 42 FR 49027, Sept. 26, 1977, as amended by CGD 78–128, 47 FR 21211, May 17, 1982; CGD 82–063b, 48 FR 4782, Feb. 3, 1983]

§ 153.1011 Changing containment systems and hoses to and from alkylene oxide service.

(a) The person in charge of cargo transfer shall make sure that:

(1) No alkylene oxide is loaded into a containment system that last carried a cargo other than an alkylene oxide unless the containment system has been cleaned and inspected to make sure it is in good condition with no heavy rust accumulations or traces of previous cargoes;

(2) No alkylene oxide is loaded into a containment system that within the previous three loadings carried a cargo listed in paragraph (b) of this section unless the containment system has been cleaned to the satisfaction of a Coast Guard Marine Inspector or a person specifically authorized by the Commandant (CG–ENG) to approve alkylene oxide tank cleaning;

(3) No cargo but an alkylene oxide is loaded into a containment system which last carried an alkylene oxide unless the containment system has been cleaned of alkylene oxide to the satisfaction of a Coast Guard Marine Inspector or person specifically authorized by the Commandant (CG–ENG) to approve alkylene oxide tank cleaning; and

(4) No hose marked "For Alkylene Oxide Transfer Only" is used for the transfer of a cargo other than an alkylene oxide.

(b) The following cargoes are particularly reactive with alkylene oxides:

(1) Non-oxidizing mineral acids (e.g. hydrochloric, phosphoric);
(2) Sulfuric acid;
(3) Nitric acid;
(4) Organic acids (e.g. acetic, formic);
(5) Halogenated organic acids (e.g. chloroacetic);
(6) Sulfonic acids (e.g. alkyl benzene sulfonic);
(7) Caustic alkalies (e.g. caustic soda, caustic potash; sodium hydrosulfide);
(8) Ammonia and ammonia solutions;
(9) Aliphatic amines;
(10) Alkanolamines; and

(11) Oxidizing substances.

[CGD 78–128, 47 FR 21211, May 17, 1982, as amended by CGD 82–063b, 48 FR 4782, Feb. 3, 1983; CGD 81–078, 50 FR 21174, May 22, 1985]

§ 153.1020 Unusually toxic cargoes.

(a) No person may load or carry a cargo referenced to this section in Table 1 unless the cargo's piping and venting systems are separated from piping and venting systems carrying cargoes not referred to this section.

(b) The master shall ensure that no heat transfer medium that has been circulated through a cargo referenced to this section in Table 1 is circulated through a cargo not referenced to this section unless he determines the medium to be uncontaminated with cargo.

(c) No person may discharge overboard condensed steam from the heating system of a cargo referenced to this section in Table 1 unless he first determines the condensate to be uncontaminated with cargo.

[CGD 73–96, 42 FR 49027, Sept. 26, 1977, as amended by CGD 78–128, 47 FR 21212, May 17, 1982]

§ 153.1025 Motor fuel antiknock compounds.

(a) No person may load or carry any other cargo in a containment system approved for motor fuel antiknock compounds containing lead alkyls except a cargo to be used solely in the manufacture of motor fuel antiknock compounds.

(b) The master shall ensure that no person enter a pumproom or void space that contains piping from a containment system approved for motor fuel antiknock compounds containing lead alkyls unless:

(1) The pumproom or void space atmosphere has been analyzed for its lead (as Pb) content and found to be less than 0.075 mg/m³; or

(2) The person follows the procedures for entering a cargo tank described in paragraph (c) of this section.

(c) No person may enter a cargo tank endorsed for motor fuel antiknock compounds containing lead alkyls without prior specific authorization from the Commandant (CG–ENG). This authorization may be obtained by calling telephone number 202–372–1420 or e-mail *hazmatstandards@uscg.mil* if the person has previously obtained approval for the cargo tank entry procedure from the Commandant (CG–ENG).

(d) No person may enter a cargo tank endorsed for motor fuel antiknock compounds if he does not follow the conditions in the authorization under paragraph (c) of this section.

[CGD 73–96, 42 FR 49027, Sept. 26, 1977, as amended by CGD 78–128, 47 FR 21212, May 17, 1982; CGD 82–063b, 48 FR 4782, Feb. 3, 1983; CGD 88–100, 54 FR 40042, Sept. 29, 1989; USCG–2006–25697, 71 FR 55747, Sept. 25, 2006; USCG–2012–0832, 77 FR 59785, Oct. 1, 2012]

§ 153.1035 Acetone cyanohydrin or lactonitrile solutions.

No person may operate a tankship carrying a cargo of acetone cyanohydrin or lactonitrile solutions, unless that cargo is stabilized with an inorganic acid.

[CGD 88–100, 54 FR 40042, Sept. 29, 1989]

§ 153.1040 Carbon disulfide.

(a) No person may load, carry, or discharge carbon disulfide unless the cargo tank has a water pad over the cargo of at least one meter (approx. 40 in.).

(b) The person in charge of a carbon disulfide transfer operation shall ensure that carbon disulfide is discharged only by displacement or intank cargo pump.

(c) No person may remove a cargo pump for a containment system that carries carbon disulfide unless:

(1) The containment system has a gas free certificate issued under the standards in § 35.01–1 of this chapter; or

(2) The vapor space in the pump well is filled with water.

§ 153.1045 Inorganic acids.

When Table 1 refers to this section, the person in charge of cargo transfer shall ensure that the legends "NO SMOKING" and "NO OPEN LIGHTS" are displayed on the warning sign required in § 153.955(a) when cargo is transferred.

§ 153.1046 Sulfuric acid.

No person may liquefy frozen or congealed sulfuric acid other than by external tank heating coils.

§ 153.1052 Carriage of other cargoes in acid tanks.

No person shall load or carry other cargoes in a cargo containment system of a U.S. flag ship endorsed to carry sulfuric acid, hydrochloric acid, or phosphoric acid with out specific authorization from the Commandant (CG–ENG).

[CGD 94–900, 59 FR 45139, Aug. 31, 1994]

§ 153.1060 Benzene.

The person in charge of a Coast Guard inspected vessel must ensure that the provisions of part 197, subpart C, of this chapter are applied.

[CGD 88–040, 56 FR 65006, Dec. 13, 1991]

§ 153.1065 Sodium chlorate solutions.

(a) No person may load sodium chlorate solutions into a containment system that previously carried another cargo unless the containment system is thoroughly washed before loading.

(b) The person in charge of cargo transfer shall make sure that spills of sodium chlorate solutions are immediately washed away.

[CGD 81–078, 50 FR 21174, May 22, 1985]

APPROVAL OF SURVEYORS AND HANDLING OF CATEGORIES A, B, C, AND D CARGO AND NLS RESIDUE

SOURCE: CGD 81–101, 52 FR 7785, Mar. 12, 1987, unless otherwise noted.

§ 153.1100 Responsibility of the person in charge.

The person in charge of the ship shall ensure that—

(a) The requirements of §§ 153.1102 through 153.1132 are met; and

(b) The procedures in the approved Procedures and Arrangements Manual are followed.

§ 153.1101 Procedures for getting a Surveyor: Approval of Surveyors.

(a) At least 24 hours before a Surveyor is needed, the person wishing the services of a Surveyor must contact the Captain of the Port or the Sector Office that has jurisdiction over the port at which the Surveyor will be needed to—

(1) Arrange for the Coast Guard to provide a Surveyor; or

(2) Inform the Coast Guard of the selection of a Surveyor from one of the organizations accepted by the Coast Guard to provide Surveyors.

(b) Organizations may be accepted by the Coast Guard to provide Surveyors if they—

(1) Are engaged, as a regular part of their business, in performing inspections or tests of bulk liquid cargo tanks or bulk liquid cargo handling equipment;

(2) Are familiar with the references in § 153.0(b) and with the requirements of this part;

(3) Are not controlled by the owners or operators of ships needing the services of the Surveyors or the facilities at which those ships would unload cargo;

(4) Are not dependent on Coast Guard acceptance under this section to remain in business; and

(5) Sign a Memorandum of Understanding with the Coast Guard.

(c) Each application for acceptance as a Surveyor must be submitted to the Commandant (CG–ENG) and must contain the following:

(1) The name and address of the organization, including subsidiaries and divisions, requesting acceptance by the Coast Guard to provide Surveyors.

(2) A statement that the organization is not controlled by the owners or operators of ships needing the services of Surveyors or the facilities at which these ships would unload, or a full disclosure of any ownership or controlling interest held by such parties.

(3) A description of the experience and qualifications of the personnel who would be performing the function of Surveyor.

(4) A statement that the persons who will be performing the function of Surveyor have been trained in and are familiar with the requirements of Annex II and the regulations in this part.

(5) A statement that the Coast Guard may verify the information submitted in the application and may examine the persons who will be performing the function of Surveyor to determine their qualifications.

(d) The acceptance of an organization may be terminated by the Commandant if the organization fails to

§ 153.1102

properly perform or supervise the inspections required in this part.

[CGD 81–101, 52 FR 7785, Mar. 12, 1987, as amended by USCG–2006–25556, 72 FR 36330, July 2, 2007]

§ 153.1102 Handling and disposal of NLS residue: Categories A, B, C, and D.

(a) Except those Category A NLS residues that must be discharged under paragraph (c) of this section, NLS residue from an NLS whose vapor pressure is 5 kPa (50 mbar) or less at 20 °C (68 °F) must be—

NOTE TO PARAGRAPH (a): The Marine Protection, Research, and Sanctuaries Act allows specific liquids to be discharged to the sea under permits issued by the EPA.

(1) Unloaded to any consignee;
(2) Returned to the shipper;
(3) Discharged to a reception facility;
(4) Retained on the ship; or
(5) Discharged to the sea under § 153.1126 or § 153.1128.

(b) Except those Category A NLS residues that must be discharged under paragraph (c) of this section, NLS residue from an NLS whose vapor pressure is greater than 5 kPa (50 mbar) at 20 °C must be—

(1) Handled in the same way as the NLS residue under paragraph (a) of this section; or

(2) Ventilated following a ventilation procedure in the approved Procedures and Arrangements Manual.

NOTE: The Clean Air Act (42 U.S.C. 7401 et seq) allows states to regulate emissions from tank ventilation. There may be other regulations, both local and Federal, that affect the use of tank ventilation for safety or environmental purposes.

(c) NLS residue containing Category A NLS in pumproom bilges and in spill trays at the manifold must be discharged to a reception facility.

[CGD 81–101, 52 FR 7785, Mar. 12, 1987, as amended by CGD 81–101, 53 FR 28975, Aug. 1, 1988 and 54 FR 12629, Mar. 28, 1989]

§ 153.1104 Draining of cargo hose: Categories A, B, C, and D.

Before a cargo hose used in discharging an NLS from a ship's cargo tank is disconnected, the hose must be drained back to the transfer terminal unless the tank unloading the cargo has a waiver under § 153.483 or § 153.491.

[CGD 81–101, 53 FR 28975, Aug. 1, 1988 and 54 FR 12629, Mar. 28, 1989]

§ 153.1106 Cleaning agents.

No tank cleaning agent other than water or steam may be used to clean an NLS residue from a cargo tank except as prescribed in the approved Procedures and Arrangements Manual.

§ 153.1108 Heated prewash for solidifying NLS, high viscosity NLS and required prewashes of NLS whose viscosity exceeds 25 mPa sec at 20 °C: Categories A, B, and C.

(a) When a high viscosity or solidifying cargo is unloaded from a cargo tank, the cargo tank must be prewashed unless § 153.1114 or paragraph (c) of this section allows the prewash to be omitted.

(b) When a prewash is required for a tank that has unloaded a solidifying cargo or a cargo having a viscosity exceeding 25 mPa sec at 20 °C, the wash water used in the prewash must leave the tank washing machine at a temperature of at least 60 °C (140 °F).

(c) The prewash required under paragraph (a) of this section may be omitted if the approved Procedures and Arrangements Manual contains a procedure for measuring the temperature of all interior cargo tank surfaces throughout unloading and under the measuring procedure the temperature of these surfaces remains above—

(1) The temperature of the cargo's melting point if the cargo is a Category B or C solidifying NLS; or

(2) The temperature at which the cargo's viscosity exceeds—

(i) 25 mPa.s, if the cargo is a high viscosity Category B NLS; or

(ii) 60 mPa.s, if the cargo is a high viscosity Category C NLS.

[81–101, 53 FR 28975, Aug. 1, 1988 and 54 FR 12629, Mar. 28, 1989]

§ 153.1112 Prewash for tanks containing Category A NLS residue.

Unless § 153.1114 allows the prewash to be omitted, a cargo tank that unloads a Category A NLS cargo must be prewashed following the procedures in § 153.1120.

§ 153.1114 Conditions under which a prewash may be omitted: Categories A, B, and C.

A prewash required by this part may be omitted if one of the following requirements is met:

(a) A Surveyor has signed a statement in the Cargo Record Book that the next cargo has been determined to be one that may be loaded without washing the tank, and the tank is not washed or ballasted before it is loaded with the next cargo.

(b) A Surveyor has signed a statement in the Cargo Record Book that the approved Procedures and Arrangements Manual contains procedures for removing the NLS residue by ventilation, and the cargo tank is not washed or ballasted before being cleaned following the ventilation procedure.

NOTE: The Clean Air Act (42 U.S.C. 7401 et seq.) allows states to regulate emissions from tank ventilation. There may be other regulations, both local and Federal, that affect the use of tank ventilation for safety or environmental purposes.

(c) The tank requiring the prewash has a waiver issued under § 153.483 or § 153.491 and the waiver states when the tank is to be prewashed.

§ 153.1116 Prewash for tanks unloaded without following the approved Procedures and Arrangements Manual: Categories B and C.

If for any reason more Category B or C NLS residue remains in a cargo tank and transfer piping of a ship after unloading than would remain after a normal discharge of the cargo when the unloading procedures in the approved Procedures and Arrangements Manual are followed, the tank must be prewashed following the procedures in § 153.1120 unless—

(a) Section 153.1114 allows the prewash to be omitted; or

(b) The residue is reduced using another procedure, and a Surveyor estimates and states in the Cargo Record Book that the cargo tank and transfer piping contain no more NLS residue than they would if discharged following the procedures in the approved Procedures and Arrangements Manual, and no other prewash is required by this part.

§ 153.1118 Prewash of Categories B and C cargo tanks not meeting stripping standards: Categories B and C.

(a) Unless § 153.1114 allows the prewash to be omitted, a cargo tank from which a Category B NLS is unloaded must be prewashed using the procedures in § 153.1120(b) if the tank—

(1) Operates under the interim standard in § 153.481(b); or

(2) Has a waiver issued under § 153.483.

(b) Unless § 153.1114 allows the prewash to be omitted, a cargo tank from which a Category C NLS is unloaded must be prewashed using the procedures in § 153.1120(b) if the tank has a waiver issued under § 153.483.

§ 153.1119 When to prewash and discharge NLS residues from a prewash; unloading an NLS cargo in a country whose Administration is not signatory to MARPOL 73/78: Categories A, B, and C.

(a) Except as allowed in paragraphs (b), (c), and (e) of this section, each prewash required by this subpart must be completed and all tank washings must be discharged to a reception facility before the ship leaves the unloading port.

(b) NLS residue from the prewash following the unloading of a Category B NLS may be transferred to a slop tank for discharge under § 153.1126 instead of being discharged under paragraph (a) of this section if the prewash is required solely under § 153.1118(a)(1).

(c) A tank that is required by this part to be prewashed may be prewashed in a port other than the unloading port if the following conditions are met:

(1) The person in charge requests permission from the Commandant (CG–ENG) (tel num; 202–372–1425) if the prewash port is a foreign port, or the Captain of the Port having jurisdiction over the unloading port if the prewash port is a U.S. port.

(2) The person in charge supplies with the request required under paragraph (c)(1) of this section—

(i) The name of the ship;

(ii) The name of the owner;

(iii) The name of the NLS;

(iv) The approximate date the tank will be prewashed if the relocation of the prewash port is for one time only;

§ 153.1120

(v) A written agreement to receive the tank washings by a reception facility in the prewash port;

(vi) When the prewash port or terminal is in a country whose Administration is signatory to MARPOL 73/78, a written attestation from the person in charge of each prewash port or terminal that the Administration has determined the port or terminal to have adequate reception facilities for the NLS residue;

(vii) Written pledges from the person in charge that—

(A) The tank to be prewashed will not be washed or ballasted before being prewashed; and

(B) The ship will be taken to the reception facility and the tank prewashed in accordance with the requirements in § 153.1120; and

(viii) Any additional information the Captain of the Port or Commandant (CG–ENG) requests to evaluate granting the permission.

(3) The Coast Guard or Commandant (CG–ENG) has granted the permission in writing, the permission is carried aboard the ship, and the person in charge of the ship has made an entry in the Cargo Record Book stating that the permission has been granted.

(d) Unless the permission granted under paragraph (c)(4) of this section includes alternate conditions of termination or revocation in writing, the permission is—

(1) Terminated after the tank is prewashed as pledged in paragraph (c)(3)(vii) of this section or loaded with another cargo;

(2) Revoked if either of the pledges in paragraph (c)(3)(vii) of this section is invalidated or the agreement in paragraph (c)(3)(v) of this section is repudiated; and

(3) Revoked at any time the ship is not operated in accordance with the pledges in paragraph (c)(3)(vii) of this section and the conditions listed with the granted permission.

(e) A U.S. ship that would otherwise be required by this part to prewash in a port without reception facilities must obtain permission from Commandant (CG–ENG) to prewash in an alternate port.

[CGD 81–101, 52 FR 7785, Mar. 12, 1987, as amended by USCG–2006–25697, 71 FR 55747, Sept. 25, 2006]

§ 153.1120 Procedures for tank prewash: Categories A, B, and C.

Except where the approved Procedures and Arrangements Manual prescribes a different procedure, each of the following steps must be done in the order listed for the Coast Guard to consider the tanks prewashed under this part:

(a) When this part requires a prewash of a tank containing Category A NLS residue and the alternative prewash procedure in paragraph (b) of this section is not used, the prewash must meet the following:

(1) The prewash may not begin until—

(i) A Surveyor is present; and

(ii) Instrumentation or equipment is available that is capable of measuring the concentration of the Category A NLS in the NLS residue and determining whether it is below 0.1 per cent by weight.

(2) The equipment specified in § 153.484 must be used as prescribed in the approved Procedures and Arrangements Manual for the prewash.

(3) The wash water must be heated if required by § 153.1108, and water or tank washings must pass through the cargo pump and piping, including any stripping equipment, during washing or during discharge of tank washings.

(4) The tank washing machine must be placed in all positions specified for the tank's Category A NLS prewash procedure in the approved Procedures and Arrangements Manual.

(5) The tank must be pumped out each time there are enough tank washings collected in the bottom of the tank for the pump to gain suction, and if the NLS is immiscible with water or is a solidifying cargo, all floating and suspended NLS must be discharged.

(6) The washing machine must be operated until samples of the discharged tank washings taken by the Surveyor are tested using the equipment required by paragraph (a)(1)(ii) of this section and the concentration of NLS is below 0.1 per cent by weight.

Coast Guard, DHS § 153.1124

(7) After the washing is stopped, the remaining tank washings must be pumped out.

(8) The Cargo Record Book must have items 12 through 14 completed and must show the Surveyor's written certification of their accuracy.

(9) The Cargo Record Book must have the Surveyor's written concurrence that the prewash procedures specified in the approved Procedures and Arrangements Manual were followed.

(b) When this part requires a prewash of a tank containing Category B or C NLS residue or when the procedure in this paragraph is used as an alternative to the prewash procedure under paragraph (a) of this section, the prewash must meet the following:

(1) If the prewash is for a Category A NLS, the prewash may not begin until a Surveyor is present.

(2) The equipment specified in § 153.484 must be used as prescribed in the approved Procedures and Arrangements Manual for the prewash.

(3) The wash water must be heated if required by § 153.1108, and water or tank washings must pass through the cargo pump and piping, including any stripping equipment, during washing or during discharge of tank washings.

(4) Except as required in paragraph (b)(5) of this section, the number of washing machine cycles specified in Table 153.1120 must be completed. If a prewash is required by a section listed under Column 1 of Table 153.1120 and another section listed under Column 2, the number of cycles in Column 1 must be completed but no additional cycles are necessary.

(5) If the approved Procedures and Arrangements Manual specifies that a tank washing machine must be moved for the prewash of a tank from which a Category A NLS or a solidifying NLS has been unloaded, the number of washing machine cycles specified in Table 153.1120 must be completed at each position to which the washing machine is moved.

(6) When the NLS is immiscible with water or is a solidifying cargo, the tank must be pumped out each time enough tank washings collect in the bottom of the tank for the pump to gain suction, or the procedures in paragraphs (b)(3), (b)(4), and (b)(5) of this section must be repeated two additional times with the tank pumped out each time, for a total of three washings.

(7) Items 12 through 14 in the Cargo Record Book must be completed and, if the prewash is for a Category A NLS, verification that the procedures specified in the approved Procedures and Arrangements Manual were followed shown by the Surveyor's endorsement in the Cargo Record Book.

TABLE 153.1120—NUMBER OF WASHING MACHINE CYCLES IN THE PREWASH PROCEDURE

	Number of washing machine cycles	
	Column 1: Prewash under § 153.1116 or for a solidifying NLS under § 153.1108	Column 2: Prewashes except those listed under column 1
Category A NLS	2	1
Category B or C NLS	1	1/2

[CGD 81–101, 52 FR 7785, Mar. 12, 1987, as amended by CGD 81–101, 53 FR 28975, Aug. 1, 1988 and 54 FR 12629, Mar. 28, 1989]

§ 153.1122 Discharges of NLS residue from tank washing other than a prewash: Categories A, B, and C.

Tank washings that do not result from a prewash and that contain Category A, B, or C NLS residues must be discharged to a reception facility or discharged to the sea under § 153.1126 or § 153.1128 except those tank washings resulting from washing a tank that has been cleaned following a ventilation procedure in the approved Procedures and Arrangements Manual.

§ 153.1124 Discharges of Category D NLS residue.

NLS residue from Category D NLSs must be discharged to a reception facility or discharged to the sea using the following procedure:

(a) Before discharge begins, drain or flush the NLS residue in the tank's piping systems into the tank.

(b) After draining or flushing, discharge the NLS residue to the sea in accordance with § 153.1128 or transfer it to a slop tank and discharge in accordance with § 153.1126.

§ 153.1126 Discharge of NLS residue from a slop tank to the sea: Categories A, B, C, and D.

NLS residue in a slop tank may not be discharged into the sea unless—

(a) The ship meets the conditions for discharging the NLS residue from a cargo tank in § 153.1128; and

(b) For Category B NLS residue transferred to the slop tank under § 153.1119(b), the NLS is discharged—

(1) Through an NLS residue discharge system with the flow recording equipment required in § 153.481(b)(2) operating; and

(2) At a rate maintained at or below Q in the following:

For tank contents that are miscible

$$Q = \frac{VKU^{1.4}L^{1.6}}{N} \times 10^{-5} \ m^3/hr$$

For tank contents that are immiscible

$Q = KU^{1.4} L^{1.6} \times 10^{-5} \ m^3/hr$

where:

Q=maximum permissible slops discharge rate in cubic meters per hour.
V=volume of slops in the tank in cubic meters.
K=4.3, except K=6.45 if Q is distributed between two NLS residue discharge outlets on opposite sides of the ship (see §§ 153.470(c) and 153.481(b)).
U=ship's speed in knots.
L=ship's length in meters.
N=number of tanks containing Category B NLS residue pumped into the slop tank.

§ 153.1128 Discharge of NLS residue from a cargo tank to the sea: Categories A. B, C, and D.

The discharge of NLS residue to the sea must be made with the ship at least 22.24 km (12 nautical miles) from the nearest land, and must meet the following additional conditions:

(a) To discharge the following the ship must be in water at least 25 m (76.2 ft) deep:

(1) Category B or C NLS residue diluted to less than 1 ppm of the NLS.

(2) Category B or C NLS residue resulting from washing a tank after the following washing procedure has been completed:

(i) If the tank is not required to be prewashed under this part, the tank must be washed following the procedures that apply to a prewash of a Category B NLS in § 153.1120 using one washing machine cycle, and the tank washings discharged to a reception facility or to the sea under § 153.1126 or paragraph (a)(1), (c) or (d) of this section.

(ii) After the tank has been prewashed or has been washed under paragraph (a)(2)(i) of this section, the tank must then be washed with one cycle of the tank washing machine, and the tank washings discharged to a reception facility or to the sea in accordance with § 153.1126 or paragraph (a)(1), (c), or (d) of this section.

(b) To discharge a Category D NLS residue to which 10 times its volume in water is added and mixed, the ship must be—

(1) If self-propelled, maintained at a speed of at least 12.97 km/hr (7 knots); and

(2) If not self-propelled, maintained at a speed of at least 7.41 km/hr (4 knots).

(c) Each ship built before July 1, 1986 that discharges Category A, B or C NLS residues before January 1, 1988 must be—

(1) In water at least 25 m (76.2 ft) deep;

(2) If discharging the residue of a Category A NLS cargo, discharging only residue created by washing the Category A NLS's cargo tank after a prewash;

(3) If discharging the residue of a Category B NLS cargo, discharging no more than the larger of 1 m³ or 1/3000th the volume of the Category B cargo loaded;

(4) If discharging the residue of a Category C NLS cargo, discharging no more than the larger of 3 m³ of or 1/1000th the volume of the Category C cargo loaded;

(5) If self-propelled, maintained at a speed of at least 12.97 km/hr (7 knots); and

(6) If not self-propelled, maintained at a speed of at least 7.41 km/hr (4 knots).

(d) To discharge Category A, B, C, or D NLS residue other than as allowed under paragraphs (a) through (c) of this section, the ship must be—

(1) In water at least 25 m (76.2 ft) deep;

(2) Discharging at a rate not exceeding that used for Q_d in § 153.470;

(3) If self-propelled, maintained at speed no less than the minimum specified in the approved Procedures and Arrangements Manual but at least 12.97 km/hr (7 knots);

(4) If not self-propelled, maintained at a speed no less than the minimum specified in the approved Procedures and Arrangements Manual but at least 7.41 km/hr (4 knots);

(5) If discharging the residue of a Category A NLS cargo, discharging only residue created by washing the Category A NLS's cargo tank after a prewash;

(6) If discharging the residue of a Category B NLS cargo, discharging no more than the larger of 1 m³ or 1/3000th the volume of the Category B cargo loaded;

(7) If discharging the residue of a Category C NLS cargo, discharging no more than the larger of 3 m³ of or 1/1000th the volume of the Category C cargo loaded;

(8) Discharging through an NLS residue discharge system meeting § 153.470.

[CGD 81–101, 52 FR 7785, Mar. 12, 1987, as amended by CGD 81–101, 53 FR 28976, Aug. 1, 1988 and 54 FR 12629, Mar. 28, 1989]

§ 153.1130 Failure of slops discharge recording equipment; operating with, reporting failures, and replacing pollution equipment: Category A, B, C, D.

(a) If equipment required in §§ 153.470 through 153.488 fails, the Coast Guard Marine Inspection Office, Sector Office, or Captain of the Port must be notified within 24 hours after the failure.

(b) No person shall replace a piece of equipment required by §§ 153.470 through 153.488 unless the replacement is—

(1) Identical to the original equipment; or

(2) Allowed as an alternative under § 153.10.

(c) The following conditions apply when discharge recording equipment required under § 153.481(b)(2) fails:

(1) No NLS residue may be discharged unless the approved Procedures and Arrangements Manual contains procedures for discharging with incapacitated discharge recording equipment while meeting the discharge restrictions of § 153.1126(b) and these procedures are followed.

(2) The failure of the discharge recording equipment must be recorded in the Cargo Record Book within 24 hours after the failure.

(3) If the ship operates under a Certificate of Inspection, the failed discharge recording equipment must be repaired or replaced within 60 days after it fails, and the repair or replacement recorded in the Cargo Record Book and reported to the Coast Guard within 24 hours after it is completed.

[CGD 81–101, 52 FR 7785, Mar. 12, 1987, as amended by USCG–2006–25556, 72 FR 36330, July 2, 2007]

§ 153.1132 Reporting spills and non-complying discharges: Category A, B, C, and D.

The following shall be reported following the procedures applying to oil in 33 CFR 151.15 (c), (d), (g), (h):

(a) All discharges of the NLS that do not meet the requirements of this part.

(b) All spills into the water.

MAINTENANCE

§ 153.1500 Venting system rupture disks.

The master shall ensure that a relief valve exposed to a cargo after the failure of a rupture disk or breaking pin is cleaned and operates properly before the next cargo is loaded into the tank.

§ 153.1502 Fixed ballast relocation.

No person may remove or relocate fixed ballast unless:

(a) The change is approved by the Commandant (CG–ENG); or

(b) The ballast is temporarily moved under the supervision of a Coast Guard Marine Inspector for examination or repair of the tankship.

[CGD 73–96, 42 FR 49027, Sept. 26, 1977, as amended by CGD 82–063b, 48 FR 4782, Feb. 3, 1983]

§ 153.1504 Inspection of personnel emergency and safety equipment.

The master shall ensure that the personnel emergency and safety equipment required by § 153.214 is inspected each 30 days and found to be in good condition and operating properly.

§ 153.1600

Subpart D—Test and Calculation Procedures for Determining Stripping Quantity, Clingage NLS Residue, and Total NLS Residue

SOURCE: CGD 81–101, 52 FR 7788, Mar. 12, 1987, unless otherwise noted.

§ 153.1600 Equipment required for conducting the stripping quantity test.

The operator shall ensure the stripping quantity test is conducted with—

(a) Equipment that maintains a backpressure of at least 100 kPa (1 atm) (gauge) at the connection of the discharge line of the tank to be tested to the cargo transfer hose, including, but not limited to, piping whose discharge is 10 m above the manifold or a constant pressure valve in the discharge line and set at 100 kPa;

(b) A container for measuring the volume of water remaining in the tank to an accuracy of ±5%;

(c) A squeegee or broom to collect standing water on the tank floor;

(d) One or more containers for collecting and transferring water; and

(e) One of the following for transferring the water remaining in the tank to the measuring container:

(1) A wet vacuum.

(2) A positive displacement pump.

(3) An eductor with an air/water separator in line.

§ 153.1602 Test procedure for determining the stripping quantity.

(a) The stripping quantity of a tank must be determined by testing the tank under the procedures in paragraph (b) of this section unless the Coast Guard agrees under the provisions of § 153.10 to accept the stripping quantity, previously determined under paragraph (b) of this section, of a tank having similar geometry, internal structure, and piping system.

(b) When testing a tank for stripping quantity, the owner or operator of the ship shall proceed as follows:

(1) Make arrangements with the Officer in Charge, Marine Inspection, for a Coast Guard Marine Inspector to witness the stripping test.

(2) Clean and gas free the tanks to be tested.

(3) Determine the least favorable values of list and trim for drainage within the range allowed by the approved Procedures and Arrangements Manual.

(4) Maintain the ship's list and trim during the test to that determined under paragraph (b)(3) of this section.

(5) Load the tank with enough water so that unloading the water simulates the final stages of unloading a full tank of cargo.

(6) Pump out the water and strip the tank using the procedures specified in the approved Procedures and Arrangements Manual.

(7) After shutting the manifold valve, open any cargo pump foot valve to allow water trapped in the cargo pump to drain into the tank.

(8) Open all valves in the piping system except the manifold valve and allow the water to drain into the tank.

(9) Squeegee or sweep the water drained under paragraphs (b)(7) and (b)(8) of this section and any water that stands in puddles on the tank floor to the tank's low point or sump and collect in the container required by § 153.1600(b) using the equipment required in § 153.1600(e).

(10) With the manifold valve still closed, drain any water remaining in the piping system on the ship's side of the cargo transfer manifold valve into containers, and add this water to that collected from the tank under paragraph (b)(9) of this section. Water collected from a cargo line serving a block of tanks may be prorated between all the tanks it serves if—

(i) The ship owner requests, under the provisions of § 153.10, that the water be prorated; and

(ii) The ship's approved Procedures and Arrangements Manual specifies that no tank in the block be washed until all the tanks in the block have been discharged.

(c) Include any water that is trapped in dead end pipe sections, either by—

(1) Draining the pipe sections and adding the water to that collected in the container under paragraphs (b)(9) and (b)(10) of this section; or

(2) Adding an estimate of the water's volume to the sum calculated in paragraph (d) of this section using the pipe's dimensions, the ship's list and

trim, and the geometry of the piping system.

(d) Measure the volume of water collected in the container under paragraphs (b)(9), (b)(10), and (c)(1) of this section and add to that volume the volume, if any, estimated under paragraph (c)(2) of this section.

§ 153.1604 Determining the stripping quantity from the test results.

(a) For a single test, the stripping quantity is the volume of water calculated under § 153.1602(d).

(b) If multiple tests are made on a tank without modifications to the tank, pumping system, or stripping procedure between the tests, the stripping quantity must be taken as the average of the stripping quantities for all of the tests.

(c) If multiple tests are made on a tank with modifications to the tank, pumping system, or stripping procedure between the tests, the stripping quantity is the stripping quantity determined under paragraph (b) of this section using only those tests performed after the last modification.

§ 153.1608 Calculation of total NLS residue and clingage NLS residue.

(a) The total NLS residue for each tank is calculated by adding the stripping quantity and the clingage NLS residue.

(b) The clingage NLS residue for each tank is calculated using the following formula:

$$Q_{clingage} = 1.1 \times 10^{-4} \, A_d + 1.5 \times 10^{-5} \, A_w + 4.5 \times 10^{-4} \, L^{1/2} \, A_b$$

where:

A_b = Area of the tank bottom added to the area in square meters of tank structural components projected on a horizontal surface

A_d = Area of the tank underdecks added to the area in square meters of tank structural components projected on a horizontal surface

A_w = Area of the tank walls added to the area in square meters of tank structural components projected on a vertical surface

L = Length of tank in meters from fore to aft

$Q_{clingage}$ = volume of clingage in cubic meters

When using the formula in this paragraph, areas that are inclined more than 30° from the horizontal may be assumed to be vertical.

NOTE: The Commandant (CG–ENG) (telephone number 202–372–1420) has information that may be useful in approximating surface areas of typical structural members for the projected area calculations under § 153.1608(b).

[CGD 81–101, 52 FR 7788, Mar. 12, 1987, as amended by USCG–2006–25697, 71 FR 55747, Sept. 25, 2006; USCG–2012–0832, 77 FR 59785, Oct. 1, 2012]

TABLE 1 TO PART 153—SUMMARY OF MINIMUM REQUIREMENTS

Cargo name	IMO Annex II Pollution Category	Haz.	Cargo containment system	Vent height	Vent	Gauge	Fire protection system	Special requirements in 46 CFR Part 153	Electrical hazard class and group
a.	b.	c.	d.	e.	f.	g.	h.	i.	j.
Acetic acid	D	S	III	4m	PV	Restr	A	.238(a), .409, .527, .554, .933	I-D
Acetic anhydride	D	S	II	4m	PV	Restr	A	.238(a), .409, .526, .527, .554, .933	I-D
Acetochlor	A	P	II	NR	Open	Open	A	.409	NA
Acetone cyanohydrin	A	S/P	II	B/3	PV	Closed	A	.238(a), .316, .336, .408, .525, .526, .527, .912(a)(2), .933, .1002, .1004, .1020, .1035.	I-D
Acetonitrile	III	S	II	B/3	PV	Restr	A	.409, .525, .526, .1020	I-D
Acrylamide solution (50% or less)	D	S	II	NR	Open	Closed	NSR	.409, .525(a), (c), (d), (e), .912(a)(1), .1002(a), .1004, .1020.	NA
Acrylic acid	D	S	II	4m	PV	Restr	A	.238(a), .409, .526, .912(a)(1), .933, .1002(a), .1004	I-D
Acrylonitrile	B	S/P	II	B/3	PV	Closed	A	.236(a), (c), (d), .316, .408, .525, .526, .527, .912(a)(1), .1004, .1020.	I-D
Adiponitrile	D	S	III	4m	PV	Restr	A	.526	I-D
Alachlor	B	S/P	III	NR	Open	Open	A, C	.238(a), .409, .440, .488, .908(a), (b)	NA
Alcohol (C6–C17) (secondary) poly(3–6)ethoxylates.	A	P	II	NR	Open	Open	A	.409	NA
Alcohol (C6–C17) (secondary) poly(7–12)ethoxylates.	B	P	III	NR	Open	Open	A	.409, .440, .908(a), (b)	NA
Alcohol(C9–C11) poly(2.5–9) ethoxylate .. see poly(...)ethoxylates.	B	P	III	NR	Open	Open	A	.409, .440, .908(a)	NA
Alcohol(C12–C15) poly(...)ethoxylates, Alcohol(C12–C16) poly(...)ethoxylates.									
Alcohol(C12–C16) poly(1–6)ethoxylates	A	P	II	NR	Open	Open	A	.409	NA
Alcohol(C12–C16) poly(7–19)ethoxylates	B	P	III	NR	Open	Open	A	.409, .440, .908(a)	NA
Alcohol(C12–C16) poly(20+)ethoxylates	C	P	III	NR	Open	Open	A	None	NA
Alkanes(C6–C9) (all isomers)	C	P	II	4m	PV	Restr	A	.409	I-D
Alkane(C14–C17) sulfonic acid, sodium salt solution (65% or less).	B	P	III	NR	Open	Open	NSR	.440, .908(a)	NA
Alkyl polyether (C9–C20)	B	P	III	NR	Open	Open	A, B	.409; (.440, .908(a))[1]	NA
Alkenyl(C16–C20) succinic anhydride	D	S	III	B/3	PV	Closed	NSR	.316, .408, .525, .526, .1020	NA
Alkyl acrylate-Vinyl pyridine copolymer in Toluene.	C	P	III	4m	PV	Restr	A	.409	NA
Alkylaryl phosphate mixtures (more than 40% Diphenyl tolyl phosphate, less than 0.02% ortho- isomer).	A	S/P	I	B/3	PV	Closed	A, B, C	.316, .408, .525, .526, .1020	NA
Alkyl(C3–C4)benzenes (all isomers)	A	P	III	4m	PV	Restr	A	.409	I-D
Alkyl(C5–C8)benzenes (all isomers)	A	P	II	NR	Open	Open	A	.409	I-D
Alkylbenzene, Alkylindane, Alkylindene mixture (each C12–C17).	A	P	II	NR	Open	Open	A	.409	NA
Alkylbenzenesulfonic acid (greater than 4%).	C	S/P	III	NR	Open	Open	A, B	.440, .908(a)	NA

246

Coast Guard, DHS — Pt. 153, Table 1

Chemical								References	
Alkylbenzenesulfonic acid, sodium salt solution.	C	P	III	NR	Open	Open	NSR	440, 903, 908(a), (b)	NA
Alkyl(C7–C9) nitrates	B	S/P	II	NR	Open	Open	A, B	409, 560, .1002	NA
Alkyl (C7–C11) phenol poly(4-12) ethoxylate.	B	P	II	NR	Open	Open	A	409, 440, 488¹, .908(a), (b)	I-D
Alkyl(C8–C9) phenylamine in aromatic solvent.	A	P	III	4m	PV	Restr	A	409	NA
Alkyl(C10–C20, saturated and unsaturated) phosphite.	C	P	III	NR	Open	Open	A	None	NA
Alkyl(C8–C10) polyglucoside solution (65% or less).	C	P	III	NR	Open	Open	NSR	440, .908(a), (b)	NA
Alkyl(C12–C14) polyglucoside solution (55% or less).	B	P	III	NR	Open	Open	NSR	409, 440, .908(a), (b)	NA
Alkyl(C8–C10)/(C12–C14): (40% or less/60% or more) polyglucoside solution (55% or less).	B	P	III	NR	Open	Open	NSR	409, 440, .908(a), (b)	NA
Alkyl(C8–C10)/(C12–C14): (50/50%) polyglucoside solution (55% or less).	C	P	III	NR	Open	Open	NSR	440, .908(a), (b)	NA
Alkyl(C8–C10)/(C12–C14): (60% or more/40% or less) polyglucoside solution (55% or less).	C	P	III	NR	Open	Open	NSR	440, .908(a), (b)	NA
Allyl alcohol	B	S/P	II	B/3	PV	Closed	A	316, .408, .525, .526, .527, .933, .1020	I-C
Allyl chloride	B	S/P	II	B/3	PV	Closed	A	316, .408, .525, .526, .527, .933, .1020	I-D
Aluminum chloride (30% or less). Hydrochloric acid (20% or less) solution.	D	S	III	4m	PV	Restr	NSR	252, .526, .527, .554, .557, .933, .1045, .1052	I-B
2-(2-Aminoethoxy) ethanol	D	S	III	NR	Open	Open	A, C, D	236(b), (c), .409	NA
Aminoethylethanolamine	D	S	III	NR	Open	Open	A	236(a), (b), (c), (g)	NA
N-Aminoethylpiperazine	D	S	III	4m	PV	Restr	A	236(b), (c), .409, .526	I-C
2-Amino-2-methyl-1-propanol (90% or less).	D	S	III	NR	Open	Open	A	236(a), (b), (c), (g)	I-D
Ammonia aqueous (28% or less), see Ammonium hydroxide (28% or less NH₃).									
Ammonium bisulfite solution (70% or less NH₃).	D	S	III	4m	PV	Restr	No	238(e), .526, .933, .1002	NA
Ammonium hydroxide (28% or less NH₃).	C	S/P	III	4m	PV	Restr	A, B, C	236(b), (c), (f), .526, .527	I-D
Ammonium nitrate solution (greater than 45% and less than 93%).	D	S	II	NR	Open	Open	NSR	238(d), .252, .336, .409, .554(a), (b)	NA
Ammonium sulfide solution (45% or less)	B	S/P	II	B/3	PV	Closed	A, C	236(a), (b), (c), (g). 316, .408, .525, .526, .527, .933, .1002, .1020.	I-D
Ammonium thiocyanate (25% or less), Ammonium thiosulfate (20% or less) solution.	C	P	III	NR	Open	Open	NSR	None	NA
Ammonium thiosulfate solution (60% or less).	C	P	III	NR	Open	Open	NSR	440, .908(b)	NA
Amyl acetate (all isomers)	C	P	III	4m	PV	Restr	A	409	I-D
tert-Amyl methyl ether	C	P	III	4m	PV	Restr	A	409	NA
Aniline	C	S/P	II	B/3	PV	Closed	A	316, .408, .525, .526, .933, .1020	I-D
Anthracene oil (Coal tar fraction), see Coal tar.									

Pt. 153, Table 1   46 CFR Ch. I (10–1–13 Edition)

Cargo name	IMO Annex II Pollution Category	Haz.	Cargo containment system	Vent height	Vent	Gauge	Fire protection system	Special requirements in 46 CFR Part 153	Electrical hazard class and group
a.	b.	c.	d.	e.	f.	g.	h.	i.	j.
Aviation alkylates .... (C8 paraffins and iso-paraffins, b. pt. 95–120 deg. C).	C	P	III	4m	PV	Restr	B	.409	I-C
Barium long chain (C11–C50) alkaryl sulfonate.	B	S/P	II	NR	Open	Open	A, D	.408, .440, .525(a), (c), (e), (d), .908(a), .1020	NA
Barium long chain alkyl (C8–C14) phenate sulfide.	[A]	P	II	NR	Open	Open	A	.409	NA
Benzene hydrocarbon mixtures [2] (having 10% Benzene or more).	C[2]	S/P	III	B/3	PV	Closed	A, B	.316, .409, .440, .526, .908(b), .933, .1060	I-D
Benzenesulfonyl chloride	D	S	III	4m	PV	Restr	A, B, D	.236(a), (b), (c), (g), .409, .526	I-D
Benzene, Toluene, Xylene mixtures [2] (having 10% Benzene or more).	@C[2]	S/P	III	B/3	PV	Closed	B	.316, .409, .440, .526, .908(b), .1060	I-D
Benzyl acetate	C	P	III	NR	Open	Open	A	None	I-D
Benzyl alcohol	C	P	III	NR	Open	Open	A	None	I-D
Benzyl chloride	B	S/P	III	B/3	PV	Closed	A, B	.316, .408, .525, .526, .527, .912(a)(2), .1004, .1020	I-D
Bromochloromethane	B	S	III	4m	Restr	Restr	NSR	.236(a), (b), (d), .526, .933	NA
Butene oligomer	B	P	III	NR	Open	Open	A	.409	NA
Butyl acetate (all isomers)	C	P	III	4m	PV	Restr	A	.409	I-D
Butyl acrylate (all isomers)	B	S/P	II	B/3	PV	Restr	A	.409, .526, .912(a)(1), .1002(a), (b), .1004	I-D
Butylamine (all isomers)	C	S/P	III	4m	PV	Restr	A	.236(b), (c), .316, .408, .525, .526, .527, .1020	I-D
Butylbenzene (all isomers), see Alkyl(C3–C4)benzenes (all isomers).	A	P	II	NR	Open	Open	A	.409	I-D
Butyl benzyl phthalate	A	P	II	NR	Open	Open	A	.409	I-D
Butyl butyrate, see Butyl butyrate (all isomers).									
Butyl butyrate (all isomers)	B	P	III	4m	PV	Restr	A, C	.372, .409, .440, .500, .526, .530(a), (c), (e)–(g), (m)–(o), .1010, .1011.	I-D
1,2-Butylene oxide	C	S/P	III	4m	PV	Restr	A, D	.409, .500, .525, .526, .1020	I-B
n-Butyl ether	C	S/P	III	B/3	PV	Restr	A	None	I-C
Butyl heptyl ketone	[C]	P	III	NR	Open	Open	A		NA
iso-Butyl isobutyrate, see Butyl butyrate (all isomers).									
Butyl methacrylate	D	P	III	4m	PV	Restr	A, D	.409, .526, .912(a)(1), .1002(a), (b), .1004	I-D
Butyl methacrylate, Decyl methacrylate, Cetyl-Eicosyl methacrylate mixture.	D	P	III	4m	PV	Restr	A, C, D	.912(a)(1), .1002(a), (b), .1004	I-D
n-Butyl propionate	C	P	III	4m	PV	Restr	A	.409	I-D
Butyl toluene	@A	S/P	III	NR	Open	Open	A	.409	I-D
Butyraldehyde (all isomers)	C	S	III	4m	PV	Restr	A	.409, .526	I-C
Butyric acid	D	S/P	III	4m	PV	Restr	A	.238(a), .554	I-D
Calcium alkyl(C9)phenol sulfide, polyolefin phosphorosulfide mixture.	A	P	II	NR	Open	Open	A, B	.409	NA

248

Coast Guard, DHS   Pt. 153, Table 1

Name									
Calcium bromide, Zinc bromide solution, see Drilling brine (containing Zinc salts).									
Calcium hypochlorite solution (15% or less).	C	S/P	III	4m	PV	Restr	NSR	.236(a), (b)	NA
Calcium hypochlorite solution (more than 15%).	B	S/P	III	4m	PV	Restr	NSR	.236(a), (b), 409	NA
Calcium long chain alkyl(C5–C10) phenate.	C	P	III	NR	Open	Open	A	None	NA
Calcium long chain alkyl salicylate (C13+)	C	P	III	NR	Open	Open	A, B	(.440, .903, .908(a))[1]	I-D
Camphor oil	B	S/P	III	4m	PV	Restr	A, B	.409	NA
Carbolic oil	A	S/P	III	B/3	PV	Closed	A	.408, .440, .525, .526, .908(b), .933, .1020	NA
Carbon disulfide	B	S/P	III	B/3	PV	Closed	C	.236(c), .252, .408, .500, .515, .520, .525, .526, .527, .1020, .1040.	I-A
Carbon tetrachloride	B	S/P	III	B/3	PV	Closed	NSR	.316, .409, .525, .526, .527, .1020	NA
Cashew nut shell oil (untreated)	D	S	III	4m	PV	Restr	A, B	.526, .933	NA
Caustic potash solution	C	S/P	III	NR	Open	Open	NSR	.236(a), (c), (g), .933	NA
Caustic soda solution	D	S	III	NR	Open	Open	NSR	.236(a), (c), (g), .933	NA
Cetyl-Eicosyl methacrylate mixture	III	S	III	NR	Open	Open	A, C, D	.912(a)(1), .1002(a), (b), .1004	NA
Chlorinated paraffins (C10–C13)	A	P	–	NR	Open	Open	A	.408	NA
Chloroacetic acid (80% or less)	C	S/P	II	B/3	PV	Closed	NSR	.238(e), .408, .440, .554, .908(b)	I-D
Chlorobenzene	B	S/P	III	4m	PV	Restr	A, B	.409, .526	NA
Chloroform	B	S	III	B/3	PV	Restr	NSR	.409, .525, .526, .527, .1020	NA
(crude) Chlorohydrins	D	S	II	B/3	PV	Closed	A	.408, .525, .526, .1020	I-D
4-Chloro-2-methylphenoxyacetic acid, di-methylamine salt solution.	C	P	III	NR	Open	Open	NSR	.236(a), (b), (c), (g)	NA
o-Chloronitrobenzene	B	S/P	II	B/3	PV	Closed	A, B, C, D	.316, .336, .408, .440, .525, .526, .908(a), (b), .933, .1020.	NA
1-(4-Chlorophenyl)-4,4-dimethyl pentan-3-one.	B	P	III	NR	Open	Open	A, B, D	.409, .440, .488, .908(a), (b)	NA
2- or 3-Chloropropionic acid	C	S/P	III	NR	Open	Open	A	.238(a), (b), .440, .554, .908(a), (b)	NA
Chlorosulfonic acid	C	S/P	–	B/3	PV	Closed	NSR	.408, .525, .526, .527, .554, .555, .602, .933, .1000, .1020, .1045.	I-B
o-Chlorotoluene	A	S/P	III	4m	PV	Restr	A, B, C	.409, .526	I-D
m-Chlorotoluene	B	S/P	III	4m	PV	Restr	A, B, C	.409, .526	I-D
p-Chlorotoluene	B	S/P	III	4m	PV	Restr	A, B, C	.409, .440, .526, .908(b)	I-D
Chlorotoluenes (mixed isomers)	A	S/P	III	4m	PV	Restr	A, B, C	.409, .526	I-D
Coal tar	B	S/P	III	4m	PV	Restr	B, D	.409, .933, .1060	I-D
Coal tar naphtha solvent	D	S	III	4m	PV	Restr	A, D	.409, .526, .933, .1060	I-D
Coal tar pitch (molten)	B	S/P	III	4m	PV	Restr	B, D	.252, .409, .933, .1060	I-D
Cobalt naphthenate in solvent naphtha	C	P	III	NR	Open	Open	A	.409, .526	NA
Coconut oil, fatty acid	[C]	P	II	NR	Open	Open	A	.440, .903, .908(a), (b)	NA
Cottonseed oil, fatty acid	A	S/P	II	NR	Open	Open	A, B	.440, .903, .908(a)	NA
Creosote (coal tar)	A	S/P	III	NR	Open	Open	A, B, D	.409	I-D
Creosote (wood)	A	S/P	II	NR	Open	Open	A, B, D	.409	NA
Cresols (all isomers)	A	S/P	II	NR	Open	Open	A, B	.409, .440, .908(b)	I-D

249

Cargo name	IMO Annex II Pollution Category	Haz.	Cargo containment system	Vent height	Vent	Gauge	Fire protection system	Special requirements in 46 CFR Part 153	Electrical hazard class and group
a.	b.	c.	d.	e.	f.	g.	h.	i.	j.
Cresols with less than 5% Phenol, see Cresols (all isomers)									
Cresols with 5% or more Phenol, see Phenol									
Cresylate spent caustic (mixtures of Cresols and Caustic soda solutions).	A	S/P	II	NR	Open	Open	NSR	.236(a), (c), .409, .933	NA
Cresylic acid, dephenolized	A	S/P	II	NR	Open	Open	A, B	.409	NA
Cresylic acid, sodium salt solution, see Cresylate spent caustic.									
Crotonaldehyde	A	S/P	II	B/3	PV	Restr	A	.316, .409, .525, .526, .527, .1020	I-C
Cumene (isopropylbenzene), see Propylbenzene (all isomers).									
1,5,9-Cyclododecatriene	A	S/P	I	4m	PV	Restr	A	.236(b), (c), .408, .526, .912(a)(1), .1002(a), (b), .1004	I-D
Cycloheptane	C	P	III	4m	PV	Restr	A	.409	I-D
Cyclohexane	C	P	III	4m	PV	Restr	A	.409, .440, .908(b)	I-D
Cyclohexanone	D	S	III	4m	PV	Restr	A	.236(a), (b), .409, .526	I-D
Cyclohexanone, Cyclohexanol mixture	D	S	III	4m	PV	Restr	A	.236(a), (b), .526	I-D
Cyclohexyl acetate	B	P	III	4m	PV	Restr	A	.409	I-D
Cyclohexylamine	C	S/P	III	4m	PV	Restr	A, C, D	.236(a), (b), (c), (g), .409, .526	I-C
1,3-Cyclopentadiene dimer (molten)	B	P	III	4m	PV	Restr	A	.409, .440, .488, .908(a), (b)	I-D
Cyclopentane	C	P	III	4m	PV	Restr	A	.409	I-D
Cyclopentene	B	P	III	4m	PV	Restr	A	.409	I-D
p-Cymene	C	P	III	4m	PV	Restr	A	.409	I-C
iso-Decaldehyde	@C	P	III	NR	Open	Open	A	None	I-C
n-Decaldehyde	@B	P	III	NR	Open	Open	A	None	I-C
Decanoic acid	C	P	III	NR	Open	Restr	A	.440, .903, .908(a), (b)	NA
Decene	B	P	III	4m	PV	Open	A	.409	I-D
Decyl acetate	B	P	III	NR	Open	Open	A, C, D	.409	NA
(iso-, n-) Decyl acrylate	A	S/P	III	NR	Open	Open	A	.236(a), (b), (c), .409, .912(a)(1), .1002(a), (b), .1004	I-D
Decyl alcohol (all isomers)	B	P	III	NR	Open	Open	A	.409, .440, .908(b)	NA
Decyloxytetrahydro-thiophene dioxide	A	S/P	II	B/3	PV	Restr	A	.409, .526	NA
Dibromomethane	C	S/P	II	4m	PV	Restr	NSR	.236(a), (b), (d), .408, .525(a), (c), (d), (e), .526, .933, .1020.	NA
Dibutylamine	C	S/P	III	4m	PV	Restr	A, B, C, D	.236(b), (c), .409, .526	I-C
Dibutyl hydrogen phosphonate	B	P	III	NR	Open	Open	A	.409, .440, .908(a)	NA
ortho-Dibutyl phthalate	A	P	II	NR	Open	Open	A	.409	I-D
Dichlorobenzene (all isomers)[1]	B	S/P	II	4m	PV	Restr	A, B, D	.236(a), (b), .409, .440, .488[1], .526, .908(a), (b)[1]	I-D
3,4-Dichloro-1-butene	B	S/P	II	B/3	PV	Closed	A, B, C	.316, .409, .525(a), (c), (d), (e), .526, .527, .933, .1020	I-D
1,1-Dichloroethane	D	S	III	4m	PV	Restr	A, B	.409, .526, .527	I-D
2,2'-Dichloroethyl ether	B	S/P	II	4m	PV	Restr	A	.236(a), (b), .409, .526	I-C
1,6-Dichlorohexane	B	S/P	II	4m	PV	Restr	A, B	.409, .526	NA

Coast Guard, DHS Pt. 153, Table 1

Name									
2,2'-Dichloroisopropyl ether	C	S/P	II	B/3	PV	Restr	A, B, C, D	236(a), (b), .316, .408(a), .440, .525, .526, .1020	I-D
Dichloromethane	D	S	III	4m	PV	Restr	NSR	.526	I-D
2,4-Dichlorophenol⁴	A	S/P	II	4m	PV	Restr	A, B, C, D	236(a), (b), (c), (g), .409, .440, .500, .501, .526, .908(b), .933	I-D
2,4-Dichlorophenoxyacetic acid, diethanolamine salt solution.	A	S/P	III	NR	Open	Open	NSR	236(a), (b), (c), (g), .409	NA
2,4-Dichlorophenoxyacetic acid, dimethylamine salt solution.	A	S/P	III	NR	Open	Open	NSR	236(a), (b), (c), (g), .409	NA
2,4-Dichlorophenoxyacetic acid, trisopropanolamine salt solution.	A	S/P	III	NR	Open	Open	NSR	236(a), (b), (c), (g), .409	NA
1,1-Dichloropropane	C	S/P	II	B/3	PV	Restr	A, B	409, .525, .526, .1020	I-D
1,2-Dichloropropane	C	S/P	II	B/3	PV	Restr	A, B	409, .525, .526, .1020	I-D
1,3-Dichloropropane	D	S	II	B/3	PV	Restr	A, B	409, .525, .526, .1020	I-D
1,3-Dichloropropene	B	S/P	II	B/3	PV	Closed	A, B	.316, .336, .408, .525, .526, .527	I-D
Dichloropropene, Dichloropropane mixtures.	B	S/P	II	B/3	PV	Closed	A, B, C, D	.316, .336, .408, .526, .527	I-D
2,2-Dichloropropionic acid	D	S	III	4m	PV	Restr	A	238(e), .266, .500, .501, .554, .933	NA
Diethanolamine	D	S	III	NR	Open	Open	A	236(b), (c)	NA
Diethylamine	C	S/P	II	B/3	PV	Restr	A	236(a), (b), (c), (g), .409, .525, .526, .527, .1020	I-C
Diethylaminoethanol, see Diethylethanolamine									
2,6-Diethylaniline	C	S/P	III	NR	Open	Open	B, C, D	236(b), .409, .440, .908(b)	NA
Diethylbenzene	A	P	III	4m	PV	Restr	A	409	I-D
Diethylenetriamine	D	S	III	NR	Open	Open	A	236(b), (c)	NA
Diethylethanolamine	C	S/P	III	4m	PV	Restr	A, C	236(a), (b), (c), (g), .409, .526	I-C
Diethyl ether, see Ethyl ether									
Di-(2-ethylhexyl) phosphoric acid	C	S/P	III	NR	Open	Open	A, B, C, D	236(b), (c)	I-D
Diethyl phthalate	C	P	III	NR	Open	Open	A	None	I-D
Diethyl sulfate	B	S/P	II	4m	PV	Closed	A, D	236(a), (c), (d), .409, .526, .933	I-D
Diglycidyl ether of Bisphenol A	B	P	III	NR	Open	Open	A	409, .440, .908(a)	NA
Diglycidyl ether of Bisphenol F	B	P	III	NR	Open	Open	A	409, .440, .908(a)	NA
Di-n-hexyl adipate	B	P	III	NR	Open	Open	A	409	NA
Diisobutylamine	C	S/P	II	4m	PV	Restr	A, B, C, D	236(a), (b), (c), (g), .409, .525(a), (c), (d), (e), .526, .1020.	I-C
Diisobutylcarbinol	@C	P	III	NR	Open	Open	A	None	I-D
Diisobutylene	B	P	III	4m	PV	Restr	A	409	I-D
Diisobutyl phthalate	B	P	III	NR	Open	Open	A	409, .440, .908(a)	I-D
Diisopropanolamine	C	P	III	NR	Open	Open	A	236(b), (c), .440, .908(a), (b)	I-C
Diisopropylamine	C	S/P	II	B/3	PV	Closed	A	236(b), (c), .408, .525, .526, .527, .1020	I-C
Diisopropylbenzene (all isomers)	A	P	III	NR	Open	Open	A	409	I-D
N,N-Dimethylacetamide	D	S	III	B/3	PV	Restr	B	236(b), .316, .525, .526, .527, .1020	I-D
N,N-Dimethylacetamide solution (40% or less).	D	S	III	B/3	PV	Restr	B	236(b), .316, .526	I-D
Dimethyl adipate	B	P	III	NR	Open	Open	A	409, .440, .908(b)	NA
Dimethylamine solution (45% or less)	C	S/P	II	B/3	PV	Restr	A, C, D	236(a), (b), (c), (g), .409, .525, .526, .527, .1020	I-C
Dimethylamine solution (over 45% but not over 55%).	C	S/P	II	B/3	PV	Closed	A, C, D	236(a), (b), (c), (g), .316, .408, .525, .526, .527, .1020	I-C

Pt. 153, Table 1 46 CFR Ch. I (10-1-13 Edition)

Cargo name	IMO Annex II Pollution Category	Haz.	Cargo containment system	Vent height	Vent	Gauge	Fire protection system	Special requirements in 46 CFR Part 153	Electrical hazard class and group
a.	b.	c.	d.	e.	f.	g.	h.	i.	j.
Dimethylamine solution (over 55% but not over 65%).	C	S/P	II	B/3	PV	Closed	A, C, D	.236(a), (b), (c), (g), .316, .372, .408, .525, .526, .527, .1020.	I-C
2,6-Dimethylaniline	[C]	S/P	III	NR	Open	Open	B, C, D	.236(b), .409, .440, .908(b)	I-D
N,N-Dimethylcyclohexylamine	C	S/P	III	B/3	PV	Restr	A, C	.236(a), (b), (c), (g), .316, .409, .525, .526, .527, .1020	NA
N,N-Dimethyldodecylamine	A	S/P	I	NR	PV	Open	B	.236(b), .408	NA
Dimethylethanolamine	D	S	III	4m	PV	Restr	A, D	.236(b), (c), .409, .526	I-C
Dimethylformamide	D	S	III	4m	PV	Restr	A, D	.236(b), .409, .526	I-D
Dimethyl glutarate	C	P	III	NR	Open	Open	A	None	NA
Dimethyl hydrogen phosphite	B	S/P	III	4m	PV	Restr	A, D	.526	NA
Dimethyl naphthalene sulfonic acid, sodium salt solution.	[A]	P	I	NR	Open	Open	NSR	.409	NA
Dimethyloctanoic acid	C	P	III	NR	Open	Open	A	.440, .903, .908(b)	I-D
Dimethyl phthalate	C	P	III	NR	Open	Open	A	None	I-D
Dimethyl succinate	C	P	III	NR	Open	Open	A	.440, .908(b)	NA
Dinitrotoluene (molten)	A	S/P	II	B/3	PV	Closed	A	.316, .408, .525, .526, .527, .1003, .1020	I-C
1,4-Dioxane	D	S	III	B/3	PV	Closed	A	.408, .525, .526, .1020	I-D
Dipentene	C	P	III	4m	PV	Restr	A	.409	I-D
Diphenyl	A	P	I	NR	Open	Open	B	.408	NA
Diphenylamine (molten)	B	P	III	NR	Open	Open	B, D	.236(b), .409, .440, .488, .908(b)	NA
Diphenylamines, alkylated	A	P	II	NR	Open	Open	A	.409	NA
Diphenylamine, reaction product with 2,2,4-Trimethylpentene.	A	S/P	I	NR	Open	Open	A	.408	NA
Diphenyl, Diphenyl ether mixtures	A	P	I	NR	Open	Open	B	.408	I-D
Diphenyl ether	A	P	III	NR	Open	Open	A	.409	I-D
Diphenyl ether, Biphenyl phenyl ether mixture.	A	P	III	NR	Open	Open	A, B	.409	NA
Diphenylmethane diisocyanate [6]	B	S/P	II	B/3	PV	Closed	A, B, C[6], D	.236(a), (b), .316, .409, .440, .500, .501, .525, .526, .602, .908(a), .1000, .1020.	NA
Diphenylol propane-epichlorohydrin resins	B	P	III	NR	Open	Open	A, B	.409, .440, .908(a)	NA
Di-n-propylamine	C	S/P	III	4m	PV	Restr	A, C	.236(b), (c), .409, .525, .526, .1020	I-C
Dithiocarbamate ester (C7–C35)	A	P	II	NR	Open	Open	A, D	.409	NA
Dodecanol	B	P	III	NR	Open	Open	A	.409, .440, .488, .908(a), (b)	I-D
Dodecene (all isomers)	B	P	III	NR	Open	Open	A	.409	I-D
Dodecyl alcohol, see Dodecanol.									
Dodecylamine, Tetradecylamine mixture	A	S/P	II	4m	PV	Restr	A, D	.236(b), (c), .409, .526	NA
Dodecyldimethylamine, Tetradecyldimethylamine mixture.	A	S/P	II	NR	Open	Open	B, C, D	.236(b), .409	NA
Dodecyl diphenyl ether disulfonate solution.	A	S/P	II	NR	Open	Open	NSR	.409	NA
Dodecyl hydroxypropyl sulfide	A	P	I	NR	Open	Open	A, C	.408	NA
Dodecyl methacrylate	III	S	III	NR	Open	Open	A, C	.236(b), (c), .912(a)(1), .1004	I-D
Dodecyl-Octadecyl methacrylate mixture	D	S	III	NR	Open	Open	A, D	.236(b), .912(a)(1), .1002(a), (b), .1004	NA

252

Coast Guard, DHS — **Pt. 153, Table 1**

Name										Notes	Code
Dodecyl-Pentadecyl methacrylate mixture	III	S			NR	Open	Open	A, C, D	.912(a)(1), .1002(a), (b), .1004		NA
Dodecyl phenol	A	P	—		NR	Open	Open	A	.408		I-D
Drilling brine (containing Zinc salts)	B	P	≡		NR	Open	Open	NSR	.409		NA
Epichlorohydrin	A	S/P	≡		B/3	PV	Closed	A	.316, .408, .525, .526, .527, .1020		I-C
Ethanolamine	D	S	≡		NR	Open	Open	A	.236(b), (c), .526		I-C
2-Ethoxyethyl acetate	D	P	≡		4m	PV	Restr	A	.409		I-D
Ethyl acrylate	A	S/P	=		4m	PV	Restr	A	.409, .526, .527, .912(a)(1), .1002(a), (b), .1004		I-D
Ethylamine	C	S/P	≡		B/3	PV	Closed	C, D	.236(b), (c), .252, .372, .409, .525, .526, .527, .1020		I-D
Ethylamine solution (72% or less)	C	S/P	≡		B/3	PV	Closed	A, C	.236(a), (b), (c), (g), .372, .408, .525(a), (c), (d), (e), .526, .527, .1020		I-D
Ethyl amyl ketone	C	P	≡		4m	PV	Restr	A	.409		I-D
Ethylbenzene	B	P	≡		4m	PV	Restr	A	.409		I-D
N-Ethylbutylamine	C	S/P	≡		4m	PV	Restr	A	.236(a), (b), (c), (g), .409, .525(a), (c), (d), (e), .526, .1020		I-C
Ethyl tert-butyl ether	C	P	≡		4m	PV	Restr	A	.409		I-C
Ethyl butyrate	C	P	≡		4m	PV	Restr	A	.409		I-D
Ethylcyclohexane	C	P	≡		4m	PV	Restr	A	.409		I-D
N-Ethylcyclohexylamine	O	P	≡		NR	PV	Open	A, C	.236(a), (b), (c), (g), .409, .526		I-C
S-Ethyl dipropylthiocarbamate	D	P	=		4m	Open	Open	A	.409		NA
Ethylene chlorohydrin	A	S/P	≡		B/3	PV	Closed	A, D	.316, .408, .525, .526, .527, .933, .1020		I-D
Ethylene cyanohydrin	D	S	≡		NR	PV	Open	A	None		NA
Ethylenediamine	D	S/P	≡		4m	Open	Restr	A	.236(b), (c), .409, .440, .525, .526, .908(b)		I-D
Ethylene dibromide	C	S/P	=		B/3	PV	Closed	NSR	.408, .440, .525, .526, .527, .908(b), .1020		NA
Ethylene dichloride	B	P	≡		4m	PV	Restr	A, B	.236(b), .408, .526		I-D
Ethylene glycol butyl ether acetate	C	P	≡		NR	Open	Open	A	None		I-C
Ethylene glycol diacetate	C	P	≡		NR	Open	Open	A	None		I-D
Ethylene glycol ethyl ether acetate, see 2-Ethoxyethyl acetate											
Ethylene glycol methyl ether acetate	C	P	≡		NR	Open	Open	A	None		I-C
Ethylene glycol monoalkyl ether	D	S	≡		4m	PV	Restr	A	.409		I-C
Including:											
2-Ethoxyethanol											
Ethylene glycol butyl ether											
Ethylene glycol tert-butyl ether											
Ethylene glycol ethyl ether											
Ethylene glycol hexyl ether											
Ethylene glycol methyl ether											
Ethylene glycol n-propyl ether											
Ethylene glycol isopropyl ether											
Ethylene oxide (30% or less), Propylene oxide mixture.	C	S/P	=		B/3	PV	Closed	A, C	.252, .372, .408, .440, .500, .525, .526, .530, .1010, .1011, .1020		I-B
Ethyl ether	III	S	≡		4m	PV	Restr	A	.236(g), .252, .372, .408, .440, .500, .515, .526, .527		I-C
Ethyl-3-ethoxypropionate	C	P	≡		4m	PV	Restr	A	.409		NA
2-Ethylhexanol	@C	P	=		NR	Open	Open	A	None		I-D
2-Ethylhexyl acrylate	B	S/P	≡		NR	PV	Restr	A	.409, .912(a)(1), .1002(a), (b), .1004		I-D
2-Ethylhexylamine	B	S/P	≡		B/3	PV	Restr	A	.236(b), (c), .409, .525, .526, .1020		I-D
Ethyl hexyl phthalate	O	P	≡		NR	Open	Open	A	None		NA
Ethylidene norbornene	B	S/P	≡		B/3	PV	Restr	A, B, C, D	.236(b), .409, .526		NA
Ethyl methacrylate	D	S	≡		4m	PV	Restr	A, B, D	.409, .526, .912(a)(1), .1002(a), (b), .1004		I-D

253

Cargo name	IMO Annex II Pollution Category	Haz.	Cargo containment system	Vent height	Vent	Gauge	Fire protection system	Special requirements in 46 CFR Part 153	Electrical hazard class and group
a.	b.	c.	d.	e.	f.	g.	h.	i.	j.
Ethylphenol	A	S/P	III	NR	Open	Open	B	409	I-D
2-Ethyl-3-propylacrolein	A	S/P	III	4m	PV	Restr	A	409, 526	I-C
Ethyl toluene	B	P	III	4m	PV	Restr	A	409	I-D
Ferric chloride solutions	C	S/P	II	NR	Open	Open	NSR	409, 440, 554, 555, 908(b), 1045	I-B
Ferric nitrate, Nitric acid solution	C	S/P	III	4m	PV	Restr	NSR	408, 526, 527, 554, 555, 559, 933, 1045	I-B
Fluorosilicic acid (30% or less)	C	S/P	III	B/3	PV	Restr	NSR	252, 526, 527, 554, 555, 933, 1045	I-B
Formaldehyde (50% or more), Methanol mixtures.	#	S/P	III	4m	PV	Closed	A	409, 526, 527	I-B
Formaldehyde solution (37% to 50%)	C	S/P	III	4m	PV	Restr	A	409, 440, 526, 527, 908(b)	I-B
Formic acid	D	S	III	4m	PV	Restr	A	238(b), (c), 409, 526, 527, 554, 933	I-D
Fumaric adduct of rosin, water dispersion	B	P	III	NR	Open	Open	NSR	409, 440, 908(a)	NA
Furfural	C	S/P	III	4m	PV	Restr	A	409, 526	I-C
Furfuryl alcohol	C	P	III	NR	Open	Open	A	None	NA
Glutaraldehyde solution (50% or less)	D	S	III	NR	Open	Open	NSR	None	NA
Glycidyl ester of C10 Trialkyl acetic acid, see Glycidyl ester of Tridecyl acetic acid.									
Glycidyl ester of Tridecyl acetic acid	B	P	III	NR	Open	Open	A	409	NA
Glyoxylic acid solution (50% or less)	D	S	III	NR	Open	Open	A, C, D	238(e), .554(a), (b), (c), .933, 1002	NA
Heptane (all isomers), see Alkanes(C6-C9) (all isomers).	C	P	III	4m	PV	Restr	A	409	I-D
Heptanol (all isomers)	C	P	III	4m	PV	Restr	A	409	I-D
Heptene (all isomers)	C	P	III	4m	PV	Restr	A	409	I-D
Heptyl acetate	B	P	III	NR	Open	Open	A	409	NA
Hexamethylenediamine (molten)	C	S/P	II	B/3	PV	Closed	C	236(a), (b), (c), (g), 316, 336, 409, 440, 525, 526, 527, .908(a), (b), .933, 1020.	NA
Hexamethylenediamine solution	C	S/P	III	4m	PV	Restr	A	236(b), (c), 409, 440, 526, .908(b)	I-D
Hexamethylene diisocyanate [6]	B	S/P	II	B/3	PV	Closed	A, C, D	238(d), 252, 316, 336, 408, 500, 501, 525, 526, 527, 602, 1000, 1020.	NA
Hexamethyleneimine	C	S/P	III	4m	PV	Restr	A, C	236(a), (b), (c), (g), 409, 526	I-C
Hexane (all isomers), see Alkanes(C6-C9).	C	P	III	4m	PV	Restr	A	409	I-D
Hexene (all isomers)	C	P	III	4m	PV	Restr	A	409	I-D
Hexyl acetate	B	P	III	4m	PV	Restr	A	409	I-D
Hydrochloric acid	D	S	III	4m	PV	Restr	NSR	252, 526, 527, 554, 557, 933, 1045, 1052	I-B
Hydrogen peroxide solutions (over 8% but not over 60%).	C	S/P	III	B/3	PV	Closed	NSR	238(a), (c), .355, 409, 440(a)(1)&(2), .500, .933, .1004(a)(2), 1500.	NA
Hydrogen peroxide solutions (over 60% but not over 70%).	C	S/P	II	B/3	PV	Closed	NSR	238(a), (c), .355, 409, 440(a)(1)&(2), .500, .933, .1004(a)(2), 1500.	NA
2-Hydroxyethyl acrylate	B	S/P	II	B/3	PV	Closed	A	408, 525, 526, .912(a)(1), .933, .1002(a), (b), .1004, .1020.	NA
N,N-bis(2-Hydroxyethyl) oleamide	B	P	II	4m	PV	Restr	A	409, 440, 488, 908(a), (b)	NA

Coast Guard, DHS   **Pt. 153, Table 1**

Chemical								
2-Hydroxy-4-(methylthio)butanoic acid	C	P	III	NR	Open	Open	A	.440, .903, .908(a)	NA
alpha-hydro-omega-Hydroxytetradeca(oxytetra methylene), see Poly(tetramethylene ether) glycols (mw 950–1050).									
Icosa (oxypropane-2,3-diyl)s	B	P	III	NR	Open	Open	A	.409, .440, .908(a)	NA
Isophorone diamine	D	S	III	4m	PV	Restr	A	.236(b), (c), .526	NA
Isophorone diisocyanate [6]	B	S/P	II	B/3	PV	Closed	A, B, C [6] D	.236(a), (b), .316, .409, .500, .501, .525, .526, .602, .1000, .1020.	NA
Isoprene	C	S/P	III	4m	PV	Restr	B	.372, .409, .440, .912(a)(1), .1002(a), (b), .1004	I-D
Isopropylbenzene, see Propylbenzene (all isomers)									
Lactonitrile solution (80% or less)	B	S/P	II	B/3	PV	Closed	A, C, D	.238(d), .252, .316, .336, .408, .440, .525, .526, .527, .908(a), .912(a)(2), .1002, .1004, .1020, .1035.	I-D
Lauric acid	B	P	III	NR	Open	Open	A	.409, .440, .488, .908(a), (b)	NA
Lauryl polyglucose (50% or less), see Alkyl(C12–C14) polyglucoside solution (55% or less).									
Long chain alkaryl polyether (C11–C20)	C	P	III	NR	Open	Open	A, B	(.440, .903, .908(a)) [1]	NA
Long chain polyetheramine in alkyl(C2–C4)benzenes.	C	P	III	4m	PV	Restr	A	.409, .440, .903, .908(a)	I-D
Magnesium long chain alkyl salicylate (C11+).	C	P	III	NR	Open	Open	A, B	(.440, .903, .908(a)) [1]	NA
Maleic anhydride [7]	D	S	III	4m	PV	Restr	[7]A, C	None	I-D
Mercaptobenzothiazol, sodium salt solution, see Sodium-2-mercaptobenzothiazol solution									
Mesityl oxide	D	S	III	4m	PV	Restr	A	.236(b), (c), .409, .526	I-D
Metam sodium solution	A	S/P	II	NR	Open	Open	NSR	.236(a), (b), (c), (g), .409	NA
Methacrylic acid	D	S	III	4m	PV	Restr	A	.238(a), .526, .912(a)(1), .1002(a), .1004	NA
Methacrylic resin in Ethylene dichloride	B	S/P	II	4m	PV	Restr	A, B	.236(b), .408, .440, .526, .908(a)	I-D
Methacrylonitrile	D	S	II	B/3	PV	Closed	A	.236(b), .316, .408, .525, .526, .527, .912(a)(1), .1002(a), .1004, .1020.	NA
N-(2-Methoxy-1-methyl ethyl)-2-ethyl-6-methyl chloroacetanilide, see Metolachlor									
Methyl acrylate	B	S/P	II	4m	PV	Restr	A, B	.409, .526, .527, .912(a)(1), .1002(a), (b), .1004	I-D
Methylamine solution (42% or less)	C	S/P	II	B/3	PV	Closed	A, C, D	.236(a), (b), (c), (g), .316, .408, .525, .526, .527, .1020	I-D
Methylamyl acetate	C	P	III	4m	PV	Restr	A	.409	I-D
Methylamyl alcohol	C	P	III	4m	PV	Restr	A	.409	I-D
Methyl butyrate	C	P	III	4m	PV	Restr	A	.409	I-D
Methylcyclohexane	C	P	III	4m	PV	Restr	A	.409	I-D
Methylcyclopentadiene dimer	B	P	III	4m	PV	Restr	B	.409	I-B
Methyl diethanolamine	D	S	III	NR	Open	Open	A	.236(b), (c)	I-C
Methylene chloride, see Dichloromethane									
2-Methyl-6-ethylaniline	C	S/P	III	NR	Open	Open	A, B, C, D	None	NA
2-Methyl-5-ethylpyridine	B	S/P	III	NR	Open	Restr	A, D	.236(b), .409	I-D
Methyl formate	D	S	II	B/3	PV	Restr	A	.372, .408, .440, .525, .526, .527, .1020	I-D
Methyl heptyl ketone	B	P	III	4m	PV	Restr	A	.409	I-D

255

Cargo name	IMO Annex II Pollution Category	Haz.	Cargo containment system	Vent height	Vent	Gauge	Fire protection system	Special requirements in 46 CFR Part 153	Electrical hazard class and group
a.	b.	c.	d.	e.	f.	g.	h.	i.	j.
2-Methyl-2-hydroxy-3-butyne	III	S	III	4m	PV	Restr	A, B, C, D	.236(b), (d), (f), (g), .409, .526	I-D
Methyl methacrylate	D	S	II	4m	PV	Restr	A, B	.409, .526, .912(a)(1), .1002(a), (b), .1004	I-D
Methyl naphthalene (molten)	A	S/P	II	4m	PV	Restr	A, D	.409	I-D
2-Methyl-1-pentene (Hexene (all isomers)), see Alkanes(C6–C9).									
4-Methyl-1-pentene (Hexene (all isomers)), see Alkanes(C6–C9).									
Methyl tert-pentyl ether, see tert-Amyl methyl ether.									
2-Methylpyridine	D	S	II	B/3	PV	Closed	A, C	.236(b), .408, .525(a), (c), (d), (e), .1020	I-D
3-Methylpyridine	C	S/P	II	B/3	PV	Closed	A, C	.236(b), .408, .525(a), (c), (d), (e), .1020	I-D
4-Methylpyridine	D	S	II	B/3	PV	Closed	A, C, D	.236(b), .408, .440, .525(a), (c), (d), (e), .526, .908(b), .1020.	I-D
Methyl salicylate	B	P	III	NR	Open	Open	A	.409	I-D
alpha-Methylstyrene	A	S/P	III	4m	PV	Restr	A, D	.409, .526, .912(a)(1), .1002(a), (b), .1004	I-D
3-(Methylthio) propionaldehyde	B	S	III	B/3	PV	Closed	B, C	.238(e), .316, .408, .525, .526, .527, .1020	NA
Metolachlor	B	P	III	NR	Open	Open	A	.409	NA
Morpholine	D	S	III	4m	PV	Restr	A	.236(b), (c), .409	NA
Motor fuel anti-knock compounds (containing lead alkyls).	A	S/P	I	B/3	PV	Closed	A, B, C	.252, .316, .336, .408, .525, .526, .527, .933, .1020, .1025.	I-D
Naphthalene (molten)	A	S/P	II	4m	PV	Restr	A, D	.409, .440, .908(b)	I-D
Naphthalene sulfonic acid, sodium salt solution (40% or less).	[A]	P	III	NR	Open	Open	NSR	.409	NA
Naphthenic acid	A	P	II	NR	Open	Open	A	.409	NA
Naphthenic acid, sodium salt solution	[A]	P	II	NR	Open	Open	NSR	.409	NA
Neodecanoic acid	C	P	III	NR	Open	Closed	A	None	NA
Nitrating acid (mixture of sulfuric and nitric acids).	C	S/P	II	B/3	PV	Closed	NSR	.316, .408, .526, .527, .554, .555, .556, .559, .602, .933, .1000, .1045.	I-B
Nitric acid (70% or less)	C	S/P	II	4m	PV	Restr	NSR	.408, .526, .527, .554, .555, .559, .933, .1045	I-B
Nitrobenzene	B	S/P	II	B/3	PV	Closed	A, D	.316, .336, .408, .440, .525, .526, .908(b), .933, .1020	I-D
Nitroethane	D	S	III	4m	PV	Restr	7A, C	.236(b), .409, .526, .1002(a), (b), .1003	I-C
Nitroethane, 1-Nitropropane (each 15% or more) mixture [7].	D	S	III	4m	PV	Restr	7A	.236(b), .409, .526, .1002	I-C
o-Nitrophenol (molten)	B	S/P	II	B/3	PV	Closed	A, C, D	.409, .440, .525, .526, .908(a), (b), .1020	NA
1- or 2-Nitropropane [7]	D	S	III	4m	PV	Restr	7A, C	.409, .526	I-C
Nitropropane (60%), Nitroethane (40%) mixture [7].	D	S	III	4m	PV	Restr	7A, C	.236(b), .409, .526	I-C
Nitropropane (20%), Nitroethane (80%) mixture [7].	D	S	III	4m	PV	Restr	7A, C	.236(b), .409, .526, .1002(a), (b), .1003	I-C
(o-, p-) Nitrotoluene	B	S/P	II	B/3	PV	Closed	A, B	.316, .408, .440, .525, .526, .908(b), .1020	I-D

Coast Guard, DHS   **Pt. 153, Table 1**

Nonane (all isomers), see Alkanes(C6–C9).								I-D
Nonene (all isomers)		P	III	4m	PV	Restr	A	.409 I-D
Nonyl acetate	B	P	III	NR	Open	Restr	A	.409 I-D
Nonyl alcohol (all isomers)	C	P	III	NR	Open	Open	A	None I-D
Nonyl phenol	C	P	=	NR	Open	Open	A	.409, 440, 488[1], 908(a), (b) I-D
Nonyl phenol poly(4-)ethoxylates	A	P	III	NR	Open	Open	A	.409, 440, 488[1], 908(a), (b) I-D
Noxious liquid, N.F., (1) n.o.s. ("trade name" contains "principal components") ST 1, Cat A.	B	P	—	NR	Open	Open	A	.408 NA
Noxious liquid, F., (2) n.o.s. ("trade name" contains "principal components") ST 1, Cat A.	A	P	I	4m	PV	Restr	A	.408 NA
Noxious liquid, N.F., (3) n.o.s. ("trade name" contains "principal components") ST 2, Cat A.	A	P	II	NR	Open	Open	A	.409 NA
Noxious liquid, F., (4) n.o.s. ("trade name" contains "principal components") ST 2, Cat A.	A	P	II	4m	PV	Restr	A	.409 NA
Noxious liquid, N.F., (5) n.o.s. ("trade name" contains "principal components") ST 2, Cat B.	B	P	II	NR	Open	Open	A	.409; (.440, .908)[1] NA
Noxious liquid, N.F., (6) n.o.s. ("trade name" contains "principal components") ST 2, Cat B, mp. equal to or greater than 15 deg. C.	B	P	II	NR	Open	Open	A	.409, 440, 488, 908(b); (.908(a))[1] NA
Noxious liquid, F., (7) n.o.s. ("trade name" contains "principal components") ST 2, Cat B.	B	P	II	4m	PV	Restr	A	.409; (.440, .908)[1] NA
Noxious liquid, F., (8) n.o.s. ("trade name" contains "principal components") ST 2, Cat B, mp. equal to or greater than 15 deg. C.	B	P	II	4m	PV	Restr	A	.409, 440, 488, 908(b); (.908(a))[1] NA
Noxious liquid, N.F., (9) n.o.s. ("trade name" contains "principal components") ST 3, Cat A.	A	P	III	NR	Open	Open	A	.409 NA
Noxious liquid, F., (10) n.o.s. ("trade name" contains "principal components") ST 3, Cat A.	A	P	III	4m	PV	Restr	A	.409 NA
Noxious liquid, N.F., (11) n.o.s. ("trade name" contains "principal components") ST 3, Cat B.	B	P	III	NR	Open	Open	A	(.409, .440, .908)[1] NA
Noxious liquid, N.F., (12) n.o.s. ("trade name" contains "principal components") ST 3, Cat B, mp. equal to or greater than 15 deg. C.	B	P	III	NR	Open	Open	A	.409, 440, 488, 908(b); (.908(a))[1] NA
Noxious liquid, F., (13) n.o.s. ("trade name" contains "principal components") ST 3, Cat B.	B	P	III	4m	PV	Restr	A	.409; (.440, .908)[1] NA

Pt. 153, Table 1   46 CFR Ch. I (10-1-13 Edition)

Cargo name	IMO Annex II Pollution Category	Haz.	Cargo containment system	Vent height	Vent	Gauge	Fire protection system	Special requirements in 46 CFR Part 153	Electrical hazard class and group
a.	b.	c.	d.	e.	f.	g.	h.	i.	j.
Noxious liquid, F., (14) n.o.s. ("trade name" contains "principal components") ST 3, Cat B, mp. equal to or greater than 15 deg. C.	B	P	III	4m	PV	Restr	A	.409, .440, .488, .908(b); .908(a)[1]	NA
Noxious liquid, N.F., (15) n.o.s. ("trade name" contains "principal components") ST 3, Cat C.	C	P	III	NR	Open	Open	A	(.440, .903, .908)[1]	NA
Noxious liquid, F., (16) n.o.s. ("trade name" contains "principal components") ST 3, Cat C.	C	P	III	4m	PV	Restr	A	(.440, .903, .908)[1]	NA
Octane (all isomers), see Alkanes(C6–C9)	C	P	III	4m	PV	Restr	A	.409	I-D
Octanol (all isomers)	C	P	III	NR	Open	Open	A	None	I-D
Octene (all isomers)	B	P	III	4m	PV	Restr	A	.409	I-D
Octyl acetate	C	P	III	NR	Open	Open	A	None	I-D
Octyl aldehydes	B	P	III	4m	PV	Restr	A	.409, .440, .908(b)	I-C
Octyl nitrates (all isomers), see Alkyl(C7–C9) nitrates.									
Olefin mixtures (C5–C7)	C	P	III	4m	PV	Restr	A	.409	I-D
Olefin mixtures (C5–C15)	B	P	III	4m	PV	Restr	A	.409	I-D
alpha-Olefins (C6–C18) mixtures	B	P	II	4m	PV	Restr	A	.409, .440, .908(a), (b)	I-D
Oleum	C	S/P	II	B/3	PV	Closed	NSR	.316, .408, .440, .526, .527, .554, .555, .556, .602, .908(a), .933, 1000, 1045, 1052.	I-B
Oleylamine	A	S/P	II	4m	PV	Restr	A	.409, .526	NA
Palm kernel acid oil	C	P	III	NR	Open	Open	A, B	.440, .903, .908(a), (b)	NA
Paraldehyde	C	S/P	III	4m	PV	Restr	A	.409, .440, .908(b)	I-C
Paraldehyde-ammonia reaction product	C	S/P	III	B/3	PV	Closed	A	.236 (a), (b), (c), (g), .525(a), (c), (e), .408, .526, 1020	NA
Pentachloroethane	B	S/P	III	B/3	PV	Restr	NSR	.316, .409, .525, .526, 1020	NA
1,3-Pentadiene	C	S/P	III	4m	PV	Restr	A, B	.409, .526, .912(a)(1), 1002, 1004	I-D
Pentane (all isomers)	C	P	III	4m	PV	Restr	A	.372, .409	I-D
n-Pentanoic acid (64%), 2-Methyl butyric acid (36%) mixture.	D	S	II	B/3	Open	Closed	A, D	.238(a), .408, .525(a), (c), (e), .554, .933, 1020	I-D
Pentene (all isomers)	C	P	III	4m	PV	Restr	A	.409	I-D
n-Pentyl propionate	C	P	III	4m	PV	Restr	A	.409	I-D
Perchloroethylene	B	S/P	III	4m	PV	Restr	NSR	.409, .526	NA
Phenol (or solutions with 5% or more Phenol).	C	S/P	II	B/3	PV	Closed	A	.408, .440, .488, .525, .526, .908(a), (b), .933, 1020	I-D
1-Phenyl-l-xylyl ethane	C	P	III	NR	Open	Open	A, B	None	NA
Phosphate esters, alkyl(C12–C14)amine	B	P	III	4m	PV	Restr	A	.409	NA
Phosphoric acid	D	S	III	NR	Open	Open	NSR	.554, .555, .558, .1045, .1052, .933	I-B
Phthalic anhydride (molten)	C	S/P	III	4m	PV	Restr	A, D	.440, .908(a), (b)	I-D
Pinene, see the alpha- or beta- isomers.									
alpha-Pinene	A	P	III	4m	PV	Restr	A	.409	I-D

258

Coast Guard, DHS — Pt. 153, Table 1

Name								References	
beta-Pinene	B	P	III	4m	PV	Restr	A	.409	I-D
Pine oil	C	P	III	NR	Open	Open	A	.440, .908(a)	I-D
Polyalkyl(C18–C22) acrylate in Xylene	C	P	III	4m	PV	Restr	A	.409, .440, .903, .908(a)	NA
Polyalkylene oxide polyol	C	P	II	NR	Open	Open	A, D	.440, .903, .908(a)	NA
Poly(2+)cyclic aromatics	A	P	III	4m	PV	Restr	A	.409	I-D
Polyethylene polyamines	C	S/P	III	NR	Open	Open	A	.236(b), (c), .400, .440, .908(b)	NA
Polyferric sulfate solution	C	S/P	III	NR	Open	Open	NSR	.238(d)	NA
Polyisobutenamine in aliphatic (C10–C14) solvent.	C	P	III	NR	Open	Open	A	.903	NA
Polymethylene polyphenyl isocyanate [6]	D	S	II	B/3	PV	Closed	A, C[6], D	.236(a), (b), .409, .500, .501, .525, .526, .602, .1000, .1020.	NA
Polyolefinamine (C28–C250)	C	P	III	NR	Open	Open	A	None	NA
Polyolefinamine in alkyl(C2–C4)benzenes	C	P	III	4m	PV	Restr	A	.409, .440, .903, .908(a)	I-D
Polyolefin phosphorosulfide, barium derivative (C28–C250).	C	P	III	NR	Open	Open	A, B	(.440, .903, .908(a)) [1]	NA
Poly(tetramethylene ether) glycols (mw 950-1050).	B	P	III	NR	Open	Open	A, D	.409, .440, .488, .908(a), (b)	NA
Potassium hydroxide solution, see Caustic potash solution									
Potassium oleate	C	P	III	NR	Open	Open	A	.409	NA
Potassium thiosulfate (50% or less)	C	P	III	NR	Open	Open	NSR	None	NA
iso-Propanolamine	C	S/P	III	NR	Open	Open	A	.236(b), (c), .440, .526, .903, .908(b)	I-D
n-Propanolamine	C	S/P	III	NR	Open	Open	A, D	.236(b), (c), .440, .526, .908(b)	NA
Propionaldehyde	C	S/P	III	4m	PV	Restr	A	.316, .409, .526, .527	I-C
Propionic acid	D	S	III	4m	PV	Restr	A	.238(a), .409, .527, .554, .933	I-D
Propionic anhydride	C	S/P	III	4m	PV	Restr	A	.238(a), .526	I-D
Propionitrile	C	P	II	B/3	PV	Closed	A, D	.252, .316, .336, .408, .525, .526, .527, .1020	I-D
iso-Propylamine	C	S/P	II	B/3	PV	Closed	C, D	.236(b), (c), .372, .408, .440, .525, .526, .527, .1020	I-D
iso-Propylamine solution (70% or less)	C	S/P	II	B/3	PV	Closed	C, D	.236(a), (b), (c), (g), .408, .440, .525, .526, .527, .1020	I-D
n-Propylamine	C	S/P	II	B/3	PV	Closed	A, C, D	.236(b), (c), .408, .500, .525, .526, .527, .1020	I-D
n-Propylbenzene, see Propylbenzene (all isomers).									
Propylbenzene (all isomers)	A	P	III	4m	PV	Restr	A	.409	I-D
n-Propyl chloride	D	S	III	4m	PV	Restr	A, B	.409	I-D
iso-Propylcyclohexane	C	P	III	4m	PV	Restr	A	.409, .440, .903, .908(a)	I-D
Propylene dimer	C	P	III	4m	PV	Restr	A	.409	NA
Propylene oxide	C	S/P	II	B/3	PV	Closed	A, C	.372, .408, .440, .500, .526, .530, .1010, .1011	I-B
Propylene tetramer	B	P	III	4m	PV	Restr	A	.409	I-D
Propylene trimer	B	P	III	4m	PV	Restr	A	.409	I-D
iso-Propyl ether	D	S	III	4m	PV	Restr	A	.409, .500, .515, .912(k)(1)	I-D
Pyridine	D	S	III	4m	PV	Restr	A	.236(b), .409	I-D
Rosin, see Rosin oil.									
Rosin oil	B	P	III	NR	Open	Open	A	.409, .440, .488, .908(a), (b)	I-D
Rosin soap (disproportionated) solution	B	P	III	NR	Open	Open	A	.409	NA
Sodium alkyl (C14-C17) sulfonates 60-65% solution, see Alkane (C14-C17) sulfonic acid, sodium salt solution.									
Sodium aluminate solution	D	S	III	NR	Open	Open	NSR	.236(a), (b), (c), (g), .933	NA
Sodium borohydride (15% or less), Sodium hydroxide solution.	C	S/P	III	NR	Open	Open	NSR	.236(a), (b), (c), (g), .440, .908(a), .933	NA

259

Cargo name	IMO Annex II Pollution Category	Haz.	Cargo containment system	Vent height	Vent	Gauge	Fire protection system	Special requirements in 46 CFR Part 153	Electrical hazard class and group
a.	b.	c.	d.	e.	f.	g.	h.	i.	j.
Sodium chlorate solution (50% or less)	III	S	III	NR	Open	Open	NSR	409, 933, 1065	NA
Sodium dichromate solution (70% or less)	C	S/P	II	B/3	Open	Closed	NSR	.236(b), (c), .408, .525, .933, .1020	NA
Sodium dimethyl naphthalene sulfonate solution, see Dimethyl naphthalene sulfonic acid, sodium salt solution.									
Sodium hydrogen sulfide (6% or less)	B	P	III	NR	Open	Open	NSR	.409	NA
Sodium hydrogen sulfite solution (45% or less).	D	S	III	NR	Open	Open	NSR	None	NA
Sodium hydrosulfide solution (45% or less).	B	S/P	III	4m	PV	Restr	NSR	409, .440, .526, .908(b), .933	NA
Sodium hydrosulfide, Ammonium sulfide solution.	B	S/P	II	B/3	PV	Closed	A, C	.236(a), (b), (c), (g), .316, .372, .408, .525, .526, .527, .933, .1002, .1020.	NA
Sodium hydroxide solution, see Caustic soda solution									
Sodium hypochlorite solution (15% or less).	C	S/P	II	4m	PV	Restr	NSR	.236(a), (b), .933	NA
Sodium long chain alkyl salicylate (C13+)	[C]	P	III	NR	Open	Open	A	(.440, .903, .908(a))[1]	NA
Sodium-2-mercaptobenzothiazol solution	B	S/P	III	NR	Open	Open	NSR	.236(a), (b), (c), (g), .409, .440, .908(b), .933	NA
Sodium N-methyldithiocarbamate solution, see Metam sodium solution.									
Sodium naphthalene sulfonate solution (40% or less), see Naphthalene sulfonic acid, sodium salt solution (40% or less).									
Sodium naphthenate solution, see Naphthenic acid, sodium salt solution.									
Sodium nitrite solution	B	S/P	II	NR	Open	Open	NSR	.408, .525(a), (c), (d), (e), .1020	NA
Sodium petroleum sulfonate	B	S/P	II	NR	Open	Open	A	.409, .440, .908(a)	NA
Sodium silicate solution	C	P	III	B/3	PV	Closed	A	None	NA
Sodium sulfide solution (15% or less)	B	S/P	III	NR	Open	Open	NSR	.236(a), (b), .409, .440, .526, .908(b)	NA
Sodium sulfite solution (25% or less)	C	P	III	NR	Open	Open	NSR	.409, .440, .908(b)	NA
Sodium tartrates, Sodium succinates solution.	D	S	III	NR	Open	Open	A, B	.238(e)	NA
Sodium thiocyanate solution (56% or less)	B	P	III	NR	Open	Open	NSR	.238(a), .409	NA
Styrene monomer	B	S/P	III	4m	PV	Restr	A, B	.236(b), .409, .912(a)(1), .1002(a), (b), .1004	I-D
Sulfohydrocarbon, long chain (C18+) alkylamine mixture.	B	P	III	NR	Open	Open	A, B	.409; (.440, .908(a))[1]	NA
Sulfur (molten)	III	S	III	NR	Open	Open	NSR	.252, .440, .526, .545	I-C
Sulfuric acid	C	S/P	III	NR	Open	Open	NSR	.440, .554, .555, .556, .602, .908(a), (b), .933, .1000, .1045, .1046, .1052.	I-B
Tall oil (crude and distilled)	B	P	III	NR	Open	Open	A	.409, .440, .488, .908(a), (b)	NA

Name									References	
Tall oil, fatty acid (*resin acids less than 20%*)	C				NR	Open	Open	A	.440, .908(a), (b)	NA
Tall oil fatty acid, barium salt	B	S/P	III		NR	Open	Open	A	.409, .440, .908(a)	NA
Tall oil soap (disproportionated) solution	B	P	III		NR	Open	Open	A	.409, .440, .908(a), (b)	NA
1,1,2,2-Tetrachloroethane	B	S/P	III		B/3	PV	Restr	NSR	.316, .409, .525, .526, .1020	NA
Tetraethylenepentamine [3]	D	P	III		NR	Open	Restr	A	.236(b), (c), (g)	I-C
Tetrahydrofuran	D	S	III		4m	PV	Open	A, D	.409, .526, .912(a)(2), .1004	I-C
Tetrahydronaphthalene	C	S	III		NR	Open	Open	A	None	I-D
Tetramethylbenzene (all isomers)	A	P	III		NR	Open	Open	A	None	I-D
Toluene	C	P	III		4m	PV	Restr	A	.409	I-D
Toluenediamine	C	S/P	II		B/3	PV	Closed	A, B, C, D	.236(a), (b), (c), (g), .316, .408, .440, .525, .526, .527, .908(a), (b), .933, .1020.	NA
Toluene diisocyanate [6]	C	S/P	II		4m	PV	Closed	A, C[6], D	.236(b), .316, .408, .440, .500, .501, .525, .526, .527, .602, .908(b), .1000, .1020.	I-D
o-Toluidine	C	S/P	II		B/3	PV	Closed	A, C	.316, .408, .525, .526, .933, .1020	I-D
Tributyl phosphate	B	P	III		NR	Open	Open	A	.409	I-D
1,2,3-Trichlorobenzene (molten)	A	S/P	I		B/3	PV	Closed	A, C, D	.316, .408, .440, .526, .908(b), .933	I-D
1,2,4-Trichlorobenzene	B	S/P	II		4m	PV	Restr	A, B,C,	.409, .440, .526, .908(b),	I-D
1,1,1-Trichloroethane	B	P	III		NR	Open	Open	A	.409	I-D
1,1,2-Trichloroethane	C	S/P	II		B/3	PV	Restr	NSR	.409, .525, .526, .933, .1020	I-D
Trichloroethylene	C	S/P	III		B/3	PV	Restr	NSR	.316, .408, .525, .526, .1020	I-D
1,2,3-Trichloropropane	C	S/P	II		B/3	PV	Closed	A, B, C, D	.316, .408, .525, .526, .933, .1020	I-D
1,1,2-Trichloro-1,2,2-trifluoroethane	C	P	III		NR	Open	Open	NSR	None	NA
Tricresyl phosphate (less than 1% of the ortho isomer).	A	P	II		NR	Open	Open	A	.409	I-D
Tricresyl phosphate (1% or more of the ortho isomer).	A	S/P	I		4m	PV	Closed	A, B	.408, .525(a), (c), (d), (e), .1020	I-D
Tridecanoic acid	B	P	III		NR	Open	Open	A	.409, .440, .488, .908(a), (b)	NA
Triethanolamine	D	S	III		NR	Open	Open	A	.236(a), (b), (c), (g)	I-C
Triethylamine	C	S/P	II		B/3	PV	Restr	A, B, C	.236(b), (c), .409, .525, .526, .527, .1020	I-C
Triethylbenzene	A	P	II		NR	Open	Open	A	.409	I-D
Triethylene glycol di-(2-ethylbutyrate)	[C]	P	III		NR	Open	Open	A	None	I-C
Triethylenetetramine	D	S	III		NR	PV	Open	A	.236(a), (b), (c)	I-C
Triethyl phosphite	B	P	II		NR	Open	Open	A, B, D	.409, .526	NA
Triisopropylated phenyl phosphates	A	S/P	II		B/3	PV	Open	A	.409	NA
Trimethylacetic acid	D	S	II		4m	PV	Restr	A, C	.238(a), .266, .554	I-D
Trimethylamine solution (30% or less)	C	S/P	II		B/3	PV	Closed	A, C	.236(a), (b), (c), (g), .372, .408, .440, .525, .526, .527, .908(b), .1020.	I-C
Trimethylbenzene (all isomers)	A	P	III		4m	PV	Restr	A, C	.409	I-D
Trimethylhexamethylenediamine (2,2,4- and 2,4,4- isomers).	D	S	III		NR	Open	Open	A, C	.236(a), (b), (c), (g), .409	NA
Trimethylhexamethylene diisocyanate (2,2,4- and 2,4,4- isomers) [6].	B	S/P	II		B/3	PV	Closed	A, C[6]	.316, .409, .500, .501, .525, .526, .602, .1000, .1020	NA
2,2,4-Trimethyl-1,3-pentanediol-1-isobutyrate.	C	P	III		NR	Open	Open	A	None	I-D
Trimethyl phosphite	#	S	III		4m	PV	Restr	A, D	.409, .526, .602, .1000	I-D
1,3,5-Trioxane	D	S	II		4m	PV	Restr	A, D	.409	I-C
Trixylenyl phosphate	A	P	I		NR	Open	Open	A	.408	NA

261

Cargo name	IMO Annex II Pollution Category	Haz.	Cargo containment system	Vent height	Vent	Gauge	Fire protection system	Special requirements in 46 CFR Part 153	Electrical hazard class and group
a.	b.	c.	d.	e.	f.	g.	h.	i.	j.
Trixylyl phosphate, *see* Trixylenyl phosphate.									
Turpentine	B	P	III	4m	PV	Restr	A	409	I-D
Undecanoic acid	B	P	III	NR	Open	Open	A	.440, .908(a), (b)	NA
1-Undecene	B	P	III	NR	Open	Open	A	409	I-D
1-Undecyl alcohol	B	P	III	NR	Open	Open	A	409, .440, .908(b)	I-D
Urea, Ammonium nitrate solution (containing more than 2% NH₃).	C	S/P	III	4m	PV	Restr	A	.236(b), .526	I-D
Valeraldehyde (all isomers)	C	S/P	III	4m	PV	Restr	A	409, .500, .526	I-C
Vinyl acetate	C	S/P	III	4m	PV	Restr	A	409, .912(a)(1), .1002(a), (b), .1004	I-D
Vinyl ethyl ether	C	S/P	II	4m	PV	Closed	A	.236(b), (d), (f), (g), .252, .372, .408, .440, .500, .515, .526, .527, .912(a)(1), .1002(a), (b), .1004.	I-C
Vinylidene chloride	D	S	II	4m	PV	Restr	B	.236(a), (b), .372, .409, .440, .500, .526, .527, .912(a)(1), .1002(a), (b), .1004.	I-D
Vinyl neodecanate	B	S/P	III	NR	Open	Open	A, B	409, .912(a)(1), .1002(a), (b), .1004	NA
Vinyltoluene	A	S/P	III	4m	PV	Restr	A, B, D	.236(a), (b), (c), (g), .409, .912(a)(1), .1002(a), (b), .1004.	I-D
White spirit (low (15–20%) aromatic)	B	P	II	4m	PV	Restr	A	409	NA
Xylenes[8] (*ortho-, meta-, para-*)	C	P	III	4m	PV	Restr	A	409, .440, .908(b)[8]	I-D
Xylenes, Ethylbenzene (10% or more) mixture.	B	P	III	4m	PV	Restr	A	409	NA
Xylenol	B	S/P	III	NR	Open	Open	A, B	409, .440, .908(a), (b)	NA
Zinc alkaryl dithiophosphate (C7–C16)	C	P	III	NR	Open	Open	A, B	(.440, .903, .908(a))[1]	NA
Zinc alkyl dithiophosphate (C3–C14)	B	P	III	NR	Open	Open	A, B	409; (.440, .908(a))[1]	NA

Column Heading Footnotes:

a. The cargo name must be as it appears in this column (see 153.900, 153.907). Words in italics are not part of the cargo name but may be used in addition to the cargo name. When one entry references another entry by use of the word "see", and both names are in roman type, either name may be used as the cargo name (e.g., Diethyl ether; *see* Ethyl ether). However, the referenced entry is preferred.

The provisions contained in 46 CFR part 197, subpart C, apply to liquid cargoes containing 0.5% or more benzene by volume.

b. This column lists the IMO Annex II Pollution Category.

    A, B, C, D—NLS Category of Annex II of MARPOL 73/78.

    III—Appendix III of Annex II (non-NLS cargoes) of MARPOL 73/78.

    #—No determination of NLS status. For shipping on an oceangoing vessel, see 46 CFR 153.900(c).

    [ ]—A NLS category in brackets indicates that the product is provisionally categorized and that further data are necessary to complete the evaluation of its pollution hazards. Until the hazard evaluation is completed, the pollution category assigned is used.

    @—The NLS category has been assigned by the U.S. Coast Guard, in absence of one assigned by the IMO. The category is based upon a GESAMP Hazard Profile or by analogy to a closely related product having an NLS assigned.

c. This column lists the hazard(s) of the commodity:

    S—The commodity is included because of its safety hazards.

    P—The commodity is included because of its pollution hazards.

    S/P—The commodity is included because of both its safety and pollution hazards.

d. This column lists the type of containment system the cargo must have (see 153.230 through 153.232).

e. This column lists the height of any vent riser required (see 153.350 and 153.351).

f. This column lists any vent control valve required (see 153.355).

g. This column lists the type of gauging system required (see 153.400 through 153.406).

h. This column lists the type of fire protection system required. Where more than one system is listed, any listed system may be used. A dry chemical system may not be substituted for either type of foam system unless the dry chemical system is listed as an alternative or the substitution is approved by Commandant (CG–ENG) (telephone number 202–372–1420) (see 153.460). The types are as follows:

A is a foam system for water soluble cargoes (polar solvent foam).
B is a foam system for water insoluble cargoes (non-polar solvent foam).
C is a water spray system.
D is a dry chemical system.
NSR means there is no special requirement applying to fire protection systems.

i. This column lists sections that apply to the cargo in addition to the general requirements of this part. The 153 Part number is omitted.
j. This column lists the electrical hazard class and group used for the cargo when determining requirements for electrical equipment under Subchapter J (Electrical Engineering) of this chapter.

A number of electrical hazard class and group assignments are based upon that which appears in "Classification of Gases, Liquids and Volatile Solids Relative to Explosion-Proof Electrical Equipment", Publication NMAB 353–5, National Academy Press, 1982, when not appearing in NFPA 497M, "Manual for Classification of Gases, Vapors and Dusts for Electrical Equipment in Hazardous (Classified) Locations."

The I-B electrical hazard does not apply to weather deck locations (see 46 CFR Part 111) for inorganic acids: Chlorosulfonic acid; Hydrochloric acid; Nitrating acid; Nitric acid (70% or less); Oleum; Phosphoric acid; Sulfuric acid.

Abbreviations used in the Table:
NR—No requirement.
NA—Not applicable.

Abbreviations for Noxious Liquid cargoes:
N.F.—non-flammable (flash point greater than 60 deg C (140 deg F) closed cup (cc)).
F.—flammable (flash point less than or equal to 60 deg C (140 deg F) closed cup (cc)).
n.o.s.—not otherwise specified.
ST—Ship type.
Cat—Pollution category.

Footnotes for Specific Cargoes:
1. Special applicability:
   153.440 and 908(a) apply to the chemical, and mixtures containing the chemical, with a viscosity of 25 mPa.s at 20 deg C (68 deg F).
   153.440 and 908(b) apply to the chemical, and mixtures containing the chemical, with a melting point of 0 deg C (32 deg F) and above.
   153.488 applies to the chemical, and mixtures containing the chemical, with a melting point of 15 deg C (59 deg F) and above.
2. Benzene containing cargoes.
   Applies to mixtures containing no other components with safety hazards and where the pollution category is C or less.
3. Diammonium salt of Zinc ethylenediaminetetraacetic acid solution; Tetraethylenepentamine.
   Aluminum is a questionable material of construction with this cargo since pitting and corrosion has been reported. The IMO Chemical Code prohibits aluminum as a material of construction for this cargo.
   Some tank pitting has been reported when this cargo is contaminated with water, including moisture in the air. The IMO Chemical Code requires that the vapor space over this cargo be kept dry.
4. 2,4-Dichlorophenol.
5. Reserved.
6. Diphenylmethane diisocyanate; Hexamethylene diisocyanate; Isophorone diisocyanate; Polymethylene polyphenyl isocyanate; Toluene diisocyanate; Trimethylhexamethylene diisocyanate (2,2,4- and 2,4,4- isomers).
   Water is effective in extinguishing open air fires but will generate hazardous quantities of gas if put on the cargo in enclosed spaces.
7. Maleic anhydride; Nitroethane; Nitromethane, 1-Nitropropane mixtures; 1- or 2-Nitropropane; Nitropropane; Nitroethane mixtures.
   Dry chemical extinguishers should not be used on fires involving these cargoes since some dry chemicals may react with the cargo and cause an explosion.
8. Xylenes.
   Special requirement 908(b) only applies to the para- (p-) isomer, and mixtures containing the para-isomer having a melting point of 0 deg C (32 deg F) or more.

[USCG 2000–7079, 65 FR 67196, Nov. 8, 2000, as amended by USCG–2012–0832, 77 FR 59785, Oct. 1, 2012]

Table 2 to Part 153—Cargoes Not Regulated Under Subchapters D or O of This Chapter When Carried in Bulk on Non-oceangoing Barges

The cargoes listed in this table are not regulated under subchapter D or O of this title when carried in bulk on non-oceangoing barges. Category A, B, or C noxious liquid substance (NLS) cargo, as defined in §153.2 of this chapter, listed in this table, or any mixture containing one or more of these cargoes, must be carried under this subchapter if carried in bulk on an oceangoing ship. Requirements for Category D NLS cargoes and mixtures of non-NLS cargoes with Category D NLS cargoes are in 33 CFR part 151.

Cargoes	Pollution Category
2-Amino-2-hydroxymethyl-1,3-propanediol solution	III
Ammonium hydrogen phosphate solution	D
Ammonium lignosulfonate solution, see also Lignin liquor	III
Ammonium nitrate solution (45% or less)	D
Ammonium nitrate, Urea solution (2% or less NH$_3$), see also Urea, Ammonium nitrate solution (2% or less NH$_3$)	D
Ammonium phosphate, Urea solution, see also Urea, Ammonium phosphate solution	D
Ammonium polyphosphate solution	D
Ammonium sulfate solution (20% or less)	D
Ammonium thiosulfate solution (60% or less)	C
Apple juice	III
Calcium bromide solution	III
Calcium carbonate slurry	III
Calcium chloride solution	III
Calcium hydroxide slurry	D
Calcium lignosulfonate solution, see also Lignin liquor	III
Calcium nitrate, Magnesium nitrate, Potassium chloride solution	III
Caramel solutions	III
Chlorinated paraffins (C14–C17) (with 52% Chlorine)	III
2-Chloro-4-ethylamino-6-isopropylamino-5-triazine solution	#
Choline chloride solution	D
Clay slurry	III
Coal slurry	III
Dextrose solution, see Glucose solution.	
Diethylenetriamine pentaacetic acid, pentasodium salt solution	III
1,4-Dihydro-9,10-dihydroxy anthracene, disodium salt solution	D
Dodecenylsuccinic acid, dipotassium salt solution	D
Drilling brine (containing Calcium, Potassium, or Sodium salts) (see also Potassium chloride solution (10% or more))	III
Drilling brine (containing Zinc salts)	B
Drilling mud (low toxicity) (if non-flammable and non-combustible)	[III]
Ethylenediaminetetraacetic acid, tetrasodium salt solution	D
Ethylene-Vinyl acetate copolymer (emulsion)	III
Ferric hydroxyethylethylenediamine triacetic acid, trisodium salt solution	D
Fish solubles (water based fish meal extracts)	III
Fructose solution	#
Glucose solution	III
Glycine, sodium salt solution	III
Hexamethylenediamine adipate solution	D
N-(Hydroxyethyl)ethylenediamine triacetic acid, trisodium salt solution	D
Kaolin clay solution	III
Kaolin slurry	III
Kraft pulping liquor (free alkali content, 1% or less) including: Black, Green, or White liquor	#
Lignin liquor (free alkali content, 1% or less) including:.	#
Ammonium lignosulfonate solution	III
Calcium lignosulfonate solution	III
Sodium lignosulfonate solution	III
Lignin sulfonic acid, sodium salt solution, see also Lignin liquor or Sodium lignosulfonate solution	III
Magnesium chloride solution	III
Magnesium hydroxide slurry	III
Milk	III
Molasses	III
Molasses residue (from fermentation)	[III]
Naphthenic acid, sodium salt solution	[A]
Noxious liquid, N.F., (1) n.o.s. ("trade name" contains "principle components") ST 1, Cat A (if non-flammable or non-combustible)	A
Noxious liquid, N.F., (3) n.o.s. ("trade name" contains "principle components") ST 2, Cat A (if non-flammable or non-combustible)	A
Noxious liquid, N.F., (5) n.o.s. ("trade name" contains "principle components") ST 2, Cat B (if non-flammable or non-combustible)	B

Cargoes	Pollution Category
Noxious liquid, N.F., (6) n.o.s. ("trade name" contains "principle components") ST 2, Cat B, mp. equal to or greater than 15 deg. C (*if non-flammable or non-combustible*)	B
Noxious liquid, N.F., (9) n.o.s. ("trade name" contains "principle components") ST 3, Cat A (*if non-flammable or non-combustible*)	A
Noxious liquid, N.F., (11) n.o.s. ("trade name" contains "principle components") ST 3, Cat B (*if non-flammable or non-combustible*)	B
Noxious liquid, N.F., (12) n.o.s. ("trade name" contains "principle components") ST 3, Cat B, mp. equal to or greater than 15 deg. C (*if non-flammable or non-combustible*)	B
Noxious liquid, N.F., (15) n.o.s. ("trade name" contains "principle components") ST 3, Cat C (*if non-flammable or non-combustible*)	C
Noxious liquid, n.o.s. (17) ("trade name," contains "principal components"), Category D (*if non-flammable or non-combustible*)	D
Non-noxious liquid, n.o.s. (18) ("trade name," contains "principal components"), Appendix III (*if non-flammable or non-combustible*)	III
Pentasodium salt of Diethylenetriamine pentaacetic acid solution, *see* Diethylenetriamine pentaacetic acid, pentasodium salt solution..	
Polyaluminum chloride solution	III
Potassium chloride solution (10% or more)(*see also* the drilling brines entry)	III
Sewage sludge, treated (*treated so as to pose no additional decompositional and fire hazard; stable, non-corrosive, non-toxic, non-flammable*)	#
Silica slurry	[III]
Sludge, treated (*treated so as to pose no additional decompositional and fire hazard; stable, non-corrosive, non-toxic, non-flammable*)	#
Sodium acetate, Glycol, Water mixture (containing 1% or less, Sodium hydroxide) (*if non-flammable or non-combustible*)	#
Sodium aluminosilicate slurry	III
Sodium carbonate solution	D
Sodium lignosulfonate solution, *see also* Lignin liquor	III
Sodium naphthenate solution (free alkali content, 3% or less), *see* Naphthenic acid, sodium salt solution..	
Sodium poly(4+)acrylate solution	III
Sodium silicate solution	C
Sodium sulfate solution	III
Sorbitol solution	III
Sulfonated polyacrylate solution	III
Tetrasodium salt of Ethylenediaminetetraaacetic acid solution, *see* Ethylenediaminetetraacetic acid, tetrasodium salt solution..	
Titanium dioxide slurry	III
1,1,1-Trichloroethane	C
1,1,2-Trichloro-1,2,2-trifluoroethane	C
Trisodium salt of N-(Hydroxyethyl)ethylenediamine triacetic acid solution, *see* N-(Hydroxyethyl)ethylenediamine triacetic acid, trisodium salt solution..	
Urea, Ammonium mono- and di-hydrogen phosphate, Potassium chloride solution	D
Urea, Ammonium nitrate solution (2% or less NH$_3$), *see also* Ammonium nitrate, Urea solution (2% or less)	D
Urea, Ammonium phosphate solution, *see also* Ammonium phosphate, Urea solution	D
Urea solution	III
Vanillan black liquor (free alkali content, 1% or less)	#
Vegetable protein solution (*hydrolysed*)	III
Water	III
Zinc bromide, Calcium bromide solution, *see* Drilling brine (containing Zinc salts).	

Explanation of Symbols: As used in this table, the following stand for:
A, B, C, D—NLS Category of Annex II of MARPOL 73/78.
I—Considered an "oil" under Annex I of MARPOL 73/78.
III—Appendix III of Annex II (non-NLS cargoes) of MARPOL 73/78.
LFG—Liquefied flammable gas.
#—No determination of NLS status. For shipping on an oceangoing vessel, see 46 CFR 153.900(c).
[ ]—A NLS category in brackets indicates that the product is provisionally categorized and that further data are necessary to complete the evaluation of its pollution hazards. Until the hazard evaluation is completed, the pollution category assigned is used.
@The NLS category has been assigned by the U.S. Coast Guard, in absence of one assigned by the IMO. The category is based upon a GESAMP Hazard Profile or by analogy to a closely related product having an NLS assigned.
 Abbreviations for Noxious liquid Cargoes:
  N.F.—non-flammable (flash point greater than 60 degrees C (140 degrees F) cc).
  n.o.s.—not otherwise specified.
  ST—Ship type.
  Cat—Pollution category.

[CGD 88–100, 54 FR 43584, Oct. 26, 1989; CGD 92–100, 59 FR 17044, Apr. 11, 1994, as amended by CGD 94–900, 59 FR 45142, Aug. 31, 1994; CGD 94–902, 60 FR 34043, June 29, 1995; CGD 95–900, 60 FR 34052, June 29, 1995; USCG 2000–7079, 65 FR 67213, Nov. 8, 2000]

EFFECTIVE DATE NOTE: By USCG–2013–0423, 78 FR 50208, Aug. 16, 2013, table 2 to part 153 was revised, effective Sept. 16, 2013. At 78 FR 56837, Sept. 16, 2013, the effectiveness was delayed until Jan. 16, 2014. For the convenience of the user, the revised text is set forth as follows:

TABLE 2 TO PART 153—CARGOES NOT REGULATED UNDER SUBCHAPTERS D OR O OF THIS CHAPTER WHEN CARRIED IN BULK ON NON-OCEANGOING BARGES

[The cargoes listed in this table are not regulated under subchapter D or O of this title when carried in bulk on non-oceangoing barges. Category X, Y, or Z noxious liquid substance (NLS) cargo, as defined in Annex II of MARPOL 73/78, listed in this table, or any mixture containing one or more of these cargoes, must be carried under this subchapter if carried in bulk on an oceangoing ship.]

Cargoes	Pollution category
Acrylic acid/ethenesulfonic acid copolymer with phosphonate groups, sodium salt solution *	Z
Aluminum sulfate solution *	Y
2-Amino-2-hydroxymethyl-1,3-propanediol solution	#
Ammonium hydrogen phosphate solution	Z
Ammonium lignosulfonate solutions, see also Lignin liquor	Z
Ammonium nitrate solution (45% or less)	#
Ammonium phosphate, urea solution, see also Urea, Ammonium phosphate solution	#
Ammonium polyphosphate solution	Z
Ammonium sulfate solution	Z
Ammonium thiosulfate solution (60% or less)	Z
Apple juice	OS
Calcium bromide solution	Z
Calcium carbonate slurry	OS
Calcium chloride solution	Z
Calcium hydroxide slurry	Z
Calcium lignosulfonate solution, see also Lignin liquor	Z
Calcium nitrate solutions (50% or less) *	Z
Calcium nitrate/Magnesium nitrate/Potassium chloride solution	Z
Caramel solutions	#
Chlorinated paraffins (C14-C17) (with 50% Chlorine or more, and less than 1% C13 or shorter chains) *	X
Chlorinated paraffins (C14-C17) (with 52% Chlorine)	#
2-Chloro-4-ethylamino-6-isopropylamino-5-triazine solution	#
4-Chloro-2-methylphenoxyacetic acid, dimethylamine salt solution *	Y
Choline chloride solutions	Z
Clay slurry	OS
Coal slurry	OS
Dextrose solution, see Glucose solution.	
Diethylenetriamine pentaacetic acid, pentasodium salt solution	Z
1,4-Dihydro-9,10-dihydroxy anthracene, disodium salt solution	#
Dodecenylsuccinic acid, dipotassium salt solution	#
Drilling brine (containing Calcium, Potassium, or Sodium salts) (see also Potassium chloride solution (10% or more))	#
Drilling brines, including: Calcium bromide solution, Calcium chloride solution and Sodium chloride solution (if non-flammable and non-combustible)	Z
Drilling brines (containing Zinc salts)	X
Drilling mud (low toxicity) (if non-flammable and non-combustible)	#
Ethylene-Vinyl acetate copolymer (emulsion)	Y
Ferric hydroxyethylethylenediamine triacetic acid, trisodium salt solution	Z
Fish solubles (water based fish meal extracts)	#
Fructose solution	#
Glucose solution	OS
Glycine, Sodium salt solution	Z
Glyphosate solution (not containing surfactant) *	Y
Hexamethylenediamine adipate solution	#
Hexamethylenediamine adipate (50% in water)	Z
N-(Hydroxyethyl)ethylenediamine triacetic acid, trisodium salt solution	Y
Kaolin clay solution	#
Kaolin slurry	OS
Kraft pulping liquor (free alkali content, 1% or less) including: Black, Green, or White liquor	#
Lignin liquor (free alkali content, 1% or less)	Z
including:	
Ammonium lignosulfonate solutions	Z
Calcium lignosulfonate solutions	Z
Sodium lignosulfonate solution	Z
Ligninsulfonic acid, Sodium salt solution	Z
Magnesium chloride solution	Z
Magnesium hydroxide slurry	Z
Magnesium sulfonate solution	#
Maltitol solution *	OS
Microsillica slurry *	OS
Milk	#
Molasses	OS
Molasses residue (from fermentation)	#
Naphthalenesulfonic acid-Formaldehyde copolymer, sodium salt solution	Z
Naphthenic acid, sodium salt solution	#
Nitrilotriacetic acid, trisodium salt solution *	Y
Noxious liquid, NF, (1) n.o.s. ("trade name" contains "principle components") ST 1, Cat X (if non-flammable and non-combustible)	X

Coast Guard, DHS — Pt. 153, Table 2, Nt.

[The cargoes listed in this table are not regulated under subchapter D or O of this title when carried in bulk on non-oceangoing barges. Category X, Y, or Z noxious liquid substance (NLS) cargo, as defined in Annex II of MARPOL 73/78, listed in this table, or any mixture containing one or more of these cargoes, must be carried under this subchapter if carried in bulk on an oceangoing ship.]

Cargoes	Pollution category
Noxious liquid, NF, (3) n.o.s. ("trade name" contains "principle components") ST 2, Cat X (if non-flammable and non-combustible)	X
Noxious liquid, NF, (5) n.o.s. ("trade name" contains "principle components") ST 2, Cat Y (if non-flammable and non-combustible)	Y
Noxious liquid, NF, (7) n.o.s. ("trade name" contains "principle components") ST 3, Cat Y (if non-flammable and non-combustible)	Y
Noxious liquid, NF, (9) n.o.s. ("trade name" contains "principle components") ST 3, Cat Z (if non-flammable and non-combustible)	Z
Noxious liquid, NF, (11) n.o.s. ("trade name" contains "principle components") Cat Z (if non-flammable and non-combustible)	Z
Noxious liquid, NF, (12) n.o.s. ("trade name" contains "principle components") Cat OS (if non-flammable and non-combustible)	OS
Orange juice (concentrated)*	OS
Orange juice (not concentrated)*	OS
Pentasodium salt of Diethylenetriamine pentaacetic acid solution, see Diethylenetriamine pentaacetic acid, pentasodium salt solution.	
Polyaluminum chloride solution	Z
Potassium chloride solution (26% or more), see Drilling brines, including: Calcium bromide solution, Calcium chloride solution and Sodium chloride solution.	
Potassium chloride solution (less than 26%)*	OS
Potassium formate solutions*	Z
Potassium thiosulfate (50% or less)*	Y
Sewage sludge, treated (treated so as to pose no additional decompositional and fire hazard; stable, non-corrosive, non-toxic, non-flammable)	#
Silica slurry	#
Sludge, treated (treated so as to pose no additional decompositional and fire hazard; stable, non-corrosive, non-toxic, non-flammable)	#
Sodium acetate, Glycol, Water mixture (containing 1% or less Sodium hydroxide) (if non-flammable or non-combustible)	#
Sodium acetate solutions	Z
Sodium alkyl (C14-C17) sulfonates (60–65% solution)*	Y
Sodium aluminosilicate slurry	Z
Sodium bicarbonate solution (less than 10%)*	OS
Sodium carbonate solution	Z
Sodium hydrogen sulfide (6% or less)/Sodium carbonate (3% or less) solution*	Z
Sodium lignosulfonate solution, see also Lignin liquor	Z
Sodium naphthenate solution (free alkali content, 3% or less), see Naphthenic acid, sodium salt solution.	
Sodium poly(4+)acrylate solutions	Z
Sodium silicate solution	Y
Sodium sulfate solutions	Z
Sodium sulfite solution (25% or less)*	Y
Sodium thiocyanate solution (56% or less)*	Y
Sorbitol solution	OS
Sulfonated polyacrylate solution	Z
Tetrasodium salt of Ethylenediaminetetraaacetic acid solution, see Ethylenediaminetetraacetic acid, tetrasodium salt solution.	
Titanium dioxide slurry	Z
1,1,1-Trichloroethane	Y
1,1,2-Trichloro-1,2,2-trifluoroethane	Y
Trisodium salt of N-(Hydroxyethyl)ethylenediamine triacetic acid solution, see N-(Hydroxyethyl)ethylenediamine triacetic acid, trisodium salt solution.	
Urea, Ammonium mono- and di-hydrogen phosphate, Potassium chloride solution	#
Urea/Ammonium nitrate solution*	Z
Urea/Ammonium phosphate solution	Y
Urea solution	Z
Vanillan black liquor (free alkali content, 1% or less)	#
Vegetable protein solution (hydrolyzed) (if non-flammable and non-combustible)	OS
Water	OS
Zinc bromide, Calcium bromide solution, see Drilling brines (containing Zinc salts).	

Explanation of Symbols Used in this Table:
X, Y, Z—NLS Category of Annex II of MARPOL 73/78.
#—No determination of NLS status. For shipping on an oceangoing vessel, see 46 CFR 153.900(c).
OS—Other substances, at present considered to present no harm to marine resources, human health, amenities or other legitimate uses of the sea when discharged into the sea from tank cleaning or deballasting operations.
    Abbreviations for Noxious Liquid Cargoes Used In This Table:
      Cat—Pollution category.
      NF—Non-flammable (flash point greater than 60 degrees C (140 degrees F) cc).
      n.o.s.—Not otherwise specified.
      ST—Ship type.
      *—From the March 2012 Annex to the 2007 IBC Code.

Appendix I to Part 153 [Reserved]

Appendix II to Part 153—Metric Units Used in Part 153

Parameter	Metric (SI unit)	Abbreviation	Equivalent to English or common metric
Force	Newton	N	0.225 lbs.
Length	Meter	m	39.37 in.
	Centimeter	cm	.3937 in.
Pressure	Pascal	Pa	1.450×10^{-4} lbs/in^2.
	Kilo-Pascal (1,000 Pascals)	kPa	0.145 lbs/in^2.
	Kilo-Pascal	kPa	1.02×10^{-2} kg/cm^2.
	......do	kPa	1×10^3 N/m^2.
Temperature	Degree Celsius	°C	5/9 (°F−32).
Viscosity	milli-Pascal second	mPa. sec	1.0 centipoise.
Volume	Cubic meter	m^3	264 gallons (gal).
	......do	m^3	35.3 ft^3.

[CGD 73–96, 42 FR 49027, Sept. 26, 1977, as amended by CGD 78–128, 47 FR 21212, May 17, 1982; CGD 81–101, 52 FR 7799, Mar. 12, 1987. Redesignated by CGD 92–100, 59 FR 17045, Apr. 11, 1994]

PART 154—SAFETY STANDARDS FOR SELF-PROPELLED VESSELS CARRYING BULK LIQUEFIED GASES

Subpart A—General

Sec.
154.1 Incorporation by reference.
154.3 Purpose.
154.5 Applicability.
154.7 Definitions, acronyms, and terms.
154.9 Issuance of documents.
154.12 Existing gas vessel: Endorsements and requirements.
154.15 U.S. flag vessel: Endorsement application.
154.17 U.S. flag vessel: Certificate of Inspection endorsement.
154.19 U.S. flag vessel: IMO certificate issuance.
154.22 Foreign flag vessel: Certificate of Compliance endorsement application.
154.24 Foreign flag vessel: IMO Certificate.
154.30 [Reserved]
154.32 Equivalents.
154.34 Special approval: Requests.
154.36 Correspondence and vessel information: Submission.
154.40 Right of appeal.

Subpart B—Inspections and Tests

EXAMINATION REQUIREMENTS FOR FOREIGN FLAG VESSELS

154.150 Examination required for a Certificate of Compliance.
154.151 Procedures for having the Coast Guard examine a vessel for a Certificate of Compliance.

Subpart C—Design, Construction, and Equipment

HULL STRUCTURE

154.170 Outer hull steel plating.
154.172 Contiguous steel hull structure.
154.174 Transverse contiguous hull structure.
154.176 Longitudinal contiguous hull structure.
154.178 Contiguous hull structure: Heating system.
154.180 Contiguous hull structure: Welding procedure.
154.182 Contiguous hull structure: Production weld test.
154.188 Membrane tank: Inner hull steel.
154.195 Aluminum cargo tank: Steel enclosure.

SHIP SURVIVAL CAPABILITY AND CARGO TANK LOCATION

154.200 Stability requirements: General.
154.235 Cargo tank location.

SHIP ARRANGEMENTS

154.300 Segregation of hold spaces from other spaces.
154.305 Segregation of hold spaces from the sea.
154.310 Cargo piping systems.
154.315 Cargo pump and cargo compressor rooms.
154.320 Cargo control stations.
154.325 Accommodation, service, and control spaces.
154.330 Openings to accommodation, service, or control spaces.
154.340 Access to tanks and spaces in the cargo area.
154.345 Air locks.
154.350 Bilge and ballast systems in the cargo area.
154.355 Bow and stern loading piping.
154.356 Cargo emergency jettisoning piping.

Coast Guard, DHS   Pt. 154

Cargo Containment Systems

154.401 Definitions.
154.405 Design vapor pressure (P_o) of a cargo tank.
154.406 Design loads for cargo tanks and fixtures: General.
154.407 Cargo tank internal pressure head.
154.408 Cargo tank external pressure load.
154.409 Dynamic loads from vessel motion.
154.410 Cargo tank sloshing loads.
154.411 Cargo tank thermal loads.
154.412 Cargo tank corrosion allowance.

Integral Tanks

154.418 General.
154.419 Design vapor pressure.
154.420 Tank design.
154.421 Allowable stress.

Membrane Tanks

154.425 General.
154.426 Design vapor pressure.
154.427 Membrane tank system design.
154.428 Allowable stress.
154.429 Calculations.
154.430 Material test.
154.431 Model test.
154.432 Expansion and contraction.

Semi-Membrane Tanks

154.435 General.
154.436 Design vapor pressure.

Independent Tank Type A

154.437 General.
154.438 Design vapor pressure.
154.439 Tank design.
154.440 Allowable stress.

Independent Tank Type B

154.444 General.
154.445 Design vapor pressure.
154.446 Tank design.
154.447 Allowable stress.
154.448 Calculations.
154.449 Model test.

Independent Tank Type C and Process Pressure Vessels

154.450 General.
154.451 Design vapor pressure.
154.452 External pressure.
154.453 Failure to meet independent tank type C standards.

Secondary Barrier

154.459 General.
154.460 Design criteria.

Insulation

154.465 General.
154.466 Design criteria.
154.467 Submission of insulation information.

Support System

154.470 General.
154.471 Design criteria.
154.476 Cargo transfer devices and means.

Cargo and Process Piping Systems

154.500 Cargo and process piping standards.
154.503 Piping and piping system components: Protection from movement.
154.506 Mechanical expansion joint: Limits in a piping system.
154.512 Piping: Thermal isolation.
154.514 Piping: Electrical bonding.
154.516 Piping: Hull protection.
154.517 Piping: Liquid pressure relief.
154.519 Piping relief valves.
154.520 Piping calculations.
154.522 Materials for piping.
154.524 Piping joints: Welded and screwed couplings.
154.526 Piping joints: Flange connection.
154.528 Piping joints: Flange type.
154.530 Valves: Cargo tank MARVS 69 kPa gauge (10 psig) or lower.
154.532 Valves: Cargo tank MARVS greater than 69 kPa gauge (10 psig).
154.534 Cargo pumps and cargo compressors.
154.536 Cargo tank gauging and measuring connections.
154.538 Cargo transfer connection.
154.540 Quick-closing shut-off valves: Emergency shut-down system.
154.544 Quick-closing shut-off valves.
154.546 Excess flow valve: Closing flow.
154.548 Cargo piping: Flow capacity.
154.550 Excess flow valve: Bypass.

Cargo Hose

154.551 Cargo hose: General.
154.552 Cargo hose: Compatibility.
154.554 Cargo hose: Bursting pressure.
154.556 Cargo hose: Maximum working pressure.
154.558 Cargo hose: Marking.
154.560 Cargo hose: Prototype test.
154.562 Cargo hose: Hydrostatic test.

Materials

154.605 Toughness test.
154.610 Design temperature not colder than 0 °C (32 °F).
154.615 Design temperature below 0 °C (32 °F) and down to -55 °C (-67 °F).
154.620 Design temperature below -55 °C (-67 °F) and down to -165 °C (-265 °F).
154.625 Design temperature below 0 °C (32 °F) and down to -165 °C (-265 °F).
154.630 Cargo tank material.

Construction

154.650 Cargo tank and process pressure vessel welding.
154.655 Stress relief for independent tanks type C.
154.660 Pipe welding.

Pt. 154

154.665 Welding procedures.

CARGO PRESSURE AND TEMPERATURE CONTROL

154.701 Cargo pressure and temperature control: General.
154.702 Refrigerated carriage.
154.703 Methane (LNG).
154.705 Cargo boil-off as fuel: General.
154.706 Cargo boil-off as fuel: Fuel lines.
154.707 Cargo boil-off as fuel: Ventilation.
154.708 Cargo boil-off as fuel: Valves.
154.709 Cargo boil-off as fuel: Gas detection equipment.

CARGO VENT SYSTEMS

154.801 Pressure relief systems.
154.802 Alternate pressure relief settings.
154.804 Vacuum protection.
154.805 Vent masts.
154.806 Capacity of pressure relief valves.

ATMOSPHERIC CONTROL IN CARGO CONTAINMENT SYSTEMS

154.901 Atmospheric control within cargo tanks and cargo piping systems.
154.902 Atmospheric control within hold and interbarrier spaces.
154.903 Inert gas systems: General.
154.904 Inert gas system: Controls.
154.906 Inert gas generators.
154.908 Inert gas generator: Location.
154.910 Inert gas piping: Location.
154.912 Inerted spaces: Relief devices.

ELECTRICAL

154.1000 Applicability.
154.1002 Definition.
154.1005 Equipment approval.
154.1010 Electrical equipment in gas-dangerous space or zone.
154.1015 Lighting in gas-dangerous space.
154.1020 Emergency power.

FIREFIGHTING

Firefighting System: Exterior Water Spray

154.1105 Exterior water spray system: General.
154.1110 Areas protected by system.
154.1115 Discharge.
154.1120 Nozzles.
154.1125 Pipes, fittings, and valves.
154.1130 Sections.
154.1135 Pumps.

Firefighting System: Dry Chemical

154.1140 Dry chemical system: General.
154.1145 Dry chemical supply.
154.1150 Distribution of dry chemical.
154.1155 Hand hose line: Coverage.
154.1160 Monitor coverage of system.
154.1165 Controls.
154.1170 Hand hose line: General.

CARGO AREA: MECHANICAL VENTILATION SYSTEM

154.1200 Mechanical ventilation system: General.
154.1205 Mechanical ventilations system: Standards.
154.1210 Hold space, void space, cofferdam, and spaces containing cargo piping.

INSTRUMENTATION

154.1300 Liquid level gauging system: General.
154.1305 Liquid level gauging system: Standards.
154.1310 Closed gauge shut-off valve.
154.1315 Restricted gauge excess flow valve.
154.1320 Sighting ports, tubular gauge glasses, and flat plate type gauge glasses.
154.1325 Liquid level alarm system: All cargo tanks.
154.1330 Liquid level alarm system: Independent tank type C.
154.1335 Pressure and vacuum protection.
154.1340 Temperature measuring devices.
154.1345 Gas detection.
154.1350 Flammable gas detection system.
154.1360 Oxygen analyzer.
154.1365 Audible and visual alarms.
154.1370 Pressure gauge and vacuum gauge marking.
154.1375 Readout for temperature measuring device: Marking.

SAFETY EQUIPMENT

154.1400 Safety equipment: All vessels.
154.1405 Respiratory protection.
154.1410 Decontamination shower.
154.1415 Air compressor.
154.1420 Stretchers and equipment.
154.1430 Equipment locker.
154.1435 Medical first aid guide.
154.1440 Antidotes.

Subpart D—Special Design and Operating Requirements

154.1700 Purpose.
154.1702 Materials of construction.
154.1705 Independent tank type C.
154.1710 Exclusion of air from cargo tank vapor spaces.
154.1715 Moisture control.
154.1720 Indirect refrigeration.
154.1725 Ethylene oxide.
154.1730 Ethylene oxide: Loading and off-loading.
154.1735 Methyl acetylene-propadiene mixture.
154.1740 Vinyl chloride: Inhibiting and inerting.
154.1745 Vinyl chloride: Transferring operations.
154.1750 Butadiene or vinyl chloride: Refrigeration system.
154.1755 Nitrogen.
154.1760 Liquid ammonia.

Coast Guard, DHS

Subpart E—Operations

154.1800 Special operating requirements under Part 35 of this chapter.
154.1801 Certificates, letters, and endorsements: U.S. flag vessels.
154.1802 Certificates, letters, and endorsements: Foreign flag vessels.
154.1803 Expiration of Certificates of Compliance.
154.1804 Document posted in wheelhouse.
154.1806 Regulations on board.
154.1808 Limitations in the endorsement.
154.1809 Loading and stability manual.
154.1810 Cargo manual.
154.1812 Operational information for terminal personnel.
154.1814 Cargo information cards.
154.1816 Cargo location plan.
154.1818 Certification of inhibition.
154.1820 Shipping document.
154.1822 Shipping document: Copy for transfer terminal.
154.1824 Obstruction of pumproom ladderways.
154.1826 Opening of cargo tanks and cargo sampling.
154.1828 Spaces containing cargo vapor: Entry.
154.1830 Warning sign.
154.1831 Persons in charge of transferring liquid cargo in bulk or preparing cargo tanks.
154.1834 Cargo transfer piping.
154.1836 Vapor venting as a means of cargo tank pressure and temperature control.
154.1838 Discharge by gas pressurization.
154.1840 Protective clothing.
154.1842 Cargo system: Controls and alarms.
154.1844 Cargo tanks: Filling limits.
154.1846 Relief valves: Changing set pressure.
154.1848 Inerting.
154.1850 Entering cargo handling spaces.
154.1852 Air breathing equipment.
154.1854 Methane (LNG) as fuel.
154.1858 Cargo hose.
154.1860 Integral tanks: Cargo colder than −10 °C (14 °F).
154.1862 Posting of speed reduction.
154.1864 Vessel speed within speed reduction.
154.1866 Cargo hose connection: Transferring cargo.
154.1868 Portable blowers in personnel access openings.
154.1870 Bow and stern loading.
154.1872 Cargo emergency jettisoning.

APPENDIX A TO PART 154—EQUIVALENT STRESS
APPENDIX B TO PART 154—STRESS ANALYSES DEFINITIONS

AUTHORITY: 46 U.S.C. 3703, 9101; Department of Homeland Security Delegation No. 0170.1.

SOURCE: CGD 74–289, 44 FR 26009, May 3, 1979, unless otherwise noted.

EDITORIAL NOTE: Nomenclature changes to part 154 appear at 60 FR 50466, Sept. 29, 1995, 61 FR 50732, Sept. 27, 1996, 74 FR 49235, Sept. 25, 2009, and at 77 FR 59785, Oct. 1, 2012.

Subpart A—General

SOURCE: CGD 77–069, 52 FR 31626, Aug. 21, 1987, unless otherwise noted.

§ 154.1 Incorporation by reference.

(a) Certain materials are incorporated by reference into this part with approval of the Director of the Federal Register in accordance with 5 U.S.C. 552(a). The Office of the Federal Register publishes a list "Material Approved for Incorporation by Reference," which appears in the Finding Aids section of this volume. To enforce any edition other than the one listed in paragraph (b) of this section, notice of change must be published in the FEDERAL REGISTER and the material made available. All approved material is on file at the Coast Guard Headquarters. Contact Commandant (CG–ENG), Attn: Office of Design and Engineering Systems, U.S. Coast Guard Stop 7509, 2703 Martin Luther King Jr. Avenue SE., Washington, DC 20593–7509; or contact the National Archives and Records Administration (NARA). For information on the availability of this material at NARA, call 202–741–6030, or go to: *http://www.archives.gov/federal_register/code_of_federal_regulations/ibr_locations.html*.

(b) The materials approved for incorporation by reference in this part are:

American Bureau of Shipping (ABS)

ABS Plaza, 16855 Northchase Drive, Houston, TX 77060
Rules for Building and Classing Steel Vessels, 1981

American National Standards Institute

11 West 42nd Street, New York, NY 10036
ANSI Z89.1–69 Safety Requirements for Industrial Head Protection, 1969
ANSI Z87.1–79 Practice for Occupational and Educational Eye and Face Protection, 1979

American Society for Testing and Materials (ASTM)

100 Barr Harbor Drive, West Conshohocken, PA 19428–2959.

ASTM A 20/A 20M–97a, Standard Specification for General Requirements for Steel Plates for Pressure Vessels—154.610

ASTM F 1014–92, Standard Specification for Flashlights on Vessels—154.1400

NOTE: All other documents referenced in this part are still in effect.

International Maritime Organization

Publications Section, 4 Albert Embankment, London SE1 7SR, United Kingdom

Resolution A.328(IX), Code for the Construction and Equipment of Ships Carrying Liquefied Gases in Bulk, 1976

Code For Existing Ships Carrying Liquefied Gases in Bulk, 1976

Medical First Aid Guide for Use in Accidents Involving Dangerous Goods

Underwriters Laboratories, Inc.

12 Laboratory Drive, Research Triangle Park, NC 27709–3995

UL No. 783–79 Standard for Safety, Electric Flashlights for Use in Hazardous Locations, Class 1, Groups C and D, 1979.

[CGD 77–069, 52 FR 31626, Aug. 21, 1987, as amended by CGD 82–042, 53 FR 17705, May 18, 1988; CGD 82–042, 53 FR 18949, May 25, 1988; CGD 88–070, 53 FR 34535, Sept. 7, 1988; CGD 96–041, 61 FR 50732, Sept. 27, 1996; CGD 97–057, 62 FR 51048, Sept. 30, 1997; USCG–1999–5151, 64 FR 67183, Dec. 1, 1999; USCG–2000–7790, 65 FR 58463, Sept. 29, 2000; 69 FR 18803, Apr. 9, 2004; USCG–2013–0671, 78 FR 60155, Sept. 30, 2013]

§ 154.3 Purpose.

The purpose of this part is to prescribe rules for new and existing gas vessels.

§ 154.5 Applicability.

This part applies to each self-propelled vessel that has on board bulk liquefied gases as cargo, cargo residue or vapor, except subpart C does not apply if the vessel meets § 154.12 (b), (c), or (d).

§ 154.7 Definitions, acronyms, and terms.

As used in this part:

"A" Class Division means a division as defined in Regulation 3 of Chapter II-2 of the 1974 Safety Convention.

Accommodation spaces means public spaces, corridors, lavatories, cabins, offices, hospitals, cinemas, game and hobby rooms, pantries containing no cooking appliances, and spaces used in a similar fashion.

Boiling point means the temperature at which a substance's vapor pressure is equal to the atmospheric barometric pressure.

Breadth (B) means the maximum width of the vessel in meters measured amidships to the molded line of the frame in a ship with a metal shell and to the outer surface of the hull in a ship with a shell of any other material.

Cargo area means that part of the vessel that contains the cargo containment system, cargo pump rooms, cargo compressor rooms, and the deck areas over the full beam and the length of the vessel above them, but does not include the cofferdams, ballast spaces, or void spaces at the after end of the aftermost hold space or the forward end of the forwardmost hold space.

Cargo containment system means the arrangement for containment of the cargo including a primary and secondary barrier, associated insulation and any intervening spaces, and adjacent structure that is necessary for the support of these elements.

Cargo service space means space within the cargo area that is more than 2 m^2 (21.5 ft.^{2}) in deck area and used for work shops, lockers, or store rooms.

Cargo tank means the liquid tight shell that is the primary container of the cargo.

Certificate of Compliance means a certificate issued by the Coast Guard to a foreign flag vessel after it is examined and found to comply with regulations in this chapter.

Cofferdam means the isolating space between two adjacent steel bulkheads or decks, which could be a void space or a ballast space.

Contiguous hull structure includes the inner deck, the inner bottom plating, longitudinal bulkhead plating, transverse bulkhead plating, floors, webs, stringers, and attached stiffeners.

Control space means those spaces in which the vessel's radio, main navigating equipment, or the emergency source of power is located or in which the fire control equipment, other than firefighting control equipment under § 154.1140 to § 154.1170, is centralized.

Design temperature means the minimum cargo temperature the Coast Guard allows for loading, unloading, or carriage.

Design vapor pressure (P_o) means the maximum gauge pressure at the top of the cargo tank for the design of the cargo tank.

Document means a Certificate of Inspection for a U.S. flag vessel or a Certificate of Compliance for a foreign flag vessel.

Existing gas vessel means a self-propelled vessel that—

(a) Is delivered on or before October 31, 1976; or

(b) Is delivered between October 31, 1976 and June 30, 1980, and is not a new gas vessel.

Flammable cargoes includes the following liquefied gases from Table 4 (follows § 154.1872):

Acetaldehyde
Butadiene
Butane
Butylene
Dimethylamine
Ethane
Ethylamine
Ethyl chloride
Ethylene
Ethylene oxide
Methane (LNG)
Methyl acetylene-propadiene mixture
Methyl bromide
Methyl chloride
Propane
Propylene
Vinyl chloride

Gas-dangerous space includes the following spaces:

(a) A space in the cargo area without arrangements to provide a safe atmosphere at all times.

(b) An enclosed space outside the cargo area through which any piping that may contain liquid or gaseous cargo passes, or within which that piping terminates, without arrangements to prevent gas from escaping into the space.

(c) A cargo containment system and cargo piping.

(d) A hold space where cargo is carried in a cargo containment system:

(1) With a secondary barrier; or

(2) Without a secondary barrier.

(e) A space separated from a hold space under paragraph (d)(1) of this definition by a single gastight boundary.

(f) A cargo pumproom and a cargo compressor room.

(g) A zone on the weather deck or a semi-enclosed space on the weather deck within 3.05 m (10 ft) of any cargo tank outlet, gas or vapor outlet, cargo pipe flange, cargo valve, or of entrances and ventilation openings to a cargo pump room or a cargo compressor room.

(h) Except for existing gas vessels, the weather deck over the cargo area and 3.05 m (10 ft) forward and aft of the cargo area on the weather deck to 2.4 m (8 ft) above the weather deck.

(i) A zone within 2.4 m (8 ft) of the outer surface of a cargo containment system where the surface is exposed to the weather.

(j) An enclosed or semi-enclosed space in which there is piping containing cargo, except those—

(1) With gas sampling lines for gas detection equipment under § 154.1350(n); or

(2) In which boil-off gas is used as fuel under § 154.703.

(k) A space for storage of cargo hoses.

(l) An enclosed or semi-enclosed space having an opening into any gas-dangerous space or zone.

Gas-safe space means a space that is not a gas-dangerous space.

Hold space means the space enclosed by the vessel's structure in which there is a cargo containment system.

IMO stands for the International Maritime Organization.

IMO Certificate means a Certificate of Fitness for the Carriage of Liquefied Gases in Bulk issued under the IMO—

(a) "Code for the Construction and Equipment of Ships Carrying Liquefied Gases in Bulk", adopted November 12, 1975 by Assembly Resolution A.328(IX), as amended;

(b) "Code for Existing Ships Carrying Liquefied Gases in Bulk", adopted November 12, 1975, as amended; or

(c) "Recommendations Concerning Ships Not Covered by the Code for the Construction and Equipment of Ships Carrying Liquefied Gases in Bulk", (Resolution A.328(IX)), adopted November 12, 1975 by Assembly Resolution A.329(IX).

Independent tank is a cargo tank that is permanently affixed to the vessel, is self-supporting, and is not part of the hull or essential to the strength or integrity of the hull.

§ 154.7

Independent tank type A is an independent cargo tank designed primarily using classification society classical ship structural analysis procedures.

Independent tank type B is an independent cargo tank designed from model tests, refined analytical tools, and analysis methods to determine stress levels, fatigue life, and crack propagation characteristics.

Independent tank type C (pressure tank) is an independent cargo tank meeting pressure vessel criteria where the dominant stress producing load is design vapor pressure.

Insulation space means a space, that could be an interbarrier space, occupied wholly or in part by insulation.

Integral tank means a cargo tank that is a structural part of the vessel's hull and is influenced in the same manner and by the same loads that stress the adjacent hull structure.

Interbarrier space means the space between a primary and a secondary barrier, with or without insulation or other material.

Length (L) is ninety-six percent of the total length in meters on a waterline at eighty-five percent of the least molded depth measured from the top of the keel or the length from the foreside of the stem to the axis of the rudder stock on the waterline, whichever is greater. In vessels having a rake of keel, the waterline is parallel to the design waterline.

Liquefied gas means a cargo having a vapor pressure of 172 kPa (25 psia) or more at 37.8 °C (100 °F).

MARVS stands for the Maximum Allowable Relief Valve Setting.

Membrane tank is a cargo tank that is not self-supporting and consists of a thin layer (membrane) supported through insulation by the adjacent hull structure.

New gas vessel means a self-propelled vessel that—

(a) Is constructed under a building contract awarded after October 31, 1976;

(b) In the absence of a building contract, has a keel laid or is at a similar stage of construction after December 31, 1976;

(c) Is delivered after June 30, 1980; or

(d) Has undergone a major conversion for which—

(1) The building contract is awarded after October 31, 1976;

(2) In the absence of a building contract, conversion is begun after December 31, 1976; or

(3) Conversion is completed after June 30, 1980.

Primary barrier means the inner boundary that contains the cargo when the cargo containment system includes two boundaries.

Process pressure vessel means a pressure vessel that is used in a reliquefaction, cargo heating, or other system that processes cargo.

Remote group alarm means an audible and visual alarm that alerts when an alarm condition exists but does not identify that condition.

Secondary barrier means the liquid resisting outer boundary of a cargo containment system when the cargo containment system includes two boundaries.

Semi-membrane tank is a cargo tank that is not self-supporting and that can expand and contract due to thermal, hydrostatic, and pressure loadings. It consists of flat surfaces, supported through insulation by the adjacent hull structure, and shaped corners that connect the flat surfaces.

Service space means a space outside the cargo area that is used for a galley, pantry containing cooking appliances, locker or store room, workshop except those in machinery spaces, and similar spaces and trunks to those spaces.

Shut-off valve is a valve that closes a pipeline and provides nominal metal to metal contact between the valve operating parts, including the disc and gate, and the valve body.

Specific gravity (p) means the ratio of the density of the cargo at the design temperature to the density of water at 4 °C (39 °F).

Tank cover is the structure protecting those parts of the cargo containment system that protrude through the weather deck and providing continuity to the deck structure.

Tank dome means the uppermost portion of the cargo tank. For below deck cargo containment systems, it means the uppermost portion of the cargo tank that protrudes through the weather deck or through the tank cover.

Toxic cargoes includes the following liquefied gases from Table 4 (follows § 154.1872):

Acetaldehyde
Ammonia, anhydrous
Dimethylamine
Ethylamine
Ethyl chloride
Ethylene oxide
Methyl bromide
Methyl chloride
Sulfur dioxide
Vinyl chloride

Vapor pressure means the absolute equilibrium pressure of the saturated vapor above the liquid, expressed in kPa (psia), at a specific temperature.

Void space means an enclosed space in the cargo area outside of the cargo containment system, except a hold space, ballast space, fuel oil tank, cargo pump or compressor room, or any space used by personnel.

1974 Safety Convention stands for the International Convention on Safety of Life at Sea, 1974, done at London, November 1, 1974.

§ 154.9 Issuance of documents.

The Coast Guard issues an endorsed Certificate of Inspection to a U.S. flag vessel or an endorsed Certificate of Compliance to a foreign flag vessel that meets this part.

§ 154.12 Existing gas vessel: Endorsements and requirements.

(a) Except an existing gas vessel under paragraph (b), (c), or (d) of this section, an existing gas vessel must meet subpart C of this part if the owner desires a document endorsed for the carriage of a cargo listed in Table 4 (follows § 154.1872).

(b) If an existing gas vessel is issued a document by the Coast Guard before November 1, 1987 that is endorsed for the carriage of a cargo listed in Table 4 (follows § 154.1872), and the owner desires the same endorsement on a reissued document, the vessel must—

(1) Continue to meet the same design and construction standards under which the Coast Guard issued the original document; and

(2) Meet paragraph (e) of this section.

(c) If an existing gas vessel is issued a document by the Coast Guard before November 1, 1987 that is endorsed for the carriage of a cargo listed in Table 4 (follows § 154.1872), and the owner desires an endorsement for a different cargo listed in that table, the vessel must—

(1) Continue to meet the same design and construction standards under which the Coast Guard issued the original document;

(2) Meet paragraph (e) of this section;

(3) Meet subpart D for the different cargo; and

(4) Meet any additional requirements of this part that the Commandant (CG-ENG) determines to be necessary for safety.

(d) If an existing gas vessel does not meet paragraph (b) or (c) of this section and the owner desires a document endorsed for the carriage of a cargo listed in Table 4 (follows § 154.1872), the vessel must—

(1) Have a letter from the Coast Guard dated before November 1, 1987 stating that—

(i) Review of the vessel's plans for the carriage of that cargo is completed; or

(ii) The vessel's IMO Certificate endorsed for the carriage of that cargo is accepted;

(2) Meet the plans that were reviewed and marked "Examined" or "Approved" by the Coast Guard, or meet the standards under which the IMO Certificate was issued;

(3) Meet paragraph (e) of this section; and

(4) Meet any additional requirements of this part that the Commandant (CG-ENG) determines to be necessary for safety.

(e) If the owner of a vessel desires any document endorsement described in paragraph (b), (c), or (d) of this section, the existing gas vessel must meet the requirements in each of the following:

(1) Section 154.310 (d) and (e).
(2) Section 154.320 (b) and (c).
(3) Section 154.330 (a) through (e).
(4) Section 154.340(d).
(5) Section 154.345 (a), (b)(1) through (b)(5), (b)(7) and (c).
(6) Section 154.476(a).
(7) Section 154.519(a)(2).
(8) Section 154.534.
(9) Section 154.538.
(10) Section 154.540 (c) and (d).

§ 154.15

(11) Section 154.556.
(12) Section 154.558.
(13) Section 154.560.
(14) Section 154.562.
(15) Section 154.703.
(16) Section 154.705.
(17) Section 154.706.
(18) Section 154.707.
(19) Section 154.708.
(20) Section 154.709.
(21) Section 154.904.
(22) Section 154.906.

(23) Section 154.908(a), unless the space is separated from the accommodation, service, or control space by a steel door that—

(i) Is watertight when tested with a firehose at not less than 207 kPa gauge (30 psig);

(ii) Has a means to self-close and does not have latches or other devices designed to hold it open; and

(iii) Has an audible and visual alarm on both sides of the door which is actuated when the door is open.

(24) Section 154.910.
(25) Section 154.912.
(26) Sections 154.1110 through 154.1130, except §§ 154.1115(b), 154.1120(b), and 154.1125 (c) and (f).
(27) Section 154.1145, except an existing gas vessel with a cargo carrying capacity of less than 2500 m^3 (88,200 ft^3) may have only one self-contained dry chemical storage unit if that unit—

(i) is installed before November 1, 1987; and

(ii) Has the capacity to meet § 154.1145 (d) and (e), and § 154.1170(e).

(28) Section 154.1150 (a) and (b).
(29) Section 154.1155.
(30) Section 154.1160.
(31) Section 154.1165 (a), (b), (d), and (f).
(32) Section 154.1170 (b) through (f).
(33) Section 154.1200 (a), (b)(1), and (b)(2).
(34) Section 154.1205(f).
(35) Section 154.1325.
(36) Section 154.1335(e).
(37) Section 154.1350 (e), (f), (i), (o), and (u).

§ 154.15 U.S. flag vessel: Endorsement application.

(a) A person who desires the endorsement required under § 154.1801 for a U.S. flag vessel must submit an application for an endorsement of the vessel's Subchapter D Certificate of Inspection under the procedures in § 91.55–15 of this chapter.

(b) The person requesting an endorsement under paragraph (a) of this section must submit to the Coast Guard, if requested—

(1) Calculations for hull design required by § 172.175 of this chapter;

(2) The plans and information listed in §§ 54.01–18, 56.01–10, 91.55–5 (a), (b), (d), (g), and (h), and 110.25–1 of this chapter;

(3) Plans for the dry chemical supply and distribution systems, including the controls; and

(4) Any other vessel information, including, but not limited to plans, design calculations, test results, certificates, and manufacturer's data, needed to determine whether or not the vessel meets the standards of this part.

§ 154.17 U.S. flag vessel: Certificate of Inspection endorsement.

The Certificate of Inspection for a U.S. flag vessel allowed to carry a liquefied gas listed in Table 4 has the following endorsement for each cargo, with the corresponding carriage requirement data inserted:

Inspected and approved for the carriage of _____ at a maximum allowable relief valve setting of _____ kPa gauge (_____ psig) with an F factor of _____, a maximum external pressure of _____ kPa gauge (_____ psig), a minimum service temperature of _____ °C (_____ °F), and a maximum specific gravity of _____. Hull type _____.

§ 154.19 U.S. flag vessel: IMO certificate issuance.

(a) Either a classification society authorized under 46 CFR part 8, or the Coast Guard Officer in Charge, Marine Inspection, issues an IMO Certificate to a U.S. flag vessel when requested by the owner or representative, if—

(1) The vessel meets the requirements of this part; and

(2) It is a new gas vessel, it meets the IMO Resolution A.328(IX), "Code for the Construction and Equipment of Ships Carrying Liquefied Gases in Bulk, 1975"; or

(3) It is an existing gas vessel, it meets the IMO "Code for Existing Ships Carrying Liquefied Gases in Bulk, 1975".

(b) The IMO Certificate expires on the same date that the vessel's Certificate of Inspection expires.

[CGD 77–069, 52 FR 31626, Aug. 21, 1987, as amended by CGD 95–010, 62 FR 67537, Dec. 24, 1997]

§ 154.22 Foreign flag vessel: Certificate of Compliance endorsement application.

(a) A person who desires an endorsed Certificate of Compliance to meet § 154.1802(a) of this part for a foreign flag vessel, whose flag administration issues IMO Certificates, must submit to the Commanding Officer (MSC), Attn: Marine Safety Center, U.S. Coast Guard Stop 7410, 4200 Wilson Boulevard Suite 400, Arlington, VA 20598–7410, in a written or electronic format, an application that includes the following:

(1) The vessel's valid IMO Certificate.
(2) A description of the vessel.
(3) Specifications for the cargo containment system.
(4) A general arrangement plan of the vessel.
(5) A midship section plan of the vessel.
(6) Schematic plans of the liquid and vapor cargo piping.
(7) A firefighting and safety plan.
(8) If the applicant is requesting an endorsement for the carriage of ethylene oxide, a classification society certification that the vessel meets § 154.1725(a) (4), (5), and (7).
(9) If the vessel is a new gas vessel, or an existing vessel that does not meet § 154.12 (b), (c), or (d)—
 (i) A certification from a classification society that the vessel—
 (A) Has enhanced grades of steel meeting § 154.170 (b)(1) and (b)(2) for crack arresting purposes in the deck stringer, sheer strake, and bilge strake; and
 (B) Meets § 154.701, or if the vessel carries methane, meets § 154.703, by having the capability of cargo tank pressure and temperature control without venting; and
 (ii) The vessel's valid SOLAS Cargo Ship Safety Construction Certificate and Cargo Ship Safety Equipment Certificate.
(10) Any additional plans, certificates, and information needed by the Commanding Officer, Marine Safety Center to determine whether or not the vessel meets this part.

(b) A person who desires an endorsed Certificate of Compliance to meet § 154.1802(b) for a foreign flag vessel, whose flag administration does not issue IMO Certificates, must submit to the Commanding Officer, Marine Safety Center the plans, calculations, and information under § 154.15(b).

[CGD 77–069, 52 FR 31626, Aug. 21, 1987, as amended by CGD 88–070, 53 FR 34535, Sept. 7, 1988; CGD 89–025, 54 FR 19571, May 8, 1989; CGD 95–072, 60 FR 50466, Sept. 29, 1995; 60 FR 54106, Oct. 19, 1995; USCG–2005–23172, 70 FR 75734, Dec. 21, 2005; USCG–2007–29018, 72 FR 53967, Sept. 21, 2007; USCG–2013–0671, 78 FR 60155, Sept. 30, 2013]

§ 154.24 Foreign flag vessel: IMO Certificate.

(a) An IMO Certificate issued under the IMO Resolution A.328(IX),"Code for the Construction and Equipment of Ships Carrying Liquefied Gases in Bulk, 1975" is usually sufficient evidence of compliance with this part for the Coast Guard to endorse a foreign flag vessel's Certificate of Compliance with the name of each cargo in Table 4 (follows § 154.1872) that is listed on the IMO Certificate, if the information listed in item 3 of the IMO Certificate shows that—

(1) The design ambient temperatures meet § 154.174 and § 154.176;
(2) The cargo tank design stress factors and resulting MARVS of independent tanks type B or C meet § 154.447 or § 154.450; and
(3) The cargo tank MARVS of a type IIPG ship meets § 172.175(c) of this chapter.

(b) If a foreign flag existing gas vessel meets § 154.12 (b), (c), or (d), the vessel's IMO Certificate issued under the IMO "Code for Existing Ships Carrying Liquefied Gases in Bulk, 1975" is usually sufficient evidence of compliance with the requirements of § 154.12(e) for the Coast Guard to endorse the Certificate of Compliance with the name of each cargo in Table 4 (follows § 154.1872) that is listed on the IMO Certificate; however if a foreign flag existing gas vessel does not meet § 154.12 (b), (c), or (d), an IMO Certificate issued under the IMO "Code for Existing Ships Carrying Liquefied Gases in Bulk, 1975" is not acceptable evidence of compliance with

§ 154.30

the requirements of this part for the endorsement of a Certificate of Compliance.

§ 154.30 [Reserved]

§ 154.32 Equivalents.

(a) A vessel that fails to meet the standards in this part for an endorsement on a Certificate of Inspection or a Certificate of Compliance may meet an alternate standard if the Commandant (CG–ENG) finds that the alternate standard provides an equivalent or greater level of protection for the purpose of safety.

(b) The Commandant (CG–ENG) considers issuance of a finding of equivalence to the standard required by this part if the person requesting the finding submits a written application to the Commandant (CG–ENG) that includes—

(1) A detailed explanation of the vessel's characteristics that do not meet the requirements in this part; and

(2) An explanation of how each substituted standard would enable the vessel to meet a level of safety that would be equivalent to or greater than the standard in this part.

(c) Operational methods or procedures may not be substituted for a particular fitting, material, appliance, apparatus, item, or type of equipment required in this part.

§ 154.34 Special approval: Requests.

Each request for special approval must be in writing and submitted to the Commandant (CG–ENG), Attn: Office of Design and Engineering Systems, U.S. Coast Guard Stop 7509, 2703 Martin Luther King Jr. Avenue SE., Washington, DC 20593–7509.

[CGD 77–069, 52 FR 31626, Aug. 21, 1987, as amended by USCG–2013–0671, 78 FR 60155, Sept. 30, 2013]

§ 154.36 Correspondence and vessel information: Submission.

Correspondence to the Coast Guard and all vessel information submitted to the Coast Guard must be in English, except—

(a) IMO Certificates may be in French; and

(b) SOLAS Certificates may be in the official language of the flag administration.

§ 154.40 Right of appeal.

Any person directly affected by a decision or action taken under this part, by or on behalf of the Coast Guard, may appeal therefrom in accordance with subpart 1.03 of this chapter.

[CGD 88–033, 54 FR 50381, Dec. 6, 1989]

Subpart B—Inspections and Tests

EXAMINATION REQUIREMENTS FOR FOREIGN FLAG VESSELS

§ 154.150 Examination required for a Certificate of Compliance.

Before a vessel receives an initial or reissued Certificate of Compliance endorsed with the name of a cargo from Table 4 of this part, the vessel must call at a United States port for an examination, during which the Officer in Charge, Marine Inspection, determines whether or not the vessel meets the requirements of this chapter.

[CGD 81–052, 50 FR 8734, Mar. 5, 1985]

§ 154.151 Procedures for having the Coast Guard examine a vessel for a Certificate of Compliance.

To have the Coast Guard examine the vessel for a Certificate of Compliance, as required in § 154.150, the owner of a foreign flag vessel must proceed as follows:

(a) After submitting an application under § 154.22, await notification by the Commanding Officer, Marine Safety Center that review of the vessel's plans or IMO Certificate and supporting documents is complete.

(b) Except when paragraph (c) of this section applies,

(1) After receiving notification from Commanding Officer, Marine Safety Center that review is complete and the application is acceptable, dispatch the vessel to a United States port;

(2) Notify the Officer in Charge, Marine Inspection, for the port where the vessel is to be inspected at least seven days before the vessel arrives and arrange the exact time and other details of the examination. This notification is

Coast Guard, DHS § 154.172

in addition to any other pre-arrival notice to the Coast Guard required by other regulations and must include:

(i) The name of the vessel's first U.S. port of call;

(ii) The date the vessel is scheduled to arrive;

(iii) The name and telephone number of the owner's local agent; and

(iv) The names of all cargoes listed in Table 4 of this part that are on board the vessel;

(3) Make sure that the following items are available on board the vessel for the use of the Marine Inspector before beginning the examination required by § 154.150:

(i) A general arrangement (including the location of firefighting, safety, and lifesaving gear); and

(ii) The cargo manual required by § 154.1810.

(c) If the vessel was accepted for U.S. service on the basis of Coast Guard plan review under § 154.22(b), the vessel owner must notify Commanding Officer, Marine Safety Center 14 days prior to the vessel's arrival at a U.S. port. This notification must include:

(1) The name of the vessel's first U.S. port of call;

(2) The date the vessel is scheduled to arrive;

(3) The name and telephone number of the owner's local agent; and

(4) The names of all cargoes listed in Table 4 of this part that are on board the vessel.

[CGD 81–052, 50 FR 8734, Mar. 5, 1985; 50 FR 15895, Apr. 23, 1985; CGD 77–069, 52 FR 31630, Aug. 21, 1987; CGD 95–072, 60 FR 50466, Sept. 29, 1995; 60 FR 54106, Oct. 19, 1995; USCG–2013–0671, 78 FR 60155, Sept. 30, 2013]

Subpart C—Design, Construction and Equipment

HULL STRUCTURE

§ 154.170 Outer hull steel plating.

(a) Except as required in paragraph (b) of this section, the outer hull steel plating, including the shell and deck plating must meet the material standards of the American Bureau of Shipping published in "Rules for Building and Classing Steel Vessels" 1981.

(b) Along the length of the cargo area, grades of steel must be as follows:

(1) The deck stringer and sheer strake must be at least Grade E steel or a grade of steel that has equivalent chemical properties, mechanical properties, and heat treatment, and that is specially approved by the Commandant (CG–ENG).

(2) The strake at the turn of the bilge must be Grade D, Grade E, or a grade of steel that has equivalent chemical properties, mechanical properties, and heat treatment, and that is specially approved by the Commandant (CG–ENG).

(3) The outer hull steel of vessels must meet the standards in § 154.172 if the hull steel temperature is calculated to be below −5 °C (23 °F) assuming:

(i) For any waters in the world, the ambient cold conditions of still air at 5 °C (41 °F) and still sea water at 0 °C (32 °F);

(ii) For cargo containment systems with secondary barriers, the temperature of the secondary barrier is the design temperature; and

(iii) For cargo containment systems without secondary barriers, the temperature of the cargo tank is the design temperature.

[CGD 74–289, 44 FR 26009, May 3, 1979, as amended by CGD 82–063b, 48 FR 4782, Feb. 3, 1983; CGD 77–069, 52 FR 31630, Aug. 21, 1987]

§ 154.172 Contiguous steel hull structure.

(a) Except as allowed in paragraphs (b) and (c) of this section, plates, forgings, forged and rolled fittings, and rolled and forged bars and shapes used in the construction of the contiguous steel hull structure must meet the thickness and steel grade in Table 1 for the temperatures under §§ 154.174(b) and 154.176(b).

(b) for a minimum temperature, determined under §§ 154,174(b) and 154.176(b), below −25 °C (−13 °F), the contiguous steel hull structure must meet § 54.25–10 for that minimum temperature.

(c) If a steel grade that is not listed in Table 1 has the equivalent chemical properties, mechanical properties, and heat treatment of a steel grade that is listed, the steel grade not listed may be specially approved by the Commandant

§ 154.174

(CG–ENG), for use in the contiguous hull structure.

TABLE 1—MINIMUM TEMPERATURE, THICKNESS, AND STEEL GRADES IN CONTIGUOUS HULL STRUCTURES

Minimum temperature	Steel thickness	Steel[1] grade
0 °C (32 °F)	All	Standards of the American Bureau of Shipping published in "Rules for Building and Classing Steel Vessels", 1981
−10 °C (14 °F)	T≤112.5 mm (½ in.)	B
	12.5<t≤25.5 mm (1 in.)	D
	>25.5 mm (1 in.)	E
−25 °C (−13 °F)	t≤112.5 mm (½ in.)	D
	>12.5 mm (½ in.)	E

[1] Steel grade of the American Bureau of Shipping published in "Rules for Building and Classing Steel Vessels", 1981.

[CGD 74–289, 44 FR 26009, May 3, 1979, as amended by CGD 82–063b, 48 FR 4782, Feb. 3, 1983; CGD 77–069, 52 FR 31630, Aug. 21, 1987]

§ 154.174 Transverse contiguous hull structure.

(a) The transverse contiguous hull structure of a vessel having cargo containment systems without secondary barriers must meet the standards of the American Bureau of Shipping published in "Rules for Building and Classing Steel Vessels", 1981.

(b) The transverse contiguous hull structure of a vessel having cargo containment systems with secondary barriers must be designed for a temperature that is:

(1) Colder than the calculated temperature of this hull structure when:

(i) The temperature of the secondary barrier is the design temperature, and

(ii) The ambient cold condition under § 154.176(b)(1)(ii) and (iii) are assumed; or

(2) Maintained by the heating system under § 154.178.

[CGD 74–289, 44 FR 26009, May 3, 1979, as amended by CGD 77–069, 52 FR 31630, Aug. 21, 1987]

§ 154.176 Longitudinal contiguous hull structure.

(a) The longitudinal contiguous hull structure of a vessel having cargo containment systems without secondary barriers must meet the standards of the American Bureau of Shipping published in "Rules for Building and Classing Steel Vessels", 1981.

(b) The longitudinal contiguous hull structure of a vessel having cargo containment systems with secondary barriers must be designed for a temperature that is:

(1) Colder than the calculated temperature of this hull structure when:

(i) The temperature of the secondary barrier is the design temperature; and

(ii) For any waters in the world except Alaskan waters, the ambient cold condition of:

(A) Five knots air at −18 °C (0 °F); and

(B) Still sea water at 0 °C (32 °F); or

(iii) For Alaskan waters the ambient cold condition of:

(A) Five knots air at −29 °C (−20 °F); and

(B) Still sea water at −2 °C (28 °F); or

(2) Maintained by the heating system under § 154.178, if, without heat, the contiguous hull structure is designed for a temperature that is colder than the calculated temperature of the hull structure assuming the:

(i) Temperature of the secondary barrier is the design temperature; and

(ii) Ambient cold conditions of still air at 5 °C (41 °F) and still sea water at 0 °C (32 °F).

[CGD 74–289, 44 FR 26009, May 3, 1979, as amended by CGD 77–069, 52 FR 31630, Aug. 21, 1987]

§ 154.178 Contiguous hull structure: Heating system.

The heating system for transverse and longitudinal contiguous hull structure must:

(a) Be shown by a heat load calculation to have the heating capacity to meet § 154.174(b)(2) or § 154.176(b)(2);

(b) Have stand-by heating to provide 100% of the required heat load and distribution determined under paragraph (a); and

(c) Meet Parts 52, 53, and 54 of this chapter.

§ 154.180 Contiguous hull structure: Welding procedure.

Welding procedure tests for contiguous hull structure designed for a temperature colder than −18 °C (0 °F) must meet §54.05–15 and subpart 57.03 of this chapter.

§154.182 Contiguous hull structure: Production weld test.

If a portion of the contiguous hull structure is designed for a temperature colder than −34 °C (−30 °F) and is not part of the secondary barrier, each 100m (328 ft.) of full penetration butt welded joints in that portion of the contiguous hull structure must pass the following production weld tests in the position that the joint is welded:

(a) Bend tests under §57.06–4 of this chapter.

(b) A Charpy V-notch toughness test under §57.06–5 of this chapter on one set of 3 specimens alternating the notch location on successive tests between the center of the weld and the most critical location in the heat affected zone.[2]

(c) If the contiguous hull structure does not pass the test under paragraph (b) of this section, the retest procedures under §54.05–5(c) must be met.

§154.188 Membrane tank: Inner hull steel.

For a vessel with membrane tanks, the inner hull plating thickness must meet the deep tank requirements of the American Bureau of Shipping published in "Rules for Building and Classing Steel Vessels", 1981.

[CGD 74–289, 44 FR 26009, May 3, 1979, as amended by CGD 77–069, 52 FR 31630, Aug. 21, 1987]

§154.195 Aluminum cargo tank: Steel enclosure.

(a) An aluminum cargo tank and its dome must be enclosed by the vessel's hull structure or a separate steel cover.

(b) The steel cover for the aluminum cargo tank must meet the steel structural standards of the American Bureau of Shipping published in "Rules for Building and Classing Steel Vessels", 1981.

(c) The steel cover for the aluminum tank dome must be:

---
[2] The most critical location in the heat affected zone of the weld is based on procedure qualification results, except austenitic stainless steel need have notches only in the center of the weld.

(1) At least 3.2 mm (⅛ in.) thick;

(2) Separated from the tank dome, except at the support points; and

(3) Thermally isolated from the dome.

[CGD 74–289, 44 FR 26009, May 3, 1979, as amended by CGD 77–069, 52 FR 31630, Aug. 21, 1987]

SHIP SURVIVAL CAPABILITY AND CARGO TANK LOCATION

§154.200 Stability requirements: General.

Each vessel must meet the applicable requirements in subchapter S of this chapter.

[CGD 79–023, 48 FR 51009, Nov. 4, 1983]

§154.235 Cargo tank location.

(a) For type IG hulls, cargo tanks must be located inboard of:

(1) The transverse extent of damage for collision penetration specified in Table 172.180 of this chapter;

(2) The vertical extent of damage for grounding penetration specified in Table 172.180 of this chapter; and

(3) 30 inches (760 mm) from the shell plating.

(b) For type IIG, IIPG, and IIIG hulls, cargo tanks must be located inboard of:

(1) The vertical extent of damage for grounding penetration specified in Table 172.180 of this chapter; and

(2) 30 inches (760 mm) from the shell plating.

(c) In vessels having membrane and semi-membrane tanks, the vertical and transverse extents of damage must be measured to the inner hull.

(d) For type IIG, IIPG, and IIIG hulls, cargo tank suction wells may penetrate into the area of bottom damage specified as the vertical extent of damage for grounding penetration in Table 172.180 of this chapter if the penetration is the lesser of 25% of the double bottom height or 13.8 in. (350 mm).

[CGD 74–289, 44 FR 26009, May 3, 1979, as amended by CGD 79–023, 48 FR 51010, Nov. 4, 1983]

Ship Arrangements

§ 154.300 Segregation of hold spaces from other spaces.

Hold spaces must be segregated from machinery and boiler spaces, accommodation, service and control spaces, chain lockers, potable, domestic and feed water tanks, store rooms and spaces immediately below or outboard of hold spaces by a:

(a) Cofferdam, fuel oil tank, or single gastight A–60 Class Division of all welded construction in a cargo containment system not required by this part to have a secondary barrier;

(b) Cofferdam or fuel oil tank in a cargo containment system required by this part to have a secondary barrier; or

(c) If there are no sources of ignition or fire hazards in the adjoining space, single gastight A-O Class Division of all welded construction.

§ 154.305 Segregation of hold spaces from the sea.

In vessels having cargo containment systems required by this part to have a secondary barrier, hold spaces must be segregated from the sea by:

(a) A double bottom if the cargo tanks meet this part for design temperatures colder than $-10\ °C\ (14\ °F)$; and

(b) Wing tanks if the cargo tanks meet this part for design temperatures colder than $-55\ °C\ (-67\ °F)$.

§ 154.310 Cargo piping systems.

Cargo liquid or vapor piping must:

(a) Be separated from other piping systems, except where an interconnection to inert gas or purge piping is required by § 154.901(a);

(b) Not enter or pass through any accommodation, service, or control space;

(c) Except as allowed under § 154.703, not enter or pass through a machinery space other than a cargo pump or compressor room;

(d) Be in the cargo area except:

(1) As allowed under § 154.703;

(2) Bow and stern loading piping; and

(3) Emergency jettisoning piping.

(e) Be above the weather deck except:

(1) As allowed under § 154.703;

(2) Pipes in a trunk traversing void spaces above a cargo containment system; and

(3) Pipes for draining, venting, or purging interbarrier and hold spaces;

(f) Connect into the cargo containment system above the weather deck except:

(1) Pipes in a trunk traversing void spaces above a cargo containment system; and

(2) Pipes for draining, venting, or purging interbarrier and hold spaces.

(g) Be inboard of the transverse cargo tank location required by § 154.235, except for athwartship shore connection manifolds not subject to internal pressure at sea.

§ 154.315 Cargo pump and cargo compressor rooms.

(a) Cargo pump rooms and cargo compressor rooms must be above the weather deck and must be within the cargo area.

(b) Where pumps and compressors are driven by a prime mover in an adjacent gas safe space:

(1) The bulkhead or deck must be gastight; and

(2) The shafting passing through the bulkhead or deck must be sealed by a fixed oil reservoir gland seal, a pressure grease seal, or another type of positive pressure seal specially approved by the Commandant (CG–ENG).

[CGD 74–289, 44 FR 26009, May 3, 1979, as amended by CGD 82–063b, 48 FR 4782, Feb. 3, 1983]

§ 154.320 Cargo control stations.

(a) Cargo control stations must be above the weather deck.

(b) If a cargo control station is in accommodation, service, or control spaces or has access to such a space, the station must:

(1) Be a gas safe space;

(2) Have an access to the space that meets § 154.330; and

(3) Have indirect reading instrumentation, except for gas detectors.

(c) Cargo control stations, including a room or area, must contain all alarms, indicators, and remote controls associated with each cargo tank that the station controls.

§ 154.325 Accommodation, service, and control spaces.

(a) Accommodation, service, and control spaces must be outside the cargo area.

(b) If a hold space having a cargo containment system, required by this part to have a secondary barrier, is separated from any accommodation, service, or control space by a cruciform joint, there must be a cofferdam providing at least 760 mm (30 inches) by 760 mm (30 inches) clearance on one side of the cruciform joint.

§ 154.330 Openings to accommodation, service, or control spaces.

(a) Entrances, forced or natural ventilation intakes and exhausts, and other openings to accommodation, service, or control spaces, except as allowed in paragraph (c) of this section, must be:

(1) At least L/25 or 3.05m (10 ft) from the athwartship bulkhead facing the cargo area, whichever is farther, except that the distance need not exceed 5m (16.4 ft); and

(2) On a house athwartship bulkhead not facing the cargo area or on the outboard side of the house.

(b) Each port light, located on the athwartship bulkhead of a house facing the cargo area or the house sides within the distance specified in paragraph (a)(1) of this section, must be a fixed type.

(c) Wheelhouse doors and windows that are not fixed may be within the distance specified in paragraph (a)(1) of this section from the athwartship bulkhead of a house facing the cargo area, if they have gaskets and pass a tightness test with a fire hose at not less than 207 kPa gauge (30 psig).

(d) Port lights in the hull plating below the uppermost continuous deck and in the first tier of the superstructure must be a fixed type.

(e) Air intakes and openings into accommodation, service, and control spaces must have metal closures that pass a tightness test with a fire hose at not less than 207 kPa gauge (30 psig).

(f) On liquefied toxic gas vessels, the closures required in paragraph (e) of this section must be capable of being closed from inside the space.

§ 154.340 Access to tanks and spaces in the cargo area.

(a) Each cargo tank must have a manhole from the weather deck, the clear opening of which is at least 600 mm by 600 mm (23.6 in. by 23.6 in.).

(b) Each access into and through a void space or other gas-dangerous space in the cargo area, except spaces described in paragraph (e) of the definition for "gas-dangerous space" in §154.7, must—

(1) Have a clear opening of at least 600 mm by 600 mm (23.6 in. by 23.6 in.) through horizontal openings, hatches, or manholes;

(2) Have a clear opening of at least 600 mm by 800 mm (23.6 in. by 31.5 in.) through bulkheads, frames or other vertical structural members; and

(3) Have a fixed ladder if the lower edge of a vertical opening is more than 600 mm (23.6 in.) above the deck or bottom plating.

(c) Each access trunk in the cargo area must be at least 760 mm (30 in.) in diameter.

(d) The lower edge of each access from the weather deck to gas-safe spaces in the cargo area must be at least 2.4 m (7.9 ft.) above the weather deck or the access must be through an air lock that meets §154.345.

(e) The inner hull in the cargo area must be accessible for inspection from at least one side without the removal of any fixed structure or fitting.

(f) The hold space insulation in the cargo area must be accessible for inspection from at least one side from within the hold space or there must be a means, that is specially approved by the Commandant, of determining from outside the hold space whether or not the hold space insulation meets this part.

[CGD 74–289, 44 FR 26009, May 3, 1979, as amended by CGD 77–069, 52 FR 31630, Aug. 21, 1987]

§ 154.345 Air locks.

(a) An air lock may be used for access from a gas-dangerous zone on the weather deck to a gas-safe space.

(b) Each air lock must:

(1) Consist of two steel doors, at least 1.5 m (4.9 ft.) but not more than 2.5 m (8.2 ft.) apart, each gasketed and tight

§ 154.350

when tested with a fire hose at not less 207 kPa gauge (30 psig);

(2) Have self-closing doors with no latches or other devices for holding them open;

(3) Have an audible and visual alarm on both sides which are actuated when both door securing devices are in other than the fully closed position at the same time;

(4) Have mechanical ventilation in the space between the doors from a gas-safe area;

(5) Have a pressure greater than that of the gas-dangerous area on the weather deck;

(6) Have the rate of air change in the space between the doors of at least 8 changes per hour; and

(7) Have the space between the doors monitored for cargo vapor leaks under § 154.1350.

(c) In addition to the requirements of paragraphs (a) and (b) of this section, no gas-safe space on a liquefied flammable gas carrier may have an air lock unless the space:

(1) Is mechanically ventilated to make the pressure in the space greater than that in the air lock; and

(2) Has a means of automatically de-energizing all electrical equipment that is not explosion-proof in the space when the pressure in the space falls to or below the pressure in the air lock.

§ 154.350 Bilge and ballast systems in the cargo area.

(a) Hold, interbarrier, and insulation spaces must have a means of sounding the space or other means of detecting liquid leakage specially approved by the Commandant (CG-ENG).

(b) Each hold and insulation space must have a bilge drainage system.

(c) Interbarrier spaces must have an eductor or pump for removing liquid cargo and returning it to the cargo tanks or to an emergency jettisoning system meeting § 154.356.

(d) Spaces in the cargo containment portion of the vessel, except ballast spaces and gas-safe spaces, must not connect to pumps in the main machinery space.

[CGD 74–289, 44 FR 26009, May 3, 1979, as amended by CGD 82–063b, 48 FR 4782, Feb. 3, 1983]

§ 154.355 Bow and stern loading piping.

(a) Bow and stern loading piping must:

(1) Meet § 154.310;

(2) Be installed in an area away from the accommodation, service, or control space on type IG hulls;

(3) Be clearly marked;

(4) Be segregated from the cargo piping by a removable spool piece in the cargo area or by at least two shut-off valves in the cargo area that have means of locking to meet § 154.1870(a);

(5) Have a means for checking for cargo vapor between the two valves under paragraph (a)(4) of this section;

(6) Have fixed inert gas purging lines; and

(7) Have fixed vent lines for purging with inert gas to meet § 154.1870(b).

(b) Entrances, forced or natural ventilation intakes, exhausts, and other openings to accommodation, service, or control spaces that face the bow or stern loading area must meet § 154.330.

§ 154.356 Cargo emergency jettisoning piping.

Emergency jettisoning piping must:

(a) Meet § 154.355(a);

(b) Be designed to allow cargo discharge without the outer hull steel temperature falling below the minimum temperatures under §§ 154.170 and 154.172; and

(c) Be specially approved by the Commandant (CG-ENG).

[CGD 74–289, 44 FR 26009, May 3, 1979, as amended by CGD 82–063b, 48 FR 4782, Feb. 3, 1983]

CARGO CONTAINMENT SYSTEMS

§ 154.401 Definitions.

As used in §§ 154.440 and 154.447:

"σ_Y" means the minimum yield strength of the tank material, including weld metal, at room temperature.

"σ_B" means minimum tensile strength of the tank material, including weld metals, at room temperature.

§ 154.405 Design vapor pressure (P_o) of a cargo tank.

(a) The design vapor pressure (P_o) of a cargo tank must be equal to or greater than the MARVS.

Coast Guard, DHS § 154.407

(b) The P_o of a cargo tank must be equal to or greater than the vapor pressure of the cargo at 45 °C (113 °F) if:

(1) The cargo tank has no temperature control for the cargo; and

(2) The vapor pressure of the cargo results solely from ambient temperature.

(c) The P_o of a cargo tank may be exceeded under harbor conditions if specially approved by the Commandant (CG–ENG).

[CGD 74–289, 44 FR 26009, May 3, 1979, as amended by CGD 82–063b, 48 FR 4782, Feb. 3, 1983]

§ 154.406 Design loads for cargo tanks and fixtures: General.

(a) Calculations must show that a cargo tank and its fixtures are designed for the following loads:

(1) Internal pressure head.

(2) External pressure load.

(3) Dynamic loads resulting from the motion of the vessel.

(4) Transient or stationary thermal loads if the design temperature is colder that −55 °C (−67 °F) or causes thermal stresses in cargo tank supports.

(5) Sloshing loads, if the cargo tank is designed for partial loads.

(6) Loads resulting from vessel's deflection.

(7) Tank weight, cargo weight, and corresponding support reaction.

(8) Insulation weight.

(9) Loads of a pipe tower and any other attachments to the cargo tank.

(10) Vapor pressure loads in harbor conditions allowed under § 154.405.

(11) Gas pressurization if the cargo tank is designed for gas pressurization as a means of cargo transfer.

(b) A cargo tank must be designed for the most unfavorable static heel angle within a 0° to 30° range without exceeding the allowable stress of the material.

(c) A hydrostatic or hydropneumatic test design load must be specially approved by the Commandant (CG–ENG).

[CGD 74–289, 44 FR 26009, May 3, 1979, as amended by CGD 82–063b, 48 FR 4782, Feb. 3, 1983]

§ 154.407 Cargo tank internal pressure head.

(a) For the calculation required under § 154.406(a)(1) and (b), the internal pressure head (h_{eq}), must be determined from the following formula:

$h_{eq} = 10\ P_o + (h_{gd})_{max}$

where:

h_{gd} (the value of internal pressure, in meters of fresh water, resulting from the combined effects of gravity and dynamic accelerations of a full tank) = $a\beta\ Z\beta\ Y$;

where:

$a\beta$ = dimensionless acceleration relative to the acceleration of gravity resulting from gravitational and dynamic loads in the β direction (see figure 1);

$Z\beta$ = largest liquid height (m) above the point where the pressure is to be determined in the β direction (see figure 2);

Y = maximum specific weight of the cargo (t/m³) at the design temperature.

§ 154.407

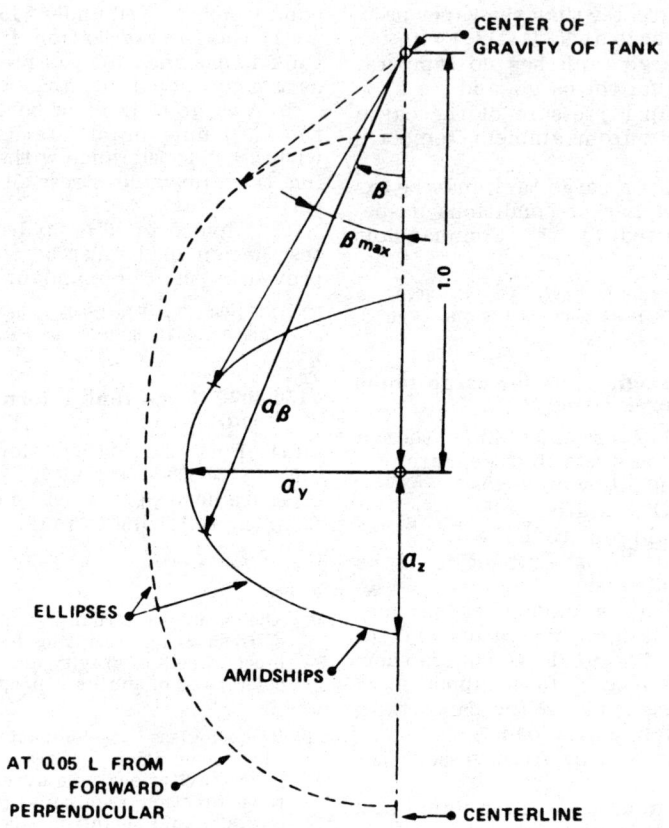

NOTE: RESULTING ACCELERATION (STATIC + DYNAMIC) = a_β IN ARBITRARY DIRECTION β.

a_y = TRANSVERSE COMPONENT OF ACCELERATION.

a_z = VERTICAL COMPONENT OF ACCELERATION.

Figure 1. Acceleration Ellipse

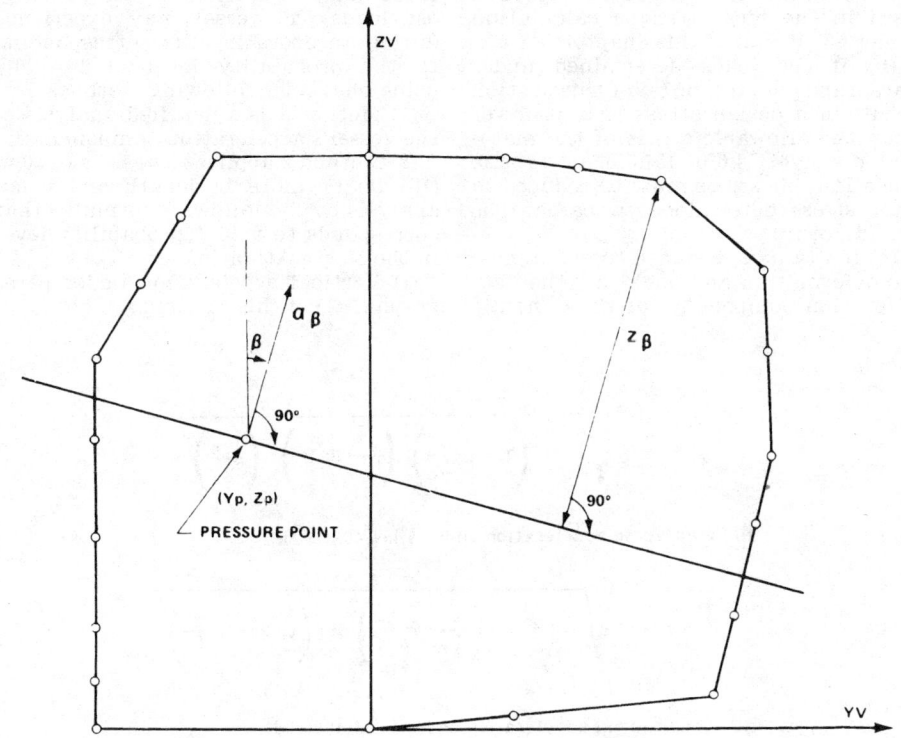

NOTE: LARGEST LIQUID HEIGHT ABOVE THE POINT WHERE THE PRESSURE IS DETERMINED = Z_β

Figure 2. Determination of Internal Pressure Heads

(b) The $(h_{gd})_{max}$ is determined for the β direction, on the ellipse in Figure 1, which gives the maximum value for h_{gd}.

(c) When the longitudinal acceleration is considered in addition to the vertical transverse acceleration, an ellipsoid must be used in the calculations instead of the ellipse contained in Figure 1.

§ 154.408 Cargo tank external pressure load.

For the calculation required under § 154.406 (a)(2) and (b), the external pressure load must be the difference between the minimum internal pressure (maximum vacuum), and the maximum external pressure to which any portion of the cargo tank may be simultaneously subjected.

§ 154.409 Dynamic loads from vessel motion.

(a) For the calculation required under § 154.406 (a)(3) and (b), the dynamic loads must be determined from the long term distribution of vessel motions, including the effects of surge, sway, heave, roll, pitch, and yaw on irregular seas that the vessel may experience during 10^8 wave encounters. The speed used for this calculation may be reduced from the ship service speed if specially approved by the Commandant

§ 154.409

(CG-ENG) and if that reduced speed is used in the hull strength calculation under § 31.10-5(c) of this chapter.

(b) If the loads determined under paragraphs (c), (d), or (e) of this section result in a design stress that is lower than the allowable stress of the material under §§ 154.610, 154.615, or 154.620, the allowable stress must be reduced to that stress determined in paragraphs (c), (d), or (e).

(c) If a tank is designed to avoid plastic deformation and buckling, then acceleration components of the dynamic loads must be determined for the largest loads the vessel may experience during an operating life corresponding to the probability level of 10^{-8} by using one of the following methods:

(1) Method 1 is a detailed analysis of the vessel's acceleration components.

(2) Method 2 applies to vessels of 50 m (164 ft) or more in length and is an analysis by the following formulae that corresponds to a 10^{-8} probability level in the North Atlantic:

(i) Vertical acceleration under paragraph (f)(1) of this section:

$$a_z = \pm a_0 \sqrt{1 + \left(5.3 - \frac{45}{L_0}\right)^2 \left(\frac{x}{L_0} + 0.05\right)^2 \left(\frac{0.6}{C_B}\right)^{3/2}}$$

(ii) Transverse acceleration under § 154.409(f)(2):

$$a_y = \pm a_0 \sqrt{0.6 + 2.5 \left(\frac{x}{L_0} + 0.05\right)^2 + K\left(1 + 0.6K\frac{z}{B}\right)^2}$$

(iii) Longitudinal acceleration under § 154.409(f)(3):

$$a_x = \pm a_0 \sqrt{0.06 + A^2} - 0.25A$$

where:

$$A = \left(0.7 - \frac{L_0}{1200} + 5\frac{z}{L_0}\right)\left(\frac{0.6}{C_B}\right)$$

L_0 = the distance in meters on the estimated summer loadline, from the fore side of the stem to the after side of the rudder-post or sternpost; where there is no rudderpost or sternpost, L_0 is to be measured to the centerline of the rudder stock, but in any case

L_o is not to be less than 96% and need not be greater than 97% of the length on the summer loadline.

C_B = block coefficent.

B = greatest moulded breadth, in meters.

x = longitudinal distance, in meters, from amidships to the center of gravity of the tank with contents (positive - forward of amidships. negative - aft of amidships).

z = vertical distance in meters, from the vessel's waterline, to center of gravity of tank with contents (positive - above, and negative - below the waterline).

$$a_o = 0.2 \frac{V}{\sqrt{L_o}} + \frac{34-(600/L_o)}{L_o}$$

V = service speed in knots.

K = 1.00 OR $\frac{13GM}{B}$, whichever is greater.

GM = metacentric height in meters.

a_x = the maximum dimensionless acceleration in the x direction, acting separately for calculation purposes, and includes the component of the static weight in the longitudinal direction due to pitching.

a_y = maximum dimensionless acceleration in the y direction, acting separately for calculation purposes, and includes the component of static weight in the transverse direction due to rolling.

a_z = maximum dimensionless acceleration in the z direction, acting separately for calculation purposes, not including the static weight.

(d) If a cargo tank is designed to avoid fatigue, the dynamic loads determined under paragraph (a) of this section must be used to develop the dynamic spectrum.

§ 154.409

(e) If a cargo tank is designed to avoid uncontrolled crack propagation, the dynamic loads are:
(1) Determined under paragraph (a) of this section; and
(2) For a load distribution for a period of 15 days by the method in Figure 3.

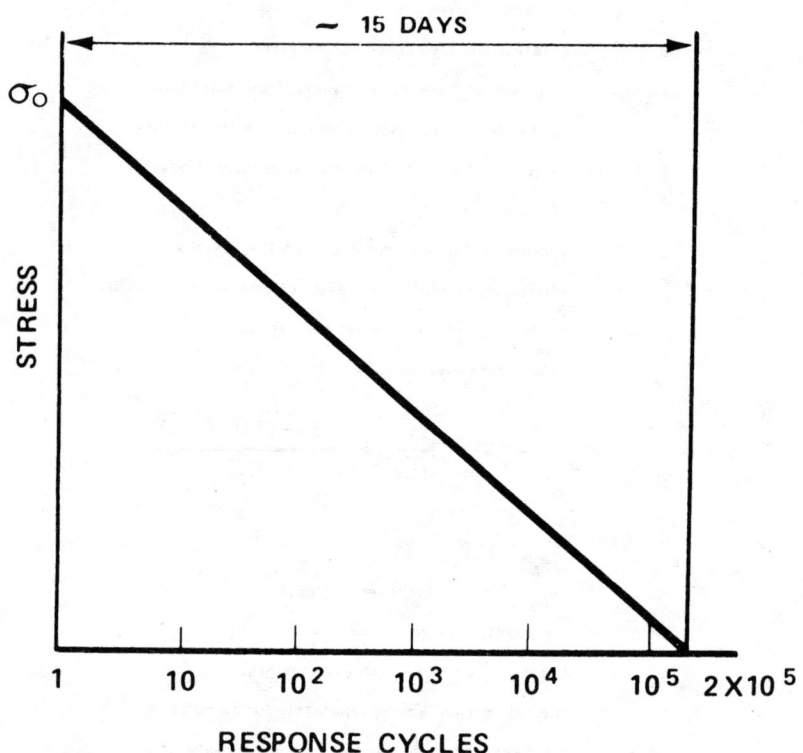

NOTE: σ_O = MOST PROBABLE MAXIMUM STRESS DURING THE LIFE OF THE VESSEL.

RESPONSE CYCLE SCALE IS LOGARITHMIC.

THE VALUE OF 2×10^5 IS GIVEN AS AN EXAMPLE OF ESTIMATE.

Figure 3. Simplified Load Distribution

(f) When determining the accelerations for dynamic loads under paragraph (a) of this section, the accelerations acting in a cargo tank must be estimated for the cargo tank's center of gravity and include the following component accelerations:

(1) Vertical accelerations, meaning the motion acceleration of heave and pitch, and of any roll normal to the vessel base that has an effect on the component acceleration.

(2) Transverse acceleration, meaning the motion acceleration of sway, yaw and roll, and gravity component of roll.

(3) Longitudinal acceleration, meaning the motion acceleration of surge and pitch and gravity component of pitch.

[CGD 74–289, 44 FR 26009, May 3, 1979, as amended by CGD 82–063b, 48 FR 4782, Feb. 3, 1983]

§ 154.410 Cargo tank sloshing loads.

(a) For the calculation required under § 154.406 (a)(5) and (b), the determined sloshing loads resulting from the accelerations under § 154.409(f) must be specially approved by the Commandant (CG–ENG).

(b) If the sloshing loads affect the cargo tank scantlings, an analysis of the effects of the sloshing loads in addition to the calculation under paragraph (a) of this section must be specially approved by the Commandant (CG–ENG).

[CGD 74–289, 44 FR 26009, May 3, 1979, as amended by CGD 82–063b, 48 FR 4782, Feb. 3, 1983]

§ 154.411 Cargo tank thermal loads.

For the calculations required under § 154.406(a)(4), the following determined loads must be specially approved by the Commandant (CG–ENG):

(a) Transient thermal loads for the cooling down periods of cargo tanks for design temperatures lower than −55 °C (−67 °F).

(b) Stationary thermal loads for cargo tanks for design temperatures lower than −55 °C (−67 °F) that cause high thermal stress.

[CGD 74–289, 44 FR 26009, May 3, 1979, as amended by CGD 82–063b, 48 FR 4782, Feb. 3, 1983]

§ 154.412 Cargo tank corrosion allowance.

A cargo tank must be designed with a corrosion allowance if the cargo tank:

(a) is located in a space that does not have inert gas or dry air; or

(b) carries a cargo that corrodes the tank material.

NOTE: Corrosion allowance for independent tank type C is contained in § 54.01–35 of this chapter.

INTEGRAL TANKS

§ 154.418 General.

An integral tank must not be designed for a temperature colder than −10 °C (14 °F), unless the tank is specially approved by the Commandant (CG–ENG).

[CGD 74–289, 44 FR 26009, May 3, 1979, as amended by CGD 82–063b, 48 FR 4782, Feb. 3, 1983]

§ 154.419 Design vapor pressure.

The P_o of an integral tank must not exceed 24.5 kPa gauge (3.55 psig) unless special approval by the Commandant (CG–ENG) allows a P_o between 24.5 kPa gauge (3.55 psig) and 69 kPa gauge (10 psig).

[CGD 74–289, 44 FR 26009, May 3, 1979, as amended by CGD 82–063b, 48 FR 4782, Feb. 3, 1983]

§ 154.420 Tank design.

(a) The structure of an integral tank must meet the deep tank scantling standards of the American Bureau of Shipping published in "Rules for Building and Classing Steel Vessels", 1981.

(b) The structure of an integral tank must be designed and shown by calculation to withstand the internal pressure determined under § 154.407.

[CGD 74–289, 44 FR 26009, May 3, 1979, as amended by CGD 77–069, 52 FR 31630, Aug. 21, 1987]

§ 154.421 Allowable stress.

The allowable stress for the integral tank structure must meet the American Bureau of Shipping's allowable stress for the vessel's hull published in

§ 154.425

"Rules for Building and Classing Steel Vessels", 1981.

[CGD 74–289, 44 FR 26009, May 3, 1979, as amended by CGD 77–069, 52 FR 31630, Aug. 21, 1987]

MEMBRANE TANKS

§ 154.425 General.

The design of the hull structure and the design of the membrane tank system, that includes the membrane tank, secondary barrier, including welds, the supporting insulation, and pressure control equipment, must be specially approved by the Commandant (CG–ENG).

[CGD 74–289, 44 FR 26009, May 3, 1979, as amended by CGD 82–063b, 48 FR 4782, Feb. 3, 1983]

§ 154.426 Design vapor pressure.

The P_o of a membrane tank must not exceed 24.5 kPa gauge (3.55 psig) unless special approval by the Commandant (CG–ENG) allows a P_o between 24.5 kPa gauge (3.55 psig) and 69 kPa gauge (10 psig).

[CGD 74–289, 44 FR 26009, May 3, 1979, as amended by CGD 82–063b, 48 FR 4782, Feb. 3, 1983]

§ 154.427 Membrane tank system design.

A membrane tank system must be designed for:

(a) Any static and dynamic loads with respect to plastic deformation and fatigue;

(b) Combined strains from static, dynamic, and thermal loads;

(c) Preventing collapse of the membrane from:

(1) Over-pressure in the interbarrier space;

(2) Vacuum in the cargo tank;

(3) Sloshing in a partially filled cargo tank; and

(4) Hull vibrations; and

(d) The deflections of the vessel's hull.

§ 154.428 Allowable stress.

The membrane tank and the supporting insulation must have allowable stresses that are specially approved by the Commandant (CG–ENG).

[CGD 74–289, 44 FR 26009, May 3, 1979, as amended by CGD 82–063b, 48 FR 4782, Feb. 3, 1983]

§ 154.429 Calculations.

The tank design load calculations for a membrane tank must include the following:

(a) Plastic deformation and fatigue life resulting from static and dynamic loads in the membrane and the supporting insulation.

(b) The response of the membrane and its supporting insulation to vessel motion and acceleration under the worst weather conditions. Calculations from a similar vessel may be submitted to meet this paragraph.

(c) The combined strains from static, dynamic, and thermal loads.

§ 154.430 Material test.

(a) The membrane and the membrane supporting insulation must be made of materials that withstand the combined strains calculated under § 154.429(c).

(b) Analyzed data of a material test for the membrane and the membrane supporting insulation must be submitted to the Commandant (CG–ENG).

[CGD 74–289, 44 FR 26009, May 3, 1979, as amended by CGD 82–063b, 48 FR 4782, Feb. 3, 1983]

§ 154.431 Model test.

(a) The primary and secondary barrier of a membrane tank, including the corners and joints, must withstand the combined strains from static, dynamic, and thermal loads calculated under § 154.429(c).

(b) Analyzed data of a model test for the primary and secondary barrier of the membrane tank must be submitted to the Commandant (CG–ENG).

[CGD 74–289, 44 FR 26009, May 3, 1979, as amended by CGD 82–063b, 48 FR 4782, Feb. 3, 1983]

§ 154.432 Expansion and contraction.

The support system of a membrane tank must allow for thermal and physical expansion and contraction of the tank.

Semi-Membrane Tanks

§ 154.435 General.

(a) The design of a semi-membrane tank, the supporting insulation for the tank, and the supporting hull structure for the tank must be specially approved by the Commandant (CG-ENG).

(b) A semi-membrane tank must be designed to meet:

(1) § 154.425 through § 154.432;
(2) § 154.437 through § 154.440; or
(3) § 154.444 through § 154.449.

[CGD 74–289, 44 FR 26009, May 3, 1979, as amended by CGD 82–063b, 48 FR 4782, Feb. 3, 1983]

§ 154.436 Design vapor pressure.

The P_o of a semi-membrane tank must not exceed 24.5 kPa gauge (3.55 psig) unless special approval by the Commandant (CG-ENG) allows a P_o between 24.5 kPa gauge (3.55 psig) and 69 kPa gauge (10 psig).

[CGD 74–289, 44 FR 26009, May 3, 1979, as amended by CGD 82–063b, 48 FR 4782, Feb. 3, 1983]

Independent Tank Type A

§ 154.437 General.

An independent tank type A must meet § 154.438 through § 154.440.

§ 154.438 Design vapor pressure.

(a) If the surface of an independent tank type A are mostly flat surfaces, the P_o must not exceed 69 kPa gauge (10 psig).

(b) If the surfaces of an independent tank type A are formed by bodies of revolution, the design calculation of the P_o must be specially approved by the Commandant (CG-ENG).

[CGD 74–289, 44 FR 26009, May 3, 1979, as amended by CGD 82–063b, 48 FR 4782, Feb. 3, 1983]

§ 154.439 Tank design.

An independent tank type A must meet the deep tank standard of the American Bureau of Shipping published in "Rules for Building and Classing Steel Vessels", 1981, and must:

(a) Withstand the internal pressure determined under § 154.407;

(b) Withstand loads from tank supports calculated under §§ 154.470 and 154.471; and

(c) Have a corrosion allowance that meets § 154.412.

[CGD 74–289, 44 FR 26009, May 3, 1979, as amended by CGD 77–069, 52 FR 31630, Aug. 21, 1987]

§ 154.440 Allowable stress.

(a) The allowable stresses for an independent tank type A must:

(1) For tank web frames, stringers, or girders of carbon manganese steel or aluminum alloys, meet $\sigma_B/2.66$ or $\sigma_Y/1.33$, whichever is less; and

(2) For other materials, be specially approved by the Commandant (CG-ENG).

(b) A greater allowable stress than required in paragraph (a)(1) of this section may be specially approved by the Commandant (CG-ENG) if the equivalent stress (σ_c) is calculated from the formula in appendix A of this part.

(c) Tank plating must meet the American Bureau of Shipping's deep tank standards, for an internal pressure head that meets § 154.439(a), published in "Rules for Building and Classing Steel Vessels", 1981.

[CGD 74–289, 44 FR 26009, May 3, 1979, as amended by CGD 82–063b, 48 FR 4782, Feb. 3, 1983; CGD 77–069, 52 FR 31630, Aug. 21, 1987]

Independent Tank Type B

§ 154.444 General.

An independent tank type B must be designed to meet §§ 154.445 through 154.449.

§ 154.445 Design vapor pressure.

If the surfaces of an independent tank type B are mostly flat surfaces, the P_o must not exceed 69 kPa gauge (10 psig).

§ 154.446 Tank design.

An independent tank type B must meet the calculations under § 154.448.

§ 154.447 Allowable stress.

(a) An independent tank type B designed from bodies of revolution must

§ 154.448

have allowable stresses[3] determined by the following formulae:

$\sigma_m \leq f$

$\sigma_L \leq 1.5\ f$

$\sigma_b \leq 1.5\ F$

$\sigma_L + \sigma_b \leq 1.5\ F$

$\sigma_m + \sigma_b \leq 1.5\ F$

where:

σ_m = equivalent primary general membrane stress[4]

σ_L = equivalent primary local membrane stress[4]

σ_b = equivalent primary bending stress[4]

f = the lesser of (σ_B/A) or (σ_Y/B)

F = the lesser of (σ_B/C) or (σ_Y/D)

A, B, C, and D = stress factors in Table 2.

TABLE 2—VALUES FOR STRESS FACTORS

Stress factors:	Nickel steel and carbon manganese steel values	Austenitic steel values	Aluminum alloy values
A	4.0	4.0	4.0
B	2.0	1.6	1.5
C	3.0	3.0	3.0
D	1.5	1.5	1.5

(b) An independent tank type B designed from plane surfaces must have allowable stresses specially approved by the Commandant (CG–ENG).

[CGD 74–289, 44 FR 26009, May 3, 1979, as amended by CGD 82–063b, 48 FR 4782, Feb. 3, 1983]

§ 154.448 Calculations.

The following calculations for an independent tank type B must be specially approved by the Commandant (CG–ENG):

(a) Plastic deformation, fatigue life, buckling, and crack propagation resulting from static and dynamic loads on the tank and its support.

(b) A three-dimensional analysis of the stress exerted by the hull on the tank, its support, and its keys.

(c) The response of the tank and its support to the vessel's motion and acceleration in irregular waves or calculations from a similar vessel.

(d) A tank buckling analysis considering the maximum construction tolerance.

---

[3] See Appendix B for stress analyses definitions.

[4] See Appendix A for equivalent stress.

(e) A finite element analysis using the loads determined under § 154.406.

(f) A fracture mechanics analysis using the loads determined under § 154.406.

(g) The cumulative effects of the fatigue load from the following formula:

$$\sum \frac{n_1}{N_1} + \frac{10^3}{N_j} \leq C_w$$

where:

n_i = the number of stress cycles at each stress level during the life of the vessel;

N_i = the number of cycles to failure for corresponding stress levels from the Wohler (S-N) curve;

N_j = the number of cycles to failure from the fatigue load by loading and unloading the tank; and

C_w = 0.5 or less. A C_w of greater than 0.5 but not exceeding 1.0 may be specially approved by the Commandant (G-MTH).

[CGD 74–289, 44 FR 26009, May 3, 1979, as amended by CGD 82–063b, 48 FR 4782, Feb. 3, 1983]

§ 154.449 Model test.

The following analyzed data of a model test of structural elements for independent tank type B must be submitted to the Commandant (CG–ENG) for special approval:

(a) Stress concentration factors.

(b) Fatigue life.

[CGD 74–289, 44 FR 26009, May 3, 1979, as amended by CGD 82–063b, 48 FR 4782, Feb. 3, 1983]

INDEPENDENT TANK TYPE C AND PROCESS PRESSURE VESSELS

§ 154.450 General.

Independent tanks type C and process pressure vessels must be designed to meet the requirements under Part 54 of this chapter, except § 54.01–40(b), and:

(a) The calculation under § 54.01–18 (b)(1) must also include the design loads determined under § 154.406;

(b) The calculated tank plating thickness, including any corrosion allowance, must be the minimum thickness without a negative plate tolerance; and

(c) The minimum tank plating thickness must not be less than:

(1) 5mm (3/16 in.) for carbon-manganese steel and nickel steel;

(2) 3mm (⅛ in.) for austenitic steels; or

(3) 7mm (9/32 in.) for aluminum alloys.

§ 154.451 Design vapor pressure.

The P_o (kPa) of an independent tank type C must be calculated by the following formula:

$$P_o = 196 + AC(\rho)^{3/2}$$

where:

$A = 1.813 \, (\sigma_m/\Delta\sigma_A)^2$;
σ_m = design primary membrane stress;
$\Delta\sigma_A$ = (allowable dynamic membrane stress for double amplitude at probability level $Q=10^{-8}$) 53.9 MPa (7821 psi) for ferritic and martensitic steels and 24.5 MPa (3555 psi) for 5083-0 aluminum;
C = a characteristic tank dimension that is the greatest of h, 0.75b, or 0.45 l;

where:

h = the height of the tank or the dimension in the vessel's vertical direction, in meters;
b = the width of the tank or the dimension in the vessel's transverse direction; in meters; and
l = the length of the tank or the dimension in the vessel's longitudinal direction, in meters; and
ρ = the specific gravity of the cargo.

§ 154.452 External pressure.

The design external pressure, P_e, for an independent tank type C must be calculated by the following formula:

$$P_e = P_1 + P_2 + P_3 + P_4$$

where:

P_1 = the vacuum relief valve setting for tanks with a vacuum relief valve, or 24.5 kPa gauge (3.55 psig) for tanks without a vacuum relief valve.
P_2 = 0, or the pressure relief valve setting for an enclosed space containing any portion of a pressure vessel.
P_3 = total compressive load in the tank shell from the weight of the tank, including corrosion allowance, weight of insulation, weight of dome, weight of pipe tower and piping, the effect of the partially filled tank, the effect of acceleration and hull deflection, and the local effect of external and internal pressure.
P_4 = 0, or the external pressure from the head of water from any portion of the pressure vessel on exposed decks.

§ 154.453 Failure to meet independent tank type C standards.

If the Commandant (CG–ENG) determines during plan review, that a tank designed as an independent tank type C fails to meet the standards under § 154.450, § 154.451, and 154.452 and can not be redesigned to meet those standards, the tank may be redesigned as an independent tank type A or B.

[CGD 74–289, 44 FR 26009, May 3, 1979, as amended by CGD 82–063b, 48 FR 4782, Feb. 3, 1983]

SECONDARY BARRIER

§ 154.459 General.

(a) Each cargo tank must have a secondary barrier that meets Table 3 and except as allowed in Table 3, the hull must not be the secondary barrier.

(b) If the Commandant (CG–ENG) specially approves an integral tank for a design temperature at atmospheric pressure lower than −10 °C (14 °F), the integral tank must have a complete secondary barrier that meets § 154.460.

(c) If the Commandant (CG–ENG) specially approves a semi-membrane tank under the requirements of an independent tank type B, the semi-membrane tank may have a partial secondary barrier specially approved by the Commandant (CG–ENG).

(d) If Table 3 allows the hull to be a secondary barrier, the vessel's hull must:

(1) Meet §§ 154.605 through 154.630; and

(2) Be designed for the stresses resulting from the design temperature.

TABLE 3—SECONDARY BARRIERS FOR TANKS

Tank type	Cargo temperature (T) at atmospheric pressure		
	T ≥ −10 °C (14 °F)	T < −10 °C (14 °F) ≥ 55 °C (−67 °F)	T < −55 °C (−67 °F)
Integral	No secondary barrier required	Tank type not usually allowed [1]	Tank type not allowed.
Membrane	......do	Complete secondary barrier [1]	Complete secondary barrier.
Semi-membrane	......do	......do	Do.
Independent:			
Type A	......do	......do	Do.
Type B	......do	Partial secondary barrier [1]	Partial secondary barrier.
Type C	......do	No secondary barrier required	No secondary barrier required.

[1] The hull may be a secondary barrier.

(14 U.S.C. 632; 46 U.S.C. 369, 375, and 416; 49 U.S.C. 1655(b); 49 CFR 1.46(b))

[CGD 74–289, 44 FR 26009, May 3, 1979, as amended by CGD 82–063b, 48 FR 4782, Feb. 3, 1983]

§ 154.460 Design criteria.

At static angles of heel up through 30°, a secondary barrier must

(a) If a complete secondary barrier is required in § 154.459, hold all of the liquid cargo in the cargo tank for at least 15 days under the dynamic loads in § 154.409(e);

(b) If a partial secondary barrier is permitted in § 154.459, hold any leakage of liquid cargo corresponding to the extent of failure under § 154.448(a) after initial detection or primary barrier leak for at least 15 days under the dynamic loads in § 154.409(e);

(c) If the primary barrier fails, prevent the temperature of the vessel's structure from falling below the minimum allowable service temperature of the steel; and

(d) Be designed so that a cargo tank failure does not cause a failure in the secondary barrier.

INSULATION

§ 154.465 General.

If the design temperature is below −10 °C (14 °F), the cargo tank insulation must prevent the temperature of the vessel's hull from cooling below the minimum temperature allowed under § 154.172.

§ 154.466 Design criteria.

(a) The insulation for a cargo tank without a secondary barrier must be designed for the cargo tank at the design temperature, and for a vessel operating in:

(1) Any waters in the world, except Alaskan waters, for the ambient cold condition of:

(i) Five knots air at −18 °C (0 °F); and

(ii) Still sea water at 0 °C (32 °F); or

(2) Alaskan waters for the ambient cold condition of:

(i) Five knots air at −29 °C (20 °F); and

(ii) Still sea water at −2 °C (28 °F).

(b) The insulation for a cargo tank with a secondary barrier must be designed for the secondary barrier at the design temperature, and the ambient cold conditions listed under paragraph (a)(1) or paragraph (a)(2) of this section.

(c) The insulation material must be designed for any loads transmitted from adjacent hull structure.

(d) Insulation for cargo tank and piping must meet § 38.05–20 of this chapter.

(e) Powder or granulated insulation must:

(1) Not compact from vibrations of the vessel;

(2) Maintain the thermal conductivity listed under § 154.467; and

(3) Not exert a static pressure greater than the external design pressure of the cargo tank under § 154.408.

§ 154.467 Submission of insulation information.

The following insulation information must be submitted for special approval by the Commandant (CG–ENG):

(a) Compatibility with the cargo.

(b) Solubility in the cargo.

(c) Absorption of the cargo.

(d) Shrinkage.

(e) Aging.

(f) Closed cell content.

(g) Density.

(h) Mechanical properties.

(i) Thermal expansion.

(j) Abrasion.

(k) Cohesion.

(l) Thermal conductivity.

(m) Resistance to vibrations.

(n) Resistance to fire and flame spread.

(o) The manufacturing and installation details of the insulation including:

(1) Fabrication;

(2) Storage;

(3) Handling;

(4) Erection; and

(5) Quality control.

[CGD 74–289, 44 FR 26009, May 3, 1979, as amended by CGD 82–063b, 48 FR 4782, Feb. 3, 1983]

SUPPORT SYSTEM

§ 154.470 General.

(a) A cargo tank must have a support system that:

(1) prevents movement of the cargo tank under the static and dynamic loads in § 154.406; and

(2) allows the cargo tank to contract and expand from temperature variation and hull deflection without exceeding the design stress of the cargo tank and the hull.

(b) The cargo tank support system must have a key that prevents rotation of the cargo tank.

(c) An independent tank must have supports with an antiflotation system that withstands the upward force of the tank without causing plastic deformation that endangers the hull structure when the tank is:

(1) Empty; and

(2) In a hold space flooded to the summer load draft of the vessel.

§ 154.471 Design criteria.

(a) The cargo tank support system must be designed:

(1) For the loads in § 154.406(a);

(2) To not exceed the allowable stress under this part at a static angle of heel of 30°;

(3) To withstand a collision force equal to at least one-half the weight of the cargo tank and cargo from forward and one-quarter the weight of the cargo tank and cargo from aft; and

(4) For the largest resulting acceleration in Figure 1, including rotational and translation effects.

(b) The cargo tank support design loads in paragraph (a) of this section may be analyzed separately.

§ 154.476 Cargo transfer devices and means.

(a) If a cargo pump in a cargo tank is not accessible for repair when the cargo tank is in use, the cargo tank must have an additional means of cargo transfer, such as another pump or gas pressurization.

(b) If cargo is transferred by gas pressurization, the pressurizing line must have a safety relief valve that is set at less than 90 percent of the tank relief valve setting.

CARGO AND PROCESS PIPING SYSTEMS

§ 154.500 Cargo and process piping standards.

The cargo liquid and vapor piping and process piping systems must meet the requirements in §§ 154.503 through 154.562, Subparts 56.01 through 56.35, §§ 56.50–20 and 56.50–105, and Subparts 56.60 through 56.97 of this chapter.

§ 154.503 Piping and piping system components: Protection from movement.

Where thermal movement and movements of the cargo tank and the hull structure may cause stresses that exceed the design stresses, the piping and piping system components and cargo tanks must be protected from movement by:

(a) Offsets;

(b) Loops;

(c) Bends;

(d) Mechanical expansion joints including:

(1) Bellows;

(2) Slip joints;

(3) Ball joints; or

(e) Other means specially approved by the Commandant (CG–ENG).

[CGD 74–289, 44 FR 26009, May 3, 1979, as amended by CGD 82–063b, 48 FR 4782, Feb. 3, 1983]

§ 154.506 Mechanical expansion joint: Limits in a piping system.

Mechanical expansion joints in a piping system outside of a cargo tank:

(a) May be installed only if offsets, loops or bends cannot be installed due to limited space or piping arrangement;

(b) Must be a bellows type; and

(c) Must not have insulation or a cover unless necessary to prevent damage.

§ 154.512 Piping: Thermal isolation.

Low temperature piping must be thermally isolated from any adjacent hull structure to prevent the temperature of that structure from dropping below the minimum temperature for the hull material under § 154.170.

§ 154.514 Piping: Electrical bonding.

(a) Cargo tanks or piping that are separated from the hull structure by thermal isolation must be electrically bonded to the hull structure by a method under paragraph (c) of this section.

(b) A pipe joint or a hose connection fitting that has a gasket must be electrically bonded by a method under paragraph (c) of this section that bonds:

(1) Both sides of the connection to the hull structure; or

(2) Each side of the connection to the other side.

(c) An electrical bond must be made by at least one of the following methods:

(1) A metal bonding strap attached by welding or bolting.

(2) Two or more bolts that give metal to metal contact between the bolts and the parts to be bonded.

(3) Metal to metal contact between adjacent parts under designed operating conditions.

§ 154.516 Piping: Hull protection.

A vessel's hull must be protected from low temperature liquid leakage by a drip pan, or other means specially approved by the Commandant (CG–ENG), at:

(a) Each piping connection dismantled on a routine basis;

(b) Cargo discharge and loading manifolds; and

(c) Pump seals.

[CGD 74–289, 44 FR 26009, May 3, 1979, as amended by CGD 82–063b, 48 FR 4782, Feb. 3, 1983]

§ 154.517 Piping: Liquid pressure relief.

The cargo loading and discharge crossover headers, cargo hoses, and cargo loading arms must have means to relieve cargo pressure and to remove liquid cargo.

§ 154.519 Piping relief valves.

(a) The liquid relief valve that protects the cargo piping system from liquid pressure exceeding the design pressure must discharge into:

(1) A cargo tank; or

(2) A cargo vent mast if that vent mast has a means for the detection and removal of the liquid cargo that is specially approved by the Commandant (CG–ENG).

(b) A relief valve on a cargo pump that protects the cargo piping system must discharge into the pump suction.

[CGD 74–289, 44 FR 26009, May 3, 1979, as amended by CGD 82–063b, 48 FR 4782, Feb. 3, 1983]

§ 154.520 Piping calculations.

A piping system must be designed to meet the allowable stress values under § 56.07–10 of this chapter and, if the design temperature is −110 °C (−166 °F) or lower, the stress analysis must be specially approved by the Commandant (CG–ENG) and must include:

(a) Pipe weight loads;

(b) Acceleration loads;

(c) Internal pressure loads;

(d) Thermal loads; and

(e) Loads from the hull.

[CGD 74–289, 44 FR 26009, May 3, 1979, as amended by CGD 82–063b, 48 FR 4782, Feb. 3, 1983]

§ 154.522 Materials for piping.

(a) The materials for piping systems must meet § 154.625 for the minimum design temperature of the piping, except the material for open ended vent piping may be specially approved by the Commandant (CG–ENG) if:

(1) The temperature of the cargo at the pressure relief valve setting is −55 °C (−67 °F) or warmer; and

(2) Liquid can not discharge to the vent piping.

(b) Materials for piping outside the cargo tanks must have a melting point of at least 925 °C (1697 °F), except for short lengths of pipes with fire resisting insulation that are attached to the cargo tanks.

§ 154.524 Piping joints: Welded and screwed couplings.

Pipe lengths without flanges must be joined by one of the following:

(a) A butt welded joint with complete penetration at the weld root except that for design temperatures colder than −10 °C (14 °F) the butt weld must be double welded or must be welded using:

(1) A backing ring that for design pressures greater than 979 kPa gauge (142 psig) must be removed after the weld is completed;

(2) A consumable insert; or

(3) An inert gas back-up on the first weld pass.

(b) A slip-on welded joint with sleeves and attachment welds is allowed for an open ended pipe with an external diameter of 50 mm (2 in.) or less and a design temperature of −55 °C (−67 °F), or warmer.

(c) A socket weld fitting with attachment welds is allowed for pipe with an external diameter of 50 mm (2 in.) or less and a design temperature of −55 °C (−67 °F) or warmer.

(d) Screwed couplings are allowed for instrumentation and control piping that meets § 56.30–20 and § 56.50–105 (a)(4) and (b)(4) of this chapter.

(e) A method or fitting specially approved by the Commandant (CG–ENG).

[CGD 74–289, 44 FR 26009, May 3, 1979, as amended by CGD 82–063b, 48 FR 4782, Feb. 3, 1983]

§ 154.526 Piping joints: Flange connection.

Flange connections for pipe joints must meet § 56.30–10 and § 56.50–105 (a)(4) and (b)(4) of this chapter.

§ 154.528 Piping joints: Flange type.

(a) A flange must be one of the following types:
(1) Welding neck.
(2) Slip-on.
(3) Socket weld.

(b) If the piping is designed for a temperature between −10 °C (14 °F) and −55 °C (−67 °F), the pipe flange may be a:
(1) Slip-on type, if the nominal pipe size is 100 mm (4 in.) or less;
(2) Socket weld, if the nominal pipe size is 50 mm (2 in.) or less; or
(3) Welding neck.

(c) If the piping is designed for a temperature lower than −55 °C (−67 °F), the pipe flange must be a welding neck type.

§ 154.530 Valves: Cargo tank MARVS 69 kPa gauge (10 psig) or lower.

(a) Except those connections for tank safety relief valves and for liquid level gauging devices other than those under §§ 154.536 and 154.1310, liquid and vapor connections on a cargo tank with a MARVS of 69 kPa gauge (10 psig) or lower must have shut-off valves that—

(1) Are located as close to the tank as practical;
(2) Are capable of local manual operation; and
(3) May be remotely controlled.

(b) The cargo piping system for a cargo tank with a MARVS of 69 kPa gauge (10 psig) or lower must have at least one remotely controlled quick-closing shut-off valve for closing liquid and vapor piping between vessel and shore that meets §§ 154.540 and 154.544.

[CGD 74–289, 44 FR 26009, May 3, 1979, as amended by CGD 77–069, 52 FR 31630, Aug. 21, 1987]

§ 154.532 Valves: Cargo tank MARVS greater than 69 kPa gauge (10 psig).

(a) Except connections for tank safety relief valves and except for liquid level gauging devices other than those under §§ 154.536 and 154.1310, liquid and vapor connections on a cargo tank with a MARVS greater than 69 kPa gauge (10 psig) must have, as close to the tank as practical, a:
(1) Stop valve capable of local manual operation; and
(2) A remotely controlled quick-closing shut-off valve.

(b) If the nominal pipe size of a liquid or vapor connection is less than 50 mm (2 in.), an excess flow valve may be substituted for the quick-closing valve under paragraph (a) of this section.

(c) One valve may be substituted for the manual controlled stop valve and the remotely controlled quick-closing shut-off valve required under paragraph (a) of this section if that valve:
(1) Meets §§ 154.540 and 154.544; and
(2) Is capable of local manual operation.

§ 154.534 Cargo pumps and cargo compressors.

Cargo pumps and cargo compressors must shut-down automatically when the quick-closing shut-off valves under §§ 154.530 and 154.532 are closed by the emergency shut-down system required under § 154.540.

§ 154.536 Cargo tank gauging and measuring connections.

Unless the outward flow from a cargo tank is less than the flow through a circular hole of 1.4 mm (0.055 in.) in diameter, cargo tank connections for

§ 154.538

gauging or measuring devices must have the excess flow, shut-off, or quick-closing shut-off valves under § 154.530 or § 154.532.

§ 154.538 Cargo transfer connection.

A cargo transfer connection must have a:

(a) Remotely controlled quick-closing shut-off valve that meets §§ 154.540 and 154.544; or

(b) Blank flange.

§ 154.540 Quick-closing shut-off valves: Emergency shut-down system.

The quick-closing shut-off valves under §§ 154.530, 154.532, and 154.538 must have an emergency shut-down system that:

(a) Closes all the valves;

(b) Is actuated by a single control in at least two locations remote from the quick-closing valves;

(c) Is actuated by a single control in each cargo control station under § 154.320; and

(d) Has fusible elements at each tank dome and cargo loading and discharge manifold that melt between 98 °C (208 °F) and 104 °C (220 °F) and actuate the emergency shut-down system.

§ 154.544 Quick-closing shut-off valves.

The quick-closing shut-off valve under §§ 154.530, 154.532 and 154.538 must:

(a) Be a shut-off valve;

(b) Close from the time of actuation in 30 seconds or less;

(c) Be the fail-closed type; and

(d) Be capable of local manual closing.

[CGD 74–289, 44 FR 26009, May 3, 1979, as amended by CGD 77–069, 52 FR 31630, Aug. 21, 1987]

§ 154.546 Excess flow valve: Closing flow.

(a) The rated closing flow of vapor or liquid cargo for an excess flow valve must be specially approved by the Commandant (CG–ENG).

(b) An excess flow valve allowed under § 154.532(b) must close automatically at the rated closing flow.

[CGD 74–289, 44 FR 26009, May 3, 1979, as amended by CGD 82–063b, 48 FR 4782, Feb. 3, 1983]

§ 154.548 Cargo piping: Flow capacity.

Piping with an excess flow valve must have a vapor or liquid flow capacity that is greater than the rated closing flow under § 154.546.

§ 154.550 Excess flow valve: Bypass.

If the excess flow valve allowed under § 154.532(b) has a bypass, the bypass must be of 1.0 mm (0.0394 in.) or less in diameter.

CARGO HOSE

§ 154.551 Cargo hose: General.

Each of the vessel's liquid and vapor cargo hose for loading or discharging cargo must meet §§ 154.552 through 154.562.

§ 154.552 Cargo hose: Compatibility.

Liquid and vapor cargo hoses must:

(a) Not chemically react with the cargo; and

(b) Withstand design temperature.

§ 154.554 Cargo hose: Bursting pressure.

Cargo hose that may be exposed to the pressure in the cargo tank, the cargo pump discharge, or the vapor compressor discharge must have a bursting pressure of at least five times the maximum working pressure on the hose during cargo transfer.

§ 154.556 Cargo hose: Maximum working pressure.

A cargo hose must have a maximum working pressure not less than the maximum pressure to which it may be subjected and at least 1034 kPa gauge (150 psig).

§ 154.558 Cargo hose: Marking.

Each cargo hose must be marked with the:

(a) Maximum working pressure; and

(b) Minimum service temperature for service at other than ambient temperature.

§ 154.560 Cargo hose: Prototype test.

(a) Each cargo hose must be of a type that passes a prototype test at a pressure of at least five times its maximum working pressure at or below the minimum service temperature.

(b) Each cargo hose must not be the hose used in the prototype test.

§ 154.562 Cargo hose: Hydrostatic test.

Each cargo hose must pass a hydrostatic pressure test at ambient temperature of at least one and a half times its specified maximum working pressure but not more than two-fifths its bursting pressure.

MATERIALS

§ 154.605 Toughness test.

(a) Each toughness test under §§ 154.610 through 154.625 must meet Subpart 54.05 of this chapter.

(b) If subsize test specimens are used for the Charpy V-notch toughness test, the Charpy V-notch energy must meet Table 54.05–20 (a) of this chapter.

§ 154.610 Design temperature not colder than 0 °C (32 °F).

Materials for cargo tanks for a design temperature not colder than 0 °C (32 °F) must meet the following:

(a) The tank materials must meet §§ 54.25–1 and 54.25–3 of this chapter.

(b) Plates, forgings, rolled and forged bars and shapes must be carbon manganese steel or other material allowed under §§ 154.615, 154.620, and 154.625.

(c) Plates must be normalized or quenched and tempered and where the thickness exceeds 20 mm (0.787 in.), made with fine grain practice, austenitic grain size of five or finer. A control rolling procedure may be substituted for normalizing if specially approved by the Commandant (CG–ENG). Plate for an independent tank type C must also meet the requirements of ASTM A 20 (incorporated by reference, see § 154.1) and § 54.01–18(b)(5) of this chapter.

(d) For integral and independent type A tanks, the American Bureau of Shipping's grade D not exceeding 20 mm (0.787 in.) in thickness, and Grade E hull structural steel are allowed if the steel meets § 54.05–10 of this chapter.

(e) The tensile properties under paragraph (a) of this section must be determined for:

(1) Each plate as rolled; and

(2) Each five short ton batch of forgings, forged or rolled fittings, and forged or rolled bars and shapes.

(f) The specified yield strength must not exceed 637 MPa (92.43 Ksi) and when it exceeds 490 MPa (71.10 Ksi), the hardness of the weld and the heat affected zone must be specially approved by the Commandant (CG–ENG).

(g) The Charpy V-notch impact energy must be determined for:

(1) Each plate as rolled; and

(2) Each five short ton batch of forgings, forged or rolled fittings and rolled or forged bars and shapes.

(h) The orientation and required impact energy of a 10 mm × 10 mm (0.394 in. × 0.394 in.) Charpy V-notch specimen must be:

(1) For plates; transverse specimen and 27.4 J (20 ft-lbs); and

(2) For forgings, forged and rolled fittings and rolled and forged bars: longitudinal specimen and 41.1 J (30 ft-lbs).

(i) The test temperature of the Charpy V-notch specimens is as follows:

Material Thickness	Test Temperature
t≤20 mm (0.788 in.)	0 °C (32 °F)
20<t<30 mm (1.182 in.)	−20 °C (−4 °F)
30<t<40 mm (1.576 in.)	−40 °C (−40 °F)

[CGD 74–289, 44 FR 26009, May 3, 1979, as amended by CGD 82–063b, 48 FR 4782, Feb. 3, 1983; USCG–1999–5151, 64 FR 67183, Dec. 1, 1999]

§ 154.615 Design temperature below 0 °C (32 °F) and down to −55 °C (−67 °F).

Plates, forgings, forged or rolled or forged bars and shapes for cargo tanks and secondary barriers for a design temperature below 0 °C (32 °F) and down to −55 °C (−67 °F) must meet § 54.25–10 of this chapter.

§ 154.620 Design temperature below −55 °C (−67 °F) and down to −165 °C (−265 °F).

Plates, forgings and forged or rolled fittings, and rolled, forged or extruded bars and shapes for cargo tanks, secondary barriers, and process pressure vessels for a design temperature below −55 °C (−67 °F) and down to −165 °C (−265 °F) must:

(a) Meet § 54.25–10(b)(2), § 54.25–15, or § 54.25–20 of this chapter; or

§ 154.625

(b) Be of an aluminum alloy that is specially approved by the Commandant (CG–ENG).

[CGD 74–289, 44 FR 26009, May 3, 1979, as amended by CGD 82–063b, 48 FR 4782, Feb. 3, 1983]

§ 154.625 Design temperature below 0 °C (32 °F) and down to −165 °C (−265 °F).

Pipes, tubes, forgings, castings, bolting, and nuts for cargo and process piping for a design temperature below 0 °C (32 °F) and down to −165 °C (−265 °F) must meet § 56.50–105 of this chapter.

§ 154.630 Cargo tank material.

(a) If a material of a cargo tank is not listed in §§ 154.610, 154.615 or § 154.620, the allowable stress of that material must be specially approved by the Commandant (CG–ENG).

(b) For cargo tanks of aluminum alloys with welded connections, the minimum tensile strength (σ_B) for the calculations under § 154.440, § 154.447 and § 154.450 must be the minimum tensile strength of the alloy in the annealed condition.

(c) Increased yield strength and tensile strength of a material at low temperature for independent tanks type A, B, and C must be specially approved by the Commandant (CG–ENG).

[CGD 74–289, 44 FR 26009, May 3, 1979, as amended by CGD 82–063b, 48 FR 4782, Feb. 3, 1983]

CONSTRUCTION

§ 154.650 Cargo tank and process pressure vessel welding.

(a) Cargo tank and process pressure vessel welding must meet Subpart 54.05 and Part 57 of this chapter.

(b) Welding consumables used in welding cargo tanks must meet § 57.02–4 of this chapter.

(c) Independent tanks must meet the following:

(1) Each welded joint of the shells must be a full penetration butt weld, except dome to shell connections may have full penetration tee welds.

(2) Each nozzle weld must be of the full penetration type, except for small penetrations on domes.

(d) Each welded joint in an independent tank type C or in a process pressure vessel must meet part 54 of this chapter, except that any backing rings must be removed unless specially approved by the Commandant (CG–OES).

(e) Each welded joint in a membrane tank must meet the quality assurance measures, weld procedure qualification, design details, materials, construction, inspection, and production testing of components developed during the prototype testing program that are specially approved by the Commandant (CG–OES) under this part.

(f) Each welded joint in a semi-membrane tank must meet paragraph (c) or (e) of this section.

[CGD 74–289, 44 FR 26009, May 3, 1979, as amended by CGD 82–063b, 48 FR 4782, Feb. 3, 1983]

§ 154.655 Stress relief for independent tanks type C.

For a design temperature colder than −10 °C (14 °F), an independent tank type C of:

(a) Carbon and carbon-manganese steel must be stress relieved by post-weld heat treatment under § 54.25–7 of this chapter or by mechanical stress relief under subpart 54.30 of this chapter; or

(b) Materials other than carbon and carbon manganese steel must be stress relieved as required under part 54 of this chapter. The procedure for stress relieving must be specially approved by the Commandant (CG–OES).

§ 154.660 Pipe welding.

(a) Pipe welding must meet part 57 of this chapter.

(b) Longitudinal butt welds, in piping that does not meet a standard or specification under § 56.60–1 of this chapter, and girth butt welds must meet the following:

(1) Butt welds of pipes made from carbon, carbon manganese, or low alloy steels must meet § 56.50–105 of this chapter, including the requirements for post-weld heat treatment.

(2) Except for piping inside an independent cargo tank type A, B, or C, butt welds must be 100% radiographically tested if the design temperature is lower than −10 °C (14 °F), and:

(i) The wall thickness is greater than 10 mm (0.394 in.); or

Coast Guard, DHS § 154.703

(ii) The nominal pipe diameter is greater than 100 mm (nominal 4 in.).

(3) If Table 4 references this section, butt welds for deck cargo piping exceeding 75 mm (3 in.) in diameter must be 100% radiographically tested.

(4) Butt welds of pipes not meeting paragraph (b)(2) or (b)(3) of this section must meet the non-destructive testing requirements under Subpart 56.95 of this chapter.

§ 154.665 Welding procedures.

Welding procedure tests for cargo tanks for a design temperature colder than 0 °C (32 °F), process pressure vessels, and piping must meet § 54.05-15 and Subpart 57.03 of this chapter.

CARGO PRESSURE AND TEMPERATURE CONTROL

§ 154.701 Cargo pressure and temperature control: General.

Except as allowed under § 154.703, cargo tanks must:

(a) Have their safety relief valves set at a pressure equal to or greater than the vapor pressure of the cargo at 45 °C (113 °F) but not greater than the MARVS under § 154.405; or

(b) Be refrigerated by a system meeting § 154.702, and each refrigerated incompatible cargo refrigerated by a separate system.

§ 154.702 Refrigerated carriage.

(a) Each refrigeration system must:

(1) Have enough capacity to maintain the cargo vapor pressure in each cargo tank served by the system below the set pressure of the relief valves under ambient temperatures of 45 °C (113 °F) still air and 32 °C (89.6 °F) still water with the largest unit in the system inoperative; or

(2) Have a standby unit with a capacity at least equal to the capacity of the largest refrigeration unit in the system.

(b) For the purpose of this section, a "refrigeration unit" includes a compressor and its motors and controls.

(c) Each refrigeration system must:

(1) Have a heat exchanger with an excess capacity of 25 percent of the required capacity; or

(2) A standby heat exchanger.

(d) Where cooling water is used in a refrigeration system:

(1) The cooling water pump or pumps must be used exclusively for the system;

(2) Each pump must have suction lines from sea chests on the port and starboard sides of the vessel; and

(3) There must be a standby pump, that may be used for:

(i) Non-essential purposes on the vessel; or

(ii) Essential purposes on the vessel, if the pump is sized to simultaneously provide for the capacity requirements for the essential purposes and the refrigeration cooling water.

(e) Each refrigeration system must use refrigerants that are compatible with the cargo and, for cascade units, with each other.

(f) The pressure of the heat transfer fluid in each cooling coil in a tank must be greater than the pressure of the cargo.

§ 154.703 Methane (LNG).

Unless a cargo tank carrying methane (LNG) can withstand the pressure build up due to boil-off for 21 days, the pressure in the cargo tank must be maintained below the set pressure of the safety relief valve for at least 21 days by:

(a) A refrigeration system that meets § 154.702;

(b) A waste heat or catalytic furnace that burns boil-off gas, and:

(1) Maintains the stack exhaust temperature below 535 °C (995 °F);

(2) Exhibits no visible flame; and

(3) Is specially approved by the Commandant (CG–OES);

(c) Boilers, inert gas generators, and combustion engines in the main propelling machinery space that use boil-off gas as fuel; or

(d) Equipment for services, other than those under paragraph (c) of this section, that use boil-off gas as fuel and that are located:

(1) In the main propelling machinery space; or

(2) a space specially approved by the Commandant (CG–OES).

[CGD 74–289, 44 FR 26009, May 3, 1979, as amended by CGD 82–063b, 48 FR 4782, Feb. 3, 1983]

§ 154.705 Cargo boil-off as fuel: General.

(a) Each cargo boil-off fuel system under § 154.703(c) must meet §§ 154.706 through 154.709.

(b) The piping in the cargo boil-off fuel system must have a connection for introducing inert gas and for gas freeing the piping in the machinery space.

(c) A gas fired main propulsion boiler or combustion engine must have a fuel oil fired pilot that maintains fuel flow as required under § 154.1854 if the gas fuel supply is cut-off.

§ 154.706 Cargo boil-off as fuel: Fuel lines.

(a) Gas fuel lines must not pass through accommodation, service, or control spaces. Each gas fuel line passing through other spaces must have a master gas fuel valve and meet one of the following:

(1) The fuel line must be a double-walled piping system with the annular space containing an inert gas at a pressure greater than the fuel pressure. Visual and audible alarms must be installed at the machinery control station to indicate loss of inert gas pressure.

(2) The fuel line must be installed in a mechanically exhaust-ventilated pipe or duct, having a rate of air change of at least 30 changes per hour. The pressure in the space between the inner pipe and outer pipe or duct must be maintained at less than atmospheric pressure. Continuous gas detection must be installed to detect leaks in the ventilated space. The ventilation system must meet § 154.1205.

(b) Each double wall pipe or vent duct must terminate in the ventilation hood or casing under § 154.707(a). Continuous gas detection must be installed to indicate leaks in the hood or casing.

§ 154.707 Cargo boil-off as fuel: Ventilation.

(a) A ventilation hood or casing must be installed in areas occupied by flanges, valves, and piping at the fuel burner to cause air to sweep across them and be exhausted at the top of the hood or casing.

(b) The hood or casing must be mechanically exhaust-ventilated and meet § 154.1205.

(c) The ventilated hood or casing must have an airflow rate specially approved by the Commandant.

§ 154.708 Cargo boil-off as fuel: Valves.

(a) Gas fuel lines to the gas consuming equipment must have two fail-closed automatic valves in series. A third valve, designed to fail-open, must vent that portion of pipe between the two series valves to the open atmosphere.

(b) The valves under paragraph (a) of this section must be arranged so that loss of boiler forced draft, flame failure, or abnormal gas fuel supply pressure automatically causes the two series valves to close and the vent valve to open. The function of one of the series valves and the vent valve may be performed by a single three-way valve.

(c) A master gas fuel valve must be located outside the machinery space, but be operable from inside the machinery space and at the valve. The valve must automatically close when there is:

(1) A gas leak detected under § 154.706(a)(2) or § 154.706(b);

(2) Loss of the ventilation under § 154.706(a)(2) or § 154.707(c); or

(3) Loss of inert gas pressure within the double-walled piping system under § 154.706(a)(1).

§ 154.709 Cargo boil-off as fuel: Gas detection equipment.

(a) The continuous gas detection system required under § 154.706(a)(2) and (b) must:

(1) Meet § 154.1350(c), (d), and (j) through (s); and

(2) Have a device that:

(i) Activates an audible and visual alarm at the machinery control station and in the wheelhouse if the methane concentration reaches 1.5 percent by volume; and

(ii) Closes the master gas fuel valve required under § 154.708(c) before the methane concentration reaches 3 percent by volume.

(b) The number and arrangement of gas sampling points must be specially approved by the Commandant (CG–OES).

[CGD 74–289, 44 FR 26009, May 3, 1979, as amended by CGD 82–063b, 48 FR 4782, Feb. 3, 1983]

Cargo Vent Systems

§ 154.801 Pressure relief systems.

(a) Each cargo tank that has a volume of 20m³ (706 ft.³) or less must have at least one pressure relief valve.

(b) Each cargo tank that has a volume of more than 20m³ (706 ft.³) must have at least two pressure relief valves of the same nominal relieving capacity.

(c) Each pressure relief valve must:

(1) Meet Subpart 162.018 of this chapter or, if the valve is also capable of vacuum relief and the MARVS is 69 kPa gauge (10 psig) or less, Subpart 162.017 of this chapter, and have at least the capacity required under § 154.806;

(2) Not be set for a higher pressure than the MARVS;

(3) Have a fitting for sealing wire that prevents the set pressure from being changed without breaking the sealing wire;

(4) Be fitted on the cargo tank to remain in the vapor phase under conditions of 15° list and of 0.015 L trim by both the bow and stern;

(5) Vent to a vent mast under § 154.805, except a relief valve may vent to a common tank relief valve header if the back pressure is included in determining the required capacity under § 154.806;

(6) Not vent to a common header or common vent mast if the relief valves are connected to cargo tanks carrying chemically incompatible cargoes;

(7) Not have any stop valves or other means of isolating the cargo tank from its relief valve unless:

(i) The stop valves are interlocked or arranged so that only one pressure relief valve is out of service at any one time;

(ii) The interlock arrangement automatically shows the relief valve that is out of service; and

(iii) The other valves have the relieving capacity required under § 154.806, or all relief valves on the cargo tank are the same size and there is a spare of the same size, or there is a spare for each relief valve on a cargo tank.

(d) The pressure relief system must:

(1) If the design temperature is below 0 °C (32 °F), be designed to prevent the relief valve from becoming inoperative due to ice formation; and

(2) Be designed to prevent chattering of the relief valve.

[CGD 74-289, 44 FR 26009, May 3, 1979; 44 FR 59234, Oct. 15, 1979]

§ 154.802 Alternate pressure relief settings.

Cargo tanks with more than one relief valve setting must have one of the following arrangements:

(a) Relief valves that:

(1) Are set and sealed under § 154.801(c);

(2) Have the capacity under § 154.806; and

(3) Are interlocked so that cargo tank venting can occur at any time.

(b) Relief valves that have spacer pieces or springs that:

(1) Change the set pressure without pressure testing to verify the new setting; and

(2) Can be installed without breaking the sealing wire required under § 154.801(c)(3).

§ 154.804 Vacuum protection.

(a) Except as allowed under paragraph (b) of this section, each cargo tank must have a vacuum protection system meeting paragraph (a)(1) of this section and either paragraph (a)(2) or (a)(3) of this section.

(1) There must be a means of testing the operation of the system.

(2) There must be a pressure switch that operates an audible and visual alarm in the cargo control station identifying the tank and the alarm condition and a remote group audible and visual alarm in the wheelhouse. Both alarms must be set at or below 80% of the maximum external design pressure differential of the cargo tanks. There must be a second, independent pressure switch that automatically shuts off all suction of cargo liquid or vapor from the cargo tank and secures any refrigeration of that tank at or below the maximum external design pressure differential.

(3) There must be a vacuum relief valve that:

(i) Has a gas flow capacity at least equal to the maximum cargo discharge rate per tank;

§ 154.805

(ii) Is set to open at or below the maximum external design pressure differential; and

(iii) Admits inert gas, cargo vapor from a source other than a cargo vapor header, or air except as prohibited under § 154.1710.

(b) A vacuum protection system does not have to be installed if the cargo tank is designed to withstand:

(1) A maximum external pressure differential exceeding 24.5 kPa gauge (3.55 psig); and

(2) The maximum external pressure differential that can be obtained:

(i) At maximum discharge rates with no vapor return to the cargo tanks;

(ii) By operation of the cargo refrigeration system; or

(iii) By drawing off vapor for use in accordance with § 154.703(c)

[CGD 74–289, 44 FR 26009, May 3, 1979; 44 FR 59234, Oct. 15, 1979]

§ 154.805 Vent masts.

Relief valves or common vent headers from relief valves must discharge to a vent mast that:

(a) Discharges vertically upward;

(b) Has a rain cap or other means of preventing the entrance of rain or snow;

(c) Has a screen with 25mm (1 inch) wire mesh or bars not more than 25mm (1 in.) apart on the discharge port;

(d) Extends at least to a height of B/3 or 6m (19.7 ft.), whichever is greater, above the weather deck and 6m (19.7 ft.) above the working level;

(e) For a cargo tank, does not exhaust cargo vapors within a radius of B or 25m (82 ft.), whichever is less, from any forced or natural ventilation intake or other opening to an accommodation, service, control station, or other gas-safe space, except that for vessels less than 90m (295 ft.) in length, shorter distances may be specially approved by the Commandant (CG–OES);

(f) For a containment system, except a cargo tank, does not exhaust vapor within a radius of 10m (32.8 ft.) or less from any forced or natural ventilation intake or other opening to an accommodation, service, control station, or other gas-safe space;

(g) Has drains to remove any liquid that may accumulate; and

(h) Prevents accumulations of liquid at the relief valves.

[CGD 74–289, 44 FR 26009, May 3, 1979, as amended by CGD 82–063b, 48 FR 4782, Feb. 3, 1983]

§ 154.806 Capacity of pressure relief valves.

Pressure relief valves for each cargo tank must have a combined relief capacity, including the effects of back pressure from vent piping, headers, and masts, to discharge the greater of the following with not more than a 20% rise in cargo tank pressure above the set pressure of the relief valves:

(a) The maximum capacity of an installed cargo tank inerting system if the maximum attainable working pressure of the cargo tank inerting system exceeds the set pressure of the relief valves.

(b) The quantity of vapors generated from fire exposure that is calculated under § 54.15–25 of this chapter.

ATMOSPHERIC CONTROL IN CARGO CONTAINMENT SYSTEMS

§ 154.901 Atmospheric control within cargo tanks and cargo piping systems.

(a) Each vessel must have a piping system for purging each cargo tank and all cargo piping.

(b) The piping system must minimize the pocketing of gas or air remaining after purging.

(c) For cargo tanks certificated to carry flammable gases, the piping system must allow purging the tank of flammable vapors before air is introduced and purging the tank of air before the tank is filled with cargo.

(d) Each cargo tank must have:

(1) Gas sampling points at its top and bottom; and

(2) Gas sampling line connections that are valved and capped above the deck.

§ 154.902 Atmospheric control within hold and interbarrier spaces.

(a) Vessels certificated to carry flammable cargo in cargo containment systems with full secondary barriers must have an inert gas system or onboard storage of inert gas that provides enough inert gas to meet the requirements of §154.1848 for 30 days consumption.

(b) Vessels certificated to carry flammable cargo in cargo containment systems with partial secondary barriers must:

(1) Have an inert gas system or on-board inert gas storage that can inert the largest hold and interbarrier space so that the oxygen concentration is 8 percent or less by volume; and

(2) Meet paragraph (a) or (c)(2) of this section.

(c) Vessels certificated to carry only nonflammable cargo in cargo containment systems with secondary barriers must:

(1) Meet paragraph (a) of this section; or

(2) Have air drying systems that reduce the dewpoint of air admitted to hold or interbarrier spaces below the temperature of any surface in those spaces or −45 °C (−49 °F), whichever is warmer.

(d) Vessels with refrigerated independent tanks type C must have inert gas or air drying systems that reduce the dewpoint of any inert gas or air admitted to the hold spaces below the temperature of any surface in those spaces or −45 °C (−49 °F), whichever is warmer.

§ 154.903 Inert gas systems: General.

(a) Inert gas carried or generated to meet §§ 154.901, 154.902, and 154.1848 must be non-flammable and non-reactive with the cargoes that the vessel is certificated to carry and the materials of construction of the cargo tanks, hold and interbarrier spaces, and insulation.

(b) The boiling point and dewpoint at atmospheric pressure of the inert gas must be below the temperature of any surface in those spaces or −45 °C (−49 °F), whichever is warmer.

(c) For the temperatures and pressures at which the gas is stored and used, storage vessels and inert gas piping must meet §§ 154.450 and 154.500 respectively.

§ 154.904 Inert gas system: Controls.

The inert gas system must have:
(a) At least one check valve in the cargo area to prevent the back flow of cargo vapor into the inert gas system, or another means specially approved by the Commandant (CG–OES);

(b) If the inert gas system is in the machinery space or another space outside the cargo area, a second check valve in the cargo area meeting paragraph (a) of this section;

(c) Automatic and manual inert gas pressure controls; and

(d) Valves to isolate each inerted space.

[CGD 74–289, 44 FR 26009, May 3, 1979, as amended by CGD 82–063b, 48 FR 4782, Feb. 3, 1983]

§ 154.906 Inert gas generators.

The inert gas generator must:

(a) Produce an inert gas containing less than 5% oxygen by volume;

(b) Have a device to continuously sample the discharge of the generator for oxygen content; and

(c) Have an audible and visual alarm in the cargo control station that alarms when the inert gas contains 5% or more oxygen by volume.

§ 154.908 Inert gas generator: Location.

(a) Except as allowed in paragraph (b) of this section, an inert gas generator must be located in the main machinery space or a space that is not in the cargo area and does not have direct access to any accommodation, service, or control space.

(b) An inert gas generator that does not use flame burning equipment may be located in the cargo area if specially approved by the Commandant (CG–OES).

[CGD 74–289, 44 FR 26009, May 3, 1979, as amended by CGD 82–063b, 48 FR 4782, Feb. 3, 1983]

§ 154.910 Inert gas piping: Location.

Inert gas piping must not pass through or terminate in an accommodation, service, or control space.

§ 154.912 Inerted spaces: Relief devices.

Inerted spaces must be fitted with relief valves, rupture discs, or other devices specially approved by the Commandant (CG–OES).

[CGD 74–289, 44 FR 26009, May 3, 1979; CGD 82–063b, 48 FR 39229, Sept. 1, 1983]

ELECTRICAL

§ 154.1000 Applicability.

Sections 154.1005 through 154.1020 apply to flammable cargo and ammonia carriers.

§ 154.1002 Definition.

For the purposes of §§ 154.1005 through 154.1020, "gas-dangerous" does not include the weather deck of an ammonia carrier.

§ 154.1005 Equipment approval.

(a) Electrical equipment that is required to be intrinsically safe or explosion proof under § 154.1010 must be specially approved by the Commandant or listed as intrinsically safe or explosion proof by an independent laboratory that is specially approved by the Commandant (CG–OES), for Class I Division I locations and the Group that is specified in Table 4 for the cargo carried.

(b) Each submerged cargo pump motor installation must be specially approved by the Commandant (CG–OES).

(c) Electrical equipment that must be intrinsically safe to meet § 154.1010 must meet the definition in § 110.15–100(i) of this chapter.

(d) Electrical equipment that must be explosion proof to meet § 154.1010 must meet § 110.15–65(e) of this chapter.

[CGD 74–289, 44 FR 26009, May 3, 1979, as amended by CGD 82–063b, 48 FR 4782, Feb. 3, 1983]

§ 154.1010 Electrical equipment in gas-dangerous space or zone.

(a) Except as allowed in this section, electrical equipment must not be installed in a gas-dangerous space or zone.

(b) Intrinsically safe electrical equipment and wiring may be in a gas-dangerous space or zone.

(c) A submerged cargo pump motor may be in a cargo tank if:

(1) Low liquid level, motor current, or pump discharge pressure automatically shuts down power to the pump motor if the pump loses suction;

(2) There is an audible and visual alarm at the cargo control station that actuates if the motor shuts down under the requirements of paragraph (c)(1) of this section; and

(3) There is a lockable circuit breaker or lockable switch that disconnects the power to the motor.

(d) A supply cable for a submerged cargo pump motor may be in a hold space.

(e) A hold space that has a tank that is not required to have a secondary barrier under § 154.459 may only have:

(1) Through runs of cable;

(2) Explosion-proof lighting fixtures;

(3) Depth sounding devices in gas-tight enclosures;

(4) Log devices in gas-tight enclosures; and

(5) Impressed current cathodic protection system electrodes in gas-tight enclosures.

(f) A space that is separated by a gas-tight steel boundary from a hold space that has a cargo tank that must have a secondary barrier, under the requirements of § 154.459, may only have:

(1) Through runs of cable;

(2) Explosion-proof lighting fixtures;

(3) Depth sounding devices in gas-tight enclosures;

(4) Log devices in gastight enclosures;

(5) Impressed current cathodic protection system electrodes in gastight enclosures;

(6) Explosion-proof motors that operate cargo system valves or ballast system valves; and

(7) Explosion-proof bells for general alarm systems.

(g) A cargo handling room may only have:

(1) Explosion-proof lighting fixtures; and

(2) Explosion-proof bells for general alarm systems.

(h) A space for cargo hose storage may only have:

(1) Explosion-proof lighting fixtures; and

(2) Through runs of cable.

Coast Guard, DHS § 154.1125

(i) A space that has cargo piping may only have:
(1) Explosion-proof lighting fixtures; and
(2) Through runs of cable.

(j) A gas-dangerous zone on the weather deck may only have:
(1) Explosion-proof equipment that is for the operation of the vessel; and
(2) Through runs of cable.

(k) A space, except those under paragraphs (e) through (j) of this section, that has a direct opening to a gas-dangerous space or zone may only have the electrical equipment allowed in the gas-dangerous space or zone.

§ 154.1015 Lighting in gas-dangerous space.

(a) Each gas-dangerous space that has lighting fixtures must have at least two branch circuits for lighting.

(b) Each switch and each overcurrent protective device for any lighting circuit that is in a gas-dangerous space must open each conductor of the circuit simultaneously.

(c) Each switch and each overcurrent protective device for lighting in a gas-dangerous space must be in a gas-safe space.

§ 154.1020 Emergency power.

The emergency generator must be designed to allow operation at the final angle of heel under § 154.230(a).

Firefighting

Firefighting System: Exterior Water Spray

§ 154.1105 Exterior water spray system: General.

Each liquefied flammable gas vessel and each liquefied toxic gas vessel must have an exterior water spray system that meets §§ 154.1110 through 154.1135.

§ 154.1110 Areas protected by system.

Each water spray system must protect:
(a) All cargo tank surfaces that are not covered by the vessel's hull structure or a steel cover;
(b) Each cargo tank dome;
(c) Each on-deck storage vessel for flammable or toxic liquefied gases;
(d) Each cargo discharge and loading manifold;

(e) Each quick-closing valve under §§ 154.530, 154.532, and 154.538, and other control valves essential to cargo flow;

(f) Each boundary facing the cargo area of each superstructure that contains accommodation, service, or control spaces;

(g) Each boundary facing the cargo area of each deckhouse that contains accommodation, service, or control spaces; and

(h) Each boundary of each deckhouse that is within the cargo area and that is manned during navigation of the vessel or during cargo transfer operations, except the deckhouse roof if it is 2.4 m (8 ft.) or higher above the cargo containing structure.

[CGD 74–289, 44 FR 26009, May 3, 1979; 44 FR 59234, Oct. 15, 1979]

§ 154.1115 Discharge.

(a) The discharge density of each water spray system must be at least:
(1) 10000 $cm^3/m^2/min$. (0.25 $gpm/ft.^2$) over each horizontal surface; and
(2) 4000 $cm^3/m^2/min$. (0.10 $gpm/ft.^2$) against vertical surface, including the water rundown.

(b) The water spray protection under § 154.1110 (d) and (e) must cover an area in a horizontal plane extending at least 0.5 m (19 in.) in each direction from the pipes, fittings, and valves, or the area of the drip tray, whichever is greater.

§ 154.1120 Nozzles.

(a) Nozzles for the water spray system must be spaced to provide the minimum discharge density under § 154.1115 in each part of the protected area.

(b) The vertical distance between water spray nozzles for the protection of vertical surfaces must be 3.7 m (12 ft.) or less.

§ 154.1125 Pipes, fittings, and valves.

(a) Each pipe, fitting, and valve for each water spray system must meet Part 56 of this chapter.

(b) Each water spray main that protects more than one area listed in § 154.1110 must have at least one isolation valve at each branch connection and at least one isolation valve downstream of each branch connection to isolate damaged sections.

§ 154.1130

(c) Each valved cross-connection from the water spray system to the fire main must be outside of the cargo area.

(d) Each pipe, fitting, and valve for the water spray system must be made of fire resistant and corrosion resistant materials, such as galvanized steel or galvanized iron pipe.

(e) Each water spray system must have a means of drainage to prevent corrosion of the system and freezing of accumulated water in subfreezing temperatures.

(f) Each water spray system must have a dirt strainer that is located at the water spray system manifold or pump.

§ 154.1130 Sections.

(a) If a water spray system is divided into sections, each section must at least include the entire deck area bounded by the length of a cargo tank and the full beam of the vessel.

(b) If a water spray system is divided into sections, the control valves must be at a single manifold that is aft of the cargo area.

§ 154.1135 Pumps.

(a) Water to the water spray system must be supplied by:

(1) A pump that is only for the use of the system;

(2) A fire pump; or

(3) A pump specially approved by the Commandant (CG–OES).

(b) Operation of a water spray system must not interfere with simultaneous operation of the fire main system at its required capacity. There must be a valved cross-connection between the two systems.

(c) Except as allowed under paragraph (d) of this section, each pump for each water spray system must have the capacity to simultaneously supply all areas named in § 154.1110.

(d) If the water spray system is divided into sections, the pump under paragraph (a) of this section must have the capacity to simultaneously supply the required discharge density under § 154.1115(a) for:

(1) The areas in §§ 154.1110(f) through (h) and 154.1115(b); and

(2) The largest section that includes the required protection under § 154.1110 (a), (b), and (c).

[CGD 74–289, 44 FR 26009, May 3, 1979, as amended by CGD 82–063b, 48 FR 4782, Feb. 3, 1983]

FIREFIGHTING SYSTEM: DRY CHEMICAL

§ 154.1140 Dry chemical system: General.

Each liquefied flammable gas carrier must have a dry chemical firefighting system that meets §§ 154.1145 through 154.1170, Part 56 and Subpart 162.039 of this chapter.

§ 154.1145 Dry chemical supply.

(a) A vessel with a cargo carrying capacity less that 1000 m^3 (35,300 ft.^{3}) must have at least one self-contained dry chemical storage unit for the cargo area with an independent inert gas pressurizing source adjacent to each unit.

(b) A vessel with a cargo carrying capacity of 1000 m^3 (35,300 ft.^{3}) or more must have at least two self-contained dry chemical storage units for the cargo area with an independent inert gas pressurizing source adjacent to each unit.

(c) A vessel with bow and stern loading and discharge areas must have at least one self-contained dry chemical storage unit with an independent inert gas pressurizing source adjacent to the unit for each area.

(d) Each dry chemical storage unit and associated piping must be designed for:

(1) Sequential discharge of each hose line and each monitor for 45 seconds; and

(2) Simultaneous discharge of all hose lines and monitors for 45 seconds.

(e) Each fully charged dry chemical storage unit must have the greater of the following:

(1) Enough dry chemical to provide for sequential discharge of each attached hose and monitor for 45 seconds.

(2) Enough dry chemical to provide for simultaneous discharge of all attached hoses and monitors for 45 seconds.

§ 154.1150 Distribution of dry chemical.

(a) All locations on the above deck cargo area and the cargo piping outside that cargo area must be protected by:

(1) At least two dry chemical hand hose lines; or

(2) At least one dry chemical hand hose line and one dry chemical monitor.

(b) At least one dry chemical storage unit and hand hose line or monitor must be at the after end of the cargo areas.

(c) Each cargo loading and discharge manifold must be protected by at least one dry chemical monitor.

§ 154.1155 Hand hose line: Coverage.

The coverage for the area for a hand hose line under § 154.1150 must not exceed the length of the hand hose line except the coverage for the protection of areas that are inaccessible to personnel must not exceed one-half the projection of the hose at its rated discharge, or 10 m (32.8 ft.), whichever is less.

§ 154.1160 Monitor coverage of system.

The coverage of each dry chemical system monitor under § 154.1150 must not exceed:

(a) 10 m (32.8 ft.) at 10 kg/sec (22 lb/sec);

(b) 30 m (98.4 ft.) at 25 kg/sec (55 lb/sec);

(c) 40 m (131.2 ft.) at 45 kg/sec (99 lb/sec);

(d) An interpolation between 10 m (32.8 ft.) at 10 kg/sec (22 lb/sec) and 30 m (98.4 ft.) at 25 kg/sec (55 lb/sec); or

(e) An interpolation between 30 m (98.4 ft.) at 25 kg/sec (55 lb/sec) and 40 m (131.2 ft.) at 45 kg/sec (99 lb/sec).

§ 154.1165 Controls.

(a) Each dry chemical hand hose line must be one that can be actuated at its hose reel or hose storage cabinet.

(b) Each dry chemical monitor must be one that can be actuated and controlled at the monitor.

(c) A dry chemical monitor for the cargo loading and discharging manifold areas must be one that can be:

(1) Actuated from a location other than the monitor and manifold area; and

(2) Except for pre-aimed monitors, controlled from a location other than the monitor and manifold area.

(d) Each dry chemical storage unit must have independent piping with a stop valve in the piping for each remote hand hose line and remote monitor where the piping connects to the storage container, if the unit has:

(1) More than one hand hose line;

(2) More than one monitor; or

(3) A combination of hand hose lines and monitors.

(e) Each stop valve under paragraph (d) of the section must be capable of:

(1) Manual operation; and

(2) Being opened from the hose reel or monitor to which it is connected.

(f) Damage to any dry chemical system hose, monitor, pipe or control circuits must not prevent the operation of other hoses, monitors, or control circuit that are connected to the same storage unit.

§ 154.1170 Hand hose line: General.

Each dry chemical hand hose line must:

(a) Not be longer than 33m (108 ft.);

(b) Be stored on a hose reel or in a hose cabinet and be one that is operable whether or not it is unwound from a hose reel or removed from a hose cabinet;

(c) Be non-kinkable;

(d) Have a nozzle with a valve to start and stop the flow of chemical;

(e) Have a capacity of at least 3.5 kg/sec (7.7 lb./sec); and

(f) Be one that can be operated by one person.

CARGO AREA: MECHANICAL VENTILATION SYSTEM

§ 154.1200 Mechanical ventilation system: General.

(a) Each cargo compressor room, pump room, gas-dangerous cargo control station, and space that contains cargo handling equipment must have a fixed, exhaust-type mechanical ventilation system.

(b) The following must have a supply-type mechanical ventilation system:

(1) Each space that contains electric motors for cargo handling equipment.

(2) Each gas-safe cargo control station in the cargo area.

(3) Each gas-safe space in the cargo area.

(4) Each space that contains inert gas generators, except main machinery spaces.

§ 154.1205 Mechanical ventilation system: Standards.

(a) Each exhaust type mechanical ventilation system required under § 154.1200 (a) must have ducts for vapors from the following:

(1) The deck level.

(2) Bilges.

(3) If the vapors are lighter than air, the top of each space that personnel enter during cargo handling operations.

(b) The discharge end of each duct under paragraph (a) of this section must be at least 10 m (32.8 ft.) from ventilation intakes and openings to accommodations, service, control station, and other gas-safe spaces.

(c) Each ventilation system under § 154.1200 (a) and (b)(1) must change the air in that space and its adjoining trunks at least 30 times each hour.

(d) Each ventilation system for a gas-safe cargo control station in the cargo area must change the air in that space at least eight times each hour.

(e) A ventilation system must not recycle vapor from ventilation discharges.

(f) Each mechanical ventilation system must have its operational controls outside the ventilated space.

(g) No ventilation duct for a gas-dangerous space may pass through any machinery, accommodation, service, or control space, except as allowed under § 154.703.

(h) Each electric motor that drives a ventilation fan must not be within the ducts for any space that may contain flammable cargo vapors.

(i) Ventilation impellers and the housing in way of those impellers on a flammable cargo carrier must meet one of the following:

(1) The impeller, housing, or both made of non-metallic material that does not generate static electricity.

(2) The impeller and housing made of non-ferrous material.

(3) The impeller and housing made of austenitic stainless steel.

(4) The impeller and housing made of ferrous material with at least 13mm (0.512 in.) tip clearance.

(j) No ventilation fan may have any combination of fixed or rotating components made of an aluminum or magnesium alloy and ferrous fixed or rotating components.

(k) Each ventilation intake and exhaust must have a protective metal screen of not more than 13mm (0.512 in.) square mesh.

§ 154.1210 Hold space, void space, cofferdam, and spaces containing cargo piping.

(a) Each hold space, void space, cofferdam, and spaces containing cargo piping must have:

(1) A fixed mechanical ventilation system; or

(2) A fixed ducting system that has a portable blower that meets § 154.1205(i) and (j).

(b) A portable blower in any personnel access opening must not reduce the area of that opening so that the opening does not meet § 154.340.

INSTRUMENTATION

§ 154.1300 Liquid level gauging system: General.

(a) If Table 4 lists a closed gauge for a cargo, the liquid level gauging system under § 154.1305 must be closed gauges that do not have any opening through which cargo liquid or vapor could escape, such as an ultrasonic device, float type device, electronic or magnetic probe, or bubble tube indicator.

(b) If Table 4 lists a restricted gauge for a cargo, the liquid level gauging system under § 154.1305 must be closed gauges that meet paragraph (a) of this section or restricted gauges that do not vent the cargo tank's vapor space, such as a fixed tube, slip tube, or rotary tube.

§ 154.1305 Liquid level gauging system: Standards.

(a) Each cargo tank must have at least one liquid level gauging system that is operable:

(1) At pressures up to, and including, the MARVS of the tank; and

(2) At temperatures that are within the cargo handling temperature range for all cargoes carried.

(b) Unless the cargo tank has one liquid gauging system that can be repaired and maintained when the tank contains cargo, each cargo tank must have at least two liquid level gauging systems that meet paragraph (a) of this section.

(c) Each liquid level gauging system must measure liquid levels from 400 mm (16 in.) or less from the lowest point in the cargo tank, except collection wells, to 100 percent full.

§ 154.1310 Closed gauge shut-off valve.

Each closed gauge that is not mounted directly on the cargo tank must have a shut-off valve that is as close to the tank as practical.

§ 154.1315 Restricted gauge excess flow valve.

Each restricted gauge that penetrates a cargo tank must have an excess flow valve unless the gauge meets § 154.536.

§ 154.1320 Sighting ports, tubular gauge glasses, and flat plate type gauge glasses.

(a) Cargo tanks may have sighting ports as a secondary means of liquid level gauging in addition to the gauges under § 154.1305, if:

(1) The tank has a MARVS that is less than 69 kPa gauge (10 psig);

(2) The port has a protective cover and an internal scale; and

(3) The port is above the liquid level.

(b) Tubular gauge glasses must not be liquid level gauges for cargo tanks.

(c) Plate type gauge glasses must not be liquid level gauges for cargo tanks, except deck tanks if the gauge connections have excess flow valves.

§ 154.1325 Liquid level alarm system: All cargo tanks.

Except as allowed under § 154.1330, each cargo tank must have a high liquid level alarm system that:

(a) Is independent of the liquid level gauging system under § 154.1305;

(b) Actuates quick-closing valves under §§ 154.530, 154.532, and 154.538 or a stop valve in the cargo tank loading line to prevent the tank from becoming 100 percent liquid full and without causing the pressure in the loading lines to exceed the design pressure; and

(c) Actuates an audible and visual alarm at the cargo control station at the liquid level at which the valves under paragraph (b) of this section are actuated or at some lower liquid level.

§ 154.1330 Liquid level alarm system: Independent tank type C.

Independent tanks type C need not have the high liquid level alarm system under § 154.1325 if:

(a) The tank volume is less than 200 m^3 (7,060 ft.^{3}); or

(b) The tank can withstand the maximum possible pressure during loading, that pressure is below the relief valve setting, and overflow of the tank cannot occur.

§ 154.1335 Pressure and vacuum protection.

(a) Each cargo tank must have the following:

(1) A pressure gauge that:

(i) Monitors the vapor space;

(ii) Is readable at the tank; and

(iii) Has remote readouts at the cargo control station.

(2) If vacuum protection is required under § 154.804, a vacuum gauge meeting paragraphs (a)(1)(i), (a)(1)(ii), and (a)(1)(iii) of this section.

(b) The vessel must have at least one high pressure alarm that:

(1) Actuates before the pressure in any cargo tank exceeds the maximum pressure specially approved by the Commandant (CG–OES); and

(2) Actuates an audible and visual alarm at the cargo control station, and a remote group alarm in the wheelhouse.

(c) If vacuum protection is required under § 154.804, the vessel must have at least one low pressure alarm that:

(1) Actuates before the pressure in any cargo tank falls below the minimum pressure specially approved by the Commandant (CG–522); and

(2) Actuates an audible and visual alarm at the cargo control station, and a remote group alarm in the wheelhouse.

(d) At least one pressure gauge must be fitted on each:

(1) Enclosed hold;

§ 154.1340

(2) Enclosed interbarrier space;
(3) Cargo pump discharge line;
(4) Liquid cargo manifold; and
(5) Vapor cargo manifold.

(e) There must be a local manifold pressure gauge between each manifold stop valve and each hose connection to the shore.

[CGD 74–289, 44 FR 26009, May 3, 1979, as amended by CGD 82–063b, 48 FR 4782, Feb. 3, 1983]

§ 154.1340 Temperature measuring devices.

(a) Each cargo tank must have devices that measure the temperature:
(1) At the bottom of the tank; and
(2) Near the top of the tank and below the maximum liquid level allowed under § 154.1844.

(b) Each device required by paragraph (a) must have a readout at the cargo control station.

(c) Except for independent tanks type C, each cargo containment system for a design temperature colder than −55 °C (−67 °F) must have temperature measuring devices that meet the following:
(1) The number and location of the devices must be specially approved by the Commandant (CG–OES).
(2) The devices must be within the cargo tank's insulation or on the adjacent hull structure.
(3) Each device must show the temperature continuously or at regular intervals of one hour or less.
(4) Each device must actuate an audible and visual alarm at the cargo control station and a remote group alarm in the wheelhouse before the temperature of the steel of the adjacent hull structure is cooled below the lowest temperature allowed for the steel under § 154.172.

(d) For each cargo tank with a design temperature colder than −55 °C (−67 °F), the number and arrangement of the devices that show the temperature of the tank during cool down procedures must be specially approved by the Commandant (CG–OES).

[CGD 74–289, 44 FR 26009, May 3, 1979, as amended by CGD 82–063b, 48 FR 4782, Feb. 3, 1983]

§ 154.1345 Gas detection.

(a) Each vessel carrying a cargo that is designated with an "I" or "I and T" in Table 4 must have:
(1) A fixed flammable gas detection system that meets § 154.1350; and
(2) Two portable gas detectors that can each measure 0 to 100% of the lower flammable limit of the cargo carried.

(b) Each vessel carrying a cargo that is designated with a "T" or "I and T" in Table 4 must have:
(1) Two portable gas detectors that show if the concentration of cargo is above or below the threshold limit value listed in 29 CFR 1910.1000 for that cargo; and
(2) Fixed gas sampling tubes in each hold space and interbarrier space with:
(i) The number of tubes specially approved by the Commandant (CG–OES);
(ii) Each tube valved and capped above the main deck unless it is connected to a fixed toxic gas detector;
(iii) If the vessel carries cargo that is heavier than the atmosphere of the space, each tube's open end in the lower part of the space;
(iv) If the vessel carries cargo that is lighter than the atmosphere of the space, each tube's open end in the upper part of the space;
(v) If the vessel carries cargo that is heavier than the atmosphere of the space and another cargo that is lighter than the atmosphere of the space, tubes with their open ends in the lower part of the space and tubes with their open ends in the upper part of the space; and
(vi) If the vessel carries cargo that can be both heavier and lighter than the atmosphere of the space, tubes with their open ends in the lower part of the space and tubes with their open ends in the upper part of the space.

(c) A vessel that carries methyl bromide or sulfur dioxide must have a fixed gas detection system that is not located in a gas-safe space.

(d) A vessel that carries sulfur dioxide must have a fixed gas detection system that meets § 154.1350 except paragraph (j).

(e) Each alarm under § 154.1350(e) on a vessel that carries methyl bromide or sulfur dioxide must be set at or below the threshold limit value listed in 29 CFR 1910.1000 for the cargo carried.

[CGD 74–289, 44 FR 26009, May 3, 1979, as amended by CGD 82–063b, 48 FR 4782, Feb. 3, 1983]

§ 154.1350 Flammable gas detection system.

(a) The vessel must have a fixed flammable gas detection system that has sampling points in:

(1) Each cargo pump room;
(2) Each cargo compressor room;
(3) Each motor room for cargo handling machinery;
(4) Each cargo control station that is not gas-safe;
(5) Each hold space, interbarrier space, and other enclosed spaces, except fuel oil or ballast tanks, in the cargo area, unless the vessel has independent tanks type C; and
(6) Each space between the doors of an air lock under § 154.345.

(b) The sampling points under paragraph (a) of this section must meet § 154.1345(b)(2) (iii) through (vi).

(c) Gas sampling lines for the flammable gas detection system must not pass through any gas-safe space, except the gas-safe space in which the gas detection equipment is located.

(d) Gas detection systems must have a readout with meters that show flammable gas concentration over the concentration or volume ranges under paragraph (t) or (u) of this section.

(e) Each flammable gas detection system must have audible and visual alarms that are actuated at a cargo concentration that is 30% or less of the lower flammable limit in air of the cargo carried.

(f) Each flammable gas detection system must have an audible and visual alarm for power failure and loss of gas sampling flow.

(g) The alarms under paragraphs (e) and (f) of this section must signal in the space where the gas detection system's readout is located and must meet § 154.1365.

(h) Remote group alarms, that indicate that one of the alarm conditions under paragraphs (e) and (f) of this section exists, must meet § 154.1365 and must be in each wheelhouse and in each cargo control station if the gas detection system's readout is not located in those spaces.

(i) Each flammable gas detection system must monitor each sampling point at 30 minute or shorter intervals.

(j) Electrical equipment for each flammable gas detection system that is in a gas-dangerous space or area must meet §§ 154.1000 through 154.1015.

(k) Each flammable gas detection system must have enough flame arrestors for all gas sampling lines to prevent flame propagation to the spaces served by the system through the sampling lines.

(l) Each flammable gas detection system must have a filter that removes particulate matter in each gas sampling line.

(m) Each filter under paragraph (l) of this section must be located where it can be removed during vessel operation, unless it can be freed by back pressure.

(n) Each flammable gas detection system in a gas-safe space must:

(1) Have a shut-off valve in each sampling line from an enclosed space, such as a hold or interbarrier space; and
(2) Exhaust gas to a safe location in the open atmosphere and away from all ignition sources.

(o) Each flammable gas detection system must not have common sampling lines, except sampling lines may be manifolded at the gas detector location if each line has an automatic valve that prevents cross-communication between sampling points.

(p) Each flammable gas detection system must have at least one connection for injecting zero gas and span gas into the system for testing and calibration.

(q) Each flammable gas detection system must have span gas for testing and calibration that is of known concentration.

(r) The calibration test procedure and type and concentration of span gas under paragraph (q) of this section must be on or in each gas analyzer cabinet.

(s) Each flammable gas detection system must have at least one flow meter capable of measuring the flow to the gas analyzer, and must provide a

§ 154.1360

means for ensuring that there is a positive flow in the right direction in each sampling line at all times.

(t) Each flammable gas detection system must measure gas concentrations that:

(1) Are at least 0% through 200% of the alarm concentration; and

(2) Allow calibration of the equipment with span gas.

(u) In each hold and each interbarrier space that contains tanks other than independent tanks type A, B, or C, the flammable gas detection system must measure cargo concentrations of 0 to 100% by volume with:

(1) An analyzer other than the one under paragraph (t) of this section; or

(2) The analyzer under paragraph (t) of this section with a scale switch that automatically returns the analyzer to the concentration range under paragraph (t) of this section when released.

§ 154.1360 Oxygen analyzer.

The vessel must have a portable analyzer that measures oxygen levels in an inert atmosphere.

§ 154.1365 Audible and visual alarms.

(a) Each audible alarm must have an arrangement that allows it to be turned off after sounding. For remote group alarms this arrangement must not interrupt the alarm's actuation by other faults.

(b) Each visual alarm must be one that can be turned off only after the fault that actuated it is corrected.

(c) Each visual alarm must be marked to show the type and, except for remote group alarms, the location of each fault that actuates it.

(d) Each vessel must have means for testing each alarm.

§ 154.1370 Pressure gauge and vacuum gauge marking.

Each pressure gauge and vacuum gauge under § 154.1335(a) must be marked with the maximum and minimum pressures that are specified on the vessel's certificate for the cargo carried.

§ 154.1375 Readout for temperature measuring device: Marking.

Each readout under § 154.1340 for a device that measures temperature in a cargo tank must be marked with the design temperature specified for the cargo tank on the vessel's certificate.

SAFETY EQUIPMENT

§ 154.1400 Safety equipment: All vessels.

(a) Instead of the equipment under § 35.30-20 of this chapter, a vessel of less than 25,000 m^3 cargo capacity must have the following personnel safety equipment:

(1) Six self-contained, pressure-demand-type, air-breathing apparatus approved by the Mining Enforcement and Safety Administration (MESA) or the National Institute for Occupational Safety and Health (NIOSH), each having at least a 30 minute capacity.

(2) Nine spare bottles of air for the self-contained air-breathing apparatus, each having at least a 30 minute capacity.

(3) Six steel-cored lifelines.

(4) Six Type II or Type III flashlights constructed and marked in accordance with ASTM F 1014 (incorporated by reference, see § 154.1).

(5) Three fire axes.

(6) Six helmets that meet ANSI Safety Requirements for Industrial Head Protection, Z-89.1 (1969).

(7) Six sets of boots and gloves that are made of rubber or other electrically non-conductive material.

(8) Six sets of goggles that meet the specifications of ANSI Practice for Occupational and Educational Eye and Face Protection, Z-87.1 (1979).

(9) Three outfits that protect the skin from scalding steam and the heat of a fire, and that have a water resistant outer surface.

(10) Three chemical protective outfits that protect the wearers from the particular personnel hazards presented by the cargo vapor.

(b) Instead of the equipment under § 35.30-20 of this chapter, a vessel of 25,000 m^3 cargo capacity or more must have the following personnel safety equipment:

(1) Eight self-contained, pressure-demand-type, air-breathing apparatus approved by the Mining Enforcement and Safety Administration (MESA) or the National Institute for Occupational Safety and Health (NIOSH), each having at least a 30 minute capacity.

(2) Nine spare bottles of air for the self-contained air-breathing apparatus, each having at least a 30 minute capacity.

(3) Eight steel-cored lifelines.

(4) Eight Type II or Type III flashlights constructed and marked in accordance with ASTM F 1014 (incorporated by reference, see §154.1).

(5) Three fire axes.

(6) Eight helmets that meet ANSI Safety Requirements for Industrial Head Protection, Z–89.1 (1969).

(7) Eight sets of boots and gloves that are made of rubber or other electrically non-conductive material.

(8) Eight sets of goggles that meet the specifications of ANSI Practice for Occupational and Educational Eye and Face Protection, Z–87.1 (1979).

(9) Five outfits that protect the skin from scalding steam and the heat of a fire, and that have a water resistant outer surface.

(10) Three chemical protective outfits that protect the wearers from the particular personnel hazards presented by the cargo vapor.

(c) When Table 4 references this section, a vessel carrying the listed cargo must have the following additional personnel protection equipment:

(1) Three self-contained, pressure-demand-type, air-breathing apparatus approved by the Mining Enforcement and Safety Administration (MESA) or the National Institute for Occupational Safety and Health (NIOSH), each having at least a 30 minute capacity.

(2) Nine spare bottles of air for the self-contained air-breathing apparatus, each having at least a 30 minute capacity.

(3) Three steel-cored lifelines.

(4) Three Type II or Type III flashlights constructed and marked in accordance with ASTM F 1014 (incorporated by reference, see §154.1).

(5) Three helmets that meet ANSI Safety Requirements for Industrial Head Protection, Z–89.1 (1969).

(6) Three sets of boots and gloves that are made of rubber or other electrically non-conductive material.

(7) Three sets of goggles that meet the specifications of ANSI Practice for Occupational and Educational Eye and Face Protection, Z–87.1 (1979).

(8) Three chemical protective outfits that protect the wearers from the particular personnel hazards presented by the cargo vapor.

[CGD 74–289, 44 FR 26009, May 3, 1979, as amended by CGD 77–069, 52 FR 31630, Aug. 21, 1987; CGD 82–042, 17705, May 18, 1988; USCG–1999–5151, 64 FR 67183, Dec. 1, 1999]

§154.1405 Respiratory protection.

When Table 4 references this section, a vessel carrying the listed cargo must have:

(a) Respiratory protection equipment for each person on board that protects the person from the cargo vapor for at least 5 minutes; and

(b) Two additional sets of respiratory protection equipment that:

(1) Are stowed in the wheelhouse; and

(2) Protects the wearer from the cargo vapor for at least 5 minutes.

§154.1410 Decontamination shower.

When Table 4 references this section, a vessel carrying the listed cargo must have a decontamination shower and an eye wash that:

(a) Are on the weatherdeck; and

(b) Have their location marked EMERGENCY SHOWER in letters:

(1) 7.6 cm (3 in.) high; and

(2) 5.1 cm (2 in.) wide.

§154.1415 Air compressor.

Each vessel must have an air compressor to recharge the bottles for the air-breathing apparatus.

§154.1420 Stretchers and equipment.

Each vessel must have:

(a) Two stretchers or wire baskets; and

(b) Equipment for lifting an injured person from a cargo tank, hold, or void space.

§154.1430 Equipment locker.

One of each item of equipment under §§154.1400 and 154.1420 must be stowed in a marked locker:

(a) On the open deck in or adjacent to the cargo area; or

(b) In the accommodation house, near to a door that opens onto the main deck.

§ 154.1435 Medical first aid guide.

Each vessel must have a copy of the *IMO Medical First Aid Guide for Use in Accidents Involving Dangerous Goods*, printed by IMO, London, U.K.

§ 154.1440 Antidotes.

Each vessel must have the antidotes prescribed in the *IMO Medical First Aid Guide for Use in Accidents Involving Dangerous Goods*, printed by IMO, London, U.K. for the cargoes being carried.

Subpart D—Special Design and Operating Requirements

§ 154.1700 Purpose.

This subpart prescribes design and operating requirements that are unique for certain cargoes regulated by this part.

§ 154.1702 Materials of construction.

When Table 4 references one of the following paragraphs in this section, the materials in the referenced paragraph must not be in components that contact the cargo liquid or vapor:

(a) Aluminum and aluminum bearing alloys.
(b) Copper and copper bearing alloys.
(c) Zinc or galvanized steel.
(d) Magnesium.
(e) Mercury.
(f) Acetylide forming materials, such as copper, silver, and mercury.

§ 154.1705 Independent tank type C.

The following cargoes must be carried in an independent tank type C that meets § 154.701(a):

(a) Ethylene oxide.
(b) Methyl bromide.
(c) Sulfur dioxide.

§ 154.1710 Exclusion of air from cargo tank vapor spaces.

When a vessel is carrying acetaldehyde, butadiene, ethylene oxide, or vinyl chloride, the master shall ensure that air is:

(a) Purged from the cargo tanks and associated piping before the cargo is loaded; and
(b) Excluded after the cargo is loaded by maintaining a positive pressure of at least 13.8 kPa gauge (2 psig) by:
(1) Introducing a gas that:
(i) Is not reactive;
(ii) Is not flammable; and
(iii) Does not contain more than 0.2% oxygen by volume; or
(2) Controlling the cargo temperature.

§ 154.1715 Moisture control.

When a vessel is carrying sulfur dioxide, the master shall ensure that:

(a) A cargo tank is dry before it is loaded with sulfur dioxide; and
(b) Air or inert gas admitted into a cargo tank carrying sulfur dioxide during discharging or tank breathing has a moisture content equal to or less than the moisture content of air with a dewpoint of −45 °C (−49 °F) at atmospheric pressure.

§ 154.1720 Indirect refrigeration.

A refrigeration system that is used to cool acetaldehyde, ethylene oxide, or methyl bromide, must be an indirect refrigeration system that does not use vapor compression.

§ 154.1725 Ethylene oxide.

(a) A vessel carrying ethylene oxide must:

(1) Have cargo piping, vent piping, and refrigeration equipment that have no connections to other systems;
(2) Have valves, flanges, fittings, and accessory equipment made of steel, stainless steel, except types 416 and 442, or other material specially approved by the Commandant (CG–OES);
(3) Have valve disk faces, and other wearing parts of valves made of stainless steel containing not less than 11% chromium;
(4) Have gaskets constructed of spirally wound stainless steel with teflon or other material specially approved by the Commandant (CG–OES);
(5) Not have asbestos, rubber, or cast iron components in the cargo containment system and piping;
(6) Not have threaded joints in cargo piping;
(7) Have a water spray system under § 154.1105 that protects the above deck cargo piping; and
(8) Have a nitrogen inerting system or on board nitrogen gas storage that can inert the vapor space of an ethylene oxide cargo tank for a period of 30

days under the condition of paragraph (e) of this section.

(b) Cargo hose used for ethylene oxide must:

(1) Be specially approved by the Commandant (CG–OES); and

(2) Be marked "For (Alkylene or Ethylene) Oxide Transfer Only."

(c) Ethylene oxide must be maintained at less than 30 °C (86 °F).

(d) Cargo tank relief valves for tanks containing ethylene oxide must be set at 539 kPa gauge (78.2 psig) or higher.

(e) The vapor space of a cargo tank carrying ethylene oxide must be maintained at a nitrogen concentration of 45% by volume.

(f) A vessel must have a method for jettisoning ethylene oxide that meets §§ 154.356 and 154.1872.

[CGD 74–289, 44 FR 26009, May 3, 1979, as amended by CGD 82–063b, 48 FR 4782, Feb. 3, 1983]

§ 154.1730 Ethylene oxide: Loading and off loading.

(a) The master shall ensure that before ethylene oxide is loaded into a cargo tank:

(1) The tank is thoroughly clean, dry, and free of rust;

(2) The hold spaces are inerted with an inert gas that meets § 154.1710(b)(1); and

(3) The cargo tank vapor space is inerted with nitrogen.

(b) Ethylene oxide must be off loaded by a deepwell pump or inert gas displacement.

(c) Ethylene oxide must not be carried in deck tanks.

§ 154.1735 Methyl acetylene-propadiene mixture.

(a) The composition of the methyl acetylene-propadiene mixture at loading must be within the following limits or specially approved by the Commandant (CG–OES):

(1) One composition is:

(i) Maximum methyl acetylene and propadiene molar ratio of 3 to 1;

(ii) Maximum combined concentration of methyl acetylene and propadiene of 65 mole percent;

(iii) Minimum combined concentration of propane, butane, and isobutane of 24 mole percent, of which at least one-third (on a molar basis) must be butanes and one-third propane; and

(iv) Maximum combined concentration of propylene and butadiene of 10 mole percent.

(2) A second composition is:

(i) Maximum methyl acetylene and propadiene combined concentration of 30 mole percent;

(ii) Maximum methyl acetylene concentration of 20 mole percent;

(iii) Maximum propadiene concentration of 20 mole percent;

(iv) Maximum propylene concentration of 45 mole percent;

(v) Maximum butadiene and butylenes combined concentration of 2 mole percent;

(vi) A minimum saturated C_4 hydrocarbon concentration of 4 mole percent; and

(vii) A minimum propane concentration of 25 mole percent.

(b) A vessel carrying a methyl acetylene-propadiene mixture must have a refrigeration system without vapor compression or have a refrigeration system with the following features:

(1) A vapor compressor that does not raise the temperature and pressure of the vapor above 60 °C (140 °F) and 1.72 MPa gauge (250 psig) during its operation and that does not allow vapor to stagnate in the compressor while it continues to run.

(2) Discharge piping from each compressor stage or each cylinder in the same stage of a reciprocating compressor that has:

(i) Two temperature actuated shutdown switches set to operate at 60 °C (140 °F) or less;

(ii) A pressure actuated shutdown switch set to operate at 1.72 MPa gauge (250 psig) or less; and

(iii) A safety relief valve set to relieve at 1.77 MPa gauge (256 psig) or less.

(3) A relief valve that vents to a mast meeting § 154.805 and that does not relieve into the compressor suction line.

(4) An alarm that sounds in the cargo control station and in the wheelhouse when any of the high pressure or high temperature switches under paragraphs (b)(2)(i) and (b)(2)(ii) of this section operate.

(c) A vessel carrying a methyl acetylene-propadiene mixture must have

§ 154.1740

separate cargo piping, vent piping, and refrigeration equipment for methyl acetylene-propadiene that are segregated from other cargo piping, vent piping and refrigeration equipment on the vessel.

[CGD 74–289, 44 FR 26009, May 3, 1979; 44 FR 59234, Oct. 15, 1979; CGD 82–063b, 48 FR 4782, Feb. 3, 1983]

§ 154.1740 Vinyl chloride: Inhibiting and inerting.

When a vessel is carrying vinyl chloride, the master shall ensure that:

(a) Section 154.1818 is met; or

(b) Section 154.1710 is met, and the oxygen content of inert gas is less than 0.1% by volume.

§ 154.1745 Vinyl chloride: Transferring operations.

A vessel carrying vinyl chloride must meet the requirements of § 151.50–34(g) through (k) of this chapter.

[CGD 95–012, 60 FR 48051, Sept. 18, 1995]

§ 154.1750 Butadiene or vinyl chloride: Refrigeration system.

A refrigeration system for butadiene or vinyl chloride must not use vapor compression unless it:

(a) Avoids any stagnation points where uninhibited liquid can accumulate; or

(b) Has inhibited liquid from the cargo tank added to the vapor upstream of the condenser.

§ 154.1755 Nitrogen.

Except for deck tanks and their piping systems, cargo containment systems and piping systems carrying nitrogen must be specially approved by the Commandant (CG–OES).

[CGD 74–289, 44 FR 26009, May 3, 1979, as amended by CGD 82–063b, 48 FR 4782, Feb. 3, 1983]

§ 154.1760 Liquid ammonia.

The master shall ensure that no person sprays liquid ammonia into a cargo tank containing more than 8% oxygen by volume.

Subpart E—Operations

§ 154.1800 Special operating requirements under Part 35 of this chapter.

Each vessel must meet the requirements of Part 35 of this chapter except § 35.30–20.

§ 154.1801 Certificates, letters, and endorsements: U.S. flag vessels.

No person may operate a U.S. flag vessel unless the vessel has a Certificate of Inspection, issued under Subchapter D of this chapter, which is endorsed with the name of the cargo that it is allowed to carry.

§ 154.1802 Certificates, letters and endorsements: Foreign flag vessels.

(a) No person may operate on the navigable waters of the United States a foreign flag vessel, whose flag administration issues IMO Certificates, unless the vessel has:

(1) An IMO Certificate issued by the flag administration that is endorsed with the name of the cargo that it is allowed to carry, and, except when entering United States waters to be examined as required by § 154.150, a Certificate of Compliance[1] issued by the Coast Guard endorsed under this part with the name of the cargo that it is allowed to carry; or

(2) Special approval under § 154.30.

(b) No person may operate on the navigable waters of the United States a foreign flag vessel, whose flag administration does not issue IMO Certificates, unless the vessel has:

(1) Except when entering United States waters to be examined as required by § 154.150, a Certificate of Compliance[1] issued by the Coast Guard endorsed under this part with the name of the cargo it is allowed to carry; or

(2) Special approval under § 154.30.

(c) No person may operate on the navigable waters of the United States a foreign flag vessel unless the vessel has

---

[1] Until the Certificate of Compliance form is developed, the Letter of Compliance with a Subchapter O endorsement for the carriage of liquefied gases will serve the purpose of the endorsed Certificate of Compliance.

onboard the following plans and information which except for the certificates under paragraph (c)(1) of this section, are in English:

(1) The vessel's Cargo Ship Safety Construction Certificate and Cargo Ship Safety Equipment Certificate issued under the International Convention for Safety of Life at Sea, 1974.

(2) A description and schematic plan of the arrangement for inerting cargo tanks, hold spaces, and interbarrier spaces.

(3) A description of the cargo tank gauging equipment.

(4) A description and instruction manual for the calibration of the cargo leak detector equipment.

(5) A schematic plan that shows the locations of leak detectors and sampling points.

(6) If the vessel carries methane, a description of the systems for cargo temperature and pressure control. (See §§ 154.703 through 154.709.)

[CGD 74–289, 44 FR 26009, May 3, 1979, as amended by CGD 81–052, 50 FR 8735, Mar. 5, 1985; CGD 77–069, 52 FR 31631, Aug. 21, 1987; CGD 90–008, 55 FR 30663, July 26, 1990]

§ 154.1803 Expiration of Certificates of Compliance.

(a) A Certificate of Compliance expires after a period not to exceed twenty-four months from the date of the examination under § 154.150.

(b) If a vessel's IMO Certificate of Fitness expires or otherwise becomes invalid, its Certificate of Compliance becomes invalid for the carriage of cargoes listed in Table 4 of this part or authorized by special approval under § 154.12. To maintain the validity of the Certificate of Compliance, the vessel's owner must submit a copy of any revised or reissued IMO Certificate to Commanding Officer, Marine Safety Center.

[CGD 81–052, 50 FR 8735, Mar. 5, 1985; CGD 95–072, 60 FR 50466, Sept. 29, 1995; 60 FR 54106, Oct. 19, 1995]

§ 154.1804 Document posted in wheelhouse.

No person may operate a U.S. flag vessel unless the documents under § 154.1801 are under glass in a conspicuous place in the wheelhouse.

§ 154.1806 Regulations on board.

No person may operate a U.S. flag vessel unless a copy of this part and a copy of Part 35 of this chapter are on board.

§ 154.1808 Limitations in the endorsement.

No person may operate a vessel unless that person complies with all limitations in the endorsement on the vessel's Certificate of Inspection or Certificate of Compliance.

[CGD 81–052, 50 FR 8735, Mar. 5, 1985]

§ 154.1809 Loading and stability manual.

(a) No person may operate a vessel unless that vessel has on board a loading and stability manual.

(b) The loading and stability manual must contain:

(1) Information that enables the master to load and ballast the vessel while keeping structural stresses within design limits; and

(2) The information required by § 170.110 of this chapter.

[CGD 74–289, 44 FR 26009, May 3, 1979, as amended by CGD 79–023, 49 FR 51010, Nov. 4, 1983]

§ 154.1810 Cargo manual.

(a) No person may operate a foreign flag vessel, whose flag administration does not issue IMO Certificates, on the navigable waters of the United States, or a U.S. flag vessel, unless the vessel has on board a cargo manual containing the following information:

(1) A description of each cargo carried, its handling hazards as a liquid or as a gas including frostbite or asphyxiation, its safety equipment and necessary first aid measures required by this part.

(2) A description of the dangers of asphyxiation from the inerting gases used on the vessel.

(3) The measures that mitigate embrittlement of steel structure in way of cargo leakage.

(4) The use of the firefighting systems on the vessel.

(5) The features of the cargo containment system that affect its operation and maintenance, including pressure

§ 154.1812

and temperature ranges and relief valve settings.

(6) Pressures, temperatures, and liquid levels for all operations.

(7) General information derived from the first loading of the vessel.

(8) Alarm settings.

(9) Descriptions of the components of the cargo system, including the following:

(i) Liquid cargo system.

(ii) Liquid recirculating or condensate return system.

(iii) Cargo tank cool-down system.

(iv) Cargo tank warm-up or vaporization system.

(v) Gas main system.

(vi) Cargo tank or compressor relief system and blocked liquid or gas relief system.

(vii) Inerting system.

(viii) Boil-off gas compressor or re-liquefaction system.

(ix) Gas detection systems.

(x) Alarm or safety indication systems.

(xi) Cargo jettisoning system.

(xii) The system for using boil-off gas as fuel.

(10) A description of cargo loading and discharge operations, including simultaneous handling of multigrades of cargo and ballast.

(11) A description of cargo operations during the voyage.

(12) A description of cargo tank cool-down and warm-up operations including purging with inert gas and air.

(13) A description of hull and cargo tank temperature monitoring systems.

(14) A description of gas detection systems and alarm or safety systems.

(15) A description of the following conditions and their symptoms, including emergency measures and corrective actions:

(i) Cargo or ballast valve malfunction.

(ii) Low cargo tank gas pressure.

(iii) High fill level shutdown.

(iv) Gas compressor shutdown.

(v) Hull cold spots.

(vi) Cargo piping leaks.

(vii) Primary or secondary barrier failure.

(viii) Hold boundary structural failure.

(ix) Fire in vent mast head.

(x) Reliquefaction plant failure.

(xi) Vaporizer malfunction or failure.

(xii) Piping or cargo valve freeze-up.

(16) Any other matters relating to operation of the cargo systems.

(17) The operational means to maintain the vessel in a condition of positive stability in accordance with the loading and stability manual under § 154.1809 through all conditions of:

(i) Loading and deballasting; and

(ii) Unloading and ballasting.

(b) The master shall ensure that the cargo manual is kept up-to-date.

§ 154.1812 Operational information for terminal personnel.

The master shall ensure that terminal personnel are told the operational information required by § 154.1810(a)(17).

§ 154.1814 Cargo information cards.

(a) No person may operate a vessel unless a cargo information card for each cargo being transported is carried either in the wheelhouse, in the ship's office, or in another location easily accessible to the person in charge of the watch.

(b) When a vessel is moored at a terminal, the master shall ensure that a set of information cards is in the possession of the terminal's person in charge of cargo transfer operations.

(c) Each card must be at least 17 cm × 24 cm (6¾ in. × 9½ in.), have printing on one side only, and must contain the following information about the cargo:

(1) Name as listed in Table 4.

(2) Appearance.

(3) Odor.

(4) Safe handling procedures, including special handling instructions, and handling hazards.

(5) Procedures to follow in the event of spills, leaks, or uncontrolled cargo release.

(6) Procedures to be followed if a person is exposed to the cargo.

(7) Firefighting procedures and materials.

§ 154.1816 Cargo location plan.

The master shall ensure that:

(a) A cargo location plan is prepared that gives:

(1) The location and number of each cargo tank; and

(2) The name of the cargo in each tank;

(b) One cargo location plan is kept with the sets of cargo information cards required under § 154.1814; and

(c) The cargo names in the cargo location plan do not differ from the names of the cargoes listed in Table 4.

§ 154.1818 Certification of inhibition.

(a) Except as provided in § 154.1740(b), no person may operate a vessel carrying butadiene or vinyl chloride without carrying in the wheelhouse written certification from the shipper that the product is inhibited.

(b) The certification required by this section must contain the following information:

(1) The name and concentration of the inhibitor.

(2) The date the inhibitor was added.

(3) The expected duration of the inhibitor's effectiveness.

(4) Any temperature limitations qualifying the inhibitor's effective lifetime.

(5) The action to be taken if the time of the voyage exceeds the inhibitor's lifetime.

§ 154.1820 Shipping document.

No person may operate a vessel without carrying a shipping document in the wheelhouse that lists for each cargo on board:

(a) The cargo tank in which the cargo is stowed;

(b) The name of the shipper;

(c) The location of the loading terminal;

(d) The cargo name as listed in Table 4; and

(e) The approximate quantity of the cargo.

§ 154.1822 Shipping document: Copy for transfer terminal.

While a vessel is moored at a transfer terminal, the master shall ensure that at least one copy of the shipping document is given to the terminal's person in charge of cargo transfer.

§ 154.1824 Obstruction of pumproom ladderways.

The master shall ensure that each cargo pumproom access is unobstructed.

§ 154.1826 Opening of cargo tanks and cargo sampling.

(a) The master shall ensure that each cargo tank opening is fully closed at all times.

(b) The master may authorize the opening of a cargo tank:

(1) During tank cleaning; and

(2) To sample a cargo that Table 4 allows to be carried in a containment system having a restricted gauging system if:

(i) The cargo tank is not being filled during sampling;

(ii) The vent system has relieved any pressure in the tank; and

(iii) The person sampling the cargo wears protective clothing.

(c) The master shall ensure that cargoes requiring closed gauging as listed in Table 4 are sampled only through the controlled sampling arrangement of the cargo tank.

§ 154.1828 Spaces containing cargo vapor: Entry.

(a) No person may enter a cargo handling space without the permission of the master or without following a safety procedure established by the master.

(b) Before allowing anyone to enter a cargo handling space, the master shall ensure that:

(1) The space is free of toxic vapors and has an oxygen concentration of at least 19.5 percent oxygen by volume; or

(2) Those entering the space wear protective equipment with breathing apparatus and an officer closely supervises the entire operation in the space.

§ 154.1830 Warning sign.

(a) The master shall ensure that a vessel transferring cargo, while fast to a dock or while at anchor in port, displays a warning sign:

(1) At the gangway facing the shore so that the sign may be seen from the shore; and

(2) Facing outboard towards the water so that the sign may be seen from the water.

(b) Except as provided in paragraph (e) of this section, each warning sign must have the following words:

(1) Warning.

(2) Dangerous Cargo.

(3) No Visitors.

(4) No Smoking.

§ 154.1831

(5) No Open Lights.

(c) Each letter in the words on the sign must:

(1) Be block style;
(2) Be black on a white background;
(3) Be 7.6 cm (3 in.) high;
(4) Be 5.1 cm (2 in.) wide, except for "M" and "W" which must be 7.6 cm (3 in.) wide, and the letter "I" which may be 1.3 cm (½ in.) wide; and
(5) Have 1.3 cm (½ in.) stroke width.

(d) The spacing between letters must be:

(1) 1.3 cm (½ in.) between letters of the same word on the sign;
(2) 5.1 cm (2 in.) between words;
(3) 5.1 cm (2 in.) between lines; and
(4) 5.1 cm (2 in.) at the borders of the sign.

(e) The words "No Smoking" and "No Open Lights" may be omitted when the cargoes on board a vessel are not flammable.

(f) When a vessel carries or transfers vinyl chloride, the warning sign under paragraph (b) of this section must also have the words "Cancer Suspect Agent."

§ 154.1831 Persons in charge of transferring liquid cargo in bulk or preparing cargo tanks.

(a) The owner and operator of the vessel, and his or her agent, and each of them, shall ensure that—

(1) Enough "Tankerman-PICs" or restricted "Tankerman-PICs", and "Tankerman-Assistants", authorized for the classification of cargo carried, are on duty to safely conduct a transfer of liquid cargo in bulk or a cooldown, warm-up, gas-free, or air-out of each cargo tank;

(2) Each transfer of liquid cargo in bulk, and each cool-down, warm-up, gas-free, or air-out of a cargo tank, is supervised by a person designated as a person in charge of the transfer that possesses the qualifications required by 33 CFR 155.710;

(3) On each foreign tankship, the person in charge of either a transfer of liquid cargo in bulk or a cool-down, warm-up, gas-free, or air-out of a cargo tank possesses the qualifications required by 33 CFR 155.710;

(4) When cargo regulated under this part is being transferred, the person in charge of the transfer has received special training in the particular hazards associated with the cargo and in all special procedures for its handling; and

(5) On each foreign vessel, the person in charge understands his or her responsibilities as described in this subchapter.

(b) Upon request by the Officer in Charge, Marine Inspection, in whose zone the transfer will take place, the owner and operator of the vessel, and his or her agent, and each of them, shall provide documentary evidence that the person in charge has received the training specified by paragraph (a)(4) of this section and is capable of competently performing the procedures necessary for the cargo.

[CGD 79–116, 60 FR 17158, Apr. 4, 1995]

§ 154.1834 Cargo transfer piping.

The person in charge of cargo transfer shall ensure that cargo is transferred to or from a cargo tank only through the cargo piping system.

§ 154.1836 Vapor venting as a means of cargo tank pressure and temperature control.

When the vessel is on the navigable waters of the United States, the master shall ensure that the cargo pressure and temperature control system under §§ 154.701 through 154.709 is operating and that venting of cargo is unnecessary to maintain cargo temperature and pressure control, except under emergency conditions.

§ 154.1838 Discharge by gas pressurization.

The person in charge of cargo transfer may not authorize cargo discharge by gas pressurization unless:

(a) The tank to be offloaded is an independent tank type B or C;

(b) The pressurizing medium is the cargo vapor or a nonflammable, nontoxic gas that is inert with the cargo; and

(c) The pressurizing line has:

(1) A pressure reducing valve that has a setting that is 90 percent or less of the tank's relief valve setting; and

(2) A manual control valve between the pressure reducing valve and the tank.

§ 154.1840 Protective clothing.

The person in charge of cargo transfer shall ensure that each person involved in a cargo transfer operation, except those assigned to gas-safe cargo control rooms, wears protective clothing.

§ 154.1842 Cargo system: Controls and alarms.

The master shall ensure that the cargo emergency shut-down system and the alarms under § 154.1325 are tested and working before cargo is transferred.

§ 154.1844 Cargo tanks: Filling limits.

(a) Unless a higher limit is specified on the certificate the master shall ensure that a cargo tank is not loaded:

(1) More than 98 percent liquid full; or

(2) In excess of the volume determined under the following formula:

$$V_L = (0.98\ V)\left(\frac{d_r}{d_L}\right)$$

where:

V_L = maximum volume to which the tank may be loaded;
V = volume of the tank;
d_r = density at the reference temperature specified in paragraph (b) of this section; and
d_L = density of the cargo at the loading temperature and pressure.

(b) The reference temperature to be used in paragraph (a)(2) of this section is the temperature corresponding to the vapor pressure of the cargo at the set pressure of the pressure relief valves.

§ 154.1846 Relief valves: Changing set pressure.

The master shall:

(a) Supervise the changing of the set pressure of relief valves under § 154.802(b);

(b) Enter the change of set pressure in the vessel's log; and

(c) Ensure that a sign showing the set pressure is posted:

(1) In the cargo control room or station; and

(2) At each relief valve.

§ 154.1848 Inerting.

(a) The master shall ensure that:

(1) Hold and interbarrier spaces on a vessel with full secondary barriers are inerted so that the oxygen concentration is 8 percent or less by volume when flammable cargoes are carried;

(2) Hold and interbarrier spaces contain only dry air or inert gas on:

(i) A vessel with partial secondary barriers;

(ii) A vessel with full secondary barriers when non-flammable cargoes are carried; and

(iii) A vessel with refrigerated independent tanks type C;

(3) When cargo tanks containing flammable vapor are to be gas freed, the flammable vapors are purged from the tank by inert gas before air is admitted; and

(4) When gas free cargo tanks are to be filled with a flammable cargo, air is purged from the tank by inert gas until the oxygen concentration in the tank is 8 percent or less by volume before cargo liquid or vapor is introduced.

(b) Inert gas must be supplied from the shore or from the vessel's inert gas system.

§ 154.1850 Entering cargo handling spaces.

(a) The master shall ensure that the ventilation system under § 154.1200 is in operation for 30 minutes before a person enters one of the following:

(1) Spaces containing cargo pumps, compressors, and compressor motors.

(2) Gas-dangerous cargo control spaces.

(3) Other spaces containing cargo handling equipment.

(b) The master shall ensure that a warning sign listing the requirement for use of the ventilation system, is posted outside of each space under paragraph (a) of this section.

(c) The master shall ensure that no sources of ignition are put in a cargo handling space on a vessel carrying flammable cargo unless the space is gas free.

§ 154.1852 Air breathing equipment.

(a) The master shall ensure that a licensed officer inspects the compressed air breathing equipment at least once each month.

§ 154.1854

(b) The master shall enter in the vessel's log a record of the inspection required under paragraph (a) of this section that includes:

(1) The date of the inspection; and

(2) The condition of the equipment at the time of the inspection.

§ 154.1854 Methane (LNG) as fuel.

(a) If methane (LNG) vapors are used as fuel in the main propulsion system of a vessel, the master shall ensure that the fuel oil fired pilot under § 154.705(c) is used when the vessel is on the navigable waters of the United States.

(b) When the methane (LNG) fuel supply is shut down due to loss of ventilation or detection of gas, the master shall ensure that the methane (LNG) fuel supply is not used until the leak or other cause of the shutdown is found and corrected.

(c) The master shall ensure that the required procedure under paragraph (b) of this section is posted in the main machinery space.

(d) The master shall ensure that the oxygen concentration in the annular space of the fuel line under § 154.706(a)(1) is 8% or less by volume before methane (LNG) vapors are admitted to the fuel line.

§ 154.1858 Cargo hose.

The person in charge of cargo transfer shall ensure that cargo hose used for cargo transfer service meets §§ 154.552 through 154.562.

§ 154.1860 Integral tanks: Cargo colder than −10 °C (14 °F).

The master shall ensure that an integral tank does not carry a cargo colder than −10 °C (14 °F) unless that carriage is specially approved by the Commandant (CG–OES).

[CGD 74–289, 44 FR 26009, May 3, 1979, as amended by CGD 82–063b, 48 FR 4782, Feb. 3, 1983]

§ 154.1862 Posting of speed reduction.

If a speed reduction is specially approved by the Commandant under § 154.409, the master shall ensure that the speed reduction is posted in the wheelhouse.

§ 154.1864 Vessel speed within speed reduction.

The master shall ensure that the speed of the vessel is not greater than the posted speed reduction.

§ 154.1866 Cargo hose connection: Transferring cargo.

No person may transfer cargo through a cargo hose connection unless the connection has the remotely controlled quick closing shut off valve required under § 154.538.

§ 154.1868 Portable blowers in personnel access openings.

The master shall ensure that a portable blower in a personnel access opening does not reduce the area of the opening so that it does not meet § 154.340.

§ 154.1870 Bow and stern loading.

(a) When the bow or stern loading piping is not in use, the master shall lock closed the shut-off valves under § 154.355(a)(4) or remove the spool piece under § 154.355(a)(4).

(b) The person in charge of cargo transfer shall ensure that after the bow or stern loading piping is used it is purged of cargo vapors with inert gas.

(c) The person in charge of cargo transfer shall ensure that entrances, forced or natural ventilation intakes, exhausts, and other openings to any deck house alongside the bow or stern loading piping are closed when this piping is in use.

(d) The person in charge of cargo transfer shall ensure that bow or stern loading piping installed in the area of the accommodation, service, or control space is not used for transfer of the following:

(1) Acetaldehyde.
(2) Ammonia, anhydrous.
(3) Dimethylamine.
(4) Ethylamine.
(5) Ethyl Chloride.
(6) Methyl Chloride.
(7) Vinyl Chloride.

§ 154.1872 Cargo emergency jettisoning.

(a) The master shall ensure that emergency jettisoning piping under § 154.356, except bow and stern loading

Coast Guard, DHS § 154.1872

and discharging piping, is only used when an emergency exists.

(b) Emergency jettisoning piping when being used may be outside of the transverse tank location under § 154.310.

(c) The master shall ensure that cargo is not jettisoned in a U.S. port.

(d) When ethylene oxide is carried, the master shall ensure that the emergency jettisoning piping with associated pumps and fittings is on-line and ready for use for an emergency.

(e) The master shall lock closed the shut-off valves under § 154.356 when the emergency jettisoning piping is not in use.

(f) The person in charge of cargo transfer shall ensure that after the emergency jettisoning piping is used it is purged of cargo vapors with inert gas.

(g) The person in charge of cargo transfer shall ensure that entrances, forced or natural ventilation intakes, exhausts, and other openings to accommodation, service, or control spaces facing the emergency jettisoning piping area and alongside the emergency jettisoning piping are closed when this piping is in use.

TABLE 4—SUMMARY OF MINIMUM REQUIREMENTS

Cargo name [1]	Ship type	Independent tank type C required	Control of cargo tank vapor space	Vapor detection [2]	Gauging [3]	Electrical hazard class and group [4]	Special requirements
Acetaldehyde	IIG/IIPG	....	Inert	I & T	C	I-C	154.1410 (c), 154.1410, 154.1710, 154.1720, 154.1870.
Ammonia, anhydrous.	IIG/IIPG	....	....	T	C	I-D	154.1000, 154.1400 (c), 154.1405, 154.1410, 154.1702 (b), (c), (e), 154.1760, 154.1870.
Butadiene	IIG/IIPG	....	Inert	I	R	I-B	154.1702 (b), (d), (f), 154.1710, 154.1750, 154.1818.
Butane	IIG/IIPG	....	....	I	R	I-D	None.
Butylene	IIG/IIPG	....	....	I	R	I-D	None.
Dimethylamine	IIG/IIPG	....	....	I & T	C	I-C	154.1400 (c), 154.1405, 154.1410, 154.1702 (b), (c), (e), 154.1870.
Ethane	IIG	....	....	I	R	I-D	None.
Ethylamine	IIG/IIPG	....	....	I & T	C	I-C	154.1400 (c), 154.1405, 154.1410, 154.1702 (b), (c), (e), 154.1870.
Ethyl Chloride	IIG/IIPG	....	....	I & T	R	I-D	154.1870.
Ethylene	IIG	....	....	I	R	I-C	None.
Ethylene oxide	IG	Yes	Inert	I & T	C	I-B	154.660 (b) (3), 154.1400 (c), 154.1405, 154.1410, 154.1702 (b), (d), (f), 154.1705, 154.1710, 154.1720, 154.1725, 154.1730, 154.1870 (a), (b).
Methane (LNG).	IIG	....	....	I	C	I-D	154.703 through 154.709, 154.1854.
Methyl acetylene-propadiene mixture.	IIG/IIPG	....	....	I	R	I	154.1735.
Methyl bromide.	IG	Yes	....	I & T	C	I-D	154.660 (b) (3), 154.1345 (c) (d), 154.1400 (c), 154.1405, 154.1410, 154.1702 (a), (d), 154.1705, 154.1710, 154.1870 (a), (b).
Methyl chloride.	IIG/IIPG	....	....	I & T	C	I-D	154.1702 (a), 154.1870.
Nitrogen	IIIG	....	....	O	C	....	154.1755.
Propane	IIG/IIPG	....	....	I	R	I-D	None.
Propylene	IIG/IIPG	....	....	I	R	I-D	None.
Refrigerant	IIIG	....	....	....	R	....	None.

TABLE 4—SUMMARY OF MINIMUM REQUIREMENTS—Continued

Cargo name [1]	Ship type	Independent tank type C required	Control of cargo tank vapor space	Vapor detection [2]	Gauging [3]	Electrical hazard class and group [4]	Special requirements
Sulfur dioxide	IG	Yes	Dry	T	C		154.660 (b) (3), 154.1345 (c), (d), 154.1400 (c), 154.1405, 154.1410, 154.1705, 154.1715, 154.1720, 154.1870 (a), (b).
Vinyl chloride	IIG/IIPG			I & T	C	I-D	154.1405, 154.1410, 154.1702 (a) (b) (d) (f), 154.1710, 154.1740, 154.1745, 154.1750, 154.1818, 154.1830 (f), 154.1870.

[1] Refrigerant gases include non-toxic, non-flammable gases such as: dichlorodifluoromethane, dichloromonofluoromethane, dichlorotetrafluoroethane, monochlorodifluoromethane, monochlorotetrafluoroethane, and monochlorotrifluoromethane.
[2] As used in this column: "I" stands for flammable vapor detection; "T" stands for toxic vapor detection; "O" stands for oxygen detection; and see §§ 154.1345 thru 154.1360.
[3] As used in this column: "C" stands for closed gauging; "R" stands for restricted gauging; and see § 154.1300.
[4] The designations used in this column are from the National Electrical Code.

[CGD 74-289, 44 FR 26009, May 3, 1979; 44 FR 59234, Oct. 15, 1979]

APPENDIX A TO PART 154—EQUIVALENT STRESS

I. Equivalent stress (σ c) is calculated by the following formula or another formula specially approved by the Commandant (CG-522) as equivalent to the following:

$$\sigma_c = \sqrt{\sigma_x^2 + \sigma_y^2 - \sigma_x \sigma_y + 3\tau_{xy}^2}$$

where:

σ_x=total normal stress in "x" direction.
σ_y=total normal stress in "y" direction.
τ_{xy}=total shear stress in "xy" plane.

II. When the static and dynamic stresses are calculated separately, the total stresses in paragraph I are calculated from the following formulae or another formulae specially approved by the Commandant (CG-522) as equivalent to the following:

$$\sigma_x = \sigma_x(\text{static}) \pm \sqrt{\sum (\sigma_x(\text{dynamic}))^2}$$

$$\sigma_y = \sigma_y(\text{static}) \pm \sqrt{\sum (\sigma_y(\text{dynamic}))^2}$$

$$\tau_{xy} = \tau_{xy}(\text{static}) \pm \sqrt{\sum (\tau_{xy}(\text{dynamic}))^2}$$

III. Each dynamic and static stress is determined from its acceleration component and its hull strain component from hull deflection and torsion.

[CGD 74-289, 44 FR 26009, May 3, 1979, as amended by CGD 82-063b, 48 FR 4782, Feb. 3, 1983]

APPENDIX B TO PART 154—STRESS ANALYSES DEFINITIONS

The following are the standard definitions of stresses for the analysis of an independent tank type B:

Normal stress means the component of stress normal to the plane of reference.

Membrane stress means the component of normal stress that is uniformly distributed and equal to the average value of the stress across the thickness of the section under consideration.

Bending stress means the variable stress across the thickness of the section under consideration, after the subtraction of the membrane stress.

Shear stress means the component of the stress acting in the plane of reference.

Primary stress means the stress produced by the imposed loading that is necessary to balance the external forces and moments. (The basic characteristic of a primary stress is that it is not self-limiting. Primary stresses that considerably exceed the yield strength result in failure or at least in gross deformations.)

Primary general membrane stress means the primary membrane stress that is so distributed in the structure that no redistribution of load occurs as a result of yielding.

Primary local membrane stress means the resulting stress from both a membrane stress, caused by pressure or other mechanical loading, and a primary or a discontinuity effect that produces excessive distortion in the transfer of loads to other portions of the structure. (The resulting stress is a primary local membrane stress although it has some characteristics of a secondary stress.) A stress region is local if:

$$S_1 \leq 0.5\sqrt{Rt}; \text{ and}$$

$$S_2 \leq 2.5\sqrt{Rt}$$

where:

S_1=distance in the meridional direction over which the equivalent stress exceeds 1.1 f.

S_2=distance in the meridional direction to another region where the limits for primary general membrane stress are exceeded.

R=mean radius of the vessel.

t=wall thickness of the vessel at the location where the primary general membrane stress limit is exceeded.

f=allowable primary general membrane stress.

Secondary stress means a normal stress or shear stress caused by constraints of adjacent parts or by self-constraint of a structure. The basic characteristic of a secondary stress is that it is self-limiting. Local yielding and minor distortions can satisfy the conditions that cause the stress to occur.

PART 155 [RESERVED]

SUBCHAPTER P—MANNING OF VESSELS [RESERVED]

FINDING AIDS

A list of CFR titles, subtitles, chapters, subchapters and parts and an alphabetical list of agencies publishing in the CFR are included in the CFR Index and Finding Aids volume to the Code of Federal Regulations which is published separately and revised annually.

Table of CFR Titles and Chapters
Alphabetical List of Agencies Appearing in the CFR
List of CFR Sections Affected

Table of CFR Titles and Chapters
(Revised as of October 1, 2013)

Title 1—General Provisions

I Administrative Committee of the Federal Register (Parts 1—49)
II Office of the Federal Register (Parts 50—299)
III Administrative Conference of the United States (Parts 300—399)
IV Miscellaneous Agencies (Parts 400—500)

Title 2—Grants and Agreements

SUBTITLE A—OFFICE OF MANAGEMENT AND BUDGET GUIDANCE FOR GRANTS AND AGREEMENTS

I Office of Management and Budget Governmentwide Guidance for Grants and Agreements (Parts 2—199)
II Office of Management and Budget Circulars and Guidance (200—299)

SUBTITLE B—FEDERAL AGENCY REGULATIONS FOR GRANTS AND AGREEMENTS

III Department of Health and Human Services (Parts 300— 399)
IV Department of Agriculture (Parts 400—499)
VI Department of State (Parts 600—699)
VII Agency for International Development (Parts 700—799)
VIII Department of Veterans Affairs (Parts 800—899)
IX Department of Energy (Parts 900—999)
XI Department of Defense (Parts 1100—1199)
XII Department of Transportation (Parts 1200—1299)
XIII Department of Commerce (Parts 1300—1399)
XIV Department of the Interior (Parts 1400—1499)
XV Environmental Protection Agency (Parts 1500—1599)
XVIII National Aeronautics and Space Administration (Parts 1800—1899)
XX United States Nuclear Regulatory Commission (Parts 2000—2099)
XXII Corporation for National and Community Service (Parts 2200—2299)
XXIII Social Security Administration (Parts 2300—2399)
XXIV Housing and Urban Development (Parts 2400—2499)
XXV National Science Foundation (Parts 2500—2599)
XXVI National Archives and Records Administration (Parts 2600—2699)
XXVII Small Business Administration (Parts 2700—2799)
XXVIII Department of Justice (Parts 2800—2899)

Title 2—Grants and Agreements—Continued

Chap.
XXX	Department of Homeland Security (Parts 3000—3099)
XXXI	Institute of Museum and Library Services (Parts 3100—3199)
XXXII	National Endowment for the Arts (Parts 3200—3299)
XXXIII	National Endowment for the Humanities (Parts 3300—3399)
XXXIV	Department of Education (Parts 3400—3499)
XXXV	Export-Import Bank of the United States (Parts 3500—3599)
XXXVII	Peace Corps (Parts 3700—3799)
LVIII	Election Assistance Commission (Parts 5800—5899)

Title 3—The President

I	Executive Office of the President (Parts 100—199)

Title 4—Accounts

I	Government Accountability Office (Parts 1—199)
II	Recovery Accountability and Transparency Board (Parts 200—299)

Title 5—Administrative Personnel

I	Office of Personnel Management (Parts 1—1199)
II	Merit Systems Protection Board (Parts 1200—1299)
III	Office of Management and Budget (Parts 1300—1399)
V	The International Organizations Employees Loyalty Board (Parts 1500—1599)
VI	Federal Retirement Thrift Investment Board (Parts 1600—1699)
VIII	Office of Special Counsel (Parts 1800—1899)
IX	Appalachian Regional Commission (Parts 1900—1999)
XI	Armed Forces Retirement Home (Parts 2100—2199)
XIV	Federal Labor Relations Authority, General Counsel of the Federal Labor Relations Authority and Federal Service Impasses Panel (Parts 2400—2499)
XV	Office of Administration, Executive Office of the President (Parts 2500—2599)
XVI	Office of Government Ethics (Parts 2600—2699)
XXI	Department of the Treasury (Parts 3100—3199)
XXII	Federal Deposit Insurance Corporation (Parts 3200—3299)
XXIII	Department of Energy (Parts 3300—3399)
XXIV	Federal Energy Regulatory Commission (Parts 3400—3499)
XXV	Department of the Interior (Parts 3500—3599)
XXVI	Department of Defense (Parts 3600— 3699)
XXVIII	Department of Justice (Parts 3800—3899)
XXIX	Federal Communications Commission (Parts 3900—3999)
XXX	Farm Credit System Insurance Corporation (Parts 4000—4099)
XXXI	Farm Credit Administration (Parts 4100—4199)

Title 5—Administrative Personnel—Continued

Chap.	
XXXIII	Overseas Private Investment Corporation (Parts 4300—4399)
XXXIV	Securities and Exchange Commission (Parts 4400—4499)
XXXV	Office of Personnel Management (Parts 4500—4599)
XXXVII	Federal Election Commission (Parts 4700—4799)
XL	Interstate Commerce Commission (Parts 5000—5099)
XLI	Commodity Futures Trading Commission (Parts 5100—5199)
XLII	Department of Labor (Parts 5200—5299)
XLIII	National Science Foundation (Parts 5300—5399)
XLV	Department of Health and Human Services (Parts 5500—5599)
XLVI	Postal Rate Commission (Parts 5600—5699)
XLVII	Federal Trade Commission (Parts 5700—5799)
XLVIII	Nuclear Regulatory Commission (Parts 5800—5899)
XLIX	Federal Labor Relations Authority (Parts 5900—5999)
L	Department of Transportation (Parts 6000—6099)
LII	Export-Import Bank of the United States (Parts 6200—6299)
LIII	Department of Education (Parts 6300—6399)
LIV	Environmental Protection Agency (Parts 6400—6499)
LV	National Endowment for the Arts (Parts 6500—6599)
LVI	National Endowment for the Humanities (Parts 6600—6699)
LVII	General Services Administration (Parts 6700—6799)
LVIII	Board of Governors of the Federal Reserve System (Parts 6800—6899)
LIX	National Aeronautics and Space Administration (Parts 6900—6999)
LX	United States Postal Service (Parts 7000—7099)
LXI	National Labor Relations Board (Parts 7100—7199)
LXII	Equal Employment Opportunity Commission (Parts 7200—7299)
LXIII	Inter-American Foundation (Parts 7300—7399)
LXIV	Merit Systems Protection Board (Parts 7400—7499)
LXV	Department of Housing and Urban Development (Parts 7500—7599)
LXVI	National Archives and Records Administration (Parts 7600—7699)
LXVII	Institute of Museum and Library Services (Parts 7700—7799)
LXVIII	Commission on Civil Rights (Parts 7800—7899)
LXIX	Tennessee Valley Authority (Parts 7900—7999)
LXX	Court Services and Offender Supervision Agency for the District of Columbia (Parts 8000—8099)
LXXI	Consumer Product Safety Commission (Parts 8100—8199)
LXXIII	Department of Agriculture (Parts 8300—8399)
LXXIV	Federal Mine Safety and Health Review Commission (Parts 8400—8499)
LXXVI	Federal Retirement Thrift Investment Board (Parts 8600—8699)
LXXVII	Office of Management and Budget (Parts 8700—8799)
LXXX	Federal Housing Finance Agency (Parts 9000—9099)
LXXXII	Special Inspector General for Iraq Reconstruction (Parts 9200—9299)

Title 5—Administrative Personnel—Continued

Chap.

LXXXIII Special Inspector General for Afghanistan Reconstruction (Parts 9300—9399)

LXXXIV Bureau of Consumer Financial Protection (Parts 9400—9499)

LXXXVI National Credit Union Administration (9600—9699)

XCVII Department of Homeland Security Human Resources Management System (Department of Homeland Security—Office of Personnel Management) (Parts 9700—9799)

XCVII Council of the Inspectors General on Integrity and Efficiency (Parts 9800—9899)

Title 6—Domestic Security

I Department of Homeland Security, Office of the Secretary (Parts 1—99)

X Privacy and Civil Liberties Oversight Board (Parts 1000—1099)

Title 7—Agriculture

SUBTITLE A—OFFICE OF THE SECRETARY OF AGRICULTURE (PARTS 0—26)

SUBTITLE B—REGULATIONS OF THE DEPARTMENT OF AGRICULTURE

I Agricultural Marketing Service (Standards, Inspections, Marketing Practices), Department of Agriculture (Parts 27—209)

II Food and Nutrition Service, Department of Agriculture (Parts 210—299)

III Animal and Plant Health Inspection Service, Department of Agriculture (Parts 300—399)

IV Federal Crop Insurance Corporation, Department of Agriculture (Parts 400—499)

V Agricultural Research Service, Department of Agriculture (Parts 500—599)

VI Natural Resources Conservation Service, Department of Agriculture (Parts 600—699)

VII Farm Service Agency, Department of Agriculture (Parts 700—799)

VIII Grain Inspection, Packers and Stockyards Administration (Federal Grain Inspection Service), Department of Agriculture (Parts 800—899)

IX Agricultural Marketing Service (Marketing Agreements and Orders; Fruits, Vegetables, Nuts), Department of Agriculture (Parts 900—999)

X Agricultural Marketing Service (Marketing Agreements and Orders; Milk), Department of Agriculture (Parts 1000—1199)

XI Agricultural Marketing Service (Marketing Agreements and Orders; Miscellaneous Commodities), Department of Agriculture (Parts 1200—1299)

XIV Commodity Credit Corporation, Department of Agriculture (Parts 1400—1499)

XV Foreign Agricultural Service, Department of Agriculture (Parts 1500—1599)

Chap.	Title 7—Agriculture—Continued
XVI	Rural Telephone Bank, Department of Agriculture (Parts 1600—1699)
XVII	Rural Utilities Service, Department of Agriculture (Parts 1700—1799)
XVIII	Rural Housing Service, Rural Business-Cooperative Service, Rural Utilities Service, and Farm Service Agency, Department of Agriculture (Parts 1800—2099)
XX	Local Television Loan Guarantee Board (Parts 2200—2299)
XXV	Office of Advocacy and Outreach, Department of Agriculture (Parts 2500—2599)
XXVI	Office of Inspector General, Department of Agriculture (Parts 2600—2699)
XXVII	Office of Information Resources Management, Department of Agriculture (Parts 2700—2799)
XXVIII	Office of Operations, Department of Agriculture (Parts 2800—2899)
XXIX	Office of Energy Policy and New Uses, Department of Agriculture (Parts 2900—2999)
XXX	Office of the Chief Financial Officer, Department of Agriculture (Parts 3000—3099)
XXXI	Office of Environmental Quality, Department of Agriculture (Parts 3100—3199)
XXXII	Office of Procurement and Property Management, Department of Agriculture (Parts 3200—3299)
XXXIII	Office of Transportation, Department of Agriculture (Parts 3300—3399)
XXXIV	National Institute of Food and Agriculture (Parts 3400—3499)
XXXV	Rural Housing Service, Department of Agriculture (Parts 3500—3599)
XXXVI	National Agricultural Statistics Service, Department of Agriculture (Parts 3600—3699)
XXXVII	Economic Research Service, Department of Agriculture (Parts 3700—3799)
XXXVIII	World Agricultural Outlook Board, Department of Agriculture (Parts 3800—3899)
XLI	[Reserved]
XLII	Rural Business-Cooperative Service and Rural Utilities Service, Department of Agriculture (Parts 4200—4299)

Title 8—Aliens and Nationality

I	Department of Homeland Security (Immigration and Naturalization) (Parts 1—499)
V	Executive Office for Immigration Review, Department of Justice (Parts 1000—1399)

Title 9—Animals and Animal Products

I	Animal and Plant Health Inspection Service, Department of Agriculture (Parts 1—199)

Title 9—Animals and Animal Products—Continued

Chap.

II	Grain Inspection, Packers and Stockyards Administration (Packers and Stockyards Programs), Department of Agriculture (Parts 200—299)
III	Food Safety and Inspection Service, Department of Agriculture (Parts 300—599)

Title 10—Energy

I	Nuclear Regulatory Commission (Parts 0—199)
II	Department of Energy (Parts 200—699)
III	Department of Energy (Parts 700—999)
X	Department of Energy (General Provisions) (Parts 1000—1099)
XIII	Nuclear Waste Technical Review Board (Parts 1300—1399)
XVII	Defense Nuclear Facilities Safety Board (Parts 1700—1799)
XVIII	Northeast Interstate Low-Level Radioactive Waste Commission (Parts 1800—1899)

Title 11—Federal Elections

I	Federal Election Commission (Parts 1—9099)
II	Election Assistance Commission (Parts 9400—9499)

Title 12—Banks and Banking

I	Comptroller of the Currency, Department of the Treasury (Parts 1—199)
II	Federal Reserve System (Parts 200—299)
III	Federal Deposit Insurance Corporation (Parts 300—399)
IV	Export-Import Bank of the United States (Parts 400—499)
V	Office of Thrift Supervision, Department of the Treasury (Parts 500—599)
VI	Farm Credit Administration (Parts 600—699)
VII	National Credit Union Administration (Parts 700—799)
VIII	Federal Financing Bank (Parts 800—899)
IX	Federal Housing Finance Board (Parts 900—999)
X	Bureau of Consumer Financial Protection (Parts 1000—1099)
XI	Federal Financial Institutions Examination Council (Parts 1100—1199)
XII	Federal Housing Finance Agency (Parts 1200—1299)
XIII	Financial Stability Oversight Council (Parts 1300—1399)
XIV	Farm Credit System Insurance Corporation (Parts 1400—1499)
XV	Department of the Treasury (Parts 1500—1599)
XVI	Office of Financial Research (Parts 1600—1699)
XVII	Office of Federal Housing Enterprise Oversight, Department of Housing and Urban Development (Parts 1700—1799)
XVIII	Community Development Financial Institutions Fund, Department of the Treasury (Parts 1800—1899)

Title 13—Business Credit and Assistance

Chap.
- I Small Business Administration (Parts 1—199)
- III Economic Development Administration, Department of Commerce (Parts 300—399)
- IV Emergency Steel Guarantee Loan Board (Parts 400—499)
- V Emergency Oil and Gas Guaranteed Loan Board (Parts 500—599)

Title 14—Aeronautics and Space

- I Federal Aviation Administration, Department of Transportation (Parts 1—199)
- II Office of the Secretary, Department of Transportation (Aviation Proceedings) (Parts 200—399)
- III Commercial Space Transportation, Federal Aviation Administration, Department of Transportation (Parts 400—1199)
- V National Aeronautics and Space Administration (Parts 1200—1299)
- VI Air Transportation System Stabilization (Parts 1300—1399)

Title 15—Commerce and Foreign Trade

SUBTITLE A—OFFICE OF THE SECRETARY OF COMMERCE (PARTS 0—29)

SUBTITLE B—REGULATIONS RELATING TO COMMERCE AND FOREIGN TRADE

- I Bureau of the Census, Department of Commerce (Parts 30—199)
- II National Institute of Standards and Technology, Department of Commerce (Parts 200—299)
- III International Trade Administration, Department of Commerce (Parts 300—399)
- IV Foreign-Trade Zones Board, Department of Commerce (Parts 400—499)
- VII Bureau of Industry and Security, Department of Commerce (Parts 700—799)
- VIII Bureau of Economic Analysis, Department of Commerce (Parts 800—899)
- IX National Oceanic and Atmospheric Administration, Department of Commerce (Parts 900—999)
- XI Technology Administration, Department of Commerce (Parts 1100—1199)
- XIII East-West Foreign Trade Board (Parts 1300—1399)
- XIV Minority Business Development Agency (Parts 1400—1499)

SUBTITLE C—REGULATIONS RELATING TO FOREIGN TRADE AGREEMENTS

- XX Office of the United States Trade Representative (Parts 2000—2099)

SUBTITLE D—REGULATIONS RELATING TO TELECOMMUNICATIONS AND INFORMATION

- XXIII National Telecommunications and Information Administration, Department of Commerce (Parts 2300—2399)

Title 16—Commercial Practices

Chap.
I   Federal Trade Commission (Parts 0—999)
II   Consumer Product Safety Commission (Parts 1000—1799)

Title 17—Commodity and Securities Exchanges

I   Commodity Futures Trading Commission (Parts 1—199)
II   Securities and Exchange Commission (Parts 200—399)
IV   Department of the Treasury (Parts 400—499)

Title 18—Conservation of Power and Water Resources

I   Federal Energy Regulatory Commission, Department of Energy (Parts 1—399)
III   Delaware River Basin Commission (Parts 400—499)
VI   Water Resources Council (Parts 700—799)
VIII   Susquehanna River Basin Commission (Parts 800—899)
XIII   Tennessee Valley Authority (Parts 1300—1399)

Title 19—Customs Duties

I   U.S. Customs and Border Protection, Department of Homeland Security; Department of the Treasury (Parts 0—199)
II   United States International Trade Commission (Parts 200—299)
III   International Trade Administration, Department of Commerce (Parts 300—399)
IV   U.S. Immigration and Customs Enforcement, Department of Homeland Security (Parts 400—599)

Title 20—Employees' Benefits

I   Office of Workers' Compensation Programs, Department of Labor (Parts 1—199)
II   Railroad Retirement Board (Parts 200—399)
III   Social Security Administration (Parts 400—499)
IV   Employees' Compensation Appeals Board, Department of Labor (Parts 500—599)
V   Employment and Training Administration, Department of Labor (Parts 600—699)
VI   Office of Workers' Compensation Programs, Department of Labor (Parts 700—799)
VII   Benefits Review Board, Department of Labor (Parts 800—899)
VIII   Joint Board for the Enrollment of Actuaries (Parts 900—999)
IX   Office of the Assistant Secretary for Veterans' Employment and Training Service, Department of Labor (Parts 1000—1099)

Title 21—Food and Drugs

Chap.
I Food and Drug Administration, Department of Health and Human Services (Parts 1—1299)
II Drug Enforcement Administration, Department of Justice (Parts 1300—1399)
III Office of National Drug Control Policy (Parts 1400—1499)

Title 22—Foreign Relations

I Department of State (Parts 1—199)
II Agency for International Development (Parts 200—299)
III Peace Corps (Parts 300—399)
IV International Joint Commission, United States and Canada (Parts 400—499)
V Broadcasting Board of Governors (Parts 500—599)
VII Overseas Private Investment Corporation (Parts 700—799)
IX Foreign Service Grievance Board (Parts 900—999)
X Inter-American Foundation (Parts 1000—1099)
XI International Boundary and Water Commission, United States and Mexico, United States Section (Parts 1100—1199)
XII United States International Development Cooperation Agency (Parts 1200—1299)
XIII Millennium Challenge Corporation (Parts 1300—1399)
XIV Foreign Service Labor Relations Board; Federal Labor Relations Authority; General Counsel of the Federal Labor Relations Authority; and the Foreign Service Impasse Disputes Panel (Parts 1400—1499)
XV African Development Foundation (Parts 1500—1599)
XVI Japan-United States Friendship Commission (Parts 1600—1699)
XVII United States Institute of Peace (Parts 1700—1799)

Title 23—Highways

I Federal Highway Administration, Department of Transportation (Parts 1—999)
II National Highway Traffic Safety Administration and Federal Highway Administration, Department of Transportation (Parts 1200—1299)
III National Highway Traffic Safety Administration, Department of Transportation (Parts 1300—1399)

Title 24—Housing and Urban Development

SUBTITLE A—OFFICE OF THE SECRETARY, DEPARTMENT OF HOUSING AND URBAN DEVELOPMENT (PARTS 0—99)

SUBTITLE B—REGULATIONS RELATING TO HOUSING AND URBAN DEVELOPMENT

I Office of Assistant Secretary for Equal Opportunity, Department of Housing and Urban Development (Parts 100—199)

Title 24—Housing and Urban Development—Continued

Chap.

II   Office of Assistant Secretary for Housing-Federal Housing Commissioner, Department of Housing and Urban Development (Parts 200—299)

III Government National Mortgage Association, Department of Housing and Urban Development (Parts 300—399)

IV   Office of Housing and Office of Multifamily Housing Assistance Restructuring, Department of Housing and Urban Development (Parts 400—499)

V   Office of Assistant Secretary for Community Planning and Development, Department of Housing and Urban Development (Parts 500—599)

VI   Office of Assistant Secretary for Community Planning and Development, Department of Housing and Urban Development (Parts 600—699) [Reserved]

VII Office of the Secretary, Department of Housing and Urban Development (Housing Assistance Programs and Public and Indian Housing Programs) (Parts 700—799)

VIII Office of the Assistant Secretary for Housing—Federal Housing Commissioner, Department of Housing and Urban Development (Section 8 Housing Assistance Programs, Section 202 Direct Loan Program, Section 202 Supportive Housing for the Elderly Program and Section 811 Supportive Housing for Persons With Disabilities Program) (Parts 800—899)

IX   Office of Assistant Secretary for Public and Indian Housing, Department of Housing and Urban Development (Parts 900—1699)

X   Office of Assistant Secretary for Housing—Federal Housing Commissioner, Department of Housing and Urban Development (Interstate Land Sales Registration Program) (Parts 1700—1799)

XII Office of Inspector General, Department of Housing and Urban Development (Parts 2000—2099)

XV   Emergency Mortgage Insurance and Loan Programs, Department of Housing and Urban Development (Parts 2700—2799)

XX   Office of Assistant Secretary for Housing—Federal Housing Commissioner, Department of Housing and Urban Development (Parts 3200—3899)

XXIV Board of Directors of the HOPE for Homeowners Program (Parts 4000—4099)

XXV Neighborhood Reinvestment Corporation (Parts 4100—4199)

Title 25—Indians

I   Bureau of Indian Affairs, Department of the Interior (Parts 1—299)

II   Indian Arts and Crafts Board, Department of the Interior (Parts 300—399)

III National Indian Gaming Commission, Department of the Interior (Parts 500—599)

IV   Office of Navajo and Hopi Indian Relocation (Parts 700—799)

V   Bureau of Indian Affairs, Department of the Interior, and Indian Health Service, Department of Health and Human Services (Part 900)

Title 25—Indians—Continued

Chap.	
VI	Office of the Assistant Secretary-Indian Affairs, Department of the Interior (Parts 1000—1199)
VII	Office of the Special Trustee for American Indians, Department of the Interior (Parts 1200—1299)

Title 26—Internal Revenue

I	Internal Revenue Service, Department of the Treasury (Parts 1—End)

Title 27—Alcohol, Tobacco Products and Firearms

I	Alcohol and Tobacco Tax and Trade Bureau, Department of the Treasury (Parts 1—399)
II	Bureau of Alcohol, Tobacco, Firearms, and Explosives, Department of Justice (Parts 400—699)

Title 28—Judicial Administration

I	Department of Justice (Parts 0—299)
III	Federal Prison Industries, Inc., Department of Justice (Parts 300—399)
V	Bureau of Prisons, Department of Justice (Parts 500—599)
VI	Offices of Independent Counsel, Department of Justice (Parts 600—699)
VII	Office of Independent Counsel (Parts 700—799)
VIII	Court Services and Offender Supervision Agency for the District of Columbia (Parts 800—899)
IX	National Crime Prevention and Privacy Compact Council (Parts 900—999)
XI	Department of Justice and Department of State (Parts 1100—1199)

Title 29—Labor

SUBTITLE A—OFFICE OF THE SECRETARY OF LABOR (PARTS 0—99)
SUBTITLE B—REGULATIONS RELATING TO LABOR

I	National Labor Relations Board (Parts 100—199)
II	Office of Labor-Management Standards, Department of Labor (Parts 200—299)
III	National Railroad Adjustment Board (Parts 300—399)
IV	Office of Labor-Management Standards, Department of Labor (Parts 400—499)
V	Wage and Hour Division, Department of Labor (Parts 500—899)
IX	Construction Industry Collective Bargaining Commission (Parts 900—999)
X	National Mediation Board (Parts 1200—1299)
XII	Federal Mediation and Conciliation Service (Parts 1400—1499)
XIV	Equal Employment Opportunity Commission (Parts 1600—1699)

Title 29—Labor—Continued

Chap.

XVII	Occupational Safety and Health Administration, Department of Labor (Parts 1900—1999)
XX	Occupational Safety and Health Review Commission (Parts 2200—2499)
XXV	Employee Benefits Security Administration, Department of Labor (Parts 2500—2599)
XXVII	Federal Mine Safety and Health Review Commission (Parts 2700—2799)
XL	Pension Benefit Guaranty Corporation (Parts 4000—4999)

Title 30—Mineral Resources

I	Mine Safety and Health Administration, Department of Labor (Parts 1—199)
II	Bureau of Safety and Environmental Enforcement, Department of the Interior (Parts 200—299)
IV	Geological Survey, Department of the Interior (Parts 400—499)
V	Bureau of Ocean Energy Management, Department of the Interior (Parts 500—599)
VII	Office of Surface Mining Reclamation and Enforcement, Department of the Interior (Parts 700—999)
XII	Office of Natural Resources Revenue, Department of the Interior (Parts 1200—1299)

Title 31—Money and Finance: Treasury

SUBTITLE A—OFFICE OF THE SECRETARY OF THE TREASURY (PARTS 0—50)

SUBTITLE B—REGULATIONS RELATING TO MONEY AND FINANCE

I	Monetary Offices, Department of the Treasury (Parts 51—199)
II	Fiscal Service, Department of the Treasury (Parts 200—399)
IV	Secret Service, Department of the Treasury (Parts 400—499)
V	Office of Foreign Assets Control, Department of the Treasury (Parts 500—599)
VI	Bureau of Engraving and Printing, Department of the Treasury (Parts 600—699)
VII	Federal Law Enforcement Training Center, Department of the Treasury (Parts 700—799)
VIII	Office of International Investment, Department of the Treasury (Parts 800—899)
IX	Federal Claims Collection Standards (Department of the Treasury—Department of Justice) (Parts 900—999)
X	Financial Crimes Enforcement Network, Department of the Treasury (Parts 1000—1099)

Title 32—National Defense

SUBTITLE A—DEPARTMENT OF DEFENSE

I	Office of the Secretary of Defense (Parts 1—399)

Title 32—National Defense—Continued

Chap.

V	Department of the Army (Parts 400—699)
VI	Department of the Navy (Parts 700—799)
VII	Department of the Air Force (Parts 800—1099)

SUBTITLE B—OTHER REGULATIONS RELATING TO NATIONAL DEFENSE

XII	Defense Logistics Agency (Parts 1200—1299)
XVI	Selective Service System (Parts 1600—1699)
XVII	Office of the Director of National Intelligence (Parts 1700—1799)
XVIII	National Counterintelligence Center (Parts 1800—1899)
XIX	Central Intelligence Agency (Parts 1900—1999)
XX	Information Security Oversight Office, National Archives and Records Administration (Parts 2000—2099)
XXI	National Security Council (Parts 2100—2199)
XXIV	Office of Science and Technology Policy (Parts 2400—2499)
XXVII	Office for Micronesian Status Negotiations (Parts 2700—2799)
XXVIII	Office of the Vice President of the United States (Parts 2800—2899)

Title 33—Navigation and Navigable Waters

I	Coast Guard, Department of Homeland Security (Parts 1—199)
II	Corps of Engineers, Department of the Army (Parts 200—399)
IV	Saint Lawrence Seaway Development Corporation, Department of Transportation (Parts 400—499)

Title 34—Education

SUBTITLE A—OFFICE OF THE SECRETARY, DEPARTMENT OF EDUCATION (PARTS 1—99)

SUBTITLE B—REGULATIONS OF THE OFFICES OF THE DEPARTMENT OF EDUCATION

I	Office for Civil Rights, Department of Education (Parts 100—199)
II	Office of Elementary and Secondary Education, Department of Education (Parts 200—299)
III	Office of Special Education and Rehabilitative Services, Department of Education (Parts 300—399)
IV	Office of Vocational and Adult Education, Department of Education (Parts 400—499)
V	Office of Bilingual Education and Minority Languages Affairs, Department of Education (Parts 500—599)
VI	Office of Postsecondary Education, Department of Education (Parts 600—699)
VII	Office of Educational Research and Improvement, Department of Education (Parts 700—799)[Reserved]

SUBTITLE C—REGULATIONS RELATING TO EDUCATION

XI	National Institute for Literacy (Parts 1100—1199)
XII	National Council on Disability (Parts 1200—1299)

Chap.

Title 35 [Reserved]

Title 36—Parks, Forests, and Public Property

I	National Park Service, Department of the Interior (Parts 1—199)
II	Forest Service, Department of Agriculture (Parts 200—299)
III	Corps of Engineers, Department of the Army (Parts 300—399)
IV	American Battle Monuments Commission (Parts 400—499)
V	Smithsonian Institution (Parts 500—599)
VI	[Reserved]
VII	Library of Congress (Parts 700—799)
VIII	Advisory Council on Historic Preservation (Parts 800—899)
IX	Pennsylvania Avenue Development Corporation (Parts 900—999)
X	Presidio Trust (Parts 1000—1099)
XI	Architectural and Transportation Barriers Compliance Board (Parts 1100—1199)
XII	National Archives and Records Administration (Parts 1200—1299)
XV	Oklahoma City National Memorial Trust (Parts 1500—1599)
XVI	Morris K. Udall Scholarship and Excellence in National Environmental Policy Foundation (Parts 1600—1699)

Title 37—Patents, Trademarks, and Copyrights

I	United States Patent and Trademark Office, Department of Commerce (Parts 1—199)
II	U.S. Copyright Office, Library of Congress (Parts 200—299)
III	Copyright Royalty Board, Library of Congress (Parts 300—399)
IV	Assistant Secretary for Technology Policy, Department of Commerce (Parts 400—599)

Title 38—Pensions, Bonuses, and Veterans' Relief

I	Department of Veterans Affairs (Parts 0—199)
II	Armed Forces Retirement Home (Parts 200—299)

Title 39—Postal Service

I	United States Postal Service (Parts 1—999)
III	Postal Regulatory Commission (Parts 3000—3099)

Title 40—Protection of Environment

I	Environmental Protection Agency (Parts 1—1099)
IV	Environmental Protection Agency and Department of Justice (Parts 1400—1499)
V	Council on Environmental Quality (Parts 1500—1599)
VI	Chemical Safety and Hazard Investigation Board (Parts 1600—1699)

Title 40—Protection of Environment—Continued

Chap.

VII Environmental Protection Agency and Department of Defense; Uniform National Discharge Standards for Vessels of the Armed Forces (Parts 1700—1799)

Title 41—Public Contracts and Property Management

SUBTITLE A—FEDERAL PROCUREMENT REGULATIONS SYSTEM [NOTE]

SUBTITLE B—OTHER PROVISIONS RELATING TO PUBLIC CONTRACTS

50 Public Contracts, Department of Labor (Parts 50–1—50–999)
51 Committee for Purchase From People Who Are Blind or Severely Disabled (Parts 51–1—51–99)
60 Office of Federal Contract Compliance Programs, Equal Employment Opportunity, Department of Labor (Parts 60–1—60–999)
61 Office of the Assistant Secretary for Veterans' Employment and Training Service, Department of Labor (Parts 61–1—61–999)
62—100 [Reserved]

SUBTITLE C—FEDERAL PROPERTY MANAGEMENT REGULATIONS SYSTEM

101 Federal Property Management Regulations (Parts 101–1—101–99)
102 Federal Management Regulation (Parts 102–1—102–299)
103—104 [Reserved]
105 General Services Administration (Parts 105–1—105–999)
109 Department of Energy Property Management Regulations (Parts 109–1—109–99)
114 Department of the Interior (Parts 114–1—114–99)
115 Environmental Protection Agency (Parts 115–1—115–99)
128 Department of Justice (Parts 128–1—128–99)
129—200 [Reserved]

SUBTITLE D—OTHER PROVISIONS RELATING TO PROPERTY MANAGEMENT [RESERVED]

SUBTITLE E—FEDERAL INFORMATION RESOURCES MANAGEMENT REGULATIONS SYSTEM [RESERVED]

SUBTITLE F—FEDERAL TRAVEL REGULATION SYSTEM

300 General (Parts 300–1—300–99)
301 Temporary Duty (TDY) Travel Allowances (Parts 301–1—301–99)
302 Relocation Allowances (Parts 302–1—302–99)
303 Payment of Expenses Connected with the Death of Certain Employees (Part 303–1—303–99)
304 Payment of Travel Expenses from a Non-Federal Source (Parts 304–1—304–99)

Title 42—Public Health

I Public Health Service, Department of Health and Human Services (Parts 1—199)
IV Centers for Medicare & Medicaid Services, Department of Health and Human Services (Parts 400—599)

Chap.
Title 42—Public Health—Continued

V Office of Inspector General-Health Care, Department of Health and Human Services (Parts 1000—1999)

Title 43—Public Lands: Interior

SUBTITLE A—OFFICE OF THE SECRETARY OF THE INTERIOR (PARTS 1—199)

SUBTITLE B—REGULATIONS RELATING TO PUBLIC LANDS

I Bureau of Reclamation, Department of the Interior (Parts 400—999)

II Bureau of Land Management, Department of the Interior (Parts 1000—9999)

III Utah Reclamation Mitigation and Conservation Commission (Parts 10000—10099)

Title 44—Emergency Management and Assistance

I Federal Emergency Management Agency, Department of Homeland Security (Parts 0—399)

IV Department of Commerce and Department of Transportation (Parts 400—499)

Title 45—Public Welfare

SUBTITLE A—DEPARTMENT OF HEALTH AND HUMAN SERVICES (PARTS 1—199)

SUBTITLE B—REGULATIONS RELATING TO PUBLIC WELFARE

II Office of Family Assistance (Assistance Programs), Administration for Children and Families, Department of Health and Human Services (Parts 200—299)

III Office of Child Support Enforcement (Child Support Enforcement Program), Administration for Children and Families, Department of Health and Human Services (Parts 300—399)

IV Office of Refugee Resettlement, Administration for Children and Families, Department of Health and Human Services (Parts 400—499)

V Foreign Claims Settlement Commission of the United States, Department of Justice (Parts 500—599)

VI National Science Foundation (Parts 600—699)

VII Commission on Civil Rights (Parts 700—799)

VIII Office of Personnel Management (Parts 800—899)

X Office of Community Services, Administration for Children and Families, Department of Health and Human Services (Parts 1000—1099)

XI National Foundation on the Arts and the Humanities (Parts 1100—1199)

XII Corporation for National and Community Service (Parts 1200—1299)

XIII Office of Human Development Services, Department of Health and Human Services (Parts 1300—1399)

Chap.
Title 45—Public Welfare—Continued

XVI Legal Services Corporation (Parts 1600—1699)
XVII National Commission on Libraries and Information Science (Parts 1700—1799)
XVIII Harry S. Truman Scholarship Foundation (Parts 1800—1899)
XXI Commission on Fine Arts (Parts 2100—2199)
XXIII Arctic Research Commission (Part 2301)
XXIV James Madison Memorial Fellowship Foundation (Parts 2400—2499)
XXV Corporation for National and Community Service (Parts 2500—2599)

Title 46—Shipping

I Coast Guard, Department of Homeland Security (Parts 1—199)
II Maritime Administration, Department of Transportation (Parts 200—399)
III Coast Guard (Great Lakes Pilotage), Department of Homeland Security (Parts 400—499)
IV Federal Maritime Commission (Parts 500—599)

Title 47—Telecommunication

I Federal Communications Commission (Parts 0—199)
II Office of Science and Technology Policy and National Security Council (Parts 200—299)
III National Telecommunications and Information Administration, Department of Commerce (Parts 300—399)
IV National Telecommunications and Information Administration, Department of Commerce, and National Highway Traffic Safety Administration, Department of Transportation (Parts 400—499)

Title 48—Federal Acquisition Regulations System

1 Federal Acquisition Regulation (Parts 1—99)
2 Defense Acquisition Regulations System, Department of Defense (Parts 200—299)
3 Health and Human Services (Parts 300—399)
4 Department of Agriculture (Parts 400—499)
5 General Services Administration (Parts 500—599)
6 Department of State (Parts 600—699)
7 Agency for International Development (Parts 700—799)
8 Department of Veterans Affairs (Parts 800—899)
9 Department of Energy (Parts 900—999)
10 Department of the Treasury (Parts 1000—1099)
12 Department of Transportation (Parts 1200—1299)
13 Department of Commerce (Parts 1300—1399)
14 Department of the Interior (Parts 1400—1499)

Title 48—Federal Acquisition Regulations System—Continued

Chap.

15	Environmental Protection Agency (Parts 1500—1599)
16	Office of Personnel Management, Federal Employees Health Benefits Acquisition Regulation (Parts 1600—1699)
17	Office of Personnel Management (Parts 1700—1799)
18	National Aeronautics and Space Administration (Parts 1800—1899)
19	Broadcasting Board of Governors (Parts 1900—1999)
20	Nuclear Regulatory Commission (Parts 2000—2099)
21	Office of Personnel Management, Federal Employees Group Life Insurance Federal Acquisition Regulation (Parts 2100—2199)
23	Social Security Administration (Parts 2300—2399)
24	Department of Housing and Urban Development (Parts 2400—2499)
25	National Science Foundation (Parts 2500—2599)
28	Department of Justice (Parts 2800—2899)
29	Department of Labor (Parts 2900—2999)
30	Department of Homeland Security, Homeland Security Acquisition Regulation (HSAR) (Parts 3000—3099)
34	Department of Education Acquisition Regulation (Parts 3400—3499)
51	Department of the Army Acquisition Regulations (Parts 5100—5199)
52	Department of the Navy Acquisition Regulations (Parts 5200—5299)
53	Department of the Air Force Federal Acquisition Regulation Supplement (Parts 5300—5399)[Reserved]
54	Defense Logistics Agency, Department of Defense (Parts 5400—5499)
57	African Development Foundation (Parts 5700—5799)
61	Civilian Board of Contract Appeals, General Services Administration (Parts 6100—6199)
63	Department of Transportation Board of Contract Appeals (Parts 6300—6399)
99	Cost Accounting Standards Board, Office of Federal Procurement Policy, Office of Management and Budget (Parts 9900—9999)

Title 49—Transportation

SUBTITLE A—OFFICE OF THE SECRETARY OF TRANSPORTATION (PARTS 1—99)

SUBTITLE B—OTHER REGULATIONS RELATING TO TRANSPORTATION

I	Pipeline and Hazardous Materials Safety Administration, Department of Transportation (Parts 100—199)
II	Federal Railroad Administration, Department of Transportation (Parts 200—299)
III	Federal Motor Carrier Safety Administration, Department of Transportation (Parts 300—399)
IV	Coast Guard, Department of Homeland Security (Parts 400—499)

Title 49—Transportation—Continued

Chap.

V National Highway Traffic Safety Administration, Department of Transportation (Parts 500—599)
VI Federal Transit Administration, Department of Transportation (Parts 600—699)
VII National Railroad Passenger Corporation (AMTRAK) (Parts 700—799)
VIII National Transportation Safety Board (Parts 800—999)
X Surface Transportation Board, Department of Transportation (Parts 1000—1399)
XI Research and Innovative Technology Administration, Department of Transportation (Parts 1400—1499)[Reserved]
XII Transportation Security Administration, Department of Homeland Security (Parts 1500—1699)

Title 50—Wildlife and Fisheries

I United States Fish and Wildlife Service, Department of the Interior (Parts 1—199)
II National Marine Fisheries Service, National Oceanic and Atmospheric Administration, Department of Commerce (Parts 200—299)
III International Fishing and Related Activities (Parts 300—399)
IV Joint Regulations (United States Fish and Wildlife Service, Department of the Interior and National Marine Fisheries Service, National Oceanic and Atmospheric Administration, Department of Commerce); Endangered Species Committee Regulations (Parts 400—499)
V Marine Mammal Commission (Parts 500—599)
VI Fishery Conservation and Management, National Oceanic and Atmospheric Administration, Department of Commerce (Parts 600—699)

CFR Index and Finding Aids

Subject/Agency Index
List of Agency Prepared Indexes
Parallel Tables of Statutory Authorities and Rules
List of CFR Titles, Chapters, Subchapters, and Parts
Alphabetical List of Agencies Appearing in the CFR

Alphabetical List of Agencies Appearing in the CFR
(Revised as of October 1, 2013)

Agency	CFR Title, Subtitle or Chapter
Administrative Committee of the Federal Register	1, I
Administrative Conference of the United States	1, III
Advisory Council on Historic Preservation	36, VIII
Advocacy and Outreach, Office of	7, XXV
Afghanistan Reconstruction, Special Inspector General for	22, LXXXIII
African Development Foundation	22, XV
Federal Acquisition Regulation	48, 57
Agency for International Development	2, VII; 22, II
Federal Acquisition Regulation	48, 7
Agricultural Marketing Service	7, I, IX, X, XI
Agricultural Research Service	7, V
Agriculture Department	2, IV; 5, LXXIII
Advocacy and Outreach, Office of	7, XXV
Agricultural Marketing Service	7, I, IX, X, XI
Agricultural Research Service	7, V
Animal and Plant Health Inspection Service	7, III; 9, I
Chief Financial Officer, Office of	7, XXX
Commodity Credit Corporation	7, XIV
Economic Research Service	7, XXXVII
Energy Policy and New Uses, Office of	2, IX; 7, XXIX
Environmental Quality, Office of	7, XXXI
Farm Service Agency	7, VII, XVIII
Federal Acquisition Regulation	48, 4
Federal Crop Insurance Corporation	7, IV
Food and Nutrition Service	7, II
Food Safety and Inspection Service	9, III
Foreign Agricultural Service	7, XV
Forest Service	36, II
Grain Inspection, Packers and Stockyards Administration	7, VIII; 9, II
Information Resources Management, Office of	7, XXVII
Inspector General, Office of	7, XXVI
National Agricultural Library	7, XLI
National Agricultural Statistics Service	7, XXXVI
National Institute of Food and Agriculture	7, XXXIV
Natural Resources Conservation Service	7, VI
Operations, Office of	7, XXVIII
Procurement and Property Management, Office of	7, XXXII
Rural Business-Cooperative Service	7, XVIII, XLII, L
Rural Development Administration	7, XLII
Rural Housing Service	7, XVIII, XXXV, L
Rural Telephone Bank	7, XVI
Rural Utilities Service	7, XVII, XVIII, XLII, L
Secretary of Agriculture, Office of	7, Subtitle A
Transportation, Office of	7, XXXIII
World Agricultural Outlook Board	7, XXXVIII
Air Force Department	32, VII
Federal Acquisition Regulation Supplement	48, 53
Air Transportation Stabilization Board	14, VI
Alcohol and Tobacco Tax and Trade Bureau	27, I
Alcohol, Tobacco, Firearms, and Explosives, Bureau of	27, II
AMTRAK	49, VII
American Battle Monuments Commission	36, IV
American Indians, Office of the Special Trustee	25, VII

Agency	CFR Title, Subtitle or Chapter
Animal and Plant Health Inspection Service	7, III; 9, I
Appalachian Regional Commission	5, IX
Architectural and Transportation Barriers Compliance Board	36, XI
Arctic Research Commission	45, XXIII
Armed Forces Retirement Home	5, XI
Army Department	32, V
Engineers, Corps of	33, II; 36, III
Federal Acquisition Regulation	48, 51
Bilingual Education and Minority Languages Affairs, Office of	34, V
Blind or Severely Disabled, Committee for Purchase from People Who Are	41, 51
Broadcasting Board of Governors	22, V
Federal Acquisition Regulation	48, 19
Bureau of Ocean Energy Management, Regulation, and Enforcement	30, II
Census Bureau	15, I
Centers for Medicare & Medicaid Services	42, IV
Central Intelligence Agency	32, XIX
Chemical Safety and Hazardous Investigation Board	40, VI
Chief Financial Officer, Office of	7, XXX
Child Support Enforcement, Office of	45, III
Children and Families, Administration for	45, II, III, IV, X
Civil Rights, Commission on	5, LXVIII; 45, VII
Civil Rights, Office for	34, I
Council of the Inspectors General on Integrity and Efficiency	5, XCVIII
Court Services and Offender Supervision Agency for the District of Columbia	5, LXX
Coast Guard	33, I; 46, I; 49, IV
Coast Guard (Great Lakes Pilotage)	46, III
Commerce Department	2, XIII; 44, IV; 50, VI
Census Bureau	15, I
Economic Analysis, Bureau of	15, VIII
Economic Development Administration	13, III
Emergency Management and Assistance	44, IV
Federal Acquisition Regulation	48, 13
Foreign-Trade Zones Board	15, IV
Industry and Security, Bureau of	15, VII
International Trade Administration	15, III; 19, III
National Institute of Standards and Technology	15, II
National Marine Fisheries Service	50, II, IV
National Oceanic and Atmospheric Administration	15, IX; 50, II, III, IV, VI
National Telecommunications and Information Administration	15, XXIII; 47, III, IV
National Weather Service	15, IX
Patent and Trademark Office, United States	37, I
Productivity, Technology and Innovation, Assistant Secretary for	37, IV
Secretary of Commerce, Office of	15, Subtitle A
Technology Administration	15, XI
Technology Policy, Assistant Secretary for	37, IV
Commercial Space Transportation	14, III
Commodity Credit Corporation	7, XIV
Commodity Futures Trading Commission	5, XLI; 17, I
Community Planning and Development, Office of Assistant Secretary for	24, V, VI
Community Services, Office of	45, X
Comptroller of the Currency	12, I
Construction Industry Collective Bargaining Commission	29, IX
Consumer Financial Protection Bureau	5, LXXXIV; 12, X
Consumer Product Safety Commission	5, LXXI; 16, II
Copyright Royalty Board	37, III
Corporation for National and Community Service	2, XXII; 45, XII, XXV
Cost Accounting Standards Board	48, 99
Council on Environmental Quality	40, V
Court Services and Offender Supervision Agency for the District of Columbia	5, LXX; 28, VIII
Customs and Border Protection	19, I

Agency	CFR Title, Subtitle or Chapter
Defense Contract Audit Agency	32, I
Defense Department	2, XI; 5, XXVI; 32, Subtitle A; 40, VII
Advanced Research Projects Agency	32, I
Air Force Department	32, VII
Army Department	32, V; 33, II; 36, III; 48, 51
Defense Acquisition Regulations System	48, 2
Defense Intelligence Agency	32, I
Defense Logistics Agency	32, I, XII; 48, 54
Engineers, Corps of	33, II; 36, III
National Imagery and Mapping Agency	32, I
Navy Department	32, VI; 48, 52
Secretary of Defense, Office of	2, XI; 32, I
Defense Contract Audit Agency	32, I
Defense Intelligence Agency	32, I
Defense Logistics Agency	32, XII; 48, 54
Defense Nuclear Facilities Safety Board	10, XVII
Delaware River Basin Commission	18, III
District of Columbia, Court Services and Offender Supervision Agency for the	5, LXX; 28, VIII
Drug Enforcement Administration	21, II
East-West Foreign Trade Board	15, XIII
Economic Analysis, Bureau of	15, VIII
Economic Development Administration	13, III
Economic Research Service	7, XXXVII
Education, Department of	2, XXXIV; 5, LIII
Bilingual Education and Minority Languages Affairs, Office of	34, V
Civil Rights, Office for	34, I
Educational Research and Improvement, Office of	34, VII
Elementary and Secondary Education, Office of	34, II
Federal Acquisition Regulation	48, 34
Postsecondary Education, Office of	34, VI
Secretary of Education, Office of	34, Subtitle A
Special Education and Rehabilitative Services, Office of	34, III
Vocational and Adult Education, Office of	34, IV
Educational Research and Improvement, Office of	34, VII
Election Assistance Commission	2, LVIII; 11, II
Elementary and Secondary Education, Office of	34, II
Emergency Oil and Gas Guaranteed Loan Board	13, V
Emergency Steel Guarantee Loan Board	13, IV
Employee Benefits Security Administration	29, XXV
Employees' Compensation Appeals Board	20, IV
Employees Loyalty Board	5, V
Employment and Training Administration	20, V
Employment Standards Administration	20, VI
Endangered Species Committee	50, IV
Energy, Department of	2, IX; 5, XXIII; 10, II, III, X
Federal Acquisition Regulation	48, 9
Federal Energy Regulatory Commission	5, XXIV; 18, I
Property Management Regulations	41, 109
Energy, Office of	7, XXIX
Engineers, Corps of	33, II; 36, III
Engraving and Printing, Bureau of	31, VI
Environmental Protection Agency	2, XV; 5, LIV; 40, I, IV, VII
Federal Acquisition Regulation	48, 15
Property Management Regulations	41, 115
Environmental Quality, Office of	7, XXXI
Equal Employment Opportunity Commission	5, LXII; 29, XIV
Equal Opportunity, Office of Assistant Secretary for	24, I
Executive Office of the President	3, I
Administration, Office of	5, XV
Environmental Quality, Council on	40, V
Management and Budget, Office of	2, Subtitle A; 5, III, LXXVII; 14, VI; 48, 99

Agency	CFR Title, Subtitle or Chapter
National Drug Control Policy, Office of	21, III
National Security Council	32, XXI; 47, 2
Presidential Documents	3
Science and Technology Policy, Office of	32, XXIV; 47, II
Trade Representative, Office of the United States	15, XX
Export-Import Bank of the United States	2, XXXV; 5, LII; 12, IV
Family Assistance, Office of	45, II
Farm Credit Administration	5, XXXI; 12, VI
Farm Credit System Insurance Corporation	5, XXX; 12, XIV
Farm Service Agency	7, VII, XVIII
Federal Acquisition Regulation	48, 1
Federal Aviation Administration	14, I
Commercial Space Transportation	14, III
Federal Claims Collection Standards	31, IX
Federal Communications Commission	5, XXIX; 47, I
Federal Contract Compliance Programs, Office of	41, 60
Federal Crop Insurance Corporation	7, IV
Federal Deposit Insurance Corporation	5, XXII; 12, III
Federal Election Commission	5, XXXVII; 11, I
Federal Emergency Management Agency	44, I
Federal Employees Group Life Insurance Federal Acquisition Regulation	48, 21
Federal Employees Health Benefits Acquisition Regulation	48, 16
Federal Energy Regulatory Commission	5, XXIV; 18, I
Federal Financial Institutions Examination Council	12, XI
Federal Financing Bank	12, VIII
Federal Highway Administration	23, I, II
Federal Home Loan Mortgage Corporation	1, IV
Federal Housing Enterprise Oversight Office	12, XVII
Federal Housing Finance Agency	5, LXXX; 12, XII
Federal Housing Finance Board	12, IX
Federal Labor Relations Authority	5, XIV, XLIX; 22, XIV
Federal Law Enforcement Training Center	31, VII
Federal Management Regulation	41, 102
Federal Maritime Commission	46, IV
Federal Mediation and Conciliation Service	29, XII
Federal Mine Safety and Health Review Commission	5, LXXIV; 29, XXVII
Federal Motor Carrier Safety Administration	49, III
Federal Prison Industries, Inc.	28, III
Federal Procurement Policy Office	48, 99
Federal Property Management Regulations	41, 101
Federal Railroad Administration	49, II
Federal Register, Administrative Committee of	1, I
Federal Register, Office of	1, II
Federal Reserve System	12, II
Board of Governors	5, LVIII
Federal Retirement Thrift Investment Board	5, VI, LXXVI
Federal Service Impasses Panel	5, XIV
Federal Trade Commission	5, XLVII; 16, I
Federal Transit Administration	49, VI
Federal Travel Regulation System	41, Subtitle F
Financial Crimes Enforcement Network	31, X
Financial Research Office	12, XVI
Financial Stability Oversight Council	12, XIII
Fine Arts, Commission on	45, XXI
Fiscal Service	31, II
Fish and Wildlife Service, United States	50, I, IV
Food and Drug Administration	21, I
Food and Nutrition Service	7, II
Food Safety and Inspection Service	9, III
Foreign Agricultural Service	7, XV
Foreign Assets Control, Office of	31, V
Foreign Claims Settlement Commission of the United States	45, V
Foreign Service Grievance Board	22, IX
Foreign Service Impasse Disputes Panel	22, XIV
Foreign Service Labor Relations Board	22, XIV
Foreign-Trade Zones Board	15, IV

Agency	CFR Title, Subtitle or Chapter
Forest Service	36, II
General Services Administration	5, LVII; 41, 105
Contract Appeals, Board of	48, 61
Federal Acquisition Regulation	48, 5
Federal Management Regulation	41, 102
Federal Property Management Regulations	41, 101
Federal Travel Regulation System	41, Subtitle F
General	41, 300
Payment From a Non-Federal Source for Travel Expenses	41, 304
Payment of Expenses Connected With the Death of Certain Employees	41, 303
Relocation Allowances	41, 302
Temporary Duty (TDY) Travel Allowances	41, 301
Geological Survey	30, IV
Government Accountability Office	4, I
Government Ethics, Office of	5, XVI
Government National Mortgage Association	24, III
Grain Inspection, Packers and Stockyards Administration	7, VIII; 9, II
Harry S. Truman Scholarship Foundation	45, XVIII
Health and Human Services, Department of	2, III; 5, XLV; 45, Subtitle A,
Centers for Medicare & Medicaid Services	42, IV
Child Support Enforcement, Office of	45, III
Children and Families, Administration for	45, II, III, IV, X
Community Services, Office of	45, X
Family Assistance, Office of	45, II
Federal Acquisition Regulation	48, 3
Food and Drug Administration	21, I
Human Development Services, Office of	45, XIII
Indian Health Service	25, V
Inspector General (Health Care), Office of	42, V
Public Health Service	42, I
Refugee Resettlement, Office of	45, IV
Homeland Security, Department of	2, XXX; 6, I; 8, I
Coast Guard	33, I; 46, I; 49, IV
Coast Guard (Great Lakes Pilotage)	46, III
Customs and Border Protection	19, I
Federal Emergency Management Agency	44, I
Human Resources Management and Labor Relations Systems	5, XCVII
Immigration and Customs Enforcement Bureau	19, IV
Transportation Security Administration	49, XII
HOPE for Homeowners Program, Board of Directors of	24, XXIV
Housing and Urban Development, Department of	2, XXIV; 5, LXV; 24, Subtitle B
Community Planning and Development, Office of Assistant Secretary for	24, V, VI
Equal Opportunity, Office of Assistant Secretary for	24, I
Federal Acquisition Regulation	48, 24
Federal Housing Enterprise Oversight, Office of	12, XVII
Government National Mortgage Association	24, III
Housing—Federal Housing Commissioner, Office of Assistant Secretary for	24, II, VIII, X, XX
Housing, Office of, and Multifamily Housing Assistance Restructuring, Office of	24, IV
Inspector General, Office of	24, XII
Public and Indian Housing, Office of Assistant Secretary for	24, IX
Secretary, Office of	24, Subtitle A, VII
Housing—Federal Housing Commissioner, Office of Assistant Secretary for	24, II, VIII, X, XX
Housing, Office of, and Multifamily Housing Assistance Restructuring, Office of	24, IV
Human Development Services, Office of	45, XIII
Immigration and Customs Enforcement Bureau	19, IV
Immigration Review, Executive Office for	8, V
Independent Counsel, Office of	28, VII
Indian Affairs, Bureau of	25, I, V

Agency	CFR Title, Subtitle or Chapter
Indian Affairs, Office of the Assistant Secretary	25, VI
Indian Arts and Crafts Board	25, II
Indian Health Service	25, V
Industry and Security, Bureau of	15, VII
Information Resources Management, Office of	7, XXVII
Information Security Oversight Office, National Archives and Records Administration	32, XX
Inspector General	
Agriculture Department	7, XXVI
Health and Human Services Department	42, V
Housing and Urban Development Department	24, XII, XV
Institute of Peace, United States	22, XVII
Inter-American Foundation	5, LXIII; 22, X
Interior Department	2, XIV
American Indians, Office of the Special Trustee	25, VII
Bureau of Ocean Energy Management, Regulation, and Enforcement	30, II
Endangered Species Committee	50, IV
Federal Acquisition Regulation	48, 14
Federal Property Management Regulations System	41, 114
Fish and Wildlife Service, United States	50, I, IV
Geological Survey	30, IV
Indian Affairs, Bureau of	25, I, V
Indian Affairs, Office of the Assistant Secretary	25, VI
Indian Arts and Crafts Board	25, II
Land Management, Bureau of	43, II
National Indian Gaming Commission	25, III
National Park Service	36, I
Natural Resource Revenue, Office of	30, XII
Ocean Energy Management, Bureau of	30, V
Reclamation, Bureau of	43, I
Secretary of the Interior, Office of	2, XIV; 43, Subtitle A
Surface Mining Reclamation and Enforcement, Office of	30, VII
Internal Revenue Service	26, I
International Boundary and Water Commission, United States and Mexico, United States Section	22, XI
International Development, United States Agency for	22, II
Federal Acquisition Regulation	48, 7
International Development Cooperation Agency, United States	22, XII
International Joint Commission, United States and Canada	22, IV
International Organizations Employees Loyalty Board	5, V
International Trade Administration	15, III; 19, III
International Trade Commission, United States	19, II
Interstate Commerce Commission	5, XL
Investment Security, Office of	31, VIII
Iraq Reconstruction, Special Inspector General for	5, LXXXVII
James Madison Memorial Fellowship Foundation	45, XXIV
Japan–United States Friendship Commission	22, XVI
Joint Board for the Enrollment of Actuaries	20, VIII
Justice Department	2, XXVIII; 5, XXVIII; 28, I, XI; 40, IV
Alcohol, Tobacco, Firearms, and Explosives, Bureau of	27, II
Drug Enforcement Administration	21, II
Federal Acquisition Regulation	48, 28
Federal Claims Collection Standards	31, IX
Federal Prison Industries, Inc.	28, III
Foreign Claims Settlement Commission of the United States	45, V
Immigration Review, Executive Office for	8, V
Offices of Independent Counsel	28, VI
Prisons, Bureau of	28, V
Property Management Regulations	41, 128
Labor Department	5, XLII
Employee Benefits Security Administration	29, XXV
Employees' Compensation Appeals Board	20, IV
Employment and Training Administration	20, V

Agency	CFR Title, Subtitle or Chapter
Employment Standards Administration	20, VI
Federal Acquisition Regulation	48, 29
Federal Contract Compliance Programs, Office of	41, 60
Federal Procurement Regulations System	41, 50
Labor-Management Standards, Office of	29, II, IV
Mine Safety and Health Administration	30, I
Occupational Safety and Health Administration	29, XVII
Office of Workers' Compensation Programs	20, VII
Public Contracts	41, 50
Secretary of Labor, Office of	29, Subtitle A
Veterans' Employment and Training Service, Office of the Assistant Secretary for	41, 61; 20, IX
Wage and Hour Division	29, V
Workers' Compensation Programs, Office of	20, I
Labor-Management Standards, Office of	29, II, IV
Land Management, Bureau of	43, II
Legal Services Corporation	45, XVI
Library of Congress	36, VII
Copyright Royalty Board	37, III
U.S. Copyright Office	37, II
Local Television Loan Guarantee Board	7, XX
Management and Budget, Office of	5, III, LXXVII; 14, VI; 48, 99
Marine Mammal Commission	50, V
Maritime Administration	46, II
Merit Systems Protection Board	5, II, LXIV
Micronesian Status Negotiations, Office for	32, XXVII
Millennium Challenge Corporation	22, XIII
Mine Safety and Health Administration	30, I
Minority Business Development Agency	15, XIV
Miscellaneous Agencies	1, IV
Monetary Offices	31, I
Morris K. Udall Scholarship and Excellence in National Environmental Policy Foundation	36, XVI
Museum and Library Services, Institute of	2, XXXI
National Aeronautics and Space Administration	2, XVIII; 5, LIX; 14, V
Federal Acquisition Regulation	48, 18
National Agricultural Library	7, XLI
National Agricultural Statistics Service	7, XXXVI
National and Community Service, Corporation for	2, XXII; 45, XII, XXV
National Archives and Records Administration	2, XXVI; 5, LXVI; 36, XII
Information Security Oversight Office	32, XX
National Capital Planning Commission	1, IV
National Commission for Employment Policy	1, IV
National Commission on Libraries and Information Science	45, XVII
National Council on Disability	34, XII
National Counterintelligence Center	32, XVIII
National Credit Union Administration	5, LXXXVI; 12, VII
National Crime Prevention and Privacy Compact Council	28, IX
National Drug Control Policy, Office of	21, III
National Endowment for the Arts	2, XXXII
National Endowment for the Humanities	2, XXXIII
National Foundation on the Arts and the Humanities	45, XI
National Highway Traffic Safety Administration	23, II, III; 47, VI; 49, V
National Imagery and Mapping Agency	32, I
National Indian Gaming Commission	25, III
National Institute for Literacy	34, XI
National Institute of Food and Agriculture	7, XXXIV
National Institute of Standards and Technology	15, II
National Intelligence, Office of Director of	32, XVII
National Labor Relations Board	5, LXI; 29, I
National Marine Fisheries Service	50, II, IV
National Mediation Board	29, X
National Oceanic and Atmospheric Administration	15, IX; 50, II, III, IV, VI
National Park Service	36, I
National Railroad Adjustment Board	29, III

Agency	CFR Title, Subtitle or Chapter
National Railroad Passenger Corporation (AMTRAK)	49, VII
National Science Foundation	2, XXV; 5, XLIII; 45, VI
Federal Acquisition Regulation	48, 25
National Security Council	32, XXI
National Security Council and Office of Science and Technology Policy	47, II
National Telecommunications and Information Administration	15, XXIII; 47, III, IV
National Transportation Safety Board	49, VIII
Natural Resources Conservation Service	7, VI
Natural Resource Revenue, Office of	30, XII
Navajo and Hopi Indian Relocation, Office of	25, IV
Navy Department	32, VI
Federal Acquisition Regulation	48, 52
Neighborhood Reinvestment Corporation	24, XXV
Northeast Interstate Low-Level Radioactive Waste Commission	10, XVIII
Nuclear Regulatory Commission	2, XX; 5, XLVIII; 10, I
Federal Acquisition Regulation	48, 20
Occupational Safety and Health Administration	29, XVII
Occupational Safety and Health Review Commission	29, XX
Ocean Energy Management, Bureau of	30, V
Offices of Independent Counsel	28, VI
Office of Workers' Compensation Programs	20, VII
Oklahoma City National Memorial Trust	36, XV
Operations Office	7, XXVIII
Overseas Private Investment Corporation	5, XXXIII; 22, VII
Patent and Trademark Office, United States	37, I
Payment From a Non-Federal Source for Travel Expenses	41, 304
Payment of Expenses Connected With the Death of Certain Employees	41, 303
Peace Corps	2, XXXVII; 22, III
Pennsylvania Avenue Development Corporation	36, IX
Pension Benefit Guaranty Corporation	29, XL
Personnel Management, Office of	5, I, XXXV; 45, VIII
Human Resources Management and Labor Relations Systems, Department of Homeland Security	5, XCVII
Federal Acquisition Regulation	48, 17
Federal Employees Group Life Insurance Federal Acquisition Regulation	48, 21
Federal Employees Health Benefits Acquisition Regulation	48, 16
Pipeline and Hazardous Materials Safety Administration	49, I
Postal Regulatory Commission	5, XLVI; 39, III
Postal Service, United States	5, LX; 39, I
Postsecondary Education, Office of	34, VI
President's Commission on White House Fellowships	1, IV
Presidential Documents	3
Presidio Trust	36, X
Prisons, Bureau of	28, V
Private and Civil Liberties Oversight Board	6, X
Procurement and Property Management, Office of	7, XXXII
Productivity, Technology and Innovation, Assistant Secretary	37, IV
Public Contracts, Department of Labor	41, 50
Public and Indian Housing, Office of Assistant Secretary for	24, IX
Public Health Service	42, I
Railroad Retirement Board	20, II
Reclamation, Bureau of	43, I
Recovery Accountability and Transparency Board	4, II
Refugee Resettlement, Office of	45, IV
Relocation Allowances	41, 302
Research and Innovative Technology Administration	49, XI
Rural Business-Cooperative Service	7, XVIII, XLII, L
Rural Development Administration	7, XLII
Rural Housing Service	7, XVIII, XXXV, L
Rural Telephone Bank	7, XVI
Rural Utilities Service	7, XVII, XVIII, XLII, L

Agency	CFR Title, Subtitle or Chapter
Saint Lawrence Seaway Development Corporation	33, IV
Science and Technology Policy, Office of	32, XXIV
Science and Technology Policy, Office of, and National Security Council	47, II
Secret Service	31, IV
Securities and Exchange Commission	5, XXXIV; 17, II
Selective Service System	32, XVI
Small Business Administration	2, XXVII; 13, I
Smithsonian Institution	36, V
Social Security Administration	2, XXIII; 20, III; 48, 23
Soldiers' and Airmen's Home, United States	5, XI
Special Counsel, Office of	5, VIII
Special Education and Rehabilitative Services, Office of	34, III
State Department	2, VI; 22, I; 28, XI
Federal Acquisition Regulation	48, 6
Surface Mining Reclamation and Enforcement, Office of	30, VII
Surface Transportation Board	49, X
Susquehanna River Basin Commission	18, VIII
Technology Administration	15, XI
Technology Policy, Assistant Secretary for	37, IV
Tennessee Valley Authority	5, LXIX; 18, XIII
Thrift Supervision Office, Department of the Treasury	12, V
Trade Representative, United States, Office of	15, XX
Transportation, Department of	2, XII; 5, L
Commercial Space Transportation	14, III
Contract Appeals, Board of	48, 63
Emergency Management and Assistance	44, IV
Federal Acquisition Regulation	48, 12
Federal Aviation Administration	14, I
Federal Highway Administration	23, I, II
Federal Motor Carrier Safety Administration	49, III
Federal Railroad Administration	49, II
Federal Transit Administration	49, VI
Maritime Administration	46, II
National Highway Traffic Safety Administration	23, II, III; 47, IV; 49, V
Pipeline and Hazardous Materials Safety Administration	49, I
Saint Lawrence Seaway Development Corporation	33, IV
Secretary of Transportation, Office of	14, II; 49, Subtitle A
Surface Transportation Board	49, X
Transportation Statistics Bureau	49, XI
Transportation, Office of	7, XXXIII
Transportation Security Administration	49, XII
Transportation Statistics Bureau	49, XI
Travel Allowances, Temporary Duty (TDY)	41, 301
Treasury Department	5, XXI; 12, XV; 17, IV; 31, IX
Alcohol and Tobacco Tax and Trade Bureau	27, I
Community Development Financial Institutions Fund	12, XVIII
Comptroller of the Currency	12, I
Customs and Border Protection	19, I
Engraving and Printing, Bureau of	31, VI
Federal Acquisition Regulation	48, 10
Federal Claims Collection Standards	31, IX
Federal Law Enforcement Training Center	31, VII
Financial Crimes Enforcement Network	31, X
Fiscal Service	31, II
Foreign Assets Control, Office of	31, V
Internal Revenue Service	26, I
Investment Security, Office of	31, VIII
Monetary Offices	31, I
Secret Service	31, IV
Secretary of the Treasury, Office of	31, Subtitle A
Thrift Supervision, Office of	12, V
Truman, Harry S. Scholarship Foundation	45, XVIII
United States and Canada, International Joint Commission	22, IV
United States and Mexico, International Boundary and Water Commission, United States Section	22, XI

Agency	CFR Title, Subtitle or Chapter
U.S. Copyright Office	37, II
Utah Reclamation Mitigation and Conservation Commission	43, III
Veterans Affairs Department	2, VIII; 38, I
Federal Acquisition Regulation	48, 8
Veterans' Employment and Training Service, Office of the Assistant Secretary for	41, 61; 20, IX
Vice President of the United States, Office of	32, XXVIII
Vocational and Adult Education, Office of	34, IV
Wage and Hour Division	29, V
Water Resources Council	18, VI
Workers' Compensation Programs, Office of	20, I
World Agricultural Outlook Board	7, XXXVIII

List of CFR Sections Affected

All changes in this volume of the Code of Federal Regulations (CFR) that were made by documents published in the FEDERAL REGISTER since January 1, 2008 are enumerated in the following list. Entries indicate the nature of the changes effected. Page numbers refer to FEDERAL REGISTER pages. The user should consult the entries for chapters, parts and subparts as well as sections for revisions.

For changes to this volume of the CFR prior to this listing, consult the annual edition of the monthly List of CFR Sections Affected (LSA). The LSA is available at *www.fdsys.gov*. For changes to this volume of the CFR prior to 2001, see the "List of CFR Sections Affected, 1949–1963, 1964–1972, 1973–1985, and 1986–2000" published in 11 separate volumes. The "List of CFR Sections Affected 1986–2000" is available at *www.fdsys.gov*.

2008
46 CFR — 73 FR Page

Chapter I
150   Tables I and II amended 56510

2009
46 CFR — 74 FR Page

Chapter I
147   Nomenclature changes............ 49235
147.5   Amended 49235
148   Nomenclature change 49235
148.01–9   (a) amended 49235
148.01–11   (b)(2) amended 49236
150   Tables I and II amended 49236
151   Nomenclature change 49236
151.03–53   Introductory text amended.................................. 11266
153   Nomenclature change 49236
153.4   (a) amended 49236
153.9   (b) amended 49236
154   Nomenclature change 49236
154.1   (a) amended 49236
154.22   (a) amended 49236
154.34   Amended............................. 49236

2010
46 CFR — 75 FR Page

Chapter I
148   Revised................................... 64591
150   Table 1 amended..................... 60003
154.30   Removed............................. 60003

2011
46 CFR — 76 FR Page

Chapter I
148   Regulation at 75 FR 64591 confirmed.. 8658

2012
46 CFR — 77 FR Page

Chapter I
147.1   Heading revised; (d) added... 33885
147.5   Amended 59783
147.7   Revised 33885
   (a) amended 59783
147.9   (a) amended 59783
147.40   Heading, (a) introductory text, (b) and (c) amended 59783
147.45   (f)(4), (5) and (6) revised 33885
147.50   (d) amended 59783
147.60   (a)(4) revised 33886
   (c)(2) amended............................ 59783
147.66   Added 33886
147.67   Added 33886
148.3   Amended 59783
148.5   (a) amended 59783
148.8   (a) amended 59783
148.15   (b) and (c) amended 59783
148.25   (b) amended 59783
148.30   Amended............................. 59783
148.55   (b)(3) and (4) amended 59783
148.115   (b) and (c) amended 59783
148.245   (a)(1) amended 59783
148.250   (a)(1) amended 59783

363

46 CFR—Continued

77 FR Page

Chapter I—Continued
148.310	(i) amended	59783
150.140	Amended	59783
150.150	Introductory text amended	59783
150.160	(a) amended	59783
150	Table I Note 1 amended	59783
	Table II Note 1 and Appendix III amended	59784
151.50-20	(i) amended	59784
151.50-22	(d) amended	59784
151.50-23	(e) amended	59784
151.50-36	(b) amended	59784
151.50-50	(n) amended	59784
151.50-75	Amended	59784
151.50-76	(b), (c) and (g) amended	59784
151.50-77	(a) amended	59784
151.50-80	(c) amended	59784
151.50-84	(e)(2) amended	59784
153.2	Amended	59784
153.4	(a) amended	59784
153.7	(b)(4) introductory text, (iii), (c)(3) introductory text, (4) introductory text, (5) and (6) amended	59784
153.10	(a)(1) introductory text, (3) and (b) introductory text amended	59784
153.15	(b)(4) amended	59784
153.16	(a) amended	59784
153.219	(b)(3) amended	59784
153.250	Amended	59784
153.336	(a)(3) amended	59784
153.353	(c) amended	59784
153.365	(a)(3) amended	59784
153.407	(b) amended	59784
153.460	(b) and (c) amended	59784
153.490	(b)(1) amended	59784
153.491	(b)(3) amended	59784
153.525	(d)(3) amended	59784
153.530	(c) introductory text, (1), (2) and (o)(1) amended	59784
153.556	(a) amended	59784
153.557	(a)(3) and (b) amended	59784
153.558	(b) amended	59785
153.921	Amended	59785
153.935a	(a)(2) amended	59785
153.1010	(b)(4) amended	59785
153.1011	(a)(2) and (3) amended	59785
153.1025	(c) amended	59785
153.1052	Amended	59785
153.1101	(c) introductory text amended	59785
153.1119	(c)(1), (2)(viii), (3) and (e) amended	59785
153.1502	(a) amended	59785

46 CFR—Continued

77 FR Page

Chapter I—Continued
153.1608	Note amended	59785
153	Table 1 footnote h amended	59785
154.1	(a) amended	59785
154.12	(c)(4) and (d)(4) amended	59785
154.32	(a) and (b) amended	59785
154.34	Amended	59785
154.170	(b)(1) and (2) amended	59785
154.172	(c) amended	59785
154.315	(b)(2) amended	59785
154.350	(a) amended	59785
154.356	(c) amended	59785
154.405	(c) amended	59785
154.406	(c) amended	59785
154.409	(a) amended	59785
154.410	(a) and (b) amended	59785
154.411	Introductory text amended	59785
154.418	Amended	59785
154.419	Amended	59785
154.425	Amended	59785
154.426	Amended	59785
154.428	Amended	59785
154.430	(b) amended	59785
154.431	(b) amended	59785
154.435	(a) amended	59785
154.436	Amended	59785
154.438	(b) amended	59785
154.440	(a)(2) and (b) amended	59785
154.447	(b) amended	59785
154.448	Introductory text amended	59785
154.449	Introductory text amended	59785
154.453	Amended	59785
154.459	(b) and (c) amended	59785
154.467	Introductory text amended	59785
154.503	(e) amended	59785
154.516	Introductory text amended	59785
154.519	(a)(2) amended	59785
154.520	Introductory text amended	59785
154.522	(a) amended	59785
154.524	(e) amended	59785
154.546	(a) amended	59785
154.610	(c) and (f) amended	59785
154.620	(b) amended	59785
154.630	(a) and (c) amended	59785
154.650	(d) and (e) amended	59785
154.655	(b) amended	59785
154.703	(b)(3) and (d)(2) amended	59785
154.709	(b) amended	59785
154.805	(e) amended	59785

List of CFR Sections Affected

46 CFR—Continued
77 FR Page

Chapter I—Continued
154.904	(a) amended	59785
154.908	(b) amended	59785
154.912	Amended	59785
154.1005	(a) and (b) amended	59785
154.1135	(a)(3) amended	59785
154.1335	(b)(1) amended	59785
154.1340	(c)(1) and (d) amended	59785
154.1345	(b)(2)(i) amended	59785
154.1725	(a)(2), (4) and (b)(1) amended	59785
154.735	(a) introductory text amended	59785
154.1755	Amended	59785
154.1860	Amended	59785

2013

(Regulations published from January 1, 2013, through October 1, 2013)

46 CFR
78 FR Page

Chapter I
147.5	Revised	60154
147.7	(a) amended	60154
147.9	(a) amended	60154
147.40	(a), (b) and (c) amended	60154
147.60	(c)(2) amended	60154
147.95	(a) and (b)(2) revised	60154

46 CFR—Continued
78 FR Page

Chapter I—Continued
148.3	Amended	60154
148.8	(a) amended	60154
148.115	(b) amended	60154
150	Note 1 table 1 amended	60155
	Note 1 table 2 amended	60155
	Appendix III amended	60155
150.160	Regulation at 78 FR 50162 eff. date delayed to 1-16-14	56837
	Regulation at 78 FR 50187 eff. date delayed to 1-16-14	56837
	Regulation at 78 FR 50205 eff. date delayed to 1-16-14	56837
150	Table I revised; interim	50162
	Table II revised; interim	50187
	Appendix I revised; interim	50205
151.03-31	Amended	60155
153.2	Amended	60155
153.4	(b) revised; (c) added	13251
	(a) amended	60155
153.9	(b) amended	60155
153	Table 2 revised; interim	50208
	Regulation at 78 FR 50208 eff. date delayed to 1-16-14	56837
154.1	(a) amended	60155
154.22	(a) amended	60155
154.34	Amended	60155
154.151	(c) amended	60155